American Historical Fiction
An Annotated Guide to Novels for Adults and Young Adults

**by
Lynda G. Adamson**

ORYX PRESS
1999

The rare Arabian Oryx is believed to have inspired the myth of the unicorn. This desert antelope became virtually extinct in the early 1960s. At that time several groups of international conservationists arranged to have 9 animals sent to the Phoenix Zoo to be the nucleus of a captive breeding herd. Today the Oryx population is over 1,000 and over 500 have been returned to the Middle East.

Library of Congress Cataloging-in-Publication Data
Adamson, Lynda G.
    American historical fiction : an annotated guide to novels for adults and young adults / by Lynda G. Adamson.
        p. cm.
    Expanded and updated ed. of: American historical fiction / A.T. Dickinson. 5th ed.
    Includes bibliographical references and indexes.
    ISBN 1-57356-067-7 (alk. paper)
    1. Historical fiction, American—Bibliography. 2. Young adult fiction, American—Bibliography. 3. American fiction—20th century--Bibliography. 4. United States—History—Fiction—Bibliography. 5. United States—In literature—Bibliography. I. Dickinson, A.T. American historical fiction. II. Title.
Z1231.F4D47 1998
[PS374.H5]
016.813'08109—dc21   98-38044
                                                              CIP

For Frank, Frank III, and Gregory

Contents

Preface

Historical fiction evokes a particular time period by focusing on a well-known person or event or on an ordinary person living in historical times. Through historical fiction, a reader can learn how people traveled, what they ate, and how they established relationships in a time other than the present. Readers often become fascinated with specific times and want to read additional titles with these settings.

The generally accepted definition of historical fiction is that it is about a time period at least 25 years before it was written. I have espoused a similar definition in other publications, but I no longer think it viable. If the setting is in a time earlier than that with which the reader is familiar, it is historical fiction. Therefore, in *American Historical Fiction: An Annotated Guide to Novels for Adults and Young Adults,* I have included a great many books with settings that are not present day, regardless of when they were written.

This book originally began as an update to the fifth edition of Dickinson's *American Historical Fiction* by Virginia Brokaw Gerhardstein (1986). It has become more. Rather than merely add titles published after 1985, I examined over 5,500 titles listed under the subject heading "Historical Fiction" in the Library of Congress catalog. Since many books that could fit the subject of "Historical Fiction" are not marked as such in the Library of Congress catalog, I also examined the subject listings under "War stories," "Detective and mystery stories," "Romantic suspense novels," "Love stories," "Christian fiction," and simply "Fiction." I also examined issues of *Library Journal, Publishers Weekly*, and *Booklist* published since 1980. After I had created my list, I checked Gerhardstein's book and decided to retain any overlapping titles that are classics, have sequels or prequels, or contain settings rarely reappearing in more recent historical fiction. As a final criterion for inclusion, books had to be either reviewed, or in the case of genres only recently earning the attention of reviewers (Christian fiction or romances, for example), appear with a summary of content in the publisher's catalog. This *Guide,* therefore, will help readers to choose from over 3,300 titles of historical fiction set within the United States in a variety of genres.

Organization

American Historical Fiction is organized by time periods from prehistory (before the arrival of European explorers) through the recent past. The novels are listed alphabetically by author within the appropriate time period. If the novel spans more than one of the designated time periods, I have sorted the entry by the dates of the time period in which the book begins. If the novel's characters remain in a specific locale, I have used that place, usually a state, as the main setting, which is listed in the Geographic Index. If they travel in a general area, such as the West, South, or East, I have designated that area as the setting.

Each entry includes the author; title; date of publication (and most recently known reprint if applicable); number of pages; brief description of the content, setting, and main characters; genre(s) if applicable; and any awards the book may have received. Annotations are descriptive rather than evaluative and include setting, character, and plot, and list relevant sequels or identify series to which books belong.

Since reprints appear erratically, I advise librarians or patrons planning to purchase books to check current citation sources for books, including those online that list and sell out-of-print titles. For almost all books that have been reprinted in large type, I have used the original date of publication and number of pages.

Young Adult Books

Books designated as "Young Adult" are, in almost all cases, books written for adults that young adults ninth grade and older might enjoy reading. I have included only a handful of books published specifically for young adults; these are excellent books giving an unusual point of view, generally set in a time period few other novels cover. Almost all of the adult books noted as appropriate for young adults come from professional educators' and reviewers' lists in *School Library Journal* and *Booklist*. Since adult mores and opinions about appropriate material for young adults vary, adults who plan to make selections for young adults from this guide and who have specific concerns about sexual content or language may wish to examine the entire novel. Similarly, other adults may discover books in the *Guide* not designated as "young adult" that they think teenagers with whom they are acquainted will appreciate. Books designated as young adult in this *Guide* will be marked with a diamond (◆) symbol, and listed alphabetically by author in Appendix II.

Appendixes and Indexes

Following the main entry section are two appendixes: a list of books that have won awards and the list of books that may be appropriate for young adults. Following these are five indexes: author, title, genre, geographic, and subject.

Genres

To say that a book of historical fiction belongs in a specific genre can be constraining and misleading. War stories can be romances, and romances can be mysteries or adventures. Therefore, a book may have more than one genre that fits its content. Genres and their general definitions for *American Historical Fiction* are

- Adventure Story—stories filled with action
- Allegory—stories that can be read on a symbolic level
- Bildungsroman (Coming-of-Age)— stories in which the protagonist matures, usually by means of some significant event
- Biographical Fiction—stories focusing on the life of a specific person in which the author creates dialogue rather than documentation
- Christian Fiction—stories without explicit sex or obscene language in which the protagonist from a Christian denomination faces challenges based on a faith in God
- Domestic Fiction—stories focusing on the home life or immediate family situations of a character
- Epic Literature—stories with a protagonist who acts heroic against a nationalistic setting
- Erotic Literature—stories with graphic sexual encounters
- Family Saga—stories about several generations of a family within the same book or over a series of books
- Fantastic Literature—stories not known to be true but using characters who have become part of legend
- Gothic Fiction—stories that include a dark atmosphere or eerie phenomena
- Humorous Fiction—stories that use humor as a basis for the characters to understand themselves and the world
- Jewish Fiction—stories focusing on Jews and Jewish culture
- Legal Story—stories with trials or lawyers as integral parts of the plot
- Love Story—stories depicting complex love affairs that are not necessarily patterned to have happy endings
- Medical Novel—stories in which one of the important characters is a healer or physician
- Musical Fiction—stories in which the protagonist is a musician

- Mystery (including Detective Fiction)—stories with an unknown factor that must be solved, such as a murder or other crime
- Picaresque Fiction—stories in which the episodic action moves from place to place without seeming to have a single climax
- Political Fiction—stories in which the protagonists must cope in some way with a hostile government, or in which political intrigue is an integral part of the plot
- Religious Fiction—stories in which members of non-Christian religions reveal their faith
- Romance—stories in which two people fall in love but must overcome difficulties before they can be together
- Satire—stories that jest about society's mores
- Sea Story—stories focusing on adventures at sea or taking place on ships at sea
- Sports Fiction—stories with protagonists interested or involved in a specific sport
- Spy Fiction—stories in which espionage drives the plot
- Time Travel—stories in which a protagonist enters a different time period, which then becomes the main setting
- War Story—stories that take place during a time of a war when a protagonist either fights on the front or remains at home waiting for a loved one to return
- Westerns—stories taking place in different locations across America as the frontier moved westward

Sample Entry

Time Period ——————————— **1815-1845**
Early Westward Expansion

Author ———————— Long, Jeff   — Publication Information
499. *Empire of Bones*. New York: Morrow, 1993. 256 pp.
Sam Houston wonders if he will be able to succeed in
Title   defeating Mexico with the motley group composing the
Texas forces of 1836.
Award(s): Western Writers of America Spur Award.———Award(s)
Description   *Genre(s):* Biographical Fiction; War Story. ————— Genre(s)

Acknowledgments

I would like to express my appreciation to Merle Jacob at the Chicago Public Library for her advice and John Bartles in my college library for his help in gathering information. I also thank Anne Thompson and Jennifer Ashley at The Oryx Press for their ideas and suggestions. Without the patience and support of my husband, this project could have never started, much less have come to completion.

MAIN ENTRY SECTION

North America before 1600

Bohnaker, Joseph J.

◆ 1. *Of Arms I Sing.* Santa Fe, NM: Sunstone, 1989.
182 pp.
Captain Villagrá, in a Seville prison cell, writes about
Don Juan de Oñate's conquest of the southwest and the
pueblo dwellers in the New World and of the fighting
among his men after Oñate becomes governor of the area.
Genre(s): Adventure Story.

Bruchac, Joseph

2. *Dawn Land.* Golden, CO: Fulcrum, 1993. 317
pp.
A snake bites Young Hunter, and when he tells the oldest
Talker, the man realizes that the snake has chosen Young
Hunter to protect the Only People as danger approaches.
Genre(s): Domestic Fiction.

Coldsmith, Don

3. *Runestone.* New York: Bantam, 1995. 489 pp.
Nils Thorsson comes to Vinland as Leif Erikssson did,
and when his companions suffer disaster, he learns to survive in the wilds with the help of a one-eyed Native
Amerian.

Conley, Robert J.

4. *The Dark Way.* New York: Doubleday, 1993.
179 pp.
When the Cherokee priest allows his homosexual lover,
Two Heads, to choose a sacrificial victim for rain, the
Cherokee are horrified, and lose faith in their priests. (*Se-
ries:* Real People, 2)
Genre(s): Adventure Story.

5. *The Peace Chief.* New York: St. Martin's Press,
1998. 336 pp.
After accidently killing his best friend, the Cherokee
Young Pupp is spiritually reborn as Comes Back to Life,
and he leads his people during troubles with the Spanish,
the French, and the Seneca.
Genre(s): Domestic Fiction.

◆ 6. *War Woman.* New York: St. Martin's Press,
1997. 384 pp.
In 1580, Whirlwind goes to Florida to find her Spanish
grandfather with her brother and husband-to-be, but the
males become dependent on Spanish liquor, and she
grows rich after her people begin mining gold.
Genre(s): Family Saga.

Fletcher, Inglis

◆ 7. *Roanoke Hundred.* Indianapolis, IN: Bobbs
Merrill, 1954. 492 pp.
Sir Richard Grenville tries to establish the colony at
Roanoke Island in 1588, but disease and discontent
thwart its completion. (*Series:* Carolina, 1)
Genre(s): Biographical Fiction; Family Saga; Romance.

Gear, Kathleen O'Neal, and W. Michael Gear

◆ 8. *People of the Lakes.* New York: Forge, 1994.
608 pp.
Mica Bird, a young warrior, finds a Mask with great powers, which the spirit of his dead grandfather warns him
not to misuse. (*Series:* First North American, 6)
Genre(s): Epic Literature; Adventure Story.

◆ 9. *People of the Lightning.* New York: Forge,
1995. 414 pp.
In prehistoric Florida, a young man in a fishing village
has the ability to tell the future. (*Series:* First North
American, 7)
Genre(s): Epic Literature; Adventure Story.

◆ 10. *People of the Mist.* New York: Tor, 1998. 432
pp.
Although Hunting Hawk knows that his granddaughter,
Red Knot, loves High Fox, he still promises her in mar-
riage to Copper Thunder, the chief of a rival clan.
Genre(s): Epic Literature; Adventure Story.

◆ 11. *People of the Silence.* New York: Forge, 1996.
496 pp.
Cornsilk and Poor Singer have secrets in their Anasazi
pasts that seem to mirror the decline of their civilization.
(*Series:* First North Americans, 8)
Genre(s): Epic Literature; Adventure Story.

Gear, W. Michael, and Kathleen O'Neal Gear

◆ 12. *People of the Earth.* New York: Tor, 1992.
608 pp.
White Ash of the Earth People clan has the responsibility
of dreaming for her people, and after their many misfortunes and enemy invasions, she advises them to go on a
year's journey to the East. (*Series:* First North American,
3)
Genre(s): Epic Literature; Adventure Story.

13. *People of the Fire.* New York: Tor, 1991. 467
pp.
The chief of the Red Hand people watches his people die
in a period of severe drought while a false dreamer is in
power. (*Series:* First North American, 2)
Genre(s): Epic Literature; Adventure Story.

◆ 14. *People of the River.* New York: Tor, 1992. 400 pp.
Near contemporary Cahokia, Illinois, around 1300, Nightshade lives with other Mississippians or Mound-Builders. (*Series:* First North American, 4)
Genre(s): Epic Literature; Adventure Story.

◆ 15. *People of the Sea.* New York: Forge, 1993. 425 pp.
When Kestrel becomes pregnant with her lover's twins, her abusive husband Lambkill kills Iceplant, her lover, with a knife, and Kestrel escapes to the coastal home of Iceplant's relatives. (*Series:* First North American, 5)
Genre(s): Epic Literature; Adventure Story.

◆ 16. *People of the Wolf.* New York: Tor, 1990. 435 pp.
Runs-in-Light and Raven Hunger, born brothers in the Ice Age clan of the The People, Children of the Father Sun, chose different paths, one being a proud, violent warrior and the other a Dreamer serving his people. (*Series:* First North American, 1)
Genre(s): Epic Literature; Adventure Story.

Gray, Robert Steele

17. *Survivor.* New York: St. Martin's Press, 1998. 336 pp.
When lightning bolts strike Mark Lewellyn, they transport him from contemporary America to AD 200 where he must survive buffalo herds and warring Native Americans.
Genre(s): Time Travel; Adventure Story.

Harrigan, Lana M.

18. *Coma.* New York: Forge, 1997. 384 pp.
Vicente de Vizcarra brings his wife Maria Angelica to New Mexico in 1598, expecting her wealth to fund his pursuit of gold, and during his long absences, she adjusts by having an affair with a Native American.
Genre(s): Political Fiction.

Harrison, Sue

19. *Brother Wind.* New York: Morrow, 1994. 494 pp.
In the sequel to *My Sister the Moon,* Kiin must abandon her tribe and one of her twin sons to return with her husband's killer to his village.
Genre(s): Family Saga.

◆ 20. *Mother Earth, Father Sky.* Garden City, NY: Doubleday, 1990. 313 pp.
Chagak flees with her grandfather when enemies destroy her Aleutian Island village in 7000 BC.
Genre(s): Family Saga.

21. *My Sister the Moon.* Garden City, NY: Doubleday, 1992. 449 pp.
In the sequel to *Mother Earth, Father Sky,* Kiin's jealous younger brother kidnaps and rapes her before trying to sell her as a slave to a distant tribe.
Genre(s): Family Saga.

Hunt, Angela Elwell

22. *Roanoke.* Wheaton, IL: Tyndale House, 1996. 488 pp.
Jocelyn White, a newlywed who dutiful accompanies her husband to the New World, is one of the settlers who founds Roanoke colony.
Genre(s): Christian Fiction; Romance.

Jekel, Pamela

23. *Columbia.* New York: St. Martin's Press, 1986. 448 pp.
A saga of the Columbia River in the Pacific Northwest begins 9000 years ago, where people such as Ilchee lived, and where archeologists currently dig.
Genre(s): Family Saga.

24. *Deepwater.* New York: Kensington, 1994. 512 pp.
Leah Hancock's female descendants in North Carolina from 1587 to Reconstruction show their courage and fortitude.
Genre(s): Family Saga.

Kaufelt, David A.

25. *American Tropic.* New York: Poseidon, 1987. 463 pp.
After John Cabot discovers Florida in the 15th century, three prisoners jailed during the Inquistion are freed and sent to the New World, and there they begin the history of Florida's inhabitants.
Genre(s): Family Saga.

Lytle, Andrew Nelson

26. *At the Moon's Inn.* 1941. Tuscaloosa: University of Alabama Press, 1990. 400 pp.
The conquistadors come with Hernando de Soto to the Florida territory in 1540 and settle.
Genre(s): Biographical Fiction.

Michener, James A.

27. *Alaska.* New York: Random House, 1988. 868 pp.
The prehistory of Alaska does not seem to prepare it for the changes beginning in the 18th century when traders and hunters began to take its resources.
Genre(s): Epic Literature.

28. *Chesapeake.* New York: Random House, 1978. 865 pp.
The Eastern shore of Maryland and Virginia evolves from prehistory into the 20th century and influences the lives of Native Americans, African Americans, and Irish immigrants who live there.
Genre(s): Epic Literature.

29. *Hawaii.* New York: Random House, 1959. 937p pp.
Hawaii's prehistory and history appears through the eyes of its natives and the missionaries and Asians who came to influence it.
Genre(s): Epic Literature.

◆ May be suitable for young adult readers

30. *Texas.* New York: Random House, 1985. 1096 pp.

Texas finds itself the site for many events from 1527 to the present, including the Battle of the Alamo.
Genre(s): Epic Literature.

Panger, Daniel

31. *Black Ulysses.* Athens, OH: Ohio State University Press, 1982. 402 pp.

Estevan, a Moorish slave, demonstrates the hardships of the Spanish expedition of 1527 when he is one of four to survive under Panfilo de Narvaez.
Genre(s): Adventure Story; Biographical Fiction.

Shuler, Linda Lay

32. *Let the Drum Speak.* New York: Morrow, 1996. 446 pp.

In the sequel to *Voice of the Eagle*, Antelope, the new seer for her tribe, her husband, and her daughter go to Oklahoma, but after her husband deserts her and she becomes the mate of the chief of the Hasinai, she decides to return to her people.
Genre(s): Epic Literature.

◆ 33. *She Who Remembers.* New York: Arbor House, 1988. 432 pp.

When the Anasazi believe Kwani to be a witch in the 13th century, they exile her, and Kokopelli rescues her and takes her to his village before she rises to the position of She Who Remembers, the woman who reveals tribal traditions.
Genre(s): Epic Literature.

◆ 34. *Voice of the Eagle.* New York: Morrow, 1992. 654 pp.

In the sequel to *She Who Remembers*, Kwani returns to the Cicuye village as the wife of Tolonqua, a hunting chief in the 13th century.
Genre(s): Epic Literature.

Speerstra, Karen

◆ 35. *The Earthshapers.* Happy Camp, CA: Naturegraph, 1980. 80 pp.

Yellow Moon, a moundbuilder in the Northwest, moves from winter home to summer village as the tribe cycles through the year in prehistoric times.
Genre(s): Domestic Fiction.

Swisher, Robert K. Jr.

36. *The Land.* Santa Fe, NM: Sunstone, 1986. 178 pp.

In the 16th century, a family begins ranching, and as the ranch changes management, a young man tries to restore the old method of ranching.
Genre(s): Western Fiction.

Taylor, Mark A.

37. *Chaco.* Santa Fe, NM: Sunstone, 1993. 282 pp.
Two friends, one Hopi and one Zuni, try to decide why the civilization in the Chaco Canyon disappeared in the 12th century.
Genre(s): Allegory.

Thom, James Alexander

◆ 38. *The Children of First Man.* New York: Ballantine, 1994. 547 pp.

In the 12th century, Madoc, the illegitimate son of a weak Welsh king, takes 10 boatloads of followers to America, where they encounter tribulations and confrontations with Native Americans.
Genre(s): Adventure Story.

Treece, Henry

◆ 39. *Westward to Vinland.* New York: S. G. Phillips, 1967. 192 pp.

Erik the Red flees Norway for Iceland in AD 960, and his son Lief the Lucky continues their exploration to America, landing on the southern coast of contemporary New England.
Genre(s): Adventure Story; Biographical Fiction.

Welch, James

◆ 40. *Fools Crow.* New York: Viking, 1986. 391 pp.
White Man's Dog, renamed Fools Crow, and some of his fellow Blackfoot try to follow the white man's ways while watching their traditions disappear.
Award(s): Los Angeles Times Book Prize.

1600-1699
The North American European Settlers

Ammerman, Mark

41. *The Rain From God.* Camp Hill, PA: Horizon, 1997. 320 pp.
Katanaquat, warrior in the Narragansett tribe, believes in many wives and gods, but when he meets Roger Williams, he learns about a different way of life.
Genre(s): Christian Fiction.

Barth, John

42. *The Sot-Weed Factor.* Garden City, NY: Doubleday, 1967. 756 pp.
Ebnezer Cooke, his twin sister, and their young tutor go from England to Maryland where they participate in the area's early years.
Genre(s): Picaresque Fiction; Satire.

Begiebing, Robert J.

43. *The Strange Death of Mistress Coffin.* Chapel Hill, NC: Algonquin, 1991. 252 pp.
An Englishman who has recently come to a New Hampshire community in the 17th century tries to find out who killed Mrs. Higgins after her husband and the accused murderer have disappeared.
Genre(s): Legal Story; Mystery.

Bernhard, Virginia

◆ 44. *A Durable Fire.* New York: Morrow, 1990. 384 pp.
In 1609, Temperance and her new husband George set off for Jamestown, and although George shipwrecks in Bermuda, Temperance reaches Virginia and discovers that the town is poorly managed and badly built.

Bigsby, Christopher

◆ 45. *Hester.* New York: Viking, 1994. 199 pp.
In a prequel to *The Scarlet Letter*, Hester Prynne flees her husband in England, and on the ship to the New World, she meets Dimmesdale and falls in love with him.
Genre(s): Romance.

Bowman, John Clarke

46. *Powhatan's Daughter.* New York: Viking, 1973. 336 pp.
Pocahontas encounters John Smith, and their constant love continues even as their lives diverge.
Genre(s): Biographical Fiction.

Boyle, T. Coraghessan

47. *World's End.* New York: Viking, 1987. 456 pp.
Seventeenth-century Dutch settlers and contemporary Native Americans reveal several centuries of social and political experiments.
Award(s): PEN/Faulkner Award for Fiction.

Cavanaugh, Jack

48. *The Puritans.* Wheaton, IL: Victor, 1994. 432 pp.
Drew Morgan, a young Englishman, has dreams of becoming a knight, but he decides to go to the New World instead. (*Series:* American Family Portrait, 1)
Genre(s): Christian Fiction; Family Saga.

Child, Lydia Maria Francis

49. *Hobomok.* New Brunswick, NJ: Rutgers, 1986. 188 pp.
A white woman and an Indian chief marry in an early-17th-century Puritan settlement.
Genre(s): Domestic Fiction.

Coleman, Terry

50. *Thanksgiving.* New York: Simon and Schuster, 1981. 408 pp.
In 1620, Wolsey Lowell settles with the Puritans, but after her marriage and her husband's disappearance, she

leaves for New Amsterdam with a sea captain and her children.

Condé, Maryse

51. *I, Tituba, Black Witch of Salem.* Charlottesville, VA: University Press of Virginia, 1992. 227 pp.
Tituba, a slave from Barbados, learns African arts of healing from her mother, which eventually leads Puritans to accuse her of witchcraft.

Conley, Robert J.

52. *The Long Way Home.* New York: Doubleday, 1994. 182 pp.
When Spaniards catch Cherokee priest Deadwood Lighter west of his home, they enslave him and take him to Havana, where he wonders about their treatment of slaves when they profess to be so religious. (*Series:* The Real People, 5)
Genre(s): Western Fiction.

Cooke, John Esten

53. *My Lady Pokahontas.* 1885. Ridgewood, NJ: Gregg, 1968. 190 pp.
John Smith has difficulties settling in Virginia until Pocahontas helps him. When she marries John Rolfe, she goes with him to England.
Genre(s): Domestic Fiction; Biographical Fiction.

Cooper, James Fenimore

◆ 54. *Wept of Wish-Ton-Wish.* 1829. New York: AMS, 1976. 251 pp.
In the 17th century, King Philip tries to protect his people from the Europeans in a 1675 war known as King Philip's War, but he loses badly.
Genre(s): War Story.

Dailey, Janet

55. *The Great Alone.* New York: Poseidon, 1986. 716 pp.
When Russian fur hunters arrive in the Aleutian Islands, Luka Kharkov takes an Aleutian woman as concubine and begins a family history lasting through statehood in 1959.
Genre(s): Family Saga.

Dillon, Eilís

◆ 56. *The Seekers.* New York: Scribner's, 1986. 136 pp.
Edward comes to Massachusetts with his fiancée Rebecca and her family in 1632, but he and Rebecca become discouraged by zealotry and disease and they return to England.
Genre(s): Christian Fiction.

Donnell, Susan

◆ 57. *Pocahontas.* New York: Berkley, 1991. 456 pp.
In 1616, Pocahontas goes to England with her husband, John Rolfe, and their child, after serving as an emissary to the white men in Virginia for her father.
Genre(s): Biographical Fiction.

Elliott, Edward E.

58. *The Devil and the Mathers.* San Francisco CA: Strawberry Hill, 1989. 375 pp.
Increase Mather urges his son to be judicious in his support of the witch hunters in Salem, but Cotton Mather sees witches everywhere.
Genre(s): Domestic Fiction.

Few, Mary Dodgen

59. *Azilie of Bordeaux.* Greenwood, SC: Carolina Editio, 1973. 335 pp.
Azilie comes to South Carolina to escape the Hugenot purge in France during the 17th century.
Genre(s): Domestic Fiction.

Fickett, Harold

60. *First Light.* Minneapolis, MN: Bethany House, 1993. 286 pp.
Abram White can escape neither his past nor the message of preacher George Whitefield in colonial America. (*Series:* Of Saints and Sinners, 1)
Genre(s): Christian Fiction; Adventure Story.

Fletcher, Inglis

◆ 61. *Bennett's Welcome.* Indianapolis: Bobbs Merrill, 1950. 451 pp.
The first settlement of North Carolina begins while the area is still part of Virginia in 1651-1652. (*Series:* Carolina, 2)
Genre(s): Family Saga; Romance.

◆ 62. *Lusty Wind for Carolina.* Indianapolis, IN: Bobbs Merrill, 1944. 562 pp.
While settlers try to stay in North Carolina, battles on the sea against pirates help to ease trade route dangers. (*Series:* Carolina, 5)
Genre(s): Romance; Family Saga.

◆ 63. *Rogue's Harbor.* Indianapolis: Bobbs Merrill, 1964. 242 pp.
In 1677, North Carolinians rebel against the local rule of the British. (*Series:* Carolina, 3)
Genre(s): Family Saga; Romance.

Fried, Albert

64. *The Prescott Chronicles.* New York: Putnam, 1976. 412 pp.
The Prescotts, a Boston family, begin their lineage in 1630 and continue to have contacts with influential government figures through 1973.
Genre(s): Family Saga; Political Fiction.

Gerson, Noel B.

65. *The Land Is Bright.* Garden City, NY: Doubleday, 1961. 356 pp.
William Bradford becomes the governor of Plymouth Colony during its first three years after a difficult life in Yorkshire and Holland.
Genre(s): Biographical Fiction.

Gross, Joel

66. *Home of the Brave.* New York: Seaview, 1982. 406 pp.

An American family with a home called Safe Haven experiences four centuries of events including revolution, slavery, civil war, and anti-Semitism.
Genre(s): Family Saga.

Hall, Oakley

67. *The Children of the Sun.* New York: Atheneum, 1983. 358 pp.

After four men survive the Narvaez expedition to Florida in the 16th century, they go with Cortes and Coronado looking for the seven cities of Cibola.
Genre(s): Biographical Fiction.

Hawthorne, Nathaniel

◆ 68. *The Scarlet Letter.* 1850. New York: Cambridge, 1997. 288 pp.

Hester Prynne is shunned from society and must wear a visible letter "A" to indicate that her daughter Pearl was born out of wedlock.

Heidish, Marcy

◆ 69. *Witnesses.* Boston: Houghton Mifflin, 1980. 235 pp.

Anne Hutchinson's struggle for religious freedom in Massachusetts during the 1630s gets her banished to Rhode Island.
Genre(s): Biographical Fiction.

Hunt, Angela Elwell

70. *Hartford.* Wheaton, IL: Tyndale House, 1996. 346 pp.

Twin brothers are rivals for their mother's love and attention while the Pequot War rages around them in 1636. (*Series:* Keepers of the Ring, 3)
Genre(s): War Story; Christian Fiction.

71. *Jamestown.* Wheaton, IL: Tyndale House, 1996. 420 pp.

Jocelyn and Thomas's grandchildren and their two friends escape a massacre but find themselves caught between their native culture and the new one. (*Series:* Keepers of the Ring, 2)
Genre(s): Christian Fiction.

Kevan, Martin

72. *Racing Tides.* New York: Beaufort, 1983. 283 pp.

The colonists react to the Native Americans and to each other from the viewpoint of a young Frenchman who poses as a seminarian but is actually a gambler fleeing his debts.
Genre(s): Adventure Story.

L'Amour, Louis

73. *Jubal Sackett.* New York: Bantam, 1985. 375 pp.

Jubal Sackett explores the West and meets a Kickapoo brave who helps him save the Natchez princess Itchakomi from a Spanish soldier. (*Series:* The Sacketts, 4)
Genre(s): Western Fiction; Adventure Story; Family Saga.

Larson, Charles R.

74. *Arthur Dimmesdale.* New York: A and W, 1983. 170 pp.

Arthur Dimmesdale gives his view of Hester Prynne and the Puritan community in *The Scarlet Letter.*
Genre(s): Domestic Fiction.

Lottman, Eileen

75. *The Brahmins.* New York: Delacorte, 1982. 416 pp.

Four women from Boston's wealthy Staffords influence their family as they become part of the social and political situations of the times from 1688 to 1970.
Genre(s): Domestic Fiction; Family Saga.

Lucas, Janice

76. *The Long Sun.* New York: Soho, 1994. 266 pp.
John Billips takes his family into the wilderness in the late 17th century after killing a drunken British soldier, and Lame Crow, a Tuscarora, helps them survive.
Genre(s): Domestic Fiction.

MacCurdy, Tim

77. *Caesar of Santa Fe.* Albuquerque, NM: Amador, 1990. 240 pp.

In 1637, Luis de Rosas is governor of colonial New Mexico while Philip IV rules Spain, and he struggles to keep peace between the church and state, Indians, Spanish, and Mestizos.
Genre(s): Biographical Fiction.

Martin, William

◆ 78. *Cape Cod.* New York: Warner Books, 1991. 652 pp.

After the *Mayflower* arrives on the Massachusetts coast, two families, the Bigelows and the Hilyards, become enemies in a rivalry that lasts for three centuries.
Genre(s): Family Saga.

Mason, F. Van Wyck

79. *The Sea Venture.* Garden City, NY: Doubleday, 1961. 349 pp.

A storm blows a group of settlers coming to Virginia and Jamestown into a Bermuda reef where they have to build another boat before continuing their journey.
Genre(s): Adventure Story.

Meyers, Maan

◆ 80. *The Dutchman.* New York: Doubleday, 1992. 306 pp.

In 1664, the British invade New Amsterdam, but settlers are also worried about a series of murders, and Pieter

Tonneman, the sheriff, wants to solve the case before the British win and take his job away.
Genre(s): Mystery.

◆ 81. *The Dutchman's Dilemma.* New York: Bantam, 1995. 254 pp.
In 1672, Pieter Tonneman, former sheriff of Manhattan Island, is married to Jewish widow Racquel and has four children, and he must investigate the murder of several animals and a man at the request of New York's first councilor.
Genre(s): Mystery.

Morris, Gilbert

82. *The Captive Bride.* Minneapolis, MN: Bethany House, 1987. 238 pp.
The Winslow family survives at Plymouth, and their descendants become involved in the Salem witch trials. (*Series:* House of Winslow, 2)
Genre(s): Domestic Fiction; Christian Fiction; Family Saga.

83. *The Honorable Imposter.* Minneapolis, MN: Bethany House, 1986. 331 pp.
The Winslow family arrives in the New World after a difficult voyage on the *Mayflower.* (*Series:* House of Winslow, 1)
Genre(s): Family Saga; Christian Fiction.

Pitre, Glen, and Michelle Benoit

84. *Great River.* Gretna, LA: Pelican, 1993. 248 pp.
Robert Cavelier comes to the New World and explores in Canada before Louis XIV approves his plan to go south to explore the Mississippi River and win it for France in 1682.
Genre(s): Biographical Fiction.

Porter, Donald Clayton

85. *The Renegade.* New York: Bantam, 1980. 369 pp.
Seneca warrior Renno, white son of the Iroquois Sachem, goes to London in 1690 to plead with the king for assistance in capturing the French fort at Louisburg. (*Series:* White Indian, 2)
Genre(s): War Story.

86. *White Indian.* New York: Bantam, 1979. 407 pp.
When Ghonka, leader of the Seneca tribe, plunders Fort Springfield, he spares the life of one infant whom he names Renno and raises as his own in the Ottawa tribe. (*Series:* White Indian, 1)
Genre(s): Domestic Fiction; War Story.

Pye, Michael

87. *The Drowning Room.* New York: Granta, 1995. 252 pp.
A child moves into Gretje Reyniers's house after the death of her husband in 1642, and she tells him the story of her life before she came to the New World.
Genre(s): Domestic Fiction.

Robards, Karen

88. *Nobody's Angel.* New York: Delacorte, 1992. 324 pp.
After Susannah Redman buys an indentured prisoner, he shaves his beard and she falls in love with him, only to find out that he is a wealthy Englishman who has been wronged.
Genre(s): Love Story.

Robson, Lucia St. Clair

89. *Mary's Land.* New York: Ballantine, 1995. 465 pp.
After three months on a ship in 1638, wealthy Catholic Margaret Brent arrives in Baltimore where she and others must adjust to a difficult and primitive life.
Genre(s): Political Fiction.

Rushing, Jane Gilmore

90. *Covenant of Grace.* Garden City, NY: Doubleday, 1982. 394 pp.
Anne Hutchinson believes that only God can grant salvation, and the Massachusetts Bay Colony tries and exiles her for defying its leaders.
Genre(s): Religious Fiction.

Sandburg, Carl

91. *Remembrance Rock.* New York: Harcourt Brace, 1948. 1067 pp.
Persons from colonial times, the Revolutionary War, and the Civil War express their views of the American dream.
Genre(s): Epic Literature.

Sedgwick, Catharine Maria

92. *Hope Leslie, or, Early Times in the Massachusetts.* New Brunswick, NJ: Rutgers University Press, 1987. 365 pp.
Puritan women and their Native American contemporaries have similar difficulties in their lives.
Genre(s): Domestic Fiction.

Seton, Anya

93. *The Winthrop Woman.* Boston: Houghton Mifflin, 1958. 586 pp.
Elizabeth Winthrop endures two bad marriages before finding love with William Hallet and a welcome exile from the Massachusetts Bay Colony.
Genre(s): Biographical Fiction; Love Story.

Sherwood, Valerie

94. *To Love a Rogue.* New York: New American Library, 1987. 426 pp.
After her mother dies, Lorraine London must indenture herself to a local innkeeper in Rhode Island during the 17th century before she joins Raile Cameron in a series of adventures.
Genre(s): Romance; Adventure Story.

Smith, Claude Clayton

◆ 95. *The Stratford Devil.* New York: Walker, 1984.
165 pp.
In 1651, adolescent Ruth Paine is missing from her home
for one week, and when she returns, she says that she was
lost in the woods and a Native American nursed her back
to health after a wolf attack, but the townspeople accuse
her of witchcraft.

Swanson, Neil Harmon

96. *The First Rebel.* New York: Farrar, Straus and
Giroux, 1937. 393 pp.
James Smith and the Scotch-Irish assert themselves politi-
cally in Pennsylvania as King George's War begins, in
the sequel to *The Judas Tree.*
Genre(s): Political Fiction.

97. *The Judas Tree.* New York: Putnam, 1933.
406 pp.
The Native Americans seize Fort Pitt in 1763, after a
lengthy and difficult battle.
Genre(s): War Story.

Vernon, John

◆ 98. *La Salle.* New York: Viking, 1986. 240 pp.
La Salle, the first white man who traveled the length of
the Mississippi River, describes his interest in nature
while his cartographer, Pierre Goupil, sees the filth and
sickness of 17th-century exploration.
Genre(s): Biographical Fiction.

Wohl, Burton

99. *Soldier in Paradise.* New York: Putnam, 1977.
345 pp.
In 1580, Captain John Smith is born and, unsuited for a
quiet life of farming, he joins the army and ends up in the
New World and Virginia.
Genre(s): Biographical Fiction.

Youmans, Marly

◆ 100. *Catherwood.* New York: Farrar, Straus and
Giroux, 1996. 163 pp.
Catherwood and her husband sail to the New World and
settle near Albany, New York, in 1676, but she and her
daughter Elizabeth become lost in the woods.
Genre(s): Adventure Story.

Zaroulis, N. L.

101. *Massachusetts.* New York: Fawcett, 1991.
709 pp.
The Revell family arrives in Massachusetts on the *Mayflower* and experiences many events in subsequent generations.
Genre(s): Family Saga.

◆ May be suitable for young adult readers

1700-1774
The American Colonies

Allen, Hervey

102. *Bedford Village.* New York: Rinehart, 1944. 305 pp.
In this sequel to *The Forest and the Fort*, Salathiel Albine, raised by Indians, moves to western Pennsylvania where he loves and loses, fights and wins.
Genre(s): War Story; Love Story; Family Saga.

103. *The Forest and the Fort.* New York: Rinehart, 1943. 344 pp.
Salathiel Albine, kidnapped and raised by Shawnee, returns to the white man's world, reassimilates, and anticipates seeing his first town.
Genre(s): War Story; Family Saga; Adventure Story.

104. *Toward the Morning.* New York: Rinehart, 1948. 485 pp.
In the sequel to *Bedford Village*, Salathiel Albine travels to Philadelphia in the winter of 1764 and hears concerns about Indians on the western frontier and the British on the eastern seaboard.
Genre(s): War Story; Family Saga; Adventure Story.

Bailey, Anthony

105. *Major André.* New York: Farrar, Straus and Giroux, 1987. 200 pp.
The capture of Major André prevents Benedict Arnold's betrayal of West Point, and André relates his point of view to his guards prior to his execution.
Genre(s): Biographical Fiction; War Story.

Bingham, Lisa

106. *Wild Serenade.* New York: Pocket Books, 1997. 320 pp.
Garrick Dalton, a ship's captain, hires Patience Pedigrue as governess for his younger sister, but after Patience and Garrick fall in love, someone trying to destroy the Dalton shipping empire kidnaps Patience.
Genre(s): Romance.

Brooks, Betty

107. *Jade.* New York: Zebra, 1997. 320 pp.
As penalty for saving herself from rape by one of the king's men, Jade Carrington is sold into indentured service, and Matthew Hunter buys her, mistakenly believing that she is supplying Native Americans with money for war.
Genre(s): Romance.

Buchan, John

108. *Salute to Adventurers.* New York: Doran, 1917. 366 pp.
A Scotsman sails to Virginia to manage an estate and finds the area to be an excitingly wild country.
Genre(s): Adventure Story.

Busbee, Shirlee

109. *A Heart for the Taking.* New York: Warner Books, 1997. 432 pp.
In 1774, Baroness Merrivale comes to America with Ellen to meet Jonathan, her intended, and when she arrives, she encounters Chance, Jonathan's cousin and enemy.
Genre(s): Romance.

Byrd, Max

◆ 110. *Jefferson.* New York: Bantam, 1993. 424 pp.
William Short, Thomas Jefferson's secretary, accompanies Jefferson to Paris where Jefferson shows his conflicting emotions by falling in love with another man's wife.
Genre(s): Biographical Fiction.

Cannon, LeGrand

111. *Look to the Mountain.* New York: Holt, Rinehart and Winston, 1942. 565 pp.
A young bride and groom make their home in the New Hampshire Grants from 1769 to 1777.

Cassel, Virginia C.

112. *Juniata Valley.* New York: Viking, 1981. 329 pp.
Five families and four Indian tribes interact in the French and Indian War during the mid-18th century.
Genre(s): War Story; Family Saga.

Cavanaugh, Jack

113. *The Colonists.* Wheaton, IL: Victor, 1995. 482 pp.
The Morgans settle in their New England home, where tests of their faith arise through their dealings with Native Americans and others. (*Series:* American Family Portrait, 2)
Genre(s): Christian Fiction; Family Saga.

Churchill, Winston

114. *Richard Carvel.* New York: Macmillan, 1899. 560 pp.
Richard Carvel grows up in Maryland and leaves to fight in the American Revolution with John Paul Jones.
Genre(s): War Story; Love Story.

Clark, Jean

115. *The Marriage Bed.* New York: Putnam, 1983. 396 pp.
Margretta Van Dyck serves as a governess to a clergyman's family in Hudson Valley during the 1740s and marries happily after choosing from three suitors.

Coffman, Virginia

116. *Mistress Devon.* New York: Arbor House, 1972. 252 pp.
In 1774, while touring with the Dantine Players in the American Colonies, Devon Howard wants to be independent, but she becomes attracted to the troupe's director.
Genre(s): Romance; Adventure Story.

Coldsmith, Don

117. *Return of the Spanish.* New York: Doubleday, 1991. 179 pp.
The Spanish try to limit the influence of the French on the Mississippi River by bringing Plains Indians who have allied with the French into camp. (Spanish Bit Saga, 18)
Genre(s): Family Saga; Western Fiction.

Cooper, James Fenimore

◆ 118. *The Deerslayer, or, the First War-Path.* New York: Lea and Blanchard, 1841. 528 pp.
Natty Bumppo, a young white hunter brought up in the Delaware Indian tribe, has to defend settlers before returning to the Iroquois who have allowed him parole.
Genre(s): Adventure Story; War Story.

◆ 119. *Last of the Mohicans.* 1826. New York: Acclaim, 1997. 352 pp.
In the sequel to *The Deerslayer*, Natty Bumppo helps with the campaign of Fort William Henry on Lake George during the French and Indian attack.
Genre(s): War Story.

◆ 120. *The Pathfinder.* 1840. Cutchogue, NY: Buccaneer, 1984. 419 pp.
In the sequel to *The Last of the Mohicans*, Natty Bumppo tries to help a small outpost on Lake Ontario.
Genre(s): Adventure Story; War Story.

◆ 121. *The Pioneers.* Albany: State University of New York, 1980. 565 pp.
In the sequel to *The Pathfinder*, Hawkeye is 70 and has returned to his boyhood home at Lake Otsego.
Genre(s): Adventure Story; War Story.

Deveraux, Jude

122. *The Raider.* New York: Pocket Books, 1987. 338 pp.
Returning to Maine before the Revolutionary War after 10 years abroad, Alexander Montgomery finds villagers distressed at the king's deputy, and he disguises himself as the black-masked Raider to stop him, but he unexpectedly falls in love with Jessica Taggert, a childhood playmate.
Genre(s): Romance; War Story.

Dubus, Elizabeth Nell

123. *Cajun.* New York: Putnam, 1983. 496 pp.
The Langlinais family and the de Clouets become neighbors in Louisiana, where they are involved in similar pursuits and problems for over 100 years.
Genre(s): Domestic Fiction; Family Saga.

Edmonds, Janet

◆ 124. *Sarah Camberwell Tring.* New York: St. Martin's Press, 1993. 232 pp.
Sarah Camberwell Tring becomes an heiress in Yorktown when she inherits her husband's land there and in England, but a French spy pursues her to England trying to intercept a message she carries to the government.
Genre(s): Romance.

125. *Turn of the Dice.* New York: St. Martin's Press, 1990. 416 pp.
Abigail sails with the man who bought her as a bond-slave to pay her father's debts, and on board, she falls in love with a former bond-slave who has become a plantation owner.
Genre(s): Romance.

Ellsberg, Edward

126. *Captain Paul.* New York: Dodd Mead, 1941. 607 pp.
Tom Folger of Nantucket tells about Captain John Paul Jones, whom he has admired since he was a privateer.
Genre(s): Biographical Fiction; Sea Story.

Erickson, Steve

127. *Arc D'X.* New York: Poseidon, 1993. 298 pp.
Thomas Jefferson visits Paris and finds himself torn between his ideals and his interest in his quadroon slave Sally Hemings, in the pursuit of happiness.
Genre(s): Adventure Story.

Fast, Howard

◆ 128. *Citizen Tom Paine.* New York: Grove Press, 1983. 341 pp.
Thomas Paine, a revolutionary by choice, travels between Paris, London, and colonial Philadelphia during the revolutionary period.
Genre(s): Biographical Fiction; Political Fiction.

Faulkner, Colleen

129. *Fire Dancer.* New York: Kensington, 1997. 320 pp.
When artist Mackenzie Daniels goes to Fort Belvadere with her fur trading father for an opportunity to paint the

French, Indian, and British participants in peace talks, she falls in love with a Shawnee, Fire Dancer, who saves her when the fort is attacked.
Genre(s): War Story; Romance.

Fickett, Harold

130. *Daybreak.* Minneapolis, MN: Bethany House, 1995. 288 pp.
When Jonathan Edwards does not fulfill a promise, Abram has problems with his marriage, his business, and his name. (*Series:* Of Saints and Sinners, 2)
Genre(s): Christian Fiction.

Fleming, Thomas

131. *Remember the Morning.* New York: Forge, 1997. 384 pp.
Senecas kidnap 17-year-old Catalyntie Van Vorst and her friend and ex-slave Clara, but the two never forget their Seneca lives, and they become business owners while loving the same man.

Fletcher, Inglis

◆ 132. *Cormorant's Brood.* Philadelphia: Lippincott, 1959. 345 pp.
The colonists in the area of Albemarle chafe under the control of greed royal governors. (*Series:* Carolina, 6)
Genre(s): Family Saga; Romance.

◆ 133. *Men of Albemarle.* Indianapolis, IN: Bobbs Merrill, 1942. 566 pp.
Indian uprisings in North Carolina between 1710 and 1720 upset the settlers. (*Series:* Carolina, 4)
Genre(s): Romance; Family Saga.

◆ 134. *Raleigh's Eden.* Indianapolis, IN: Bobbs Merrill, 1940. 598 pp.
Upper class families help to develop the plantation life in the rich fertile land along North Carolina's coast from 1765 through the American Revolution. (*Series:* Carolina, 7)
Genre(s): Family Saga; Romance.

◆ 135. *The Scotswoman.* Indianapolis, IN: Bobbs Merrill, 1954. 532 pp.
Flora MacDonald comes to North Carolina after helping Bonnie Prince Charlie in the Jacobite Rebellion and sides with the British, in duty to her husband. (*Series:* Carolina, 9)
Genre(s): Biographical Fiction; Family Saga; Romance.

◆ 136. *The Wind in the Forest.* Indianapolis, IN: Bobbs Merrill, 1975. 416 pp.
A young member of the North Carolina governor's staff supports the rebellious colonists as they rail against unjust taxes and abuse of power. (*Series:* Carolina, 8)
Genre(s): Romance; Family Saga.

Follett, Ken

137. *A Place Called Freedom.* New York: Crown, 1995. 407 pp.
In 1766, after Sir George Jamisson mistreats Mack and others in the mines of Scotland, Mack flees to London before deportation to the American colonies where he finds work on Jamisson's son's Virginia plantation.
Genre(s): Romance; Adventure Story.

Fowler, Robert H.

◆ 138. *Jason McGee.* New York: Harper and Row, 1979. 322 pp.
In the mid-18th century, Jason McGee goes to find the brother that Native Americans kidnapped in a raid during which they killed his mother and he gains two traveling companions, a Quaker missionary and a fur trader.
Genre(s): War Story.

139. *Jeremiah Martin.* New York: St. Martin's Press, 1988. 348 pp.
Patriot Jeremiah Martin serves in several capacities during the American Revolution that include traveling to London, France, and Barbados, while he denounces slavery and wants the Native Americans to keep their lands.
Genre(s): War Story.

Gabaldon, Diana

140. *Drums of Autumn.* New York: Delacorte, 1997. 880 pp.
From 1767 to 1770, Claire, a 20th-century woman, and her 18th-century Scottish husband, struggle to set up their home in South Carolina.
Genre(s): Time Travel; Fantastic Literature; Romance.

Gerson, Noel B.

141. *Give Me Liberty.* Garden City, NY: Doubleday, 1966. 347 pp.
When Patrick Henry discovers law, his life focuses, and he becomes a dedicated patriot.
Genre(s): Biographical Fiction; Political Fiction.

Giles, Janice Holt

142. *The Enduring Hills.* 1950. Boston: Houghton Mifflin, 1971. 256 pp.
Hod Pierce loves the Kentucky mountains but wants to explore further.
Genre(s): Adventure Story.

Gramling, Lee

143. *Trail From St. Augustine.* Sarasota, FL: Pineapple, 1993. 266 pp.
John MacKenzie goes trapping in 18th-century colonial times, and when he returns to Florida, he helps a young woman indentured to the leader of local vigilantes.
Genre(s): Western Fiction.

Grey, Zane

144. *George Washington, Frontiersman.* Lexington, KY: University Press of Kentucky, 1994. 268 pp.
George Washington's adventures as a young man and the support of his wife prepare him to take command of the Continental Army in 1775.
Genre(s): Biographical Fiction.

Grimes, Roberta

◆ 145. *My Thomas.* New York: Doubleday, 1993. 320 pp.
Martha Jefferson keeps a diary about her 10-year marriage to Thomas before she dies in 1784 following childbirth.
Genre(s): Biographical Fiction; Love Story.

Haley, Alex

◆ 146. *Roots.* New York: Doubleday, 1976. 379 pp.
Captured in Africa, Kunta Kinte, a tribal prince, becomes a slave, and eventually generations of his family survive to become free again.
Genre(s): Family Saga.

Houston, James A.

147. *Ghost Fox.* New York: Harcourt Brace, 1977. 302 pp.
In the 1750s, Abnaki Algonquians abduct Sarah Wells (Ghost Fox), 17, from her farm home.
Genre(s): War Story.

Hunt, Angela Elwell

148. *Rehoboth.* Wheaton, IL: Tyndale House, 1997. 374 pp.
When Daniel Bailie takes his children, Mojag and Aiyana, to minister to Christian Indians, Mojag feels that he should serve the non-Christian Indians planning to make war with the colonists. (*Series:* Keepers of the Ring, 4)
Genre(s): War Story.

Jarrett, Miranda

149. *The Secrets of Catie Hazard.* New York: Harlequin, 1997. 352 pp.
Catie Willman becomes pregnant just before her soldier lover leaves for England, so she marries an innkeeper, but the soldier returns to fight for the British eight years later.
Genre(s): Romance.

Johnston, Coleen L.

150. *The Founders.* New York: St. Martin's Press, 1993. 356 pp.
In 1750, Scots-Irish migrant Thomas Gairden moves from Pennsylvania to Charles Town, Carolina, to start a weaving shop.
Genre(s): Domestic Fiction.

Kilian, Michael

151. *Major Washington.* New York: St. Martin's Press, 1998. 368 pp.
When Thomas Tick Morley, a shipowner who likes the wrong women and has little ambition, meets George Washington in 1753, Morley thinks he has a good influence on Washington but is concerned about the rise in the slave trade.
Genre(s): Adventure Story.

Koen, Karleen

152. *Now Face to Face.* New York: Random House, 1995. 733 pp.
In the sequel to *Through a Glass Darkly*, Barbara Devane, a widow at 20 returns to Virginia and her grandmother's property before going back to England and an unwilling involvement in a Jacobite plot.
Genre(s): Political Fiction.

Laity, Sally, and Dianna Crawford

153. *Fires of Freedom.* Wheaton, IL: Tyndale House, 1996. 449 pp.
During hostilities between the colonists and the English in 1774, the English arrest Daniel Haynes for helping his brother-in-law desert the British army. (*Series:* Freedom's Holy Light, 4)
Genre(s): Christian Fiction; Romance.

154. *The Gathering Dawn.* Wheaton, IL: Tyndale House, 1994. 357 pp.
In 1770, Susannah comes to the colonies with her friend Julie, but after Julie dies in childbirth, Susannah must make her way alone until she meets Dan, a Presbyterian who makes her think about both love and religion. (*Series:* Freedom's Holy Light, 1)
Genre(s): Christian Fiction; Romance.

155. *The Kindled Flame.* Wheaton, IL: Tyndale House, 1994. 298 pp.
Susannah's life with Dan continues in the colonies during the American Revolution. (*Series:* Freedom's Holy Light, 2)
Genre(s): Christian Fiction; Romance.

L'Amour, Louis

156. *Sackett's Land.* New York: Saturday Review, 1974. 198 pp.
Barnabas Sackett owns land in Cambridgeshire, but he flees from a hostile aristocrat to London and then to America where he becomes a fur trapper. (*Series:* The Sacketts, 1)
Genre(s): Western Fiction; Family Saga.

157. *To the Far Blue Mountains.* New York: Saturday Review, 1976. 156 pp.
Barnabas Sackett returns from London, sails up the James River, and begins raising his children. (*Series:* The Sacketts, 2)
Genre(s): Western Fiction; Family Saga.

Levin, Benjamin H.

◆ 158. *To Spit against the Wind.* New York: Citadel, 1970. 569 pp.
Thomas Paine often suffers because he has ideas that are ahead of the times in which he lives.
Genre(s): Biographical Fiction.

Marshall, Joe

159. *Winter of the Holy Iron.* Santa Fe, NM: Red Crane, 1994. 295 pp.
Henri Bruneaux shoots Gaston de la Verendrye while attempting to steal his gold, and Whirlwind, war leader of the Wolf Tail Lakota, takes de la Verendrye back to his camp for healing while fearing the consequences of his people finding out about guns in the mid-18th century.
Genre(s): War Story.

Mason, F. Van Wyck

160. *Brimstone Club.* Boston: Little, Brown, 1971. 338 pp.
Jeremy Brett, a New Hampshire shipbuilder, goes to London to secure contracts, and he comes in contact with the Brimstone Club, a group of wealthy men who like sex with their politics.
Genre(s): Political Fiction.

161. *Three Harbours.* Philadelphia: Lippincott, 1938. 694 pp.
In the stages before the American Revolution, merchants ship goods by sea, and Bermuda is an important place.
Genre(s): War Story.

McCarry, Charles

162. *The Bride of the Wilderness.* New York: New American Library, 1988. 438 pp.
Fanny, who is half French and half English, goes with her godfather to Connecticut to claim his inheritance, but Indians kidnap her.
Genre(s): Adventure Story.

McFarland, Philip

163. *Seasons of Fear.* New York: Schocken, 1984. 250 pp.
In 1741, when Charles Alexander Corimer arrives in the New World, his slave escapes, and when fires and a burglary occur in the area, Manhattan dwellers see a slave plot and plan to hang all of the insurgents.
Genre(s): Adventure Story; Political Fiction.

Meyers, Maan

164. *The Kingsbridge Plot.* New York: Doubleday, 1993. 321 pp.
Pieter Tonneman helps a young doctor try to solve a series of brutal murders in New York City near the time when someone attempts to murder George Washington.
Genre(s): Mystery; Romance.

Michaels, Kasey

165. *The Homecoming.* New York: Pocket Books, 1996. 324 pp.
In 1763, an Irish orphan marries for convenience, and she and her gentleman husband become involved with the Lenni-Lenape Indians.
Genre(s): Romance.

Morris, Gilbert

166. *The Indentured Heart.* Minneapolis, MN: Bethany House, 1988. 288 pp.
The Winslow family hears Jonathan Edwards preach in pre-Revolutionary New England. (*Series:* House of Winslow, 3)
Genre(s): Christian Fiction; Domestic Fiction; Family Saga.

◆ 167. *Sound the Trumpet.* Minneapolis, MN: Bethany House, 1995. 316 pp.
Daniel and Lyna Bradford leave England after Daniel becomes indentured to his enemy, but in America, he falls

in love with the enemy's wife as the Revolution begins. (*Series:* The Liberty Bell, 1)
Genre(s): Christian Fiction; War Story.

Moss, Robert

168. *The Firekeeper.* New York: Forge, 1995. 512 pp.
Sir William Johnson gains the trust of Mohawk Indians and leads them into battle against the French during the colonial period.
Genre(s): War Story.

◆ 169. *The Interpreter.* New York: Tor, 1997. 352 pp.
In 1710, German Conrad Weiser arrives in the New World expecting land promised by Queen Anne, but when he becomes an indentured servant instead, he organizes others and learns enough Mohawk to become an interpreter and colony leader.

Oates, Joyce Carol

170. *My Heart Laid Bare.* New York: Dutton, 1998. 420 pp.
During colonial times, a family of con artists thrives.
Genre(s): Family Saga.

O'Toole, G. J. A.

◆ 171. *Poor Richard's Game.* New York: Delacorte, 1982. 309 pp.
When Benjamin Franklin is accused of being a traitor, a double agent, and a licentious man, an Irish soldier goes to Paris to uncover the truth.
Genre(s): Biographical Fiction; War Story.

Porter, Donald Clayton

172. *Ambush.* New York: Bantam, 1983. 310 pp.
The Seneca Ghonkaba, half-white son of Ja-gonh and grandson of Sachem Renno, sneaks into the fortressed city of Quebec to rescue an Erie woman captured into prostitution. (*Series:* White Indian)
Genre(s): War Story.

Pynchon, Thomas

173. *Mason and Dixon.* New York: Henry Holt, 1997. 773 pp.
Surveyors in the 18th century go south to the Cape of Good Hope and west to America, where they draw the boundary that becomes the arbitrary division between north and south.
Genre(s): Biographical Fiction.

Richter, Conrad

◆ 174. *A Country of Strangers.* New York: Knopf, 1966. 169 pp.
Stone Girl, kidnapped by Indians at five, grows up in the tribe and has a child, but when she is traded back into the white world, it will not accept her and her Indian child, in the sequel to *The Light in the Forest.*

◆ 175. *The Light in the Forest.* New York: Knopf, 1953. 179 pp.

Kidnapped at four by the Delaware Indians, John Butler returns to his family 11 years later, only to escape and be rejected by the Indians after an ambush fails.

Riefe, Barbara

176. *For Love of Two Eagles.* New York: Forge, 1995. 378 pp.

In the sequel to *The Woman Who Fell from the Sky*, Margaret Addison loves Two Eagles, her Oneida chief husband and must decide if she should return to England when an Englishman, searching at her father's request, finds her.

Genre(s): Domestic Fiction.

177. *Mohawk Woman.* New York: Forge, 1996. 378 pp.

Mohawk woman Singing Brook devotes herself to her husband, Sky Toucher, and she bravely rescues him from the French after they capture him in Queen Anne's War during 1710.

Genre(s): War Story.

Roberts, Carey, and Rebecca Seely

178. *Tidewater Dynasty.* New York: Harcourt Brace, 1981. 435 pp.

The history of the Lees of Stratford Hall spans the eras of Governor Tom Lee, founder of the dynasty in 1720, to General Light Horse Harry Lee, who abandoned Stratford in 1810.

Genre(s): Biographical Fiction.

Roberts, Kenneth Lewis

◆ 179. *Boon Island.* Garden City, NY: Doubleday, 1956. 275 pp.

The British galley *Nottingham*, loaded with cheese and butter, crashes off the Maine coast on December 10, 1710, and 24 men survive without shelter, food, or fresh water for 24 days.

Genre(s): Sea Story.

◆ 180. *Northwest Passage.* Garden City, NY: Doubleday, 1937. 709 pp.

Major Robert Rogers dreams of an overland passage to the Pacific, and a budding painter from Maine wants to follow him and paint the Indians realistically.

Seifert, Shirley

181. *The Medicine Man.* Philadelphia: Lippincott, 1972. 360 pp.

Dr. Antoine Saugrain serves as an army doctor and tries to find a way to handle the perishable smallpox vaccine.

Genre(s): Biographical Fiction; Medical Novel.

Sessions, Richard

182. *Island Woman.* New York: Arch Grove, 1997. 295 pp.

Abbie finds herself transported to 1704 off the coast of California where an Englishman she met in a later century has returned to change the history of Spanish colonization in the New World.

Genre(s): Time Travel; Adventure Story.

Simms, William Gilmore

183. *The Yemassee.* 1835. New York: Twayne, 1964. 415 pp.

Native Americans watch the white settlers moving into their lands, a process leading to the Yemassee War in the early 1700s.

Genre(s): Romance; War Story.

Statham, Frances Patton

◆ 184. *Call the River Home.* New York: Fawcett, 1991. 408 pp.

Mary Musgrove, a Creek princess, serves as a liaison and interpreter for James Oglethorpe in Georgia as he establishes and settles Savannah in the early 18th century.

Genre(s): Biographical Fiction.

Stone, Irving

185. *Those Who Love.* Garden City, NY: Doubleday, 1965. 662 pp.

Abigail Smith marries John Adams and faces the country's struggle for independence with him.

Genre(s): Love Story; Biographical Fiction.

Swann, Lois

186. *The Mists of Manittoo.* New York: Scribner's, 1976. 455 pp.

Elizabeth Dowland, daughter of a wealthy landowner, falls in love with Wakwa, a Native American who finds her lost and sick in the forest.

Genre(s): Romance.

187. *Torn Covenants.* New York: Scribner's, 1981. 401 pp.

In 1748, Elizabeth Dowland marries Wakwa, a Massachuset, as his second wife and bears him a son, only to face the hostilities of her white neighbors, in the sequel to *The Mists of Manitoo.*

Genre(s): Love Story.

Swanson, Neil Harmon

188. *The Silent Drum.* New York: Farrar, Straus and Giroux, 1940. 503 pp.

In the sequel to *The First Rebel*, families live on the Pennsylvania frontier before the Revolution begins.

Genre(s): War Story.

◆ 189. *Unconquered.* Garden City, NY: Doubleday, 1947. 440 pp.

In the sequel to *The Silent Drum*, Chris Holden returns from London and tries to warn frontier forts of an attack, which later is called Pontiac's Conspiracy.

Thackeray, William Makepeace

190. *The Virginians.* New York: Fields, Osgood, 1869. 809 pp.

In the sequel to *The History of Henry Esmond, Esquire*, Henry comes to Virginia, where his grandsons fight on different sides in the Revolution.

Genre(s): War Story.

◆ May be suitable for young adult readers

Thane, Elswyth

191. *Dawn's Early Light.* New York: Duell, Sloane, and Pearce, 1943. 317 pp.
Fatherless Julian Day stays in Williamsburg after arriving from London, and when St. John Sprague befriends him, Day becomes intrigued with the cause of the Continental Army.
Genre(s): War Story; Family Saga.

Thom, James Alexander

192. *Follow the River.* New York: Ballantine, 1981. 416 pp.
After being captured in an Indian raid during 1755, Mary Draper Ingles follows the Ohio River for 1,000 miles to return home to Virginia by herself.
Genre(s): Adventure Story.

Unsworth, Barry

193. *Sacred Hunger.* Garden City, NY: Doubleday, 1992. 629 pp.
William Kemp wants to recoup economic losses from cotton by entering the slave trade, while his nephew serves as a doctor on a slave ship before leading a revolt against the crew.
Genre(s): Sea Story.

Williams, Carol

◆ 194. *The Switzers.* Virginia Beach, VA: Donning, 1981. 310 pp.
Johannes and Madlee come to South Carolina from Switzerland in the 1750s and try to establish a home and a family.
Genre(s): Domestic Fiction.

Wilson, Dorothy Clarke

◆ 195. *Lady Washington.* Garden City, NY: Doubleday, 1984. 376 pp.
Martha Washington, widow of Daniel Custis, supports George Washington in all that he does, including spending the winter with him at Valley Forge.
Genre(s): Biographical Fiction; Political Fiction.

Wright, Don

196. *The Woodsman.* New York: Tor, 1984. 406 pp.
Morgan Patterson helps three Englishwomen escape from the French after the French defeat the British forces in the French and Indian Wars.
Genre(s): War Story.

Wyckoff, Nicholas Elston

◆ 197. *The Braintree Mission.* New York: Macmillan, 1957. 184 pp.
William Pitt, Earl of Chatham, offers John Adams a title and a seat in Parliament in the hope that the move will stop the colonies from going to war.
Genre(s): Biographical Fiction.

1775-1783
The American Revolution

Arnow, Harriette Louisa Simpson

◆ 198. *The Kentucky Trace: A Novel of the American Revolution.* New York: Knopf, 1974. 288 pp.
Surveyor William David Leslie Collins struggles with other settlers to live in the Kentucky wilderness.
Genre(s): War Story.

Barker, Shirley

199. *Strange Wives.* New York: Crown, 1963. 377 pp.
Reuben Bravo, a Portuguese Jew, and Jenny Tupper, a Christian, try to find religious freedom in Rhode Island.
Genre(s): Jewish Fiction; Love Story.

Barry, Jane

◆ 200. *The Carolinians.* Garden City, NY: Doubleday, 1959. 318 pp.
Loyalists in South Carolina help one of the wounded officers from Morgan's Raiders.
Genre(s): War Story.

◆ 201. *The Long March.* New York: Appleton, 1955. 316 pp.
Daniel Morgan defeats the British and Lord Cornwallis on the border of South Carolina at the Battle of Cowpens in 1781.
Genre(s): War Story.

Benet, Stephen Vincent

202. *Spanish Bayonet.* New York: Doran, 1926. 268 pp.
Indentured servants on a Florida plantation face Spanish oppression.
Genre(s): War Story; Domestic Fiction.

Benzoni, Juliette

203. *Lure of the Falcon.* New York: Putnam, 1978. 408 pp.
Gilles Goelo comes to America to fight in the Revolution with Lafayette and returns with a title and an estate.
Genre(s): War Story; Romance.

Beyea, Basil

204. *The Golden Mistress.* New York: Simon and Schuster, 1975. 380 pp.
Betsy Bowen, raised in a Rhode Island house of prostitution in the 18th century, learns how to trade sex for favors, and after disappointment in love, she goes to New York and becomes close friends with such men as Aaron Burr.
Genre(s): Biographical Fiction.

Boyd, James

205. *Drums.* New York: Scribner's, 1928. 409 pp.
The Fraser family from Scotland lives in North Carolina and serves the community, but its members do not forget Culloden.
Genre(s): War Story.

Brick, John

206. *Eagle of Niagara.* Garden City, NY: Doubleday, 1955. 279 pp.
The Indian Joseph Brant captures David Harper, a Continental soldier.
Genre(s): War Story.

207. *The King's Rangers.* Garden City, NY: Doubleday, 1954. 290 pp.
Colonel Butler leads a group of woodsmen in a New York state Loyalist cause.
Genre(s): War Story.

208. *The Rifleman.* Garden City, NY: Doubleday, 1953. 349 pp.
Tim Murphy, an Indian fighter, woodsrunner, and lover helps Morgan win the battle at Saratoga.
Genre(s): War Story.

209. *The Strong Men.* Garden City, NY: Doubleday, 1959. 360 pp.
Baron von Steuben, a professional soldier, forms a strong army of colonial volunteers at Valley Forge.
Genre(s): War Story.

Bristow, Gwen

210. *Celia Garth.* New York: Crowell, 1959. 406 pp.
Celia Garth, an orphan working as a dressmaker in Charleston, sees the British siege the city and becomes a rebel spy.
Genre(s): War Story.

Callahan, North

211. *Peggy.* New York: Cornwall, 1983. 241 pp.
Empty-headed Peggy Shippen grows up in Philadelphia before marrying the greedy Benedict Arnold.
Genre(s): Biographical Fiction.

◆ May be suitable for young adult readers

Caudill, Rebecca

◆ 212. *Tree of Freedom.* New York: Viking, 1949. 279 pp.
Stephanie's family moves to Kentucky from Carolina in 1780, and she takes apple seeds from her French great-grandmother's tree to symbolize her freedom.
Award(s): New York Herald Tribune Award.
Genre(s): Western Fiction.

Cavanaugh, Jack

213. *The Patriots.* Wheaton, IL: Victor, 1995. 530 pp.
Esau and Jacob Morgan's rivalry reaches a climax when they fight on two different sides during the American Revolution. (*Series:* American Family Portrait, 3)
Genre(s): Christian Fiction; War Story; Family Saga.

Churchill, Winston

214. *The Crossing.* New York: Macmillan, 1899. 598 pp.
David Ritchie's father dies in the American Revolution, and David joins George Rogers Clark's campaign before studying law and traveling to New Orleans.
Genre(s): War Story; Adventure Story.

Cooper, James Fenimore

215. *The Pilot.* New York: C. Wiley, 1823. 357 pp.
During the Revolutionary War, some attempt to abduct prominent Englishmen to exchange for American prisoners.
Genre(s): Sea Story.

216. *The Red Rover.* New York: Lea and Blanchard, 1828. 2 vols.
A sea captain, once a pirate, fights in the War of Independence.
Genre(s): Adventure Story; Sea Story.

217. *The Spy.* 1821. Laurel, NY: Lightyear Press, 1976. 471 pp.
Harvey Birch spies during the American Revolution.
Genre(s): Adventure Story; Spy Fiction.

Cornwell, Bernard

218. *Redcoat.* New York: Viking, 1988. 405 pp.
Sam Gilpin and Jonathan Becket transfer allegiance from the Loyalists to the Patriots, each for very different reasons.
Genre(s): War Story.

Davis, Mildred, and Katherine Davis

219. *Lucifer Land.* New York: Random House, 1977. 326 pp.
Cassie and her family become suspicious of their neighbors and worry about the news during the Revolutionary War in Bedford, New York.
Genre(s): War Story.

Eastman, Edward Roe

220. *The Destroyers.* Ithaca, NY: American Agricultural Press, 1946. 250 pp.
In 1779, Tories and Native Americans attack Cherry Valley.
Genre(s): War Story.

Eberhart, Mignon G.

221. *Enemy in the House.* New York: Random House, 1962. 216 pp.
On the night after Amity marries Simon in Savannah, the parson and a lawyer who attended their wedding are murdered, forcing the two to leave immediately, Amity going to Jamaica with her Tory father and Simon to fight.
Genre(s): Mystery; War Story.

Eckert, Allan W.

222. *The Court-Martial of Daniel Boone.* Boston: Little, Brown, 1973. 309 pp.
When Captain Daniel Boone is accused of treason in 1778, he declares himself not guilty and defends himself with advice from two lawyers, finally able to prove his innocence after cross-examination.
Genre(s): Biographical Fiction; Legal Story.

Edmonds, Walter D.

◆ 223. *Drums along the Mohawk.* Boston: Little, Brown, 1936. 592 pp.
Gil Martin and his wife clear a place for their home in the Mohawk River Valley and, along with others, try to ignore the Indian raids and British invasions of the world outside.
Genre(s): War Story.

224. *In the Hands of the Senecas.* Boston: Little, Brown, 1947. 213 pp.
After Burgoyne's surrender at Saratoga, families at Dygartobush, feeling secure, do not build a stockade, and Senecas attack and capture them.
Genre(s): Adventure Story.

Ehle, John

225. *The Land Breakers.* New York: Harper and Row, 1964. 407 pp.
After Mooney Wright and his wife settle on the Carolina-Tennessee border in 1779, other people move into the area who have different desires and expectations.
Genre(s): Family Saga.

Fast, Howard

◆ 226. *April Morning.* New York: Crown, 1961. 184 pp.
Adam Cooper, 15, observes the events in Lexington and Concord on April 19, 1775.
Genre(s): War Story.

◆ 227. *The Hessian.* New York: Morrow, 1972. 192 pp.
A Quaker family hides a Hessian involved in an inconsequential action near the end of the American Revolution, but the townspeople find and hang him.
Genre(s): War Story.

◆ 228. *Seven Days in June.* Secaucus, NJ: Carol, 1994. 191 pp.
The week before the Battle of Bunker Hill, Evan Feversham, an English surgeon living in Connecticut, is at the center of the action.
Genre(s): War Story.

Fleming, Thomas

229. *Liberty Tavern.* New York: Doubleday, 1976. 502 pp.
Jonathan Gifford, ex-British soldier and owner of Liberty Tavern, dislikes living with people who use patriotism as a pretense for spite.
Genre(s): War Story.

Fletcher, Inglis

◆ 230. *Toil of the Brave.* Indianapolis, IN: Bobbs Merrill, 1946. 547 pp.
Angela Ferrier falls in love with Captain Peter Huntley in Albemarle County before the defeat of the British at the Battle of King's Mountain. (*Series:* Carolina, 10)
Genre(s): War Story; Romance; Family Saga.

◆ 231. *Wicked Lady.* New York: Bantam, 1962. 254 pp.
The British wife of a German landowner uses her wiles to support the British in the Revolution. (*Series:* Carolina, 11)
Genre(s): Family Saga; Romance; War Story.

Ford, Paul Leicester

232. *Janice Meredith.* New York: Dodd, Mead, 1899. 536 pp.
Janice Meredith falls in love with an indentured servant who becomes a general in the Revolutionary Army and enemy of her Tory father.
Genre(s): War Story; Romance.

Forman, James

◆ 233. *The Cow Neck Rebels.* New York: Farrar, Straus and Giroux, 1969. 272 pp.
The Cameron family divides with the locals about the American Revolution before the Battle of Long Island in 1776.

Giles, Janice Holt

234. *Hannah Fowler.* Boston: Houghton Mifflin, 1956. 219 pp.
In 1778, Hannah Moore's father dies while they travel to Boonesborough, and a frontiersman helps her reach Logan's Fort.
Genre(s): Family Saga; Western Fiction.

Glover, Douglas

235. *The Life and Times of Captain N.* New York: Knopf, 1993. 185 pp.
Captain Hendrick Nellis serves the British army in New York City during the American Revolution, while his son longs to be a good patriot.
Genre(s): War Story.

Hatcher, Maynard

236. *Liberty Pole.* Desert, ME: Windswept House, 1987. 200 pp.
In 1775, Luke Cole, 17, works in a sawmill making lumber for the British Navy, but he finds himself on the American ship *Unity* when it engages the British ship *Margaretta* during the Revolution's first naval battle.
Genre(s): War Story.

Heckert, Eleanor

237. *The Golden Rock.* New York: Doubleday, 1971. 232 pp.
The Dutch West Indies offer a trading link for the Americans during the Revolution, especially on St. Eustatius Island.
Genre(s): War Story.

Hodge, Jane Aiken

◆ 238. *Judas Flowering.* New York: Coward-McCann, 1976. 316 pp.
The American Revolution separates Mercy Purchis from her husband, and she has to cope with storms and men who make unwelcome advances.
Genre(s): Romance.

◆ 239. *Wide Is the Water.* New York: Coward-McCann, 1981. 240 pp.
The sequel to *Judas Flowering* finds Mercy and Hart Purchis separated by the Revolution with Hart a prisoner in England and Mercy traveling from Boston to Philadelphia and London to reunite with him.
Genre(s): Romance; War Story.

Jones, Douglas C.

240. *Shadow of the Moon.* New York: Henry Holt, 1995. 470 pp.
Sergeant Bobby, an English immigrant, meets Nalambigi when fighting in Quebec, and he goes West with her after the war.
Genre(s): War Story; Love Story.

Kantor, MacKinlay

241. *Valley Forge.* New York: Evans, 1975. 339 pp.
During the American Revolution, leaders show their courage and their fortitude, especially George Washington.
Genre(s): War Story.

Laity, Sally, and Dianna Crawford

242. *The Embers of Hope.* Wheaton, IL: Tyndale House, 1996. 387 pp.
Emily's life goes up in flames during the American Revolution, and she must rebuild her life and love. (*Series:* Freedom's Holy Light, 5)
Genre(s): Christian Fiction; War Story.

243. *The Torch of Triumph.* Wheaton, IL: Tyndale House, 1997. 421 pp.
After Native Americans capture Evelyn Thomas while she is spying for the American colonies, only her beloved can save her.
Genre(s): War Story; Christian Fiction; Spy Fiction.

◆ May be suitable for young adult readers

Lambdin, Dewey

◆ 244. *The French Admiral.* New York: Donald I.
Fine, 1990. 414 pp.
Alan Lewrie, although unhappy with the Royal Navy in
the sequel to *The King's Coat,* gains a sense of duty as he
participates in the American Revolution.
Genre(s): War Story; Sea Story.

Lancaster, Bruce

245. *The Big Knives.* Boston: Little, Brown, 1964.
371 pp.
George Rogers Clark leads a group of 200 into the Northwest Territory during 1778 to destroy the British supply
headquarters at Detroit.
Genre(s): Adventure Story.

246. *Guns of Burgoyne.* New York: Stokes, 1939.
424 pp.
In 1777, Kurt Ahrens, a young Hessian soldier, takes
command of some of the British General Burgoyne's
guns.
Genre(s): War Story.

247. *The Secret Road.* Boston: Little, Brown,
1952. 259 pp.
Townsend and Andre have activities on Long Island related to their secret service responsibilites in 1780.
Genre(s): War Story.

Martin, William

248. *Annapolis.* New York: Warner Books, 1996.
685 pp.
The Stafford family sends its sons to sea and battles the
Parrish family's desire to recover their Annapolis home,
lost to the Staffords during the Revolution.
Genre(s): Family Saga; War Story; Sea Story.

Mason, F. Van Wyck

249. *Eagle in the Sky.* Philadelphia: Lippincott,
1948. 500 pp.
Three men graduate from medical school in 1780, in the
sequel to *Rivers of Glory,* and continue their careers in
different ways during the American Revolution.
Genre(s): Medical Novel; War Story.

250. *Guns for Rebellion.* Garden City, NY: Doubleday, 1977. 400 pp.
In 1775, Andrew Hunter's loyalty to the British crown is
tested when his assignment is to shell his hometown during the Battle of Bunker Hill.
Genre(s): War Story.

251. *Rivers of Glory.* Philadelphia: Lippincott,
1042. 572 pp.
In the sequel to *Stars on the Sea,* Andrew Warren commands a merchant ship and poses as a Tory so that he can
get supplies in Jamaica.
Genre(s): War Story.

252. *Stars on the Sea.* Philadelphia: Lippincott,
1940. 720 pp.
The sequel to *Three Harbours* features Timothy Bennett,
a young privateersman, as he travels from Rhode Island
to the Bahamas during the Revolution.
Genre(s): Sea Story; War Story.

253. *Wild Horizon.* Boston: Little, Brown, 1966.
399 pp.
A group of people travel west to create a settlement before the battle at King's Mountain, North Carolina.
Genre(s): War Story.

McCrumb, Sharyn

254. *She Walks These Hills.* New York: Scrib-
ner's, 1995. 336 pp.
In the Appalachian wilderness, a pioneer woman mur-
dered in the 18th century meets a present-day escaped
convict.
Award(s): Agatha Award; Anthony Award; Macavity
Award.
Genre(s): Mystery.

Morgan, Robert

255. *The Hinterlands.* Chapel Hill, NC: Algonquin, 1994. 356 pp.
A settler takes his bride into Kentucky in 1771, and as
they develop the land, they raise their family until their
great grandsons build a turnpike in 1845.
Genre(s): Domestic Fiction.

Morris, Gilbert

256. *Arrow of the Almighty.* Minneapolis, MN:
Bethany House, 1997. 320 pp.
Michah Bradford falls in love with a Patriot supporter
and joins the Continental Army, but he simultaneously is
forced to protect a woman of ill repute. (*Series:* Liberty
Bell, 4)
Genre(s): War Story; Romance; Christian Fiction.

257. *The Gentle Rebel.* Minneapolis, MN: Be-
thany House, 1988. 285 pp.
The Winslow family takes part in the American Revolu-
tion. (*Series:* House of Winslow, 4)
Genre(s): Domestic Fiction; Christian Fiction; Family
Saga.

258. *The Holy Warrior.* Minneapolis, MN: Be-
thany House, 1989. 288 pp.
The sons of Nathan Winslow head west on different
trails, where they have both adventure and frustration.
(*Series:* House of Winslow, 6)
Genre(s): Christian Fiction; Family Saga; Adventure
Story.

259. *The Saintly Buccaneer.* Minneapolis, MN:
Bethany House, 1988. 299 pp.
During the American Revolution, the Winslow family
demonstrates both its conflicts and its belief in God. (*Se-
ries:* House of Winslow, 5)
Genre(s): Domestic Fiction; Christian Fiction; Family
Saga; War Story.

260. *Song in a Strange Land.* Minneapolis, MN:
Bethany House, 1996. 320 pp.
Patriotism and a woman tear the Bradford cousins apart.
(*Series:* Liberty Bell, 2)
Genre(s): War Story; Christian Fiction.

261. *Tread upon the Lion.* Minneapolis, MN: Bethany House, 1996. 302 pp.
Sir Leo Rochester hires Abigail Howland of the Winslow family to lure Matthew Bradford into his evil schemes while Clive Gordon falls in love with a Patriot spy and causes conflict in the two branches of the Bradford family. (*Series:* The Liberty Bell, 3)
Genre(s): Christian Fiction.

Nelson, James L.

262. *By Force of Arms.* New York: Pocket Books, 1996. 324 pp.
Isaac Biddlecomb commands his vessel after rising through the ranks before the American Revolution and fights off Captain James Wallace, commander of the *Rose.*
Genre(s): Sea Story; War Story.

263. *The Maddest Idea.* New York: Pocket Books, 1997. 417 pp.
Captain Isaac Biddlecomb leads the British on a chase while searching for powder for Washington's army, after which Major Fitzgerald searches for the traitor who revealed Biddlecomb's route.
Genre(s): Sea Story; War Story.

Oakley, Don

◆ 264. *The Adventure of Christian Fast.* Marietta, GA: Eyrie, 1989. 267 pp.
Christian Fast fights with George Rogers Clark against the British at Detroit, but after Delaware Indians capture him, he eventually becomes a warrior and a member of a raid against his Pennsylvania home during the Revolutionary War.

Page, Elizabeth

265. *The Tree of Liberty.* New York: Holt, Rinehart and Winston, 1939. 985 pp.
Matthew Howard, frontiersman, and his wife, an aristocrat of Tidewater, Virginia, marry before the American Revolution and continue to disagree for the next 30 years as the country grows.
Genre(s): War Story; Domestic Fiction.

Partington, Norman

266. *The Sunshine Patriot.* New York: St. Martin's Press, 1975. 221 pp.
Benedict Arnold undergoes experiences from the beginning of the Revolutionary War leading up to his treason at West Point in 1780.
Genre(s): Biographical Fiction.

Porter, Donald Clayton

267. *Seneca.* New York: Bantam, 1984. 295 pp.
Ghonkaba, a white settler raised by Native Americans, breaks with his Seneca tribe to fight on the side of the American colonists under Washington by forming an elite scouting unit that his daughter Ena joins. (*Series:* White Indian)
Genre(s): War Story; Domestic Fiction; Family Saga.

Pottle, Russ

268. *Patriot Royal.* Williamsburg, VA: Chestnut Hill, 1996. 355 pp.
Charles Royal, scion of a wealthy Boston family, joins the Colonial army during the American Revolution.
Genre(s): Family Saga; War Story; Romance.

Rao, Linda Rae

◆ 269. *Eagles Flying High.* Grand Rapids, MI: Revell, 1995. 301 pp.
Jessica McClaren's father has made a contract, and she must uphold it by giving a mare to a hostile Tory.
Genre(s): Christian Fiction; War Story.

Rayner, William

270. *The World Turned Upside Down.* New York: Morrow, 1970. 223 pp.
A British soldier fighting during the Revolution realizes that he wants nothing to do with the war after his men are ambushed, but he has to undergo several unpleasant situations before he finally reaches the British army as it surrenders at Yorktown.
Genre(s): War Story; Adventure Story.

Roberts, Kenneth Lewis

◆ 271. *Arundel.* Garden City, NY: Doubleday, 1933. 632 pp.
Steven Nason goes to Quebec with Benedict Arnold from Arundel, the Maine province where Nason lives.
Genre(s): War Story.

◆ 272. *Rabble in Arms.* Garden City, NY: Doubleday, 1935. 586 pp.
In the sequel to *Arundel,* the American Congress becomes the enemy of Benedict Arnold's heroics during the campaign ending with the battle of Saratoga.
Genre(s): War Story.

Settle, Mary Lee

273. *O Beulah Land.* New York: Viking, 1956. 368 pp.
The Virginia gentleman Jonathan Lacey scouts and surveys the mountains in 1775, leading a group into an area that the New Light preacher accompanying him calls Beulah, in the sequel to *Prisons.*
Genre(s): Family Saga.

Sherman, Dan

◆ 274. *The Traitor.* New York: Donald I. Fine, 1987. 263 pp.
Patriots become upset with George Washington in 1780, and when Matty Grove investigates the murders of an English officer and his mistress, he finds a conspiracy to use the Revolution for financial gain.
Genre(s): War Story; Spy Fiction.

St. Clare, Katherine

275. *To Tell Me Terrible Lies.* Emmaus, PA: Wainwright, 1993. 335 pp.
Serena Wainwright wants to become the ironmaster on her father's iron plantation, but when she realizes that he

will not make her his heir, she runs away. (*Series:* Wainwright Chronicles, 1)
Genre(s): Romance; War Story.

Thompson, Maurice

276. *Alice of Old Vincennes.* 1900. Bloomington: Indiana University Press, 1985. 419 pp.
In the Northwest Territory, near Vincennes, Native Americans battle the pioneers in 1778.
Genre(s): War Story.

Turnbull, Agnes Sligh

277. *The Day Must Dawn.* New York: Macmillan, 1942. 483 pp.
A Scots-Irish family of western Pennsylvania finds itself in the middle of the Revolutionary War.
Genre(s): War Story; Domestic Fiction.

278. *The King's Orchard.* Boston: Houghton Mifflin, 1963. 467 pp.
James O'Hara emigrates to America before the Revolution, becomes an officer, and makes a fortune in land and industry.
Genre(s): War Story.

Wheeler, Guy

279. *Cato's War.* New York: Macmillan, 1980. 320 pp.
An officer sent from England to America during the Revolution witnesses battles in the Carolinas and at Yorktown.
Genre(s): War Story.

White, Richard

◆ 280. *Jordan Freeman Was My Friend.* New York: Four Walls Eight Windows, 1994. 223 pp.
Freed slave Jordan Freeman becomes Billy Latham's friend when Jordan saves him from a bull, and Billy is the water boy at Fort Griswald when Jordan is massacred.
Genre(s): War Story.

Williams, Ben Ames

281. *Come Spring.* Boston: Houghton Mifflin, 1940. 866 pp.
Although the Revolution rages to the south, the people in Union, Maine, worry more about Indian raids.
Genre(s): War Story.

Wilson, Dorothy Clarke

282. *Queen Dolley.* Garden City, NY: Doubleday, 1987. 373 pp.
Dolley Madison, disowned by Quakers for marrying a nonbeliever, is the appropriate wife for her quiet husband.
Genre(s): Biographical Fiction.

Winter, J. D.

283. *First Trail Drive.* New York: M. Evans, 1994. 204 pp.
A New Orleans businessman hires Ben Cross and his uncle to gather a herd of Texas longhorns and drive them to Mississippi to feed Spanish and American forces fighting the British.
Genre(s): Western Fiction.

Wolf, William J.

284. *Benedict Arnold.* Ashfield, MA: Paideia, 1990. 413 pp.
Filled with contradictory behavior, Benedict Arnold showed himself to have superb leadership qualities and incontrollable hostily toward those he thought had insulted him.
Genre(s): Biographical Fiction; War Story.

Wright, Don

285. *The Captives.* New York: Tor, 1987. 448 pp.
In the sequel to *The Woodsman*, the British attack two Kentucky settlements, and their Native American allies capture Susan Patterson and her daughter, but her husband tracks them.
Genre(s): War Story.

1784-1814
The Early United States

Ankenbruck, John

286. *The Voice of the Turtle.* Fort Wayne, IN: News, 1974. 164 pp.
In the late 18th century, Little Turtle functions as the chief of the Miami tribe in Michigan.
Genre(s): Biographical Fiction.

Anness, Milford E.

287. *Song of Metamoris.* New York: Caxton, 1964. 304 pp.
In 1811, Tecumseh and his brother Metamoris try to protect their lands from the whites who want them, but they lose at the battle of Tippecanoe.
Genre(s): Biographical Fiction; War Story.

Atherton, Gertrude Franklin Horn

288. *Rezanov.* New York: Cupples, 1906. 320 pp.
The Russian Rezanov goes to California in 1806 and tries to gain control of trade in San Francisco.
Genre(s): Biographical Fiction; Western Fiction.

Benchley, Nathaniel

289. *Portrait of a Scoundrel.* Garden City, NY: Doubleday, 1979. 300 pp.
After the American Revolution, James Greenleaf, a well-connected Bostonian, joins a financier in an attempt to gain a monopoly of the unbuilt national capital's real estate.
Genre(s): Biographical Fiction.

Beyea, Basil

290. *Notorious Eliza.* New York: Simon And Schuster, 1978. 351 pp.
Betsy Bowen arrives in New York in 1794 and changes her name to Eliza before she becomes the mistress of men including Alexander Hamilton and Aaron Burr, and tricks Stephen Jumel into marrying her, in the sequel to *The Golden Mistress.*
Genre(s): Biographical Fiction; Domestic Fiction.

Bontemps, Arna

291. *Black Thunder.* 1935. Boston: Beacon, 1992. 224 pp.
Gabriel Prosser, a slave in Virginia, organizes a revolt to avenge the death of another slave around 1800.

Brick, John

292. *Rogues' Kingdom.* Garden City, NY: Doubleday, 1965. 301 pp.
Horse thieves in upper New York state prosper until members of the family fall in love.
Genre(s): Love Story.

Bristow, Gwen

293. *Deep Summer.* New York: Crowell, 1937. 258 pp.
Judith Sheramy travels south to Louisiana with her Puritan Connecticut farmer family, falls in love with the son of an aristocratic South Carolina family, and marries him.
Genre(s): Family Saga.

Brown, Dee Alexander

294. *Creek Mary's Blood.* New York: Holt, Rinehart and Winston, 1980. 401 pp.
Creek Mary's grandson Dane tells her story when he is 90—the story of frontiersmen crushing the Native Americans through battle and sweet lies.
Genre(s): Western Fiction.

Brown, Rita Mae

◆ 295. *Dolley.* New York: Bantam, 1994. 382 pp.
Dolley Madison helps to defend Washington from the British during 1814.
Genre(s): War Story.

296. *Murder at Monticello: Or, Old Sins.* New York: Bantam, 1994. 288 pp.
Mary Minor Harry Haristeen, postmistress of Crozet, Virginia, finds the journals a murdered archaeologist had discovered in the course of his work at Monticello, and uses them to solve a 200-year-old mystery.
Genre(s): Mystery.

Burland, Brian

297. *Stephen Decatur, the Devil, and the Endymion.* London: Allen and Unwin, 1975. 128 pp.
Stephen Decatur fights on the sea during the War of 1812.
Genre(s): Biographical Fiction; Sea Story.

Burns, Ron

298. *Enslaved.* New York: St. Martin's Press, 1994. 262 pp.
Thomas Jefferson asks Harrison Hull, a soldier and frontier adventurer, to find the two missing slaves that belong to his nephew.
Genre(s): Mystery.

299. *The Mysterious Death of Meriwether Lewis.* New York: St. Martin's Press, 1992. 242 pp.
Neither ornithologist Alexander Wilson nor explorer Harrison Hull believe that Meriwether Lewis committed suicide in 1809 at a Tennessee inn, and they travel to the area to investigate.
Genre(s): Mystery.

Carmer, Carl Lamson

300. *Genesee Fever.* New York: Farrar and Rinehart, 1941. 360 pp.
Nathan Hart, a schoolteacher who participated in the Whiskey Rebellion, seeks refuge in New York State's Genesee region with Colonel Williamson.
Genre(s): War Story.

Charbonneau, Louis

301. *Trail.* New York: Doubleday, 1989. 506 pp.
The story of Lewis and Clark comes not only from themselves but from the dog on their expedition named Seaman.
Genre(s): Adventure Story.

Chase-Riboud, Barbara

◆ 302. *The President's Daughter.* New York: Crown, 1994. 467 pp.
Harriet, daughter of Thomas Jefferson and his slave Sally Hemings in the sequel to *Sally Hemings*, passes as a white person in post-Revolutionary Philadelphia but fears danger for her husband and her children.
Genre(s): Domestic Fiction.

303. *Sally Hemings.* New York: Viking, 1979. 348 pp.
Sally Hemings lives with Thomas Jefferson as his quadroon slave for 38 years, bearing him many children.
Genre(s): Biographical Fiction; Love Story.

Clague, Maryhelen

304. *So Wondrous Free.* New York: Stein and Day, 1978. 314 pp.
To escape the lechery of a master, Nabby Colson, an indentured servant, moves between the two armies of the American Revolution, with lovers on both sides.
Genre(s): War Story.

Coldsmith, Don

305. *Thunderstick.* New York: Doubleday, 1993. 182 pp.
Singing Wolf assumes that he will marry Rain after he has become a man in his first hunt, but White Feathers shows up with a thunderstick, or a musket, that attracts Rain.
Genre(s): Western Fiction.

Cooper, James Fenimore

◆ 306. *The Prairie.* New York: Dodd Mead, 1827. 566 pp.
The sequel to *The Pioneers* finds Natty going West and opposing the destruction of the land of the animals.
Genre(s): War Story.

Courlander, Harold

307. *The African.* New York: Crown, 1967. 311 pp.
Sold into slavery in his native Dahomey, Hwesuhunu travels to Georgia in 1802, and after his experiences there, plans an escape to Ohio.

Davis, John

308. *The Post-Captain.* 1806. New York: Garland, 1977. 300 pp.
Native Americans capture Thomas Keith in 1794 from his post as fort captain.
Genre(s): Biographical Fiction.

De Blasis, Celeste

309. *Wild Swan.* New York: Bantam, 1984. 574 pp.
In 1810, Alexandria Thaine Falcomer comes to Maryland from Kent with her husband to start a horse-breeding farm.
Genre(s): Romance; Family Saga.

Delmar, Vina

310. *A Time for Titans.* San Diego, CA: Harcourt Brace, 1974. 336 pp.
The slave revolt of Toussaint L'Ouverture in Haiti against Napoleon's French regime changes the course of American history under the presidency of Thomas Jefferson.
Genre(s): Political Fiction.

Deveraux, Jude

311. *River Lady.* New York: Pocket Books, 1985. 390 pp.
In the late 18th century, Leah Simmons tries to change her downtrodden and abused life by dreaming about Wesley Stanford, a wealthy plantation owner who loves someone else, but he is forced to marry Leah, and when he takes her to Kentucky from Virginia, he begins to appreciate her.
Genre(s): Romance.

Eagle, Sarah

312. *Lady Vengeance.* New York: Harper, 1995. 341 pp.
Celia Tregaron goes from Baltimore to England to kill the Earl of Ashmore for murdering her brother, and she falls in love instead.
Genre(s): Romance.

Ehle, John

313. *The Journey of August King.* New York: Harper and Row, 1971. 218 pp.
August King, a community leader in North Carolina, helps a young runaway female slave in 1810 in the sequel to *The Land Breakers*.
Genre(s): Family Saga.

Fine, Warren

◆ **314.** *In the Animal Kingdom.* New York: Knopf, 1971. 256 pp.
A young man goes westward in the late 18th century to look at the beauty of America.
Genre(s): Adventure Story.

Forbes, Esther

315. *The Running of the Tide.* Boston: Houghton Mifflin, 1948. 632 pp.
The Inmans, a family of Salem ship owners, rise to wealth, but their fortunes decline after the War of 1812.

Fowler, Robert H.

316. *Voyage to Honor.* Mechanicsburg, PA: Stackpole, 1996. 552 pp.
Lovejoy Martin boards Admiral Perry's ship at the Battle of Lake Erie, and after sailing to Washington, defends the Baltimore shipyards in the War of 1812.
Genre(s): War Story; Sea Story.

Fuller, Iola

317. *The Loon Feather.* San Diego: Harcourt Brace, 1940. 456 pp.
Oneta, an Ojibwa and daughter of Tecumseh, chief of the Loon tribe, tells of the busiest fur trading years on Mackinac Island in the early 1800s.
Genre(s): Western Fiction.

Gerson, Noel B.

318. *Clear for Action!* Garden City, NY: Doubleday, 1970. 254 pp.
David Farragut becomes a midshipman at 10 years old, takes his first command, albeit temporary, at 13, and learns everything possible about ships and the sea on his rise to admiral.
Genre(s): Biographical Fiction; War Story; Sea Story.

319. *Old Hickory.* Garden City, NY: Doubleday, 1964. 372 pp.
Andrew Jackson hates the English and loves both his wife and Tennessee as he leads troops against the British.
Genre(s): Biographical Fiction; War Story.

Giles, Janice Holt

320. *Johnny Osage.* Boston: Houghton Mifflin, 1960. 350 pp.
Johnny Fowler, son of Hannah Fowler, in the sequel to *The Believers*, moves west and earns the name Osage because of his close relationship to the Osage Indians.
Genre(s): Adventure Story; Family Saga.

Gulick, Bill

321. *Distant Trails, 1805-1836.* Garden City, NY: Doubleday, 1988. 179 pp.
Fur traders want Indian furs, and missionaries want to convert them before Matt Crane and the Nez Percé Moon Bird have a son called Tall Bird.
Genre(s): Western Fiction.

Hale, Edward Everett

322. *Man Without a Country.* 1863. Englewood Cliffs, NJ: Prentice Hall, 1987. 106 pp.
Philip Nolan, an officer in the United States Army, is tried as part of the Aaron Burr conspiracy and is convicted to life on a naval vessel where he stays for 57 years.
Genre(s): Sea Story.

Harris, Cyril

323. *Street of Knives.* Boston: Little, Brown, 1950. 370 pp.
Aaron Burr journeys westward to Mexico in 1805 with his wife.
Genre(s): Biographical Fiction.

Hart, Catherine

324. *Charmed.* New York: Zebra, 1996. 408 pp.
Nichole Swan goes to Ohio in 1813 and finds herself in the presence of Silver Thorn, Tecumseh's handsome twin brother, who wants to know the future of the Shawnee.
Genre(s): Time Travel; Romance.

Heidish, Marcy

◆ **325.** *Miracles.* New York: New American Library, 1984. 312 pp.
A priest gathering information about Elizabeth Seton to support her nomination to sainthood at first doubts her worthiness.
Genre(s): Christian Fiction; Biographical Fiction.

Henke, Shirl

326. *Deep as the Rivers.* New York: St. Martin's Press, 1997. 400 pp.
After his marriage ends, Colonel Samuel Shelby goes west on a secret mission for President Madison, and he meets independent beauty Olivia St. Etienne, who saves him from assassins but who is not interested in becoming his mistress.
Genre(s): War Story; Romance.

Henry, Will

327. *The Gates of the Mountains.* New York: Random House, 1963. 306 pp.
A Native American of mixed heritage joins the Lewis and Clark expedition for the adventure.
Award(s): Western Writers of America Spur Award.
Genre(s): Adventure Story; Western Fiction.

Hill, Ruth Beebe

328. *Hanta Yo.* Garden City, NY: Doubleday, 1979. 834 pp.
The Teton Sioux make their seasonal moves across the plains from 1794 through 1835 during which two males find a lasting friendship.
Genre(s): Western Fiction.

Hodge, Jane Aiken

◆ 329. *Savannah Purchase.* Garden City, NY: Doubleday, 1971. 205p pp.
Two French cousins who look like twins trade places in Savannah while one of them plots to free Napoleon with a ship and a few men in the sequel to *Wide Is the Water.*
Genre(s): Romance.

Hoff, B. J.

330. *Cloth of Heaven.* Wheaton, IL: Tyndale House, 1997. 400 pp.
Not as successful in America as he would like, Cavan Sheridan cannot bring his sister from Ireland, but after another Irish immigrant hires him, he has hopes of success. (*Series:* Song of Erin, 1)
Genre(s): Christian Fiction; Romance.

Hoffmann, Peggy

331. *My Dear Cousin.* New York: Harcourt Brace, 1970. 435 pp.
The British Ambassador to the United States falls in love with an American woman even though he has vowed not to do so.
Genre(s): War Story; Romance.

Hotchkiss, Bill

332. *Ammahabas.* New York: Norton, 1983. 350 pp.
In the sequel to *The Medicine Calf,* Jim Beckwourth continues his life as a mountain man, Native American chief, and African American hero.
Genre(s): Biographical Fiction.

333. *The Medicine Calf.* New York: Norton, 1981. 408 pp.
The Crow make Jim Beckwourth, son of a Virginia aristocrat and a half-white slave, their chief and call him Medicine Calf only five years after they capture him.
Genre(s): Biographical Fiction; Western Fiction.

Hotchner, A. E.

334. *Louisiana Purchase.* New York: Carroll and Graf, 1996. 383 pp.
Guy Laroule, a friend of Louis XV's mistress, Madame de Pompadour, is banished to the French territory of Louisiana, where he marries, loses his holdings, and goes up the river toward the to-be-founded St. Louis.

House, R. C.

◆ 335. *Warhawk.* New York: M. Evans, 1993. 196 pp.
When Jacob Lyman, a mountain man and a trapper, rescues widowed Rachel England from a bear, he falls in love with her and vows to find her son, who was captured by Native Americans five years earlier.
Genre(s): Western Fiction; Love Story; Adventure Story.

Houston, James A.

336. *Eagle Song.* San Diego, CA: Harcourt Brace, 1983. 362 pp.
From 1803 to 1805, a survivor from the Nootkan massacre of an English trading ship crew watches the tribe's migrations, trading, whale hunts, and potlatches.

Hubbard, L. Ron

◆ 337. *Buckskin Brigades.* 1937. Los Angeles: Bridge, 1987. 316 pp.
In the early 19th century, Alexander McGlincy tries to defeat Yellow Hair, a white youth raised as a Blackfoot, in the fur trade.
Genre(s): Western Fiction.

Huston, James A.

338. *Counterpoint.* Lawrenceville, VA: Brunswick, 1987. 629 pp.
William Henry Harrison and Tecumseh, both born in the mid-1700s, rise among their respective people to become leaders, but the two men meet at the Battle of the Thames in Canada in 1813.
Genre(s): War Story; Political Fiction; Biographical Fiction.

Innis, Pauline B.

339. *Gold in the Blue Ridge.* Washington, DC: Devon, 1973. 249 pp.
Thomas Jefferson Beale went with a group of men to the West to find gold and silver, and after Native Americans killed them, someone took their treasure back to Bedford County, Virginia, and hid it in a cave.
Genre(s): Mystery; Western Fiction.

Johnston, Terry C.

340. *Carry the Wind.* New York: Delacorte, 1982. 571 pp.
Joshiah Paddock kills his lover's fiancé and flees to the West where an old mountain man protects him.
Genre(s): Western Fiction.

◆ 341. *Dance on the Wind.* New York: Bantam, 1995. 517 pp.
In 1810, Titus Bass decides that he cannot tolerate farming or his father so he leaves his Kentucky home to find out what lies in the West.
Genre(s): Western Fiction; Bildungsroman (Coming of Age).

Jones, Douglas C.

◆ 342. *This Savage Race.* New York: Henry Holt, 1993. 320 pp.
The Fawley family settles in Arkansas after the Revolutionary War, surviving their first winter by eating the dog given them by a Cherokee, but they begin to prosper after moving when the New Madrid earthquake destroys their land.
Genre(s): Western Fiction.

Judd, Cameron

◆ 343. *Crockett of Tennessee.* New York: Bantam, 1994. 528 pp.
Davy Crockett begins to roam at 14 when he goes on a cattle drive to Virginia and continues wandering as an explorer, soldier, and politician.
Genre(s): Biographical Fiction.

Kunstler, James Howard

344. *An Embarrassment of Riches.* New York: Dial, 1985. 276 pp.
In 1803, Samuel, 19, accompanies his famous uncle William Walker, a botanist, when President Jefferson requests that Walker explore the wilderness between the Ohio River and the Gulf of Mexico to find a megatherium (*Series:* giant sloth)
Genre(s): Adventure Story; Humorous Fiction.

Laity, Sally, and Dianna Crawford

◆ 345. *The Tempering Blaze.* Wheaton, IL: Tyndale House, 1995. 392 pp.
Two couples become involved in the Boston Tea Party episode before the American Revolution, and it changes their lives. (*Series:* Freedom's Holy Light, 3)
Genre(s): Christian Fiction; War Story.

Lamb, Arnette

346. *True Heart.* New York: Pocket Books, 1998. 307 pp.
In post-Revolutionary America, Virignia is sold into indentured servitude, and when she is freed after 10 years, she reunites with Cameron, and they return to Scotland, where he tries to get her to marry him.
Genre(s): Romance.

Lawrence, Margaret K.

347. *Blood Red Roses.* New York: Avon, 1997. 336 pp.
In 1785, midwife Hannah Trevor tries to protect her daughter from becoming an indentured servant after the death of her husband.
Genre(s): Mystery.

348. *Hearts and Bones.* New York: Avon, 1996. 307 pp.
In 1786, Hannah Trevor, a midwife and healer in Rufford, Maine, becomes the female witness to ensure that murdered Anthea Emory's body is treated properly, and she begins investigating the death since one of the men accused is the father of her deaf child.
Genre(s): Mystery.

Mackin, Jeanne

◆ 349. *The Frenchwoman.* New York: St. Martin's Press, 1989. 387 pp.
As a seamstress in the court of Queen Marie Antoinette, Julienne marries a young officer who fought with Lafayette in America, and when he dies, she flees to Pennsylvania where Royalists try to recreate their lives in France.
Genre(s): War Story.

Mason, David P.

350. *Five Dollars a Scalp.* Huntsville, AL: Strode, 1975. 202 pp.
In the Creek War of 1813, a massacre at Fort Mims, Alabama, decimates the tribe's power.
Genre(s): War Story.

Meyers, Maan

◆ 351. *The High Constable.* New York: Doubleday, 1994. 336 pp.
In the early 19th century, the New York high constable contacts physician John Tonneman when a man is suffocated after being buried alive and the skull of a young woman is discovered near his body.
Genre(s): Mystery.

Miller, Isabel

352. *Patience and Sarah.* New York: McGraw Hill, 1972. 192 pp.
Patience and Sarah meet in the early 19th century, and when they fall in love, family pressures force them to leave their homes and buy a farm together.
Genre(s): Bildungsroman (Coming of Age); Love Story.

Moore, Ruth

353. *Sarah Walked over the Mountain.* New York: Morrow, 1979. 252 pp.
Sarah Thomas Scott follows her husband to the New World from Wales and eventually discovers that he has another wife.
Genre(s): Domestic Fiction.

Morris, Gilbert, and Aaron McCarver

354. *Beyond the Quiet Hills.* Minneapolis, MN: Bethany House, 1997. 351 pp.
Hawk Spencer, who settles in Tennessee on the frontier, and his stepbrother fall in love with the same woman. (*Series:* Spirit of Appalachia, 2)
Genre(s): Christian Fiction; Western Fiction.

355. *Over the Misty Mountain.* Minneapolis, MN: Bethany House, 1997. 334 pp.
After his wife dies in childbirth, Josh Hawk Spencer goes west into the wilderness where he meets another pioneer, Elizabeth MacNeal. (*Series:* The Spirit of Appalachia, 1)
Genre(s): Western Fiction; Christian Fiction.

Mourning Dove

◆ 356. *Cogewea, the Half Blood.* Lincoln, NE: University of Nebraska Press, 1981. 302 pp.
Cogewea, half Okinaga, grows up worrying whether she should live with the Okanagans or with the whites, but she never feels part of either group.
Genre(s): Domestic Fiction.

Munn, Vella

357. *Wind Warrior.* New York: St. Martin's Press, 1998. 384 pp.
Corporal Sebastian Rodriguez, a Spanish military man who abuses his wife and children, confronts Black Wolf,

a Chumash warrior trying to save his people from the invaders.
Genre(s): Political Fiction; War Story.

Nevin, David

358. *1812.* New York: Forge, 1996. 445 pp.
Players in the War of 1812 and after include Dolley and James Madison, Andrew and Rachel Jackson, and Winfield Scott.
Genre(s): War Story.

Nissenson, Hugh

359. *The Tree of Life.* New York: Harper and Row, 1985. 224 pp.
Thomas Keene keeps a diary around the time of the War of 1812 in Ohio in which two prominent figures are Fanny Cooper, the woman he loves, and John Chapman, now known as Johnny Appleseed.
Genre(s): Biographical Fiction.

O'Neal, Reagan

360. *The Fallon Pride.* New York: Forge, 1996. 384 pp.
Captain Robert Fallon sails around the world as merchant, patriot, and lover of many, including his sister, with the pirate, Murad Reis, following him.
Genre(s): Sea Story; War Story; Romance.

Peck, Richard

361. *This Family of Women.* New York: Delacorte, 1983. 393 pp.
Five women present four generations of their family as they either go West or east to London, and experience the upheavals of settlement and relationships with men.
Genre(s): Family Saga.

Phillips, Caryl

362. *Crossing the River.* New York: Knopf, 1994. 237 pp.
Three children leave Africa in the 18th century to become slaves, and the life of each one is recounted.
Genre(s): Domestic Fiction.

Price, Eugenia

◆ 363. *Bright Captivity.* Garden City, NY: Doubleday, 1991. 631 pp.
Anne Couper falls in love with a British lieutenant in the early 19th century on St. Simons Island.
Genre(s): War Story; Romance.

◆ 364. *Don Juan McQueen.* Philadelphia: Lippincott, 1974. 384 pp.
Jon McQueen comes to Florida after the American Revolution, and when his wife joines him, they settle in St. Augustine.
Genre(s): Romance.

◆ 365. *Lighthouse.* Philadelphia: Lippincott, 1971. 342 pp.
James Gould leaves Massachusetts for St. Simons Island to survey timber for the new American navy in 1791,

stays to marry a Savannah woman, and realizes a dream when he has a chance to build a lighthouse on the island.
Genre(s): Romance; Family Saga.

◆ 366. *Savannah.* Garden City, NY: Doubleday, 1983. 595 pp.
Mark Browning enjoys the gracious society of Savannah in the early 19th century and becomes involved in several questionable relationships. (*Series:* Savannah Quartet, 1)
Genre(s): Family Saga; Domestic Fiction; Romance.

Prose, Francine

367. *Marie Laveau.* New York: Putnam, 1977. 342 pp.
Marie Laveau, the New Orleans voodoo queen, is healer magician, and enchantress until her death in 1881.
Genre(s): Biographical Fiction.

Rao, Linda Rae

368. *Of Eagles and Ravens.* Grand Rapids, MI: Revell, 1996. 288 pp.
The Macklins endure the trauma of the War of 1812.
Genre(s): War Story; Christian Fiction; Romance.

369. *Ordeal at Iron Mountain.* Grand Rapids, MI: Revell, 1995. 200 pp.
Cherokees battle greedy speculators who want their land after the American Revolution in North Carolina's Chalequah Valley.
Genre(s): War Story; Christian Fiction.

Receveur, Betty Layman

370. *Kentucky Home.* New York: Ballantine, 1995. 409 pp.
Kitty Gentry recollects life in 1792 when she and her second husband, Roman, came to Washington, DC, after his election as Kentucky's first senator.
Genre(s): Family Saga.

Rhodes, Jewell Parker

371. *Voodoo Dreams.* New York: St. Martin's Press, 1993. 448 pp.
Marie Laveau comes to New Orleans with her grandmother, a former slave, where she marries Jacques, a black sailor, to escape being killed for her voodoo powers, and when she eventually accepts them, she becomes independent.
Genre(s): Biographical Fiction.

Richter, Conrad

◆ 372. *The Fields.* New York: Knopf, 1946. 288 pp.
In the sequel to *The Trees*, Sayward makes a farm out of the wilderness of southern Ohio and raises her family there.
Genre(s): Domestic Fiction.

◆ 373. *The Town.* New York: Knopf, 1950. 433 pp.
The sequel to *The Fields* shows Sayward Wheeler and her husband moving from a cabin into a mansion and their children moving into their own homes.
Award(s): Pulitzer Prize.
Genre(s): Family Saga.

◆ 374. *The Trees.* New York: Knopf, 1940. 302 pp.
Sayward, the oldest daughter in the Luckett family, becomes determined that the family will survive in the wilderness of Ohio.
Genre(s): Domestic Fiction; Family Saga.

Rikhoff, Jean

375. *Buttes Landing.* New York: Dial, 1973. 440 pp.
In 1807, Odder Buttes begins building in the Adirondak Mountains and marries Emily, only to have her die during childbirth.

Roberts, Kenneth Lewis

◆ 376. *Captain Caution.* Garden City, NY: Doubleday, 1934. 310 pp.
In the sequel to *The Lively Lady*, the merchant ship *Olive Branch* is captured, and Dan Marvin tries to save the daughter of the dead captain.
Genre(s): War Story.

◆ 377. *The Lively Lady.* Garden City, NY: Doubleday, 1931. 374 pp.
In the sequel to *Rabble in Arms*, Richard, the son of Steven Nason from Arundel, captains the *Lively Lady* and becomes a prisoner in England.
Genre(s): War Story; Sea Story.

◆ 378. *Lydia Bailey.* Garden City, NY: Doubleday, 1947. 499 pp.
A Maine lawyer goes to Haiti to rescue a girl just as Napoleon attempts to overtake the government and the slaves begin their revolt.
Genre(s): War Story; Sea Story.

Robson, Lucia St. Clair

379. *Light a Distant Fire.* New York: Ballantine, 1988. 431 pp.
Osceola leads the Seminole tribe against the Army until he dies in prison in 1838.
Genre(s): Biographical Fiction.

Roesch, E. P.

◆ 380. *Ashana.* New York: Random House, 1990. 404 pp.
The Russian Alexander Baranof takes Ashana, an Alaskan native engaged to Jabila, hostage in 1790, along with 1,000 others, to serve him and the other Russians.
Genre(s): Family Saga.

Ross, Dana Fuller

◆ 381. *Westward.* New York: Bantam, 1992. 477 pp.
Clay and Jefferson Holt leave the Ohio Valley for the West in the early 1800s after a local feud. (*Series:* Wagons West, 1)
Genre(s): Western Fiction; Adventure Story.

Schreiner, Samuel Agnew

382. *The Possessors and the Possessed.* New York: Arbor House, 1980. 500 pp.
The Van Alens are a force in New York City business and society between the years of Washington and Lincoln.
Genre(s): Domestic Fiction; Family Saga.

Sherman, Jory

◆ 383. *The Medicine Horn.* New York: Tor, 1991. 278 pp.
In 1793, Lem, a farmer, and his wife Roberta, a lover of pleasure, leave Virginia for Kentucky where they have a child, Morgan, and when Morgan is 16, he and his father go west. (*Series:* The Buckskinners Trilogy, 1)
Award(s): Western Writers of America Spur Award.
Genre(s): Western Fiction.

384. *Trapper's Moon.* New York: Forge, 1994. 286 pp.
Lem Hawkes and his son Morgan head for the Rockies from St. Louis to become trappers. (*Series:* The Buckskinner Trilogy, 2)
Genre(s): Adventure Story.

Simms, William Gilmore

385. *The Cassique of Kiawah.* 1859. Gainesville, GA: Magnolia, 1990. 600 pp.
The members of Charleston, South Carolina, society reveal their greed and hypocrisy in the early 19th century.
Genre(s): Domestic Fiction.

Slate, Sam J.

386. *As Long as the Rivers Run.* New York: Doubleday, 1972. 306 pp.
The Cherokee try to build a separate nation for themselves within the boundaries of contemporary Georgia from 1813 to 1828, but Andrew Jackson decides to take their land for white settlers and move them out.
Genre(s): Political Fiction.

387. *Satan's Back Yard.* New York: Doubleday, 1974. 254 pp.
James Madison serves as president as the United States acquires the Florida territory after vying with Britain, Spain, and Mexico.
Genre(s): Political Fiction.

Street, James

388. *Oh, Promised Land.* New York: Dial, 1940. 816 pp.
After Indians kill their parents, Sam Dabney and Honoria travel from their parents' grave into Mississippi.

Tallant, Robert

389. *The Voodoo Queen.* 1956. Gretna, LA: Pelican, 1983. 314 pp.
Marie Laveau, a beautiful quadroon in New Orleans, weaves her voodoo spells as "America's last witch."
Genre(s): Biographical Fiction.

Thom, James Alexander

◆ 390. *Panther in the Sky.* New York: Ballantine, 1989. 655 pp.
Tecumseh, born under a shooting star, becomes the leader of tribes who want to fight for their freedom in the late 18th and early 19th century.
Award(s): Western Writers of America Spur Award.
Genre(s): Biographical Fiction.

◆ May be suitable for young adult readers

Thornton, Lawrence

◆ 391. *Ghost Woman.* New York: Ticknor and Fields, 1992. 302 pp.
After a friar arranges for a native woman to come from an island to the California mainland as an example of a converted Christian, her host rapes her.

Trell, Max

392. *The Small Gods and Mr. Barnum.* New York: McCall, 1971. 230 pp.
P.T. Barnum makes people believe almost anything with his hype about his "Greatest Show on Earth."
Genre(s): Biographical Fiction; Fantastic Literature.

Turner, William Oliver

393. *Call the Beast Thy Brother.* New York: Doubleday, 1973. 206 pp.
Primitive Haida tribesmen capture and hold missionary Alexander Cargo and his assistant as their slaves during the 19th century, and both begin to adjust to the Haida ways.
Genre(s): Adventure Story.

Vidal, Gore

394. *Burr.* New York: Random House, 1973. 430 pp.
Aaron Burr tells his biographer details of his life, including his duel with Alexander Hamilton and his two marriages. (*Series:* American Chronicle, 1)
Genre(s): Biographical Fiction.

Wellman, Paul Iselin

395. *The Iron Mistress.* Garden City, NY: Doubleday, 1951. 404 pp.
James Bowie lives a hard but full life in the West.
Genre(s): Biographical Fiction; Western Fiction.

Wideman, John Edgar

396. *The Cattle Killing.* New York: Mariner, 1996. 212 pp.
An African American novelist dreams his way into 1793, during which an epidemic of yellow fever sweeps the city, and white citizens blame the blacks for the pestilence.
Genre(s): Domestic Fiction; Medical Novel.

Williams, Bronwyn

397. *The Warfield Bride.* New York: New American Library, 1994. 384 pp.
Penn Warfield wants all of his brothers married, so he chooses a mail-order bride for his brother, but when the pregnant widow arrives on the Outer Banks of North Carolina, he himself falls in love with her.
Genre(s): Romance.

Wilson, Dorothy Clarke

◆ 398. *Lincoln's Mothers.* Garden City, NY: Doubleday, 1981. 423 pp.
Two women in Abe Lincoln's life, his mother Nancy Hanks and his stepmother Sally Bush, encourage him to educate himself.
Genre(s): Biographical Fiction; Domestic Fiction.

Worcester, Donald Emmet

399. *Gone to Texas.* New York: M. Evans, 1993. 214 pp.
Ellis Bean leaves Tennessee in 1800 for Texas, but after Spanish soldiers capture him, he becomes deeply involved in Mexico's political life.
Genre(s): Biographical Fiction; Western Fiction.

Zelazny, Roger, and Gerald Hausman

400. *Wilderness.* New York: Forge, 1994. 304 pp.
In amazing escapes, Jack Colter runs over mountains barefoot for 150 miles in 1808 trying to escape Blackfoot warriors, and in 1823, a bear mauls Hugh Glass, and he must crawl a long way to civilization.
Genre(s): Adventure Story.

1815-1845
Early Westward Expansion

Adams, Samuel Hopkins

401. *Canal Town.* New York: Random House, 1944. 465 pp.
When a young doctor tries to improve sanitary conditions in Palmyra while men build the Erie Canal, he faces the hostility of townspeople.
Genre(s): Medical Novel.

Agnew, James B.

402. *Eggnog Riot.* San Rafael, CA: Presidio, 1979. 211 pp.
In 1826, on Christmas Day at West Point, 90 cadets tear the barracks apart and face court martials.
Genre(s): Adventure Story; Legal Story; Political Fiction.

Alter, Judy

403. *Jessie.* New York: Bantam, 1995. 436 pp.
Jessie Benton leaves home at 17 to marry John Fremont, and after going West with him, she supports his various political aspirations.
Genre(s): Biographical Fiction; Western Fiction.

Berry, Don

404. *Moontrap.* New York: Viking, 1962. 339 pp.
A mountain man comes to Oregon Territory, marries an Indian, and attempts to farm.
Award(s): Western Writers of America Spur Award.
Genre(s): Western Fiction; Adventure Story.

405. *To Build a Ship.* New York: Viking, 1963. 209 pp.
A small community trying to survive on the Oregon Territory coast decides to build a ship as a vehicle for communicating with others.
Genre(s): Adventure Story; Sea Story.

406. *Trask.* New York: Viking, 1969. 373 pp.
Elbridge Trask records his experiences as a homesteader in Oregon Territory who negotiated with the native Americans there, the Killamooks and the Clatsops.
Genre(s): Western Fiction; Adventure Story.

Bryan, Jack Yeaman

407. *Come to the Bower.* New York: Viking, 1963. 462 pp.
A young lawyer describes the Texas war for independence beginning in 1835.
Genre(s): War Story.

Byrd, Max

◆ 408. *Jackson.* New York: Bantam, 1997. 421 pp.
David Chase has the task of writing a biography of Andrew Jackson in 1828, and when he uncovers information that would kill Jackson's bid for the presidency, he must decide what to do.
Genre(s): Biographical Fiction.

Cable, Mary

409. *Avery's Knot.* New York: Putnam, 1981. 238 pp.
Ephraim K. Avery is the first clergyman in the United States tried for murder in the case of Sarah Maria Cornell, who was found in a hayfield in 1832.
Genre(s): Legal Story.

Capps, Benjamin

410. *Woman Chief.* Garden City, NY: Doubleday, 1979. 229 pp.
Absaroka Amazon, a woman captured at 10 by the Crow, becomes a leader in the tribe in the early 19th century.
Genre(s): Biographical Fiction; Western Fiction.

Carlisle, Henry

411. *Voyage to the First of December.* New York: Putnam, 1972. 256 pp.
On December 1, 1842, a midshipman (son of the Secretary of War) and two seamen were hanged on the brig *Somers* for mutiny, and no one knows if they were actually guilty of the accusation.
Genre(s): Sea Story.

Charbonneau, Eileen

◆ 412. *Rachel LeMoyne.* New York: Forge, 1998. 320 pp.
In 1832, Rachel LeMoyne, half Choctaw, takes the Trail of Tears before going to Ireland with corn during the potato famine as a tribal representative and marrying a widower, who returns with her and accompanies on the 1848 Wagon Trail to Oregon.
Genre(s): Western Fiction; Domestic Fiction.

Chase-Riboud, Barbara

◆ 413. *Echo of Lions.* New York: Morrow, 1989. 416 pp.
In 1839, Joseph Cinque, captured African sculptor and warrior, leads a rebellion on the slave ship on which he is imprisoned, and he is tried in the United States.

Clarkson, Ewan

◆ 414. *The Many-Forked Branch.* New York: Dutton, 1980. 144 pp.
Broken Knife, an Ojibwa hunter, and a lone wolf whose pack has been killed by the Dakota meet in confrontation.
Genre(s): Western Fiction.

Coffman, Elaine

415. *If You Love Me.* New York: Fawcett, 1997. 375 pp.
Plains Indians kidnap Margery Mackinnon in 1836 and sell her into slavery several times before William Woodville, a visiting English lord, purchases her, takes her to England, and deserts her, but when he returns two years later, he finds a beautiful young woman disinterested in him.
Genre(s): Romance.

Coldsmith, Don

416. *Tallgrass.* New York: Bantam, 1997. 464 pp.
After the Santa Fe Trail opens, white settlers begin to take away the lands of the Pawnee and other tribes.
Genre(s): Family Saga; Western Fiction.

Coleman, Lonnie

417. *Beulah Land.* Garden City, NY: Doubleday, 1973. 495 pp.
The Kendrick family owns Beulah Land and participates in the life of the antebellum South.
Genre(s): Romance.

Conley, Robert J.

◆ 418. *Mountain Windsong.* Norman: University of Oklahoma Press, 1992. 218 pp.
Waguli must go on the government-enforced march with other Cherokee while his betrothed Oconeechee remains behind in the mountains, and they wait four years to reunite.
Genre(s): Love Story; Political Fiction.

Crook, Elizabeth

◆ 419. *Promised Land.* New York: Doubleday, 1994. 511 pp.
Comanches murder all but two of the Scottish immigrant Mackay family as the Texas rebellion begins in 1836, and the Kenner family looking after the baby Mackay must leave their land during the fray.
Genre(s): Domestic Fiction; War Story.

420. *The Raven's Bride.* Garden City, NY: Doubleday, 1991. 369 pp.
Sam Houston, a young, independent, and handsome man, marries Eliza Allen, but she leaves him after 11 weeks.
Genre(s): Biographical Fiction.

Cummings, Betty Sue

421. *Say These Names (Remember Them).* Englewood, FL: Pineapple, 1984. 286 pp.
During the second Seminole War in Florida during the 1830s, a young Miccosukee woman, See-ho-hee, sees the genocide of her tribe and begins to hate the hostile whites.
Genre(s): War Story.

Dailey, Janet

◆ 422. *The Proud and the Free.* Boston: Little, Brown, 1994. 322 pp.
In the 1830s Temple Gordon thinks that he and his wife will be forced to leave their Cherokee Nation home, and he tries to persuade her to leave voluntarily.
Genre(s): Love Story.

Dana, Richard

423. *Two Years Before the Mast.* Boston: Houghton Mifflin, 1840. 173 pp.
A sailor describes his voyage on a sailing vessel.
Genre(s): Sea Story.

Davenport, Kiana

424. *Shark Dialogues.* New York: Atheneum, 1994. 469 pp.
In 1834, a Yankee sailor marries a Tahitian princess in Hawaii, and their descendants are called together by Pono, a seer, who reveals the family's past.
Genre(s): Family Saga.

Daves, Francis M.

425. *Cherokee Woman.* Atlanta, GA: Cherokee, 1973. 444 pp.
In 1834, David Graham goes to Georgia to claim land won by his father in a lottery, and he falls in love with a gracious Cherokee woman after dealing with crude white landowners.
Genre(s): Political Fiction.

De Hartog, Jan

◆ 426. *The Peculiar People.* New York: Pantheon, 1992. 321 pp.
In the sequel to *The Peaceable Kingdom,* during the 1830s, the Quakers living in the Midwest worry about the slaves and the Native Americans in addition to their own difficulties.

Derleth, August William

427. *Bright Journey.* New York: Scribner's, 1940. 424 pp.
Hercules Dousman, an agent for John Jacob Aster in the Northwest territory, arrives in Wisconsin to trade his furs.
Genre(s): Western Fiction.

428. *The Hills Stand Watch.* New York: Duell, Sloane, and Pearce, 1958. 337 pp.
In a Wisconsin lead-mining town in the 1840s, as political troubles rise and the area considers statehood, a woman becomes unhappy in her marriage.
Genre(s): Western Fiction; Political Fiction.

429. *Restless Is the River.* New York: Scribner's, 1939. 514 pp.
A Hungarian immigrant settles in Wisconsin and tries to raise grapes for wine around 1839.
Genre(s): Western Fiction.

430. *Wind over Wisconsin.* New York: Scribner's, 1938. 391 pp.
In Wisconsin during the 1830s fur traders change into farmers after the Black Hawk Wars.
Genre(s): Western Fiction; War Story.

Downes, Anne Miller

431. *The Pilgrim Soul.* 1952. Etna, NH: Durand, 1997. 277 pp.
Dolly Copp becomes a pioneer in the White Mountains of New Hampshire during the 19th century.
Genre(s): Adventure Story; Biographical Fiction.

Duval, John C.

432. *Early Times in Texas.* 1936. Lincoln, NE: University of Nebraska, 1986. 284 pp.
In 1835, pioneers settle the Texas land and try to make themselves autonomous by separating from Mexico.
Genre(s): Biographical Fiction; Western Fiction.

Edmonds, Walter D.

◆ 433. *The Big Barn.* Boston: Little, Brown, 1930. 333 pp.
In the sequel to *Rome Haul*, farm family members along the Erie Canal fall in love.
Genre(s): Love Story.

◆ 434. *Chad Hanna.* Boston: Little, Brown, 1940. 548 pp.
Chad Hanna needs to escape after someone connects him with a runaway slave reaching Canada and the Underground Railroad, so he joins a traveling circus.

◆ 435. *Erie Water.* Boston: Little, Brown, 1933. 506 pp.
Jerry Fowler, a young carpenter, helps build the Erie Canal and falls in love with Mary from Albany.
Genre(s): Love Story.

436. *The Wedding Journey.* Boston: Little, Brown, 1947. 118 pp.
On their honeymoon via an Erie Canal boat, a couple learns unwelcome lessons in 1835.
Genre(s): Love Story.

Erdman, Loula Grace

437. *Many a Voyage.* New York: Dodd, Mead, 1967. 309 pp.
A wife views the troubled Midwest through the eyes of her husband, Edmund G. Ross, a crusading newspaperman.
Genre(s): Biographical Fiction; Political Fiction; Western Fiction.

Estleman, Loren D.

438. *Murdock's Law.* Garden City, NY: Doubleday, 1982. 184 pp.
Deputy Marshal Page Murdock accepts the job of town marshal in Breen, Montana, but he finds that he must deal with a range war between the large and small ranchers of the area.
Genre(s): Western Fiction.

Field, Rachel

439. *All This, and Heaven Too.* New York: Macmillan, 1938. 596 pp.
After Mademoiselle D is acquitted in a French murder trial, she decides to come to America, where she marries a minister and keeps a salon in Gramercy Park hosting such visitors as William Cullen Bryant, Harriet Beecher Stowe, Samuel Morse, and Fanny Kemble.
Genre(s): Domestic Fiction.

440. *And Now Tomorrow.* New York: Macmillan, 1942. 350 pp.
In a New England mill town, Emily Blair has enjoyed money from her family's mills, but a sudden illness makes her deaf, and she loses her boyfriend to her younger sister.
Genre(s): Domestic Fiction.

Fisher, Vardis

441. *Children of God.* New York: Harper, 1939. 769 pp.
Joseph Smith founds the Mormons, and Brigham Young organizes them as they go west and settle.
Genre(s): Religious Fiction.

Forbes, Esther

442. *O, Genteel Lady!* 1926. Chicago: Academy, 1986. 296 pp.
The literary circle of Longfellow, Wadsworth, Emerson, and Thoreau meets in Concord and Boston to discuss their philosophical theories.
Genre(s): Domestic Fiction.

Forman, James

443. *So Ends this Day.* New York: Farrar, Straus and Giroux, 1970. 247 pp.
A captain takes his children with him on a whaling voyage in the mid-19th century, and they rescue a family enemy off the coast of Africa, who tries to convince them that slaves, not whales, are the source of wealth.
Genre(s): Sea Story.

Fuller, Iola

444. *The Shining Trail.* New York: Duell, Sloane, and Pearce, 1943. 442 pp.
Black Hawk and the Sauk try to save themselves when the whites encroach on their lands and betray them.
Genre(s): Biographical Fiction.

◆ May be suitable for young adult readers

Garwood, Julie

445. *Prince Charming*. New York: Pocket Books, 1994. 587 pp.

After Lady Stapleton marries Lucas Ross, a man she had not previously met, to save her nieces from their uncle, she and Ross go to America where they must stay married longer than she had planned.

Genre(s): Romance.

Gavin, Thomas

446. *Kingkill*. New York: Random House, 1977. 398 pp.

When William Schlumberger becomes the automatic chess player for mechanical gadget maker Johann Gavin in the early 19th century, he finally realizes that he is being duped and takes action.

Genre(s): Biographical Fiction.

Gear, W. Michael

447. *The Morning River*. New York: Forge, 1996. 382 pp.

In 1825, Harvard student Richard Hamilton must deliver $30,000 to someone in St. Louis for his father or lose his inheritance, but on his journey, someone steals the money and sells him into indenture.

Genre(s): Bildungsroman (Coming of Age); Western Fiction.

Gerson, Noel B.

448. *The Slender Reed*. Garden City, NY: Doubleday, 1965. 394 pp.

Although serving only one term as president, James Knox Polk demonstrates his political courage.

Genre(s): Biographical Fiction; Political Fiction.

449. *The Yankee from Tennessee*. Garden City, NY: Doubleday, 1960. 382 pp.

The self-educated Andrew Johnson faces impeachment charges when he becomes president of the United States.

Genre(s): Biographical Fiction.

Giles, Janice Holt

450. *The Believers*. Boston: Houghton Mifflin, 1957. 214p pp.

Rebecca Fowler dutifully accompanies her husband to a Shaker colony in Kentucky in the early 1800s, but when she does not become a believer, she must leave him and the group in this sequel to *Hannah Fowler*.

Genre(s): Family Saga.

451. *Savanna*. 1961. New York: Avon, 1977. 304 pp.

Hannah Fowler's granddaughter becomes a widow while still young, and she must fight to preserve her indepdence in Arkansas during 1824.

Genre(s): Western Fiction.

452. *Voyage to Santa Fe*. Boston: Houghton Mifflin, 1962. 327 pp.

In the sequel to *Savanna*, Johnny Fowler and his wife set out in 1823 for Santa Fe, a journey that tests their marriage.

Genre(s): Adventure Story; Family Saga; Western Fiction.

Glancy, Diane

◆ 453. *Pushing the Bear*. New York: Harcourt Brace, 1996. 241 pp.

Different people tell their stories of being removed along with over 10,000 other Cherokee from their homes to Oklahoma beginning in 1838 on the Trail of Tears.

Genre(s): War Story.

Graham, Heather

◆ 454. *Runaway*. New York: Delacorte, 1994. 445 pp.

Tara Brent flees Boston for New Orleans, and then, with her new gambler husband, to Florida in the 1830s, where the Seminoles fight the white settlers.

Genre(s): Love Story.

Greber, Judith

◆ 455. *Mendocino*. New York: Crown, 1988. 356 pp.

In 1842 Russian immigrant Nicolai Beriankov decides to stay in California with his Native American wife and children, where he must hide from gold rushers and slavers before he and his family go to Mendocino and watch in dismay while a town grows up around them.

Genre(s): Family Saga.

Gulick, Bill

456. *Gathering Storm, 1837-1868*. Garden City, NY: Doubleday, 1988. 186 pp.

Matt Crane's son John meets his half brother, Tall Bird, whose mother is a Nez Percé, and they become involved in the government's persecution of the Indians in the sequel to *Distant Trails 1805-1836*.

Genre(s): Western Fiction.

Guthrie, A. B.

457. *The Way West*. Boston: Houghton Mifflin, 1949. 340 pp.

Dick Summers and others travel the Oregon Trail from Independence, Missouri, to Oregon in the sequel to *The Big Sky*.

Award(s): Pulitzer Prize.

Genre(s): Western Fiction.

Hambly, Barbara

◆ 458. *Fever Season*. New York: Bantam, 1998. 336 pp.

After black free man of color, Benjamin January, returns to New Orleans to end a 16-year absence, he must treat victims of the cholera epidemic, but when he realizes that other free blacks are disappearing, he investigates.

Genre(s): Medical Novel; Mystery.

◆ 459. *A Free Man of Color.* New York: Bantam, 1997. 320 pp.
Ben January, free man of color, returns to New Orleans in the 19th century, only to find that nothing has changed for African Americans, and when a woman is murdered, whites in the community want to blame him.
Genre(s): Mystery.

Harper, Karen

◆ 460. *Circle of Gold.* New York: Dutton, 1992. 393 pp.
After Rebecca Blake's mother dies, her father leaves her with Shakers, but she cannot follow their ways and marries a British labor activist visting in the community.
Genre(s): Religious Fiction.

461. *River of Sky.* New York: Dutton, 1994. 407 pp.
After her husband, trader Clive Craig, dies, Kate finds that he owes many debts and has a second wife, Blue Wing, whom she befriends when abandoned by St. Louis society in 1835.
Genre(s): Romance.

Hawthorne, Nathaniel

462. *The Blithedale Romance.* 1852. Boston: Bedford, 1996. 512 pp.
Several members of the Transcendentalists begin the Brook Farm socialistic experiment in 1841.

463. *The House of the Seven Gables.* 1851. New York: Oxford, 1991. 328 pp.
After 30 years in prison for a murder he did not commit, Clifford Pyncheon and his sister Hepzibah continue to worry about the power of the real murderer, their cousin Judge Pyncheon.
Genre(s): Domestic Fiction.

Hogan, Linda

◆ 464. *Power.* New York: Norton, 1998. 192 pp.
Omishto, the One Who Watches, is 16 when the government tries to take her Taiga tribe's Florida lands, and only one woman seems to have the spiritual forces to help the Taiga overcome their plight.
Genre(s): Political Fiction; Bildungsroman (Coming of Age).

Hogan, Ray

465. *Soldier in Buckskin.* Thorndike, ME: Five Star Western, 1996. 296 pp.
Kit Carson leads trapping parties and fights against the Blackfoot and Ute while marrying Singing Grass, an Arapaho, and after her death, Spanish aristocrat Josefa Jaramillo.
Genre(s): Biographical Fiction; Western Fiction.

Holland, Cecelia

◆ 466. *The Bear Flag.* Boston: Houghton Mifflin, 1990. 422 pp.
Catharine Reilly eventually reaches Sutter's Fort after the death of her husband on the trip to California, and she

falls in love with a Russian agent working for the Mexicans who rule California.
Genre(s): Western Fiction.

◆ 467. *Pacific Street.* Garden City, NY: Doubleday, 1992. 260 pp.
Frances Hardheart (Mammy), an escaped slave, knows how to use people in the early days of San Francisco, and she sets up a stage show and bar with a white woman.

Humphrey, William

468. *No Resting Place.* New York: Delacorte, 1989. 249 pp.
Amos Ferguson (Noquisi) is a half Cherokee who travels on the Trail of Tears 30 years after the Cherokees are exiled from their first home.
Genre(s): Bildungsroman (Coming of Age).

Hunter, Evan

◆ 469. *The Chisholms.* New York: Harper and Row, 1976. 208 pp.
The Chisholm family leaves Virginia for a better life in California.
Genre(s): Western Fiction.

Jakes, John

470. *North and South.* New York: Harcourt Brace, 1982. 740 pp.
The rice-growing Mains family from South Carolina meets the iron-producing Hazards from Pennsylvania at West Point in 1842.
Genre(s): Family Saga.

Johnson, Charles Richard

471. *Middle Passage.* New York: Atheneum, 1990. 209 pp.
Rutherford Calhoun, a newly freed slave living in New Orleans, is forced into marrying a Boston schoolteacher but escapes that horror for another when he stows away on a ship bound for Africa.
Award(s): National Book Award.
Genre(s): Adventure Story; Sea Story.

Johnson, Dorothy M.

472. *Buffalo Woman.* Lincoln, NE: University of Nebraska Press, 1995. 247 pp.
Whirlwind recounts the life of the Oglala Sioux from 1820 through the Battle of Wounded Knee.
Genre(s): Western Fiction; War Story.

Johnston, Terry C.

473. *Buffalo Palace.* New York: Bantam, 1996. 405 pp.
Titus Bass from *Dance on the Wind* goes to the Rockies and joins dishonest fur trappers who leave him to be attacked by Blackfeet and rescued by Shosones.
Genre(s): Western Fiction.

474. *One-Eyed Dream.* Ottawa, IL: Jameson, 1988. 592 pp.
In 1833, Titus Bass and orphan Josiah Paddock take their Native American wives to New Mexico for the winter,

where they find that the men who stole Titus's furs 10 years prior are still around, in the sequel to *Borderlords*.
Genre(s): Western Fiction.

Johnstone, William W.

475. *Eyes of Eagles.* New York: Kensington, 1993. 478 pp.
Jamie MacAllister, kidnapped by the Shawnee, flees from his enemies with Kate to Texas, where he is pressed into service to fight at the Alamo in 1836.
Genre(s): Western Fiction; Romance.

Jones, Robert F.

476. *Deadville.* New York: St. Martin's Press, 1998. 288 pp.
Dillon Griffith and his brother Owen head to the West in 1833 for adventure, and while they face hostile Arikara Indians, Jim Beckwourth rescues them.
Genre(s): Western Fiction; Adventure Story.

Jordan, Jan

477. *Dim the Flaring Lamps.* Englewood Cliffs, NJ: Prentice Hall, 1972. 282 pp.
John Wilkes Booth meets with Jefferson Davis and others, and when Lincoln fails to stop the execution of Booth's friend John Beall, he decides to assassinate Lincoln.
Genre(s): Biographical Fiction.

Juárez, Tina

478. *South Wind Come.* Houston, TX: Arte Publico, 1998. 384 pp.
Teresa Sestos y Abrantes idolizes Sam Houston in the newly independent Texas, while Carmen and Coalter Owens introduce her to the abolitionist movement which she fully embraces.
Genre(s): War Story; Political Fiction.

Kane, Harnett T.

479. *The Lady of Arlington.* Garden City, NY: Doubleday, 1953. 288 pp.
The great-granddaughter of Martha Washington marries the impoverished Robert E. Lee against her parents' wishes.

Katchor, Ben

480. *The Jew of New York.* New York: Pantheon, 1998. 104 pp.
In 1825, a New York politician and playwright tries to establish a Jewish state on an island near Buffalo.
Genre(s): Political Fiction; Jewish Fiction.

Keyes, Frances Parkinson

481. *Dinner at Antoine's.* New York: Simon and Schuster, 1948. 422 pp.
In 1840, eight people dine at Antoine's, and eight hours later, one of them dies.
Genre(s): Mystery.

King, Joan

482. *Sarah M. Peale.* Brookline Village, MA: Branden, 1987. 296 pp.
Sarah Peale defies convention and her father by supporting herself doing portraits, including subjects General Lafayette and Daniel Webster, and still lifes at a time when women are not supposed to be artists.
Genre(s): Biographical Fiction.

Kipling, Rudyard

483. *Captains Courageous.* 1896. New York: Bantam, 1963. 184 pp.
Fishermen from Gloucester bravely sail to the Grand Banks to catch fish on windy seas.
Genre(s): Sea Story; Adventure Story.

Lafferty, R.A.

484. *Okla Hannali.* New York: Doubleday, 1972. 216 pp.
Hannali Innominee, member of the Okla Hannali clan, is relocated to Oklahoma in the 1830s, remains neutral in the Civil War, loses his home in the 1860s, and watches the erosion of his Choctaw culture as the century wanes.
Genre(s): Family Saga.

L'Amour, Louis

485. *The Daybreakers.* New York: Bantam, 1960. 290 pp.
Tyrel and Orrin Sackett travel from Tennessee to Santa Fe. (*Series:* The Sacketts, 6)
Genre(s): Western Fiction; Family Saga.

486. *Hondo.* New York: Omnibus, 1953. 192 pp.
Apaches capture a man traveling west.
Genre(s): Western Fiction; Family Saga.

487. *Rivers West.* New York: Saturday Review, 1975. 192 pp.
Jean Talon leaves the Gaspé Peninsula in 1821 for Pittsburgh and meets Tabitha Majoribanks who has unknowingly hired criminals to crew a steamboat taking her to St. Louis. (*Series:* The Talons, 2)
Genre(s): Western Fiction; Family Saga.

Landis, Jill Marie

488. *Just Once.* New York: Warner Books, 1997. 384 pp.
Jemma O'Hurley decides not to be forced into marriage in 1817 and runs off to New Orleans where a buckskinned Hunter Boone rescues her.
Genre(s): Romance.

Levy, Joann

489. *Daughter of Joy.* New York: Tor, 1998. 320 pp.
Ah Toy travels to California during the Gold Rush in the 1840s with her master, but he dies on shipboard, and she wonders who will tell her what to do when she arrives, and with few alternatives available to her, she becomes a prostitute.
Genre(s): Legal Story; Domestic Fiction.

Long, Jeff

490. *Empire of Bones.* New York: Morrow, 1993. 256 pp.
Sam Houston wonders if he will be able to succeed in defeating Mexico with the motley group composing the Texas forces of 1836.
Award(s): Western Writers of America Spur Award.
Genre(s): Biographical Fiction; War Story.

Ludwig, Charles

491. *Levi Coffin and the Underground Railroad.* Scottdale, PA: Herald, 1975. 184 pp.
Levi Coffin becomes an important link in the Underground Railroad during the 19th century.
Genre(s): Political Fiction.

Martin, Larry Jay

◆ 492. *Against the 7th Flag.* New York: Bantam, 1991. 224 pp.
In the 1840s, John Clinton Ryan fights with Kit Carson and others against Mexico for the control of California.
Genre(s): Western Fiction; War Story.

Matthews, Jack

493. *Sassafras.* Boston: Houghton Mifflin, 1983. 288 pp.
Thaddeus Burke, a phrenologist, meets criminals, townsfolk, and others as he practices his trade from the Ohio River to Kansas Territory in the 1840s.
Genre(s): Adventure Story.

McCord, Christian

494. *Across the Shining Mountains.* Ottawa, IL: Jameson, 1986. 330 pp.
Nathaniel Wyeth leaves Massachusetts in 1832 for Oregon, where he plans to set up trading posts, but even though he fails, others follow his lead.
Genre(s): Adventure Story.

McCrumb, Sharyn

◆ 495. *Ballad of Frankie Silver.* New York: Dutton, 1998. 400 pp.
While Sheriff Spencer Arrowood recuperates from a gunshot wound, he begins to investigate the hanging of Frankie Silver in 1832 for the murder of her husband.
Genre(s): Mystery.

McElroy, Lee

496. *Eyes of the Hawk.* Garden City, NY: Doubleday, 1981. 182 pp.
Thomas Canfield, a poor rancher, becomes involved with a newcomer to Texas who follows the carting trade.
Genre(s): Western Fiction.

McMurtry, Larry

◆ 497. *Dead Man's Walk.* New York: Simon and Schuster, 1995. 480 pp.
In the prequel to *Lonesome Dove*, Woodrow Call and Gus McCrae are novice Texas Rangers who, while going to Santa Fe to take it from the Mexicans, come of age.
Genre(s): Western Fiction; Bildungsroman (Coming of Age).

Michener, James A.

◆ 498. *The Eagle and the Raven.* Austin, TX: State House, 1990. 214 pp.
Sam Houston, governor of Texas, and Santa Anna, president of Mexico, meet at the battle of San Jacinto, after which the United States is in a position to annex Texas.

Miller, Caroline

499. *Lamb in His Bosom.* Atlanta, GA: Peachtree, 1933. 324 pp.
Lonzo Smith brings Cean Carver to Georgia during pre-Civil War days to the cabin he has built for her, and she lives there until old enough to welcome her second husband back from the war.
Award(s): Pulitzer Prize.
Genre(s): Domestic Fiction; War Story.

Moore, Barbara

500. *The Fever Called Living.* Garden City, NY: Doubleday, 1976. 350 pp.
When Edgar Allen Poe goes to New York with his wife Virginia and her mother, he struggles to earn money for her tuberculosis treatment, while his literary rival and executor, Reverend Dr. Rufus Wilmot Griswold, does much to malign his name.
Genre(s): Biographical Fiction.

Morsi, Pamela

501. *The Love Charm.* New York: Avon, 1996. 384 pp.
Although Armand Sonnier and Aida Gaudet have loved each other for years, neither will believe it until the local seer, Orva Landry, shows them the way.
Genre(s): Romance.

Murray, Earl

◆ 502. *Spirit of the Moon.* New York: Forge, 1996. 304 pp.
While Spirit of the Moon, a young Nez Percé woman, travels with her adopted French trapper father to meet her husband, a British trader, she meets another man with whom she falls in love.
Genre(s): Adventure Story.

Nelson, Betty Palmer

503. *Private Knowledge.* New York: St. Martin's Press, 1990. 256 pp.
Molly becomes pregnant by a married man in Tennessee during the 1830s, and after his oldest friend marries her, their love grows.
Genre(s): Domestic Fiction.

◆ May be suitable for young adult readers

Ogilvie, Elisabeth

◆ 504. *Jennie Glenroy.* Camden, ME: Down East, 1993. 511 pp.
In the sequel to *The World of Jenny G.*, Jennie and her husband Alick raise five children on a Maine farm 50 years after the Declaration of Independence.
Genre(s): Domestic Fiction; Family Saga.

Olsen, Theodore V.

505. *Summer of the Drums.* New York: Doubleday, 1972. 152 pp.
In 1832, during the Black Hawk War, a family of trappers lives in Prairie du Chien, and one of them wounds and then becomes friends with Black Hawk's grandson.
Genre(s): Western Fiction.

506. *There Was a Season.* Garden City, NY: Doubleday, 1972. 444 pp.
Jefferson Davis falls in love with Knoxie Taylor, a strong woman whose father disapproves of him, and he fights in the Black Hawk War during his early years before gaining renown as the president of the Confederacy.
Genre(s): Biographical Fiction; Romance.

O'Neal, Reagan

507. *The Fallon Legacy.* New York: Forge, 1998. 384 pp.
Robert Fallon and the son he never knew, James, become involved through both friends and enemies as one struggles for freedom in Texas beginning in 1822 and the other fights in Charleston.
Genre(s): Sea Story; War Story; Romance.

Paul, Raymond

508. *The Thomas Street Horror.* New York: Viking, 1982. 322 pp.
In 1835, reporter Davy Corder becomes friends with lawyer Lon Quinncannon. When Quinncannon's mistress is murdered, Corder helps him find the murderer.
Genre(s): Mystery.

509. *The Tragedy at Tiverton.* New York: Viking, 1984. 352 pp.
Ephraim Avery, the first minister tried in America, is accused of killing a mill worker and her unborn child in 1832, and Lon Quincannon, an Irish lawyer, defends him.
Genre(s): Legal Story.

Peart, Jane

◆ 510. *Fortune's Bride.* Grand Rapids, MI: Zondervan, 1990. 288 pp.
Graham Montrose, widowed after three months, becomes Avril's guardian, and when Avril turns 16 and is introduced to society, he realizes that he has fallen in love with her. (*Series:* Brides of Montclair, 3)
Genre(s): Christian Fiction; Romance; Family Saga.

Pella, Judith, and Tracie Peterson

511. *Distant Dreams.* Minneapolis, MN: Bethany House, 1997. 320 pp.
In 1835, Carolina Adams, 15, and her tutor are interested in the new railroad and in each other, but the tutor becomes engaged to her sister, as expected, and when they

break up, Carolina follows him west. (*Series:* Ribbons of Steel, 1)
Genre(s): Christian Fiction.

512. *A Hope Beyond.* Minneapolis, MN: Bethany House, 1997. 350 pp.
When Carolina Adams faces tragedy in her family and thinks that she has lost her one love, she uses her faith to find hope. (*Series:* Ribbons of Steel, 2)
Genre(s): Christian Fiction; Romance.

513. *A Promise for Tomorrow.* Minneapolis, MN: Bethany House, 1998. 352 pp.
Carolina Adams finally marries James Baldwin, and when they move to a small Allegheny Mountain town, James oversees the construction of the B & O Railroad. (*Series:* Ribbons of Steel, 3)
Genre(s): Christian Fiction; Romance.

Pesci, David

◆ 514. *Amistad.* New York: Marlowe, 1997. 240 pp.
In 1839, slaves who took over a slave ship but could not sail it back to Africa go on trial in Connecticut, and John Quincy Adams represents them before the Supreme Court.
Genre(s): Legal Story.

Peters, Ray

515. *The Lafitte Case.* Aurora, CO: Write Way, 1997. 247 pp.
Edward Livingston tries to interest his grandson in a difficult case in which he must convince the Lafitte Society of the existence of two Jean Lafittes living in the early 19th century.
Genre(s): Mystery.

Powell, James

516. *The Malpais Rider.* Garden City, NY: Doubleday, 1981. 184 pp.
When hired killers shoot Cam Stallings's horse and leave him for dead, he decides to help a young woman rancher, two Navajos, and an aged Mexican.
Genre(s): Western Fiction.

Powers, Richard

517. *Gain.* New York: Farrar, Straus and Giroux, 1998. 356 pp.
Laura thinks her ovarian cancer stems from the unhealthy environment of a local soap and chemical company, and she examines the history of the company from its beginnings in Boston in the 1820s.
Genre(s): Domestic Fiction; Political Fiction.

Price, Eugenia

◆ 518. *To See Your Face Again.* Garden City, NY: Doubleday, 1985. 546 pp.
The sequel to *Savannah* focuses on Natalie Browning who is on board the *Pulaski* when it explodes and has to spend five days in the water with Burke Latimer before being rescued. (*Series:* Savannah Quartet, 2)
Genre(s): Domestic Fiction; Family Saga; Romance.

◆ 519. *Where Shadows Go.* Garden City, NY: Doubleday, 1993. 646 pp.
The sequel to *Bright Captivity* reveals the charmed life of John and Anne Fraser and their family from 1825, when the two return to St. Simons Island from London.
Genre(s): Romance; Family Saga.

Rae, Catherine M.

520. *The Hidden Cove.* New York: St. Martin's Press, 1995. 183 pp.
In the 1840s, Emily Adair's Uncle John, a seaman, cares for her after the death of her widowed mother, but he is murdered and a pirate king kidnaps and trains her to pickpocket until she grows up and asserts herself.
Genre(s): Mystery.

521. *The Ship's Clock.* New York: St. Martin's Press, 1993. 298 pp.
Philip Mesner takes his family's heirloom clock from Hamburg in 1810 and brings it to America where he assumes a new identity, but his father's curse on his sons follows him.
Genre(s): Mystery.

Rao, Linda Rae

522. *The Eagle Stirs Her Nest.* Ada, MI: Revell, 1997. 224 pp.
In 1841, after Chad Macklin joins the Texas Rangers, he finds both adventure and love. (*Series:* Eagle Wings, 4)
Genre(s): Christian Fiction; Western Fiction.

Rhyne, Nancy

◆ 523. *Alice Flagg.* Gretna, LA: Pelican, 1990. 255 pp.
Alice Flagg dies of black vomit (hemorrhagic fever) after her brother refuses to let her marry a lumbermen, but people report her ghost searching for her lover in the pre-Civil War South and in California during the Gold Rush.
Genre(s): Biographical Fiction; Gothic Fiction.

Robson, Lucia St. Clair

524. *Fearless.* New York: Ballantine, 1998. 416 pp.
Sarah Borginnis Bowman follows her husband to the Mexican War and stays to fight after he dies.
Genre(s): War Story.

525. *Ride the Wind.* New York: Ballantine, 1982. 562 pp.
A Comanche family adopts Cynthia Parker after kidnapping her in 1836, and she gradually becomes one of them, marrying her captor.
Award(s): Western Writers of America Spur Award.
Genre(s): Biographical Fiction.

◆ 526. *Walk in My Soul.* New York: Ballantine, 1985. 644 pp.
Tiana, a Cherokee, falls in love with the young Sam Houston before her people are forcibly moved into Oklahoma Territory in the 1830s.
Genre(s): Love Story.

Ross, Dana Fuller

527. *Expedition!* New York: Bantam, 1992. 464 pp.
In the sequel to *Westward*, Clay Holt falls in love with a Sioux woman as he and his brother try to evade a killer who is trailing them. (Wagons West, 2)
Genre(s): Adventure Story; Western Fiction; Family Saga.

◆ 528. *Independence!* New York: Bantam, 1979. 432 pp.
Wagon master Whip Holt and his children leave Independence in 1837 to begin their wagon train careers. (*Series:* Wagons West, 1)
Genre(s): Western Fiction; Adventure Story.

◆ 529. *Nebraska!* New York: Bantam, 1982. 382 pp.
Whip Holt travels with a wagon train across the plains to Nebraska. (*Series:* Wagons West, 2)
Genre(s): Western Fiction; Adventure Story.

◆ 530. *Nevada!* New York: Bantam, 1981. 336 pp.
The wagon train under Whip Holt's leadership crosses Nevada. (*Series:* Wagons West, 8)
Genre(s): Western Fiction; Adventure Story.

◆ 531. *Oregon!* New York: Bantam, 1980. 369 pp.
Whip Holt leads the first wagon train of settlers into Oregon in 1839 with his new wife, a southern belle, and they conflict with Russians and rogue Native Americans. (*Series:* Wagons West, 4)
Genre(s): Western Fiction; Adventure Story.

◆ 532. *Outpost.* New York: Bantam, 1993. 434 pp.
In the sequel to *Expedition*, Clay and Jefferson Holt form a dynasty while the French, Spanish, and Native Americans fight each other. (*Series:* Wagons West, 3)
Genre(s): Western Fiction.

◆ 533. *Texas!* New York: Bantam, 1980. 356 pp.
Whip Holt's wagon train witnesses the Texas War for Independence. (*Series:* Wagons West, 5)
Genre(s): Western Fiction; Adventure Story.

◆ 534. *Wyoming!* New York: Bantam, 1979. 355 pp.
Whip Holt leads wagons along the trail into Wyoming. (*Series:* Wagons West, 3)
Genre(s): Western Fiction.

Ross, David William

535. *Eye of the Hawk.* New York: Simon and Schuster, 1992. 512 pp.
In 1841, Seth and Isabelle Redmond start a horse ranch south of San Antonio, and during the next 25 years, they must battle Mexicans, Native Americans, and other white settlers.
Genre(s): Western Fiction.

Rossner, Judith

536. *Emmeline.* New York: Simon and Schuster, 1980. 331 pp.
In 1839, Emmeline Mosher, 13, goes to Lowell, Massachusetts, to work in the cotton mills where in her life's first calamity, an overseer seduces her and she gives birth without her family knowing.
Genre(s): Bildungsroman (Coming of Age).

Sanders, Leonard

537. *Star of Empire.* New York: Delacorte, 1992. 448 pp.
Tad Logan, interested in politics in Texas, and his wife Corrie, concerned about family, come to Texas before the revolution in 1835, where their divergent interests conflict.
Genre(s): War Story; Domestic Fiction; Legal Story.

Seton, Anya

538. *Dragonwyck.* Boston: Houghton Mifflin, 1944. 336 pp.
When Mrs. Van Ryn dies on her estate of Dragonwyck, the governess Miranda becomes the second wife and faces the horrors of the house.
Genre(s): Romance; Gothic Fiction.

Sherman, Jory

539. *Song of the Cheyenne.* New York: Doubleday, 1987. 179 pp.
A Cheyenne warrior is destined for greatness from his tribe's point of view.
Genre(s): Western Fiction.

Skimin, Robert

540. *Apache Autumn.* New York: St. Martin's Press, 1993. 426 pp.
In 1821, Lazaro becomes the stepson of the Chihenne Apache chief and its destined leader but cannot gain the love of the Mexican woman captured to be his wife.
Genre(s): Adventure Story.

541. *Ulysses.* New York: St. Martin's Press, 1994. 448 pp.
Ulysses S. Grant attends West Point, fights in the Mexican War and gains his reputation, becomes a general, and finally becomes president.
Genre(s): War Story; Biographical Fiction.

Smith, Lee

542. *The Devil's Dream.* New York: Putnam, 1992. 315 pp.
In 1833, Moses Bailey, the preacher's son who thinks music is the voice of the devil, marries Kate, whose family plays the fiddle, and their descendants tell a story of country music's development.
Genre(s): Christian Fiction.

Stambaugh, Sara

543. *The Sign of the Fox.* Intercourse, PA: Good Books, 1991. 182 pp.
Strict Mennonite Catherine goes to work at the inn of the Carpenters, a family separated from the old traditions, after Mr. Carpenter out-maneuvers her father in a land deal.
Genre(s): Domestic Fiction; Christian Fiction.

Statham, Frances Patton

544. *Trail of Tears.* New York: Fawcett, 1993. 427 pp.
Laurel MacDonald, part Scottish, is a member of the Cherokee nation, teaching in its capital, when the government demands that the Cherokee leave.
Genre(s): Political Fiction.

Steelman, Robert J.

545. *Call of the Arctic.* New York: Coward-McCann, 1960. 316 pp.
A Harvard student joins Charles Francis Hall in his expedition to the Arctic between 1860 and 1873.
Genre(s): Biographical Fiction; Western Fiction.

Steward, Barbara, and Dwight Steward

546. *Evermore.* New York: Morrow, 1978. 202 pp.
Edgar Allan Poe takes the identity of detective Henri Le Rennet and goes to Europe, where he investigates the deaths of Austria's Crown Prince Rudolph and Baroness Mary Vetsera at the royal hunting lodge.
Genre(s): Mystery.

Stone, Irving

547. *The President's Lady.* Garden City, NY: Doubleday, 1951. 338 pp.
Rachel Donelson divorces her first husband and begins her happy marriage to Andrew Jackson.
Genre(s): Biographical Fiction.

Stowe, Harriet Beecher

548. *Uncle Tom's Cabin.* 1852. New York: Random House, 1996. 494 pp.
Uncle Tom's master sells him, separating him from his wife, and he becomes attached to the gentle daughter of his new owner, but after her death, he is sold to the evil Simon Legree.
Genre(s): Domestic Fiction.

Styron, William

◆ 549. *The Confessions of Nat Turner.* New York: Random House, 1967. 429 pp.
Nat Turner leads a group of slaves in an insurrection during 1831 in Virginia.
Award(s): Pulitzer Prize; Howells Medal.
Genre(s): Political Fiction; Biographical Fiction.

Swarthout, Glendon

◆ 550. *The Homesman.* New York: Weidenfeld and Nicolson, 1988. 239 pp.
A woman feeling desolate in Missouri returns to Iowa under the care of a young school teacher and a land-grabber whom she saved from lynching.
Award(s): Western Writers of America Spur Award.
Genre(s): Western Fiction.

Taylor, Robert Lewis

551. *Niagara.* New York: Putnam, 1980. 500 pp.
Morrison, a reporter, goes to Niagara in the early 19th century to investigate a scandal and, after meeting a motley group of people, becomes a vintner.

Tryon, Thomas

552. *The Wings of the Morning.* New York: Knopf, 1990. 567 pp.
The Talcott and the Grimes family feud in Pequot Landing while the miller's daughter serves as the link between them.
Genre(s): Family Saga.

Turner, William Oliver

553. *Thief Hunt.* New York: Doubleday, 1973. 167 pp.
Bass Pattee, part Cherokee, helps to rescue an ancient deerskin calendar robe after the Trail of Tears.
Genre(s): Western Fiction.

Twain, Mark

554. *The Adventures of Huckleberry Finn.* New York: Cambridge, 1995. 384 pp.
Huckleberry Finn, an abused outcast, rafts with Jim, a runaway slave, down the Mississippi River, where they have a variety of experiences.
Genre(s): Bildungsroman (Coming of Age); Picaresque Fiction.

555. *The Adventures of Tom Sawyer.* New York: Dodd, Mead, 1876. 216 pp.
Tom, shrewd and adventurous, makes friends with Huck Finn, and they accidentally witness a murder.
Genre(s): Adventure Story; Picaresque Fiction.

Warren, Robert Penn

556. *World Enough and Time.* New York: Random House, 1950. 512 pp.
Jeremiah Beaumont, accused of murder, tries to justify the murder before he repents of it.
Genre(s): Love Story.

Wellman, Paul Iselin

557. *Magnificent Destiny.* Garden City, NY: Doubleday, 1962. 479 pp.
Andrew Jackson and Sam Houston forge a strong friendship based on common interests and patriotism.
Genre(s): Adventure Story.

Wells, Marian

558. *Morning Star.* Minneapolis, MN: Bethany House, 1986. 304 pp.
Jenny searches for the truth and finds it in the words of Jesus. (*Series:* Starlight Trilogy, 3)
Genre(s): Christian Fiction.

559. *Star Light, Star Bright.* Minneapolis, MN: Bethany House, 1986. 256 pp.
Jenny continues her story as a Mormon. (*Series:* Starlight Trilogy, 2)
Genre(s): Christian Fiction.

560. *The Wishing Star.* Minneapolis, MN: Bethany House, 1985. 288 pp.
A young girl becomes fascinated with the power of God through a series of experiences as a Mormon. (*Series:* Starlight Trilogy, 1)
Genre(s): Christian Fiction.

Wescott, Glenway

561. *The Grandmothers.* 1927. New York: Arbor House, 1986. 388 pp.
Some pioneers have secrets they need to hide, including dishonesty and cowardice.
Genre(s): Domestic Fiction; Bildungsroman (Coming of Age).

West, Jessamyn

562. *Except for Me and Thee.* New York: Harcourt Brace, 1969. 309 pp.
The Birdwell family moves to Indiana from Ohio, where Jess becomes a conductor on the Underground Railway.
Genre(s): Religious Fiction.

563. *Leafy Rivers.* New York: Harcourt Brace, 1967. 310 pp.
Leafy changes from a lighthearted homesteader to a practical woman who drives a herd of pigs to Cincinnati to earn money to pay for her land.
Genre(s): Domestic Fiction.

◆ 564. *The Massacre at Fall Creek.* New York: Harcourt Brace, 1975. 373 pp.
In 1824, white settlers murder nine Native Americans, mostly women and children, on the Indiana frontier and hang for their deed.
Genre(s): War Story; Western Fiction.

White, Stewart Edward

565. *Folded Hills.* New York: Doubleday, 1934. 479 pp.
Andy Burnett becomes a hidalgo on his ranch, which he enjoys until the Americans occupy California during the War with Mexico. (*Series:* Andy Burnett Saga, 3)
Genre(s): Western Fiction; Adventure Story.

566. *The Long Rifle.* 1932. Missoula, MT: Mountain, 1990. 375 pp.
Andy Burnett begins to explore the Rocky Mountains in the 1820s. (*Series:* Andy Burnett Saga, 1)
Genre(s): Western Fiction.

567. *Ranchero.* New York: Doubleday, 1933. 302 pp.
Andy Burnett crosses the mountains to California in 1832, where he meets and wins a wife among the Spanish settlers he encounters. (*Series:* Andy Burnett Saga, 2)
Genre(s): Western Fiction; Adventure Story.

Wilder, Robert

568. *Bright Feather.* New York: Putnam, 1948. 408 pp.
Clay Hammond, plantation heir, uses his friendship with the Indian Asseola to cheat Indians out of their Florida lands.
Genre(s): Political Fiction.

◆ May be suitable for young adult readers

Williams, Lawrence

569. *I, James McNeill Whistler.* New York: Simon and Schuster, 1972. 383 pp.
After his birth in Massachusetts, Whistler spent most of his life abroad, and although he did not bother to finish the autobiography he began, if he had, it would have vividly portrayed his personality and wit.
Genre(s): Biographical Fiction.

Yerby, Frank

570. *A Darkness at Ingraham's Crest.* New York: Dial, 1979. 581 pp.
In the sequel to *The Dahomean*, Wes Parks (Hwesu to his African tribal members) tries to escape from his master on the plantation.
Genre(s): Political Fiction.

571. *The Foxes of Harrow.* New York: Dial, 1946. 534 pp.
Stephen Fox establishes a vast plantation in Louisana during the mid-19th century, but the Civil War destroys his home.
Genre(s): Domestic Fiction; War Story.

Zaroulis, N. L.

572. *Call the Darkness Light.* New York: Soho, 1993. 560 pp.
An orphan goes to work in one of the mills in Lowell, Massacusetts, during the 19th century.
Genre(s): Domestic Fiction.

1846-1860
Slavery, Abolitionists, and Women's Rights

Adams, Jane

◆ 573. *Seattle Green.* New York: Arbor House, 1987. 305 pp.
When Abel Blanchard goes with his bride to Seattle, he builds a business over the objections of his brother, and subsequent generations support his endeavors until his granddaughter breaks away.
Genre(s): Romance; Family Saga.

Adleman, Robert H.

574. *Sweetwater Fever.* New York: McGraw Hill, 1984. 500 pp.
Collis Gibbs, 18, moves with his father, a doctor, to an Oregon mining camp in 1853 and becomes involved with thieves, a militia, and girls.
Genre(s): Adventure Story.

Aldrich, Bess Streeter

◆ 575. *A White Bird Flying.* New York: Appleton, 1931. 335 pp.
Laura Deal must decide between literary ambition or marriage.
Genre(s): Love Story; Domestic Fiction.

Allen, Jordan

576. *Cavern of Silver.* New York: Walker, 1983. 180 pp.
Don Warren goes to Virginia City, Nevada, to investigate the race of two mining companies to gain control of a large lode of silver.
Genre(s): Western Fiction.

Allen, T. D.

577. *Doctor in Buckskin.* New York: Harper, 1951. 277 pp.
Marcus and Narcissa Whitman serve as the physician and teacher for Native Americans living in the Oregon Territory.
Genre(s): Biographical Fiction; Medical Novel; Western Fiction.

Alter, Judy

578. *Libbie.* New York: Bantam, 1994. 404 pp.
Libbie Custer's mother dies when Libbie is 12, and she meets her future husband, visiting nearby, but does not marry him until he graduates from West Point.
Genre(s): Biographical Fiction.

Arnold, Elliott

579. *Blood Brother.* New York: Duell, Sloane, and Pearce, 1947. 452 pp.
Cochise, chief of the Chiracahua Apaches, and Tom Jeffords negotiate from the time of the Gadsden Purchase in 1856 until the Indian wars end in 1870.
Genre(s): War Story; Western Fiction.

Bacheller, Irving

580. *Eben Holden.* New York: Lothrop, 1900. 432 pp.
A servant on a farm in the Adirondacks gains love and respect.
Genre(s): Domestic Fiction.

Baker, Calvin

◆ 581. *Naming the New World.* New York: St. Martin's Press, 1997. 128 pp.
As soon as the new slave Ampofo arrives, Sally, a slave breeder, kills him so that he will always be free.
Genre(s): Family Saga.

Banks, Russell

582. *Cloudsplitter.* New York: HarperCollins, 1998. 768 pp.
John Brown preaches against slavery, and he plans to overtake the arsenal at Harper's Ferry.
Genre(s): Biographical Fiction; War Story.

Basso, Hamilton

583. *The View from Pompey's Head.* Garden City, NY: Doubleday, 1954. 409 pp.
When a lawyer goes to a southern town to investigate a literary claim, he renews old friendships and begins to understand himself better.
Genre(s): Legal Story.

◆ May be suitable for young adult readers

Bechko, P. A.

◆ 584. *Blown to Hell*. New York: Doubleday, 1976. 186 pp.
Elias McPherson builds a windwagon and takes his grand-daughter toward California's gold fields, but they encounter a group of people who join them, and they stop in a place called Hell.
Genre(s): Western Fiction.

Becnel, Roxanne

585. *When Lightning Strikes*. New York: Dell, 1995. 416 pp.
In 1855, Abigail Bliss and her father leave Missouri on a wagon train to Oregon under an assumed name, a decision Abby does not understand, until one man kidnaps her to keep another from killing her.
Genre(s): Romance.

Berkman, Ted

586. *To Seize the Passing Dream*. Garden City, NY: Doubleday, 1972. 431 pp.
James Abbott McNeill Whistler lives in the United States and Europe during his artistic career; his most famous pieces including *Arrangement in Grey and Black No. 1* (*Whistler's Mother*) and the ornate *Peacock Room*.
Genre(s): Biographical Fiction.

Bittner, Rosanne

587. *Thunder on the Plains*. New York: Doubleday, 1992. 464 pp.
When Bo Landers hires Colt Travis to guide his party along a possible route for a railroad, his daughter Sunny falls in love with Travis, but because of their different backgrounds, they wait 12 years before admitting their feelings.
Genre(s): Love Story; Western Fiction; Romance.

Blake, James Carlos

588. *In the Rogue Blood*. New York: Avon, 1997. 352 pp.
In 1845, Edward and John Little depart their dysfunctional Florida home for the Mexican border, and when the Rio Grande separates them, they end up fighting on different sides during the Mexican War.
Award(s): Los Angeles Times Book Prize.
Genre(s): War Story.

Blake, Jennifer

589. *Arrow to the Heart*. New York: Fawcett, 1993. 325 pp.
In Louisiana before the Civil War, the disabled Giles goes to extreme lengths to have his wife bear an heir which he is incapable of siring.
Genre(s): Domestic Fiction.

590. *Midnight Waltz*. 1984. New York: Severn House, 1996. 343 pp.
Amalie Peschier begins to question her relationship with her husband on their Louisiana plantation.
Genre(s): Romance.

591. *Wildest Dreams*. Thorndike, ME: Thorndike, 1992. 628 pp.
The only person who knows the family perfume recipe dies without divulging it, and Joletta must go to Europe from her New Orleans shop to search for it.
Genre(s): Romance.

Blakely, Mike

592. *Shortgrass Song*. New York: Forge, 1994. 448 pp.
Ab Holcomb takes his family to Colorado before the Civil War, but his wife soon dies and a freed black man helps the three sons focus on becoming wealthy ranchers.
Genre(s): Western Fiction; Family Saga.

Blevins, Winfred

593. *Stone Song*. New York: Forge, 1995. 400 pp.
Crazy Horse has mystical experiences as a young boy that motivate him throughout his life.
Award(s): Western Writers of America Spur Award.
Genre(s): Biographical Fiction.

Bly, Stephen

594. *Sweet Carolina*. Wheaton, IL: Crossway, 1998. 224 pp.
When Carolina Cantrell arrives in Montana Territory to settle her brother's estate, his partner tries to cheat her, so she stays to run his business herself. (*Series:* Heroines of the Golden West, 1)
Genre(s): Romance; Western Fiction.

Bonner, Sherwood

595. *Like Unto Like*. Columbia, SC: University of South Carolina Press, 1997. 190 pp.
Blythe Herndon must marry an abolitionist who does not think that women should be free from the husband's will.
Genre(s): Domestic Fiction.

Bowers, Terrell L.

◆ 596. *Ride Against the Wind*. New York: Walker, 1996. 192 pp.
The feud between the Danmyer and Cates families continues, but when Jerrod Danmyer rescues Marian Cates after an accident, they fall in love.
Genre(s): Western Fiction.

Bradley, David

597. *The Chaneysville Incident*. New York: Harper and Row, 1981. 432 pp.
John Washington, an African American historian, begins to examine his past after his last conversation with the man who raised him covers the Chaneysville incident when 13 slaves were killed in rural Pennsylvania as they tried to escape from the South.

Brand, Max

598. *Drifter's Vengeance*. New York: Dodd, Mead, 1932. 219 pp.
After a gambler robs Piers Morgan of his gold mining claim, a drifter musician tries to clean the town of its lawlessness.
Genre(s): Western Fiction.

Bristow, Gwen

◆ 599. *Calico Palace.* New York: Crowell, 1970. 589 pp.
Kendra Morgan lives in San Francisco during the gold mining days, and she and her friend Marny, proprietor of the Calico Palace gambling hall, eventually find happiness.
Genre(s): Romance.

Brown, Wesley

600. *Darktown Strutters.* New York: Cane Hill, 1994. 225 pp.
Jim Crow, adopted by a slave who teaches him to dance, is leased from his owner to a minstrel show owner, and as the only African American in a white troupe he faces discrimination, but after the Civil War, he and two African American women create their own troupe.

Caldwell, Taylor

601. *Captains and the Kings.* Garden City, NY: Doubleday, 1972. 640 pp.
Joseph Armagh desires wealth and success for himself and for his children as he builds his empire beginning in 1850, but the second generation of his family seems cursed.
Genre(s): Domestic Fiction; Political Fiction.

Capps, Benjamin

602. *A Woman of the People.* New York: Duell, Sloane, and Pearce, 1966. 247 pp.
The Comanches raise two young girls captured by the tribe.
Genre(s): Western Fiction.

Carroll, Lenore

603. *Annie Chambers.* Wichita, KS: Watermark, 1990. 195 pp.
Annie's father turns her out for a minor reason, and after the death of her husband and two children within a year, her only option is prostitution.
Genre(s): Domestic Fiction.

Cary, Lorene

604. *The Price of a Child.* New York: Knopf, 1995. 317 pp.
Slave Ginnie contacts members of the Underground Railroad in 1855 just as her master plans to take her and her two children to Nicaragua, and she escapes to Philadelphia where she becomes a freedwoman speaking for abolition.
Genre(s): Political Fiction.

Cather, Willa

605. *Sapphira and the Slave Girl.* New York: Knopf, 1940. 295 pp.
Sapphira Colbert proceeds to persecute a once happy slave girl, Nancy, when Sapphira suspects her husband admires Nancy.
Genre(s): War Story.

Cendrars, Blaise

606. *Gold.* Trans. Nina Rootes. New York: M. Kesend, 1984. 128 pp.
General John Sutter, a Swiss, helps to settle California during the Gold Rush.
Genre(s): Biographical Fiction; Western Fiction.

Chaikin, Linda

607. *Empire Builders.* Minneapolis, MN: Bethany House, 1994. 334 pp.
A Northwest lumberman who loves railroad heiress Ember Ridgeway helps her overcome her extravagances.
Genre(s): Christian Fiction; Western Fiction.

Charyn, Jerome

608. *Darlin' Bill.* New York: Primus, 1980. 300 pp.
After Sally's mother forces her to marry the schoolmaster, she and her husband move from Kansas to South Dakota, where Sally meets and falls in love with Wild Bill Hickock.
Genre(s): Biographical Fiction; Western Fiction; Love Story.

Clarke, William Kendall

609. *The Robber Baroness.* New York: St. Martin's Press, 1979. 347 pp.
Hetty Robinson refuses to succumb to male-dominated society so she uses money as a means to power in the 1850s and 60s and earns a seat on the Stock Exchange.
Genre(s): Biographical Fiction.

Cliff, Michelle

610. *Free Enterprise.* New York: Dutton, 1993. 213 pp.
Mary Ellen Pleasant, a 19th-century African American abolitionist and businesswoman corresponds with Annie, a Jamaican abolitionist, who forsakes her wealth in favor of antislavery.

Coldsmith, Don

◆ 611. *Bearer of the Pipe.* New York: Doubleday, 1995. 258 pp.
In the sequel to *Child of the Dead*, the enemies of the Elk-dog People, the Head Splitters, become their allies after Wolf Pup is born and shows his spiritual perception.
Genre(s): Bildungsroman (Coming of Age).

612. *Child of the Dead.* New York: Doubleday, 1995. 245 pp.
In the mid-19th century, the widow Running Deer moves into a death camp where the only resident is a little girl who survived the pox, and the two of them begin to protect each other.
Genre(s): Domestic Fiction; Western Fiction.

◆ 613. *Elk-Dog Heritage.* New York: Doubleday, 1982. 181 pp.
The Elk-Dogs and the Head Splitters fight when the younger warriors such as Badger want to make names for themselves, while Heads Off and his wife, Tall One, try to stop them.
Genre(s): Western Fiction.

◆ May be suitable for young adult readers

◆ 614. *Moon of Thunder.* Garden City, NY: Doubleday, 1985. 179 pp.
Rabbit, 17, has a vision in which he sees a strange and beautiful horse, and he leaves his tribe to find the animal. (*Series:* Spanish Bit Saga, 7)
Genre(s): Western Fiction.

615. *South Wind.* New York: Bantam, 1998. 464 pp.
In the sequel to *Tallgrass*, Jed Sterling returns to Kansas in 1846 with a new wife, a black slave he bought in New Orleans.
Genre(s): Western Fiction.

Coleman, Jane Candia

616. *Doc Holliday's Woman.* New York: Warner Books, 1995. 325 pp.
Kate Elder, lover of both Doc Holliday and Wyatt Earp, first meets Doc after the death of her husband and son.
Genre(s): Biographical Fiction; Western Fiction.

Comfort, Will Levington

617. *Apache.* New York: Dutton, 1931. 274 pp.
Mangus Colorado, an Apache chief, tries to drive away the white intruders on his land.
Genre(s): Biographical Fiction; Western Fiction.

Conroy, Sarah Booth

618. *Refinements of Love.* New York: Pantheon, 1993. 301 pp.
Clover Adams must conceal her literary and artistic talents after marrying the vain Henry Adams, and when she refuses to acquiesce, she suffers a rapid, mysterious demise.
Genre(s): Biographical Fiction; Mystery.

Cooper, J. California

◆ 619. *Family.* New York: Doubleday, 1991. 240 pp.
A slave mother, distraught that her children, sired by her master, might be sold away from her, attempts to poison them all.
Genre(s): Domestic Fiction.

Coyle, Harold

◆ 620. *Look Away.* New York: Simon and Schuster, 1995. 495 pp.
Edward Banner wants to protect his wealth in divided New Jersey in 1859, so he sends one son to Virginia Military Institute and the other to the New Jersey militia, but the sons meet at the Battle of Gettysburg.
Genre(s): Domestic Fiction; War Story.

D'Aguiar, Fred

◆ 621. *The Longest Memory.* New York: Pantheon, 1994. 137 pp.
In Virginia before the Civil War, a young male slave tries to escape, is caught, and dies while his master punishes him.
Award(s): Whitbread Book of the Year Award.

Davies, June Wyndham

622. *Golden Destiny.* New York: St. Martin's Press, 1993. 352 pp.
In 1855, Alicia Langdon and her Chinese companion apply for jobs at Jack Cornish's ranch, and after he eventually hires them, Cornish falls in love with Alice.
Genre(s): Domestic Fiction.

Davis, H. L.

623. *Beulah Land.* New York: Morrow, 1949. 314 pp.
Evan Warne escapes the North Carolina mountains after killing a man, taking with him a Cherokee woman and a white youth raised as an Indian.
Genre(s): Western Fiction.

Dawson, Geralyn

624. *The Wedding Raffle.* New York: Pocket Books, 1996. 338 pp.
Since Honor Duvall needs money, she raffles her horse, but when the winner shows up to claim the prize, the horse has died.
Genre(s): Romance; Western Fiction.

De Blasis, Celeste

625. *The Proud Breed.* New York: Coward-McCann, 1978. 578 pp.
Tessa, a beautiful Anglo-Hispanic woman, marries a Yankee with whom she raises horses and many children in California during the mid-19th century.
Genre(s): Love Story.

626. *Swan's Chance.* New York: Bantam, 1985. 547 pp.
Alexandria enjoys her Maryland horse farm in the sequel to *Wild Swan* before the onslaught of the Civil War.
Genre(s): Romance; Family Saga.

Dolman, David

627. *The Bluestocking.* New York: St. Martin's Press, 1994. 287 pp.
Catherine Norton Sinclair Forrest and Edwin Forrest, an actor, accuse each other of adultery and any other sin that will support their argument for divorce in their 19th-century trial.
Genre(s): Legal Story.

Derleth, August William

628. *The House on the Mound.* 1958. Verona, WI: E.V.A., 1973. 335 pp.
Hercules Dousman, fur trader and railroad builder, attempts to gain custody of his illegitimate son.
Genre(s): Biographical Fiction.

629. *Still Is the Summer Night.* New York: Scribner's, 1937. 356 pp.
Lumber rafts float down the Wisconsin River near Sac Prairie in the early days of the settlers.
Genre(s): Western Fiction.

630. *The Wind Leans West.* Irving, CA: Candle-light, 1969. 323 pp.
Real estate and financial problems arise for those who try to settle Wisconsin near Milwaukee.
Genre(s): Western Fiction.

Deveraux, Jude

◆ **631.** *Mountain Laurel.* New York: Pocket Books, 1990. 312 pp.
In 1859, Madalyn Worth, known as LaReina, is an opera singer who goes to Denver to entertain the gold miners, where she looks for her kidnapped sister.
Genre(s): Western Fiction; Romance.

Doig, Ivan

632. *The Sea Runners.* New York: Atheneum, 1982. 279 pp.
Among indentured servants in Alaska of 1853 were Scandanavians who had served the czar for seven years, and four of them steal a boat in an escape attempt from New Archangel (now Sitka) to Astoria, Washington.

Easton, Robert Olney

633. *Power and Glory.* Santa Barbara, CA: Capra, 1989. 374 pp.
In 1853, Madame St. Clair and David Venable arrive in San Francisco, where they observe the political turmoil of the time.
Genre(s): Family Saga; Western Fiction.

Edmonds, Walter D.

634. *Rome Haul.* Boston: Little, Brown, 1929. 347 pp.
A young farmer becomes a boatman when he inherits the *Sarsey Sal* and experiences the life of the canal in the sequel to *Erie Water.*
Genre(s): Adventure Story.

Egan, Ferol

635. *The Taste of Time.* New York: McGraw Hill, 1977. 211 pp.
In 1859, widower Jedidiah Wright, 70, sells his farm and goes west to search for gold.
Genre(s): Western Fiction.

Eggleston, Edward

636. *The Graysons.* 1888. New York: AMS, 1970. 362 pp.
Attorney Abraham Lincoln presents arguments at a murder trial in Illinois before becoming president.
Genre(s): Biographical Fiction.

Ehrlich, Leonard

637. *God's Angry Man.* New York: Simon and Schuster, 1932. 401 pp.
Either fanatic or martyr, John Brown thinks that God has called him to wipe out slavery.
Genre(s): Biographical Fiction.

Eidson, Tom

◆ **638.** *St. Agnes' Stand.* New York: Putnam, 1994. 224 pp.
In 1858, when a murderer en route to California saves three nuns and seven orphans, St. Agnes decides that God has sent him, and she helps him.
Award(s): Western Writers of America Spur Award.
Genre(s): Western Fiction.

Epstein, Leslie

639. *Pinto and Sons.* Boston: Houghton Mifflin, 1990. 419 pp.
Pinto, a former Harvard medical student, comes to California during the Gold Rush and tries to find a rabies vaccine and a gun machine.
Genre(s): Medical Novel; Family Saga; Adventure Story.

Farr, Judith

640. *I Never Came to You in White.* Boston: Houghton Mifflin, 1996. 225 pp.
One of Emily Dickinson's teachers at Miss Lyons's Academy writes to Thomas Wentworth Higginson to chastize him for supporting Dickinson's poetry.
Genre(s): Biographical Fiction.

Feldhake, Susan C.

641. *In Love's Own Time.* Grand Rapids, MI: Zondervan, 1993. 176 pp.
Sue Ellen Stone keeps her faith and attracts Alton Wheeler, a frontiersman who is surprised by her strength.
(*Series:* Enduring Faith, 1)
Genre(s): Christian Fiction; Western Fiction.

Fisher, Vardis

642. *Mountain Man.* New York: Morrow, 1965. 305 pp.
The trapper builds Kate Bowden a cabin after Indians massacre her family, and then he falls in love with a Flathead whom the Crow later murder.
Award(s): Western Writers of America Spur Award.
Genre(s): Western Fiction.

Foreman, Paul

643. *Quanah, the Serpent Eagle.* Flagstaff, AZ: Northland, 1983. 151 pp.
When Quanah Parker, Comanche warrior, faces Colonel MacKenzie at Adobe Walls in Texas, MacKenzie kills the tribe's horses and defeats the Comanche.
Genre(s): Biographical Fiction.

Fraser, George MacDonald

644. *Flashman and the Angel of the Lord.* New York: Knopf, 1995. 394 pp.
In the sequel to *Flashman and the Mountain of Light,* Harry Paget Flashman goes to Harpers Ferry, West Virginia, during John Brown's raid.
Genre(s): Adventure Story.

Fuller, Jamie

◆ 645. *The Diary of Emily Dickinson.* San Francisco: Mercury House, 1993. 215 pp.
A diary supposedly found in Emily Dickinson's home recreates her 37th year.
Genre(s): Biographical Fiction.

Galloway, David

646. *Tamsen.* San Diego, CA: Harcourt Brace, 1983. 429 pp.
Tamsen Donner, wife of the Donner party's leader, suffers in 1846 as the group tries to find a way across the Sierra Nevadas in the snow.
Genre(s): Western Fiction.

Garwood, Julie

647. *For the Roses.* New York: Pocket Books, 1995. 528 pp.
When a gang of orphans finds Mary Rose discarded in a picnic basket in New York City, they take her to Montana for a better life, and their unusual family functions for 19 years until an English nobleman shows up to claim her.
Genre(s): Romance.

Giardina, Denise

◆ 648. *Storming Heaven.* New York: Norton, 1987. 277 pp.
In the Battle of Blair Mountain, West Viriginia, in the early 20th century, coal miners fight for unionization under the leadership of Rondal Lloyd and Carrie Bishop, a nurse who helps him before and after her husband's death.

Giles, Janice Holt

649. *Six-Horse Hitch.* Boston: Houghton Mifflin, 1969. 436 pp.
Joe Fowler, 19, becomes a stagecoach reinsman in 1859 and drives the Overland Stage west for 10 years before the railroad arrives in this sequel to *Shady Grove.*
Genre(s): Adventure Story; Family Saga; Western Fiction.

Gillmor, Frances

650. *Windsinger.* Santa Fe, NM: University of New Mexico Press, 1930. 218 pp.
The Navajo prophet Windsinger, orphaned as a child, becomes the leader of tribal chants, a position of importance, and believes he is destined to help his people survive.
Genre(s): Western Fiction.

Goede, William

651. *Quantrill.* Montreal: Quadrant, 1982. 246 pp.
Kit Dalton writes about his experiences with Confederate cavalry captain William Clarke Quantrill and says that if Quantrill had been a Greek, he would have been considered a god rather than a human butcher.
Genre(s): Biographical Fiction; War Story.

Goldreich, Gloria

◆ 652. *West to Eden.* New York: Macmillan, 1987. 418 pp.
Emma leaves Amsterdam after her father's death for Galveston, Texas, where she runs a boardinghouse until leaving for Phoenix, Arizona.
Genre(s): Domestic Fiction.

Gonzalez, Jovita, and Eve Raleigh

653. *Caballero.* College Station: Texas A & M University Press, 1996. 350 pp.
A Mexican patriarch Don Santiago de Mendoza y Soria tries to keep his daughters from anything American, but thy both fall in love with Texas Rangers before the war with Mexico in 1848.
Genre(s): War Story.

Gordon, Leo V., and Richard Vetterli

654. *Powderkeg.* Novato, CA: Presidio, 1991. 361 pp.
In 1857, President Buchanan hears false reports about an uprising in Utah, and he sends an army there to quell it, but the real purpose is for the army to keep traveling into California and encourage sympathy for secession.
Genre(s): Family Saga.

Graver, Elizabeth

655. *Unravelling.* Boston: Hyperion, 1997. 352 pp.
Aimee Slater leaves her New Hampshire family for Lowell, Massachusetts, and independence, but she finds that her hastiness has made her lonely.
Genre(s): Bildungsroman (Coming of Age).

Green, Julian

◆ 656. *The Distant Lands.* Trans. Barbara Beaumont. New York: M. Boyars, 1991. 902 pp.
Elizabeth Escridge and her mother arrive at Dimwood Plantation from England with no money in 1850, and in what seems to be a land where nothing happens, Elizabeth finds much tension under the superficial politeness.
Genre(s): Adventure Story.

Greenough, Malcolm W.

657. *Dear Lily.* Dublin, NH: Yankee, 1987. 239 pp.
An old lady, Lily Violett, writes letters to her great nephew about the life of her family in New Orleans from 1859 to 1935.
Genre(s): Biographical Fiction; Love Story; Domestic Fiction.

Grey, Zane

658. *The Last of the Plainsmen.* New York: Grosset & Dunlap, 1911. 314 pp.
A trip across the Arizona desert with Buffalo Jones reveals the beauty of the area.
Genre(s): Biographical Fiction; Western Fiction.

Grove, Fred

659. *The Child Stealers.* New York: Doubleday, 1973. 205 pp.
In 1860, a cavalry officer tries to find a Native American who supposedly is leading a child kidnapping ring in the southwest.
Genre(s): Western Fiction.

Guthrie, A. B.

660. *Fair Land, Fair Land.* New York: Houghton Mifflin, 1982. 262 pp.
In the sequel to *The Way West*, Dick Summers enjoys Montana in 1845, hunting and trapping, but after the gold rush and new settlers, game becomes scarce.
Genre(s): Western Fiction.

661. *These Thousand Hills.* New York: Houghton Mifflin, 1956. 346 pp.
In the sequel to *Fair Land, Fair Land*, when Lat Evans drives a herd of cattle to Montana, he decides to stay and get his own ranch.
Genre(s): Western Fiction.

Hannah, Kristin

662. *Waiting for the Moon.* New York: Fawcett, 1995. 374 pp.
Someone brings an unconscious and bruised woman to Dr. Ian Carrick's home in 19th century Maine, and although he tries to save her, she ends up saving him.
Genre(s): Romance; Gothic Fiction; Medical Novel.

Harper, M. A.

◆ 663. *For the Love of Robert E. Lee.* New York: Soho, 1992. 325 pp.
A young girl works on a school report in the 1960s about Robert E. Lee and falls in love with him.
Genre(s): Time Travel; Love Story; Biographical Fiction.

Hartman, Jane E.

◆ 664. *Cougar Woman.* Santa Fe, NM: Sunstone, 1983. 127 pp.
Cougar Woman is taken hostage and made a slave in the Crow society, but she rises in ranks to become a shaman and finally a leader in her tribe.
Genre(s): Biographical Fiction.

Hatvary, George Egon

◆ 665. *The Murder of Edgar Allan Poe.* New York: Carroll and Graf, 1997. 211 pp.
When Auguste Dupin receives a letter in 1849 while in Paris that Edgar Allan Poe has died, possibly murdered, he goes to America to investigate.
Genre(s): Biographical Fiction; Mystery.

Heidish, Marcy

◆ 666. *A Woman Called Moses.* Boston: Houghton Mifflin, 1976. 308 pp.
Harriet Tubman earns the name of Moses while conducting hundreds of African American slaves along the Underground Railroad.
Genre(s): Biographical Fiction.

Hepler, Don

667. *Frontier Justice: Virginia.* New York: Thomas Bouregy, 1996. 192 pp.
Katie Withrow becomes a teacher in a small Virginia frontier town after her father is murdered.

Herrin, Lamar

668. *The Unwritten Chronicles of Robert E. Lee.* New York: St. Martin's Press, 1989. 248 pp.
Robert E. Lee and Stonewall Jackson express their thoughts about their lives and their participation in the Civil War battles leading to Chancellorsville.
Genre(s): Biographical Fiction.

Hoff, B. J.

669. *Dawn of the Golden Promise.* Minneapolis, MN: Bethany House, 1994. 194 pp.
The Irish come to America to escape the difficult 19th-century conditions of their homeland. (*Series:* Emerald Ballad, 5)
Genre(s): Christian Fiction.

670. *Heart of the Lonely Exile.* Minneapolis, MN: Bethany House, 1991. 384 pp.
In New York City, the Kavanaghs, Irish immigrants, find a new life. (*Series:* Emerald Ballad, 2)
Genre(s): Christian Fiction.

671. *Land of a Thousand Dreams.* Minneapolis, MN: Bethany House, 1992. 400 pp.
A family struggles for a new life and survival as immigrants in America. (*Series:* Emerald Ballad, 3)
Genre(s): Christian Fiction.

672. *Sons of an Ancient Glory.* Minneapolis, MN: Bethany House, 1993. 396 pp.
Families separated by the Irish potato famine either remain in Ireland or work in America. (*Series:* Emerald Ballad, 4)
Genre(s): Christian Fiction; Romance.

Holland, Cecelia

◆ 673. *Railroad Schemes.* New York: Forge, 1997. 272 pp.
In New Mexico during the 1850s, Spanish families believe the land belongs to them, but Lilly, daughter of one robber and expected wife of another, decides to find a different way of life.
Genre(s): Western Fiction; Love Story; Mystery.

Holm, Stef Ann

674. *Crossings.* New York: Pocket Books, 1995. 368 pp.
Helena Gray must manage the Pony Express station after her father dies, and in order to get necessary supplies, she marries a recluse who wants a piece of land.
Genre(s): Western Fiction; Romance.

Hough, Emerson

675. *The Covered Wagon.* New York: Appleton, 1922. 378 pp.
In 1848, two thousand people move from Missouri to Oregon in a wagon train.
Genre(s): Western Fiction.

Johnson, Charles Richard

676. *Oxherding Tale.* Bloomington: Indiana University Press, 1982. 176 pp.
Educated Andrew Hawkins, son of his master's wife and a house slave, searches for a place of spiritual and physical freedom.
Genre(s): Adventure Story.

Johnson, Janice Kay

677. *The Island Snatchers.* New York: Forge, 1997. 384 pp.
Anne Cartwright is unhappily married to missionary John Cartwright in Hawaii during the 1800s, but she did not want to stay in her family home, and when he soon dies, she makes herself invaluable to the indigenous people and missionaries as nurse and midwife.
Genre(s): Medical Novel.

Kane, Harnett T.

678. *The Gallant Mrs. Stonewall.* Garden City, NY: Doubleday, 1957. 320 pp.
Anna Morrison Jackson has a short but happy marriage to the Confederate leader, Stonewall Jackson.
Genre(s): Biographical Fiction; War Story; Domestic Fiction.

Kantor, MacKinlay

679. *Spirit Lake.* New York: World, 1961. 957 pp.
Marauding Indians massacre 30 settlers near Spirit Lake, Iowa, in 1857, leaving horrified survivors.
Genre(s): Western Fiction.

Kelley, Leo P.

680. *Morgan.* Garden City, NY: Doubleday, 1986. 192 pp.
Shad leaves Connecticut for California during the Gold Rush, hoping to make a fortune, but he becomes the target of con men and claim jumpers.
Genre(s): Adventure Story.

Kennedy, William

681. *Quinn's Book.* New York: Viking, 1988. 289 pp.
Daniel Quinn, a star journalist of the Civil War, remembers his prewar years pursuing Maud Fallon, an actress known for her interpretations of Byron and Keats while nude.

Keyes, Frances Parkinson

682. *The Chess Players.* New York: Farrar, Straus and Cuhady, 1960. 533 pp.
Paul Charles Morphy becomes a chess player and, at 21 in the mid-19th century, gains fame as the world's greatest player.
Genre(s): Biographical Fiction.

King, Joan

◆ 683. *Impressionist: A Novel of Mary Cassatt.* New York: Beaufort, 1983. 320 pp.
Mary Cassatt, a strong woman, decides to leave her family in Pittsburgh to study and paint in France, and there she joins with the group creating a new style of art.
Genre(s): Biographical Fiction.

Kiraly, Marie

684. *Madeline.* New York: Berkley, 1996. 407 pp.
In 1849, Pamela asks Poe's help with her search for her mother and kidnapped son, and during their travels, they meet Madeline Usher, survivor of her collapsed home.
Genre(s): Mystery.

Kirkpatrick, Jane

◆ 685. *Love to Water My Soul.* Sisters, OR: Questar, 1996. 368 pp.
Modocs find and raise Asiam, a young girl left at a watering hole by her family traveling west, until they trade her to a group of Paiutes, where she undergoes their rituals for arriving at womanhood.
Genre(s): Christian Fiction.

Lamb, Eleanor, and Douglas Stewart

686. *Against a Crooked Sky.* New York: Bantam, 1976. 119 pp.
In the 1850s, Sam Isaac Sutter, 11, goes with a Russian trapper to search for his kidnapped sister, and although he finds her, he cannot trade his life for hers.
Genre(s): Western Fiction.

Lambert, Page

◆ 687. *Shifting Stars.* New York: Tor, 1997. 352 pp.
Skye, daughter of Gregory McDonald (a bagpipe-playing trapper who escaped Scottish Highland persecution), and the deceased Breathcatcher (a Lakota Sioux), returns to her grandmother for instruction in her heritage and discovers that Caws Like Magpie loved her mother and still hates her father.
Genre(s): Romance; Western Fiction.

L'Amour, Louis

688. *Comstock Lode.* New York: Bantam, 1981. 404 pp.
In Virginia City, Nevada, during the 1860s heroes and heroines fight villains over the Comstock Lode.
Genre(s): Western Fiction.

◆ 689. *The Lonesome Gods.* New York: Bantam, 1983. 450 pp.
Johannes Verne is abandoned in the desert as a child in the 1840s, and he spends his life avoiding his enemies, including his grandfather.
Genre(s): Western Fiction.

690. *The Man from the Broken Hills.* New York: Bantam, 1975. 224 pp.
Milo Talon, a Sackett relative, rides the outlaw trail and searches for a man who betrayed the family. (*Series:* The Talons, 1)
Genre(s): Western Fiction.

691. *The Tall Stranger.* New York: Omnibus, 1957. 128 pp.
After a wagon train heads west, the party discovers that their guide is a killer.
Genre(s): Western Fiction.

Lee, W. W.

692. *Rogue's Gold.* New York: Walker, 1989. 192 pp.
Jefferson Birch, a former Texas Ranger, must rid Grant's Pass, Oregon, of the men robbing the gold miners and payroll keepers for the logging camps.
Genre(s): Western Fiction.

Lee, Wendi

693. *The Overland Trail.* New York: Forge, 1996. 320 pp.
America Hollis becomes pregnant, marries a man she barely knows so that her Philadelphia family will not be embarrassed, and leaves with him for the West via the Overland Trail.
Genre(s): Western Fiction.

Longley, Ralph L.

694. *Cabin on the Second Ridge.* New York: Vantage, 1976. 166 pp.
A family pioneers in Iowa during the 19th century.
Genre(s): Biographical Fiction; Domestic Fiction.

Lovelace, Maud Hart

695. *Early Candlelight.* New York: John Day, 1929. 322 pp.
Delia DuGay, daughter of a voyageur, lives on the frontier in Minnesota where she falls in love with fur trader Jasper Page.
Genre(s): Western Fiction; Love Story.

MacDougall, Ruth Doan

696. *The Flowers of the Forest.* New York: Atheneum, 1981. 278 pp.
The MacLornes and their neighbors emigrate to America from Scotland in the 1860s and settle in New Hampshire where they begin a sheep farm, only to lose it in unusual circumstances.
Genre(s): Domestic Fiction.

MacLean, Amanda

697. *Everlasting.* Sisters, OR: Palisades, 1996. 316 pp.
Sheridan O'Brien arrives in San Francisco from Ireland in 1855 to search for her lost twin who disappeared during the gold rush, and she hires a newspaper editor pretending to be a detective to help her.
Genre(s): Christian Fiction; Love Story; Western Fiction.

Magnuson, James, and Dorothea G. Petrie

698. *Orphan Train.* New York: Dial, 1978. 307 pp.
In 1853, Emma Symns of the Children's Aid Society takes 20 orphans west into Illinois on the train.

Marlowe, Stephen

699. *The Lighthouse at the End of the World.* New York: Dutton, 1995. 324 pp.
Poe's actions during the five days he disappeared in 1849 before he died become the focus of this investigation.
Genre(s): Mystery.

Martin, Kat

700. *Midnight Rider.* New York: St. Martin's Press, 1996. 372 pp.
Caralee McConnell's uncle claims Rancho del Robles after the Mexican War, but to keep it in his family, Ramon de la Guerra raids the ranch and captures Caralee.
Genre(s): Romance; War Story.

Martin, Larry Jay

◆ **701.** *El Lazo.* New York: Bantam, 1991. 192 pp.
In the mid-1850s, Native Americans rescue John Clinton Ryan from a shipwreck, but when his captain accuses him of causing the wreck, Ryan becomes a vaquero who always looks for his spiteful captain.
Genre(s): Western Fiction.

Masterton, Graham

702. *A Man of Destiny.* New York: Simon and Schuster, 1981. 384 pp.
Collis Edmonds, playboy son of a bankrupt financier, must go to California to seek his fortune, and there he falls in love with women and railroads.
Genre(s): Western Fiction.

Matthews, Greg

◆ **703.** *The Further Adventures of Huckleberry Finn.* New York: Crown, 1983. 500 pp.
In a sequel to *Huckleberry Finn*, Huck and Jim go west during the gold rush where they encounter a variety of unsavory characters while fleeing from a persistent detective.
Genre(s): Adventure Story.

◆ **704.** *Heart of the Country.* New York: Norton, 1986. 532 pp.
Half-white Joe Cobden's mother died giving birth to him on the Kansas prairie in 1855, and he lives in St. Louis with a doctor until age 16, when his physical disability (a hunchback) causes him to feel like an outsider, and he leaves the life he has known.
Genre(s): Medical Novel.

McCarthy, Cormac

705. *Blood Meridian, or, The Evening Redness in the West.* New York: Random House, 1985. 337 pp.
A 15-year-old runaway travels west and joins killers who have a contract for Apache scalps.
Genre(s): Western Fiction.

McCarthy, Gary

706. *The Gringo Amigo.* Garden City, NY: Doubleday, 1991. 182 pp.
Michael Callahan, in California in the early 1850s searching for gold, supports Mexicans required to pay special taxes when staking a mining claim and becomes friends with Joaquin Murieta.
Genre(s): Biographical Fiction; Western Fiction.

Mead, Robert Douglas

◆ 707. *Heartland.* Garden City, NY: Doubleday, 1986. 635 pp.
In 1859, Issac Pride leaves Iowa to find gold at Pike's Peak but spends the next 19 years in Kansas hunting buffalo, trading with the Native Americans, and becoming a businessman.
Genre(s): Western Fiction.

Medawar, Mardi Oakley

708. *People of the Whistling Waters.* Encampment, WY: Affiliated Writers of America, 1993. 442 pp.
Renee DeGeer, a French Canadian living with the tribe of his Crow wife, adopts Egbert Higgins after his parents die, and Egbert follows the Crow ways.
Genre(s): Western Fiction.

Mitchell, Paige

709. *Wild Seed.* Garden City, NY: Doubleday, 1982. 528 pp.
After Ben Calder and Anna Bellinger marry and leave Prussia for Texas in 1845, they begin a four-generation dynasty of ranches and plantations, love and hate.
Genre(s): Family Saga.

Monfredo, Miriam Grace

◆ 710. *Blackwater Spirits.* New York: St. Martin's Press, 1995. 328 pp.
The Jewish doctor Neva Cardoza arrives in Seneca Falls in 1857, and she and Glynis Tryon hear a farmer's concern for his life before he is poisoned, and when other murders follow, they investigate.
Genre(s): Mystery.

711. *North Star Conspiracy.* New York: St. Martin's Press, 1993. 352 pp.
Glynis Tryon decides not to marry, staying in Seneca Falls, and when her landlady's son Niles appears with Kiri, a slave he convinced to escape and whom he plans to marry, Glynis helps to defend Niles at his southern trial and to investigate several unexplained deaths.
Genre(s): Mystery.

◆ 712. *Seneca Falls Inheritance.* New York: St. Martin's Press, 1992. 259 pp.
Glynis Tryon, librarian in Seneca Falls, New York, investigates the murder of a woman claiming to be the illegitimate daughter of a recently deceased man prior to the First Women's Rights Convention in 1848.
Genre(s): Mystery.

713. *Through a Gold Eagle.* New York: Berkley, 1996. 386 pp.
Glynis Tryon, a Seneca Falls librarian in the 19th century, becomes involved with a murder investigation while reading of Lincoln's wife, Mary Todd, and John Brown's abolitionist ideas.
Genre(s): Mystery.

Morris, Gilbert

714. *The Reluctant Bridegroom.* Minneapolis, MN: Bethany House, 1990. 303 pp.
Sky Winslow leads a wagon train of brides from New York to Oregon. (*Series:* House of Winslow, 7)
Genre(s): Domestic Fiction; Family Saga; Christian Fiction.

Mountjoy, Roberta Jean

715. *Night Wind.* New York: Coward-McCann, 1981. 356 pp.
Marcus Opalgate loves Night Wind but not enough to prevent him from taking the giant California redwoods for lumber during the California Gold Rush era.
Genre(s): Love Story.

Murray, Earl

716. *Flaming Sky.* New York: Forge, 1995. 382 pp.
Adam Garret, undercover journalist hired by Ulysses S. Grant to find evil things about Custer, tells the story of Custer's Last Stand in the summer of 1876.
Genre(s): Biographical Fiction; War Story.

Names, Larry D.

717. *Boomtown.* Garden City, NY: Doubleday, 1981. 172 pp.
Prospector Russ Nichols teams with a newspaperman to create a boomtown called Carthage City, but hired killers interfere with their plans.
Genre(s): Western Fiction.

Nelson, Betty Palmer

718. *The Weight of Light, 1849-1890.* New York: St. Martin's Press, 1992. 302 pp.
In the sequel to *Private Knowledge*, the Nolans, Hendersons, and Fowlers continue to live in Tennessee with forays into Louisiana and Texas.
Genre(s): Domestic Fiction.

Nevin, David

719. *Dream West.* New York: Putnam, 1983. 639 pp.
John Fremont suffers while trying to help his country succeed as he explores the West and aids California.
Genre(s): Western Fiction; Biographical Fiction.

Olds, Bruce

◆ 720. *Raising Holy Hell.* New York: Henry Holt, 1995. 335 pp.
The source of John Brown's fanatical attempt to end slavery might have been his interest in abstract justice rather

than a concern for slaves, but an important influence in his life was the death of his mother when he was a child. *Genre(s):* Biographical Fiction.

Orde, Lewis

721. *Dreams of Gold.* New York: Zebra, 1993. 524 pp.
Two orphans escape from their London uncle to New Orleans, where a typhoid epidemic occurs before the Civil War starts.
Genre(s): Romance.

Parker, F. M.

722. *The Assassins.* New York: New American Library, 1989. 256 pp.
In the 1840s, thieves shoot Tim Wollfolk as he arrives in New Orleans to inherit his uncle's business and throw him into the Mississippi, but he survives, only to find that an ex-Texas Ranger has assumed his identity in order to take the inheritance.
Genre(s): Western Fiction.

723. *The Predators.* San Diego, CA: Harcourt Brace, 1990. 352 pp.
In 1859, Mormon women walk from Nebraska to Utah harnessed to handcarts with only a few men protecting them, encountering Indians wanting blonde wives and Texans wanting wives of any kind.
Genre(s): Western Fiction.

724. *The Shadow Man.* New York: New American Library, 1988. 256 pp.
When a Texas senator sees the value of Mexican holdings in the Pecos River Valley, his henchmen kill all residents, but Jacob Tamarron joins a Comanche for revenge.
Genre(s): Political Fiction; Western Fiction.

Peart, Jane

725. *A Distant Dawn.* Grand Rapids, MI: Zondervan, 1995. 240 pp.
Sunny Lyndall and her brother Tracy set out for California, but after they are robbed, they take jobs with the Pony Express. (*Series:* Westward Dreams, 3)
Genre(s): Western Fiction; Christian Fiction.

◆ 726. *Folly's Bride.* Grand Rapids, MI: Zondervan, 1990. 192 pp.
Sara, thoughtless and impertinent, becomes calm under the influence of family scion and master of Montclair, Clayborn Montrose. (*Series:* Brides of Montclair, 4)
Genre(s): Christian Fiction; Romance.

727. *Promise of the Valley.* Grand Rapids, MI: Zondervan, 1995. 282 pp.
A woman travels from Virginia to Napa Valley, California, to start a new life. (*Series:* Westward Dreams)
Genre(s): Romance; Christian Fiction.

◆ 728. *Runaway Heart.* Grand Rapids, MI: Zondervan, 1994. 231 pp.
Holly Lambeth goes to visit her cousins in Oregon after her engagement ends, but when they do not welcome her, she must survive alone. (*Series:* Westward Dreams, 1)
Genre(s): Christian Fiction; Romance.

◆ 729. *Where Tomorrow Waits.* Grand Rapids, MI: Zondervan, 1995. 221 pp.
A young woman who lives on the Oregon frontier makes her own life. (*Series:* Westward Dreams, 3)
Genre(s): Christian Fiction; Western Fiction.

Perry, Frederick E.

730. *Thunder on the Mountains.* Philadelphia: Dorrance, 1973. 166 pp.
Chief Joseph tries to lead his people away from the white soldiers into Canada during the late 19th century.
Genre(s): Biographical Fiction.

Phillips, Michael R.

◆ 731. *Daughter of Grace.* Minneapolis, MN: Bethany House, 1990. 299 pp.
The Hollister father, a widower, decides that he must find a new wife. (*Series:* Journals of Corrie Belle Hollister, 2)
Genre(s): Christian Fiction; Western Fiction.

◆ 732. *On the Trail of the Truth.* Minneapolis, MN: Bethany House, 1991. 319 pp.
When Corrie's father remarries, her siblings have a mother to care for them and she is free to think about her future. (*Series:* Journals of Corrie Belle Hollister, 3)
Genre(s): Christian Fiction; Western Fiction.

◆ 733. *A Place in the Sun.* Minneapolis, MN: Bethany House, 1991. 300 pp.
The Hollister family has both internal and external struggles. (*Series:* Journals of Corrie Belle Hollister, 4)
Genre(s): Christian Fiction; Western Fiction.

Phillips, Michael R., and Judith Pella

◆ 734. *My Father's World.* Minneapolis, MN: Bethany House, 1990. 286 pp.
The five Hollister children must find their way to California when their mother dies on the wagon train. (*Series:* Journals Of Corrie Belle Hollister, 1)
Genre(s): Christian Fiction; Western Fiction.

Preston, Don, and Sue Preston

735. *Crazy Fox Remembers.* Englewood Cliffs, NJ: Prentice Hall, 1981. 228 pp.
Jackie Knight, a remittance man, wanders through the West with Crazy Fox, guarding him during the late 19th century.
Genre(s): Western Fiction.

Price, Eugenia

◆ 736. *Beauty From Ashes.* New York: Doubleday, 1995. 627 pp.
The sequel to *Where Shadows Go* shows Anne Fraser struggling to rebuild her family even though she has lost her husband, two daughters, and her mother within six years around the time of the Civil War.
Genre(s): Romance.

737. *Before the Darkness Falls.* Garden City, NY: Doubleday, 1987. 455 pp.
In the sequel to *To See Your Face Again*, three families in Georgia have hardships and joys as they make difficult

choices in their lives prior to the Civil War. (*Series:* Savannah Quartet, 3)
Genre(s): Domestic Fiction; Family Saga; Romance.

◆ 738. *Margaret's Story.* Philadelphia: Lippincott, 1980. 394 pp.
In the sequel to *Maria*, Margaret Fleming raises her family at Hibernia, and her sons fight on both sides of the Civil War.
Genre(s): Romance; War Story.

◆ 739. *New Moon Rising.* Philadelphia: Lippincott, 1969. 281 pp.
In the sequel to *Lighthouse*, Horace Bunch Gould is dismissed from Yale for rebelling and returns to St. Simons Island where he runs his plantation and worries about slavery.
Genre(s): Romance; Family Saga; War Story.

◆ 740. *Stranger in Savannah.* Garden City, NY: Doubleday, 1989. 755 pp.
In the sequel to *Before the Darkness Falls*, three prominent Savannah families hear the first sounds of secession in 1854. (*Series:* Savannah Quartet, 4)
Genre(s): Domestic Fiction; Romance; Family Saga.

◆ 741. *The Waiting Time.* New York: Doubleday, 1997. 384 pp.
After Abbie Allyn marries and moves to a Georgia rice plantation, her husband dies, leaving her with 100 slaves and management of the land, but her young overseer helps her succeed.
Genre(s): Romance.

Proctor, George W.

◆ 742. *Walks Without a Soul.* New York: Doubleday, 1990. 183 pp.
In antebellum Texas, Nate and his family are slave sharecroppers, but when Comanches kidnap Nate's wife, he is able to travel freely among them in search of her because they only recognize men who are white.
Genre(s): Western Fiction.

Rhodes, Richard

743. *The Ungodly; a Novel of the Donner Party.* New York: Charterhouse, 1973. 371 pp.
In 1846, pioneers on their way to California become trapped in the Sierra Nevada during winter snow, and some resort to cannibalism.
Genre(s): Western Fiction.

Rice, Anne

744. *The Feast of All Saints.* New York: Simon and Schuster, 1979. 571 pp.
In antebellum New Orleans, quadroons who are children of a white plantation owner and his mistress grow up in style, but their mixed blood excludes them from society.

Riefe, Barbara

◆ 745. *Against all Odds.* New York: Tor, 1997. 288 pp.
Lucy Mitchum agrees to sell all and go with her husband on a wagon train to California to find gold, and she and other women on the journey keep the men focused.
Genre(s): Western Fiction.

Ripley, Alexandra

746. *New Orleans Legacy.* New York: Macmillan, 1987. 435 pp.
When Mary McAlister leaves home at 16 after her father's death to find her mother's family in New Orleans, she becomes involved in numerous unexpected situations.
Genre(s): Romance.

Roddy, Lee

747. *Giants on the Hill.* Dallas: Word, 1994. 313 pp.
Aldar Laird brings his innocent Eastern bride to San Francisco during the Gold Rush, and she begins to draw strength from and influence the people she meets.
Genre(s): Christian Fiction; Western Fiction; Allegory.

Roderus, Frank

748. *J.A. Whitford and the Great California Gold Hunt.* New York: Doubleday, 1990. 186 pp.
In 1859, J.A. Whitford sells passage to nonexistent gold fields in Baja, California, but when he loses the money, he cannot abandon the men in Florida as he had planned.
Genre(s): Western Fiction.

Rogers, Gayle

749. *The Second Kiss.* New York: McKay, 1972. 315 pp.
Blackfoot Indians capture Maria Frame in 1846 while her family is traveling to Oregon, and after she understands their ways, she falls in love with Nakoa, her captor, but she will not accept his offer to be his second wife.
Genre(s): Love Story.

Ross, Ann T.

750. *The Pilgrimage.* New York: Macmillan, 1987. 304 pp.
Emma Louise, 12, and her 17-year-old sister become members of the Donner party and survive the 1846 debacle as they answer God's call to serve the Indians in Oregon as missionaries.
Genre(s): Adventure Story.

Ross, Dana Fuller

◆ 751. *California!* New York: Bantam, 1981. 384 pp.
Whip Holt, his son Toby, daughter Cindy and their best friend observe the gold rush. (*Series:* Wagons West, 6)
Genre(s): Western Fiction; Adventure Story.

◆ 752. *Colorado!* New York: Bantam, 1981. 275 pp.
Whip Holt and his children lead a wagon train through Colorado. (*Series:* Wagons West, 7)
Genre(s): Western Fiction; Adventure Story.

◆ 753. *Idaho!* New York: Bantam, 1984. 338 pp.
Whip Holt takes a northerly route for his wagon train going to Idaho. (*Series:* Wagons West, 13)
Genre(s): Western Fiction; Adventure Story.

◆ 754. *Louisiana!* New York: Bantam, 1986. 337 pp.
Whip Holt's wagon train enters Louisana and encounters several unexpected situations. (*Series:* Wagons West, 16)
Genre(s): Western Fiction; Adventure Story.

◆ 755. *Mississippi!* New York: Bantam, 1985. 334 pp.
Whip Holt becomes wagon master for a wagon train bound for Mississippi. (*Series:* Wagons West, 15)
Genre(s): Western Fiction; Adventure Story.

◆ 756. *Missouri!* New York: Bantam, 1985. 334 pp.
Whip Holt starts his wagon train in Missouri. (*Series:* Wagons West, 14)
Genre(s): Western Fiction; Adventure Story.

◆ 757. *Montana!* New York: Bantam, 1983. 384 pp.
Taking a northern route, Whip Holt, his children, and a friend go to the lands of Montana. (*Series:* Wagons West, 10)
Genre(s): Western Fiction; Adventure Story.

◆ 758. *Tennessee!* New York: Bantam, 1986. 305 pp.
Whip Holt becomes wagon master for a train driving through Tennessee. (*Series:* Wagons West, 17)
Genre(s): Western Fiction; Adventure Story.

◆ 759. *Utah!* New York: Bantam, 1984. 304 pp.
Whip Holt, his children, and friends travel into Utah. (*Series:* Wagons West, 12)
Genre(s): Western Fiction; Adventure Story.

◆ 760. *Washington!* New York: Bantam, 1982. 352 pp.
Whip Holt's wagon train arrives in Washington state. (*Series:* Wagons West, 9)
Genre(s): Western Fiction; Adventure Story.

Ross, James R.

761. *I, Jesse James.* Los Angeles: Dragon, 1989. 280 pp.
While the James brothers exhibit their violence, they are devoted to family and even are heroic in some situations.
Genre(s): Biographical Fiction; Western Fiction.

Rowe, Jack

762. *Brandywine.* New York: Watts, 1984. 394 pp.
The Gallaghers, Irish immigrants, try to adapt themselves to their new home in Wilmington, Delaware, in the early 19th century, and one of their members becomes involved with a guest of the Du Pont family.
Genre(s): Biographical Fiction; Epic Literature.

Sanchez, Thomas

763. *Rabbit Boss.* New York: Knopf, 1973. 468 pp.
Four generations of a Washo family—Gayabuc who saw the white men of the Donner Party eat their own flesh, and his children and grandchildren—see their livelihood disappear in the second half of the 19th century.

Schulte, Elaine L.

764. *Eternal Passage.* Colorado Springs, CO: Chariot, 1989. 279 pp.
Louise Abigail Setter takes a ship to California via Panama to flee the abuses of her past. (*Series:* California Pioneer)
Genre(s): Christian Fiction; Adventure Story.

765. *Golden Dreams.* Colorado Springs, CO: Chariot, 1989. 253 pp.
After her fiancé dies, Rose Wilmington takes a ship to California, and on board, she meets a handsome passenger. (*Series:* California Pioneer)
Genre(s): Christian Fiction; Adventure Story.

766. *The Journey West.* Colorado Springs, CO: Chariot, 1989. 274 pp.
Abby Windsor Talbot finds that she is bankrupt after her father dies, and she decides to join a wagon train going west. (*Series:* California Pioneer)
Genre(s): Christian Fiction; Western Fiction; Adventure Story.

767. *Mercies So Tender.* Elgin, IL: Life Journey, 1995. 286 pp.
Kate Talbot and her family try to help slaves along the Underground Railway in Missouri before the Civil War, but slaveholders drive them away, and Kate falls in love with the slaveowner on the plantation where they find shelter. (*Series:* California Pioneer)
Genre(s): Christian Fiction; War Story.

768. *Peace Like a River.* Colorado Springs, CO: Chariot, 1993. 275 pp.
Callie Murray participates in a deceptive plan that she hopes will help reunite her family with their Talbot relatives in California.
Genre(s): Western Fiction; Adventure Story; Christian Fiction.

769. *With Wings as Eagles.* Colorado Springs, CO: Chariot, 1990. 297 pp.
Betsy Talbot becomes part of the Gold Rush but faces both danger and disappointment. (*Series:* California Pioneer)
Genre(s): Christian Fiction; Adventure Story; Western Fiction.

Settle, Mary Lee

770. *Know Nothing.* 1960. New York: Scribner's, 1988. 334 pp.
In the sequel to *O Beulah Land*, families in West Virginia become involved in the controversy of slavery in the 20 years before the Civil War begins.
Genre(s): Family Saga; Political Fiction.

Shaara, Jeff

◆ 771. *Gods and Generals.* New York: Ballantine, 1996. 498 pp.
Two Confederate and two Union generals (Lee, Jackson, Hancock, and Chamberlain) examine their careers leading to Fredericksburg and Chancellorsville in a prequel to *The Killer Angels*.
Genre(s): War Story.

Shelton, Gene

772. *Last Gun.* New York: Doubleday, 1991. 178 pp.
John Selman's career as an outlaw and rustler begins after he deserts the Confederate Army and continues until 1896 when an enemy finds him.
Genre(s): Biographical Fiction; Western Fiction.

Sherburne, James

◆ 773. *Hacey Miller.* Boston: Houghton Mifflin, 1971. 306 pp.
In 1845, Hacey, 13, leaves Kentucky for Boston and college where he becomes a staunch abolitionist.

Sherman, Jory

774. *The Barons of Texas.* New York: Forge, 1997. 319 pp.
When Martin Baron leaves New Orleans for Texas, lured by stories of vast land and cattle herds, Juanito Salazar, an Argentinian cowboy, guides him, but they must face hostile Apache warriors who want them to leave.
Genre(s): Western Fiction.

Sickels, Noelle

◆ 775. *Walking West.* New York: St. Martin's Press, 1995. 308 pp.
In 1852, women on the small Muller wagon train traveling from Indiana to California face weather, disease, and deaths in their families.
Genre(s): Western Fiction.

Sinclair, Bertha

776. *The Gringos.* Boston: Little, Brown, 1913. 350 pp.
A Spanish grandee protests the U.S. government's claim to his California lands, while three males fall in love with his daughter but realize in time that she is too shallow to pursue.
Genre(s): Western Fiction.

Smiley, Jane

◆ 777. *The All-True Travels and Adventures of Lidie Newton.* New York: Knopf, 1998. 448 pp.
In Quincy, Illinois, Lidie, 20, marries abolitionist Thomas Newton and goes with him to Kansas, but when Thomas is murdered, she disguises herself to get revenge.
Genre(s): Western Fiction; War Story.

Smith, Bobbi

778. *Beneath Passion's Skies.* New York: Kensington, 1993. 445 pp.
Angel Windsor flees her brutal brother-in-law before kidnapping her nephew and hiring a gunfighter to take her west to California.
Genre(s): Romance; Western Fiction.

Sorensen, Michele

779. *Broken Lance.* Salt Lake City, UT: Deseret, 1997. 285 pp.
When Angus and Callie McCraken travel to Utah in 1857 to become Mormons, Cheyenne attack their wagon train and kill Angus, but a wounded Cheyenne warrior helps Callie and her three children.
Genre(s): Christian Fiction.

Spencer, LaVyrle

780. *November of the Heart.* New York: Putnam, 1993. 381 pp.
Lorna Barnett falls in love with the young man building her father's yacht, but their class differences make their emotions ill-advised.
Genre(s): Romance.

Stevenson, Janet

781. *Departure.* San Diego, CA: Harcourt Brace, 1985. 280 pp.
Amanda Bright's captain husband attempts to teach her navigation on one of their voyages in 1851, but not until all on board who can navigate are ill or dead does she begin to earnestly study Bowditch's *The American Practical Navigator.*
Genre(s): Sea Story; Adventure Story.

Stevenson, Paul R.

782. *Cross a Wide River.* Santa Fe, NM: Sunstone, 1989. 315 pp.
John Bolt weds a woman of mixed heritage in Georgia before the Civil War, and afterward, they go to New Mexico with other family members to start a new life.
Genre(s): War Story; Adventure Story; Family Saga.

Stone, Irving

783. *Love Is Eternal.* Garden City, NY: Doubleday, 1954. 468 pp.
Mary Todd Lincoln devotes herself to family and to her husband Abraham Lincoln.
Genre(s): Biographical Fiction; Domestic Fiction.

Street, James

784. *Tap Roots.* New York: Dial, 1942. 593 pp.
The sequel to *Oh, Promised Land* places the Dabneys in southern Mississippi from 1858 to 1865 where slavery-hating Southerners try to build a Free state.
Genre(s): Domestic Fiction.

Streshinsky, Shirley

785. *Hers.* New York: Putnam, 1982. 360 pp.
Disabled Lena lives with her sister Willa and Willa's husband on a huge California ranch, but after Lena goes to China, she falls in love.
Genre(s): Family Saga.

Sutton, Stack

786. *End of the Tracks.* Garden City, NY: Doubleday, 1981. 183 pp.
Creed Weatherall begins work with the Central Pacific Railroad when it competes with the Union Pacific in laying track, and he faces murderers and saboteurs.
Genre(s): Western Fiction.

Taylor, Robert Jr.

787. *Fiddle and Bow.* Chapel Hill, NC: Algonquin, 1985. 270 pp.
Baxter tries to recreate the story of his family in Oklahoma and Tennessee, where two governors ran against each other in the War of the Roses.
Genre(s): Domestic Fiction; Political Fiction.

Taylor, Robert Lewis

788. *The Travels of Jaimie McPheeters.* Garden City, NY: Doubleday, 1958. 478 pp.
Jaimie McPheeters, 14, leaves Louisville with his father in 1849 for California and the gold fields.
Award(s): Pulitzer Prize.
Genre(s): Adventure Story.

789. *Two Roads to Guadalupe.* Garden City, NY: Doubleday, 1964. 428 pp.
Two half brothers serve with Colonel Doniphan's Volunteers during the Mexican War of 1846 to 1848.
Genre(s): War Story; Adventure Story.

Thoene, Brock

790. *Hope Valley War.* Nashville, TN: Thomas Nelson, 1997. 228 pp.
John Thornton, a drifter, hears that his brother Lucky has been lynched, and when he returns to help Lucky's widow and children, he finds out that gamblers posing as vigilantes are responsible.
Genre(s): Western Fiction; Christian Fiction.

Thorp, Roderick

791. *Jenny and Barnum.* Garden City, NY: Doubleday, 1981. 375 pp.
Although dates do not coincide with those in Barnum's and Lind's lives, the facts that Lind came to America, went on a concert tour, and delighted her audiences do.
Genre(s): Biographical Fiction; Musical Fiction.

Tremblay, William

792. *The June Rise.* Logan: Utah State University, 1994. 233 pp.
Fur trapper Antoine Janis goes West to try to save it by living with the Oglala, the Arapaho, and the Cheyenne before marrying First Elk Woman, but the government eventually asks him to choose between his wife or his country, and he chooses his wife.
Genre(s): Biographical Fiction; War Story.

Vernam, Glenn R.

793. *Pioneer Breed.* New York: Doubleday, 1972. 180 pp.
In 1852, orphans help each other survive through a winter in an isolated cabin by searching for food, completing chores, coping with illnesses, and eventually, falling in love.
Genre(s): Western Fiction.

Vernon, John

794. *Peter Doyle.* New York: Random House, 1991. 417 pp.
Peter Doyle, friend of Walt Whitman, ends up with Napoleon's penis, a part removed by a British doctor and for which several people avidly search.
Genre(s): Mystery.

Vidal, Gore

◆ 795. *Lincoln.* New York: Random House, 1984. 647 pp.
Abraham Lincoln overcomes almost insurmountable odds to show his leadership during the Civil War. (*Series:* American Chronicle, 2)
Genre(s): Biographical Fiction.

Walker, Mildred

796. *If a Lion Could Talk.* 1970. Lincoln, NE: University of Nebraska Press, 1995. 275 pp.
A young missionary couple in Massachusetts tries to convert the Blackfoot Indians to Christianity before Preacher Marcus falls in love with a Blackfoot woman.
Genre(s): Christian Fiction.

Warren, Patricia Nell

◆ 797. *One Is the Sun.* New York: Ballantine, 1991. 512 pp.
In 1857, Helle, a Mayan priestess who has escaped from a temple massacre in Yucatan, establishes a mystical site in Montana where she reveals Mayan philosophy to two 13-year-old girls.
Genre(s): Western Fiction; Religious Fiction.

Warren, Robert Penn

798. *Band of Angels.* New York: Random House, 1955. 375 pp.
Amantha Starr, summoned from her Oberlin studies at her father's death, finds out that she is a slave and most be sold.
Genre(s): Domestic Fiction.

Webb, Lucas

799. *Eli's Road.* New York: Doubleday, 1971. 384 pp.
Eli Russell, raised in Kansas before the Civil War, goes into the wilderness with Ginny, but after her pregnancy, they return to civilization, and he leaves to lead a group west into Wyoming where he settles and becomes a marshal.
Genre(s): Western Fiction; Bildungsroman (Coming of Age).

Wells, Marian

800. *Colorado Gold.* Minneapolis, MN: Bethany House, 1988. 336 pp.
A family decides to forgive and restore itself during the Gold Rush. (*Series:* Treasure Quest, 2)
Genre(s): Christian Fiction.

801. *The Silver Highway.* Minneapolis, MN: Bethany House, 1989. 368 pp.
Alexander Duncan and Matthew Thomas risk their lives trying to save slaves as abolitionists on the Underground Railway. (*Series:* Treasure Quest, 1)
Genre(s): Christian Fiction.

Wendorf, Patricia

802. *Double Wedding Ring.* New York: David and Charles, 1990. 496 pp.
Rhoda Greypaul arrives in New York to marry her dead cousin's husband and look after their infant son, but George Salter dies young, and she takes the children to a Wisconsin farm where she falls in love again.
Genre(s): Domestic Fiction; War Story.

Wheeler, Richard S.

◆ 803. *Sierra.* New York: Forge, 1996. 380 pp.
Ulysses McQueen leaves his wife in Iowa to go to California's goldfields, where he eventually meets Steven Jarvis and suggests using his land to grow produce for the hungry miners.
Award(s): Western Writers of America Spur Award.
Genre(s): Western Fiction.

◆ 804. *Where the River Runs.* Boston: Little, Brown, 1990. 180 pp.
In 1849, when Captain Jed Owen leads a group to talk to the Native Americans, he is the only survivor after cholera hits, and his fiancé Susannah searches for him along the Missouri River although everyone else thinks he is dead.
Genre(s): Romance; Western Fiction.

White, Richard

◆ 805. *Mister Grey of the Further Adventures of Huckleberry Finn.* New York: Four Walls Eight Windows, 1992. 249 pp.
Charles Prescott matures with the help of a black male school teacher and the sheriff, Huck Finn.
Genre(s): Adventure Story; Bildungsroman (Coming of Age).

White, Stewart Edward

806. *Gold.* New York: Doubleday, 1913. 437 pp.
Four men form a partnership as they come through the Panama Canal on their way to the Gold Rush, and they support each other through their gains and their losses in the fields. (*Series:* California Trilogy, 1)
Genre(s): Western Fiction; Adventure Story.

807. *The Gray Dawn.* New York: Doubleday, 1915. 395 pp.
Citizens must band together as vigilantes when threatened in San Francisco during the 1850s. (*Series:* California Trilogy, 2)
Genre(s): Western Fiction; Adventure Story.

808. *Stampede.* New York: Doubleday, 1942. 176 pp.
In the sequel to *The Folded Hills*, landowners and squatters conflict after California becomes a state in 1850. (*Series:* Andy Burnett Saga, 4)
Genre(s): Western Fiction; Adventure Story.

Whitson, Stephanie Grace

809. *Walks the Fire.* Nashville, TN: Thomas Nelson, 1995. 301 pp.
Jesse King loses her husband on the Oregon Trail, and when Sioux rescue her, she adopts the tribe until she falls in love with a missionary.
Genre(s): Western Fiction; Christian Fiction; Romance.

Wilbee, Brenda

810. *Sweetbriar Summer.* Grand Rapids, MI: Revell, 1997. 199 pp.
The David Denny family faces hostility during the Gold Rush in Seattle when the Native Americans become unhappy with the arrival of untrustworthy whites.
Genre(s): Western Fiction; Christian Fiction.

Wilson, P. B.

811. *Night Come Swiftly.* Eugene, OR: Harvest House, 1997. 350 pp.
In 1851, a white child, Meredith, and a slave, Tilly, are born on the Douglas plantation, Meredith educates Tilly before Tilly escapes, Meredith marries poorly, and they are reunited during the Reconstruction.
Genre(s): Christian Fiction; Family Saga.

Wimberly, Clara

812. *Gentle Hearts.* New York: Zebra, 1996. 380 pp.
Lida Reinhart dislikes John Sexton when he comes to her Amish community as an Underground Railroad worker, and after he and her brother are shot, she must care for his wounds.
Genre(s): Romance.

Windle, Janice Woods

◆ 813. *True Women.* New York: Putnam, 1993. 451 pp.
The Woods, King, and Lawshe families of Texas reveal a legacy of visits from Sam Houston and Santa Ana, Civil War participation, and other events in their 100-year legacy.
Genre(s): Domestic Fiction; Family Saga.

Winston, Daoma

814. *The Fall River Line.* New York: St. Martin's Press, 1984. 495 pp.
Augusta Wakefield is born on the day the first ship leaves the Fall River pier for New York in 1847, and her descendants in some way connect to the shipping line.
Genre(s): Family Saga.

Wiseman, Stan

815. *Cody's Ride.* New York: Walker, 1993. 216 pp.
By pretending that Native Americans are coming, white men rob and murder other whites until one robber spares Jenny to take her to Texas with him, and the man who loves her happens to be a sharp-shooting Pony Express rider.
Genre(s): Western Fiction.

Wulf, Jessica

816. *Hunter's Bride.* New York: Zebra, 1996. 480 pp.
In 1849, Sarah Hancock tells her dying mother that she will go to Fort Charles and marry Adam Rutledge although she does not love him.
Genre(s): Romance.

Yerby, Frank

817. *Devilseed.* Garden City, NY: Doubleday, 1984. 323 pp.
Mirielle Duclos goes to San Francisco at 15 and has various life experiences as a saloon girl, a high-class prostitute, a lesbian, and a wife.
Genre(s): Western Fiction.

Zavala, Ann

818. *San Francisco Gold.* New York: Forge, 1995. 286 pp.
When Sophie arrives in San Francisco searching for her sister Annabelle, she finds Annabelle the owner of a brothel and gaming parlor, and Annabelle falls for Ruari McKay, the pirate and gentleman who saves Sophie and her cargo.
Genre(s): Western Fiction; Romance.

1861-1865
The Civil War

Adicks, Richard

◆ 819. *A Court for Owls.* Sarasota, FL: Pineapple, 1989. 269 pp.
Lewis Powell, a soldier in the Confederate Army, was one of four persons hung for a part in the assassination of Abraham Lincoln.
Genre(s): War Story.

Auchincloss, Louis

820. *Watchfires.* Boston: Houghton Mifflin, 1982. 348 pp.
Dexter Fairchild, a lawyer, and his wife, members of New York elite, struggle through their marriage and other moral concerns during the Civil War.
Genre(s): Domestic Fiction; War Story.

Austell, Diane

821. *While the Music Plays.* New York: Bantam, 1996. 452 pp.
Yankee Chase Girard recruits Laura Chandler, a young widow in Richmond, to become a spy for the Union.
Genre(s): Romance; War Story.

Bahr, Howard

◆ 822. *The Black Flower.* Baltimore, MD. Nautical & Avia, 1997. 230 pp.
Bushrod Carter stoically awaits each Civil War battle until the Battle of Franklin, during which the Union forces defeat Carter and the Army of Tennessee.
Genre(s): War Story.

Bannister, Don

823. *Long Day At Shiloh.* New York: Knopf, 1981. 288 pp.
General Grant struggles to control the unexpected battle at Shiloh by helping his fighting soldiers gain victory.
Genre(s): War Story.

Bass, Cynthia

◆ 824. *Sherman's March.* New York: Villard, 1994. 228 pp.
Three people, a woman whose house the Union soldiers burn, a Union soldier who thinks Sherman is a genius, and Sherman himself, tell about his march across Georgia in 1864.
Genre(s): War Story.

Basso, Hamilton

825. *The Light Infantry Ball.* Garden City, NY: Doubleday, 1959. 476 pp.
A Carolina planter watches Southern society deteriorate with scandal and smuggling while he works for the Confederate government.
Genre(s): War Story; Romance.

Batchelor, John Calvin

826. *American Falls.* New York: Norton, 1985. 574 pp.
In 1864, Confederates attack New York City with fire after much espionage on both sides.
Genre(s): War Story.

Bean, Frederic

827. *Lorena.* New York: Forge, 1996. 284 pp.
Nurses Lorena Blaire and Clara Brooks go South during the Civil War to become spies, but Lorena falls in love with a Confederate surgeon and thinks her emotions may jeopardize their mission.
Genre(s): War Story.

Becker, Stephen D.

828. *When the War Is Over.* New York: Random House, 1969. 240 pp.
On May 11, 1865, a Confederate teenager shoots Max Catto, a United States army officer, and becomes entangled in the chaotic brutality following the war and Lincoln's assassination.
Genre(s): War Story.

Bittner, Rosanne

829. *Tender Betrayal.* New York: Bantam, 1994. 512 pp.
Southern slave owner Audra Brennan falls in love with her voice instructor's son Lee, a Northerner, and although they disagree over the issue of slavery, they have one night together before Audra must face the war in the South.
Genre(s): Romance.

Borland, Hal

830. *The Amulet.* Philadelphia: Lippincott, 1957. 224 pp.
Quincy Scott leaves Denver, joins the Confederates, and fights in the battle of Wilson Creek.
Genre(s): War Story.

Boyd, James

831. *Marching On.* New York: Scribner's, 1927. 426 pp.

James Fraser, son of a poor farmer, goes to fight in the Confederate army and spends time in a federal prison.
Genre(s): War Story; Love Story.

Brady, Joan

◆ 832. *Theory of War.* New York: Knopf, 1993. 257 pp.

Four-year-old Jonathan Carrick, white, is sold in 1865 to a Kansas farmer who treats him inhumanely and whose son is jealous of Jonathan's value to his father.
Award(s): Whitbread Book of the Year Award.
Genre(s): Biographical Fiction.

Brand, Max

833. *Ambush at Torture Canyon.* New York: Dodd, Mead, 1931. 252 pp.

Silas Durfee takes the job of protecting the nephew of a wealthy rancher from the outlaw, Spot Lester, who has threatened his life.
Genre(s): Western Fiction.

Brick, John

834. *Jubilee.* Garden City, NY: Doubleday, 1956. 320 pp.

A West Point graduate, Jeff Barnes, sacrifices everything in his devotion to duty during the battles of Gettysburg, Chattanooga, and Atlanta, but the farmers in his unit show their love of life.
Genre(s): War Story.

835. *The Richmond Raid.* Garden City, NY: Doubleday, 1963. 279 pp.

When the Northern army tries to raid and cripple Richmond, it suffers from its own inefficiency and the South's strong opposition.
Genre(s): War Story.

836. *Troubled Spring.* New York: Farrar, Straus and Giroux, 1950. 279 pp.

When a Union soldier returns from the Andersonville prison, he finds that his sweetheart has married his brother.
Genre(s): War Story.

Brown, Dee Alexander

◆ 837. *Conspiracy of Knaves.* New York: Wings, 1996. 393 pp.

In the Northwest Conspiracy, Confederate agents and Northern Copperheads plan to free rebel prisoners in Chicago.
Genre(s): War Story; Spy Fiction.

◆ 838. *The Way to Bright Star.* New York: Forge, 1998. 384 pp.

In the 1860s, during the Civil War, a young man travels from Kansas to Bright Star, Indiana.
Genre(s): War Story; Bildungsroman (Coming of Age).

Brown, Rita Mae

839. *High Hearts.* New York: Bantam, 1986. 464 pp.

Geneva Chatfield disguises herself as a male in the Civil War to fight with her husband for the Confederates.
Genre(s): War Story.

Carr, John Dickson

840. *Papa La-Bas.* New York: Harper, 1968. 277 pp.

Judah P. Benjamin, active for the Confederates during the Civil War, becomes involved in a murder.
Genre(s): Mystery.

Cavanaugh, Jack

841. *The Adversaries.* Wheaton, IL: Victor, 1996. 544 pp.

During the Civil War, Jeremiah Morgan's daughter goes to New York City to write tracts for homesick soldiers, and his sons fight, but their main enemy is banker Caleb McKenna. (*Series:* American Family Portrait, 4)
Genre(s): Family Saga; Christian Fiction; War Story.

Churchill, Winston

842. *The Crisis.* 1901. Cutchogue, NY: Buccaneer, 1984. 432 pp.

In the sequel to *Richard Carvel*, Stephen Brice, an abolitionist New Englander, meets southerner Virginia Carvel, falls in love with her, but faces rejection until she overcomes her political background.
Genre(s): War Story; Love Story.

Clark, L. D.

843. *A Bright Tragic Thing.* El Paso, TX: Cinco Puntos, 1992. 302 pp.

In Gainesville, Texas, during the Civil War, Confederates lynch 20 Union men while a young man tries to save his father.
Genre(s): War Story; Romance.

Collier, Louise W.

844. *Pilgrimage, A Tale of Old Natchez.* Memphis, TN: St. Luke's, 1982. 408 pp.

John Walworth's family leaves Natchez when the Union soldiers arrive, and when they return home to "The Burn," the children mature under Aunt Clara's watchful eye.
Genre(s): Domestic Fiction; War Story.

Cooke, John Esten

845. *Mohun.* New York: Dillingham, 1893. 509 pp.

Lee's Army of North Virginia suffers before the conclusion of the war at Appomattox.
Genre(s): War Story.

◆ May be suitable for young adult readers

Cornwell, Bernard

846. *The Bloody Ground.* New York: HarperCollins, 1996. 343 pp.
Nate Starbuck fights at Antietam in 1862, one of the Civil War's bloodiest battles. (*Series:* Starbuck Chronicles, 4)
Genre(s): War Story.

847. *Copperhead.* New York: HarperCollins, 1994. 375 pp.
In the sequel to *Rebel*, the Northerner Nate Starbuck fights with the Rebels in the Civil War because of his interest in the challenge of war.
Genre(s): War Story.

848. *Rebel.* New York: HarperCollins, 1993. 308 pp.
Nate Starbuck flees the North after helping a woman steal money she claimed as her own where he begins to fight for the Confederacy.
Genre(s): War Story.

Cotton, Ralph W.

◆ 849. *Powder River.* New York: St. Martin's Press, 1995. 325 pp.
Jeston Nash goes to Wyoming with stolen horses, and after having many conflicts, decides to trade with the Sioux Red Cloud because he seems to be the only decent man in the area.
Genre(s): Adventure Story; Western Fiction.

Coyle, Harold

850. *Until the End.* New York: Simon and Schuster, 1996. 462 pp.
The sequel to *Look Away* finds the estranged brothers, Kevin and James Bannon, in the final battles of the Civil War.
Genre(s): War Story; Domestic Fiction.

Crane, Stephen

851. *The Red Badge of Courage.* 1895. New York: Penguin, 1991. 220 pp.
Henry Fleming, a young Union soldier, struggles with his conflicting emotions about violence, death, and the nature of bravery in this ironic, skeptical account of the Civil War.
Genre(s): War Story.

Crane, Teresa

852. *Freedom's Banner.* New York: St. Martin's Press, 1995. 416 pp.
Mattie Henderson goes to Georgia to her new husband's plantation, but the Civil War changes everything in her life and reveals secrets about her husband's family, including the existence of his half brother.
Genre(s): War Story; Domestic Fiction.

Cullinan, Thomas

853. *The Besieged.* New York: Horizon, 1970. 285 pp.
After Union soldiers hang a Confederate lieutenant for a crime he may not have committed in South Carolina dur-

ing the Civil War, the lieutenant's sister begins her revenge.
Genre(s): War Story; Domestic Fiction.

Curtis, Jack

◆ 854. *Pepper Tree Rider.* New York: Walker, 1994. 180 pp.
Dave Cameron reports to Elizabeth that her husband has died in the Civil War and then stays to help her on the ranch, but Elizabeth needs to grieve before she can become involved with someone new.
Genre(s): Western Fiction.

Cutler, Bruce

855. *The Massacre at Sand Creek.* Norman: University of Oklahoma, 1995. 252 pp.
Colonel John Chivington, a former Methodist minister claiming to be part Indian, leads a group of soldiers in attacking a quiet Cheyenne village on Sand Creek, killing more than 200 people.
Genre(s): War Story.

Dailey, Janet

856. *Legacies.* Boston: Little, Brown, 1995. 394 pp.
Lije Stuart and his Cherokee family side with the Confederates, but his fiancé Diane belongs to a family with Union loyalties, and the family standoff occurs in battle between her father and Lije's uncle.
Genre(s): Romance; War Story.

Dann, Jack

857. *The Silent.* New York: Bantam, 1998. 301 pp.
When Edmund McDowell, 13, sees his mother raped in 1862, he becomes mute, but in 1864, he records his memory of that and his other experiences during the Civil War.
Genre(s): War Story; Bildungsroman (Coming of Age).

Delman, David

858. *Ain't Goin' to Glory.* New York: St. Martin's Press, 1991. 225 pp.
When the government draws the name of the first man to be drafted into the Civil War, riots start in New York City and last for three days until federal troops come from Gettysburg to help.
Genre(s): War Story.

Devon, Louis

859. *Aide to Glory.* New York: Crowell, 1952. 246 pp.
John A. Rawlins becomes General Ulysses S. Grant's aide-de-camp and then Grant's Secretary of War when Grant becomes president.
Genre(s): Biographical Fiction; War Story.

Dowdey, Clifford

860. *Bugles Blow No More.* Boston: Little, Brown, 1937. 497 pp.
In Richmond, the intensity of the Civil War becomes visible between 1861 and 1864.
Genre(s): War Story.

861. **The Proud Retreat.** New York: Doubleday, 1953. 318 pp.
The Confederates try to save their treasury after their defeat in the Civil War.
Genre(s): War Story.

862. **Where My Love Sleeps.** Boston: Little, Brown, 1945. 298 pp.
Residents of the area of Virginia around Richmond and Petersburg cope with the fighting near the end of the Civil War.
Genre(s): War Story.

Dubus, Elizabeth Nell

863. **Twilight of the Dawn.** New York: St. Martin's Press, 1989. 416 pp.
During the Civil War, Tom and Gabriele Cannon find themselves accused of disloyalty because of the people they love.
Genre(s): War Story; Romance.

Dyja, Tom

864. **Play for a Kingdom.** New York: Delacorte, 1997. 416 pp.
Near Spotsylvania, Virginia, a Union troop discovers a baseball field and a Confederate troop emerges from the woods ready to play a game.
Genre(s): War Story; Sports Fiction.

Dykeman, Wilma

865. **The Tall Woman.** New York: Henry Holt, 1962. 315 pp.
Lydia McQueen's husband fights for the Union in the Civil War against her father and brother, and she faces the results of still other wartime heartaches for the next 30 years.
Genre(s): War Story.

Eberhart, Mignon G.

866. **Family Fortune.** New York: Random House, 1976. 248 pp.
Lucinda's joint ownership of her father's land with her brother and his wife becomes difficult to hold when they try to sell the property before she comes of age after the Civil War.
Genre(s): Romance.

Ehle, John

◆ 867. **Time of Drums.** New York: Harper and Row, 1970. 328 pp.
In the sequel to *The Journey of August King*, southern troops in the third year of the Civil War face Gettysburg and the split loyalties of families who support freeing the slaves.
Genre(s): Family Saga; War Story.

Estleman, Loren D.

868. **Billy Gashade.** New York: Forge, 1997. 352 pp.
The only son of a wealthy businessman flees New York after the draft riots of 1863 and goes west where he adopts the name Billy Gashade before he finds a home in

a Kansas brothel playing the piano and is captured by Quantrill's Raiders.
Genre(s): Western Fiction; Bildungsroman (Coming of Age); War Story.

Eulo, Elena Yates

◆ 869. **A Southern Woman.** New York: St. Martin's Press, 1993. 371 pp.
Elizabeth, a teenage mother who is shunned when her husband joins the Union Army, is accused of his murder after shooting his murderer in the back.
Genre(s): War Story.

Farris, Jack

◆ 870. **Me and Gallagher.** New York: Simon and Schuster, 1982. 192 pp.
In 1863, vigilante groups begin in Virginia City, and Grubber Graves, 15, and his friend see some ruthless actions.
Genre(s): Western Fiction.

Faulkner, William

◆ 871. **The Unvanquished.** New York: Random House, 1938. 304 pp.
Bayard Sartoris returns from the battlefields of the Civil War and tries to build his family and his fortune.
Genre(s): War Story.

Fowler, Robert H.

872. **Jim Mundy.** New York: Harper and Row, 1977. 470 pp.
After Jim Mundy joins Confederate forces, he loses an eye at Gettysburg and is sent to prison, but escapes to Canada before returning to his losing side.
Genre(s): War Story.

Fox, John, Jr.

873. **The Trail of the Lonesome Pine.** New York: Scribner's, 1903. 421 pp.
The people in the Kentucky mountains fight on both sides during the Civil War.
Genre(s): War Story; Romance.

Frazier, Charles

◆ 874. **Cold Mountain.** New York: Atlantic Monthly, 1997. 356 pp.
After Inman escapes from a war hospital in 1864 and starts walking to Cold Mountain, Ada struggles to save her mountain farm with the elp of Ruby, an illiterate but efficient farmer.
Award(s): National Book Award.
Genre(s): War Story.

Gaffney, Virginia

875. **Carry Me Home.** Eugene, OR: Harvest House, 1997. 450 pp.
Carrie Cromwell gets unexpected help while trying to save her plantation home near Richmond as the Civil War approaches (*Series:* Richmond Chronicles, 2)
Genre(s): War Story; Christian Fiction.

876. *Magnolia Dreams.* Eugene, OR: Harvest House, 1998. 400 pp.
The honeymoon of Carrie Cromwell and Robert Borden is cut short when he is called back to duty, and while he fights, Carrie nurses the wounded. (*Series:* Richmond Chronicles, 4)
Genre(s): Romance; Christian Fiction; War Story.

877. *The Tender Rebel.* Eugene, OR: Harvest House, 1997. 400 pp.
Carrie, determined to become a nurse, must also contend with the proslavery Lieutenant Borden's love for her during the Civil War. (*Series:* Richmond Chronicles, 3)
Genre(s): Christian Fiction; War Story; Romance.

◆ 878. *Under the Southern Moon.* Eugene, OR: Harvest House, 1996. 427 pp.
Carrie must make an important decision about her best friend, the slave Rose, when the Underground Railroad comes to her plantation. (*Series:* Richmond Chronicles, 1)
Genre(s): Christian Fiction; Domestic Fiction.

Gaines, Ernest J.

◆ 879. *The Autobiography of Miss Jane Pittman.* New York: Dial, 1971. 241 pp.
Miss Jane Pittman is 110 when she recalls her childhood and the arrival of both Union and Confederate troops on the plantation where she lived.
Genre(s): Domestic Fiction.

Garfield, Brian

880. *Wild Times.* New York: Simon and Schuster, 1978. 477 pp.
Colonel Hugh Cardiff relates his memoirs, which include people he knew, such as Buffalo Bill Cody, and the variety of occupations in which he participated.
Genre(s): Western Fiction.

Gear, Kathleen O'Neal

◆ 881. *Thin Moon and Cold Mist.* New York: Tor, 1996. 587 pp.
Robin Walkingstick Heatherton, a half-Cherokee Confederate spy posing as an African American, must escape the east and certain death, so she takes her son to Colorado to claim land that she won at poker.
Genre(s): Western Fiction.

Gibbons, Kaye

◆ 882. *On the Occasion of My Last Afternoon.* New York: Putnam, 1998. 208 pp.
A woman who loves the South but hates slavery goes North after the Civil War ends.
Genre(s): War Story; Domestic Fiction.

Gordon, Noah

◆ 883. *Shaman.* New York: Dutton, 1992. 519 pp.
Rob J. Cole leaves Scotland and his medical career for political reasons and comes to Boston to work with Oliver Wendell Holmes, but opportunities in Illinois lure him farther West where he meets a Native American medicine woman.
Genre(s): Medical Novel.

Graham, Heather

884. *Rebel.* New York: Fawcett, 1998. 384 pp.
Alaina McMann, a southern spy known as the Moccasin, meets Union Major Ian McKinnon, the Panther.
Genre(s): War Story; Romance.

885. *Surrender.* New York: Topaz, 1998. 381 pp.
Jerome McKenzie captains a boat named for Jefferson Davis's wife out of Florida, and when he meets a Union general's daughter nursing the wounded, the two hate each other's allegiances, but fall for each other.
Genre(s): War Story; Romance.

Greeley, Andrew M.

◆ 886. *Irish Lace.* New York: Tor, 1996. 304 pp.
Nuala Anne McGrail thinks she hears screams of dead Confederate prisoners in Chicago's Camp Douglas and asserts that they would have been pardoned if the wardens had found the letter Lincoln wrote on the night he died.
Genre(s): Mystery.

Green, Julian

887. *The Stars of the South.* Trans. Robin Buss. New York: Marion Boyars, 1996. 651 pp.
Elizabeth Escridge's husband and lover kill each other, and she has difficulty finding a reason to live until her former love and cousin returns during the Civil War.
Genre(s): War Story.

Gurganus, Allan

888. *Oldest Living Confederate Widow Tells All.* New York: Knopf, 1989. 718 pp.
Lucille Marsden, 99, recalls her husband (whom she married when she was 15 and he was over 45) and his experiences in the Civil War and afterward during Reconstruction.
Genre(s): War Story.

Haas, Ben

889. *The Foragers.* New York: Simon and Schuster, 1962. 317 pp.
A Confederate officer must steal food for his desperate soldiers.
Genre(s): War Story.

Heath, Lorraine

890. *Always to Remember.* New York: Jove, 1997. 336 pp.
After being drafted into the Confederate Army, Clayton Holland spends nine months in prison when he refuses to fight and almost dies, and when he returns home, he is treated like a coward until townspeople realize that he is the only one capable of carving monuments for their fallen relatives.
Award(s): Romance Writers of America RITA Award.
Genre(s): War Story; Romance.

Henry, Will

891. *Journey to Shiloh.* New York: Random House, 1960. 242 pp.
Young and inexperienced Confederate soldiers fight in the Civil War under General Bragg.
Genre(s): War Story.

Herschler, Mildred Barger

◆ 892. *The Walk Into Morning.* New York: Tor, 1993. 320 pp.
The literate Chad Creel runs away from his owner to join the Union army in New Orleans, and Anna, another slave, follows him before he goes north, but she is returned to the plantation.
Genre(s): War Story.

Higgins, Joanna

893. *A Soldier's Book.* Sag Harbor, NY: Permanent Press, 1998. 192 pp.
After Ira Cahill Stevens is captured during the Battle of the Wilderness in 1864, he keeps a diary about his experience in the Andersonville prison, including descriptions of the people he encounters.
Genre(s): War Story.

Hunt, Irene

◆ 894. *Across Five Aprils.* New York: Follett, 1964. 212 pp.
Jethro's family becomes divided over the Civil War when his brothers fight on opposite sides and his father becomes ill.
Genre(s): War Story.

Jakes, John

895. *Love and War.* New York: Harcourt Brace, 1984. 1019 pp.
In the sequel to *North and South*, the Hazards of Pennsylvania and the Mains of South Carolina fight in the Civil War.
Genre(s): Family Saga.

Johnston, Mary

896. *Cease Firing.* Boston: Houghton Mifflin, 1911. 457 pp.
Richard Cleave, a Confederate artillery commander, begins service in the Civil War in the sequel to *The Long Roll*.
Genre(s): War Story.

897. *The Long Roll.* 1912. Baltimore, MD: Johns Hopkins University Press, 1996. 638 pp.
In the Civil War, Richard Cleave serves as an artillery commander in the Shenandoah Valley Campaign with Stonewall Jackson.
Genre(s): War Story.

Johnston, Terry C.

898. *Cry of the Hawk.* New York: Bantam, 1992. 391 pp.
The Confederate Jonah Hook volunteers to go West and fight Indians in return for freedom from a Union prison during the Civil War.
Genre(s): Adventure Story; Western Fiction; War Story.

Jones, Douglas C.

◆ 899. *The Barefoot Brigade.* New York: Holt, Rinehart and Winston, 1982. 313 pp.
A small group of Arkansas natives join the Confederate infantry.
Genre(s): War Story.

◆ 900. *Elkhorn Tavern.* New York: Holt, Rinehart and Winston, 1980. 311 pp.
Ore Hasford and her two teenagers try to preserve their Arkansas farm from marauders.
Genre(s): Domestic Fiction; War Story.

◆ 901. *Season of Yellow Leaf.* New York: Holt, Rinehart and Winston, 1983. 323 pp.
Comanches abduct Morfanna Perry, 10, and kill her parents before naming her Chosen and raising her as one of their tribe.
Genre(s): Western Fiction.

Jones, Ted

◆ 902. *The Fifth Conspiracy.* Novato, CA: Lyford Books, 1995. 394 pp.
In the sequel to *Hard Road to Gettysburg*, Samuel Wade, a Union leader, tries to rescue his Confederate brother Simon from a Civil War prison in 1863.
Genre(s): War Story.

903. *Grant's War.* Novato, CA: Presidio, 1992. 314 pp.
When a World War I soldier researches the Civil War, he decides that Grant's contribution was the death of two Union soldiers for every Confederate soldier.
Genre(s): Biographical Fiction; War Story.

◆ 904. *Hard Road to Gettysburg.* Novato, CA: Presidio, 1993. 320 pp.
Twins, separated at birth and unaware of each other's existence, meet on different sides of the Civil War at Gettysburg.
Genre(s): War Story.

Judd, Cameron

905. *The Shadow Warriors.* New York: Bantam, 1997. 464 pp.
Mountaineers continue to support the Union after their states secede, and Amy Deacon risks all to help on the Underground Railroad and work as a spy, but others massacre Unionists in Shelton Laurel, North Carolina, in 1862.
Genre(s): War Story; Domestic Fiction.

◆ May be suitable for young adult readers

Kafka, F.L.

906. *Tunnel to Glory.* Novato, CA: Lyford, 1992. 249 pp.
In Petersburg, Grant planned to defeat Lee and capture Richmond, but the Confederates were prepared and undefeated until a Union engineer suggested a tunnel.
Genre(s): War Story.

Kantor, MacKinlay

907. *Andersonville.* New York: World, 1955. 897 pp.
A senile general administering Andersonville Prison in Georgia during the Civil War allows many Union soldiers to suffer from exposure, disease, and starvation.
Award(s): Pulitzer Prize.
Genre(s): War Story.

908. *Long Remember.* New York: Coward-McCann, 1934. 411 pp.
In 1863, as citizens of Gettysburg continue the routine of their daily lives, war rapidly engulfs and changes them.
Genre(s): War Story.

Keneally, Thomas

909. *Confederates.* New York: Harper and Row, 1980. 427 pp.
White farm boys who fight for the Confederacy worry about the people they have left at home during the war.
Genre(s): War Story.

Keyes, Frances Parkinson

910. *Steamboat Gothic.* New York: Messner, 1952. 562 pp.
The Louisana plantation and family home called Cindy Lou is the center of a family's life from the Civil War until 1930, when it becomes a community center.
Genre(s): Domestic Fiction; Family Saga.

King, Benjamin

911. *A Bullet for Lincoln.* Gretna, LA: Pelican, 1993. 301 pp.
J.P. Morgan wants investments to go West instead of South; therefore, he hires Anderson, a spy, to kill Lincoln, and Anderson, in turn, gets John Wilkes Booth to do the job.
Genre(s): War Story; Mystery.

◆ **912.** *A Bullet for Stonewall.* Gretna, LA: Pelican, 1990. 267 pp.
Stonewall Jackson's men accidentally shoot him during the Civil War, which means that the Civil War might have ended differently.
Genre(s): War Story; Mystery.

Lacy, Al

913. *A Heart Divided.* Sisters, OR: Multnomah, 1993. 353 pp.
Captain McGraw loves both an army nurse and the wife who abandoned him but wants him back. (*Series:* Battle of Destiny, 2)
Genre(s): War Story; Romance; Christian Fiction.

914. *Joy from Ashes.* Sisters, OR: Questar, 1995. 306 pp.
After Layne Dalton leaves his pregnant wife, Melody, to fight for the Confederates in the Civil War, Steve Heglund comes to his house and beats Melody to avenge his father's murder by her father, and she loses her child.
Genre(s): War Story; Christian Fiction; Love Story.

LaDuke, Winona

◆ **915.** *Last Standing Woman.* Stillwater, MN: Voyageur, 1997. 241 pp.
Seven generations of women in the Ojibwa tribe of the Anishinaabe face racism and oppression from the 1860s into the present.
Genre(s): Family Saga.

Lancaster, Bruce

916. *Night March.* Boston: Little, Brown, 1958. 341 pp.
In 1863, after the Fitzpatrick-Dahlgren Raid on Richmond to free Union soldiers from Libby Prison, two Union captains escape.
Genre(s): War Story.

917. *No Bugles Tonight.* Boston: Little, Brown, 1948. 325 pp.
In 1862, a Union officer becomes involved with a Tennessee woman who supports the Union.
Genre(s): War Story.

918. *Roll Shenandoah.* Boston: Little, Brown, 1956. 316 pp.
Ellery Starr, wounded and honorably discharged from the army returns to report on the war and sees General Sheridan's campaign of 1865 in the Shenandoah Valley.
Genre(s): War Story.

Langan, Ruth

919. *Dulcie's Gift.* New York: Harlequin, 1996. 276 pp.
Dulcie and her group of survivors flee Charleston for an island where the Jermain brothers and their aunt also suffer from the Civil War.
Genre(s): War Story; Romance.

Leekley, John

◆ **920.** *The Blue and the Gray.* New York: Dell, 1982. 303 pp.
When Union soldiers fire on Fort Sumter, the Geyser and the Hale families split, with John Geyser becomes a war correspondent so that he need not commit to either side.
Genre(s): War Story.

Lentz, Perry

921. *The Falling Hills.* Columbia, SC: University Of South Carolina Press, 1994. 468 pp.
At Fort Pillow, Tennessee, Confederate forces slaughter Union soldiers during the Civil War.
Genre(s): War Story.

922. *It Must Be Now the Kingdom Coming.* New York: Crown, 1973. 310 pp.
Yankees take over Malory's plantation, free the slaves, and try to hang Malory before he escapes.
Genre(s): War Story.

Lytle, Andrew Nelson

923. *The Long Night.* Indianapolis: Bobbs Merrill, 1936. 331 pp.
Gangsters in Alabama murder Cameron McIvor's father in 1859, and Cameron devotes himself to revenge.
Genre(s): War Story.

MacDonald, Robert S.

924. *The Catherine.* New York: Van Nostrand Reinhold, 1982. 356 pp.
William Saunders captains a Union ship in the Civil War that rescues people or runs Confederate ships aground while trying to decide between his wife and a New Orleans widow.
Genre(s): War Story; Sea Story.

Madden, David

925. *Sharpshooter.* Knoxville: University of Tennessee, 1996. 160 pp.
After Willis Carr goes to war at 13 in 1861, he becomes a sharpshooter for the Confederate Army, serving under General Longstreet.
Genre(s): War Story.

Mallon, Thomas

926. *Henry and Clara.* New York: Ticknor and Fields, 1994. 362 pp.
Stepsiblings Henry Rathbone and Clara Harris sit in President Lincoln's box on the night he is assassinated, and afterward, they marry and have children.
Genre(s): Biographical Fiction; Love Story.

Manfred, Frederick Feikema

927. *Scarlet Plume.* New York: New American Library, 1975. 317 pp.
The Sioux rise up against the government in 1862 and capture a white woman for bargaining.
Genre(s): War Story; Western Fiction.

Mason, F. Van Wyck

928. *Our Valiant Few.* Boston: Little, Brown, 1956. 436 pp.
A newspaper editor wants to expose the Southern war profiteers during the South's struggle to break the Union blockade around Charleston.
Genre(s): War Story.

929. *Proud New Flags.* Philadelphia: Lippincott, 1951. 493 pp.
Sam Seymour fights for the Confederate Navy against his father in the Civil War.
Genre(s): War Story.

McCaig, Donald

930. *Jacob's Ladder.* New York: Norton, 1998. 528 pp.
When a Works Project Administration writer interviews an old woman in 1934, he learns the secrets of a prominent Virginia family before and during the Civil War.
Genre(s): War Story.

McCarthy, Gary

931. *The Mustangers.* Garden City, NY: Doubleday, 1987. 179 pp.
Pete Sills, 19, breaks wild mustangs on the Cross T Ranch until the owner decides he needs more land for cattle grazing during the years of the Civil War.
Genre(s): War Story; Western Fiction.

McCrumb, Sharyn

◆ **932.** *MacPherson's Lament.* New York: Ballantine, 1992. 260 pp.
Elizabeth MacPherson returns from Scotland to help her brother Bill and his new partner Amy Powell (A.P.) Hill investigate a woman's death and the confiscation of a Confederate treasury.
Genre(s): Mystery.

McLeay, Alison

933. *Sea Change.* New York: Simon and Schuster, 1992. 416 pp.
Kate Summerbee lives on board her father's riverboat docked in New Orleans, and when the Yankees come in the summer of 1862, she meets Englishman Matthew Oliver.
Genre(s): War Story; Romance.

McLellon, Waldron Murrill

934. *Leather and Soul.* Fern Park, FL: Butternut, 1994. 513 pp.
James Claudius Shaw, a slave owner, fights for the Union in the Civil War, and when he escapes from Confederate prison with black dye on his face, he takes Hannibal, a slave, to help him find his way in a different world.
Genre(s): War Story.

Meriwether, Louise

935. *Fragments of the Ark.* New York: Pocket Books, 1994. 342 pp.
In 1862, Peter Mango loads his family and friends into a Confederate gunboat and sails out of Charleston harbor to deliver himself to the Union, saying that he may have been born a slave but he thinks of himself as a man.
Genre(s): War Story.

Minatra, MaryAnn

936. *The Tapestry.* Eugene, OR: Harvest House, 1993. 402 pp.
Believing that events weave a tapestry in their lives, members of a Christian family in Illinois during the Civil War try to find safety in various ways.
Genre(s): Christian Fiction; War Story.

Minton, Charles Ethrige

937. *Juan of Santo Nino.* Santa Fe, NM: Sunstone, 1973. 184 pp.

During the years 1863-1864, Juan lives in Santo Nino where he combats problems with the land.
Genre(s): Western Fiction.

Mitchell, Kirk

938. *Fredericksburg.* New York: St. Martin's Press, 1996. 364 pp.

Six Irish soldiers tell about the Civil War battle in Fredericksburg on December 13, 1862.
Genre(s): War Story.

939. *Shadow On the Valley.* New York: St. Martin's Press, 1994. 342 pp.

In the Civil War during 1864, a battle rages on the field as well as behind the scenes as someone murders pacifist farmers in the area, and Simon Wolfe, a one-armed Union surgeon, blames the wrong man.
Genre(s): War Story.

Mitchell, Margaret

◆ 940. *Gone with the Wind.* New York: Macmillan, 1936. 1037 pp.

Scarlett O'Hara faces and survives the Civil War and Reconstruction and marries Rhett Butler for his money because her true love has married someone else.
Award(s): Pulitzer Prize.
Genre(s): War Story.

Moberg, Vilhelm

941. *Unto a Good Land.* St. Paul: Minnesota Historical Society, 1995. 371 pp.

The Nilssons, in the sequel to *The Emigrants*, arrive in America, travel to Minnesota, and begin to build a home.
Genre(s): Family Saga.

Monfredo, Miriam Grace

942. *The Stalking Horse.* New York: Berkley, 1998. 352 pp.

Glynis Tryon's niece Llyr tries to stop an attempt to assassinate Abraham Lincoln in 1861.
Genre(s): Mystery; War Story.

Morris, Gilbert

943. *Chariots in the Smoke.* Wheaton, IL: Tyndale House, 1997. 350 pp.

After enlisting in the Confederate Army to impress a young woman, David Rocklin realizes that he does not have the courage to be a soldier. (*Series:* Appomattox Saga, 9)
Genre(s): Christian Fiction; War Story.

944. *A Covenant of Love.* Wheaton, IL: Tyndale House, 1992. 361 pp.

Cousins Clay and Gideon Rocklin find themselves on different sides of the Civil War conflict but in love with the same woman. (Appomattox Saga, 1)
Genre(s): War Story; Christian Fiction; Romance.

945. *The Dixie Widow.* Minneapolis, MN: Bethany House, 1991. 318 pp.

Belle and Davis Winslow are cousins who support opposing sides during the Civil War. (*Series:* House of Winslow, 9)
Genre(s): Domestic Fiction; Christian Fiction; Family Saga.

946. *Gate of His Enemies.* Wheaton, IL: Tyndale House, 1992. 337 pp.

Although Deborah Steele, a Northerner, and Dent Rocklin, a Confederate soldier, are in love, each strongly supports a different side during the Civil War, jeopardizing their personal happiness. (*Series:* Appomattox Saga, 2)
Genre(s): War Story; Christian Fiction; Romance.

947. *Land of the Shadow.* Wheaton, IL: Tyndale House, 1993. 338 pp.

Frankie Ames, a northern woman forced to spy for the Union, becomes an assistant to Confederate photographer Paul Ristol. (*Series:* Appomattox Saga, 4)
Genre(s): War Story; Christian Fiction; Romance.

948. *The Last Confederate.* Minneapolis, MN: Bethany House, 1990. 333 pp.

During the Civil War, two factions of the Winslow family fight against each other. (*Series:* House of Winslow, 8)
Genre(s): Christian Fiction; Domestic Fiction; Family Saga.

949. *Out of the Whirlwind.* Wheaton, IL: Tyndale House, 1994. 316 pp.

Burke Rocklin contracts amnesia and falls in love with a Union nurse without either of them knowing that he is a Confederate soldier. (*Series:* Appomattox Saga, 5)
Genre(s): Christian Fiction; War Story; Romance.

950. *The Shadow of His Wings.* Wheaton, IL: Tyndale House, 1994. 352 pp.

Lowell Rocklin, seriously injured trying to lead the Southern cause in the Civil War, must also face the tragedy about the woman he loves. (*Series:* Appomattox Saga, 6)
Genre(s): War Story; Christian Fiction; Romance.

951. *Stars in Their Courses.* Wheaton, IL: Tyndale House, 1995. 350 pp.

To avoid conscription into the Federal Army, Frank Rocklin serves the North as a spy by acting in a theater troupe performing for the Confederates. (*Series:* Appomattox Saga, 8)
Genre(s): Christian Fiction; War Story.

952. *Wall of Fire.* Wheaton, IL: Tyndale House, 1995. 352 pp.

As Mark Rocklin lies close to death, he continues to hope for reunification with his estranged daughter Allyn. (*Series:* Appomattox Saga, 7)
Genre(s): Christian Fiction; War Story.

953. *Where Honor Dwells.* Wheaton, IL: Tyndale House, 1993. 355 pp.

When Vince Franklin asks Jake Hardin to help him inherit his family's fortune, he does not expect Hardin to fall in love with his sister. (*Series:* Appomattox Saga, 3)
Genre(s): Christian Fiction; War Story; Romance.

954. *The Wounded Yankee.* Minneapolis, MN: Bethany House, 1991. 304 pp.
A woman's courage helps a man overcome his bitterness from the Civil War. (*Series:* House of Winslow, 10)
Genre(s): Domestic Fiction; Christian Fiction; Family Saga.

Morrow, Honoré

955. *With Malice Toward None.* New York: Morrow, 1928. 342 pp.
Abraham Lincoln and Charles Sumner disagree about Reconstruction policies during the last two years of the Civil War in the sequel to *Forever Free.*
Genre(s): War Story.

Morrow, Honore

956. *Forever Free.* New York: Morrow, 1927. 405 pp.
In the early years of the Civil War, Abraham Lincoln's wife does not suspect Miss Ford, a beautiful Southern spy who lives in the White House.
Genre(s): War Story.

957. *Last Full Measure.* New York: Morrow, 1930. 337 pp.
In the sequel to *With Malice Toward None,* during the last months of Abraham Lincoln's life, he faces the complications of what to do to restore the South.
Genre(s): War Story.

Nicole, Christopher

958. *Iron Ships, Iron Men.* Hampton, NH: Severn House, 1989. 325 pp.
After Lieutenant Rod Bascom loses his ship he goes to New York, where he must chose between two friends, the abolitionist McGann or the slave-owning Grahame, before he is commissioned into the Confederate Navy at the beginning of the war, in the sequel to *The Sea and the Sand.*
Genre(s): Romance; Adventure Story; War Story; Sea Story.

Noble, Hollister

959. *Woman with a Sword.* Garden City, NY: Doubleday, 1948. 395 pp.
Anna Ella Carroll gains fame during the Union army's Civil War Tennessee campaign as a brilliant writer and newspaperwoman.
Genre(s): War Story; Biographical Fiction.

O'Brien, Judith

960. *Ashton's Bride.* New York: Pocket Books, 1995. 346 pp.
Margaret Garnett begins teaching at a Tennessee university and writes a letter to a Confederate general, Ashton Johnson, to tell him that his lover is fickle, and when the letter disappears into the past, she does too.
Genre(s): Romance; War Story.

Panger, Daniel

◆ **961.** *Soldier Boys.* San Jose, CA: Resource, 1988. 240 pp.
Josh, 19, and his friend Luke leave their Alabama farm home in 1862 to join the Confederate Army in Virginia.
Genre(s): War Story.

Pauley, Barbara Anne

962. *Blood Kin.* New York: Doubleday, 1972. 206 pp.
Twins, one loyal to the Confederacy and the other to the Union, become involved with their cousin, orphan Leslie Day Hallem, during the Civil War in Tennessee.
Genre(s): Gothic Fiction; Romance.

Peart, Jane

◆ **963.** *The Pledge.* Grand Rapids, MI: Zondervan, 1996. 256 pp.
Jo Beth Davidson, daughter of Johanna Davidson in *The Pattern,* falls in love with a Union supporter, and after Lincoln is assassinated, she creates her own quilt about their love. (*Series:* American Quilt 2)
Genre(s): War Story; Christian Fiction.

964. *Yankee Bride and Rebel Bride.* Grand Rapids, MI: Zondervan, 1990. 188 pp.
During the Civil War, two women strive to keep their ideals and dreams but have difficulty overcoming their hostility toward each other.
Genre(s): War Story; Christian Fiction.

Pennell, Joseph Stanley

965. *History of Rome Hanks and Kindred Matters.* New York: Scribner's, 1944. 361 pp.
A surgeon tells about his experiences in the Civil War to his friend Rome Hanks's great-grandson.
Genre(s): War Story.

Phillips, Michael R.

◆ **966.** *Into the Long Dark Night.* Minneapolis, MN: Bethany House, 1992. 297 pp.
Corrie becomes involved in her support of the Northern cause during the Civil War. (*Series:* The Journals of Corrie Belle Hollister, 6)
Genre(s): Christian Fiction; War Story.

◆ **967.** *Land of the Brave and the Free.* Minneapolis, MN: Bethany House, 1993. 317 pp.
When Corrie is wounded during the Civil War, she finds herself in the care of a strange man. (*Series:* The Journals of Corrie Belle Hollister, 7)
Genre(s): Christian Fiction; War Story.

◆ **968.** *Sea to Shining Sea.* Minneapolis, MN: Bethany House, 1992. 320 pp.
Corrie's world changes as the Civil War influences California. (*Series:* Journals of Corrie Belle Hollister, 5)
Genre(s): Christian Fiction; War Story.

Plain, Belva

◆ 969. *Crescent City.* New York: Delacorte, 1984. 429 pp.
Miriam Raphael's Jewish family flees from Europe to Louisiana during the Civil War and becomes divided in its loyalties.
Genre(s): War Story.

Price, Charles F.

970. *Hiwassee.* Chicago: Academy, 1996. 188 pp.
Of the three Curtis brothers in western North Carolina, two fight in the Battle of Chickamauga (Georgia) in 1863, and another, wounded in battle, must hide on the family farm when plundering Union soldiers arrive in the area.
Genre(s): War Story.

Quinn, Peter

971. *Banished Children of Eve.* New York: Viking, 1994. 612 pp.
During the New York draft riots of 1863, native-born people and immigrants exhibit intense hostilities.
Genre(s): War Story.

Randle, Kevin D.

◆ 972. *Spanish Gold.* Boston: Little, Brown, 1990. 148 pp.
During the Civil War, David Travis hears about Spanish gold supposedly lost in West Texas two centuries before, and he joins an old prospector's daughter to look for it.
Genre(s): War Story; Western Fiction.

Reed, Ishmael

973. *Flight to Canada.* New York: Atheneum, 1976. 179 pp.
Raven Quickskill runs away from his master during the Civil War but cannot reach the Canadian border until the war has ended because his master is determined to capture him.
Genre(s): War Story; Satire.

Renek, Morris

974. *Bread and Circus.* New York: Weidenfeld and Nicolson, 1987. 323 pp.
In 1863, Boss Tweed works to make New York citizens believe he is their savior during the Civil War Draft Riots while he goes to Tammany Hall to auction city jobs to the highest briber and meets his mistress for afternoon liaisons.
Genre(s): Biographical Fiction; Political Fiction.

Reno, Marie R.

975. *When the Music Changed.* New York: New American Library, 1980. 530 pp.
Miranda Chase has an unhappy marriage that she periodically escapes in an affair with a married man, but as the Civil War begins, it affects all her family.
Genre(s): War Story; Love Story; Family Saga.

Richards, Dusty

976. *Noble's Way.* New York: Evans, 1992. 190 pp.
Noble McCurtain moves to Kansas in 1864 and establishes a trading post that flourishes after the Civil War with the patronage of Native Americans and settlers.
Genre(s): War Story.

Rising, Clara

977. *In the Season of the Wild Rose.* New York: Villard, 1986. 899 pp.
John Hunt Morgan, cavalryman, forms his company, Morgan's Raiders, to fight for the Confederacy when Kentucky refuses to secede from the Union.
Genre(s): Biographical Fiction; War Story.

Robertson, David

◆ 978. *Booth.* New York: Doubleday, 1998. 320 pp.
D.W. Griffith asks John H. Surratt to relate his part in the assassination of Abraham Lincoln in 1916, and Surratt reviews his diary to recall his involvement with John Wilkes Booth during that fateful time.
Genre(s): Biographical Fiction.

Robertson, Don

979. *By Antietam Creek.* Englewood Cliffs, NJ: Prentice Hall, 1960. 268 pp.
The battle of Antietam, one of the Civil War's fiercest, costs 5000 lives and affects scores of others.
Genre(s): War Story.

980. *Prisoners of Twilight.* New York: Crown, 1989. 224 pp.
In April, 1865, a group of Confederates drag toward Appomattox Court House.
Genre(s): War Story.

Safire, William

981. *Freedom.* Garden City, NY: Doubleday, 1987. 1125 pp.
Lincoln suspends habeas corpus at the beginning of the Civil War and events unfold until he signs the Emancipation Proclamation.
Genre(s): Biographical Fiction; War Story.

Schaefer, Jack

982. *Company of Cowards.* Boston: Houghton Mifflin, 1957. 143 pp.
Company Q of the Union Army gains a reputation for refusing to cooperate but earns a chance to show its bravery in battle.
Genre(s): War Story.

Schultz, Duane P.

983. *Glory Enough for All.* New York: St. Martin's Press, 1993. 360 pp.
Colonel Pleasants leads a group of Pennsylvania miners into Petersburg, Virginia, during the Civil War to dig a mine shaft under the Confederate fort to blow it up.
Genre(s): War Story.

Scott, Evelyn

984. *The Wave.* 1929. Baton Rouge: Louisiana State University Press, 1996. 624 pp.
The Civil War sweeps over the South.
Genre(s): War Story.

Shaara, Jeff

985. *The Last Full Measure.* New York: Ballantine, 1998. 512 pp.
The two sides of the country go to war in the last of the trilogy that includes *Killer Angels* and *Gods and Generals.*
Genre(s): War Story.

Shaara, Michael

986. *The Killer Angels.* New York: McKay, 1974. 374 pp.
Robert E. Lee and James Longstreet tell the Southern view of the battle at Gettysburg while Colonel Joshua Chamberlain and General John Buford present the Northern view.
Award(s): Pulitzer Prize.
Genre(s): War Story.

Sherburne, James

987. *The Way to Fort Pillow.* Boston: Houghton Mifflin, 1972. 260 pp.
In the sequel to *Hacey Miller*, Hacey is an Emancipationist with a family and joins the Union Cavalry in one of the all-African American units and survives the massacre at Fort Pillow.
Genre(s): War Story.

Sinclair, Harold

988. *The Cavalryman.* New York: Harper and Row, 1958. 342 pp.
In the sequel to *The Horse Soldiers*, General Jack Marlowe goes to North Dakota in 1864 to campaign against the Sioux Nation at their annual Kildeer Mountain gathering.
Genre(s): War Story.

989. *The Horse Soldiers.* New York: Harper and Row, 1956. 336 pp.
Colonel Jack Marlowe tries to cut the South's supply line to Vicksburg.
Genre(s): War Story.

Skvorecky, Josef

990. *The Bride of Texas.* Trans. Kaca Polackova-Henley. New York: Knopf, 1996. 436 pp.
Czech immigrants Kapsa, Cyril, and Cyril's sister Lida look for happiness during the Civil War after escaping the strife of their own country.
Genre(s): War Story.

Slaughter, Frank G.

991. *The Stonewall Brigade.* New York: Pocket Books, 1976. 500 pp.
A male field hospital nurse has connections with leaders of the Civil War, and he assesses the weakening of the South long before Appomattox.
Genre(s): War Story.

Slotkin, Richard

992. *The Crater.* New York: Atheneum, 1980. 558 pp.
The Battle of the Crater near Petersburg, Virginia, lasts for six weeks in the summer of 1864, with northern soldiers planning to dig a mine while their generals engage in pettiness, and the Confederates aim their rifles at blacks.
Genre(s): War Story.

Smith, William Ferguson

◆ 993. *The Rival Lovers.* Atlanta, GA: Peachtree, 1980. 186 pp.
William Ferguson Smith gladly defends Georgia during the Civil War, but 12 years later, he recalls lost lives and loves.
Genre(s): War Story; Biographical Fiction.

Steelman, Robert J.

◆ 994. *The Galvanized Reb.* New York: Doubleday, 1977. 178 pp.
Confederates try to turn Native Americans against the Union so that the North will have to protect itself on two fronts.
Genre(s): Western Fiction; War Story; Spy Fiction.

Steward, Barbara, and Dwight Steward

995. *The Lincoln Diddle.* New York: Morrow, 1979. 251 pp.
Edgar Allan Poe attempts, as Henri Le Rennet, to foil the assassination of Lincoln by using his power of reason.
Genre(s): Mystery.

Stewart, Fred Mustard

996. *A Rage Against Heaven.* New York: Viking, 1978. 628 pp.
When Lew survives Andersonville Prison, he turns to banditry in Mexico to obtain money to kill the politician who tried to kill him, but his wife leaves for Paris where she marries his best friend.
Genre(s): War Story.

Straight, Michael Whitney

997. *A Very Small Remnant.* 1963. Albuquerque: University of New Mexico, 1976. 232 pp.
In 1864, John M. Chivington massacres a group of Cheyenne under Chief Black Kettle at Sand Creek near Fort Lyon.
Genre(s): Political Fiction; Biographical Fiction.

Stribling, T. S.

998. *The Forge.* New York: Doubleday, 1931. 525 pp.

A middle-class Alabama family, the Vaidens, live in the South until the Civil War begins and their lives are changed dramatically.
Genre(s): War Story.

Thane, Elswyth

999. *Yankee Stranger.* New York: Duell, Sloan, and Pearce, 1944. 306 pp.

In the sequel to *Dawn's Early Light*, Cabot Murray meets Eden Day and falls in love.
Genre(s): War Story; Family Saga.

Thoene, Brock, and Bodie Thoene

1000. *Cannons of the Comstock.* Minneapolis, MN: Bethany House, 1992. 208 pp.

Tom Dawson exposes a Confederate plot to draw California into the Civil War. (*Series:* Saga of the Sierras, 5)
Genre(s): War Story; Christian Fiction.

Thomsen, Robert

1001. *Carriage Trade.* New York: Simon and Schuster, 1972. 512 pp.

During the Battle of Gettysburg, a bordello becomes a hospital, and while the prostitutes serve as nurses, the 16-year-old daughter of the madam discovers her vocation.
Genre(s): War Story.

Tracy, Don

1002. *The Last Boat out of Cincinnati.* New York: Trident, 1970. 221 pp.

Hank Champelle, 16, comes to Cincinnati from Louisiana to buy horses for his father and wanders around town instead of doing business, and when the Civil War begins, no one will trade with him because he is a southerner.
Genre(s): War Story; Bildungsroman (Coming of Age).

Vogt, Esther Loewen

1003. *The Enchanted Prairie.* Camp Hill, PA: Horizon House, 1992. 271 pp.

Barbara Temple moves from Georgia to Kansas during the Civil War after her family dies, a place with strange ways that she has difficulty accepting.
Genre(s): War Story; Christian Fiction.

Walker, Jack

1004. *West of Fort Worth.* Austin, TX: Thorp Springs, 1990. 246 pp.

Fauntleroy Finch, recruited by the Texas Rangers in 1862, decides four years later to settle down on a ranch, and as he drives cattle to the Canadian River, he learns that African Americans are good cowboys.
Genre(s): Western Fiction.

Walker, Mildred

1005. *The Quarry.* New York: Harcourt Brace, 1947. 339 pp.

Several generations of miners work and live in Vermont from the Civil War to World War I.
Genre(s): War Story; Family Saga.

Wallace, Willard M.

1006. *The Raiders.* Boston: Little, Brown, 1970. 448 pp.

In England, Scott Pettigrew asks the British to stop construction on the Confederate raider *Alabama*, but when he is unsuccessful, he boards the ship and spies for the Union.
Genre(s): War Story; Adventure Story; Sea Story.

Warren, Robert Penn

1007. *Wilderness.* New York: Random House, 1961. 310 pp.

Adam Rosenzweig, a German Jew, wants to serve in the Union Army, but on shipboard to America, someone sees his deformed foot, and he has to escape from pursuers.
Genre(s): War Story.

Wells, Marian

1008. *Jewel of Promise.* Minneapolis, MN: Bethany House, 1990. 384 pp.

When Alex is missing in the Civil War, Olivia searches the military hospitals to locate him. (*Series:* Treasure Quest)
Genre(s): War Story; Christian Fiction.

1009. *Out of the Crucible.* Minneapolis, MN: Bethany House, 1988. 320 pp.

In the West during the Civil War, people must show their love and their loyalty. (*Series:* Treasure Quest, 2)
Genre(s): Christian Fiction; War Story.

Wicker, Tom

1010. *Unto this Hour.* New York: Viking, 1984. 642 pp.

In Manassas, Virginia, the Battle of Bull Run shocks those who have come to watch it as entertainment.
Genre(s): War Story.

Williams, Ben Ames

1011. *House Divided.* Boston: Houghton Mifflin, 1947. 1514 pp.

Since the Currain family owns plantations in the south, it must support the Confederates.
Genre(s): War Story.

1012. *The Unconquered.* Boston: Houghton Mifflin, 1963. 689 pp.

In the sequel to *House Divided*, the Currain family goes to New Orleans after the war and becomes involved in Louisiana politics.
Genre(s): Biographical Fiction; War Story.

Woodiwiss, Kathleen E.

1013. *Ashes In The Wind.* 1979. New York: Avon, 1996. 580 pp.

Jacques Dubonn begins a rumor that Alaina MacGaren is a traitor, forcing her to leave her family's Virginia plantation for New Orleans, where she dons several disguises before meeting the Yankee captain Cole Lattimer.

Genre(s): Romance; War Story.

Yerby, Frank

1014. *McKenzie's Hundred.* Garden City, NY: Doubleday, 1985. 377 pp.

Rose Ann McKenzie comes back to Virginia from Boston but returns north to become a Rebel spy in New York.

Genre(s): War Story.

Yevish, I.

1015. *The Smoke of Summer.* Cape May Point, NJ: Yevish, 1991. 320 pp.

In a New Jersey resort community during the horrors of the Civil War, Willacassa Harrah falls in love.

Genre(s): War Story; Romance.

Young, Stark

1016. *So Red the Rose.* New York: Scribner's, 1934. 431 pp.

Families on two plantations in Mississippi come into contact with the Civil War in a variety of subtle but powerful ways.

Genre(s): Domestic Fiction; War Story.

Zimmer, Michael

1017. *Dust and Glory.* New York: Walker, 1989. 237 pp.

Jesse Ross, 18, joins the Missouri Rangers during the Civil War, and helps them fight although he never enjoys killing.

Genre(s): War Story.

1866-1889
Reconstruction and
Development of the West

Adams, Andy

1018. *The Log of a Cowboy.* Boston: Houghton Mifflin, 1903. 387 pp.
A cowboy keeps a journal of a large cattle drive from Texas to the Blackfoot Agency in Montana.
Genre(s): Western Fiction.

Adams, Clifton

1019. *Biscuit-Shooter.* New York: Doubleday, 1971. 182 pp.
A naive Texas cowboy breaks the leg of a notorious gunman in a barroom brawl and joins a cattle drive as its inexperienced cook to escape him.
Genre(s): Western Fiction.

◆ 1020. *Hassle and the Medicine Man.* New York: Doubleday, 1973. 188 pp.
Hassle Jones, 11, likes California Sam, and he becomes his sidekick just as someone accuses Sam of using his Wa-Hoe Electric Hair Restorer to cheat him.
Genre(s): Western Fiction.

Adleman, Robert H.

1021. *The Bloody Benders.* New York: Stein and Day, 1970. 224 pp.
In the 1870s, Kate Bender's family robs and murders at least 11 guests in their Kansas roadside inn and then buries them on their farm, but the family disappears before authorities can apprehend its members.
Genre(s): Western Fiction; Mystery.

Aggeler, Geoffrey

1022. *Confessions of Johnny Ringo.* New York: Dutton, 1987. 310 pp.
Ringo, who carries the classics in his saddlebags, writes his memoirs while hiding in Arizona from Wyatt Earp, until Earp kills him in 1882 when Ringo reemerges from hiding.
Genre(s): Biographical Fiction; Western Fiction.

Aldrich, Bess Streeter

1023. *A Lantern In Her Hand.* New York: Appleton, 1928. 433 pp.
A young husband and wife cross the country to Nebraska by covered wagon to start a homestead.
Genre(s): Domestic Fiction.

1024. *The Lieutenant's Lady.* New York: Appleton, 1942. 275 pp.
Linnie Colsworth loves her cousin's fiancé in Omaha just after the Civil War.
Genre(s): Western Fiction.

◆ 1025. *Spring Came on Forever.* New York: Appleton, 1935. 332 pp.
Amalia Stolz falls in love, but her father takes her from Illinois to Nebraska via covered wagon, and the man she loves arrives too late to marry her.
Genre(s): Love Story; Domestic Fiction.

Allen, Clay

◆ 1026. *Range Trouble.* New York: Walker, 1982. 159 pp.
As Martin Ballinger tries to keep his ranch going through a terrible winter, an outlaw gunman arrives needing shelter and joins Ballinger against another rancher who wants his land.
Genre(s): Western Fiction.

Alter, Judy

1027. *Mattie.* Garden City, NY: Doubleday, 1988. 181 pp.
Dr. Mattie becomes the first female student in the Omaha Medical College in 1885, and she continues to show her courage throughout her life.
Award(s): Western Writers of America Spur Award.
Genre(s): Medical Novel; Western Fiction.

Altman, Stephen

1028. *Bowhunter.* New York: Walker, 1988. 191 pp.
Tory Bowhunter, 19 and in love with young Josie Meeker, observes the Utes' destruction of the White River Agency and the Meeker Massacre in 1879 after Nathan Meeker tried to force the Utes act like whites.
Genre(s): Western Fiction.

Andersen, Richard

1029. *Muckaluck.* New York: Delacorte, 1980. 206 pp.
In 1873, Oregon Muckalucks face starvation until they win a hard-fought battle against the United States Calvary.
Genre(s): Western Fiction; War Story.

Anderson, Catherine

1030. *Simply Love.* New York: Avon, 1997. 384 pp.
Wealthy Luke Taggart decides to pay Cassandra Zerek to become his companion after he loses interest in loose women, but after she moves in, he realizes that he wants more from her.
Genre(s): Romance.

Anderson, Sherwood

◆ 1031. *Tar: A Midwest Childhood.* New York: Boni and Liveright, 1926. 346 pp.
Tar, a character based on Sherwood Anderson, grows from four to early adolescence in a small Ohio town.
Genre(s): Domestic Fiction; Biographical Fiction.

Appel, Allen

◆ 1032. *Twice Upon a Time.* New York: Carroll and Graf, 1988. 351 pp.
Alex, historian, is transported back in time to the Philadelphia Exposition of 1876, where he becomes involved with a group converging at Little Big Horn.
Genre(s): Time Travel.

Archer, Ellen

1033. *Darling.* New York: Zebra, 1996. 352 pp.
During the 19th century, after a man returns Selena to her husband from New York City streets, the husband divorces her, and the servants fear her.
Genre(s): Romance.

Argiri, Laura

1034. *The God in Flight.* New York: Random House, 1994. 478 pp.
Simion Satterwhite attends Yale in the 1880s where he and an art professor begin a homosexual love affair.
Genre(s): Romance.

Armen, M.A.

◆ 1035. *The Hanging of Father Miguel.* New York: Evans, 1989. 131 pp.
Wounded by a young gunman, Glint McClain obtains help from Father Miguel, and after he gets well, McClain offers to help the priest's parish free themselves from the local mining despot.
Genre(s): Western Fiction.

Arnold, Elliott

1036. *The Camp Grant Massacre.* New York: Simon and Schuster, 1976. 447 pp.
Although an army officer and a warrior make peace, settlers invading the Apache village ruin their agreement.
Genre(s): Western Fiction; War Story.

Ashour, Linda Phillips

1037. *Joy Baby.* New York: Simon and Schuster, 1992. 544 pp.
Laydelle Hanks wonders why she is poor when her grandfather was an oil tycoon, and she learns about her family's history since 1884.
Genre(s): Epic Literature.

Askew, Rilla

1038. *The Mercy Seat.* New York: Viking, 1997. 432 pp.
Forced to leave Kentucky in 1888 because of her uncle's illegal acitivities, Mattie Lodi, 11, and her family go to the Indian Territory of Oklahoma; but by the time of arrival, two are dead and one is brain-damaged and Mattie must try to keep the rest together.
Genre(s): Western Fiction; Bildungsroman (Coming of Age).

Bailey, Paul Dayton

1039. *The Claws of the Hawk.* Tucson, AZ: Westernlore, 1966. 358 pp.
Wahker, chieftain of the Utes, helps his people survive by stealing horses.
Genre(s): Biographical Fiction.

Baker, A. A.

1040. *A Noose for the Marshal.* New York: Major Books, 1977. 160 pp.
Billy Arleigh, cattle rustler in Texas and Arizona, shoots a lawman who trails him.
Genre(s): Western Fiction.

Bakst, Harold

◆ 1041. *Prairie Widow.* New York: M. Evans, 1992. 120 pp.
In the late 1870s, Walter and Jennifer Vandermeer take their two children from Ohio to the Kansas prairie, and when Walter dies shortly afterwards, Jennifer must find ways to care for the family.
Genre(s): Western Fiction; Domestic Fiction.

Ballard, Willis Todhunter

1042. *The Sheriff of Tombstone.* Garden City, NY: Doubleday, 1977. 187 pp.
A Texan tries to coerce an Arizona town into raising cattle, but he first has to clear his brother-in-law's name by finding a thief.
Genre(s): Western Fiction.

1043. *Trails of Rage.* New York: Doubleday, 1975. 184 pp.
Marauders posing as either Confederate soldiers or Union troops cause chaos in Kansas and Colorado, and a former Union officer comes from the Army of the Potomac to stop them.
Award(s): Western Writers of America Spur Award.
Genre(s): Western Fiction.

Bandelier, Adolph Francis Alphonse

1044. *The Delight Makers.* 1916. New York: Harcourt Brace, 1971. 490 pp.
Pueblos follow their daily lives in the deserts of New Mexico.
Genre(s): Western Fiction.

Barr, Nevada

◆ 1045. *Bittersweet.* New York: St. Martin's Press, 1984. 339 pp.
Teacher Imogene Grelznik protects her pupil, Sarah Tolstonadge, from her abusive husband, and the two fall in love but have to move from Pennsylvania to Nevada to stay together.
Genre(s): Western Fiction.

Barrett, Bob

◆ 1046. *Pembrook vs. the West.* Garden City, NY: Doubleday, 1978. 185 pp.
Walker Pembrook, a teacher, moves to Arizona Territory to find his fortune.
Genre(s): Western Fiction.

Barry, Jane

◆ 1047. *Maximilian's Gold.* Garden City, NY: Doubleday, 1966. 281 pp.
Former Confederate soldiers from Missouri head to Mexico in search of a cave of gold, but a wagon train carrying Maximilian's treasure hinders their journey.
Genre(s): Western Fiction.

◆ 1048. *A Shadow of Eagles.* Garden City, NY: Doubleday, 1964. 408 pp.
When a cattle-drive boss falls in love with the daughter of a Spanish rancher, he has to examine his future.
Genre(s): Love Story; Western Fiction.

◆ 1049. *A Time in the Sun.* Garden City, NY: Doubleday, 1966. 378 pp.
Apaches capture a colonel's daughter during their campaigns of the 1870s.
Genre(s): War Story; Western Fiction.

Bartlett, Stephanie

1050. *Highland Flame.* New York: Doubleday, 1992. 392 pp.
A doctor woos a widowed Scottish-born woman who is running a Texas ranch.
Genre(s): Western Fiction; Romance.

Barton, Wayne

1051. *Ride Down the Wind.* Garden City, NY: Doubleday, 1981. 184 pp.
Jess Faver, an army scout, must search for his friend, Apache scout Nantahe, and either turn him in to prison or kill him.
Genre(s): Western Fiction.

Barton, Wayne, and Stan Williams

1052. *Lockhart's Nightmare.* New York: Forge, 1998. 384 pp.
Civil War veteran James Lockhart and drifter Marian Taylor escape from prison after being falsely accused of theft and begin to chase the real criminals across the west.
Genre(s): Western Fiction; Adventure Story.

Bass, Milton

1053. *Jory.* New York: Putnam, 1969. 255 pp.
Jory kills the man who murdered his father and leaves for Texas where he uses his guns to survive.
Genre(s): Western Fiction.

◆ 1054. *Mistr Jory.* New York: Putnam, 1976. 253 pp.
In the sequel to *Jory*, Jory wants to stop using his guns, but first he must kill two men taking advantage of a weak but wealthy rancher.
Genre(s): Western Fiction.

Bean, Amelia

◆ 1055. *The Feud.* New York: Doubleday, 1960. 287 pp.
In Arizona, the Graham-Tewksbury feud erupts after the Civil War.
Genre(s): Western Fiction.

1056. *Time for Outrage.* New York: Doubleday, 1967. 445 pp.
Corrupt local officials fight with frontiersmen in Lincoln County, New Mexico, during 1878.
Genre(s): Western Fiction.

Bean, Frederic

1057. *Eden.* New York: Bantam, 1997. 304 pp.
As the only King offspring concerned about others, Matthew King relates events leading to his older brother's murder.
Genre(s): Western Fiction; Domestic Fiction.

Bechko, P. A.

1058. *The Eye of the Hawk.* Unity, ME: Five Star, 1998. 213 pp.
Ethan Torregrossa loses his memory after being kidnapped from a riverboat and remembers only that he might be a gunfighter.
Genre(s): Western Fiction.

◆ 1059. *The Winged Warrior.* Garden City, NY: Doubleday, 1978. 186 pp.
Omaha Jones, educated in the East, returns to the West as half Sioux and half white, to make his dreams reality.
Genre(s): Western Fiction.

Beck, Harry

1060. *The Scarlet Hills.* New York: Walker, 1982. 160 pp.
Rustlers stealing the Bryan family's cattle are found dead, and young Bert Bryan, who seems the likely suspect, must work to keep the ranch and to clear his name.
Genre(s): Western Fiction.

Bennett, Dwight

1061. *The Cheyenne Encounter.* New York: Doubleday, 1976. 185 pp.
John Isely, a rancher in Wyoming, lives in Cheyenne since his wife hates the ranch, and when he becomes partners with the wrong man, the man who runs his ranch must extricate Isely from the mess.
Genre(s): Western Fiction.

Berger, Thomas

1062. *Little Big Man.* New York: Delacorte, 1964. 440p pp.
An elderly white man tells about his life as an adopted Cheyenne when he was a scout, gunfighter, buffalo hunter, and survivor of Custer's last stand.
Genre(s): Western Fiction; Humorous Fiction; Adventure Story.

Bickham, Jack M.

1063. *The Apple Dumpling Gang.* New York: Doubleday, 1971. 189 pp.
A 40-year-old aging sheriff must cope with three gangs, criticism of his performance, and five children suddenly in his care.
Genre(s): Western Fiction.

1064. *Baker's Hawk.* New York: Doubleday, 1974. 233 pp.
Billy Baker, 11, asks a crazy man on the mountain to help him with an injured hawk because his father has refused to let him bring more animals home.
Genre(s): Western Fiction; Domestic Fiction.

1065. *Jilly's Canal.* New York: Doubleday, 1971. 192 pp.
A young engineer comes from the East into cattle country and announces that he will bring water to a town threatened with drought.
Genre(s): Western Fiction.

1066. *Katie, Kelly, And Heck.* New York: Doubleday, 1973. 184 pp.
A staid young woman from Ohio falls in love with an Arizona town's saloon owner, who also runs the local bordello and gambling establishment in the 1880s.
Genre(s): Western Fiction; Romance.

Bittner, Rosanne

1067. *Chase the Sun.* New York: Bantam, 1995. 480 pp.
Zack Myers at 10 watched Indians murder his family, and as a U.S. army officer, he wants revenge, but he finds himself siding with the Nez Percé instead.
Genre(s): Western Fiction; Romance.

1068. *Tame the Wild Wind.* New York: Bantam, 1996. 384 pp.
Gabriel Beaumont, known to the Sioux as Tall Bear, rescues pregnant widow Faith Sommers and decides to live as a white man again.
Genre(s): Romance; Western Fiction.

1069. *Texas Embrace.* New York: Kensington, 1997. 320 pp.
After Texas Ranger John Hawkins rescues Tess Carey, she returns the favor by rescuing him, but he is part Native American and she is white, so their romance cannot proceed until she asks him to marry her.
Genre(s): Romance; Western Fiction.

Blair, Clifford

◆ 1070. *The Guns of Sacred Heart.* New York: Walker, 1991. 192 pp.
Tom and Sharon Langston come to Oklahoma Territory to start a ranch.
Genre(s): Western Fiction.

1071. *Storm over the Lightning.* New York: Walker, 1993. 228 pp.
In the sequel to *The Guns of Sacred Heart*, Tom and Sharon Langston struggle to keep their ranch from an Easterner who wants their land and water rights.
Genre(s): Western Fiction.

Blake, James Carlos

1072. *The Pistoleer.* New York: Berkley, 1995. 352 pp.
John Wesley Hardin became the most infamous mankiller in Texas after killing his first man at 13 and following with Union Occupation troops, state policemen, or those who insulted him or his family.
Genre(s): Biographical Fiction; Western Fiction.

Blake, Jennifer

1073. *Golden Fancy.* Hampton, NH: Severn House, 1997. 416 pp.
When Serena Walsh flees from a wagon train, saloonkeeper Ward Dunbar's rescue of her irritates his female friend.
Genre(s): Western Fiction.

1074. *Silver-Tongued Devil.* New York: Fawcett, 1995. 336 pp.
Angelica Carew awakens after a riverboat explosion and finds herself married to her rescuer, Renold Harden, the stepson of the owner of a plantation that her father won at cards.
Genre(s): Romance.

Blake, Michael

1075. *Dances with Wolves.* New York: Fawcett, 1988. 320 pp.
A former army officer establishes a relationship with a lone wolf who visits his camp, then he becomes friends with the Native Americans in the area.
Genre(s): Western Fiction.

1076. *Marching to Valhalla.* New York: Villard, 1996. 288 pp.
General George Custer keeps a journal about his life at West Point, the battles fought in the Civil War, his marriage, his campaigns, and his court martial.
Genre(s): Western Fiction; Biographical Fiction.

Blakely, Mike

1077. *Baron of the Sacramentos.* New York: M. Evans, 1991. 258 pp.
Bart Young drops out of law school in 1870 and leaves Louisiana for New Mexico, and using his expert forging ability, builds a fortune on deceit.
Genre(s): Adventure Story.

1078. *The Snowy Range Gang.* New York: M. Evans, 1992. 190 pp.
After Claude Deval leaves Texas for Wyoming, he helps hunt for Brahma cattle rustlers while trying to fulfill a personal vendetta.
Genre(s): Mystery; Western Fiction.

Blevins, Winfred

1079. *The Misadventures of Silk and Shakespeare.* Ottawa, IL: Jameson, 1985. 250 pp.
Silk, 16, goes in search of his father with a former actor named Shakespeare.
Genre(s): Western Fiction; Adventure Story.

1080. *The Rock Child.* New York: Tor, 1998. 416 pp.
Mark Twain joins explorer Sir Richard Burton in rescuing Asie, a Native American-English savant and Sun Moon, a Tibetan nun prostitute.
Genre(s): Western Fiction; Picaresque Fiction.

Bly, Stephen

1081. *It's Your Misfortune and None of My Own.* Wheaton, IL: Crossway, 1994. 192 pp.
Tap Andrews and Pepper Paige help their dying friends on their way to arranged marriages and take their friends' identities so that they can marry the women instead. (*Series:* Code of the West)
Genre(s): Western Fiction; Christian Fiction; Romance.

1082. *My Foot's in the Stirrup . . . My Pony Won't Stand.* Wheaton, IL: Crossway, 1996. 192 pp.
Tap Andrews, formerly a gunslinger, only wants to settle down with his wife, but when he agrees to escort a Texas man to ranch sites, he realizes that he has been hired as a gunfighter.
Genre(s): Christian Fiction; Western Fiction.

◆ 1083. *Standoff at Sunrise Creek.* Wheaton, IL: Crossway, 1993. 192 pp.
Stuart Brannon, a rancher and minister, helps the Apache and settlers in the Yavapai County War when developers try to take their lands.
Genre(s): Christian Fiction; Western Fiction.

1084. *Stay Away from That City.* Wheaton, IL: Crossway, 1996. 192 pp.
After Tap Andrews and his wife move to Cheyenne, Wyoming, he becomes marshal and tries to keep order among the gold diggers and the cattle drivers.
Genre(s): Christian Fiction; Western Fiction.

1085. *Where the Deer and the Antelope Play.* Wheaton, IL: Crossway, 1995. 192 pp.
In 1882, Tap Andrews plans to marry Pepper Paige at his ranch, but several difficulties with cattle rustlers and outlaws threaten their plans. (Code of the West, 3)
Genre(s): Christian Fiction; Western Fiction.

Boggs, Johnny D.

1086. *Riding with Hannah and the Horseman.* New York: Avalon, 1998. 192 pp.
Ranch-owner Hannah Scott and her Greek ouzo-drinking, college-educated cowboy boyfriend join Buddy Pecos in a stagecoach operation during the 1880s.
Genre(s): Western Fiction; Romance.

Bojer, Johan

1087. *The Emigrants.* Trans. A.G. Jayne. New York: Appleton, 1925. 351 pp.
Erik Foss's colony of Norwegians in the Red River Valley of North Dakota fight drought, poverty, frost, and homesickness.

Bonds, Parris Afton

1088. *For All Time.* New York: HarperCollins, 1994. 346 pp.
Stacie awakens in 1872 as Anastasia Wysee, her great-grandmother, where she falls in love with the mixed-breed Joseph Muldoon and hesitates to return to the present.
Genre(s): Western Fiction; Time Travel.

Bonner, Cindy

◆ 1089. *Lily.* Chapel Hill, NC: Algonquin, 1992. 336 pp.
Lily Delony at 15 falls in love with a member of an outlaw family instead of the son of the 1880s Texas area's wealthy family.
Genre(s): Western Fiction; Love Story.

◆ 1090. *Looking after Lily.* Chapel Hill, NC: Algonquin, 1994. 326 pp.
In the sequel to *Lily*, Lily's husband Marion goes to jail for two years just as his brother is released, and Marion asks him to watch out for Lily.
Genre(s): Western Fiction; Love Story.

◆ 1091. *The Passion of Dellie O'Barr.* Chapel Hill, NC: Algonquin, 1996. 353 pp.
Dellie, married for two years at 20, falls in love with a political organizer in the 1880s and commits a crime for which she pays heavily.
Genre(s): Love Story.

Borland, Hal

◆ 1092. *The Seventh Winter.* Philadelphia: Lippincott, 1959. 256 pp.
A cattle rancher fights to survive during the fierce Colorado winter.
Genre(s): Western Fiction.

Bowen, Peter

1093. *Kelly Blue.* New York: Crown, 1991. 268 pp.
Luther Sage Kelly tries to support the Plains Indians but is thwarted in a variety of ways.
Genre(s): Western Fiction; Humorous Fiction.

1094. *Yellowstone Kelly.* Ottawa, IL: Jameson, 1987. 282 pp.
Luther Sage Kelly, scout for the colonel who killed Nez Percé Chief Joseph, takes a British duke on an expedition with Buffalo Bill in 1877, and when the duke dies, Kelly escapes to South Africa to fight the Zulus.
Genre(s): War Story; Adventure Story.

Bowering, George

◆ 1095. *Caprice.* New York: Viking, 1988. 266 pp.
Caprice, a redheaded young woman, searches for a desperado while her boyfriend, a schoolteacher, patiently waits for her.
Genre(s): Western Fiction.

Bowman, Doug

1096. *Houston.* New York: Tor, 1998. 288 pp.
Drovers murder Camp Houston's friend John Calloway, and he searches Texas to bring them to justice.
Genre(s): Western Fiction.

Boyer, Glenn C.

1097. *The Guns of Morgette.* New York: Walker, 1982. 192 pp.
Dolf Morgette goes from an undeserved prison sentence back to Pinebluff, hoping that his enemies have left, but they have not.
Genre(s): Western Fiction.

1098. *The Return of Morgette.* New York: Walker, 1985. 185 pp.
When Dolf Morgette returns to Pinebluff for his son's wedding, his son has been shot and the sheriff supports the outlaws.
Genre(s): Western Fiction.

Brand, Max

1099. *Fightin' Fool.* New York: Dodd, Mead, 1933. 186 pp.
A cowboy recklessly incites others to challenge his shooting skills.
Genre(s): Western Fiction.

1100. *Fugitives' Fire.* New York: Putnam, 1991. 184 pp.
Paul Torridon remains prisoner to the Cheyenne because he brings good luck to them.
Genre(s): Western Fiction.

1101. *The Gentle Desperado.* New York: Dodd, Mead, 1985. 195 pp.
Robert Fernald belies his innocent demeanor when he decides to protect Beatrice Larkin from Tom Gill and his men.
Genre(s): Western Fiction.

1102. *Gold Mining.* New York: Dodd, Mead, 1922. 200 pp.
Jim Curry had to become an outlaw because of circumstances, and he changes again for the same reason.
Genre(s): Western Fiction.

1103. *Gunman's Reckoning.* 1921. New York: Dodd, Mead, 1976. 160 pp.
Donnegan, a superb gunman, must demonstrate his quick draw to survive.
Genre(s): Western Fiction.

1104. *Gunmen's Feud.* New York: Dodd, Mead, 1982. 165 pp.
Jerry Peyton has respect from ranchers, but farmers torture him for stealing horses until the real horse thief appears.
Genre(s): Western Fiction.

◆ 1105. *The Last Showdown.* New York: Dodd, Mead, 1975. 251 pp.
A bank robber trying to reform attempts to bury a companion in a churchyard, but the preacher is against the idea.
Genre(s): Western Fiction.

1106. *The Legend of Thunder Moon.* Lincoln, NE: University of Nebraska Press, 1996. 160 pp.
Big Hard Face, a Cheyenne warrior, has no sons after three marriages, so he captures a white child and names him Thunder Moon.
Genre(s): Western Fiction.

1107. *The Long, Long Trail.* New York: Dodd, Mead, 1921. 251 pp.
Hunted for the murder of his father's killer, Jess Dreer has to decide if he will risk his freedom to destroy a hired gunman.
Genre(s): Western Fiction.

1108. *The Making of a Gunman.* New York: Dodd, Mead, 1983. 192 pp.
Tommy Mayo seems stupid until he meets Harry Grant, a thief fleeing others, and he becomes a deadly gunman.
Genre(s): Western Fiction.

1109. *Man from Savage Creek.* New York: Dodd, Mead, 1977. 215 pp.
A lawman and gunman meet in the West.
Genre(s): Western Fiction.

◆ 1110. *Mountain Guns.* New York: Dodd, Mead, 1985. 224 pp.
Peter Messenger looks for Summer Day, a Blackfoot medicine man, and after Summer Day lies that he saved Messenger's life, his pursuit continues.
Genre(s): Western Fiction.

1111. *Rawhide Justice.* New York: Dodd, Mead, 1975. 186 pp.
Reata, a thief, picks the wrong pocket in Rusty Gulch, and he must make a deal with his victim to save himself.
Genre(s): Western Fiction.

1112. *Red Wind and Thunder Moon.* Lincoln, NE: University of Nebraska Press, 1996. 164 pp. Thunder Moon, white son of a Cheyenne chief, allies with Red Wind.
Genre(s): Western Fiction.

1113. *Rogue Mustang.* New York: Dodd, Mead, 1984. 182 pp.
When Paradise Al's jailers think that he looks like a Pendleton agent, he is freed to help them in their feud against Sheriff Drayton's people, but although he shoots with the best, he embarasses them with his poor horsemanship.
Genre(s): Western Fiction.

1114. *Thunder Moon and the Sky People.* Lincoln, NE: University of Nebraska Press, 1996. 210 pp.
Thunder Moon, captured son of a Cheyenne chief, fights for his adopted tribe when the whites try to take their land.
Genre(s): Western Fiction.

1115. *Thunder Moon Strikes.* New York: Warner Books, 1982. 217 pp.
Randolph and Ruth Sutton, Thunder Moon's parents, confront him after he has become a great Cheyenne warrior, and he must decide if he will return to the white world or remain a Cheyenne, in the sequel to *Thunder Moon's Challenge.*
Genre(s): Western Fiction.

1116. *Thunder Moon's Challenge.* New York: Dodd, Mead, 1927. 235 pp.
Thunder Moon seems the likely successor to his adopted father's role as chief, but he has white ancestry, a problematic background for all.
Genre(s): Western Fiction.

◆ **1117. *Wild Freedom.*** New York: Dodd, Mead, 1981. 231 pp.
Tommy Parks, 12, must learn to survive in the wilderness after his father dies.
Genre(s): Western Fiction; Adventure Story.

Brandewyne, Rebecca

1118. *Desperado.* 1993. New York: Severn House, 1996. 370 pp.
A Mexican kidnaps Araminta Winthrop from her Texas ranch, and instead of escaping, she falls in love with him and joins his renegade band.
Genre(s): Western Fiction; Romance.

1119. *Heartland.* New York: Warner Books, 1991. 297 pp.
Rachel Wilder worries about the eight children of her deceased friend and their shiftless father until their uncle, a gunslinger, arrives and claims custody of them.
Genre(s): Romance; Western Fiction.

1120. *The Outlaw Hearts.* Hampton, NH: Severn House, 1993. 480 pp.
On her way to Missouri after the Civil War has destroyed the family home, Jenny Colter meets Luke Morgan, an outlaw, marries him, and helps reform him into a politician.
Genre(s): Romance.

Braun, Matthew

1121. *The Kincaids.* New York: Putnam, 1976. 508 pp.
Two sons in a wealthy family take separate paths, one becoming an outlaw and the other, a lawman.
Award(s): Western Writers of America Spur Award.
Genre(s): Western Fiction.

Brewer, James D.

1122. *No Bottom.* New York: Walker, 1994. 256 pp.
Luke Williams, captain of a Mississippi steamboat with a reputation for good food and efficiency, investigates the sinking of his friend and partner's ship in Natchez while the insurance company sends an alcoholic to question survivors.
Genre(s): Mystery.

1123. *No Escape.* New York: Walker, 1998. 246 pp.
While a yellow fever epidemic is killing 2,000 people in Memphis during 1873 and a murderer is at large, someone embezzles from a private relief agency.
Genre(s): Mystery.

1124. *No Remorse.* New York: Walker, 1997. 272 pp.
Luke Williamson works as a steamboat pilot on the Mississippi during Reconstruction and partners with Masey Baldridge, a detective, to investigate the murder of one of Williamson's business competitors.
Genre(s): Mystery.

1125. *No Virtue.* New York: Walker, 1995. 232 pp.
In 1873, a paddle wheeler's captain finds a murdered prostitute on the Mississippi River bank, and when the Memphis police arrive, they hastily arrest the trusted African American first mate.
Genre(s): Mystery.

Bristow, Gwen

1126. *The Handsome Road.* New York: Crowell, 1938. 268 pp.
In the sequel to *Deep Summer*, Corrie May works in the Larne plantation home, and although jealous of their wealth, eventually realizes that her honest illegitimate child is more fortunate than the Larne son.
Genre(s): Family Saga.

1127. *Jubilee Trail.* New York: Crowell, 1950. 564 pp.
A New York girl completes finishing school and goes west to the Santa Fe trail.
Genre(s): Western Fiction; Adventure Story.

Brock, Darryl

1128. *If I Never Get Back.* New York: Crown, 1990. 424 pp.

A disenchanted journalist steps off the train into 1869 where he becomes a member of the Cincinnati Red Stockings as the team begins play.

Genre(s): Sports Fiction; Time Travel.

Bromael, Robert

1129. *The Bank Robber.* New York: Ballantine, 1985. 155 pp.

Kirby gets the woman that both he and his friend Swede love, but Swede robs a bank, a decision that seems justified after the revelation that the bank owners swindled and possibly killed his parents.

Genre(s): Western Fiction.

Brooks, Bill

1130. *Buscadero.* New York: Evans, 1993. 210 pp.

Robber, killer, and gambler Johnny Montana, caught with a woman who loves him, goes to Arkansas for trial, and when someone chases him on the way, Texas Ranger Henry Dollar tries to protect him.

Genre(s): Western Fiction.

Broome, H. B.

1131. *Gunfighter's Revenge.* Garden City, NY: Doubleday, 1987. 180 pp.

Tom English from *The Meanest Man in West Texas* moves to Montana Territory with his family in the 1880s, but his reputation follows him.

Genre(s): Western Fiction.

Brouwer, S. W.

◆ 1132. *Moon Basket.* Colorado Springs, CO: Victor, 1994. 314 pp.

When Samuel Keaton becomes the marshal in Laramie, Wyoming, in 1874, he must solve a series of murders.

(Series: Ghost Rider, 2)

Genre(s): Western Fiction; Christian Fiction.

◆ 1133. *Morning Star.* Colorado Springs, CO: Victor, 1994. 312 pp.

Samuel Keaton enters Laramie, Wyoming, as a man is beating a Native American, and Keaton shoots him, causing the sheriff to help him, while Morning Star, pretending to be a man, falls in love with him. *(Series:* Ghost Rider, 1)

Genre(s): Western Fiction; Christian Fiction; Mystery.

Brown, Dee Alexander

◆ 1134. *Killdeer Mountain.* New York: Holt, Rinehart and Winston, 1983. 279 pp.

Sam Morrison, a reporter for the *Saint Louis Herald*, goes to Dakota Territory where he finds conflicting stories about a supposed Civil War hero and Indian fighter.

Genre(s): Western Fiction.

Brown, Diana

◆ 1135. *The Hand of a Woman.* New York: St. Martin's Press, 1984. 528 pp.

After Damaris Fanshawe's father dies in the Civil War, she must become a servant to support her mother, but through the years, she rises until she studies medicine in an American university.

Genre(s): War Story; Medical Novel; Romance.

Brown, Linda Beatrice

1136. *Crossing over Jordan.* New York: Ballantine, 1995. 304 pp.

In a series of generations after the Civil War, a matriarchal family hides its legacy of slavery.

Genre(s): Family Saga.

Brown, Sam

1137. *The Big Lonely.* New York: Walker, 1992. 216 pp.

Tatum Staggs asks cowpunch Casey Wills to turn away when he steals cattle, but Casey refuses.

Genre(s): Western Fiction.

1138. *The Crime of Coy Bell.* New York: Walker, 1992. 176 pp.

Coy Bell falls in love with a rancher's wife, tries to forget her, but when he comes back in three years, he finds an imposter in her place and himself blamed for murder.

Genre(s): Western Fiction; Love Story.

◆ 1139. *The Long Season.* New York: Walker, 1987. 208 pp.

Jesse Coldiron comes to Texas in 1884 to gather his cattle, scattered in a winter storm, where he encounters both a thief, J. W. Cain, and a beauty, Tracey James.

Genre(s): Western Fiction.

◆ 1140. *The Trail to Honk Ballard's Bones.* New York: Walker, 1990. 223 pp.

Honk Ballard (alias Will Smith) goes to Burl's homestead to take his money, but when he finds Burl's lovely widow, he marries her instead.

Genre(s): Western Fiction.

Browne, Lydia

1141. *Snowflake Wishes.* New York: Jove, 1997. 336 pp.

Rachel wants to keep her seven-year-old brother from following the family outlaw trade so she settles with him in Brooklyn, Missouri, where she starts teaching and becomes interested in the local newspaper editor.

Genre(s): Romance; Western Fiction.

Brownley, Margaret

1142. *Buttons and Beaus.* New York: Topaz, 1997. 352 pp.

Amanda Blackwell owns a cycling school in New York City during 1880, protects her mentally disabled younger brother, and challenges Damian Newcastle's plan to build a 20-story building next door.

Genre(s): Romance.

Brunner, John

1143. *The Great Steamboat Race.* New York: Random House, 1983. 592 pp.
Enemies plan a race on the Mississippi River between New Orleans and St. Louis in 1870.
Genre(s): Adventure Story.

Bryant, Will

◆ 1144. *The Big Lonesome.* New York: Doubleday, 1971. 360 pp.
When Andrew and Tobin Shattuck fail to find gold in California, they go to Idaho on a tip from an old trapper, and after finding gold, they have a series of misfortunes before they settle down.
Genre(s): Western Fiction; Adventure Story.

Buck, Jerry

1145. *Wheeler's Choice.* New York: Holt, Rinehart, and Winston, 1989. 192 pp.
Ben Wheeler, after fighting as a Confederate in the Civil War, sets up his law office in Texas, but after bank robbers kill his wife, he chases them into Dodge City, Kansas, and shows his skill as a gunman.
Genre(s): Western Fiction.

Burchardt, Bill

1146. *Black Marshal.* Garden City, NY: Doubleday, 1981. 183 pp.
Marshal Gar Rutherford has an intuitive sense when tracking criminals which he must use to find his own son.
Genre(s): Western Fiction.

1147. *The Mexican.* New York: Doubleday, 1977. 186 pp.
Justino Guzmán, hired to clean up an Oklahoma town, ends up adding arson and murder instead.
Genre(s): Western Fiction.

Bushnell, O. A.

1148. *Molokai.* New York: World, 1963. 503 pp.
Father Damien, a priest from Belgium, devotes his life to the lepers at the Molokai colony of Hawaii.
Genre(s): Christian Fiction; Biographical Fiction.

Cabell, James Branch

1149. *The Rivet in Grandfather's Neck.* New York: R.M. McBride, 1925. 368 pp.
Patricia Stapylton seems to want to leave the South, but her loyalty keeps her with Col. Musgrave.
Genre(s): Domestic Fiction.

Cabot, Robert

1150. *The Joshua Tree.* Berkeley, CA: North Atlantic, 1988. 244 pp.
Bill Keys, whose ranch becomes the Joshua Tree National Monument, lives in the Mohave desert in the 1860s.
Genre(s): Western Fiction.

Camp, Candace

1151. *Rain Lily.* New York: HarperPaperbacks, 1993. 337 pp.
Maggie Whitcomb struggles to keep the family farm in Arkansas after her husband returns from the Civil War with the mind of a child, and when handsome Reid Prescott begins working for her, she faces a dilemma.
Genre(s): Western Fiction; Romance.

Camp, Deborah

1152. *Belle Starr.* New York: Harmony, 1987. 344 pp.
After the Civil War, Confederates continue their war in the West by robbing banks, and Belle Shirley (The Bandit Queen) rides with the Younger brothers and the Starrs.
Genre(s): Biographical Fiction; Romance; Western Fiction.

Canham, Marsha

1153. *Straight for the Heart.* New York: Dell, 1995. 400 pp.
Amanda Courtland tries gambling under the name of Montana Rose as a method of getting money to keep her family's plantation from an unscrupulous Yankee.
Genre(s): Romance.

Capps, Benjamin

1154. *The True Memoirs of Charley Blankenship.* Philadelphia: Lippincott, 1972. 252 pp.
In the 1880s, Charley travels around cattle country and experiences the variety of people and landscapes that it offers.
Genre(s): Western Fiction.

1155. *The Warren Wagontrain Raid.* New York: Dial, 1974. 304 pp.
Although Chief Satanta of the Kiowa leads an attack on a supply wagon train in May, 1871, events prior indicate that William T. Sherman may have caused racial tensions that the Kiowa could not ignore.
Genre(s): Western Fiction.

Carroll, Lenore

◆ 1156. *Abduction from Fort Union.* New York: Walker, 1988. 155 pp.
Cavalry trooper Lee Bridge steals a racing mare to pursue the kidnappers of his love, Maggie, and during the chase, he discovers the gang that has been stealing horses from the army.
Genre(s): Western Fiction.

Carter, Forrest

1157. *The Vengeance Trail of Josey Wales.* New York: Delacorte, 1976. 202 pp.
When people kill his friend Rose, and Captain Jesus Escobedo and his Rurales kidnap Ten Spot, Josey Wales changes from hunted to hunter in 1868.
Genre(s): Western Fiction.

◆ 1158. *Watch for Me on the Mountain.* New York: Delacorte, 1978. 305 pp.
Geronimo tries to follow higher laws than those espoused by the whites who decimate his tribe.
Genre(s): Biographical Fiction; Western Fiction.

Carter, Nevada

1159. *Frontier Steel.* New York: Walker, 1982. 159 pp.
Dallas Wayne becomes a powerful citizen of Virginia City until a drunken cowboy passing through town mentions Wayne's questionable conduct in the Civil War.
Genre(s): Western Fiction.

Case, David

1160. *Plumb Drillin'.* New York: Stein and Day, 1975. 201 pp.
Luke Adam DeCaire's wife's lover, the Apache Terremoto, frames him, and he waits three years for revenge.
Genre(s): Western Fiction.

Castle, Linda

1161. *Abbie's Child.* New York: Harlequin, 1996. 304 pp.
In 1882, Abigail Cooprel gives birth to a stillborn in a mining camp, and another woman dies while her son lives, but the man who delivers the children neglects to tell Abigail that the boy is not her biological child.
Genre(s): Romance; Western Fiction.

Cather, Willa

◆ 1162. *Death Comes for the Archbishop.* New York: Knopf, 1927. 303 pp.
The archbishop in Santa Fe aids in the growth and development of the Southwest.
Award(s): Howells Medal.

1163. *My Antonia.* Boston: Houghton Mifflin, 1954. 371 pp.
Antonia works as a servant for her neighbors after her father's death, elopes, and then returns to marry a Bohemian farmer.
Genre(s): Domestic Fiction.

Catto, Max

1164. *King Oil.* New York: Simon and Schuster, 1970. 287 pp.
A Texas oilman marries a Spanish woman and contends with her personality as well as his business.
Genre(s): Western Fiction.

Cavanaugh, Jack

1165. *The Pioneers.* Wheaton, IL: Victor, 1996. 432 pp.
Jessie Morgan escapes to the Midwest from New York and finds that he must trust someone other than himself to survive as a pioneer. (*Series:* American Family Portrait, 5)
Genre(s): Christian Fiction; Family Saga.

Chaikin, Linda

1166. *Winds of Allegiance.* Minneapolis, MN: Bethany House, 1996. 298 pp.
Savana MacKenzie wonders if Trace Wilder is a traitor because of his allegiance to America in a land that three nations want. (*Series:* Great Northwest, 2)
Genre(s): Christian Fiction; Western Fiction.

Champlin, Tim

◆ 1167. *King of the Highbinders.* New York: Ballantine, 1989. 192 pp.
Jay McGraw is hired to deliver a load of beer but is actually carrying gold coins which a Chinese gang leader steals, but Jay escapes and starts searching for Yen Ching.
Genre(s): Western Fiction.

1168. *The Survivor.* Old Tappen, NJ: Thorndike, 1996. 240 pp.
Jay McGraw tries to deliver to a New York publisher Marcel Dupré's manuscript about his horrible experience in a French prison before his 1883 escape and the French try to stop him.
Genre(s): Western Fiction.

Chastain, Sandra

1169. *Raven and the Cowboy.* New York: Bantam, 1996. 304 pp.
Raven Alexander, an Irish and Arapaho spirit woman, has visions in the Rio Grade during 1877.
Genre(s): Romance; Western Fiction.

1170. *Shotgun Groom.* New York: Fanfare, 1998. 336 pp.
In 1875, Lily arrives in Blue Station, Texas, expecting to marry Matt Logan, but his dying brother Jim wants her to marry him instead, then take care of Matt, the ranch, and Jim's two children after his death.
Genre(s): Western Fiction; Romance.

Chiaventone, Frederick J.

1171. *A Road We Do Not Know.* New York: Simon and Schuster, 1996. 333 pp.
When Custer fears that his enemy may have spotted smoke from a cooking fire on June 25, 1876, he attacks the Sioux and Cheyenne.
Genre(s): War Story; Political Fiction.

Christilian, J. D.

◆ 1172. *Scarlet Women.* New York: Donald I. Fine, 1996. 294 pp.
In 1871, when police find a prostitute with her throat slit wearing the clothes of a missing aristocrat, they turn the case over to Harp, who knows all of the seedy places and shadowy people in the city.
Genre(s): Mystery.

Clark, Walter Van Tilburg

1173. *The Ox-Bow Incident.* New York: Random House, 1940. 309 pp.
When cattle rustlers murder a citizen of Bridger's Gulch, others form a posse and illegally lynch them.
Genre(s): Western Fiction.

Clarke, Richard

◆ 1174. *The Arizona Panhandle.* New York: Walker, 1989. 206 pp.
Richard Ashe Colby carries a wanted poster to disguise his role as an undercover Arizona ranger while he tries to find a band of counterfeiters.
Genre(s): Western Fiction.

◆ 1175. *The Arrowhead Cattle Company.* New York: Walker, 1988. 202 pp.
Cowhand Ben Moore wins a ranch at poker, and when he arrives to stake his claim, he finds two orphan boys and land-hungry neighbors.
Genre(s): Western Fiction.

1176. *The Copperdust Hills.* New York: Walker, 1983. 120 pp.
After John Forrest's murder, his brother Mark relentlessly pursues the murderers.
Genre(s): Western Fiction.

1177. *The Guns of Peralta.* New York: Walker, 1993. 168 pp.
Marshal Lee Custis easily maintains order in his small town of Peralta, until he rides out of town to surprise killers coming through the area as they sneak into town a different way.
Genre(s): Western Fiction.

◆ 1178. *The Homesteaders.* New York: Walker, 1986. 193 pp.
Constable Cutler, wounded and unable to get out of bed, uses two women to help him rid his New Mexico town of rustlers.
Genre(s): Western Fiction.

◆ 1179. *The Undertaker.* New York: Walker, 1991. 256 pp.
Marshall Frank Butler has to figure out how to keep maurading Mexicans fueled on the Revolution from coming to his town of Peralty, and El Cajonera, a man who has helped wronged Mexicans of Peralta for over a century, is also concerned.
Genre(s): Western Fiction.

Clarke, Tom

1180. *Billy Bayes.* New York: Avalon, 1995. 183 pp.
Billy Bayes, wrangler for the Rocking J Ranch, meets his owner's sister and daughter, who bring with them an Arabian stallion, but when the horse runs for the hills, Bayes has to fight outlaws to get it.
Genre(s): Western Fiction.

Cleary, Rita

1181. *Goldtown.* Santa Fe, NM: Sunstone, 1996. 269 pp.
Lee Cameron, a former Confederate cavalry captain turned gambler, goes to Varina, Montana in 1867, looking for his pre-Civil War sweetheart, Emma Dubois.
Genre(s): Western Fiction; Romance.

Coleman, Jane Candia

1182. *I, Pearl Hart.* Unity, ME: Thorndike, 1998. 243 pp.
After Pearl Taylor marries gambler Frank Hart, she endures abuse, and to survive, she robs a stagecoach, for which she spends time in the Yuma Territorial Prison.
Genre(s): Western Fiction.

Coleman, Lonnie

1183. *The Legacy of Beulah Land.* Garden City, NY: Doubleday, 1980. 430 pp.
In the sequel to *Look Away, Beulah Land*, a poor farmer threatens those expecting to inherit the Kendricks' plantation.
Genre(s): Romance.

1184. *Look Away, Beulah Land.* Garden City, NY: Doubleday, 1977. 492 pp.
The Kendricks family of Beulah Land and the Davis family of Oaks, the plantation next door, take revenge on a Union sergeant during the painful adjustment after the Civil War in the sequel to *Beulah Land*.
Genre(s): Romance.

Combs, Harry

1185. *Brules.* Novato, CA: Lyford, 1992. 521 pp.
In 1867, Cat Brules kills a man before fleeing into Comanche territory where he continues his murderous ways.
Genre(s): Western Fiction.

1186. *The Scout.* New York: Delacorte, 1995. 602 pp.
Cat Brules tells about his life in the Indian wars of the 1870s and 1880s.
Genre(s): Western Fiction.

Conley, Robert J.

◆ 1187. *Go-Ahead Rider.* Boston: Little, Brown, 1990. 159 pp.
When half-Cherokee George Tanner returns to the Cherokee Nation with a Harvard degree after the Civil War, the sheriff deputizes him in anticipation of trouble over a projected railroad.
Genre(s): Western Fiction.

1188. *Killing Time.* New York: Evans, 1988. 176 pp.
Bluff Luton serves for 15 years as an Iowa town marshal, but when he finds out that the outlaws who killed his brother have put a bounty on his head, he sets out for Texas to confront them.
Genre(s): Western Fiction.

1189. *Ned Christie's War.* New York: Evans, 1990. 175 pp.
Ned Christie, leader of the Cherokee nation in the late 1880s, is blamed for killing a marshal, and as he becomes a hunted man, a legend about his exploits grows.
Genre(s): Biographical Fiction; Western Fiction.

◆ 1190. *Quitting Time.* New York: Evans, 1990. 161 pp.
Oliver Colfax wants to quit his occupation as a hired gun, but he needs money, so when someone offers him the chance to investigate a cattle-rustling ring, he takes the

job, after finding that a Shakespeare troupe will be playing in the area.
Genre(s): Western Fiction.

◆ 1191. *Strange Company.* New York: Pocket Books, 1991. 176 pp.
Confederate Captain Harm Early mistreats Dhu Walker and Ben Lacy in a Civil War prison camp, but Dhu and Ben convince others to help them find Early when he steals a shipment of gold at the end of the war.
Genre(s): Western Fiction.

Cook, Will

1192. *Bandit's Trail.* New York: Doubleday, 1974. 185 pp.
Jacob Spaniard, angry over his imprisonment, decides to get revenge and works to meet Texas Ranger Finley Burkhauser in a gun battle.
Genre(s): Western Fiction.

Cooke, John Byrne

1193. *The Snowblind Moon.* New York: Simon and Schuster, 1985. 688 pp.
When General Crook begins his campaign to round up the Sioux onto reservations in 1876, some Sioux and some whites join to thwart the impending hostilities.
Award(s): Western Writers of America Spur Award.
Genre(s): Family Saga.

Cooley, Lee

1194. *Judgment At Red Creek.* New York: M. Evans, 1992. 188 pp.
Jake Harmer, a ranch foreman, kills 14 people in cold blood for their land and water in New Mexico during the 1870s, and Clayton Adams determines that justice will work against them.
Genre(s): Western Fiction.

Cooper, J. California

1195. *In Search of Satisfaction.* New York: Doubleday, 1994. 368 pp.
In the years following the Civil War, the descendants of Josephus, a former slave, become involved repeatedly with the town's rich white Befoe family.
Genre(s): Domestic Fiction.

Copeland, Lori

1196. *Angelface and Amazing Grace.* New York: Fawcett, 1996. 313 pp.
When April Truitt sells her concoction to help women with their monthly problems, its high alcoholic content causes complications that the new doctor in town would prefer to avoid.
Genre(s): Romance; Medical Novel.

1197. *The Courtship of Cade Kolby.* New York: Avon, 1997. 384 pp.
Cade Kolby returns to his Kansas hometown and finds that the woman looking after his deceased sister's children is the woman he loved before he left 17 years before.
Genre(s): Western Fiction; Romance.

1198. *Promise Me Forever.* New York: Ballantine, 1994. 288 pp.
When Comanches chase the McDougal sisters, three men rescue them, but Union spy Morgan Kane must rescue Amelia again when she almost becomes part of a white slavery ring.
Genre(s): Romance; Western Fiction.

Copp, DeWitt S.

1199. *The Man They Called Mistai.* New York: Doubleday, 1971. 184 pp.
Drucie becomes enamored with Rick Owen when he helps her family escape a raid by Native Americans, but his connections with the Native Americans make him unacceptable to Drucie's father.
Genre(s): Western Fiction; Romance.

Cotton, Ralph W.

1200. *While Angels Dance.* New York: St. Martin's Press, 1994. 327 pp.
After fighting with Quantrill's Raiders in the Civil War and having his father killed, Jesse Nash, one of the James brothers' cousins, joins the Younger gang and searches for the former Kansas militia man who killed his daughter.
Genre(s): Western Fiction; War Story.

Cowan, Debra

1201. *If Only.* New York: Dell, 1997. 388 pp.
Elise Worthen murdered to save her parents and worries about being discovered, and when she begins to trust her brother's old friend, she finds that he is tracking the man she murdered.
Genre(s): Romance.

Cox, William R.

1202. *Cemetery Jones.* New York: Ballantine, 1985. 166 pp.
After Cemetery Jones becomes the marshal of Sunrise, he meets the Coleman brothers again.
Genre(s): Western Fiction.

Crane, Stephen

1203. *Maggie, a Girl of the Streets.* 1893. New York: Norton, 1979. 258 pp.
Maggie works in a collar factory in New York City, and as a child of a brutal father and a drunken mother, she allows her brother's friend to seduce her, and to survive afterward, becomes a prostitute.

Crawford, Max

1204. *Lords of the Plain.* New York: Atheneum, 1985. 307 pp.
In the 1870s, the Texas and Indian wars begin when the Army pursues the Comanches, but Army captain Philip Chapman remains ethically compromised by the slaughter.
Genre(s): War Story; Western Fiction.

Creel, Catherine

1205. *Wildsong.* New York: Fawcett, 1996. 328 pp.
When newly divorced Winnie Sinclair and her husband's lawyer are thrown off a houseboat, they find themselves in Oklahoma territory in the late 19th century.
Genre(s): Romance; Western Fiction; Time Travel.

Crider, Bill

1206. *Medicine Show.* New York: Evans, 1990. 184 pp.
While traveling with a medicine show, Ray Storey functions as a sharpshooter and publicity manager, but his real motive is to find the Hawkins brothers and avenge his mentally handicapped brother's death.
Genre(s): Mystery; Western Fiction.

◆ 1207. *Ryan Rides Back.* New York: Evans, 1988. 181 pp.
When returning to town after an unexplained absence of three years, Ryan tries to find out who beat his sister to death, not believing the man who has been tried and convicted.
Genre(s): Western Fiction.

Criswell, Millie

1208. *Dangerous.* New York: Warner Books, 1998. 384 pp.
Texas Ranger Ethan Bodine looks for his little brother, Rafe, who has supposedly shot a man and killed his wife, and on the trail he meets horticulturist Wilhemina Granville.
Genre(s): Romance; Western Fiction.

1209. *Desperate.* New York: Warner Books, 1997. 368 pp.
Emmaline St. Joseph goes to California to establish an orphanage, and when she becomes stranded, ex-Texas Ranger Rafe Bodine, on a mission to kill the man who raped and murdered his pregnant wife, rescues her.
Genre(s): Romance; Western Fiction.

1210. *Sweet Laurel.* New York: Warner Books, 1996. 346 pp.
Laurel Marin travels to Denver to become an opera singer although she knows nothing about singing, but gambler Chance Rafferty hires her to perform in his saloon.
Genre(s): Romance.

Critser, David

1211. *Border Town Law.* New York: Walker, 1994. 180 pp.
Joe Trento is falsely accused of murder, and to save his ranch and show his innocence, he and his friends fight the Milstead gang and others.
Genre(s): Western Fiction.

Cullman, Heather

1212. *Tomorrow's Dreams.* New York: Topaz, 1996. 384 pp.
Seth Tyler learns he is the son of an incestuous union, and breaks his engagement with a pregnant opera singer, only to find her several years later in a Denver dance hall.
Genre(s): Western Fiction; Romance.

Culp, John H.

1213. *Born of the Sun.* New York: William Sloane, 1959. 344 pp.
Kid Martin, an orphan, goes on the first cattle drive from Texas to Abilene in 1870, and afterwards, he returns to the Tail End Ranch in northwest Texas.
Genre(s): Western Fiction.

1214. *The Bright Feathers.* New York: Holt, Rinehart and Winston, 1965. 283 pp.
Three young cowboys return to Texas after a cattle drive to Kansas and encounter a variety of people from different social strata and career pursuits.
Genre(s): Western Fiction; Adventure Story.

1215. *Oh, Valley Green!* New York: Henry Holt, 1972. 304 pp.
Carey Key travels on the Santa Fe Trail to New Mexico and then the entire west where he encounters numerous adventures with cowboys, criminals, Native Americans, and the weather.
Genre(s): Western Fiction; Adventure Story.

1216. *The Restless Land.* New York: Sloane, 1962. 438 pp.
In the sequel to *Born of the Sun*, Martin Cameron, 15, inherits the Texas Tail End Ranch in the 1870s, and he must unite the Comanches, Comancheros, and cowboys who work for him.
Genre(s): Western Fiction; Adventure Story.

1217. *The Treasure of the Chisos.* New York: Holt, Rinehart and Winston, 1971. 272 pp.
A young man of mixed English and Spanish heritage travels from St. Louis to New Mexico to reclaim his family's land.
Genre(s): Western Fiction.

Cummings, Jack

◆ 1218. *Escape from Yuma.* New York: Walker, 1990. 192 pp.
In 1887, Opal Hartman tries to rob a stagecoach, but she is arrested, sentenced, and imprisoned before she escapes with criminals. Ridge Conley, U.S. marshal, has the job of finding her.
Genre(s): Western Fiction.

1219. *Lynch's Revenge.* New York: Walker, 1985. 189 pp.
After Comanches murder Sam Lynch's family and keep him captive for many years, he vows to kill every Comanche he sees, a quest that disrupts the Texas panhandle.
Genre(s): Western Fiction.

◆ 1220. *The Surrogate Gun.* New York: Walker, 1990. 177 pp.
After Rufe Canton shoots at newspaper editor Bret Holt and disgraces his possible lover, Canton leaves town, and Holt writes a novel about a local cowboy who wants to look as effective as the legend he has become.
Genre(s): Western Fiction.

1221. *Tiger Butte.* New York: Walker, 1986. 178 pp.

Marshal John Leslie kills The Bodie Kid in the late 1870s and then goes to California to rescue the love of his youth who has become a widow and needs money to pay her mortgage.
Genre(s): Western Fiction.

Curtis, Jack

1222. *Christmas in Calico.* New York: St. Martin's Press, 1998. 196 pp.

When a blizzard hits the Nevada prairie and their poor horse ranch, the widow Rose Cameron and her son Tommy must ask for help in the nearby small town, Calico.
Genre(s): Western Fiction.

◆ 1223. *The Sheriff Kill.* New York: Pocket Books, 1991. 295 pp.

When Kiowa investigates the death of his friend Paddy, he finds out that the sheriff is a killer who satisfies his urges on ordinary citizens if no villains are present.
Genre(s): Western Fiction.

Dailey, Janet

1224. *Calder Born, Calder Bred.* New York: Pocket Books, 1983. 345 pp.

In the sequel to *Stands a Calder Man*, Ty Calder comes to his father's ranch as a teenager after having lived with his mother in California, and although he brings his parents back together, he decides to go to college, marry a Texas tycoon's daughter, and reject the ranch, only to find that after his parents die accidentally he cannot execute his plans.
Genre(s): Romance; Family Saga.

1225. *This Calder Range.* New York: Pocket Books, 1982. 335 pp.

In the sequel to *This Calder Sky*, Benteen Calder and his wife Lorna move from Texas to Montana, and face difficult times with the land and learning about each other.
Genre(s): Family Saga; Romance.

1226. *This Calder Sky.* New York: Pocket Books, 1981. 340 pp.

Maggie, carrying Chase Calder's son, runs away after Chase's father hangs her father, and when their son Tyrone is 15, he returns to Montana and helps his parents reunite.
Genre(s): Romance; Family Saga.

Daniels, Dorothy

1227. *Whistle in the Wind.* New York: Pocket Books, 1976. 173 pp.

On a poor Louisiana plantation after the Civil War, Carolyn Taylor searches for the cause of her father's and several others' death.
Genre(s): Gothic Fiction; Romance.

Davenport, Marcia

1228. *The Valley of Decision.* New York: Scribner's, 1942. 790 pp.

Owners of the Scott Iron Works in Pittsburgh run their business with the help and confidence of immirants from 1873 to the bombing of Pearl Harbor.
Genre(s): Domestic Fiction.

Davies, June Wyndham

1229. *Storm Before Sunrise.* New York: St. Martin's Press, 1994. 455 pp.

Melisande appears at Dr. Kingsley's house in Albany, New York, and after he treats her for malnutrition, she leaves to become a teacher but eventually returns.
Genre(s): Love Story; Medical Novel.

Davis, Cliff

1230. *The Bushwackers.* New York: Major Books, 1977. 160 pp.

The four Garmon brothers track the Murrell gang after murder, rape, and ambush.
Genre(s): Western Fiction.

Davis, W. E.

◆ 1231. *The Gathering Storm.* Wheaton, IL: Crossway, 1996. 384 pp.

Matt Page goes West to find his fortune, and in Bodie, California, he meets his father who supposedly died in the Civil War. (*Series:* Valley of the Peacemaker, 1)
Genre(s): Christian Fiction; Western Fiction.

◆ 1232. *The Proving Ground.* Wheaton, IL: Crossway, 1996. 367 pp.

Matt Page acts as sheriff of Mono County and has problems coping with the disappointment of his wife's miscarriage. (*Series:* Valley of the Peacemaker, 2)
Genre(s): Western Fiction; Christian Fiction.

◆ 1233. *The Refining Fire.* Wheaton, IL: Crossway, 1997. 352 pp.

Matthew Page fills in as sheriff while his father-in-law recovers from a wound, but his life is disrupted when a Native American man is found dead in a burned building. (*Series:* Valley of the Peacemaker, 3)
Genre(s): Western Fiction; Mystery.

Dawkins, Cecil

1234. *The Live Goat.* New York: Harper, 1971. 374 pp.

Ten people chase the mentally deficient killer of a young girl, and when they apprehend him, they begin to assess their own behavior and face who is the more guilty, he or they.

Day, Robert

1235. *The Last Cattle Drive.* New York: Putnam, 1977. 221 pp.

Spangler Tukle takes his 250 steers 250 miles to Kansas City with the help of his tough wife, an old ranch hand, and a greenhorn schoolteacher.
Genre(s): Western Fiction; Adventure Story.

De Blasis, Celeste

1236. *A Season of Swans.* New York: Bantam, 1989. 676 pp.

The sequel to *Swan's Chance* reveals that Gincie Culhane has murdered her evil half brother and must flee from the horse farm.

Genre(s): Romance; Family Saga.

1237. *The Tiger's Woman.* New York: Delacorte, 1981. 680 pp.

The wealthy businessman Jason Drake becomes intrigued with a mysterious dancing girl in 1869 who will not reveal her past but offers personal favors in exchange for Drake's protection.

Genre(s): Western Fiction.

Dell, George

1238. *The Earth Abideth.* Athens, OH: Ohio State University Press, 1986. 342 pp.

Thomas Linthorne and Kate Harewell settle in Ohio in 1866 and begin to raise their family on a farm until Thomas dies in 1917.

Genre(s): War Story; Domestic Fiction.

Deloria, Ella Cara

◆ 1239. *Waterlily.* Lincoln, NE: University of Nebraska Press, 1988. 244 pp.

The daily rituals of the Yankton Sioux in the Dakotas during the 19th century reveal their traditional values.

Dempsey, Al

1240. *Path of the Sun.* New York: Tor, 1993. 320 pp.

James Jerome Hill, a 19th century railroad mogul, envisions the country united by the railroad, and another railroad owner, Zack Horton of Philadelphia, wants to make the idea become a reality.

Genre(s): Adventure Story.

Denker, Henry

◆ 1241. *The Healers.* New York: Morrow, 1983. 451 pp.

David Lilliendahl immigrates to America from Austria so that he can practice medicine as he wishes and marries Mary Sinclair, another physician, with whom he then establishes Mount Sinai hospital.

Genre(s): Medical Novel.

Deveraux, Jude

1242. *Eternity.* New York: Pocket Books, 1992. 340 pp.

Joshua Greene, an unsuccessful farmer in 1865 Colorado, needs help, and Carrie Montgomery, a New England matchmaker, aids him in more ways than she anticipates.

Genre(s): Romance; Western Fiction.

1243. *The Temptress.* New York: Pocket Books, 1987. 249 pp.

Christiana Montgomery's father hires Tynan, an outlaw, and Asher Prescott, a prospective husband, to bring her back to Washington territory, but she falls in love with the wrong man.

Genre(s): Romance; Western Fiction.

DeVries, Laura

1244. *Promise Me.* New York: Dell, 1998. 384 pp. Miranda Dare escapes from Atlanta after the Civil War with freed slave Cinthy, and when she has to steal for food on their way to Denver, Clayton Sloane catches her.

Genre(s): Western Fiction; Romance.

Dexter, Pete

1245. *Deadwood.* New York: Random House, 1986. 365 pp.

When Wild Bill Hickok takes a wagon train of prostitutes through Deadwood, a pimp hires someone to kill him.

Genre(s): Western Fiction; Humorous Fiction.

Dieter, William

1246. *The White Land.* New York: Knopf, 1970. 288 pp.

Bliss Griffith arrives at Marc Robbarde's Montana ranch with a herd of cattle, but he and Marc do not communicate well, and during a blizzard, when many of the cattle die, they have to deal with their differences.

Genre(s): Western Fiction; Gothic Fiction.

Dillard, Annie

◆ 1247. *The Living.* New York: HarperCollins, 1992. 392 pp.

When Native Americans help two struggling pioneer families in Washington, the behavior and attitudes of both groups change.

Genre(s): Domestic Fiction.

Dinneen, Joseph F.

1248. *Ward Eight.* New York: Harper And Row, 1936. 329 pp.

The old Irish colony in Boston in the shadow of the Old North Church is in Ward Eight, where Hughie Donnelly serves as ward boss and Timothy O'Flaherty opposes him.

Genre(s): Biographical Fiction; Political Fiction.

Dixon, Thomas

1249. *The Clansman.* 1905. Louisville: University Press of Kentucky, 1970. 374 pp.

The Invisible Empire of the Ku Klux Klan begins to rise as soon as the Civil War ends, in the sequel to *The Leopard's Spots.*

Genre(s): Domestic Fiction.

1250. *The Leopard's Spots.* New York: Wessels, 1908. 465 pp.

Whites in the South, furious at the end of slavery, begin a vigilante group.

Genre(s): Domestic Fiction.

1251. *The Traitor.* New York: Doubleday, 1907. 331 pp.

The influence of the Ku Klux clan seems to decline in the sequel to *The Clansman.*

Genre(s): Domestic Fiction.

Doctorow, E. L.

◆ 1252. *Waterworks.* New York: Random House, 1994. 253 pp.
When journalist Martin Pemberton thinks he has seen his dead father on a horse-drawn omnibus, he contacts Edmund Donne, the only honest New York policeman.
Genre(s): Mystery.

Dodd, Susan M.

◆ 1253. *Mamaw.* New York: Viking, 1988. 350 pp.
The mother of Frank and Jesse James was in a convent before she bore her two infamous sons.
Genre(s): Biographical Fiction.

Donati, Sara

1254. *Into the Wilderness.* New York: Bantam, 1998. 624 pp.
An Englishwoman comes to the American frontier and unexpectedly falls in love.
Genre(s): Western Fiction; Romance.

Douglas, Barbara

◆ 1255. *Fair Wind of Love.* New York: Doubleday, 1980. 175 pp.
Sarah Kinglsey becomes the guardian of two children after their mother dies aboard the ship, and in America, she must marry for convenience to a man who is probably a spy for the United States.
Genre(s): Sea Story; Romance.

Douglas, Thorne

◆ 1256. *Night Riders.* New York: Fawcett, 1975. 176 pp.
After the Civil War, four people own Rancho Bravo, a cattle ranch in Texas, and Elias Whitton, an ex-slave and excellent horse wrangler, leads the group.
Genre(s): Western Fiction.

Drake, Shannon

1257. *No Other Love.* New York: Avon, 1997. 384 pp.
When Sabrina Connor becomes pregnant with half-Sioux Major Sloan Trelawny's child, he makes her marry him and become a cavalry wife.
Genre(s): Romance; Western Fiction.

Duberstein, Larry

1258. *The Handsome Sailor.* Sag Harbor, NY: Permanent Press, 1998. 268 pp.
In 1882, Herman Melville works as a customs inspector and has an affair with Cora whom he meets at work while his wife cares for their children at home.
Genre(s): Domestic Fiction.

Durham, Marilyn

1259. *Dutch Uncle.* New York: Harcourt Brace, 1973. 303 pp.
When gunslinger and cardshark Jake Hollander gains responsibility for the delivery of two orphans, his life changes.
Genre(s): Western Fiction.

1260. *The Man Who Loved Cat Dancing.* New York: Harcourt Brace, 1972. 246 pp.
Jay Wesley plans to rob a train for money to find his son when he becomes involved with Catherine, who wants to catch the same train in her escape from her husband.
Genre(s): Western Fiction.

Eagle, Kathleen

1261. *Sunrise Song.* New York: Avon, 1996. 384 pp.
Two people of different ages but with links of blood and of Wounded Knee fall in love during the Depression.
Genre(s): Romance.

Eckert, Allan W.

◆ 1262. *Incident at Hawk's Hill.* Boston: Little, Brown, 1971. 173 pp.
Ben, six, has better rapport with the animals on his farm in 1870 than he does with his family, and he takes refuge in a badger's den during a June storm, where he stays until August when his brother finds him.
Genre(s): Domestic Fiction.

1263. *Johnny Logan.* Boston: Little, Brown, 1983. 217 pp.
Spemica Lawba, adopted by American General Benjamin Logan, tries to get his tribe to assimilate with the whites, but his uncle Tecumseh disagrees with him.
Genre(s): Biographical Fiction.

1264. *The Scarlet Mansion.* Boston: Little, Brown, 1985. 500 pp.
Herman W. Mudgett, alias H.H. Holmes, murders between 30 and 127 persons in Philadelphia during the period 1871 to 1896 before he is executed.
Genre(s): Biographical Fiction.

Edmonds, Janet

◆ 1265. *Rivers of Gold.* New York: St. Martin's Press, 1991. 304 pp.
Amity Jones wants to have a better life so she becomes a mail-order bride in Alaska's Yukon during the gold fever of the 19th century.
Genre(s): Adventure Story.

Edwards, Cassie

1266. *White Fire.* New York: Topaz, 1997. 376 pp.
Reshelle Flame Russell plans to marry Samuel White Fire Dowling, and after White Fire loses his first wife and white people take his son, she must console him.
Genre(s): Romance.

Ehle, John

1267. *The Road.* New York: Harper and Row, 1967. 401 pp.
In the sequel to *Time of Drums,* in the 1870s, several different types of men come to North Carolina mountain country to build the railroad and interact with the inhabitants.
Genre(s): Family Saga.

Eickhoff, Randy Lee

1268. *The Fourth Horseman.* New York: Tor, 1998. 416 pp.

After John Henry "Doc" Holliday shoots a carpetbagger who boasted of raping Holliday's mother, Holliday's father sends him west, and after becoming involved in crime, Holliday meets the Earp brothers.

Genre(s): Biographical Fiction; Western Fiction.

Eidson, Tom

◆ 1269. *The Last Ride.* New York: Putnam, 1995. 304 pp.

The half-white Maggie wants to avoid her dying Apache father and his mysticism, but she must engage his help when Apaches capture her daughter Lily.

Genre(s): Western Fiction.

Elfman, Blossom

1270. *The Strawberry Fields of Heaven.* New York: Crown, 1983. 373 pp.

Since Katherine does not know how to support herself, she goes to live with her husband Peter and children in the Oneida Community rather than divorce him.

Genre(s): Domestic Fiction.

Ell, Flynn J.

1271. *Dakota Scouts.* New York: Walker, 1992. 144 pp.

John Benson, an army scout, joins his black muleteer friend Isaiah Dorman to fight Lone Bear, a Sioux warrior.

Genre(s): Western Fiction.

Ellis, Peter Berresford

1272. *The Rising of the Moon.* New York: St. Martin's Press, 1987. 640 pp.

When Captain Gavin Devlin and Lieutenant John-Joe Devlin return to the north after the Civil War, John-Joe rushes to Ireland to help organize The Brotherhood, and Gavin goes to Canada, where the Fenians (Brotherhood) are organizing a stronghold and planning a Fenian uprising along the border in 1867.

Genre(s): War Story.

Engstrom, Elizabeth

1273. *Lizzie Borden.* New York: Tor, 1991. 342 pp.

Lizzie Borden, raised in a dysfunctional family, has her independence thwarted by her possessive father until she decides to free herself from both him and her overbearing stepmother by murdering them.

Genre(s): Biographical Fiction.

Erdman, Loula Grace

1274. *The Edge of Time.* New York: Dodd Mead, 1950. 275 pp.

A young couple start their married life as homesteaders in Texas panhandle country around 1885.

Genre(s): Western Fiction.

1275. *The Far Journey.* New York: Dodd Mead, 1955. 282 pp.

After Edward goes to stake a claim in Texas, Catherine follows in a wagon with her son (and uncle until he dies in an accident) across threatening terrain.

Genre(s): Western Fiction.

Erdrich, Louise

1276. *The Antelope Wife.* New York: HarperCollins, 1998. 256 pp.

A United States Cavalry officer saves an Ojibwa girl after her village is destroyed and raises her as his own, but after her mother finds her, she spends time with antelope and creates complex relationships with them.

Genre(s): War Story; Domestic Fiction.

Estleman, Loren D.

1277. *Bloody Season.* New York: Bantam, 1988. 231 pp.

In 1881, men including Doc Holliday and Wyatt Earp, become involved in a shootout at the O.K. Corral in Tombstone.

Genre(s): Western Fiction.

◆ 1278. *City of Widows.* New York: Forge, 1994. 254 pp.

When U.S. Marshal Page Murdock goes to New Mexico to retrieve murderers, he purchases a saloon for cover but finds that one of the killers is the local sheriff.

Genre(s): Western Fiction.

1279. *Journey of the Dead.* New York: Forge, 1998. 256 pp.

Pat Garrett, killer of Billy the Kid and an old Spanish alchemist tell about their lives after Billy the Kid dies in 1881.

Genre(s): Western Fiction.

1280. *This Old Bill.* Garden City, NY: Doubleday, 1984. 203 pp.

William Cody's first experience on a trail when he is 11 lures him into rough riding before he earns the name of Buffalo Bill in a buffalo-slaying contest.

Genre(s): Biographical Fiction.

Everett, Percival

1281. *God's Country.* New York: Faber and Faber, 1994. 220 pp.

When white men dressed as Indians abduct the racist Curt Marder's wife, he hires a black man to help him find her, and they begin a series of ironic adventures.

Genre(s): Western Fiction; Satire.

Fackler, Elizabeth

1282. *Billy the Kid.* New York: Forge, 1995. 512 pp.

When lawyer Alexander McSween arrives in Lincoln County in the late 1870s, he confronts gunman Jimmy Dolan, while Billy the Kid shows both his amiability and his deadliness.

Genre(s): Western Fiction; Biographical Fiction.

1283. *Blood Kin.* New York: M. Evans, 1992. 204 pp.
A lecherous killer confronts his opponent, the Ranger, and takes advantage of an innocent girl of 16.
Genre(s): Western Fiction.

1284. *Road From Betrayal.* New York: M. Evans, 1994. 228 pp.
Seth Strummar looks after his five-year-old son in 1881, in the sequel to *Backtrail*, while he and his partner Joaquin Ascarate try to rescue a friend unjustly jailed by a dishonest sheriff.
Genre(s): Western Fiction.

Fall, Thomas

1285. *The Ordeal of Running Standing.* New York: McCall, 1970. 312 pp.
Joe Standing, a Kiowa born too late to feel Native American, attends school and heads east while his Cheyenne wife goes home to teach, and when he returns, he has played the white man's game and gained his own rights.
Genre(s): Political Fiction.

Farraday, Tess

1286. *Shadows in the Flame.* New York: Jove, 1997. 368 pp.
Molly Gallagher, herb doctor and fortune-teller, fears men, and when Lightfoot O'Deigh peddles his cats in Virginia City, he tries to change her mind.
Genre(s): Western Fiction; Romance.

Farrell, Cliff

1287. *Patchsaddle Drive.* New York: Doubleday, 1972. 184 pp.
A weak crew and Native Americans threaten a cattle drive from Texas to Missouri.
Genre(s): Western Fiction.

Fast, Howard

◆ 1288. *Freedom Road.* New York: Duell, Sloan and Pearce, 1944. 263 pp.
Gideon Jackson, a freedman after the Civil War, rises from illiteracy to become a member of Congress.

Feldhake, Susan C.

1289. *For Ever and Ever.* Grand Rapids, MI: Zondervan, 1993. 191 pp.
Pioneer wife Lizzie risks losing her faith in the pursuit of happiness. (*Series:* Enduring Faith, 3)
Genre(s): Christian Fiction; Western Fiction.

1290. *From This Day Forward.* Grand Rapids, MI: Zondervan, 1994. 208 pp.
When Molly Wheeler realizes that the man she loves is in love with her sister, she decides to become a mail-order bride. (*Series:* Enduring Faith, 5)
Genre(s): Western Fiction; Christian Fiction.

1291. *Hope for the Morrow.* Grand Rapids, MI: Zondervan, 1993. 192 pp.
Lizzie's friend Brad realizes that he can ask no more of her than she can give. (*Series:* Enduring Faith, 4)
Genre(s): Christian Fiction; Western Fiction.

1292. *Seasons of the Heart.* Grand Rapids, MI: Zondervan, 1993. 200 pp.
When Sue and Alton marry, they face an uncertain future filled with danger. (*Series:* Enduring Faith, 2)
Genre(s): Christian Fiction; Romance.

Fenady, Andrew J.

◆ 1293. *Claws of the Eagle.* New York: Walker, 1984. 204 pp.
During the Apache Wars of 1880, three men, Al Sieber and his adopted sons, try to capture Geronimo.
Genre(s): Biographical Fiction; Western Fiction.

Ferber, Edna

1294. *Saratoga Trunk.* Garden City, NY: Doubleday, 1941. 352 pp.
In the 1880s, the daughter of a New Orleans aristocrat and his French mistress join with a Texas cowboy to enter society.
Genre(s): Domestic Fiction.

1295. *Show Boat.* Cutchogue, NY: Buccaneer, 1992. 620 pp.
The Hawks-Ravenal family in the 1870s is linked to the *Cotton Blossom*, a floating palace theater on the Mississippi River from New Orleans to Pennsylvania.

1296. *So Big.* Garden City, NY: Doubleday, 1924. 212 pp.
Selina DeJong, a teacher in the Dutch settlement of High Prairie after her father's death, marries one of the farmers.
Award(s): Pulitzer Prize.
Genre(s): Bildungsroman (Coming of Age); Western Fiction.

Fergus, Jim

◆ 1297. *One Thousand White Women.* New York: St. Martin's Press, 1998. 320 pp.
In a secret government project, white women go west to marry Native Americans and assimilate them into white civilization.
Genre(s): Western Fiction.

Ferro, Robert

1298. *The Blue Star.* New York: Dutton, 1985. 244 pp.
Chase, one of the men in a contemporary friendship, is the descendent of Frederick Law Olmsted, a man who built an underground hall for Chase's great-grandfather in which to revive the Order of Knights Templar.
Genre(s): Adventure Story.

Field, Rachel

1299. *Time Out of Mind.* New York: Macmillan, 1935. 462 pp.
Kate, daughter of the Fortune family's housekeeper, grows up with the children and watches their wealth decline as steamships take over sailing vessels.
Genre(s): Domestic Fiction.

Finch, Phillip

1300. *Birthright.* New York: Seaview, 1979. 344 pp.
In the 1860s, Joshua Belden, a card shark, and Elizabeth Burgess, a prostitute, begin to create a relationship after their own individual adventures in California.
Genre(s): Romance; Western Fiction.

Finney, Jack

1301. *Time and Again.* New York: Simon and Schuster, 1970. 399 pp.
Simon Morley moves into the Dakota apartments and returns to the year 1882 under hypnosis, where he falls in love and refuses to change records for the government agency controlling his experiment.
Genre(s): Time Travel; Love Story.

Fleming, Thomas

1302. *The Spoils of War.* New York: Putnam, 1985. 524 pp.
Jonathan, a Northern politician, and his Southern wife Cynthia reveal the impact of the Civil War on a group of Northerners.
Genre(s): Family Saga; Love Story; Political Fiction.

Fowler, Karen Joy

1303. *Sarah Canary.* New York: Henry Holt, 1991. 291 pp.
In 1873, Chin Ah Kin finds Sarah Canary on the outskirts of his camp, and since she only speaks nonsense, he tries to take her to an asylum, but on the way she disappears and he becomes a victim of racism.
Genre(s): Adventure Story.

Fox, John, Jr.

1304. *The Heart of the Hills.* 1913. Louisville: University of Kentucky Press, 1996. 326 pp.
The mountain folk are concerned about preserving their land while those in the towns after the Civil War aim toward progress at any cost.

1305. *The Little Shepherd of Kingdom Come.* New York: Scribner's, 1908. 322 pp.
In the area around the mountains of Virginia and Kentucky, those who live in towns have differing ideas about the process of Reconstruction than those living in the hills.
Genre(s): War Story.

Friend, Charles E.

◆ 1306. *The Savage Trail.* Santa Barbara, CA: Fithian, 1992. 128 pp.
Marshall Grant Starbuck returns from apprending cattle rustlers to find his family murdered, and he goes after the gang with the help of a widow whose husband the gang members also murdered.
Genre(s): Western Fiction.

Gabbert, Dean

1307. *The Log of the Jessie Bill.* New York: M. Evans, 1993. 168 pp.
In 1880, Peter Sherman, mud clerk on the Mississippi River raft boat *Jessie Bill* keeps a log of his experiences and the people with whom he works.
Genre(s): Western Fiction; Adventure Story.

Gaffney, Patricia

1308. *Outlaw in Paradise.* New York: Topaz, 1997. 384 pp.
Cady McGill owns the saloon in Paradise, and when gunslinger Gault comes to town, she wants to know why.
Genre(s): Western Fiction; Romance.

Gall, Grant

1309. *Apache.* Santa Fe, NM: Sunstone, 1987. 114 pp.
Apaches capture a Mexican boy of nine, and he becomes a part of their culture until he is returned to his village by American troops that defeat the Apaches.
Genre(s): Western Fiction.

García y Robertson, R.

1310. *American Woman.* New York: St. Martin's Press, 1998. 352 pp.
Intelligent and independent Sarah Kilroy leaves her job in a factory to go west and civilize the Lakota, but when she arrives, she meets and falls in love with Yellow Legs and begins to respect his culture.
Genre(s): War Story; Western Fiction.

1311. *American Women.* New York: Tor, 1998. 352 pp.
A young Quaker woman, Sarah Kilory, who comes West and marries a Cheyenne leader named Yellow Legs, lives with the Custer family in 1874, but is horrified by the Battle of Little Big Horn in 1876.
Genre(s): War Story.

Gardiner, John Rolfe

1312. *Great Dream from Heaven.* New York: Dutton, 1974. 352 pp.
In the late 1880s, Eugene Daniels tries to organize Tennessee miners but can overcome neither the independence of the miners nor the owner's refusal to change.
Genre(s): Political Fiction.

Garfield, Brian

1313. *Manifest Destiny.* New York: Penzler, 1989. 408 pp.
Theodore Roosevelt goes to the Badlands after his mother and his wife die, but when he sees how the local ranchers bully those around him, he returns to politics.
Genre(s): Biographical Fiction; Political Fiction.

Garlock, Dorothy

1314. *Larkspur.* New York: Warner Books, 1997. 416 pp.
In the 1880s, Kristin Anderson comes to Big Timber, Montana, where rancher Buck Lenning rescues her after a Native American kidnaps her.
Genre(s): Western Fiction; Romance.

1315. *Wild Sweet Wilderness.* New York: Popular Library, 1985. 394 pp.
Berry Warfield's drunken father takes her and his pregnant bondswoman west, and when he decides to open a tavern, Berry and Rachel leave, but after her father is found dead, Berry realizes that the frontier is a difficult place for unprotected women.
Genre(s): Romance; Western Fiction.

Garwood, Julie

1316. *Come the Spring.* New York: Pocket Books, 1997. 384 pp.
The Claybornes continue to marry until each one has chosen the right bride. (*Series:* Clayborne Brides, 4)
Genre(s): Western Fiction; Romance.

1317. *One Pink Rose.* New York: Pocket Books, 1997. 150 pp.
Travis Clayborne, opposed to marriage, has the task of delivering Emily Finnegan to her future husband and finds that marriage seems interesting after all. (*Series:* Clayborne Brides, 1)
Genre(s): Romance; Western Fiction.

1318. *One Red Rose.* New York: Pocket Books, 1997. 150 pp.
Adam Clayborne, a former slave, scholar, and oldest Clayborne brother, meets Genevieve Perry, beautiful and strong-willed, and falls in love.
Genre(s): Western Fiction; Romance.

1319. *One White Rose.* New York: Pocket Books, 1997. 150 pp.
Douglas Clayborne comes to an old ranch to get the horse he has bought but ends up acting as midwife to and then a protector of the widow whose recently deceased husband sold the horse. (*Series:* Clayborne Brides, 2)
Genre(s): Western Fiction; Romance.

Gast, Kelly P.

1320. *Murphy's Trail.* New York: Doubleday, 1976. 185 pp.
When Michael Murphy jumps ship, he expects to be in California, and he is, but it is Baja, and he encounters Mexican revolutionaries before he gets a job to save the Maclain ranch by herding cattle to San Diego.
Genre(s): Western Fiction.

Gerson, Noel B.

1321. *T. R.* Garden City, NY: Doubleday, 1970. 441 pp.
Theodore Roosevelt, a state legislator and a police commisioner, becomes governor of New York and then president of the United States.
Genre(s): Biographical Fiction.

Gilman, George C.

1322. *Edge: Rhapsody in Red.* New York: Pinnacle, 1977. 148 pp.
The Devil's Disciples and the hero clash at an outdoor concert.
Genre(s): Western Fiction.

Gilroy, Frank Daniel

1323. *From Noon till Three.* New York: Doubleday, 1973. 116 pp.
Amanda, a young widow and sometime member of the Buck Bowers gang, reveals her three-hour love affair with the oulaw Graham in 1881 to the newspaper, and he tells his version of the romance before dying from a posse's gunshot one year later.
Genre(s): Western Fiction; Satire.

Gipson, Fred

◆ 1324. *Old Yeller.* New York: Harper and Row, 1956. 158 pp.
In the 1860s, Travis looks after the family while his father goes on a cattle drive and takes in a stray dog that he names Old Yeller.
Genre(s): Western Fiction; Bildungsroman (Coming of Age).

Goodman, Jo

1325. *Forever in My Heart.* New York: Kensington, 1994. 346 pp.
Rancher Connor Holiday impregnates heiress Maggie Dennehy, though she has no memory of how it happened, but their marriage would provide Connor a ranch and Maggie a chance to pursue her medical studies.
Genre(s): Romance.

Gordon, Walt

1326. *Boothill Showdown.* Chatsworth, CA: Major Books, 1976. 175 pp.
When John Saddler's half-brother Mitch's men murder Shortie, Saddler's partner, Shortie lets Saddler know that Mitch has stolen his inheritance.
Genre(s): Western Fiction.

Gorman, Edward

1327. *Death Ground.* New York: Henry Holt, 1988. 157 pp.
In the 1880s, Leo Guild searches for a killer, and as he finds his man, he also encounters cholera in the same settlement.
Genre(s): Western Fiction.

Goss, Barbara Masci

1328. *Captured Heart.* Grand Rapids, MI: Revell, 1994. 160 pp.
A young woman must make her way alone in the Wild West when her family dies from cholera, but a Native American scout rescues her after other Native Americans kidnap her.
Genre(s): Western Fiction; Christian Fiction; Romance.

◆ May be suitable for young adult readers

1329. *Forbidden Legacy*. Grand Rapids, MI: Revell, 1994. 159 pp.

When a young woman goes West to the ranch her grandfather has left her, a half-Comanche caretaker contests her claim.

Genre(s): Western Fiction; Romance; Christian Fiction.

Gramling, Lee

1330. *Riders of the Suwanee*. Sarasota, FL: Pineapple, 1993. 290 pp.

Tate Barkley comes home to Florida in 1875 after gaining fame for his gunplay in Texas and Arizona, and he supports a young widow during a flare of old fights.

Genre(s): Western Fiction.

Grandower, Elissa

◆ **1331. *The Secret Room of Morgate House*.** Garden City, NY: Doubleday, 1977. 288 pp.

Leslie Marsh, 20, arrives in 1876 at the Chicago mansion of her only relative and discovers a locked room that holds the answer to the tension in the household.

Genre(s): Romance.

Grant, Jean

1332. *The Promise of the Willows*. Nashville: Thomas Nelson, 1994. 221 pp.

When Sam McLean takes his family to Fort Romie Colony, a Salvation Army settlement to help poor families, he knows he is taking a chance, but he wants a better life for his children.

Genre(s): Domestic Fiction; Christian Fiction.

Grayson, Elizabeth

1333. *So Wide the Sky*. New York: Avon, 1997. 384 pp.

When Cassandra Morgan and Drew Reynolds lost their families in a wagon train massacre, the Cheyenne captured Cassandra, and Drew became an army captain, and in 1867, when Cassandra is traded back, the two marry although both carry the burdens of the past.

Genre(s): Western Fiction; Romance.

Greenberg, Joanne

◆ **1334. *Simple Gifts*.** New York: Henry Holt, 1986. 198 pp.

When the government suggests that the Fleuris change their ranch into an 1880s homestead for paying guests, they like the idea until they do it.

Genre(s): Domestic Fiction.

Grey, Zane

1335. *Ambush for Lassiter*. New York: Pocket Books, 1985. 256 pp.

Lassiter avenges the death of his friend Timmy Borling and becomes interested in Borling's widow and son.

Genre(s): Western Fiction.

1336. *The Arizona Clan*. New York: Harper and Row, 1958. 150 pp.

Dodge Mercer looks for thieves taking his sorghum at night and becomes interested in an opposing clan's lovely daughter during the day.

Genre(s): Western Fiction.

1337. *The Border Legion*. New York: Harper and Row, 1916. 366 pp.

A gang of desperadoes captures a young girl in southern Idaho.

Genre(s): Western Fiction.

1338. *Desert Gold*. 1913. New York: Harper and Row, 1993. 372 pp.

Armies on both the Mexican and United States borders fight for territory.

Genre(s): Western Fiction.

1339. *Fighting Caravans*. 1929. New York: Harper, 1992. 343 pp.

A pioneer falls in love while traveling on the Santa Fe Trail.

Genre(s): Western Fiction.

1340. *The Hash Knife*. New York: Harper and Row, 1933. 200 pp.

A Missouri tenderfoot tries to outsmart a gang of desperados.

Genre(s): Western Fiction.

1341. *Heritage of the Desert*. 1910. New York: Tor, 1997. 278 pp.

Mormons, Navajos, and cattle rustlers conflict in the Arizona desert.

Genre(s): Western Fiction.

1342. *Knights of the Range*. New York: Harper and Row, 1939. 250 pp.

An eastern girl inherits her father's cattle empire and has to overcome outlaw bands of cattle rustlers.

Genre(s): Western Fiction.

1343. *Lassiter*. New York: Pocket Books, 1985. 252 pp.

Among Lassiter's accomplishments are rescuing prostitutes and saving a friend's ranch.

Genre(s): Western Fiction.

1344. *Riders of the Purple Sage*. New York: Harper and Row, 1912. 280 pp.

In 1871, Mormons take vengeance against those who have wronged them.

Genre(s): Western Fiction.

1345. *The Thundering Herd*. New York: Harper and Row, 1925. 350 pp.

A group of men wants to make a quick fortune from buffalo hides.

Genre(s): Western Fiction.

1346. *To the Last Man*. New York: Harper, 1922. 300 pp.

Two men carry their feud from Texas to Arizona and start the Pleasant Valley war which destroys all but one member of each family.

Genre(s): Western Fiction.

1347. *The Trail Driver.* New York: Harper and Row, 1936. 300 pp.
A large cattle drive between Texas and Kansas occurs in 1871.
Genre(s): Western Fiction.

1348. *The U.P. Trail.* New York: Harper and Row, 1918. 409 pp.
While workers build the Union Pacific Railway, the United States Army fights the Native Americans.
Genre(s): Western Fiction.

◆ 1349. *The Vanishing American.* 1925. New York: Pocket Books, 1984. 342 pp.
Nophaie, a Native American educated in white society, falls in love with a white woman, but when he returns to the reservation, he finds that missionaries and government officials have brought disease and crime to his people.
Genre(s): Western Fiction.

1350. *West of the Pecos.* New York: Harper and Row, 1937. 300 pp.
Colonel Terrill is brutally murdered, and Pecos Smith rides to rescue his daughter from the desperados.
Genre(s): Western Fiction.

1351. *Western Union.* 1939. New York: Harper, 1991. 311 pp.
Settlers face all of the problems of frontier life as they move into the West.
Genre(s): Western Fiction.

Groseclose, Elgin Earl

1352. *The Kiowa.* Elgin, IL: Cook, 1978. 187 pp.
Sanjak, a Kiowa brave, becomes attracted to Ileeta, a captured Mexican woman, and to the crucifix Ileeta wears around her neck in the 1860s.
Genre(s): Western Fiction; Love Story; Christian Fiction.

Grote, JoAnn A.

1353. *The Unfolding Heart.* Uhrichsville, OH: Barbour, 1997. 192 pp.
Millicent Strong attends her brother's wedding in the West and falls in love with the minister, but she wants neither God nor the wilderness, so she must make difficult decisions.
Genre(s): Western Fiction; Romance; Christian Fiction.

Grove, Fred

◆ 1354. *Bush Track.* Garden City, NY: Doubleday, 1978. 186 pp.
In the sequel to *The Great Horse Race*, the con artists find another victim to bet against Coyote Walking riding on Judge Blair, a good horse.
Genre(s): Western Fiction.

◆ 1355. *Deception Trail.* New York: Doubleday, 1988. 180 pp.
Horseracers from *Bush Track* continue to set up horse races with their nag, Judge Blair, until someone steals him.
Genre(s): Western Fiction.

◆ 1356. *A Far Trumpet.* Garden City, NY: Doubleday, 1985. 183 pp.
Scott William Durham goes to New Mexico after a dishonorable discharge from the army, and while trying understand what he wants in life, he begins pursuing Apache renegades, a job he soon grows to dislike.
Genre(s): Western Fiction.

1357. *The Great Horse Race.* Garden City, NY: Doubleday, 1977. 188 pp.
Three men working quarter-horse match races look for places to make money racing Judge Blair, their horse.
Award(s): Western Writers of America Spur Award.
Genre(s): Western Fiction.

1358. *Phantom Warrior.* Garden City, NY: Doubleday, 1981. 180 pp.
When Lieutenant Ewing Mackay is ready to attack the Apache warrior, Victorio, his commanding officer makes charges against him.
Genre(s): Western Fiction.

Guhrke, Laura Lee

1359. *Conor's Way.* New York: HarperCollins, 1996. 416 pp.
When Olivia Maitland need help to save her Louisiana plantation after the Civil War, she reluctantly engages Conor Branigan, a former boxer from Ireland.
Award(s): Romance Writers of America RITA Award.
Genre(s): Romance.

Gulick, Bill

1360. *Hallelujah Train.* Garden City, NY: Doubleday, 1963. 192 pp.
The Walsingham train destined for Denver carries French champagne and whiskey, which different groups of people covet for varied reasons.
Genre(s): Western Fiction.

Guthrie, A. B.

◆ 1361. *The Big Sky.* New York: Sloane, 1947. 500 pp.
Boone Caudill, 17, leaves his Kentucky home and family and settles in Big Sky, Montana.
Genre(s): Western Fiction; Adventure Story.

1362. *Wild Pitch.* Boston: Houghton Mifflin, 1972. 224 pp.
A gentle sheriff and his 17-year-old assistant must search for the murderer of a rancher at a community picnic.
Genre(s): Western Fiction.

Hackenberry, Charles

1363. *Friends.* New York: M. Evans, 1993. 238 pp.
Sheriff Clete Shannon and his loyal deputy, Willie Goodwin, traverse the Dakota Territory in 1877 on the trail of a particularly brutal killer.
Award(s): Western Writers of America Spur Award.
Genre(s): Western Fiction.

◆ May be suitable for young adult readers

Hackler, Micah S.

1364. *Dark Canyon.* New York: Dell, 1997. 288 pp.
After three murders, Sheriff Lansing asks scholars to intepret his great-great grandfather's journal from 1871, and they find an interesting tale.
Genre(s): Mystery.

Hall, Oakley

1365. *Apaches.* New York: Simon and Schuster, 1986. 464 pp.
Cavalry officer Patrick Cutler comes to Fort McLain and trains a diverse group of Native Americans to help him patrol the frontier, and he and they soon become part of an Apache uprising and a vicious war among white settlers.
Genre(s): Western Fiction; Adventure Story.

1366. *Separations.* Reno: University of Nevada Press, 1997. 288 pp.
In the 19th century, the new owner of a California literary magazine wants to go into the Grand Canyon to discredit John Wesley Powell's work, and a San Francisco woman suggests that he rescue her sister from the Hoya Indians on his journey.
Genre(s): Adventure Story.

1367. *Warlock.* 1958. Reno: University of Nevada Press, 1996. 471 pp.
Life in a frontier mining town during the 1880s becomes violent.
Genre(s): Western Fiction.

Hansen, Ron

1368. *The Assassination of Jesse James by the Coward, Robert Ford.* New York: Knopf, 1983. 304 pp.
Robert Ford rides with Jesse James for eight months before he shoots James in the back.
Genre(s): Western Fiction; Biographical Fiction.

Harington, Donald

1369. *Butterfly Weed.* San Diego, CA: Harcourt Brace, 1996. 369 pp.
Colvin Swain, doctor in Stay More, Arkansas, uses herbal remedies and other cures and also visits his patients at night on an astral plane, but the one he cannot save is the love of his life.
Genre(s): Domestic Fiction; Love Story.

Harmon, Susan

◆ 1370. *Colorado Ransom.* New York: Walker, 1992. 176 pp.
Richard Bates goes to Well Springs, Colorado, in the 1870s after hearing that his uncle has been murdered there, and he helps his uncle's mistress save the land and mine belonging to them.
Genre(s): Western Fiction.

1371. *Spirit of a Bear.* New York: Walker, 1994. 192 pp.
When Elizabeth Butler arrives as the mail-order bride matched to Trap McRae, he still considers himself married to Blue Flower, the Ute mother of his son, but later Elizabeth and Blue Flower unite to foil plans of Blue Flower's Indian husband.
Genre(s): Western Fiction.

Harris, Frank

1372. *The Bomb.* Chicago: University of Chicago Press, 1963. 332 pp.
A young German, Rudolph Schnaubelt, drifts to Chicago from Munich, and, bitter about his plight, agrees to throw the bomb that kills eight policemen in 1886.
Genre(s): Political Fiction.

Harris, Marilyn

1373. *American Eden.* Garden City, NY: Doubleday, 1987. 593 pp.
In 1889, in the sequel to *Eden Rising*, Mary Eden Stanhope and her family live in social isolation outside Mobile as a result of her husband's progressive beliefs until a vigilante group abducts Eve, 17.

Harson, Dylan

◆ 1374. *Kansas Blue.* New York: Donald I. Fine, 1993. 282 pp.
Austin Bourke leads a wagon train across Kansas, and he falls in love with a woman married to a Civil War survivor and fights cholera, thieves, and murderers.
Genre(s): Western Fiction; Romance.

Harvey, James Alphonsus

1375. *Blood Hunt.* New York: Doubleday, 1977. 156 pp.
Mike Brady searches for Ben Murdock, African American, and two other men.
Genre(s): Western Fiction.

Haseloff, Cynthia

◆ 1376. *Man Without Medicine.* New York: Five Star, 1996. 227 pp.
Kiowa warrior Daha-den, Man Without Medicine, and his adopted outcast, Thomas Young Man, must pursue horse thieves after being confined to a reservation in Oklahoma.
Genre(s): Western Fiction.

Hatcher, Robin Lee

1377. *Chances Are.* New York: HarperCollins, 1996. 352 pp.
Faith Butler, stranded in Dead Horse, Wyoming, by an unfaithful husband, becomes a housekeeper for recluse Drake Rutledge to support her two children.
Genre(s): Romance; Western Fiction.

1378. *Liberty Blue.* New York: Pocket Books, 1995. 528 pp.
Olivia Vanderhoff escapes her father and an arranged marriage with a man 35 years her senior by leaving San Francisco for a sheep farm in Idaho.
Genre(s): Romance.

Havill, Steven

1379. *Timber Blood.* New York: Walker, 1985. 146 pp.

Someone accuses Bert Schmidt, a lumberman in the 1880s, of rustling cattle, and although the town does not believe he is guilty, it wants to know who is because that person is also a murderer.
Genre(s): Western Fiction.

Haycox, Ernest

1380. *Bugles in the Afternoon.* Boston: Little, Brown, 1944. 306 pp.

A member of General Custer's army wonders about the choices of his commander.
Genre(s): Biographical Fiction; Western Fiction; War Story.

Hayes, Penny

1381. *Kathleen O'Donald.* Tallahassee, FL: Naiad, 1994. 233 pp.

After Kathleen O'Donald arrives from Ireland and passes through Ellis Island, she meets Rose Stewart from England and begins a friendship.
Genre(s): Domestic Fiction.

1382. *The Long Trail.* Tallahassee, FL: Naiad, 1986. 232 pp.

Blanche Irene Bartholomew meets Teresa, a prostitute, with whom she falls in love, and on the morning of her wedding in post-Civil War Texas, she and Teresa make their way to Blanche's lesbian aunt's home.
Genre(s): Western Fiction; Romance.

Heath, Lorraine

1383. *Texas Destiny.* New York: Topaz, 1997. 384 pp.

When mail-order bride Amelia Carson arrives in Fort Worth, her intended husband has a broken leg and sends his brother Houston, who lost an eye in the Civil War, to fetch her, and Houston falls in love with Amelia.
Genre(s): Romance.

Heck, Peter J.

◆ 1384. *A Connecticut Yankee in Criminal Court.* New York: Berkley, 1996. 311 pp.

Samuel L. Clemens (Mark Twain) and his secretary meet George Washington Cable in New Orleans and help him defend a friend accused of poisoning the wealthy man for whom he cooked.
Genre(s): Mystery.

◆ 1385. *The Prince and the Prosecutor.* New York: Berkley, 1997. 336 pp.

Rudyard Kipling helps Mark Twain and Twain's secretary, Wentworth Cabot, solve the murder of a wealthy victim on a ship en route to London.
Genre(s): Mystery.

Heidish, Marcy

◆ 1386. *The Secret Annie Oakley.* New York: New American Library, 1983. 233 pp.

Annie Oakley, star of the Wild West shows, has a dark secret in her past.
Genre(s): Biographical Fiction.

Heitzmann, Kristen

1387. *Honor's Pledge.* Minneapolis, MN: Bethany House, 1998. 288 pp.

Monte must set aside his love for Abbie Morgan when he must fullfil a wartime pledge and pay a family debt after the Civil War. (*Series:* Rocky Mountain Legacy, 1)
Genre(s): Christian Fiction; Western Fiction.

Helm, Thomas Monroe

1388. *Desert Ghost.* New York: Doubleday, 1977. 185 pp.

Snipe and Kes Morgan prospect for six years, and they experience both failure and success as they capture those who rob them.
Genre(s): Western Fiction.

Henke, Shirl

1389. *The Endless Sky.* New York: St. Martin's Press, 1997. 448 pp.

After Chase Remington falls in love with Stephanie Summerfield, his allegiance to his Native American tribe is tested in the 1870s before the Battle of Little Bighorn.
Genre(s): Western Fiction; Romance.

Henry, L. D.

1390. *Terror at Hellhole.* New York: M. Evans, 1994. 168 pp.

When prisoners break out of a prison and rape the wives of the Quechuan Indians tracking them, the women mete out justice when the local judge refuses to do so.
Genre(s): Western Fiction.

Henry, Will

1391. *Alias Butch Cassidy.* New York: Random House, 1968. 209 pp.

Butch Cassidy, as a teenager, teams up with an old rustler and accompanies him to Utah's Robber's Roost, a hideout.
Genre(s): Western Fiction; Biographical Fiction.

1392. *The Bear Paw Horses.* Philadelphia: Lippincott, 1973. 214 pp.

The Dakota Sioux attempt to help the Nez Percé escape into Canada, and a Sioux and his granddaughter recover a band of horses stolen by thieves as they go to the meeting place in the Bear Paw mountains.
Genre(s): Western Fiction.

1393. *Custer's Last Stand.* New York: Chilton, 1966. 177 pp.

General Custer destroys the Washita Native American camp in 1868 before he fights Little Big Horn in 1876 and Crazy Horse dies in 1877.
Genre(s): Western Fiction; Biographical Fiction.

1394. *From Where the Sun Now Stands.* New York: Random House, 1959. 279 pp.
Chief Joseph tries to lead the Nez Percé to Canada in a safe retreat from their Northwest home, but the whites have other ideas.
Award(s): Western Writers of America Spur Award.
Genre(s): Biographical Fiction; Western Fiction; War Story.

◆ 1395. *I, Tom Horn.* Philadelphia: Lippincott, 1975. 339 pp.
Tom Horn gives a personal account of his last days and nights in a Cheyenne, Wyoming, jail before he succumbs to his fate.
Genre(s): Biographical Fiction; War Story; Western Fiction.

1396. *One More River to Cross.* New York: Random House, 1967. 247 pp.
An African American emancipated by Lincoln finds that freedom is not as available as he expected in the West.
Genre(s): Western Fiction.

Highland, Monica

1397. *Lotus Land.* New York: Coward-McCann, 1983. 383 pp.
Three people, from China, Mexico, and Baltimore, meet in Los Angeles in the 1880s and continue to keep in touch through World War II.

Hinger, Charlotte

1398. *Come Spring.* New York: Simon and Schuster, 1986. 323 pp.
Homesteaders and town developers with railroad interests conflict in Kansas in 1881 while married Aura Lee becomes attracted to Graham, and Lucinda eyes Aura Lee's husband.
Genre(s): Western Fiction.

Hirt, Douglas

1399. *Devil's Wind.* New York: Doubleday, 1989. 180 pp.
Matt Kendell trails a gang of outlaws that has killed his wife and captured others, but his pursuit is complicated when he has to take two children whose parents were also killed by the gang.
Genre(s): Western Fiction.

Hoff, B. J.

◆ 1400. *The Winds of Graystone Manor.* Minneapolis, MN: Bethany House, 1995. 318 pp.
On Staten Island, after the Civil War, Roman St. Clare marries, but someone murders his wife.
Genre(s): Romance; Christian Fiction.

Hoffman, Lee

1401. *Fox.* New York: Doubleday, 1976. 186 pp.
When James Fox arrives in Stick City, he plans to swindle the biggest rancher so that he can settle down and change his life, but his plan becomes complicated by murder, blackmail, and the rancher's daughter.
Genre(s): Western Fiction.

1402. *Sheriff of Jack Hollow.* New York: Dell, 1977. 223 pp.
Two prostitutes plan a bank robbery for three males to execute, and their efforts change Sheriff Tuck Tobin's life.
Genre(s): Western Fiction.

Hogan, Ray

1403. *Conger's Woman.* New York: Doubleday, 1973. 188 pp.
When a woman is condemned to hanging for murdering her husband, a drifter gallantly helps her escape.
Genre(s): Western Fiction.

1404. *The Doomsday Bullet.* Garden City, NY: Doubleday, 1981. 182 pp.
John Rye goes to Crisscross, New Mexico, to face the outlaws assembled there, and since his reputation precedes him, he must first kill a man.
Genre(s): Western Fiction.

1405. *The Doomsday Marshal.* New York: Doubleday, 1975. 185 pp.
John Rye's reputation for bringing in his man either in the saddle or lying over it is challenged when he must deliver Luke Braden, a killer sentenced for hanging and whose wife has vowed to rescue him.
Genre(s): Western Fiction.

1406. *The Doomsday Posse.* New York: Doubleday, 1977. 180 pp.
When John Rye searches for an outlaw gang in a canyon, a deputy aims at him instead of the gang.
Genre(s): Western Fiction.

◆ 1407. *The Glory Trail.* New York: Doubleday, 1978. 175 pp.
Luther Pike is a cowboy who wants to be a lawman, and when he gets the chance, his first duty is to take a convicted cattle rustler (who happens to be a woman) to jail.
Genre(s): Western Fiction.

◆ 1408. *The Proving Gun.* New York: Doubleday, 1975. 157 pp.
Although he has never shot his gun, Tom Sutton will become sheriff of Mimbres Crossing when Luke Jones retires, but when a local gang decides to kidnap the teacher and five female students, Sutton has an unwanted chance to prove himself.
Genre(s): Western Fiction.

◆ 1409. *Solitude's Lawman.* New York: Doubleday, 1988. 182 pp.
Horse dealer Cole Dagget loses his money in a bank robbery and he decides to pursue the robbers on his own while the town tries to gather a posse.
Genre(s): Western Fiction.

Holm, Stef Ann

1410. *Forget Me Not.* New York: Pocket Books, 1997. 353 pp.
In 1874, Josephine Whittaker has lost wealth and station so she goes west from New York City but is stranded in Wyoming before a rancher finally hires her as a cook.
Genre(s): Western Fiction.

1411. *Harmony.* New York: Pocket Books, 1997. 420 pp.
A schoolmistress and an outdoorsman find that they own the same piece of property in Harmony, Montana, each with a different plan for its use. (*Series:* Brides for All Seasons)
Genre(s): Romance; Western Fiction.

1412. *Portraits.* New York: Pocket Books, 1996. 336 pp.
Wyatt Holloway meets a photographer when he returns to Eternity, Colorado, and her photograph of him causes his criminal background to surface.
Genre(s): Romance; Western Fiction.

Holmes, Llewellyn Perry

1413. *Rawhide Creek.* New York: Ace, 1975. 188 pp.
Cleve Ellerson does not sell his gun even though he has no money for food, and when he needs to use it in a camp in which treacherous men want gold he understands why.
Genre(s): Western Fiction.

Hong, Edna Hatlestad

◆ 1414. *The Way of the Sacred Tree.* Minneapolis, MN: Augsburg, 1983. 204 pp.
In the 19th century, Kaduza's birth seems to announce good times for the Dakota, but the white man encroaches, and when Kaduza matures, he is imprisoned for participating in a Dakota uprising.
Genre(s): War Story.

Honig, Donald

1415. *The Ghost of Major Pryor.* New York: Scribner's, 1997. 285 pp.
Captain Thomas Maynard, based in Washington after the Civil War, must go to Montana to try to raise a ghost.
Genre(s): Mystery.

1416. *The Ghost of Mayor Pryor.* New York: Scribner's, 1997. 288 pp.
Captain Thomas Maynard travels to Montana Territory in 1869 to investigate the rumor that Major Andrew Pryor, supposedly killed in the Civil War, is alive so that he can arrest him for desertion.
Genre(s): Western Fiction.

1417. *The Sword of General Englund.* New York: Scribner's, 1996. 288 pp.
In 1876, someone murders General Alfred Englund in Fort Larkin in Dakota Territory, an act surprising to no one, and Colonel Thomas Maynard must come from Philadelphia to find the guilty party.
Genre(s): Western Fiction; Mystery.

Horgan, Paul

1418. *A Distant Trumpet.* New York: Farrar, Straus and Cuhady, 1960. 629 pp.
During the Apache Indian wars of the 1870s and 1880s, Lieutenant Matthew Hazard, officers, and wives try to stay alive at the army outpost.
Genre(s): Western Fiction.

Horsley, Kate

1419. *A Killing in New Town.* Albuquerque, NM: La Alameda, 1996. 271 pp.
Eliza, tired of her town's small-mindedness and her husband's lack of attention while laying track for the new railroad, escapes by drinking and having an affair, but when her two children are kidnapped, her life shifts.
Award(s): Western States Book Award for Fiction.
Genre(s): Mystery.

House, R. C.

1420. *The Sudden Gun.* New York: M. Evans, 1991. 208 pp.
Harry Sanders has become a cold killer since outlaws murdered his parents, and until a lawman kills him in 1904, he remains a murderer and a thief.
Genre(s): Western Fiction.

Howard, Linda

1421. *The Touch of Fire.* New York: Pocket Books, 1992. 312 pp.
Outlaw Rafe McCay forces Annie Parker, the only doctor in Silver Mesa, to leave town with him and heal his gunshot wound, and she forces him to help her treat sick Apaches.
Genre(s): Western Fiction; Medical Novel; Romance.

Howell, Hannah

1422. *Wild Roses.* New York: Zebra, 1998. 352 pp.
After Ella Carson flees from her uncle in Philadelphia to her aunt in Wyoming, Harrigan Mahoney arrives to take her back, and she realizes that she must either seduce him or escape.
Genre(s): Western Fiction; Romance.

Howells, William Dean

1423. *The Rise of Silas Lapham.* 1885. New York: Oxford, 1996. 390 pp.
The uneducated Silas Lapham makes a fortune, and his family tries to penetrate Boston society with unpleasant results.
Genre(s): Domestic Fiction.

Hoyt, Edwin Palmer

◆ 1424. *The Last Stand.* New York: Forge, 1995. 316 pp.
Custer's life of contradictions with the press loving him and his men hating him leads him to make the mistake of fighting at Little Bighorn in 1876.
Genre(s): Biographical Fiction; War Story.

Huffaker, Clair

1425. *The Cowboy and the Cossack.* New York: Trident, 1973. 352 pp.
Cowboys take cattle from Montana to Vladivostok, and Cossacks join them to drive the cattle across Siberia.
Genre(s): Western Fiction.

◆ May be suitable for young adult readers

Hunsburger, H. Edward

◆ 1426. *Crossfire.* New York: Walker, 1985. 142 pp.
When Matt Cordell searches for Paul Talbert, an artist, he
finds a dead body and corruption on his way.
Genre(s): Western Fiction.

Hunter, Evan

1427. *Lizzie.* New York: Arbor House, 1984. 430
pp.
The seeds for Lizzie Borden's murder of her parents ger-
minate on a European trip two years prior to the event.
Genre(s): Biographical Fiction.

Jac, Cherlyn

1428. *Timeswept Love.* New York: Zebra, 1996.
347 pp.
A present-day police officer falls off a cliff in Arizona
while trying to find her sister's killer, time-travelling
back to 1881 where she becomes a peace officer in Tucson also on the trail of a killer.
Genre(s): Western Fiction; Romance; Time Travel.

Jacobs, Harvey

1429. *American Goliath.* New York: St. Martin's
Press, 1997. 352 pp.
In 1869, someone discovers the Cardiff Giant on a New
York farm, but after experts certify its validity, the story
of its being carved in Chicago becomes known.
Genre(s): Humorous Fiction.

Jakes, John

1430. *The Americans.* New York: Pyramid, 1980.
800 pp.
Gideon Kent's youngest son Will moves from Theodore
Roosevelt's Medora ranch to practice medicine in New
York City's tenement slums in the 1880s. (*Series:* Kent
Family Chronicles, 7)
Genre(s): Family Saga; Adventure Story.

1431. *Heaven and Hell.* New York: Harcourt
Brace, 1987. 700 pp.
The Civil War displaces Charles in the sequel to *Love
and War*, and his wife dies, so he takes his infant son out
West to start a new life.
Genre(s): Adventure Story.

James, Will

◆ 1432. *Sand.* New York: Scribner's, 1929. 328 pp.
A young boy captures and tames a black stallion on the
plains.
Genre(s): Western Fiction.

Jamison, Janelle

◆ 1433. *Beyond Today.* Uhrichsville, OH: Barbour,
1994. 170 pp.
Amy and Angie, twin sisters in Kansas, fall in love with a
circuit-riding preacher and must learn to control their jealousy of each other.
Genre(s): Christian Fiction; Western Fiction.

Jennings, Gary

1434. *Spangle.* New York: Atheneum, 1987. 869
pp.
As the Civil War ends, two Confederates leaving Appomattox stumble across a tiny circus under the leadership
of an Alsatian named Florian who wants to go back to
Europe, and they cast their lot with him, go to Europe,
and enter the circus world.
Genre(s): Picaresque Fiction; Adventure Story.

Jennings, William Dale

1435. *The Cowboys.* New York: Stein and Day,
1971. 242 pp.
In 1877, schoolboys help cowboys drive cattle for 400
miles from Montana to Dakota.
Genre(s): Western Fiction.

Johnson, Dorothy M.

1436. *All the Buffalo Returning.* New York:
Dodd, Mead, 1979. 248 pp.
A Sioux family separates after the massacre at Little Big
Horn, each going to seek a fortune.
Genre(s): Western Fiction.

Johnston, Joan

1437. *Maverick Heart.* New York: Dell, 1995. 387
pp.
After Lady Verity Talbot must marry to save her lover
Miles, she goes to Wyoming and discovers something
about the ranch on which she lives.
Genre(s): Romance; Western Fiction.

Johnston, Mary

1438. *Michael Forth.* New York: Harper, 1919.
363 pp.
After the Civil War, in the sequel to *Cease Firing*, the
protagonist grows up on a plantation destroyed in battle.
Genre(s): Domestic Fiction.

Johnston, Terry C.

1439. *Dream Catcher.* New York: Bantam, 1994.
464 pp.
After searching for 10 years, Jonah Hook finds his kidnapped wife, Gritta, at the home of Mormon zealot Jub-
liee Usher, in the sequel to *Winter Rain*.
Genre(s): Western Fiction.

1440. *Winter Rain.* New York: Bantam, 1993. 560
pp.
Jonah Hook searches the West for 10 years trying to find
his family that was captured by Mormons, and he finally
finds his daughter and one son in the sequel to *Cry of the
Hawk*.
Genre(s): Western Fiction; Adventure Story.

Johnston, Velda

1441. *The Late Mrs. Fonsell.* New York: Dodd,
Mead, 1972. 214 pp.
In the 1870s, a young girl's father and husband die, and
she marries her brother-in-law to give her child a name,
while a number of mysterious deaths occur.
Genre(s): Romance; Mystery.

Jones, Douglas C.

◆ 1442. *Arrest Sitting Bull.* New York: Scribner's, 1977. 249 pp.
When orders to arrest Sitting Bull reach the military unit responsible, its members bungle the situation.
Genre(s): Biographical Fiction; Western Fiction.

◆ 1443. *Come Winter.* New York: Holt, Rinehart and Winston, 1989. 418 pp.
Roman, in the sequel to *Roman*, friend to Native Americans and blacks, decides to buy his Arkansas town, and his decision eventually costs him more than he wants to pay.
Genre(s): Domestic Fiction.

◆ 1444. *Gone the Dreams and Dancing.* New York: Holt, Rinehart, and Winston, 1984. 323 pp.
Liverpool Morgan, son of a Comanche woman in the sequel to *Season of Yellow Leaf*, tries to help tribal members accustom themselves to the reservation.
Award(s): Western Writers of America Spur Award.
Genre(s): Western Fiction.

◆ 1445. *Roman.* New York: Holt, Rinehart, and Winston, 1986. 389 pp.
In 1868, after Roman has left his Arkansas town in the sequel to *Winding Stair*, he battles Cheyennes at the Battle of Beecher Island but survives and becomes a business tycoon in Leavenworth.
Award(s): Western Writers of America Spur Award.
Genre(s): War Story.

◆ 1446. *The Search for Temperance Moon.* New York: Henry Holt, 1991. 325 pp.
Jewel Moon, madam of Fort Smith's most famous brothel, asks a deputy marshal to investigate the murder of her mother Temperance in the Indian Nation across the river, and the interviews during his search reveal a complex woman.
Genre(s): Western Fiction; Mystery.

Jones, Hettie

◆ 1447. *Mustang Country.* New York: Pocket Books, 1976. 189 pp.
Eleven-year-olds Don Treego and Nika try to catch a wild stallion, using a dog to demonstrate that Don is the best cowboy of all.
Genre(s): Western Fiction.

Jones, Kathy

1448. *Wild Western Desire.* New York: Zebra, 1993. 270 pp.
Katy Halliday wants to write dime novels about the West, but she must leave New York for Dodge City to find out about the atmosphere, and there she meets Bat Masterson and Wyatt Earp.
Genre(s): Romance; Western Fiction.

Jones, Robert F.

◆ 1449. *Tie My Bones to Her Back.* New York: Farrar, Straus and Giroux, 1996. 271 pp.
Jenny Dousmann and her brother travel west after the panic of 1873 expecting to live on the buffalo trade, but they encounter serious problems before members of the

Cheyenne tribe rescue them and incorporate them into the tribe.
Genre(s): Adventure Story.

Judd, Cameron

◆ 1450. *Beggar's Gulch.* New York: Bantam, 1990. 154 pp.
After killing the man who murdered his father, Matt McAllison serves time in prison, and when he goes to Montana to become a ranch hand afterward, he worries that someone will reveal his past.
Genre(s): Western Fiction.

1451. *Bitterroot.* New York: Bantam, 1989. 160 pp.
After finding all of the marauding Union soldiers who killed his wife and son, Simon Caine has to deal with his brother, who has bounty hunters chase him.
Genre(s): Western Fiction.

◆ 1452. *The Hanging at Leadville.* New York: Bantam, 1991. 240 pp.
Reporter-illustrator Brady Kenton travels to Leadville, Colorado, where Confederate night rider Briggs Garrett may be hiding.
Genre(s): Western Fiction.

Kane, Kathleen

1453. *This Time for Keeps.* New York: St. Martin's Press, 1998. 320 pp.
Transported from the 20th century, Tracy Hill finds a new life in Montana during 1875 when she realizes that she must find common ground with her possible lovers.
Genre(s): Time Travel; Western Fiction.

Kelley, Leo P.

1454. *Bannock's Brand.* New York: Doubleday, 1991. 185 pp.
Bannock fights a group of Mexican cattle rustlers who brand him in one of their battles.
Genre(s): Western Fiction.

◆ 1455. *Luke Sutton.* Garden City, NY: Doubleday, 1982. 188 pp.
Luke Sutton searches for the three men who murdered his brother and must go to Mexico to find one of them.
Genre(s): Western Fiction.

1456. *Thunder Gods' Gold.* New York: Henry Holt, 1989. 192 pp.
When an Apache gives surgeon Ralph Barclay a secret lode of gold for saving his wife, Barclay tells others, and when they rush to the site, murder follows.
Genre(s): Western Fiction.

Kelley, Ray

◆ 1457. *Blue Rock Range.* New York: St. Martin's Press, 1978. 156 pp.
Bill Nash finds a Native American baby in a bush, and after a fight, he wins custody of both the baby and the mother.
Genre(s): Western Fiction.

◆ May be suitable for young adult readers

Kelton, Elmer

◆ 1458. *The Far Canyon.* Garden City, NY: Doubleday, 1994. 323 pp.
In the sequel to *Slaughter*, Jeff Layne returns from killing buffalo to find that his enemy has stolen his girlfriend and his land, and after he departs for Texas, he encounters unhappy Comanches escaping from the new reservation.
Award(s): Western Writers of America Spur Award.
Genre(s): Western Fiction.

◆ 1459. *The Good Old Boys.* Garden City, NY: Doubleday, 1978. 253 pp.
When Hewey Callahan returns to his brother's ranch in west Texas after a two-year absence, he has difficulty adjusting and wants to leave soon after arrival.
Genre(s): Western Fiction.

◆ 1460. *Manhunters.* Fort Worth: Texas Christian University Press, 1994. 196 pp.
After the Mexican Fernandez shoots a sheriff, at least 300 men chase him through Texas, not all of them seeking lawful justice.
Genre(s): Western Fiction.

◆ 1461. *The Pumpkin Rollers.* New York: Forge, 1996. 320 pp.
Trey McLean, a pumpkin roller (farmer), wants to become a cattleman, but after he leaves home he encounters frustration and danger on the way to his goal.
Genre(s): Western Fiction; Bildungsroman (Coming of Age).

◆ 1462. *Slaughter.* Garden City, NY: Doubleday, 1992. 369 pp.
Several people, including Jeff Layne, meet on the Great Plains after the Civil War, where the whites want buffalo profits and the Indians need the buffalo for survival.
Award(s): Western Writers of America Spur Award.
Genre(s): Adventure Story; Western Fiction.

◆ 1463. *The Wolf and the Buffalo.* Garden City, NY: Doubleday, 1980. 420 pp.
Gray Horse Running and ex-slave Gideon Ledbetter, a buffalo soldier, continue to cross paths as they fight in the Texas Comanche wars.
Genre(s): Western Fiction.

Kennelly, Ardyth

1464. *The Peaceable Kingdom.* Boston: Houghton Mifflin, 1949. 375 pp.
After feeling jealous of her husband's first wife, the Mormon Linnea, mother of five children, uses her courage and good sense to overcome her troubles.
Genre(s): Domestic Fiction.

Keyes, Frances Parkinson

1465. *Blue Camellia.* New York: Messner, 1957. 432 pp.
Brent Winslow moves his family from Illinois to Louisiana in the 1880s looking for cheap land, and he finds more than he expects.
Genre(s): Family Saga; Romance.

Kitzmiller, Chelley

1466. *Embrace the Wind.* New York: New American Library, 1997. 380 pp.
Ginny goes with her father to Tucson after her mother's death to write honest articles for the newspaper, even about half-Apache Bonner Kincade, son of a wealthy rancher.
Genre(s): Romance; Western Fiction.

Klem, Kaye

1467. *Touch the Sun.* New York: Doubleday, 1971. 240 pp.
In the 1870s, John Donahan, strong and honest, struggles to control his Virginia City holding and keep it from a San Francisco banker, with the help of an unpredictable partner.
Genre(s): Western Fiction; Romance.

Knott, Will C.

1468. *Caulder's Badge.* New York: Ace, 1977. 184 pp.
While Wolf Caulder works as a lawman in Green River, Reno shoots him in the leg, and although Reno escapes initially, Wolf quickly pursues him.
Genre(s): Western Fiction.

1469. *The Vengeance Seeker #1.* New York: Ace, 1975. 190 pp.
When Wolf Caulder was a boy, five men murdered his family and destroyed one of his eyes, and as an adult he kills the first three, but the fourth almost kills Caulder before Ellen Bowman intervenes.
Genre(s): Western Fiction.

1470. *The Vengeance Seeker #2.* New York: Ace, 1975. 190 pp.
Wolf Caulder promises the dying Kathy Blackmann that he will find her son Josh, but what he finds is Josh's father greedily driving out the neighbors so that he can enlarge his ranch.
Genre(s): Western Fiction.

1471. *The Vengeance Seeker #3.* New York: Ace, 1976. 202 pp.
After surviving the Tipton Train Massacre, Wolf Caulder searches for Weed Leeper, the killer, when a bribed jury lets Leeper and other gang members go free.
Genre(s): Western Fiction.

Knowles, Ardeana Hamlin

1472. *Pink Chimneys.* Gardiner, ME: Tilbury, 1987. 320 pp.
In 19th century Bangor, Maine, Pink Chimneys is the town's best brothel.
Genre(s): Domestic Fiction.

Kruger, Mary

1473. *Death on the Cliff Walk.* New York: Kensington, 1994. 277 pp.
Rosalind Sinclair, daughter of one of Newport's wealthy summer families but dressed like a maid, is discovered

murdered on the Cliff Walk, and detective Matt Devlin with his friend Brooke Cassidy of Belle Mer investigate.
Genre(s): Mystery.

1474. *Masterpiece of Murder.* New York: Kensington, 1996. 273 pp.
After being married for three months, Brooke Devlin dislikes life as a society woman, and when her friend asks for help in solving the murder of her father several months before, she happily obliges.
Genre(s): Mystery.

La Farge, Oliver

1475. *Laughing Boy.* Boston: Houghton Mifflin, 1929. 302 pp.
Slim Girl returns to her Navajo tribe after American schooling, and with her love Laughing Boy, tries to re-enter its life.
Genre(s): Western Fiction.

La Fountaine, George

◆ 1476. *The Scott-Dunlap Ring.* New York: Coward-McCann, 1978. 268 pp.
Jim Dunlap and Bob Scott team up to rob banks in the late 19th century.
Genre(s): Biographical Fiction.

Lamb, F. Bruce

1477. *Kid Curry: Life and Times of Harvey Logan and the Wild Bunch.* Boulder, CO: Johnson, 1991. 369 pp.
Harvey Logan and his ranching partner, Jim Thornkill, tell Logan's story of his association with Butch Cassidy and the Sundance Kid.
Genre(s): Biographical Fiction; Western Fiction.

L'Amour, Louis

◆ 1478. *Bendigo Shafter.* New York: Dutton, 1979. 324 pp.
Ben Shafter helps his brother, his sister Lorna, and Ethan Sackett found a town in Wyoming while trying to learn more about Native Americans as well as whites.
Genre(s): Western Fiction.

1479. *The Californios.* New York: Saturday Review, 1974. 188 pp.
When Eileen Mulkerin is about to lose her ranch, an old Indian leads her to hidden gold.
Genre(s): Western Fiction.

1480. *The Cherokee Trail.* New York: Bantam, 1982. 179 pp.
A Southerner, Mary Breydon, is the only woman managing a station on the Cherokee Trail in the 1860s.
Genre(s): Western Fiction.

1481. *The Ferguson Rifle.* New York: Bantam, 1973. 180 pp.
The Chantry family continues its frontier life during and after the Civil War. (*Series:* The Chantrys, 2)
Genre(s): Family Saga; Western Fiction; Adventure Story.

1482. *Kilkenny.* New York: Omnibus, 1954. 160 pp.
Kilkenny seems to attract thieves, violence, and death.
Genre(s): Western Fiction.

1483. *Lonely on the Mountain.* New York: Bantam, 1980. 194 pp.
Tyrel and Tell Sackett herd 1,000 steers across Dakota to British Columbia., (*Series:* The Sacketts, 14)
Genre(s): Family Saga; Western Fiction; Adventure Story.

1484. *Over on the Dry Side.* New York: Saturday Review, 1975. 184 pp.
In 1886, after returning from the Civil War, Owen Chantry discovers that his brother has been murdered on his Colorado homestead, and Chantry wants to find the murderer. (*Series:* The Chantrys, 3)
Genre(s): Western Fiction; Family Saga.

◆ 1485. *The Riders of High Rock.* New York: Bantam, 1993. 271 pp.
Hopalong Cassidy fights a gang of cattle rustlers.
Genre(s): Western Fiction.

◆ 1486. *The Rustlers of West Fork.* New York: Bantam, 1991. 259 pp.
Hopalong Cassidy helps the inhabitants of a western area with a cattle rustling problem.
Genre(s): Western Fiction.

1487. *Showdown at Yellow Butte.* New York: Omnibus, 1953. 192 pp.
Townspeople hire Tom Kendrick to stop a band of murderers.
Genre(s): Western Fiction.

◆ 1488. *The Trail to Seven Pines.* New York: Bantam, 1992. 244 pp.
Hopalong Cassidy tries to help after a stagecoach robbery and murder, only to be accused of the crime himself.
Genre(s): Western Fiction.

1489. *Trouble Shooter.* New York: Bantam, 1994. 254 pp.
When Hopalong Cassidy arrives in New Mexico to help his friend Pete Melford, Melford is dead and his ranch has disappeared.
Genre(s): Western Fiction; Mystery.

1490. *Westward the Tide.* New York: Bantam, 1995. 216 pp.
Matt Bardoul decides to join a wagon train going west, but those organizing it are secretive about its destination and warn him that he will not return alive.
Genre(s): Western Fiction.

◆ May be suitable for young adult readers

Lane, Rose Wilder

◆ 1491. *Let the Hurricane Roar.* New York: Long-mans, 1933. 118 pp.
Molly and David face the difficulties of pioneer life with grace.

Law, Susan Kay

1492. *Home Fires.* New York: HarperCollins, 1995. 305 pp.
Amanda Sellington and her stepson flee to the West from her abusive husband with only her diamonds, and after Amanda meets Helga in Minnesota, Helga starts match-making.
Genre(s): Romance; Western Fiction.

Le May, Alan

◆ 1493. *The Unforgiven.* New York: Harper and Row, 1957. 245 pp.
In the 1870s, a widow and her children try to stop Indian attacks.
Genre(s): Western Fiction.

Leaton, Anne

1494. *Pearl.* New York: Knopf, 1985. 256 pp.
The Outlaw Queen, Belle Starr, is Pearl's mother, but Pearl is madam of the best whorehouse in Fort Smith, Ar-kansas.
Genre(s): Biographical Fiction; Western Fiction.

Ledbetter, Suzann

1495. *Pure Justice.* New York: Signet, 1998. 352 pp.
Halley joins Texas Rangers to trail John Wesley Hardin after Hardin murders her brother.
Genre(s): Western Fiction.

Lee, W. W.

◆ 1496. *Outlaw's Fortune.* New York: Walker, 1993. 156 pp.
Widower Jefferson Birch is both a ranch hand and an agent for Tisdale Investigations when the Santa Fe Rail-road hires the firm to catch a robber who happens to be Birch's estranged father.
Genre(s): Western Fiction.

◆ 1497. *Rancher's Blood.* New York: Walker, 1991. 138 pp.
Jefferson Birch finds and captures Clem Johnston, ac-cused of killing his boss, and although Birch does not be-lieve that Johnston is guilty, he must bring him to trial.
Genre(s): Western Fiction; Mystery.

◆ 1498. *Rustler's Venom.* New York: Walker, 1990. 159 pp.
Jefferson Birch thinks that one of two men murdered Montana ranch widow Mattie Quinn's husband, but when that man is murdered, he revises his search.
Genre(s): Western Fiction.

Lee, Wayne C.

1499. *Law of the Lawless.* New York: Ace, 1977. 184 pp.
Jasper Dovel and his nephews plan to take land from the homesteaders, but the deputy marshal goes to Nevermore to establish order and almost succumbs to Dovel's plans.
Genre(s): Western Fiction.

Lehrer, Kate

1500. *Out of Eden.* New York: Harmony, 1996. 339 pp.
Two young women from Paris look for independence on the Kansas prairie in the 19th century.
Genre(s): Adventure Story.

L'Engle, Madeleine

1501. *The Other Side of the Sun.* New York: Far-rar, Straus and Giroux, 1971. 344 pp.
Stella, 19, goes to the South while her new husband trav-els to Africa on a secret mission after the Civil War ends.
Genre(s): Romance.

Lesley, Craig

◆ 1502. *River Song.* Boston: Houghton Mifflin, 1989. 352 pp.
Danny Kachiah and his son Jack become involved with the Nez Percé as they fight for their rights along the Co-lumbia River in the Pacific Northwest.

Levin, Meyer

1503. *The Architect.* New York: Simon and Schus-ter, 1981. 413 pp.
Andrew Lane lives similiarly to the architect Frank Lloyd Wright with his revolutionary ideas and personal relation-ships in the first part of the 20th century.
Genre(s): Biographical Fiction.

Linder, Steven

◆ 1504. *The Measure of Justice.* New York: Walker, 1992. 204 pp.
When Ulysses Rule comes to Bannon, he plans to hang mining official Tom McAllister for killing soldiers in the Civil War, but a boy who accompanies Rule hears all of the evidence before the judge arrives and questions Rule's motives.
Genre(s): Western Fiction.

Lindsey, Johanna

1505. *Brave the Wild Wind.* New York: Avon, 1984. 216 pp.
Jessie Blair manages her deceased father's ranch in Wyo-ming during the 1800s, and when her mother arrives to become her guardian, Jessie is angry, but then she falls in love with the man her mother has brought with her.
Genre(s): Romance; Western Fiction.

1506. *Heart of Thunder.* New York: Avon, 1983. 359 pp.
In 1870 in Denver, Samantha Kingsley shoots whoever bothers her, and when Hank Chavez takes her virginity, she fires at him before returning to her father's ranch,

which belonged to the Chavez family before Juárez troops took it during the revolution.
Genre(s): Romance; Western Fiction.

1507. *Savage Thunder.* New York: Avon, 1990. 503 pp.
Jocelyn Fleming travels across the country to escape a murderous detective, and she meets half-Cheyenne Colt Thunder who seems to dislike women.
Genre(s): Romance; Western Fiction.

Linz, Cathie

1508. *A Wife in Time.* New York: Silhouette, 1995. 204 pp.
Susannah Hall goes back to Savannah in 1884 to solve a mystery and to allow the present to change.
Genre(s): Romance; Time Travel; Mystery.

Llewellyn, Michael

1509. *Twelfth Night.* New York: Kensington, 1997. 372 pp.
Creole Justice Blancard chafes at her loveless marriage in 19th-century New Orleans, and she decides to have an affair while her husband entertains his mistress.
Genre(s): Romance.

Logan, Jake

1510. *Across the Rio Grande.* New York: Playboy, 1976. 206 pp.
John Slocum plans to kill a sadistic sheriff after he has seduced the sheriff's bride.
Genre(s): Western Fiction.

1511. *Ride for Revenge.* New York: Playboy, 1977. 156 pp.
John Slocum has to battle Wells Fargo agents, card players, and a crazy woman who owns a cattle empire.
Genre(s): Western Fiction.

1512. *Slocum's Woman.* New York: Playboy, 1976. 206 pp.
John Slocum buys horses and guns for a renegade Mexican general with whom he decides to ride until one of the general's men kills the general.
Genre(s): Western Fiction.

1513. *White Hell.* New York: Playboy, 1977. 190 pp.
John Slocum works in a salt mine with a chain around his neck after capture, but he manages to escape.
Genre(s): Western Fiction.

Longstreet, Stephen

1514. *The Pembroke Colors.* New York; Putnam, 1981. 324 pp.
The Pembrokes of Virginia include the patriarch Tjaden, whose life spans from the Civil War to the Depression.
Genre(s): Family Saga; Domestic Fiction.

Loveday, John

1515. *Halo.* San Diego, CA: Harcourt Brace, 1994. 292 pp.
Poetic Scrag tells about his experiences in the wilderness on a wagon train going to Oregon with Lorelei, her daughter Justly, and Sylvester (*Series:* a photographer)
Award(s): David Hingham Prize; McKitterick Prize.
Genre(s): Bildungsroman (Coming of Age); Western Fiction.

Lowell, Elizabeth

1516. *Only Love.* New York: Avon, 1995. 416 pp.
Whip Moran defends Shannon Smith, a customer in the general store, from the crude Culpepper brothers, and he discovers that her supposed husband (actually uncle) has died.
Genre(s): Western Fiction.

1517. *Winter Fire.* New York: Avon, 1997. 400 pp.
After her parents die in a flood, Sarah goes with her brother to Utah as a mail-order bride, and after her husband dies unmourned, she and Case Maxwell begin to notice each other.
Genre(s): Romance; Western Fiction.

Lutz, Giles A.

1518. *The Feud.* Garden City, NY: Doubleday, 1982. 178 pp.
The bank president of Landers, Wyoming, realizes that he can make money if he rekindles a feud between sheep ranchers and cattlemen.
Genre(s): Western Fiction.

1519. *The Lonely Ride.* New York: Doubleday, 1971. 179 pp.
In the 1870s, Portugee Phillips, a civilian scout, must make a 236-mile ride through a blizzard to get help after Sioux attack and kill half the people in Fort Kearney.
Genre(s): Western Fiction.

1520. *The Stubborn Breed.* New York: Doubleday, 1975. 159 pp.
Although Lou Manard wants to be a farmer, he has trouble focusing on his goal until a plague of grasshoppers arrives on his Kansas land.
Genre(s): Western Fiction.

1521. *A Time for Vengeance.* New York: Ace, 1977. 224 pp.
While Jonse Kirby searches for his wife's murderer, a mountain lion mauls him, and a Mexican woman who nurses him to health is involved in a family feud.
Genre(s): Western Fiction.

1522. *The Way Homeward.* New York: Doubleday, 1977. 186 pp.
Andy Bagley returns to Hays, Kansas, after a stint in prison for a prank, and he has problems before meeting the sheriff's daughter.
Genre(s): Western Fiction.

MacLean, Alistair

1523. *Breakheart Pass.* Garden City, NY: Doubleday, 1974. 178 pp.

After the Civil War, an army relief train takes supplies to an Indian fort, and its passengers suffer mysterious accidents.

Genre(s): Adventure Story.

Margason, Roger

1524. *Stagecoach to Nowhere.* New York: Major Books, 1976. 175 pp.

Calico Williams joins a brother and sister in his search for the man who kills the only person he loves, and they endure blackmail and arson before achieving success.

Genre(s): Western Fiction.

Marquand, John P.

1525. *The Late George Apley.* New York: the Modern Library, 1940. 354 pp.

George Apley, a wealthy Bostonian, finds only frustration and unfulfillment in the conservative life expected of him.

1526. *Sincerely, Willis Wayde.* Boston: Little, Brown, 1955. 511 pp.

Willis Wayde steps on several wealthy industrial families on his way to prosperity in the late 19th century.

Marshall, Catherine

◆ 1527. *Julie.* New York: McGraw Hill, 1984. 364 pp.

Julie Wallace, at 18, has the chance to write for her father's newspaper in Pennsylvania after they move from Alabama during the time of the steel magnates.

Genre(s): Christian Fiction.

Marshall, William Leonard

1528. *The New York Detective.* New York: Mysterious Press, 1989. 282 pp.

Detective Virgil Tillman finds a link to a murder in a city playhouse to a group of old Civil War friends in 1883.

Genre(s): Mystery.

Mason, Connie

1529. *To Love a Stranger.* New York: Avon, 1997. 384 pp.

The misogynist Pierce, running from vigilantes, saves Zoey from a banker who wants both her and her ranch.

Genre(s): Romance; Western Fiction.

Mason, F. Van Wyck

1530. *Trumpets Sound No More.* Boston: Little, Brown, 1975. 297 pp.

Colonel Tilt decides to take his group of soldiers called Company Z to Mexico in search of money to support his Virginia estate and his dependants.

Genre(s): Adventure Story.

Matheson, Richard

◆ 1531. *Journal of the Gun Years.* New York: M. Evans, 1991. 204 pp.

After the Civil War, Clay Halser goes West and keeps a journal about his progress from worker to renowned gunman about whom newspapers write and in whom he begins to believe.

Award(s): Western Writers of America Spur Award.

Genre(s): Western Fiction.

Mathews, John Joseph

1532. *Sundown.* 1934. Norman, OK: University of Oklahoma Press, 1988. 312 pp.

Chal Windzer, born on the Osage reservation in the early 20th century, goes to college and serves as an aviator before returning to the decadent life of the people who have discovered oil on their land and become irresponsibly wealthy.

Genre(s): Western Fiction.

Matthews, Greg

◆ 1533. *Power in the Blood.* New York: HarperCollins, 1993. 848 pp.

Clayton, Zoe, and Drew Dugan leave New York on an orphan train where three different families adopt them, and they spend the rest of their lives wandering the West, looking for somewhere to belong.

Genre(s): Western Fiction; Picaresque Fiction.

May, Karl Friedrich

1534. *Winnetou.* Trans. Michael Shaw. New York: Seabury, 1977. 749 pp.

Karl accompanies an Apache chief who searches for the goldseekers who murdered his father and sister.

Genre(s): Western Fiction.

Mayerson, Evelyn Wilde

1535. *Dade County Pine.* New York: Dutton, 1994. 464 pp.

From the 1880s, five Florida families struggle to build homes for themselves, to keep their property, or to start new lives, as Miami transforms from a small town to a large city.

Genre(s): Family Saga.

1536. *Miami.* New York: Dutton, 1994. 450 pp.

Five families, including African Americans, whites, Seminoles, and Latinos, develop the city of Miami from 1886 through Hurricane Andrew in 1992.

Genre(s): Family Saga.

McBride, Mary

1537. *Darling Jack.* New York: Harlequin, 1996. 344 pp.

When Jack Hazard needs a wife for his cover as a detective for Allan Pinkerton, he chooses a clerk who seems shy but who changes with his attentions.

Genre(s): Romance; Mystery.

McCarthy, Gary

◆ 1538. *Sodbuster.* Garden City, NY: Doubleday, 1988. 153 pp.
Zachariah and his sister Carrie flee their father in 1870s Wyoming for Texas farmland.
Genre(s): Western Fiction.

McCord, John S.

1539. *Montana Horseman.* New York: Doubleday, 1990. 256 pp.
Darnell Baynes and his sons kill men trying to conscript them into the Confederate army and escape to Montana where they rescue a miner and his lovely daughter with whom the youngest son falls in love. (*Series:* The Baynes Clan, 1)
Genre(s): War Story; Western Fiction.

1540. *Texas Comebacker.* New York: Doubleday, 1991. 184 pp.
In 1868, Milt Baynes rides into Louisiana to clear the name of his clan, but he meets Cris Mills and her brother Win, and together they begin to defend the ranchers against outlaws and corruption. (*Series:* The Baynes Clan, 2)
Genre(s): Western Fiction.

◆ 1541. *Walking Hawk.* New York: Doubleday, 1989. 183 pp.
Dan Walker's father is white and his mother a deceased Iroquois, and after he kills a man while defending his stepbrother, he leaves for Montana without knowing if he is cleared of the charges.
Genre(s): Western Fiction.

1542. *Wyoming Giant.* New York: Doubleday, 1992. 181 pp.
Luke Baynes goes east to study law, and when he returns to the West, he becomes a federal judge in Wyoming and must battle unlawful ranching practices. (*Series:* The Baynes Clan, 3)
Genre(s): Western Fiction; Adventure Story.

McCrumb, Sharyn

1543. *If I'd Killed Him When I Met Him.* New York: Ballantine, 1995. 320 pp.
Donna Jean Morgan's decision to poison her husband in Danville, Virginia, is only one of several murders that occur in the town, and after Donna Jean tells her lawyer Bill MacPherson that her mother was the famous Lethal Lucy Todhunter, Bill calls in his sister Elizabeth to investigate how Lucy poisoned her husband.
Award(s): Agatha Award.
Genre(s): Mystery.

McCunn, Ruthanne Lum

1544. *Thousand Pieces of Gold.* San Francisco: Design, 1981. 308 pp.
The family of Polly Bemis (Lalu Nathoy) sells her to bandits and a Chinese saloon keeper, but she ends up married to an American and homesteading in Idaho.
Genre(s): Biographical Fiction.

McEachin, James

◆ 1545. *Tell Me a Tale.* Novato, CA: Lyford, 1996. 252 pp.
Moses, a former slave of 17 and son of a white plantation owner and his black mistress, poses as a proslavery journalist and returns to his small town to tell the story of a burning to four white men who want slavery to return.

McGinnis, Bruce

1546. *Reflections in Dark Glass.* Denton, TX: University Of Northern Texas, 1996. 180 pp.
John Wesley Harden kills his first man in 1868, and during his lifetime, he kills 40 more, and his friends seem to tolerate his actions.
Genre(s): Biographical Fiction; Western Fiction.

McKinney, Meagan

1547. *Fair Is the Rose.* New York: Delacorte, 1993. 336 pp.
In 1875, Christabel Van Alen, wrongly accused of murdering her parents, goes west to earn money for a lawyer to prosecute her guilty uncle, but when outlaws capture her, she fears that her secret will be revealed.
Genre(s): Western Fiction; Romance.

1548. *The Fortune Hunter.* New York: Kensington, 1998. 352 pp.
During the 1880s, Lavinia Murphy suffers abuse and poverty, and when her career as a spiritualist allows her to make enough money to create a home for others like her, she fights to keep it from Edward Stuyvestant-French.
Genre(s): Romance.

McMurtry, Larry

◆ 1549. *Anything for Billy.* New York: Simon and Schuster, 1988. 382 pp.
The dime novelist Ben Sippy tells the story of Billy Bone whom he named Billy the Kid after meeting him in 1878.
Genre(s): Biographical Fiction; Western Fiction.

◆ 1550. *Buffalo Girls.* New York: Simon and Schuster, 1990. 351 pp.
Calamity Jane writes letters to her daughter, and Bill Cody runs his Wild West show during the days of the cowboys.
Genre(s): Biographical Fiction; Western Fiction.

1551. *Comanche Moon.* New York: Simon and Schuster, 1997. 752 pp.
As Buffalo Hump becomes older, his Comanche children rise to power, but his son Blue Duck breaks away to form a renegade group favoring guns over bows and arrows.
Award(s): Western Writers of America Spur Award.
Genre(s): Western Fiction.

◆ 1552. *Lonesome Dove.* New York: Simon and Schuster, 1985. 843 pp.
Former Texas Rangers leave their unsuccessful cattle business when they hear of good opportunities in newly opened territory.
Award(s): Pulitzer Prize; Western Writers of America Spur Award.
Genre(s): Western Fiction.

◆ May be suitable for young adult readers

1553. *Streets of Laredo.* New York: Simon and Schuster, 1993. 589 pp.
In the sequel to *Lonesome Dove*, Gus McCrae's old partner Woodrow Call, a railroad accountant, and a Texas deputy pursue a Mexican train robber.
Genre(s): Western Fiction.

McNab, Tom

◆ 1554. *The Fast Men.* New York: Simon and Schuster, 1988. 345 pp.
Sprinters Billy Joe and Buck are put through their paces by their trainer Moriarty as they prepare for races in the West.
Genre(s): Western Fiction; Sports Fiction.

McNamee, Thomas

1555. *A Story of Deep Delight.* New York: Viking, 1990. 421 pp.
After the Chickasaw near Memphis lose their lands to the whites and the Civil War ends, they have to cope with Ku Klux Klan members, and later a young man tries to befriend their descendants.
Genre(s): Family Saga.

McNickle, D'Arcy

◆ 1556. *The Surrounded.* New York: Dodd, Mead, 1936. 297 pp.
Archilde, son of a Spaniard and a Native American woman in Montana, wants more in his life than is offered by his tribe.
Genre(s): Western Fiction.

◆ 1557. *Wind from an Enemy Sky.* San Francisco: Harper and Row, 1978. 256 pp.
The Little Elk People lose their sacred bundle to a museum and their sacred water to a new dam, two traumas precipitated by Adam Pell, a wealthy engineer with no understanding of Native American spiritual values.
Genre(s): Western Fiction.

Meade, Richard

1558. *Gaylord's Badge.* New York: Doubleday, 1975. 183 pp.
In Colter County during the 1880s, Frank Gaylord thinks that he is an honest lawman, but when he looks closely, he sees differently.
Genre(s): Western Fiction.

Medawar, Mardi Oakley

◆ 1559. *Death at Rainy Mountain.* New York: St. Martin's Press, 1996. 262 pp.
A Kiowa medicine man uses his skills to find a killer in the 1860s.
Genre(s): Mystery; Western Fiction.

1560. *Witch of the Palo Duro.* New York: St. Martin's Press, 1997. 272 pp.
Tay-Bodal, a 19th-century Kiowa medicine man, must find out who is causing the deaths in winter camp for which his wife is being blamed.
Genre(s): Mystery; Western Fiction.

Medeiros, Teresa

1561. *Nobody's Darling.* New York: Bantam, 1998. 400 pp.
Esmeralda Fine plans to murder gunman Billy Darling when she reaches Calamity, New Mexico, but she meets a handsome outlaw and other interesting characters instead.
Genre(s): Romance; Western Fiction.

Michener, James A.

1562. *Centennial.* New York: Random House, 1974. 909 pp.
The story of Centennial, Colorado, begins when the earth formed the area and ends in the 1970s with human disregard for its benefits and beauties, and also tells the history of relations between the white settlers and Native Americans.
Genre(s): Western Fiction; Epic Literature.

Miller, Dawn

1563. *The Journal of Callie Wade.* New York: Pocket Books, 1996. 330 pp.
Callie Wade writes letters telling of the difficulties for women traveling west, including childbirth between storms and the forlorn despair of Native Americans watching their world come to an end.
Genre(s): Western Fiction.

Miller, Janice

1564. *McCannon's Country.* Chicago: Moody, 1996. 277 pp.
A wealthy businessman's daughter comes west to Colorado where she falls in love with an adventurous fur trader. (*Series:* Elk Head Creek, 2)
Genre(s): Christian Fiction; Western Fiction; Adventure Story; Romance.

1565. *Winter's Fire.* Chicago: Moody, 1995. 312 pp.
Courtney McCannon tries to thwart the outlaws who threaten his family, but he worries that he will lose his soul in the violence of the West. (*Series:* Elk Head Creek, 1)
Genre(s): Western Fiction; Christian Fiction.

Miller, Jim

1566. *Campaigning.* New York: Ballantine, 1985. 176 pp.
After Native Americans ambush him and take the supply wagon he is driving on the Santa Fe Trail, Callahan returns to his boss, who does not seem to mind that his wife is also missing as he entrusts Callahan with another wagon.
Genre(s): Western Fiction.

Miller, Linda Lael

1567. *Daniel's Bride.* New York: Pocket Books, 1992. 502 pp.
Jolie Mckibben, accused of murder, is waiting to be hanged when Dan Beckham offers to marry her under the

local terms, and with the two orphans hiding in his wagon, Jolie starts an unusual family with Beckham.
Genre(s): Romance; Western Fiction.

1568. *My Outlaw.* New York: Pocket Books, 1997. 352 pp.
Young Keighly Barrow looks from the 20th century through the mirror in her grandmother's 19th-century salon and sees Darby Elder, a little boy, and for 20 years they comfort each other, but when Keighly inherits the house, she finds diaries and photographs showing that she married Darby less than a year before his death in 1887.
Genre(s): Time Travel; Western Fiction.

Millett, Larry

◆ 1569. *Sherlock Holmes and the Red Demon.* New York: Viking, 1996. 318 pp.
Sherlock Holmes and Dr. Watson travel to Minnesota at the request of railroad tycoon James J. Hill when someone calling himself the Red Demon threatens to set the railway on fire.
Genre(s): Mystery.

Mills, Anita

1570. *Comanche Rose.* New York: New American Library, 1996. 384 pp.
Although Texas Ranger Hap Walker could not stop Comanches from capturing widow Annie Bryce, he finds her again in 1873 and agrees to help her locate her daughter.
Genre(s): Romance; Western Fiction.

Mills, Carla J.

1571. *Three Rivers.* New York: St. Martin's Press, 1988. 320 pp.
In 1878, Doreen Anderson goes from Chicago to Wyoming when she inherits Three Rivers Ranch, and she hires Laramie Smith to protect her from rustlers.
Genre(s): Western Fiction.

Mills, Charles K.

1572. *A Mighty Afternoon.* Garden City, NY: Doubleday, 1980. 183 pp.
The Seventh Cavalry fights at Little Big Horn under General Custer.
Genre(s): Biographical Fiction; War Story.

Mittman, Stephanie

1573. *The Courtship.* New York: Dell, 1998. 384 pp.
A wheelchair-bound attorney, his attorney wife, and his businessman brother form an unusual triangle in Oakland in the late 19th century.
Genre(s): Romance.

1574. *The Marriage Bed.* New York: Dell, 1996. 400 pp.
Farmer Spencer Williamson finally agrees to marry again after losing his family to diphtheria but thinks that his new bride will be unaware that he is not ejaculating when they have sex.
Genre(s): Romance.

Moberg, Vilhelm

1575. *The Last Letter Home.* New York: Simon and Schuster, 1961. 383 pp.
In the sequel to *Unto a Good Land*, the Nilssons change from wilderness pioneers to established American citizens.
Genre(s): Family Saga.

1576. *The Settlers.* St. Paul: Minnesota Historical Society, 1995. 399 pp.
The Nilssons settle in Minnesota and work to become members of American society in the sequel to *Last Letter Home*.
Genre(s): Domestic Fiction; Family Saga.

Moffat, Gwen

1577. *The Buckskin Girl.* New York: David and Charles, 1982. 191 pp.
After Comanches kill Helen Weir's parents, she joins her aunt and uncle's wagon train to California.
Genre(s): Western Fiction.

Moore, Arthur

1578. *Track of the Killer.* New York: Ace, 1975. 221 pp.
Wade Odell and his sidekick, Kizzie, agree to race their chestnut sorrel in Ryville, but the man who killed a rancher steals the horse.
Genre(s): Western Fiction.

Moore, Barbara

◆ 1579. *Hard on the Road.* New York: Doubleday, 1974. 299 pp.
Pepper Fairchild, 15, drives a mule team and wagon for his photographer cousin from Texas to California in the 1880s.
Genre(s): Western Fiction.

Moquist, Richard

◆ 1580. *Eye of the Agency.* New York: St. Martin's Press, 1997. 224 pp.
Sadie Greenstreet, newspaper columnist and reformed con artist, and her husband, a Pinkerton agent with a past, investigate the death of Elcid Hardacre, the owner of a steamboat company.
Genre(s): Mystery.

Moran, Moore

◆ 1581. *Across the Mesas.* New York: Ballantine, 1985. 154 pp.
When Joel Hollings returns to the family ranch, Apaches have killed his brother and kidnapped his father, but a young Apache woman and a ranch hand help him discover that his main enemy is the local town's law officers.
Genre(s): Western Fiction.

◆ May be suitable for young adult readers

Morgan, Speer

1582. *Belle Star.* Boston: Little, Brown, 1979. 311 pp.
Belle Starr tries to sabatoge the attempted settlement of Cherokee land in Oklahoma during the last months of her life.
Genre(s): Biographical Fiction; Western Fiction.

Morris, Alan B.

1583. *Imperial Intrigue.* Wheaton, IL: Tyndale House, 1996. 225 pp.
After Katy Steele and Sam Bronte take an Austrian prince and princess to their land in Texas, they have to fight for both the land and their lives. (*Series:* Katy Steele Adventures, 2)
Genre(s): Mystery; Western Fiction; Christian Fiction.

Morris, Alan B., and Gilbert Morris

◆ 1584. *Tracks of Deceit.* Wheaton, IL: Tyndale House, 1996. 233 pp.
The Central Pacific Railroad hires Katy Steele to investigate the death of her own father, and she finds deceit and dishonesty.
Genre(s): Mystery; Christian Fiction; Western Fiction.

Morris, Gilbert

1585. *Boomtown.* Wheaton, IL: Tyndale House, 1992. 261 pp.
Reno must try to stop a group of cutthroats from forcing miners in Virginia City to relinquish their claims. (*Series:* Reno Western Saga, 4)
Genre(s): Western Fiction; Christian Fiction.

1586. *The Crossed Sabres.* Minneapolis, MN: Bethany House, 1993. 317 pp.
Tom Winslow is a natural-born soldier whose destiny crosses with that of George Custer. (*Series:* House of Winslow, 13)
Genre(s): Christian Fiction; Domestic Fiction; Family Saga.

1587. *The Final Adversary.* Minneapolis, MN: Bethany House, 1992. 301 pp.
Barney Winslow, a prizefighter who has lost his relationship with God, revives it and goes to Africa as a missionary. (*Series:* House of Winslow, 12)
Genre(s): Domestic Fiction; Christian Fiction; Family Saga.

1588. *The Jeweled Spur.* Minneapolis, MN: Bethany House, 1994. 299 pp.
Laurie Winslow falls in love with an ex-convict and must find out for herself if he is guilty or innocent. (*Series:* House of Winslow, 16)
Genre(s): Christian Fiction; Western Fiction; Mystery; Family Saga.

1589. *Lone Wolf.* Wheaton, IL: Tyndale House, 1995. 236 pp.
Jim Reno tries to find Simon Meade's son in Dakota after Native Americans abduct him. (*Series:* Reno Western Saga, 6)
Genre(s): Western Fiction; Christian Fiction.

1590. *Reno.* Wheaton, IL: Tyndale House, 1992. 258 pp.
Jim Reno makes a promise to a dying farmer that stops the domination of the Carrs of Skull Ranch over the farmers and ranchers in the valley. (*Series:* Reno Western Saga, 1)
Genre(s): Western Fiction; Christian Fiction.

1591. *Ride the Wild River.* Wheaton, IL: Tyndale House, 1992. 339 pp.
Jim Reno rides west on a wagon train with a teenager who is trying to escape an abusive stepfather. (*Series:* Reno Western Saga, 3)
Genre(s): Western Fiction; Christian Fiction.

1592. *Rimrock.* Wheaton, IL: Tyndale House, 1992. 257 pp.
A saloon owner and a gunslinger want to kill the newly appointed lawman, Jim Reno. (*Series:* Reno Western Saga, 2)
Genre(s): Western Fiction; Christian Fiction.

1593. *The Union Belle.* Minneapolis, MN: Bethany House, 1992. 334 pp.
Mark Winslow and Lola Montez deal with the gunslingers of the West as the railroad expands. (*Series:* House of Winslow, 11)
Genre(s): Domestic Fiction; Christian Fiction; Family Saga.

1594. *The Valiant Gunman.* Minneapolis, MN: Bethany House, 1993. 320 pp.
A powerful rancher overtakes the smaller ranch owners until a Winslow man arrives and challenges him. (*Series:* House of Winslow, 14)
Genre(s): Christian Fiction; Western Fiction.

1595. *Valley Justice.* Wheaton, IL: Tyndale House, 1995. 256 pp.
When Major Reynolds purchases a ranch, he wants Jim Reno to take his family there in safety. (*Series:* Reno Western Saga, 5)
Genre(s): Western Fiction; Christian Fiction.

Morris, Gilbert, and Lynn Morris

◆ 1596. *The Stars for a Light.* Minneapolis, MN: Bethany House, 1994. 315 pp.
When Cheney Duvall graduates from medical school after the Civil War, she has difficulty finding a job, so she takes a three-month voyage around Cape Horn to Seattle with 100 women. (*Series:* Cheney Duvall, M.D., 1)
Genre(s): Christian Fiction.

Morris, Lynn

◆ 1597. *Secret Place of Thunder.* Minneapolis, MN: Bethany House, 1996. 335 pp.
When Cheney Duvall discovers that sharecroppers and servants living on her aunt's plantation have a strange sickness, she experiences unexpected threats (*Series:* Cheney Duvall, M.D., 5)
Genre(s): Medical Novel; Christian Fiction.

Morris, Lynn, and Gilbert Morris

1598. *A City Not Forsaken.* Minneapolis, MN: Bethany House, 1995. 335 pp.
When physician Cheney Duvall returns to New York and finds a cholera epidemic, she joins her former suitor in private practice to help the homeless and destitute, those most affected by the disease. (*Series:* Cheney Duvall, M.D., 3)
Genre(s): Medical Novel; Christian Fiction.

◆ 1599. *In the Twilight, in the Evening.* Minneapolis, MN: Bethany House, 1996. 320 pp.
Cheney Duvall fights with the hospital staff about the treatment of the poor of San Francisco with the support of only one other person, Shiloh Irons. (*Series:* Cheney Duvall, M.D., 6)
Genre(s): Christian Fiction; Medical Novel.

1600. *Shadow of the Mountain.* Minneapolis, MN: Bethany House, 1994. 336 pp.
Dr. Cheney Duvall goes to Arkansas after the Civil War to help her friend deliver her baby, but she has difficulty becoming used to the supersitions and unscientific practices of the mountain folk, in the sequel to *The Stars for a Light.* (*Series:* Cheney Duvall, M.D., 2)
Genre(s): Christian Fiction; Medical Novel.

◆ 1601. *Toward the Sunrising.* Minneapolis, MN: Bethany House, 1996. 368 pp.
Cheney Duvall and her male nurse, Shiloh Irons, work in Charleston during Reconstruction where they reveal unscrupulous merchants and white supremacists. (*Series:* Cheney Duvall, M.D., 4)
Genre(s): Christian Fiction; Medical Novel.

Morris, Suzanne

1602. *Wives and Mistresses.* Garden City, NY: Doubleday, 1986. 584 pp.
In 1879, Alvareda escapes her brutal father and marries Neal Garrard, whose business partnership with David Leider begins troubles for both families that last nearly a century.
Genre(s): Family Saga.

Morrison, Toni

1603. *Beloved.* New York: Knopf, 1987. 275 pp.
After the Civil War ends, Sethe longingly recalls the two-year-old daughter whom she killed when threatened with recapture after escaping from slavery 18 years before.
Award(s): Anisfield-Wolf Book Award on Race Relations; Pulitzer Prize.

Morsi, Pamela

1604. *Wild Oats.* New York: Jove, 1994. 336 pp.
For eight years after Cora Briggs's divorce from the only son of her town's matriarch, she is shunned by the community, so when the handsome undertaker comes calling, Cora is suprised.
Genre(s): Romance; Western Fiction.

Mortimer, John L.

1605. *Song of the Pedernales.* Austin, TX: Madrona, 1975. 393 pp.
Cowboys and soldiers who have returned from the Civil War rebuild their lives in Texas during Reconstruction.
Genre(s): Western Fiction.

Muir, Rae

1606. *The Lieutenant's Lady.* New York: Harlequin, 1997. 298 pp.
Lieutenant Matt Hull wants to be a lawyer and to marry the wealthy daughter of a local merchant, but he seems too lowly until she falls in love with him. (*Series:* Wedding Trail)
Genre(s): Romance.

Muller, Charles G.

1607. *Bloody Sundown.* New York: Major Books, 1977. 159 pp.
Pete Paul Coons searches for the three men who went to his ranch, tied up his mother, and raped his sisters, and with the help of Uncle Spike Ewing, Pete finds them.
Genre(s): Western Fiction.

Munn, Vella

1608. *Spirit of the Eagle.* New York: Forge, 1996. 352 pp.
Luash, a lovely young Modoc woman and niece of the Modoc chief, meets army officer Jed Britton and falls in love, even though she hates whites, as the Modoc War begins in 1872.
Genre(s): Western Fiction.

Murray, Earl

◆ 1609. *Blue Savage.* New York: Walker, 1985. 164 pp.
Adoped as a child by the Oglala tribe, Harper is traded to an army troop as an adult and he has difficulty adjusting before returning to the tribe.
Genre(s): Western Fiction.

1610. *Thunder in the Dawn.* New York: Tor, 1993. 400 pp.
In 1876, Private Mason Hall hates the army, and when he meets Ghostwind, a Native American seer, before the Battle of Rosebud Creek, he decides to fight on the side in which he believes.
Genre(s): Western Fiction.

Murray, Stuart

1611. *Judith's Dime Novel.* New York: Avalon, 1998. 345 pp.
After the Civil War, a young woman takes a stagecoach ride from St. Louis to California.
Genre(s): Western Fiction.

Nesbitt, John D.

1612. *One-Eyed Cowboy Wild.* New York: Walker, 1994. 180 pp.
Zeke kills Charlie Bickford after Bickford picks a fight with him, and Gene helps Zeke cover up the death, a decision which affects his relationships with those he knows.
Genre(s): Western Fiction.

Newton, Dwight Bennett

1613. *Legend in the Dust.* New York: Doubleday, 1970. 202 pp.
Rim Adams stops in Kansas while traveling west in the late 1860s and helps Frank Keyhoe establish law and order.
Genre(s): Western Fiction.

Nofziger, Lyn

◆ **1614.** *Tackett.* Washington, DC: Regnery Gateway, 1993. 180 pp.
Esmeralda Rankin hires Tackett to protect her ranch from cattle rustlers, and he falls in love with her.
Genre(s): Western Fiction.

1615. *Tackett and the Saloon Keeper.* Washington, DC: Tumbleweed, 1994. 233 pp.
Del Tackett wins the Staghorn Saloon while playing poker, and he forms a business partnership with Annie Laurie Burns, but he has to help the wounded sheriff before learning how to be a saloonkeeper.
Genre(s): Western Fiction.

◆ **1616.** *Tackett and the Teacher.* Washington, DC: Regnery Gateway, 1994. 186 pp.
Del Tackett finds Liddy Doyle in Abilene, and after falling in love with her, discovers that someone else has decided to marry her for her money.
Genre(s): Western Fiction.

Norris, Frank

1617. *The Octopus.* Garden City, NY: Doubleday, 1901. 652 pp.
When the railroad owners try to rob farmers of their crops, one farmer compromises his beliefs and suffers in the late 19th century.
Genre(s): Epic Literature; Western Fiction; Allegory.

1618. *The Pit: A Story of Chicago.* Garden City, NY: Doubleday, 1903. 386 pp.
In the sequel to *The Octopus*, Curtis Jadwin works so hard to make money on the Chicago stock exchange that he ignores his loving wife.
Genre(s): Domestic Fiction.

Oates, Joyce Carol

1619. *A Bloodsmoor Romance.* New York: Dutton, 1982. 615 pp.
In inventor Zinn's family during the 19th century, one daughter is an actress and Mark Twain's mistress, another is a medium, and the third runs away on her wedding night.
Genre(s): Domestic Fiction.

1620. *Mysteries of Winterthurn.* New York: Dutton, 1984. 482 pp.
Xavier Kilgarven has three baffling cases in his upper New York state 19th-century home, all of which are failures.
Genre(s): Mystery.

Oke, Janette

◆ **1621.** *A Bride for Donnigan.* Minneapolis, MN: Bethany House, 1993. 223 pp.
Kathleen O'Malley crosses the ocean from Ireland to meet a stranger and become a mail-order bride. (*Series:* Women of the West, 7)
Genre(s): Christian Fiction; Western Fiction.

◆ **1622.** *A Gown of Spanish Lace.* Minneapolis, MN: Bethany House, 1995. 251 pp.
A band of outlaws captures Ariana Benson, but the boss's son Laramie rescues her, and they fall in love, only to find that they are brother and sister.
Genre(s): Christian Fiction; Western Fiction.

1623. *Heart of the Wilderness.* Minneapolis, MN: Bethany House, 1993. 239 pp.
Kendra lives with her grandfather in the wilderness until everything changes. (*Series:* Women of the West, 8)
Genre(s): Christian Fiction; Western Fiction.

◆ **1624.** *Love Comes Softly.* Minneapolis, MN: Bethany House, 1979. 192 pp.
When a couple joins in a marriage of convenience, they discover that they have much in common. (*Series:* Love Comes Softly, 1)
Genre(s): Christian Fiction; Family Saga; Romance.

◆ **1625.** *Love's Enduring Promise.* Minneapolis, MN: Bethany House, 1980. 206 pp.
A married couple continues their life on the prairie. (*Series:* Love Comes Softly, 2)
Genre(s): Christian Fiction; Family Saga; Romance.

◆ **1626.** *Love's Long Journey.* Minneapolis, MN: Bethany House, 1982. 207 pp.
A family works together on the prairie. (*Series:* Love Comes Softly, 3)
Genre(s): Christian Fiction; Romance; Family Saga.

1627. *The Measure of the Heart.* Minneapolis, MN: Bethany House, 1992. 222 pp.
Anna Trent feels inadequate as she tries to make her way in an unfamiliar environment, but she discovers that she has unknown strength. (*Series:* Women of the West, 6)
Genre(s): Christian Fiction; Western Fiction.

1628. *Once Upon a Summer.* Minneapolis, MN: Bethany House, 1981. 203 pp.
When an orphan boy's aunt leaves him to marry, he must find his support within himself and God. (*Series:* Seasons of the Heart, 1)
Genre(s): Christian Fiction.

1629. *Spring's Gentle Promise.* Minneapolis, MN: Bethany House, 1989. 224 pp.
Josh decides that he will take over the family farm and the responsibility of the family. (*Series:* Seasons of the Heart, 4)
Genre(s): Christian Fiction; Domestic Fiction.

1630. *They Called Her Mrs. Doc.* Minneapolis, MN: Bethany House, 1992. 222 pp.
Cassandra is unprepared for the lack of culture and manners in the West. (*Series:* Women of the West, 5)
Genre(s): Christian Fiction; Romance; Medical Novel.

1631. *Too Long a Stranger.* Minneapolis, MN: Bethany House, 1994. 383 pp.
When mothers and daughters have to separate, it tests their ability to retain common beliefs. (*Series:* Women of the West, 9)
Genre(s): Christian Fiction; Western Fiction.

1632. *Winter Is Not Forever.* Minneapolis, MN: Bethany House, 1988. 218 pp.
As Josh decides what to do with his life, he becomes more confident in his decisions. (*Series:* Seasons of the Heart, 3)
Genre(s): Christian Fiction.

1633. *A Woman Named Damaris.* Minneapolis, MN: Bethany House, 1991. 287 pp.
A young girl decides that she will no longer tolerate the abuse of her alcoholic father. (*Series:* Women of the West, 4)
Genre(s): Christian Fiction; Domestic Fiction.

Olsen, Theodore V.

1634. *Blood of the Breed.* New York: Simon and Schuster, 1982. 185 pp.
Ike Banner has willed his ranch to his three sons, but rather than work together, each wants the entire ranch for himself.
Genre(s): Western Fiction.

1635. *Mission to the West.* New York: Doubleday, 1973. 181 pp.
When Lt. Stennis Fry leads the First Regiment of the U.S. Dragoons in an intimidation of the Plains Indians, he is disturbed by the unexpected casualties.
Genre(s): War Story.

1636. *Starbuck's Brand.* New York: Doubleday, 1973. 238 pp.
Yankee Perry Starbuck reveals his ambition to a vaquero who hates gringos, and the two of them conflict, but not until Starbuck has time to fall in love and marry.
Genre(s): Western Fiction.

Olson, James Robert

1637. *Ulzana.* Boston: Houghton Mifflin, 1973. 307 pp.
Ulzana, an Apache, serves as a warrior for his people, but near the end of his life, his hopes for his tribe fade.
Genre(s): Biographical Fiction; Western Fiction.

Orcutt, Jane

1638. *The Fugitive Heart.* Colorado Springs, CO: WaterBrook, 1998. 352 pp.
When Samantha Martin reunites with Nathan Hamilton six years after the Civil War, Samantha has become religious while Nathan tends toward larceny.
Genre(s): Romance; Christian Fiction.

Osborn, Karen

1639. *Between Earth and Sky.* New York: Morrow, 1996. 306 pp.
Abigail Conklin goes West with her husband in 1867 and writes her sister for over 60 years about their experiences on the journey and their life in New Mexico.
Genre(s): Western Fiction.

Osborne, Maggie

1640. *The Seduction of Samantha Kincade.* New York: Warner Books, 1995. 384 pp.
Samantha Kincaide searches for Hannibal Cotwell, the man who killed her family, but when she uses an innocent man as a lure, he saves her life, and she must, in turn, prevent him from hanging.
Genre(s): Romance; Western Fiction.

Overholser, Stephen

◆ **1641.** *Molly and the Confidence Man.* New York: Doubleday, 1975. 159 pp.
Molly Owens goes to Colorado to find Charley Castle, a con man, but someone kills her brother, a rider for the Circle 7 Ranch, and Molly decides to look for his killer while Charley looks for her.
Genre(s): Western Fiction; Mystery.

◆ **1642.** *Search for the Fox.* New York: Doubleday, 1976. 181 pp.
John Fox, Confederate general, robs a Richmond, Virginia, bank and goes west to become Colorado's most notorious outlaw, and in 1882, his son promises his mother that he will find him.
Genre(s): Western Fiction.

Overholser, Wayne D.

1643. *The Dry Gulcher.* New York: Dell, 1977. 167 pp.
A cattle baron plans to take land from a homesteader, but Dan Matson, a strong rancher, fights his cash and his guns.
Genre(s): Western Fiction.

Pace, DeWanna

1644. *Our Town.* New York: Jove, 1996. 288 pp.
In 1882, Rachel Sloane travels to Valiant, Texas, where she pretends to be her nasty employer, Johanna Tharp, recently moved to Virginia, and she falls in love with Ben McGuire, the man Johanna rejected.
Genre(s): Romance; Western Fiction.

Paine, Lauran

1645. *Bannon's Law.* New York: Walker, 1982. 160 pp.
Sheriff Tom Carland and physician Joshua Bannon have unusual ideas about keeping peace in the New Mexico Territory, and they put them into action.
Genre(s): Western Fiction.

◆ May be suitable for young adult readers

1646. *Cache Cañon.* Unity, ME: Thorndike, 1998. 170 pp.
Sheriff Charley Bent must cope with a stagecoach robbery and the murder of a cowhand, and he suspects strangers looking for buried Spanish treasure.
Genre(s): Western Fiction.

1647. *Custer Meadow.* New York: Walker, 1988. 182 pp.
When Ellis Bowman arrives with $12,000 cash in his moneybelt, people think he has robbed a bank, but he recovers the real money to exonerate himself.
Genre(s): Western Fiction.

1648. *The Marshal.* New York: Walker, 1985. 154 pp.
A Western town has to deal with a very efficient marshal who murders if necessary to keep law and order.
Genre(s): Western Fiction.

1649. *The New Mexico Heritage.* New York: Walker, 1987. 190 pp.
Someone shoots Maria Antonia, the heir to Lord Land, at the funeral of its owner, and the doctor who saves her falls in love.
Genre(s): Western Fiction.

1650. *Nightrider's Moon.* New York: Walker, 1988. 160 pp.
Old Jorge Medina and his daughter nurse Frank Tennant, wounded on the range, back to health, but since he has $30,000 in his saddle bag, they think Tennant may be a thief, although Tennant claims his uncle stole the money from his mother.
Genre(s): Western Fiction.

◆ 1651. *The Open Range Men.* New York: Walker, 1990. 196 pp.
Since the citizens of Harmonville dislike open range cattlemen, they look the other way when their marshal is involved with the killings of two of Boss Spearman's cattlemen, and Spearman has to achieve justice for himself.
Genre(s): Western Fiction.

1652. *The Prairieton Raid.* New York: Walker, 1994. 168 pp.
Although three men arrive separately in Prairieton, they plan to rob the bank together, but other dishonest men get in their way.
Genre(s): Western Fiction.

◆ 1653. *Skye.* New York: Walker, 1984. 178 pp.
When Frank Cutler and Sam Morton become partners in the west, they argue, fall in love with local women, and search for horse thieves.
Genre(s): Western Fiction.

◆ 1654. *Spirit Meadow.* New York: Walker, 1987. 188 pp.
When an old mountain man forces rangeman Joe Brian to take in a half-Native American boy, Joe carries the child to his widowed, childless sister, but an Indian agent who has made unwelcome advances toward her tries to claim the boy.
Genre(s): Western Fiction.

◆ 1655. *Tanner.* New York: Walker, 1984. 200 pp.
When Will Tanner and his ranch hands search for the Native Americans who stole his cattle, they become hunted by a posse themselves.
Genre(s): Western Fiction.

1656. *The Taurus Gun.* New York: Walker, 1989. 218 pp.
When Native Americans finally let Henry Burke into the foothills around his land, an interloper's hired gun kills Burke's foreman and believes Burke is dead as well.
Genre(s): Western Fiction.

◆ 1657. *Thunder Valley.* New York: Walker, 1993. 204 pp.
Widow Anna Marie Miller dislikes mustanger Ken Castleton until he helps her foil the sheriff's plan for stealing her cattle.
Genre(s): Western Fiction.

Palmer, Catharine

1658. *Prairie Rose.* Wheaton, IL: Tyndale House, 1997. 272 pp.
Orphan Rosie Mills saves the life of a widower homesteader with a young son and helps them overcome their strong anger while they work the farm. (*Series:* A Town Called Hope, 1)
Genre(s): Christian Fiction.

Paretti, Sandra

1659. *Tenants of the Earth.* Trans. Ruth Hein. New York: Evans, 1976. 363 pp.
Craig Matlock's strong rivalry with his father makes him determined to unseat him from the family money after the Civil War, and Matlock obtains his own railway during his quest.

Parker, F. M.

1660. *The Shanghaiers.* Garden City, NY: Doubleday, 1987. 182 pp.
Tom Galatin does not like to kill but considers it as he rescues a Chinese slave girl in San Francisco in 1870 before she returns the favor by keeping him from being shanghaied.
Genre(s): Western Fiction.

Parker, Laura

1661. *Beguiled.* New York: Dell, 1993. 362 pp.
Philadelphia Hunt thinks that her father committed suicide because someone made his bank fail in 1875, and while she investigates, she works for Eduardo Tavares, modeling his Brazilian jewelry in New York while pretending to be a Frenchwoman.
Genre(s): Mystery.

Parr, Delia

1662. *By Fate's Design.* New York: St. Martin's Press, 1996. 358 pp.
An evil guardian decides to sell Shaker Sister JoHannah Sims to the highest bidder.
Genre(s): Romance.

Parry, Richard

1663. *The Winter Wolf.* New York: Forge, 1996. 380 pp.

Wyatt Earp's illegitimate son, raised in a Denver orphanage, hears that his mother has been dead 10 years, but that she has gold for him if he tracks down and kills his no-good father, Wyatt Earp.

Genre(s): Biographical Fiction; Western Fiction.

Patten, Lewis B.

1664. *Ambush at Soda Creek.* New York: Doubleday, 1976. 159 pp.

Hiram Shaver lost his Apache wife and two sons when Colonel Hans Detrick raided his village, and when he encounters Detrick on his way to find Apaches who have taken Detrick's wife, Shaver decides to help.

Genre(s): Western Fiction.

1665. *A Death in Indian Wells.* New York: Doubleday, 1971. 138 pp.

Three buffalo hunters shoot a young Cheyenne brave, and not until the sheriff's son, whose mother is Cheyenne, takes the body home does anyone seem to care.

Genre(s): Western Fiction.

◆ 1666. *Death Rides a Black Horse.* Garden City, NY: Doubleday, 1978. 187 pp.

Jealous foreman Rafe Joslin is next in line after Frank to inherit Frank Halliday's father's land, so Frank must avoid Joslin's plans to kill him.

Genre(s): Western Fiction.

◆ 1667. *The Gallows at Graneros.* New York: Doubleday, 1975. 188 pp.

When Sheriff Thorpe Stedman returns to Graneros after a business trip, he discovers a hanged Apache, and he must find out who did it and why.

Genre(s): Western Fiction.

1668. *Hunt the Man Down.* New York: Doubleday, 1977. 185 pp.

When Mike Logan rides out to see Martha, the widow he plans to marry, during a blizzard, he finds Reese Diamond trying to rape her, and he kills Reese and sets off Reese's family's revenge.

Genre(s): Western Fiction.

1669. *The Killings at Coyote Springs.* New York: Doubleday, 1977. 185 pp.

U.S. Marshal Frank Cole investigates the murders of Arapaho Indians after Custer is defeated at Little Big Horn.

Genre(s): Western Fiction.

1670. *Man Outgunned.* Garden City, NY: Doubleday, 1976. 188 pp.

After criminals come into Placita on July 4, rob the bank, and kidnap, and later kill, a girl, the sheriff vows to track the murderers to hell.

Genre(s): Western Fiction.

1671. *The Ordeal of Jason Ord.* New York: Doubleday, 1973. 183 pp.

Jason Ord, 16, escapes his abusive father, and begins working on a large ranch, but a ranch hand sleeping with the new boss's wife murders his boss within a week, and the two blame Jason for the deed.

Genre(s): Western Fiction.

◆ 1672. *Red Runs the River.* New York: Doubleday, 1970. 181 pp.

A Kansas homesteader looks for the men who killed his family and stole his money in the late 1860s.

Genre(s): Western Fiction.

1673. *Ride a Crooked Trail.* New York: Signet, 1976. 144 pp.

Union soldiers kill Jason's parents in front of him shortly after the Civil War ends, and Jason searches for the three men for revenge.

Genre(s): Western Fiction.

◆ 1674. *Ride a Tall Horse.* New York: Doubleday, 1980. 181 pp.

Jason Cole, 18, works for the deputy marshal while he is gone, and a gunman robs and kills so Jason must work to apprehend the suspect with the help of an Apache girl.

Genre(s): Western Fiction.

1675. *The Tired Gun.* New York: Doubleday, 1973. 162 pp.

In 1879 a man wanted for killing another man's brother returns to the Kansas town where he was once the marshal.

Genre(s): Western Fiction.

◆ 1676. *Trail of the Apache Kid.* New York: Doubleday, 1979. 186 pp.

The Apache Kid is a renegade Native American who wants revenge on Frank Healy, the man who put him in jail, and he starts with Healy's wife.

Genre(s): Western Fiction.

1677. *The Trial of Judas Wiley.* New York: Doubleday, 1972. 161 pp.

A judge and jury confront a small town that has its own law, and when the judge's daughter is kidnapped, the situation becomes violent.

Genre(s): Western Fiction.

Paul, Raymond

1678. *The Bond Street Burlesque.* New York: Norton, 1987. 363 pp.

Quincannon investigates the murder of Dr. Burdell in 19th-century Manhattan after an orphan from Virginia arrives to begin a law career and learn the identity of his biological father.

Genre(s): Mystery.

Pauley, Barbara Anne

1679. *Voices Long Hushed.* Garden City, NY: Doubleday, 1976. 181 pp.

In Boston during the 1880s, a young woman is spurned in love, so she returns to the family home in Mississippi where she finds that her mother is not dead, but has been released from an asylum, and that other unusual things are happening.

Genre(s): Gothic Fiction.

Paulsen, Gary

1680. *Murphy's Gold.* New York: Walker, 1988. 143 pp.

Al Murphy, sheriff of Clincherville, would like to leave the old mining town, but he has no money, and he must find out what happened to Wangsu, the town's Chinese laundryman, in the sequel to *Murphy.*
Genre(s): Western Fiction; Adventure Story.

1681. *Murphy's Herd.* New York: Walker, 1989. 118 pp.

Al Murphy marries Midge, the owner of the Clincherville cafe, and they decide to move to Casper, Wyoming, where someone kills Midge while Murphy is away from the ranch, in the sequel to *Murphy's Gold.*
Genre(s): Western Fiction; Adventure Story.

◆ 1682. *Murphy's Stand.* New York: Walker, 1993. 128 pp.

In the sequel to *Murphy's War,* Al Murphy has settled for alcohol after the death of his love, but when Christine McCormick hires him to protect her supply wagon, he finds renewed interest in life.
Genre(s): Western Fiction.

1683. *Murphy's War.* New York: Walker, 1991. 152 pp.

Sheriff Al Murphy moves to Fletcher, Wyoming, after his wife dies, and when he tries to help a cowhand, a mob beats him and lynches the man in the sequel to *Murphy's Herd.*
Genre(s): Western Fiction; Adventure Story.

Paulsen, Gary, and Brian Burks

◆ 1684. *Murphy's Trail.* New York: Walker, 1996. 144 pp.

Risa Villabisencio asks for Al Murphy's help in finding her husband and two sons who disappeared on their way to Vera Cruz, in the sequel to *Murphy's Stand.*
Genre(s): Western Fiction.

Peart, Jane

◆ 1685. *Destiny's Bride.* Grand Rapids, MI: Zondervan, 1991. 224 pp.

Druscilla Montrose works through her difficulties to get married. (*Series:* Brides of Montclair, 8)
Genre(s): Family Saga; Christian Fiction; Romance.

◆ 1686. *Dreams of a Longing Heart.* Grand Rapids, MI: Revell, 1990. 192 pp.

When orphan Kit Ternan begins working for a family with five boys, she must choose between her faith and an opportunity. (*Series:* Orphan Train West)
Genre(s): Western Fiction; Christian Fiction.

◆ 1687. *The Heart's Lonely Secret.* Grand Rapids, MI: Revell, 1994. 239 pp.

A young girl leaves the circus to join other young people headed west on the orphan trains, hoping to be adopted.
Genre(s): Christian Fiction; Western Fiction.

◆ 1688. *Homeward the Seeking Heart.* Old Tappan, NJ: Revell, 1990. 192 pp.

When Mrs. Vale takes Toddy to look after her invalid daughter, the community will not accept her socially. (*Series:* Orphan Train West)
Genre(s): Christian Fiction; Western Fiction.

◆ 1689. *The Pattern.* Grand Rapids, MI: Zondervan, 1996. 239 pp.

When Johanna Shelby returns home from boarding school in the late 19th century, she meets and marries Ross Davidson, a newcomer, and begins a quilt after their marriage. (*Series:* American Quilt 1)
Genre(s): Christian Fiction; Love Story.

◆ 1690. *The Promise.* Grand Rapids, MI: Zondervan, 1996. 233 pp.

The daughter of JoBeth Davidson of *The Pledge* creates her quilt at the end of her story like her mother and grandmother before her. (*Series:* American Quilt 3)
Genre(s): Christian Fiction; Family Saga.

Pelham, Howard

◆ 1691. *Judas Guns.* New York: Walker, 1990. 192 pp.

When Native Americans capture Janna Dupard's son in a raid, she hires Levi Piddington, an army colonel, to help her find him.
Genre(s): Western Fiction.

Pella, Judith

1692. *Frontier Lady.* Minneapolis, MN: Bethany House, 1993. 398 pp.

Deborah Graham learns on her wedding night that her escape from the Civil War to Texas is worse than she could have imagined. (*Series:* Lone Star Legacy, 1)
Genre(s): Western Fiction; Christian Fiction.

1693. *Stoner's Crossing.* Minneapolis, MN: Bethany House, 1994. 383 pp.

Carolyn Killion comes to Stoner's Crossing to look for her father's legacy and discovers that it is not what she had expected. (*Series:* Lone Star Legacy, 2)
Genre(s): Western Fiction; Christian Fiction.

Pendleton, Tom

1694. *The Seventh Girl.* New York: McGraw Hill, 1970. 224 pp.

The noncombative hero merely wants to marry, but a villain interrupts his plans with his six-guns.
Genre(s): Western Fiction.

Perdue, Tito

1695. *Opportunities in Alabama Agriculture.* Dallas: Baskerville, 1994. 222 pp.

Ben grows up in an Alabama town in the 1870s, marries, gets jobs, and has children, without revealing that he has any interior reflection in his life.
Genre(s): Domestic Fiction.

Perks, Micah

1696. *We Are Gathered Here.* New York: St. Martin's Press, 1996. 291 pp.
When epileptic Regina Sartwell's engagement ends, humiliating the whole family, she leaves home for the Adirondacks, where she meets Olive Honsiger, a miner's wife, who suffers the intensity of their love affair and the political atmosphere of the times.
Genre(s): Domestic Fiction; Political Fiction.

Phillips, Michael R.

◆ 1697. *Grayfox.* Minneapolis, MN: Bethany House, 1993. 304 pp.
Zack Hollister becomes a man and gains a new name.
Genre(s): Christian Fiction; Adventure Story.

◆ 1698. *A Home for the Heart.* Minneapolis, MN: Bethany House, 1994. 313 pp.
When Corrie returns to Miracle Springs, she brings with her a marriage proposal from Christopher. (*Series:* Journals of Corrie Belle Hollister, 9)
Genre(s): Christian Fiction.

Phillips, Thomas Hal

1699. *The Bitterweed Path.* Chapel Hill, NC: University of North Carolina Press, 1996. 314 pp.
After the Civil War in Mississippi, two boys become involved in a homosexual relationship.
Genre(s): Love Story.

Plumb, Charles

1700. *The Tattooed Gun Hand.* New York: Major Books, 1977. 176 pp.
The one man who can defend Lee Barton is shot.
Genre(s): Western Fiction.

Plumlee, Harry James

◆ 1701. *Shadow of the Wolf.* Norman: University of Oklahoma Press, 1997. 206 pp.
Nakaidoklinni, an Apache warrior, becomes a medicine man in the White Mountain Apache band, and as he grows old, whites ruin the way of his people.
Genre(s): Biographical Fiction.

Pomerance, Bernard

1702. *We Need to Dream All This Again.* New York: Viking, 1987. 101 pp.
Crazy Horse and the Sioux battle for their land in the Black Hills with whites who want the gold known to be there.
Genre(s): War Story.

Porter, Donald Clayton

◆ 1703. *Jubilee Jim and the Wizard of Wall Street.* New York: Dutton, 1990. 480 pp.
Jay Gould and Jim Fisk, greedy Gilded Age industrialists, manipulate the stock market during the Great Erie War, but they fail to corner the gold market.

Portis, Charles

◆ 1704. *True Grit.* New York: Simon and Schuster, 1968. 215 pp.
With the help of a disreputable marshal and a Texas Ranger, Mattie Ross, 14, rushes after the man who robbed and killed her father in the 1870s.
Genre(s): Western Fiction.

Potter, Patricia

1705. *Defiant.* New York: Bantam, 1995. 448 pp.
A Colorado rancher wants a stranger to stay and help her so she promises him a horse when the ranch is established, but he feels unworthy.
Genre(s): Romance; Western Fiction.

1706. *Diablo.* New York: Bantam, 1996. 345 pp.
When Kane O'Brien agrees to go to Sanctuary, an outlaw hideout, in return for his life, he does not expect to find an innocent female.
Genre(s): Western Fiction; Romance.

Powell, James

1707. *The Mule Thieves.* New York: Walker, 1986. 192 pp.
Kel O'Day owns a small mining claim in New Mexico, but someone steals his mules, and while searching for them, he meets Ella.
Genre(s): Western Fiction.

◆ 1708. *A Summer with Outlaws.* New York: Walker, 1984. 173 pp.
T.G. Shannon, 18, spends the summer with outlaws who captured him from a train because he could identify them, and he falls in love with the leader's sister.
Genre(s): Western Fiction.

Price, Eugenia

◆ 1709. *The Beloved Invader.* Philadelphia: Lippincott, 1965. 284 pp.
In the sequel to *New Moon Rising*, Anson Dodge helps rebuild a St. Simons Island church vandalized during the Civil War after he comes to look after his wealthy family's business.
Genre(s): Romance; Family Saga.

Prince, Peter

1710. *The Great Circle.* New York: Random House, 1997. 288 pp.
In 1865, 13 diverse passengers on the steamer *Laurentia* cross from Boston to London via Halifax and find out secret things about each other.
Genre(s): Sea Story; Mystery.

◆ May be suitable for young adult readers

Proctor, George W.

1711. *Enemies.* Garden City, NY: Doubleday, 1983. 184 pp.
Gray Horse Running and ex-slave Gideon Ledbetter, a buffalo soldier, continue to encounter one another as they fight in the Texas Comanche wars.
Genre(s): Western Fiction; War Story.

Pronzini, Bill

1712. *The Gallows Land.* New York: Walker, 1983. 159 pp.
In 1879, Roy Boone seeks a new life after the death of his wife and arrives in Arizona only to find a young woman whose husband has brutally beaten her.
Genre(s): Western Fiction; Mystery.

Rølvaag, O. E.

1713. *Giants in the Earth.* New York: Harper and Row, 1927. 465 pp.
Per Hansa and his wife come to the Dakota prairie from Norway, each having a different reaction to the open expanse of land.
Genre(s): Family Saga.

1714. *Peder Victorious.* Trans. Nora O. Solum. New York: Harper and Row, 1929. 350 pp.
In the sequel to *Giants in the Earth*, Peder Victorious adjusts to the family's life in the Dakotas, but his mother refuses to change.
Genre(s): Family Saga.

1715. *Their Father's God.* Trans. Trygve M. Ager. New York: Harper and Row, 1931. 338 pp.
Peder from *Peder Victorious*, completely adapted as a Norwegian American, marries an Irish Catholic girl.
Genre(s): Family Saga.

Rae, Catherine M.

◆ 1716 *Sarah Cobb.* New York: St. Martin's Press, 1990. 181 pp.
Spinster sisters dislike their brother's attitudes and the way he has handled Millicent's illegitimate son, and when he is murdered, they become suspects.
Genre(s): Mystery.

Randisi, Robert J.

1717. *Targett.* New York: M. Evans, 1991. 170 pp.
Targett, a stranger in town, seems to be in between the lawful and the lawless.
Genre(s): Western Fiction.

Rattray, Everett T.

1718. *The Adventures of Jeremiah Dimon.* New York: Pushcart, 1985. 250 pp.
Jeremiah Dimon, 16, grows up in America during the late 19th century, going on picnics and whale hunts and trying sex for the first time.
Award(s): Editor's Book Award from Pushcart Press.
Genre(s): Domestic Fiction.

Rayner, William

1719. *Seth and Belle and Mr. Quarles and Me.* New York: Simon and Schuster, 1973. 157 pp.
While Missouri Fynn awaits execution for a justifiable murder, he tells about being betrayed.
Genre(s): Western Fiction.

Reese, John Henry

◆ 1720. *Halter-Broke.* Garden City, NY: Doubleday, 1977. 183 pp.
Alec, Esther, and Monte help each other to get more out of life on the ranch.
Genre(s): Western Fiction.

1721. *Sequoia Shootout.* New York: Doubleday, 1977. 181 pp.
Former Pinkerton agent Jefferson Hewitt becomes a white slaver named Durango Slim before kidnapping and murdering his old friend's daughter.
Genre(s): Western Fiction.

1722. *A Sheriff for All the People.* New York: Doubleday, 1976. 180 pp.
Sheriff Rodgerson Downey wants to be lieutenant governor of Wyoming if he can find a political gimmick, but other problems, including his wife's interest in a new man in town, sidetrack him.
Genre(s): Western Fiction.

1723. *Springfield.* New York: Doubleday, 1972. 183 pp.
A criminal uses a Springfield gun to kill two men, and after his escape into Mexico, the gun comes to a young deputy about to be sheriff.
Genre(s): Western Fiction.

1724. *Weapon Heavy.* New York: Doubleday, 1973. 159 pp.
A private detective who once worked for Pinkerton has several aliases, but he manages to investigate three cases at one time in Kansas during the late 1800s.
Genre(s): Western Fiction.

1725. *Wes Hardin's Gun.* New York: Doubleday, 1975. 182 pp.
Although people in School Hill, Nebraska, want to hang a young immigrant, Albrecht Raue, for a murder, private investigator Jefferson Hewitt is not convinced that Raue is guilty.
Genre(s): Western Fiction; Mystery.

Reynolds, Clay

1726. *Franklin's Crossing.* New York: Dutton, 1992. 608 pp.
As members of a wagon train cross northern Texas shortly after the Civil War, they face Comanche attacks, the weather, and conflicts with each other.
Genre(s): Western Fiction.

Rhode, Robert

1727. *Sandstone.* New York: Walker, 1982. 130 pp.
Seth March, a cowboy, meets Liz Castle, and they team up to recover stolen goods.
Genre(s): Western Fiction; Romance.

Rhodes, Eugene Manlove

1728. *Bransford in Arcadia.* Norman: University of Oklahoma, 1975. 237 pp.
A western man and an eastern woman meet and fall in love.
Genre(s): Western Fiction; Romance.

Richardson, H.L.

◆ 1729. *The Devil's Eye.* Dallas: Word, 1995. 299 pp.
Sam Dodd fears God but uses his ability to shoot accurately to protect his people in the West.
Genre(s): Western Fiction; Christian Fiction; Mystery.

Richter, Conrad

◆ 1730. *The Lady.* Lincoln, NE: University of Nebraska Press, 1957. 191 pp.
In the 1880s, Ellen Sessions survives a feud with her sister's wicked husband to find that other men in her family have disappeared.
Genre(s): Western Fiction.

◆ 1731. *The Sea of Grass.* New York: Knopf, 1937. 149 pp.
Lutie Brewton leaves her husband and children on the cattle ranch to return to the city, but 20 years later, after desperadoes kill her son, she returns.

Riefe, Barbara

1732. *Desperate Crossing.* New York: Forge, 1997. 320 pp.
After Jenny Pryor survives her capture by Oglala Sioux in 1865, she is forced to become the wife of Chief Ottawa, and the only hope she sustains of returning to her real husband is through a sympathetic Sioux raised by Jesuits.
Genre(s): Western Fiction.

Rikhoff, Jean

1733. *One of the Raymonds.* New York: Dial, 1974. 370 pp.
In the sequel to *Buttes Landing*, Mason Raymond goes to North Carolina to become initiated into manhood.
Genre(s): Bildungsroman (Coming of Age).

1734. *The Sweetwater.* New York: Dial, 1976. 406 pp.
In the sequel to *One of the Raymonds*, John Buttes goes West with his cousin Mason Raymond and they join a black cowpoke and a female outcast on their journey.
Genre(s): Western Fiction.

Riley, Eugenia

1735. *Waltz in Time.* New York: Avon, 1997. 384 pp.
Stephanie Sergeant finds herself in Natchez during 1887, where someone mistakes her for the governess of widower Andre Goddard's five children, and although she herself is attracted to him, she tries to play matchmaker for him.
Genre(s): Romance; Time Travel.

Ripley, Alexandra

1736. *Charleston.* Garden City, NY: Doubleday, 1981. 501 pp.
Two families, the Ansons and the Tradds, cope with the remnants of the Civil War and with Reconstruction as Lizzie Tradd matures into a businesswoman.
Genre(s): Domestic Fiction; Family Saga.

◆ 1737. *Scarlett.* New York: Warner Books, 1991. 823 pp.
In a sequel to Margaret Mitchell's *Gone with the Wind*, Scarlett O'Hara encounters Rhett before going to Ireland to find her family's heritage.
Genre(s): Love Story.

Ritchie, James A.

1738. *Kerrigan.* New York: Walker, 1993. 192 pp.
After Kerrigan has to kill two brothers in Texas, he escapes their father by joining a cattle drive to Alaska where the miners will buy beef at inflated prices.
Genre(s): Western Fiction.

1739. *Over on the Lonesome Side.* New York: Walker, 1991. 192 pp.
Sharpshooter Jim Darnell goes to New Mexico to help a friend keep his ranch from a land grabber, but the marshall is corrupt in the town in which he settles, and the town council appoints him as the sheriff to clean things up.
Genre(s): Western Fiction.

Rochlin, Harriet

◆ 1740. *The Reformer's Apprentice.* Santa Barbara, CA: Fithian, 1996. 224 pp.
Frieda Levie's father, a Polish Orthodox Jewish immigrant, dislikes Frieda's rancher boyfriend and also disapproves of her plans to become a schoolteacher.
Genre(s): Western Fiction.

Roderus, Frank

◆ 1741. *Hell Creek Cabin.* New York: Doubleday, 1979. 183 pp.
Three people caught in a blizzard take shelter with a couple, and the intruders decide on a showdown for gold and for the wife.
Genre(s): Western Fiction.

Ross, Dana Fuller

◆ 1742. *Arizona!* New York: Bantam, 1988. 303 pp.
Traveling through Arizona on the wagon train, Whip Holt encounters Native American parties. (*Series:* Wagons West, 21)
Genre(s): Western Fiction; Adventure Story.

◆ 1743. *California Glory.* New York: Bantam, 1991. 324 pp.
The Holt family works in California to keep out the nefarious men who would destroy the West. (*Series:* An American Dynasty, 4)
Genre(s): Western Fiction; Adventure Story.

◆ 1744. *Carolina Courage.* New York: Bantam, 1991. 353 pp.
In the Carolinas, the Holt family helps to keep the peace. (*Series:* An American Dynasty, 3)
Genre(s): Domestic Fiction.

◆ 1745. *Celebration!* New York: Bantam, 1989. 339 pp.
Whip Holt and his family celebrate the centennial of the United States. (*Series:* Wagons West, 24)
Genre(s): Western Fiction; Adventure Story.

◆ 1746. *Dakota!* New York: Bantam, 1984. 306 pp.
Whip Holt, his children, and friend go through the Dakotas with their wagon train. (*Series:* Wagons West, 11)
Genre(s): Western Fiction; Adventure Story.

1747. *Hawaii Heritage.* New York: Bantam, 1991. 337 pp.
The Holt family examines its contacts in Hawaii. (An American Dynasty, 5)
Genre(s): Domestic Fiction.

1748. *Homecoming.* New York: Bantam, 1994. 370 pp.
The Holts continue their family saga. (*Series:* An American Dynasty, 9)
Genre(s): Western Fiction; Adventure Story.

◆ 1749. *Illinois!* New York: Bantam, 1986. 304 pp.
As wagon train master Whip Holt goes through Chicago, he encounters the Chicago fire of 1871. (*Series:* Wagons West, 18)
Genre(s): Western Fiction; Adventure Story.

◆ 1750. *Kentucky!* New York: Bantam, 1987. 291 pp.
Whip Holt takes a wagon train through Kentucky. (*Series:* Wagons West, 20)
Genre(s): Western Fiction; Adventure Story.

◆ 1751. *New Mexico!* New York: Bantam, 1988. 272 pp.
Whip Holt rolls through New Mexico with his wagon train. (*Series:* Wagons West, 22)
Genre(s): Western Fiction; Adventure Story.

◆ 1752. *Oklahoma!* New York: Bantam, 1989. 304 pp.
The wagon train led by Whip Holt winds through Oklahoma and the Cherokee lands. (*Series:* Wagons West, 23)
Genre(s): Western Fiction; Adventure Story.

◆ 1753. *Oklahoma Pride.* New York: Bantam, 1989. 309 pp.
The Holt family works to overcome men trying to destroy the West. (*Series:* An American Dynasty, 2)
Genre(s): Western Fiction; Domestic Fiction.

◆ 1754. *Oregon Legacy.* New York: Bantam, 1989. 352 pp.
The Holt family members help keep peace among new settlers who followed the Oregon Trail to the West. (*Series:* An American Dynasty, 1)
Genre(s): Domestic Fiction; Western Fiction.

◆ 1755. *Sierra Triumph.* New York: Bantam, 1992. 342 pp.
In the Sierra Nevada, the Holt family continues its quest for justice. (*Series:* An American Dynasty, 6)
Genre(s): Western Fiction; Adventure Story; Domestic Fiction.

◆ 1756. *Wisconsin!* New York: Bantam, 1987. 305 pp.
Whip Holt, his children, and their friend Major Henry Blake travel through Wisconsin. (*Series:* Wagons West, 19)
Genre(s): Western Fiction; Adventure Story.

Rowe, Jack

1757. *Fortune's Legacy.* New York: Watts, 1988. 358 pp.
In the sequel to *Dominion* Alfred du Pont's parents die, and he and his siblings stay together rather than be separated among relatives while they continue the gunpowder works in Brandywine.
Genre(s): Biographical Fiction; Family Saga.

Ruiz de Burton, Maria Amparo

1758. *Who Would Have Thought It?* 1872. Houston, TX: Arte Publico, 1995. 367 pp.
Dr. Norval returns from a trip west with Lola, 10-year-old daughter of a kidnapped Mexican woman, and the townspeople accuse her of being either Indian or black until they find out that she is wealthy.
Genre(s): Satire.

Rushing, Jane Gilmore

1759. *Mary Dove: A Love Story.* Garden City, NY: Doubleday, 1974. 209 pp.
Mary Dove's father has protected her from the prejudice her black blood would cause in West Texas during the early 19th century, but after his death, she can no longer escape discrimination.
Genre(s): Western Fiction; Love Story.

Ryan, Nan

1760. *Because You're Mine.* New York: Topaz, 1995. 384 pp.
Sabella Rios wants the rancho that should have been her inheritance, so she plans to destroy the estate's current owner and ends up falling in love.
Genre(s): Romance; Western Fiction.

1761. *Outlaw's Kiss.* New York: HarperCollins, 1997. 416 pp.
Mollie Rogers finds gold taken from hard-working folk while falling in love with bounty hunter Lew Hatton
Genre(s): Romance; Western Fiction.

Sale, Richard

1762. *The White Buffalo.* New York: Simon and Schuster, 1975. 253 pp.
Wild Bill Hickok and Crazy Horse, two legends, meet as they both pursue a third legend, the white buffalo, in the final days of the Wild West.
Genre(s): Western Fiction; Adventure Story.

Sandoz, Mari

1763. *Son of the Gamblin' Man.* Lincoln, NE: University of Nebraska Press, 1976. 333 pp.
The family of Robert Henri goes west to found a town, endure frontier hardships, and finally settle in Nebraska.
Genre(s): Biographical Fiction; Domestic Fiction; Western Fiction.

Sanford, John A.

◆ 1764. *The Song of the Meadowlark.* New York: Harper and Row, 1986. 297 pp.
The Nez Percé under Chief Joseph leave their home in the Pacific Northwest in 1877 on their 1,700 mile journey to Canada to escape the United States army.
Genre(s): War Story.

Santee, Ross

◆ 1765. *Cowboy.* 1928. Lincoln, NE: University of Nebraska Press, 1977. 257 pp.
A cowboy leaves his East Texas farm to work on a cattle ranch.
Genre(s): Western Fiction.

Santmyer, Helen Hooven

◆ 1766. *. . . And Ladies of the Club.* New York: Putnam, 1982. 1176 pp.
In 1868, a group of women form a literary club in a small Ohio town that lasts for 64 years as the members and the town endure a series of upheavals and changes.
Genre(s): Domestic Fiction.

Savage, Douglas

1767. *Cedar City Rendevous.* New York: M. Evans, 1995. 168 pp.
To rid their town of lawless gunmen, the people of Cedar City, Utah, organize a five-mile race in which the men can shoot all they want and win gold and the governor's pardon.
Genre(s): Western Fiction.

1768. *The Court Martial of Robert E. Lee.* Conshohocken, PA: Combined, 1993. 475 pp.
A Confederate Congress inquires about General Lee's decisions at Gettysburg, and his answers reveal that James Longstreet should not be blamed for Pickett's charge.
Genre(s): Biographical Fiction; Political Fiction.

1769. *The Sons of Grady Rourke.* New York: Evans, 1995. 277 pp.
When Grady Rouke leaves his son Sean out of his will, his other sons Patrick and Liam become the focus of Sean's anger in the Lincoln County War of 1878.
Genre(s): Western Fiction.

Schaefer, Jack

1770. *The Canyon.* Boston: Houghton Mifflin, 1953. 131 pp.
A young Cheyenne hates war and decides to leave his tribe to live in a sheltered canyon.
Genre(s): Western Fiction.

1771. *Monte Walsh.* Boston: Houghton Mifflin, 1963. 442 pp.
Monte, a runaway, becomes a trail hand and then a cowhand, but on his rise to bronco buster, he fails and becomes a saddle bum.
Genre(s): Western Fiction.

◆ 1772. *Shane.* 1947. Boston: Houghton Mifflin, 1982. 214 pp.
Shane rides into the valley where Bob Starrett's family lives, and Bob, 15, tells about Shane's winning ways.
Genre(s): Western Fiction.

Schofield, Susan Clark

1773. *Refugio, They Named You Wrong.* Chapel Hill, NC: Algonquin, 1991. 201 pp.
The law wants Peter Jack Costello, a cattle driver, for the murder of his father and brother, and everywhere he goes, he realizes that he is a wanted man.
Genre(s): Western Fiction.

Scholefield, Alan

◆ 1774. *The Lost Giants.* New York: St. Martin's Press, 1989. 352 pp.
Native Americans capture a visiting Scotswoman, and after the militia rescues her, she has to learn to live in the country with her daughter.

Seelye, John

1775. *The Kid.* New York: Viking, 1972. 119 pp.
When an African American kills a young white male who is bullying him in a small Wyoming town, the trial reveals that the male is actually a female and that four more murders have occurred.
Genre(s): Western Fiction; Mystery.

Segal, Harriet

1776. *Susquehanna.* New York: Doubleday, 1984. 461 pp.
Isaac Hillman emigrates to the Susquehanna River Valley in 1876 from Russia, and he watches two generations of his Jewish family mature.
Genre(s): Family Saga; Jewish Fiction.

Seton, Anya

1777. *Foxfire.* Boston: Houghton Mifflin, 1951. 346 pp.
Unhappy with the isolation of an Arizona mining town, Amanda finally realizes that her marriage to a part-Apache mining engineer is more important than returning East.
Genre(s): Romance.

1778. *The Hearth and Eagle.* Boston: Houghton Mifflin, 1948. 464 pp.
A house built in the 17th century continues to serve as a haven for its inhabitants, including Hesper, who leaves it

twice in the 19th century to marry before returning permanently.

Shelton, Gene

1779. *Tascosa Gun.* New York: Doubleday, 1992. 179 pp.
Cowboy Jim East becomes engaged and plans to settle down, but when he joins a posse following Billy the Kid, he decides to run for sheriff.
Genre(s): Biographical Fiction; Western Fiction.

Sherburne, James

1780. *Death's Pale Horse.* Boston: Houghton Mifflin, 1980. 194 pp.
In Saratoga during the 1880s, the naked dead man discovered in a hotel dumbwaiter leads to intrigues in the racing world involving horses, jockeys, and owners.
Genre(s): Mystery.

Shirreffs, Gordon D.

1781. *The Apache Hunter.* New York: Fawcett, 1976. 240 pp.
Lee Kershaw hunts Yanozha, an Apache who must kill him to restore the great medicine that became imbalanced when Kershaw captured him.
Genre(s): Western Fiction.

Shivers, Louise

◆ 1782. *A Whistling Woman.* Marietta, GA: Longstreet, 1993. 160 pp.
After the end of the Civil War, Georgeanna's mother protects Georgeanna's reputation while she is pregnant, claiming that the new baby in the house is hers.
Genre(s): Gothic Fiction.

Shreve, Susan Richards

◆ 1783. *Daughters of the New World.* New York: Doubleday, 1992. 471 pp.
When Anna goes West with her master's son, her daughter Amanda grows up with the Chippewa, disguises herself as a man, and goes to France as a photographer in World War I.
Genre(s): Domestic Fiction; Family Saga.

Sickels, Nöelle

1784. *The Shopkeeper's Wife.* New York: St. Martin's Press, 1998. 416 pp.
The maid Hanna Willer becomes a suspect when her pregnant employer's shopkeeper husband dies mysteriously in 1886.
Genre(s): Mystery; Domestic Fiction.

Skinner, Gloria Dale

1785. *Cassandra.* New York: Pocket Books, 1998. 310 pp.
Cass has chosen lawyer Dustin Bennett after seeing him in Kansas City in 1889, but she lets him seduce her the day before their wedding, and he leaves her at the altar.
Genre(s): Western Fiction; Romance.

Sledge, Linda Ching

◆ 1786. *A Map of Paradise.* New York: Bantam, 1997. 416 pp.
In the sequel to *Empire of Heaven*, Rulan and Pao An, Chinese exiles in Hawaii during the late 1800s, are separated in what they expect to be paradise with Rulan pregnant in Hawaii while Pao An is alone in California.
Genre(s): Family Saga.

Snelling, Lauraine

1787. *A Land to Call Home.* Minneapolis, MN: Bethany House, 1997. 317 pp.
The Bjorklunds face other challenges in their Dakota community after they establish their farm. (*Series:* Red River of the North, 3)
Genre(s): Family Saga; Christian Fiction.

1788. *A New Day Rising.* Minneapolis, MN: Bethany House, 1996. 368 pp.
As the widow Ingeborg Bjorklund tries to survive in Dakota Territory during 1883, her husband's distant cousin arrives to help.
Genre(s): Christian Fiction; Love Story.

1789. *The Reapers' Song.* Minneapolis, MN: Bethany House, 1998. 368 pp.
The Bjorklund family and their neighbors finally reap the harvests they have so carefully planted as the railroads come, but an accident almost ruins their accomplishments. (*Series:* Red River of the North, 4)
Genre(s): Christian Fiction; Family Saga.

1790. *An Untamed Land.* Minneapolis, MN: Bethany House, 1996. 352 pp.
The Bjorklund family comes through New York from Norway to North Dakota, where they struggle to create a farm through a difficult first winter. (*Series:* Red River of the North, 1)
Genre(s): Christian Fiction; Western Fiction.

Somtow, S.P.

1791. *Darker Angels.* New York: St. Martin's Press, 1998. 384 pp.
When the British widow of the Reverend Grainger comes to his New York viewing and meets Walt Whitman, he tells her of Civil War horrors and the dark magic of Reverend Grainger's previously unknown secret life.
Genre(s): Gothic Fiction.

Southard, W. W.

1792. *Season of Vengeance.* New York: Bantam, 1981. 192 pp.
Jessie Ramming relentlessly pursues the murderer of his wife and unborn child in New Mexico.
Genre(s): Western Fiction.

Spanbauer, Tom

1793. *The Man Who Fell in Love with the Moon.* New York: Atlantic Monthly, 1991. 384 pp.
Near the end of Idaho's gold rush, Duivichi-un-Dua, known as Shed, lives in a town with people who seem

crazed, but he trusts his own inner strength, which he calls "killdeer."
Genre(s): Bildungsroman (Coming of Age); Western Fiction.

Spellman, Cathy Cash

1794. *Paint the Wind.* New York: Delacorte, 1989. 713 pp.
After Fancy Deverell loses her parents in the Civil War, she joins a circus train and travels westward.
Genre(s): Western Fiction.

Spencer, LaVyrle

1795. *Forgiving.* New York: Putnam, 1991. 381 pp.
When Sarah Merritt arrives in Deadwood in 1876, she plans to find her sister Addie and use her sister's printing press to start a newspaper.
Genre(s): Western Fiction; Love Story; Romance.

Stambaugh, Sara

◆ 1796. *I Hear the Reaper's Song.* Intercourse, PA: Good Books, 1984. 221 pp.
In a Pennsylvania Mennonite community, the Hershey family's tragedies in the 19th century lead them to take respite in their faith.
Genre(s): Christian Fiction.

Stark, Cruce

1797. *Chasing Uncle Charley.* Dallas: Southern Methodist University Press, 1992. 371 pp.
Bo Johnson, 17, leaves his Texas hometown to find his Uncle Charley, who had left years before after shooting two people.
Genre(s): Western Fiction; Bildungsroman (Coming of Age).

Steel, Danielle

1798. *Thurston House.* New York: Dell, 1983. 500 pp.
In the 1880s, Jeremiah Thurston begins to love again in his forties after the death of his fiance, and after marrying the very young Camille, he finds himself in his Nob Hill mansion with a daughter to raise after Camille runs away.
Genre(s): Romance; Family Saga.

Steelman, Robert J.

1799. *The Prairie Baroness.* Garden City, NY: Doubleday, 1981. 182 pp.
When Baron de Fleury, who lives in a lovely chateau, is accused of murdering his friend Emile, young Lutie's life undergoes change.
Genre(s): Western Fiction.

◆ 1800. *Sun Boy.* New York: Doubleday, 1975. 204 pp.
Kiowas capture Philip Rainbolt, ex-Confederate officer and accused killer, convinced that he is Pai Talyi, the Sun Boy sent by the gods.
Genre(s): Western Fiction.

Stegner, Wallace Earle

1801. *Angle of Repose.* Garden City, NY: Doubleday, 1971. 569 pp.
Susan and her engineer husband live rough lives in mining camps during the late 19th century, and their marriage cannot survive.
Award(s): Pulitzer Prize.
Genre(s): Western Fiction.

Stensland, Doris

1802. *Haul the Water, Haul the Wood.* Aberdeen, SD: North Plains, 1977. 209 pp.
The Overseths go to South Dakota and live the difficult life of a pioneer family in the 19th century.
Genre(s): Biographical Fiction.

Stevenson, Melody

1803. *The Life Stone of Singing Bird.* Boston: Faber And Faber, 1996. 175 pp.
India dies and tells about her family from the grave, especially about the Life Stone, given to her mother by the Native American woman whose child her own mother adopted and named Boy Found.
Genre(s): Western Fiction; Domestic Fiction.

Stewart, Fred Mustard

1804. *The Young Savages.* New York: Tor, 1998. 304 pp.
Justin Savage's half-Chinese daughter leaves the snobbishness of New York for San Francisco and marriage to a gambler, while his son Johnny explores with Theodore Roosevelt before Johnny joins his sister to wander around Europe in the 1880s.
Genre(s): Adventure Story.

Stone, Irving

1805. *Adversary in the House.* Garden City, NY: Doubleday, 1947. 432 pp.
Because of disagreements with his wife, Eugene Debs thinks that his main adversary lives in the same house with him.
Genre(s): Biographical Fiction.

1806. *Immortal Wife.* Garden City, NY: Doubleday, 1944. 450 pp.
Jessie Benton marries John Charles Fremont at 16 and focuses her energy on her husband's career for the rest of her life.
Genre(s): Biographical Fiction.

Storm, Hyemeyohsts

1807. *Seven Arrows.* New York: Harper and Row, 1972. 371 pp.
The Cheyenne, a peaceful people, resist the advances of the white man and continue their pre-Christian Sun Dance religion.
Genre(s): Religious Fiction.

Stover, Deb

1808. *Almost An Angel.* New York: Pinnacle, 1997. 384 pp.
Hilary Brown has to help someone else to get into heaven, and in the streets of Columbine, Colorado, she meets the right person, but she ends up in the town with him during the 19th century.
Genre(s): Romance; Time Travel; Western Fiction.

Streshinsky, Shirley

1809. *Birds of Prey.* New York: Putnam, 1982. 360 pp.
Disabled Lena Kerr goes west to live with her sister in California in the 1880s, and the lives of family and friends change as the land around them develops.
Genre(s): Domestic Fiction.

Stribling, T. S.

1810. *The Store.* New York: Doubleday, 1932. 571 pp.
In 1884, in the sequel to *The Forge*, Colonel Miltiades Vaiden settles down to a boring life after fighting at Shiloh and leading a group of the Klan during Reconstruction.
Genre(s): Domestic Fiction.

1811. *The Unfinished Cathedral.* New York: Doubleday, 1934. 305 pp.
Colonel Milt Vaiden, an old man and one of the wealthiest citizens in Florence, Alabama, has a nephew, Jerry Catlin, who becomes a Methodist minister, in the sequel to *The Store*.
Genre(s): Domestic Fiction.

Stuart, Anne

◆ 1812. *Cameron's Landing.* New York: Doubleday, 1977. 224 pp.
Lorna MacDougall becomes a companion to an old woman on a private island on the Maine coast who wants her to investigate the murder of her husband.
Genre(s): Romance; Mystery.

Stuart, Colin

1813. *Walks Far Woman.* New York: Dial, 1976. 342 pp.
In 1940, 90-year-old Walks Far tells her grandson about the exploits of her Blackfoot people, including the Battle of Little Big Horn.
Genre(s): Adventure Story.

Sutcliffe, Katherine

1814. *Jezebel.* New York: Jove, 1997. 336 pp.
Rafael de Bastitas takes shelter from a storm inside a cabin where Charity Bell, the preacher's widow, is giving birth, and he looks after her and the baby before becoming a gunslinger.
Genre(s): Western Fiction; Romance.

Svee, Gary D.

1815. *Incident at Pishkin Creek.* New York: Walker, 1989. 192 pp.
Catherine O'Dowd arrives from Ireland in Montana via Boston to answer Max Bass's advertisement for a wife, shocked to find her home a dugout, but finds that she and Max are equal in temperament.
Genre(s): Western Fiction.

◆ 1816. *Sanctuary.* New York: Walker, 1990. 192 pp.
Itinerant preacher Mordecai arrives in Sanctuary preaching "love for all humans" and annoys the local reverend as well as the wealthy rancher who detests the Indians.
Award(s): Western Writers of America Spur Award
Genre(s): Western Fiction; Allegory.

◆ 1817. *Single Tree.* New York: Walker, 1994. 191 pp.
In 1884, vigilantes are killing anyone in Montana, and Samuel Wilders arrives with his family only to disappear forever, but a Cree rescues those remaining.
Genre(s): Western Fiction.

Swan, Susan Elizabeth

1818. *The Biggest Modern Woman of the World.* New York: Ecco, 1986. 340 pp.
Anna Swan, daughter of Nova Scotia crofters, becomes an attraction in P.T. Barnum's circus in the 1860s because of her 7-foot, 6-inch height.
Genre(s): Biographical Fiction.

Tarkington, Booth

1819. *The Magnificent Ambersons.* Garden City, NY: Doubleday, 1918. 516 pp.
George Amberson Minafer, an arrogant third-generation member of his family, becomes a man during the early days of the automobile.
Genre(s): Domestic Fiction.

Taylor, Janelle

1820. *Chase the Wind.* New York: Kensington, 1994. 391 pp.
Bethany Wind and Navarro Breed marry so that they can travel together as government agents to uncover illegal gunrunning, and they discover in the course of their search that their marriage is more than a coverup.
Genre(s): Romance; Western Fiction.

1821. *Taking Chances.* New York: Severn House, 1996. 559 pp.
Kirsten Lowry tries to forget her past by moving West and restarting her life.
Genre(s): Western Fiction; Romance.

Taylor, Robert Lewis

1822. *Journey to Matecumbe.* New York: McGraw Hill, 1961. 424 pp.
Davey, his uncle, and a black servant escape down the Mississippi River from Kentucky to Key West in 1875, trying to evade the Ku Klux Klan.
Genre(s): Adventure Story.

◆ 1823. *A Roaring in the Wind.* New York: Putnam, 1978. 347 pp.
Ross Nickerson, with money given him by his aunt, goes West to make a fortune, but discovers that money is illusive.
Genre(s): Western Fiction.

Thoene, Bodie

1824. *Sequoia Scout.* Minneapolis, MN: Bethany House, 1991. 240 pp.
Caught in a clash of cultures, a young trader must decide what is right. (*Series:* Saga of the Sierras, 3)
Genre(s): Christian Fiction; Western Fiction.

1825. *Shooting Star.* Minneapolis, MN: Bethany House, 1993. 208 pp.
The first cattle drive in California occurs with the help of Andrew Jackson Sinnickson. (*Series:* Saga of the Sierras, 7)
Genre(s): Christian Fiction; Western Fiction.

1826. *The Year of the Grizzly.* Minneapolis, MN: Bethany House, 1992. 192 pp.
Will Reed becomes involved in a California land war. (*Series:* Saga of the Sierras, 6)
Genre(s): Christian Fiction; Western Fiction.

Thoene, Brock

1827. *Gold Rush Prodigal.* Minneapolis, MN: Bethany House, 1991. 223 pp.
When David Bollin goes to California expecting great wealth, he gains it in the gold fields but loses it just as quickly. (*Series:* Saga of the Sierras, 3)
Genre(s): Christian Fiction; Western Fiction.

1828. *The Legend of Storey County.* Nashville, TN: Thomas Nelson, 1995. 238 pp.
Seth Townsend comes to Virginia City, Nevada, where he meets elderly ex-slave Jim Canfield, and Canfield's story is so interesting that Seth writes about the Jim who was saved by Sam, a riverboat captain, and fought in Civil War battles.
Genre(s): Christian Fiction; Western Fiction.

1829. *The Man from Shadow Ridge.* Minneapolis, MN: Bethany House, 1990. 239 pp.
When Tom Dunlap decides to go West, he thinks that he has left the Civil War, but an incident brings it back to him. (*Series:* Saga of the Sierras, 1)
Genre(s): Christian Fiction; Western Fiction.

1830. *Riders of the Silver Rim.* Minneapolis, MN: Bethany House, 1990. 204 pp.
Joshua Roberts goes West to seek his fortune, but he finds trouble instead. (*Series:* Saga of the Sierras, 2)
Genre(s): Christian Fiction; Western Fiction.

Thomas, Jodi

◆ 1831. *To Tame a Texan's Heart.* New York: Berkley, 1994. 320 pp.
When her publisher demands that True McCormick, who writes dime novels under a pseudonym, do a book tour, she hires a man to impersonate her.
Award(s): Romance Writers of America RITA Award.
Genre(s): Romance.

Thompson, Thomas

1832. *Outlaw Valley.* Garden City, NY: Doubleday, 1987. 183 pp.
With the help of a prison parolee and a drifter, Opal Sprague herds mules for the army over the Sierra Nevadas to save her ranch.
Genre(s): Western Fiction.

Tippette, Giles

1833. *The Bank Robber.* New York: Macmillan, 1970. 224 pp.
Wilson Young wants to do one last bank robbery before settling down with a wife in Mexico.
Genre(s): Western Fiction.

Toepfer, Ray

1834. *The Stage from Deadwood.* New York: M. Evans, 1993. 168 pp.
Charlie Poker Pearse escorts Mary Lou Reilly, who carries money for her fiancé, from Deadwood to Julesburg, Colorado, and a couple wanting the money pursues them.
Genre(s): Western Fiction.

Traver, Robert

1835. *Laughing Whitefish.* New York: McGraw Hill, 1965. 312 pp.
An Ojibwa girl files a lawsuit against a powerful mining company in Marquette, Michigan, during 1873.
Genre(s): Legal Story; Political Fiction.

Trevanian

1836. *Incident at Twenty Mile.* New York: St. Martin's Press, 1998. 320 pp.
When a stranger arrives in Twenty Mile, a town near nowhere, he begins events which lead to a major showdown.
Genre(s): Western Fiction.

Trump, Gary

1837. *Roughshod.* Independence, OR: Tag, 1990. 314 pp.
Randal, a sheriff, has only an inexperienced officer to help him overcome the villains in his Oregon town.
Genre(s): Western Fiction.

Tryon, Thomas

1838. *In the Fire of Spring.* New York: Knopf, 1992. 609 pp.
In the sequel to *The Wings of the Morning*, runaway slave Rose Mills finds safety with the Talcotts, who infuriate the slave-owning Grimes family by opening a school for young black women.
Genre(s): Family Saga.

Turnbull, Agnes Sligh

1839. *The Rolling Years.* New York: Macmillan, 1936. 436 pp.
Jeannie and her daughter Connie live in a Scottish Presbyterian community in western Pennsylvania after the Civil War.
Genre(s): Domestic Fiction.

Turner, Nancy E.

◆ 1840. *These Is My Words: The Diary of Sarah Agnes Prine.* New York: HarperCollins, 1998. 384 pp.

In 1881, Sarah Agnes Prine, 17, goes from New Mexico to Texas and back, protecting her family with her rifle, and then becoming ranch manager while her second husband serves as a Texas Ranger.

Genre(s): Western Fiction; Domestic Fiction.

Ulyatt, Kenneth

1841. *North against the Sioux.* Englewood Cliffs, NJ: Prentice Hall, 1967. 224 pp.

Soldiers build Fort Phil Kearny, but Chief Red Cloud leads a group of Sioux, Cheyenne, and Arapaho that destroys it.

Genre(s): War Story; Western Fiction.

Underwood, Phillip

◆ 1842. *Ben Cooper, U.S. Marshal.* New York: Walker, 1990. 192 pp.

Marshal Cooper oversees Mexican Hat until Deke Chambers and his sons arrive and try to capture anyone they think may know where a treasure is hidden.

Genre(s): Western Fiction.

◆ 1843. *Lee Tanner.* New York: Walker, 1989. 189 pp.

Lee Tanner wants to establish a small horse ranch, and banker John Tate wants to help him and get him married to his daughter, but murder intervenes in the post-Civil War West.

Genre(s): Western Fiction; Mystery.

Vance, William E.

◆ 1844. *Law and Outlaw.* Garden City, NY: Doubleday, 1982. 179 pp.

U. S. Marshal Will Titus searches for Bart Laney, and although they were raised like brothers, they face each other in a showdown.

Genre(s): Western Fiction.

Vernam, Glenn R.

1845. *Redman in White Moccasins.* New York: Doubleday, 1973. 181 pp.

Young Native American Tom Little Bear and a ranch-hand go trapping in a dangerous canyon.

Genre(s): Western Fiction.

Vernon, John

1846. *All for Love: Baby Doe and Silver Dollar.* New York: Simon and Schuster, 1995. 235 pp.

Baby Doe, a selfish social climber, loves and marries Horace Tabor, a mine owner in Colorado, in 1883, but he loses all their money.

Genre(s): Western Fiction; Biographical Fiction.

Vestal, Stanley

◆ 1847. *Happy Hunting Grounds.* 1928. Norman, OK: University of Oklahoma Press, 1975. 219 pp.

A wounded Mandan to whom Whirlwind, a Cheyenne chief, has given shelter, betrays him by killing Whirl-

wind's son, taking one of his wives, and beginning a battle with the Sioux.

Genre(s): Western Fiction.

Vidal, Gore

1848. *1876.* New York: Random House, 1976. 364 pp.

In the sequel to *Burr*, Charlie Schuyler, a political journalist, loses money in the crash of 1872 and returns from France, where he has lived for four decades, to New York. (*Series:* American Chronicle, 3)

Genre(s): Political Fiction.

Vories, Eugene C.

1849. *Saddle a Whirlwind.* New York: Walker, 1990. 208 pp.

When her brother hurts his ankle, Becky Major manages the family ranch, and Clint Austin comes to help her.

Genre(s): Western Fiction.

Waldo, Anna Lee

1850. *Prairie.* New York: Berkley, 1987. 1120 pp.

Charles B. Irwin, a successful and influential farmer, produces a Wild West show and becomes superintendent of the Union Pacific Railroad at the turn of the century.

Genre(s): Biographical Fiction.

Walker, James

1851. *The Desert Hawks.* Minneapolis, MN: Bethany House, 1996. 336 pp.

When Zac Cobb finds out that his bandit brother is guilty of robbing army payrolls and murdering army escorts, he faces the dilemma of family versus duty. (*Series:* Wells Fargo Trail, 5)

Genre(s): Western Fiction; Christian Fiction.

1852. *The Dreamgivers.* Minneapolis, MN: Bethany House, 1994. 224 pp.

Zac Cobb becomes involved in a series of payroll robberies, which places him in a confrontation with figures from the underworld. (*Series:* Wells Fargo Trail, 1)

Genre(s): Western Fiction; Christian Fiction.

1853. *The Nightriders.* Minneapolis, MN: Bethany House, 1994. 271 pp.

When innocent men are hanged, Zachary Cobb arrives seeking vengeance with his sawed-off shotgun. (*Series:* Wells Fargo Trail, 2)

Genre(s): Western Fiction; Christian Fiction.

1854. *The Oyster Pirates.* Minneapolis, MN: Bethany House, 1996. 336 pp.

While Zac Cobb investigates disappearing gold shipments, his adopted son and a young oyster pirate are kidnapped. (*Series:* Wells Fargo Trail, 6)

Genre(s): Western Fiction; Christian Fiction.

◆ 1855. *The Rail Kings.* Minneapolis, MN: Bethany House, 1995. 301 pp.

When the Chicago Pacific Company tries to kidnap the family of General Sydney Roberts, president of the Denver and Rio Grande Railroad, Zac Cobb rescues them but becomes involved with the race for railroad revenues. (*Series:* Wells Fargo Trail, 3)

Genre(s): Western Fiction; Christian Fiction.

1856. *The Rawhiders.* Minneapolis, MN: Bethany House, 1995. 334 pp.
Four sisters drive their father's herd of longhorns from Texas to Kansas while trying to save the family ranch. (*Series:* Wells Fargo Trail, 4)
Genre(s): Western Fiction; Christian Fiction.

1857. *The Warriors.* Minneapolis, MN: Bethany House, 1997. 336 pp.
In the 1870s, the Secret Service asks Zac Cobb and his brothers to go to Mexico to rescue their outlaw brother, and Zac begins to suspect the government's motives. (*Series:* Wells Fargo Trail, 7)
Genre(s): Western Fiction; Christian Fiction.

Walker, Jim

1858. *The Ice Princess.* Minneapolis, MN: Bethany House, 1998. 336 pp.
Zac Cobb follows his love Jenny to Sitka where she has gone to find her sister, and he discovers that someone wanting to destroy Jenny's family has poisoned her uncle Ian. (*Series:* Wells Fargo Trail, 8)
Genre(s): Christian Fiction; Western Fiction.

Walker, Margaret

1859. *Jubilee.* Boston: Houghton Mifflin, 1966. 497 pp.
In the South, freed people, poor whites, and landowners survive the Civil War and begin Reconstruction.
Genre(s): War Story.

Ward, Jonas

1860. *Buchanan's Texas Treasure.* New York: Fawcett, 1977. 158 pp.
Tom Buchanan helps widow Molly Cuesta defend herself against a ruthless neighbor and find a family treasure.
Genre(s): Western Fiction.

Washburn, L. J.

◆ 1861. *Red River Ruse.* New York: M. Evans, 1991. 179 pp.
In the 1880s, Billy Cambridge, a retired Texas Ranger turned lawyer is robbed on a stagecoach, he and Nacho Graves set out to find the thieves.
Genre(s): Western Fiction.

Waters, Frank

1862. *Pike's Peak.* Athens, OH: Swallow, 1971. 743 pp.
When Joseph Rogier comes to live near Pike's Peak in the 1870s, he works as a contractor and prospers, but he loses everything when he pursues his dreams.
Genre(s): Epic Literature.

Watkins, Emerson

1863. *The Story of a Forgotten Hero.* New York: Oxford, 1995. 240 pp.
Tippy Pendarvis, last known survivor of the U.S. Tenth Calvary, escapes his slave-like conditions on a southern potato plantation in 1880.
Genre(s): Domestic Fiction.

Watson, Peter

1864. *Capo.* New York: Trafalgar Square, 1997. 464 pp.
The Mafia comes to power in New Orleans during the 19th century.
Genre(s): Political Fiction.

Wellman, Paul Iselin

1865. *The Comancheros.* Garden City, NY: Doubleday, 1952. 286 pp.
Paul Regret leaves New Orleans after a duel and joins the Texas Rangers.
Genre(s): Western Fiction.

Wells, Marian

1866. *The Wedding Dress.* Minneapolis, MN: Bethany House, 1982. 263 pp.
Rebecca thinks that marriage will be good for her widowed mother.
Genre(s): Christian Fiction.

1867. *With this Ring.* Minneapolis, MN: Bethany House, 1995. 224 pp.
A mother takes her daughter's advice and remarries.
Genre(s): Christian Fiction; Romance.

Welty, Eudora

1868. *Delta Wedding.* New York: Harcourt Brace, 1979. 247 pp.
The Fairchild family, living on their Mississippi delta plantation, plans for the wedding of Dabney, a favorite child.
Genre(s): Domestic Fiction.

West, Jessamyn

1869. *The Friendly Persuasion.* New York: Harcourt Brace, 1945. 214 pp.
The Birdwell family of Quakers lives in Indiana following the Civil War, in the sequel to *Except for Me and Thee.*

Wharton, Edith

1870. *The Age of Innocence.* New York: Simon and Schuster, 1998. 320 pp.
Wealthy New Yorkers in the 1870s have difficulties breaking free from social codes they hate.
Award(s): Pulitzer Prize.
Genre(s): Domestic Fiction; Love Story.

Wheeler, Richard S.

1871. *Cashbox.* New York: Forge, 1994. 381 pp.
Beginning in 1888, Cashbox, Montana, site of silver mining, becomes the place for many different people hoping for money to finance their dreams.
Genre(s): Western Fiction

◆ 1872. *Dodging Red Cloud.* New York: Evans, 1987. 198 pp.
When the U.S. Army withdraws from Sioux territory in Montana during 1868, Wiley Smart, Hannah Holt, and 12-year-old Linc find themselves joined as Crow captives.
Genre(s): Western Fiction; War Story.

◆ May be suitable for young adult readers

1873. *Flint's Truth.* New York: Forge, 1998. 352 pp.

In 1870, Sam Flint sets up his newspaper in Oro Blanco, New Mexico, a gold-mining town, and as he looks for stories, he finds a conspiracy involving almost everyone in town.

Genre(s): Western Fiction.

◆ 1874. *Montana Hitch.* New York: Evans, 1990. 174 pp.

Albert Dent tries to please his wife, who thinks he is weak, but when a Civil War survivor comes and makes advances toward his ranch and his wife, Dent patiently fights back.

Genre(s): Western Fiction.

◆ 1875. *Richard Lamb.* New York: Walker, 1987. 168 pp.

Richard Lamb, trader and friend of the Blackfoot, pays a price for trying to protect them from two ambitious white brothers.

Genre(s): Western Fiction.

1876. *Stop.* New York: Evans, 1988. 197 pp.

Sheriff Elmer Dudley convenes a posse of gold miners to confront brothers who plan to take over Ben Waldorf's productive gold mine.

Genre(s): Western Fiction.

White, Carolyn

◆ 1877. *Ghostroad.* Berkeley, CA: Creative Arts, 1989. 264 pp.

In 1882, Helen Fleur shoots her husband, a man she never should have married, and escapes a posse as she travels through Wyoming with the help of Sioux as she slowly becomes mentally unbalanced.

Genre(s): Western Fiction; Adventure Story.

White, Stewart Edward

1878. *Rose Dawn.* New York: Doubleday, 1920. 369 pp.

In California during the 1880s, small fruit orchard owners begin to threaten the big rancheros, and Colonel Peyton gains the help of his staff and neighbors in trying to preserve his ranch, Corona del Monte. (*Series:* California Trilogy, 3)

Genre(s): Western Fiction; Adventure Story.

Wick, Lori

1879. *Donovan's Daughter.* Eugene, OR: Harvest House, 1994. 312 pp.

After Patrick's daughter Marcail becomes a schoolteacher in Willits, she is snowed in with the bachelor doctor at his home, and the townspeople condemn her for the unavoidable situation. (*Series:* The Californians, 4)

Genre(s): Christian Fiction.

1880. *Sean Donovan.* Eugene, OR: Harvest House, 1993. 269 pp.

When Sean Donovan is sentenced to hang after his first bank robbery, Charlotte Cooper decides to save him by marrying him. (Californians, 3)

Genre(s): Christian Fiction; Romance.

Wiggs, Susan

1881. *Lightkeeper.* New York: Harlequin, 1997. 377 pp.

Solitary Jesse Morgan tends the lighthouse at Cape Disappointment in Washington territory around 1876 where he rescues a pregnant young Irishwoman, Mary Dare, who changes his life.

Genre(s): Romance; Western Fiction.

Wilder, Robert

1882. *God Has a Long Face.* New York: Putnam, 1940. 461 pp.

After the Civil War, G. Basil Wallis Burgoyne deserts and goes to Florida where he marries and starts a family before returning to his hometown of Cincinnati.

Genre(s): Domestic Fiction; Adventure Story.

Willard, Tom

1883. *Buffalo Soldiers.* New York: Forge, 1996. 331 pp.

In 1869, August Sharps, free from Kiowa captors, enlists in the Tenth U. S. Cavalry and spends his days as a soldier at Fort Wallace, Kansas, until he and his wife retire to Arizona.

Genre(s): Western Fiction; War Story.

Williams, Jeanne

◆ 1884. *Home Mountain.* New York: St. Martin's Press, 1990. 400 pp.

In 1880, orphaned Katie McLeod takes her siblings, livestock, and Irish harp to Arizona from Texas, where she plans to succeed on a ranch.

Award(s): Western Writers of America Spur Award.

Genre(s): Romance; Western Fiction.

1885. *Wind Water.* New York: St. Martin's Press, 1997. 352 pp.

Julie roams over the plains with her adoptive father building windmills, but after tragedy, she has to settle in Oklahoma territory and try to keep her land as well as that of her neighbors from the greedy Colonel Chandless.

Genre(s): Bildungsroman (Coming of Age).

Williamson, Penelope

1886. *Heart of the West.* New York: Simon and Schuster, 1995. 591 pp.

In Montana during the 1880s, Clementine runs off with Gus McQueen to escape her parents, but when she arrives at his ranch, she becomes more interesed in his brother.

Genre(s): Western Fiction.

1887. *The Outsider.* New York: Simon and Schuster, 1996. 464 pp.

Widowed Rachel Yoder, who lives with her young son on a sheep ranch, takes in a wounded gunman and nurses him to health.

Genre(s): Western Fiction; Love Story.

1888. *The Passions of Emma.* New York: Warner Books, 1997. 422 pp.

Emma Tremayne expects to avoid scandal and marry well until a young boy dies working in the mill of her fi-

ancé's father and she meets Irish activist Shay McKenna during the late 19th century.
Genre(s): Romance.

Wilson, Dorothy Clarke

◆ 1889. *Alice and Edith.* New York: Doubleday, 1989. 400 pp.
Alice Lee and Edith Carow marry Theodore Roosevelt, one after the death of the other, and both live at Sagamore Hill.
Genre(s): Biographical Fiction.

Wise, John S.

◆ 1890. *The Lion's Skin.* 1905. North Stratford, NH: Ayers, 1940. 404 pp.
Powatan Carrington fights for the Confederacy and after turning Republican, leaves Richmond for New York and success.

Wisler, G. Clifton

1891. *Antelope Springs.* New York: Walker, 1986. 192 pp.
In the 1880s, killers take Everett Raymond and his family hostage while planning a stagecoach robbery.
Genre(s): Western Fiction.

◆ 1892. *Boswell's Luck.* New York: Evans, 1990. 168 pp.
Orphan Rat Hadley gets a job as a guard for the Western Stage Company, and his ability to use a gun and his instinct for detecting trouble gain him respect in his hometown.
Genre(s): Western Fiction.

1893. *Lakota.* New York: Henry Holt, 1989. 180 pp.
Tacante, a Lakota, learns about war against the Crow and Snake tribes, but they do not prepare him for defending tribal land against the whites who want it, including Custer.
Genre(s): War Story.

◆ 1894. *The Return of Caulfield Blake.* New York: Henry Holt, 1988. 180 pp.
After the Civil War, Caulie Blake returns to Simpson, Texas, and after becoming the sheriff, he hangs land baron Henry Simpson's son for murdering a judge and loses almost everything, including his wife.
Genre(s): Western Fiction.

1895. *The Trident Brand.* Garden City, NY: Doubleday, 1982. 179 pp.
Willie Delamer wants to return to his Texas ranch after the Civil War, but his ambitious brother has decided that he will keep ownership of the ranch at any cost.
Genre(s): Western Fiction.

Wister, Owen

◆ 1896. *The Virginian.* 1902. New York: Pocket, 1977. 364 pp.
Americans show their faith as they work to survive in the Wyoming frontier.
Award(s): Western Writers of America Spur Award.
Genre(s): Western Fiction.

Wolfe, Lois

1897. *Mask of Night.* New York: Doubleday, 1993. 384 pp.
Kate Henslowe's 19th-century traveling theater needs bookings, and her brother gets one in St. Louis, where he has a contact with unscrupulous Julian Gates, a man who needs connections to opium and drugs to save his business.
Genre(s): Romance.

Woods, E. Z.

◆ 1898. *The Bloody Sands.* New York: New American Library, 1988. 185 pp.
Jess McClaren helps Joe Ed Whitley find out who is rustling his cattle in New Mexico.
Genre(s): Western Fiction.

Worcester, Donald Emmet

1899. *The War in the Nueces Strip.* New York: Doubleday, 1989. 182 pp.
The governor of Texas directs Captain Lee McNelly, former Confederate soldier, to clean up the areas around the Nueces Strip in the mid-1870s, and he hires hardened men to help him.
Genre(s): Western Fiction; Biographical Fiction.

Yarbro, Chelsea Quinn

1900. *Charity, Colorado.* New York: M. Evans, 1994. 240 pp.
Jason Russell, sheriff of Charity, Colorado, formerly of England and Australia, works to settle a Spanish land-grant dispute and catch a serial killer, in the sequel to *The Law in Charity*.
Genre(s): Western Fiction; Adventure Story.

Yarnall, Sophia

1901. *The Clark Inheritance.* New York: Walker, 1981. 237 pp.
The Clark family tries to improve the family coal mine in Pennsylvania beginning in 1871 and continuing to 1902.
Genre(s): Political Fiction.

Yerby, Frank

1902. *Western.* New York: Dial, 1982. 447 pp.
Ethan Lovejoy leaves New England for Kansas after the death of his brother in the Civil War and tries to create a prairie farm with his wife and son.
Genre(s): Western Fiction.

Yorgason, Blaine M.

◆ 1903. *Massacre at Salt Creek.* Garden City, NY: Doubleday, 1979. 183 pp.
Mentally deranged Inepegut, a small group of Utes, and five Mormons meet on a June afternoon, and only a baby survives a massacre after the mother is scalped.
Genre(s): Western Fiction; Christian Fiction.

Young, Agatha

1904. *The Hospital.* New York: Simon and Schuster, 1970. 320 pp.
In 1887, Dr. Sue Ward joins the staff of the hospital where her father and fiancé, work, and after her fiancé

dies from cocaine addition, she defies hospital regulations to deliver the child of an unmarried hospital worker and almost loses her job.
Genre(s): Medical Novel.

Young, Carter Travis

1905. *The Pocket Hunters.* New York: Doubleday, 1972. 191 pp.
When a young man returns to a mining ghost town to avenge the death of his family, the villains ambush him, expecting him to reveal the location of the missing gold.
Genre(s): Western Fiction.

1906. *Winter of the Coup.* New York: Doubleday, 1972. 185 pp.
The white community in Wyoming, including the U.S. Cavalry, confront Chief White Wolf and his people.
Genre(s): Western Fiction.

Zimmer, Michael

◆ 1907. *Sundown.* New York: Walker, 1988. 297 pp.
Luke Howard, a gunman hired to stop cattle rustlers, becomes involved with gold prospectors who want nearby farmland.
Genre(s): Western Fiction.

Zollinger, Norman

1908. *Corey Lane.* New York: Ticknor and Fields, 1981. 393 pp.
Sheriff Corey Lane first battles the Apache Chief Victorio before joining him to fight against the white man.
Genre(s): Western Fiction.

Zumwalt, Eva

1909. *Masquerade of Evil.* New York: Ace, 1975. 237 pp.
After the Civil War, Sarah York moves in with southern relatives who have suffered many tragedies, including having a blind son, and Sarah tries to help the son.
Genre(s): Romance; Gothic Fiction.

1890-1940 Progressive Era, World War I, and the Great Depression

Adams, Alice

1910. *A Southern Exposure.* New York: Knopf, 1995. 305 pp.
Harry takes his wife and daughter to North Carolina during the Depression, and instead of the trials from which they hope to escape, they find another code of life in the southern town.
Genre(s): Domestic Fiction.

Adams, Clifton

1911. *Hard Times and Arnie Smith.* New York: Doubleday, 1972. 186 pp.
In 1892, Arnie inherits his uncle's general store, and he learns quickly about the merchandise needed in a backcountry store serving sodbusters.
Genre(s): Western Fiction.

Adams, Harold

1912. *The Barbed Wire Noose.* New York: Mysterious Press, 1987. 184 pp.
After someone finds Arthur Foote hanging from a barbed wire noose during a South Dakotan winter, Carl Wilcox investigates because the town's policeman has pneumonia.
Genre(s): Mystery.

◆ 1913. *The Ditched Blonde.* New York: Walker, 1995. 157 pp.
Four years after it happens, sign painter Carl Wilcox begins investigating the murder of a pregnant teenager in Greenhill, South Dakota, in the 1930s and finds political motivations.
Genre(s): Mystery.

1914. *The Fourth Widow.* New York: Mysterious Press, 1986. 195 pp.
Carl Wilcox becomes the suspect when the corpse of a local beauty appears behind his parents' South Dakota hotel, and he must solve the mystery.
Genre(s): Mystery.

◆ 1915. *Hatchet Job.* New York: Walker, 1996. 168 pp.
Carl Wilcox becomes the temporary town policeman for Mustard after someone murders the previous policeman, Lou Dupree, with an ax, and he finds that no one in town liked Dupree.
Genre(s): Mystery.

1916. *The Man Who Met the Train.* New York: Mysterious Press, 1988. 229 pp.
In the summer of 1933, Carl Wilcox plans to work as a sign painter, but when he comes upon a train wreck, he rescues a young woman, the sole survivor, whose father also died when hit by a train.
Genre(s): Mystery.

◆ 1917. *The Man Who Missed the Party.* New York: Mysterious Press, 1989. 192 pp.
In the 1930s, Carl Wilcox manages the hotel in Corden, South Dakota, where the football team has its reunion, and during the party, the former quarterback who had a string of girlfriends is murdered.
Genre(s): Mystery.

◆ 1918. *The Man Who Was Taller Than God.* New York: Walker, 1992. 168 pp.
Carl Wilcox must stop his sign painting in the 1930s to look into the homicide of a man who left a South Dakota town 15 years before but has been found in the town's sandpit, shot in the head.
Award(s): Shamus Award.
Genre(s): Mystery.

◆ 1919. *The Naked Liar.* New York: Mysterious Press, 1985. 265 pp.
Carl Wilcox, former thief, bum, and cowboy, becomes a private detective in his leisure time and helps a widow accused of murdering her con man husband.
Genre(s): Mystery.

◆ May be suitable for young adult readers

◆ 1920. *A Way with Widows.* New York: Walker, 1994. 156 pp.
When Stella Feist is arrested for the murder of her husband during the Depression, Carl Wilcox's sister calls him to help Stella.
Genre(s): Mystery.

Adler, Elizabeth

1921. *Fortune Is a Woman.* New York: Delacorte, 1992. 433 pp.
A young woman inherits money from her grandfather while her mother runs the family business.
Genre(s): Romance.

Agee, James

◆ 1922. *A Death in the Family.* New York: McDowell Obolensky, 1957. 339 pp.
When Jay Follet dies in a car accident, his Knoxville family gathers during the days before his funeral.
Award(s): Pulitzer Prize.

Albert, Bill

◆ 1923. *Castle Garden.* Sag Harbor, NY: Permanent Press, 1996. 351 pp.
While Meyer Lieberman sits in a Idaho jail accused of a crime he did not commit, he writes of attackers leaving him mute in 1897, having members of Buffalo Bill's Wild West Show rescue him, and becoming Wild Bill's letter writer.
Genre(s): Western Fiction.

Aldrich, Bess Streeter

◆ 1924. *Miss Bishop.* New York: Appleton, 1933. 336 pp.
After her one love marries a cousin, Ella Bishop continues teaching and selflessly helping community children and grandchildren.
Genre(s): Domestic Fiction.

Alexander, Lawrence

◆ 1925. *The Big Stick.* New York: Doubleday, 1986. 349 pp.
When Theodore Roosevelt investigates a series of robberies, he discovers that all of the crime victims were passengers on a luxury liner.
Genre(s): Mystery.

◆ 1926. *The Strenuous Life.* New York: Knightsbridge, 1991. 304 pp.
When Theodore Roosevelt is New York City's police commissioner in 1895, he faces a robbery at the 71st Armory and connects Geronimo with John D. Rockefeller.
Genre(s): Mystery.

Alfieri, Richard

1927. *Ricardo: Diary of a Matinee Idol.* Santa Barbara, CA: John Daniel, 1989. 216 pp.
Ricardo, an Italian Jew from New York whose real name is Wayne Gould, becomes an idol like Valentino in 1925 and records his exploits in his diary.
Genre(s): Erotic Literature.

Algren, Nelson

1928. *A Walk on the Wild Side.* New York: Farrar, Straus and Giroux, 1956. 346 pp.
During the Depression, people living on a slum street in New Orleans try to survive.

Allen, Charlotte Vale

1929. *Mood Indigo.* Norwalk, CT: Island Nation, 1998. 288 pp.
Honoria Barlow, a script editor in Manhattan during the 1930s, investigates the murder of her best friend's son's fiancée, and finds that the girl had unsavory connections.
Genre(s): Mystery.

1930. *Time/Steps.* New York: Atheneum, 1986. 558 pp.
At 14, Beatrice Crane starts on Broadway and then moves to Hollywood during the 1930s to become a star.

Alter, Judy

◆ 1931. *Cherokee Rose.* New York: Bantam, 1996. 308 pp.
Tommy Jo Burns, alias Cherokee Rose, performs her riding and roping talents for Theodore Roosevelt and begins starring in Wild West shows.
Genre(s): Western Fiction.

Ames, Francis H.

◆ 1932. *The Callahans' Gamble.* New York: Doubleday, 1970. 240 pp.
Tom Conway, 18, helps his father save their cattle from rustlers on a cattle drive and protects their Montana homestead around 1910.
Genre(s): Western Fiction; Adventure Story.

Andersen, Doris

1933. *Ways Harsh and Wild.* Vancouver, BC: J.J. Douglas, 1973. 239 pp.
Dill Walker becomes one of the settlers in Alaska's Yukon Territory during the Gold Rush days.
Genre(s): Biographical Fiction.

Anderson, Edward

◆ 1934. *Hungry Men.* 1935. New York: Penguin, 1985. 275 pp.
Acel Stecker, a musician with no work, goes on the road as a hobo during the 1930s.

Anderson, Sherwood

◆ 1935. *Poor White.* 1920. New York: New Direction, 1993. 363 pp.
Hugh McVey is an inventor in Ohio in the early 20th century.

Applewhite, Cynthia

1936. *Summer Dreams and the Kleig Light Gas Company.* New York: Seaview, 1982. 215 pp.
Three women in White River, Missouri, during the 1930s dream about more than they have but find that preachers, revivalists, and politicians have unexpected influences.
Genre(s): Domestic Fiction.

Argers, Helen

1937. *The Gilded Lily.* New York: St. Martin's Press, 1998. 320 pp.
Because of her bad experiences with males in her family, Nina De Bonnard rapidly chooses and rejects suitors in New York during the late 1800s, but Jordan Houghton Windsor refuses to be discarded.
Genre(s): Romance.

Arleo, Joseph

1938. *The Grand Street Collector.* New York: Walker, 1970. 224 pp.
In New York during the 1930s, both Americans and Fascists ask Natale Sbagliato to assassinate Carlo Tresca, a controversial labor organizer, and Sbagliato refuses until those asking threaten his six-year-old son.
Genre(s): Political Fiction.

Arnout, Susan

1939. *The Frozen Lady.* New York: Arbor House, 1983. 581 pp.
In Alaska, Flame Ryan's family and her husband's family are involved in the political and social issues of the day in the decades before the territory gains statehood in 1959.

Aronson, Harvey

1940. *The Golden Shore.* New York: Putnam, 1982. 288 pp.
Not until 1912 is Miami Beach dredged, and avocado farmer Amos Breed and his son see the possibilities for a resort there.

Athas, Daphne

1941. *Entering Ephesus.* New York: Viking, 1971. 442 pp.
Each of the three Bishop girls chooses a method of coping with change after they move from a New England mansion to a shack in the South during the Depression.
Genre(s): Domestic Fiction.

Atwell, Lester

1942. *Life with its Sorrow, Life with its Tear.* New York: Simon and Schuster, 1971. 416 pp.
When orphaned as he enters high school, Paul lives with his uncle, a lawyer, who has welcomed other family members during the Depression and who continues to conceal his true social status while his income flounders.
Genre(s): Bildungsroman (Coming of Age).

Auchincloss, Louis

1943. *The Book Class.* Boston: Houghton Mifflin, 1984. 212 pp.
The grandson of a Park Avenue debutante of 1908 tells her story and that of the other members of a book group in which she participated.

1944. *The Country Cousin.* Boston: Houghton Mifflin, 1978. 239 pp.
A young country cousin becomes a society matron's paid companion, has an affair with a married relative, and marries a lawyer who has a similar guilt.

1945. *The Education of Oscar Fairfax.* Boston: Houghton Mifflin, 1995. 225 pp.
Oscar Fairfax has a degree from a prestigious school and becomes a member of his father's firm but, he soon begins to reject his conservative background.
Genre(s): Legal Story.

1946. *The Embezzler.* Boston: Houghton Mifflin, 1966. 277 pp.
Guy Prime serves time in prison for his Wall Street embezzlements in 1936 about which he, his best friend, and his wife reveal conflicting viewpoints.

1947. *Fellow Passengers.* Boston: Houghton Mifflin, 1989. 223 pp.
As Dan Ruggles, an attorney, recalls family and friends, he tells a story of New York society in the 1930s.

1948. *The House of Five Talents.* Boston: Houghton Mifflin, 1960. 369 pp.
A granddaughter reveals the results of enormous wealth on her family and those who married into it during the later 19th and early 20th centuries.

1949. *The House of the Prophet.* Boston: Houghton Mifflin, 1980. 275 pp.
Felix Leitner, writer, political analyst, presidential advisor, and family man becomes a legend through the work of his biographer, Roger Cutter.
Genre(s): Political Fiction.

1950. *The Lady of Situations.* Boston: Houghton Mifflin, 1990. 274 pp.
To regain her family's lost social status, Natica Chauncey marries three times to help her attain her goal in New York during the late 1930s.
Genre(s): Domestic Fiction.

1951. *Portrait in Brownstone.* Boston: Houghton Mifflin, 1962. 371 pp.
The Denisons, a New York City family, live behind their brownstones, clinging to their name while engaging in intense internal feuds.

Austin, Doris Jean

1952. *After the Garden.* New York: New American Library, 1987. 336 pp.
Elzina Tompkins marries athlete Jesse James when she becomes pregnant in 1939, and after he spends five years in prison, they try to rebuild their family.
Genre(s): Bildungsroman (Coming of Age); Domestic Fiction.

Austin, Mary

1953. *The Ford.* 1917. Berkeley: University of California, 1997. 440 pp.
The battle for water rights in California begins in the early 20th century.
Genre(s): Political Fiction.

Bagni, Gwen, and Paul Dubov

1954. *Backstairs at the White House.* Englewood Cliffs, NJ: Prentice Hall, 1978. 469 pp.
Lillian Rogers Parks, a White House maid whose years of service spanned the presidencies of Taft to Eisenhower, describes some of the White House events outside the public view.
Genre(s): Biographical Fiction.

Baker, Elliott

◆ 1955. *The Penny Wars.* New York: Putnam, 1968. 255 pp.
Although thinking that he ought to be fighting Hitler, Tyler, at 16, finds that he must first overcome his adolescent problems in his upper New York state home town.

Bamford, Susannah

1956. *The Gilded Cage.* New York: M. Evans, 1991. 424 pp.
In 1890, Lawrence Birch, an anarchist, arrives at the house of Columbine Nash, a reformer, and affects her life and those of her two housemates, while Emma Goldman and Johan Most espouse their radical doctrines in the background.
Genre(s): Romance.

Banis, Victor

1957. *The Earth and All It Holds.* New York: St. Martin's Press, 1980. 364 pp.
The de Brussac family struggles to keep its vineyards in California.
Genre(s): Family Saga.

Barber, Phyllis

1958. *And the Desert Shall Blossom.* Salt Lake City: University of Utah, 1991. 281 pp.
In the early 1930s, Mormons Alf and Esther Jensen move their family to find construction work on the Boulder Dam.
Genre(s): Domestic Fiction.

Barnes, Joanna

1959. *Silverwood.* New York: Linden, 1985. 349 pp.
Wealthy Ada Prudhomme's sons, relatives, friends, and nanny tell her story of privilege in Los Angeles.

Bart, Sheldon

1960. *Ruby Sweetwater and the Ringo Kid.* New York: McGraw Hill, 1981. 341 pp.
In 1901, the Ringo Kid arrives in New York from Colorado, expecting to stop his waywardness, but his friends, including Ruby Sweetwater and Butch Cassidy, expect him to continue his scams.
Genre(s): Adventure Story.

Bass, Cynthia

◆ 1961. *Maiden Voyage.* New York: Villard, 1996. 257 pp.
For his return to America from London, Sumner Jordan, 12, has passage on the *Titanic*, and he locks himself in his stateroom to prove his manhood as the ship sinks.
Genre(s): Sea Story; Bildungsroman (Coming of Age).

Battle, Lois

1962. *Storyville.* New York: Viking, 1993. 435 pp.
The lives of suffragist Julia Randsome and madam Kate Cavanaugh interwine when Julia's son meets 15-year-old Kate prior to his death in the Spanish-American war.
Genre(s): Domestic Fiction.

Bauer, Douglas

1963. *The Very Air.* New York: Morrow, 1993. 378 pp.
After Luther's mother dies and his father abandons him, he joins his uncle's traveling show, but circumstances eventually lead him to Hollywood and the beginnings of the pornography industry.
Genre(s): Western Fiction.

Baxt, George

1964. *The Alfred Hitchcock Murder Case.* New York: St. Martin's Press, 1986. 277 pp.
When Alfred Hitchcock films his first movie in Munich, several murders occur, and not until 11 years later does he begin to find who the 1930s murderers were.
Genre(s): Mystery.

1965. *The Clark Gable and Carole Lombard Murder Case.* New York: St. Martin's Press, 1997. 208 pp.
Carole Lombard and Clark Gable continue to attend parties and make movies while helping Herb Villon find a kidnap victim for whom Lombard is mentor.
Genre(s): Mystery.

1966. *The Dorothy Parker Murder Case.* New York: St. Martin's Press, 1984. 284 pp.
In 1926, Dorothy Parker and Alexander Woolcott help find the murderer of a woman in George F. Kaufman's apartment.
Genre(s): Mystery.

1967. *The Humphrey Bogart Murder Case.* New York: St. Martin's Press, 1995. 200 pp.
Humphrey Bogart joins Herb Villon to find murderers pursuing a horn of plenty that Marco Polo took to Europe.
Genre(s): Mystery.

1968. *The Mae West Murder Case.* New York: St. Martin's Press, 1993. 196 pp.
Herb Villon tries to find who has killed four of Mae West's impersonators in 1936.
Genre(s): Mystery.

1969. *The Marlene Dietrich Murder Case.* New York: St. Martin's Press, 1993. 218 pp.
On New Year's Eve in 1931, Marlene Dietrich's main attraction is Mai Mai Chu who dies from poison in her champagne, and Herb Villon must find the murderer among the politically connected guests.
Genre(s): Mystery.

1970. *The William Powell and Myrna Loy Murder Case.* New York: St. Martin's Press, 1996. 196 pp.
After their movie, *The Thin Man*, succeeds, Myrna Loy and William Powell find themselves investigating the deaths of a Hollywood madam's secretary and assistant after the madam said she would reveal the names of her customers.
Genre(s): Mystery.

Bean, Frederic

1971. *Black Gold.* New York: Forge, 1997. 384 pp.
When Bill Dodd makes a strike in the oil fields of Longview, Texas, in the 1930s, he is murdered before he can file his claim, and Lee Garrett, Texas Ranger, investigates a motley group of people collected in the boom town.
Genre(s): Mystery.

1972. *Tom Spoon.* New York: Walker, 1990. 158 pp.
Tom Spoon serves 12 years for murder, but he keeps his vow never to use another gun until railroad owners ruthlessly try to take land from a friend's ranch.
Genre(s): Western Fiction.

Beck, K. K.

1973. *Death in a Deck Chair.* New York: Walker, 1984. 168 pp.
In the late 1920s, Mr. Twist, a professor's aid, is stabbed in his deck chair on board an ocean liner, and a young American girl investigates with the help of a reporter.
Genre(s): Mystery; Sea Story.

1974. *Murder in a Mummy Case.* New York: Walker, 1986. 165 pp.
Iris Cooper tries to solve the murder of a boorish student and a pseudo-Egyptologist in California during the 1920s.
Genre(s): Mystery.

◆ **1975.** *Peril Under the Palms.* New York: Walker, 1989. 192 pp.
Iris Cooper and her Aunt Hermione go to Hawaii on vacation in 1928, but instead of rest, she helps her friend locate her presumed-dead mother and investigates the murder of a Boston woman.
Genre(s): Mystery.

Becker, Stephen D.

1976. *A Covenant with Death.* New York: Atheneum, 1964. 240 pp.
The young judge Ben Lewis has to decide if Bryan Talbot is guilty of killing the hangman trying to execute Talbot for murdering his wife when he did not commit the crime.
Genre(s): Western Fiction; Mystery; Legal Story.

Behrman, S. N.

1977. *The Burning Glass.* Boston: Little, Brown, 1968. 396 pp.
Stanley Grant, a Jewish dramatist, rises in the theater world while Nazism overtakes Austria.
Genre(s): War Story; Love Story; Jewish Fiction.

Bellamann, Henry

1978. *King's Row.* New York: Simon and Schuster, 1940. 674 pp.
In the 1890s, Parris Mitchell grows from a young boy to become his Missouri town's psychiatrist who sees its dark side in his patients.

1979. *Parris Mitchell of Kings Row.* New York: Simon and Schuster, 1948. 301 pp.
Parris Mitchell becomes his town's psychiarist and falls in love with another woman while trying to remain faithful to his wife.
Genre(s): Medical Novel.

Belland, F. W.

1980. *The True Sea.* New York: Henry Holt, 1984. 289 pp.
In 1909, the inhabitants in Doctor's Arm, a small town in the Florida Keys, look forward to the future, but by the late 1920s, none of their dreams have materialized.
Genre(s): Bildungsroman (Coming of Age).

Benchley, Nathaniel

1981. *All Over Again.* Garden City, NY: Doubleday, 1981. 240 pp.
The plans of several different people change drastically at the moment of the San Francisco earthquake in 1906.
Genre(s): Adventure Story.

1982. *Speakeasy.* Garden City, NY: Doubleday, 1982. 321 pp.
A small family speakeasy in New York City becomes the place where people gather in the 1920s, including a non-drinking reporter, Butterworth.
Genre(s): Domestic Fiction.

Benet, Stephen Vincent

1983. *James Shore's Daughters.* St. Claire Shores, MI: Scholar, 1934. 277 pp.
Violet Shore, daughter of a copper king, meets Gareth Grant, a young American who has been an expatriate most of his life, in the late 19th century.
Genre(s): Domestic Fiction.

Berg, Patti

1984. *If I Can't Have You.* New York: Avon, 1998. 384 pp.
In 1938, on July 4, when Trevor Montgomery becomes the suspect for the murder of his co-star, he drowns himself, and when he reappears 50 years later to fan Adriana Howard, she finds him less appealing in the flesh.
Genre(s): Time Travel; Mystery.

Berger, Thomas

1985. *The Feud.* New York: Delacorte, 1983. 265 pp.
When Dolf Beeler goes into Bullard's hardware store one Saturday and leaves humiliated, things that happen to the Bullards and to the Beelers indicate a grudge feud.
Genre(s): Domestic Fiction; Allegory.

1986. *Sneaky People.* New York: Simon and Schuster, 1975. 315 pp.
During the 1930s, a used-car salesman, Buddy Sandifer, plots to have his wife murdered so that he can marry his waitress mistress.
Genre(s): Humorous Fiction.

Bergon, Frank

1987. *Shoshone Mike.* New York: Viking, 1987. 290 pp.
Mike Daggett, known as Shoshone Mike, escapes his reservation with his family in 1911 after they kill a white rustler, and stockmen hunt them down.
Genre(s): Western Fiction.

Berlin, Ellin

1988. *The Best of Families.* Garden City, NY: Doubleday, 1970. 330 pp.
After their mother's death, four wealthy sisters grow up before and during World War I in New York City, each choosing a different path.
Genre(s): Domestic Fiction.

Bezzi, Tom

1989. *Hubble Time.* San Francisco: Mercury House, 1987. 255 pp.
In the 1920s and 1930s, Edwin Hubble and his wife live in Los Angeles and enjoy their circle of friends, including film stars, writers, and scientists, as Hubble pursues his many interests, including science.
Genre(s): Biographical Fiction.

Bissell, Elaine

1990. *Family Fortunes.* New York: St. Martin's Press, 1985. 452 pp.
One day in 1932, socialite Elizabeth Stuart gives a parlormaid a ride, and the two become close friends, linking their families through World War II.
Genre(s): Domestic Fiction; Family Saga.

Bittle, Camilla R.

1991. *Dear Family.* New York: St. Martin's Press, 1991. 272 pp.
When Ed Beane loses his job in 1935, his wife, two children, and widowed mother must go to live with Dorothy's mother on her farm, where they continue to support each other through a series of family celebrations.
Genre(s): Domestic Fiction.

Bjorn, Thyra Ferre

1992. *Dear Papa.* New York: Holt, Rinehart, and Winston, 1963. 191 pp.
As the family regards their father in the sequel to *Mama's Way*, they see an earnest clergyman with both foibles and strengths.
Genre(s): Humorous Fiction.

1993. *Mama's Way.* New York: Holt, Rinehart, and Winston, 1959. 214 pp.
In the sequel to *Papa's Wife*, Maria, the mother of eight children and the wife of a clergyman, demonstrates how she can manipulate her family.
Genre(s): Humorous Fiction.

1994. *Papa's Daughter.* New York: Holt, Rinehart, and Winston, 1958. 196 pp.
After Maria and her husband move to New England from Sweden, they have a daughter and seven more children in the sequel to *Papa's Wife*.
Genre(s): Humorous Fiction.

◆ 1995. *Papa's Wife.* New York: Holt, Rinehart and Winston, 1955. 305 pp.
A young Swedish housemaid marries her pastor, comes with him to New England from Swedish Lapland in the early 1900s, and raises their family.
Genre(s): Domestic Fiction.

Black, Jonathan

1996. *Oil.* New York: Morrow, 1974. 404 pp.
James Northcutt fights to retain his independent oil company while fighting major companies to survive.
Genre(s): Political Fiction.

Blair, Leona

1997. *With This Ring.* New York: Delacorte, 1984. 416 pp.
Jesse Slayter marries Madelyn for her money in 1904, takes her to New York, and refuses to let her dominate him as women dominated his father, but she tires of needing more than he will give.
Genre(s): Domestic Fiction.

Blakenship, William D.

1998. *Yukon Gold.* New York: Dutton, 1977. 280 pp.
In 1898, gold diggers and Hannah Young confront Canadian Mountie Brian Bonner.
Genre(s): Western Fiction.

Bliss, Alice

1999. *The Withrows.* Atlanta, GA: Bozart, 1994. 237 pp.
In Atlanta during 1932, Evelyn and her husband Fred reunite after spending years apart and begin to readjust.
Genre(s): Domestic Fiction.

Bogen, Nancy

2000. *Bobe Mayse: A Tale of Washington Square.*
New York: Twickenham, 1993. 321 pp.
In 1911, Russian Jewish Martha quits secretarial school
and begins working at the Triangle Shirtwaist Factory
and participates in union strikes before the big fire.
Genre(s): Political Fiction.

Bonds, Parris Afton

◆ 2001. *Blue Moon.* New York: Fawcett, 1985. 276
pp.
In 1916, Roxana Van Buren's family disowns her independent ways, and she becomes a Pinkerton detective
while trying to interview Pancho Villa and be recognized
as a reporter.
Genre(s): Biographical Fiction; War Story.

Bonham, Frank

2002. *The Eye of the Hunter.* New York: M.
Evans, 1989. 180 pp.
Henry Logan, a gunsmith, goes to Arizona in 1900 to in-
vestigate Frances Parrish and decide if she is a widow
and if she has murdered someone.
Genre(s): Western Fiction.

Borland, Hal

◆ 2003. *When the Legends Die.* Philadelphia: Lippincott, 1963. 288 pp.
A young Ute grows up in Colorado from 1910 to 1920,
and when he becomes civilized, his actions reflect his
conflicts.
Genre(s): Western Fiction.

Bowen, Peter

2004. *Imperial Kelly.* New York: Crown, 1992.
210 pp.
Luther Kelly, reluctant army major, continues to follow
Theodore Roosevelt's orders to search for imperial inter-
ests, and he goes to Cuba, China, and South Africa.
Genre(s): Picaresque Fiction; Adventure Story.

Bowers, Terrell L.

◆ 2005. *The Secret of Snake Canyon.* New York:
Walker, 1993. 168 pp.
One hundred workers of the Chinese labor broker Kim
Lee disappear, and with the help of a mountain man and a
half-Asian indentured servant, Deputy Marshall Reese
Corbett looks for them.
Genre(s): Western Fiction.

Boyd, Brendan C.

◆ 2006. *Blue Ruin.* New York: Norton, 1991. 339 pp.
Sport Sullivan begins the scam that fixes the 1919 World
Series between the Chicago White Sox and the Cincin-
nati Reds.
Genre(s): Sports Fiction.

Boyle, T. Coraghessan

2007. *Riven Rock.* New York: Viking, 1998. 496
pp.
After marrying Stanley McCormick, brilliant son of the
inventor of the McCormick reaper, Katherine Dexter,

graduate of MIT, discovers after they do not consummate
the marriage that he is a schizophrenic sex maniac who
must be kept separate from women.
Genre(s): Medical Novel; Domestic Fiction.

2008. *The Road to Wellville.* New York: Viking,
1993. 476 pp.
Dr. Kellogg, one of his patients, and a sleazy businessman meet at the Kellogg sanitarium in 1907.
Genre(s): Humorous Fiction.

Boyne, Walter J.

◆ 2009. *Trophy for Eagles.* New York: Crown,
1989. 455 pp.
Bruno Hafner destroys Frank Bandfield's plane as he prepares to race to Paris in 1927, and the rivalry begun between the two men ends when Bandfield shoots down
Hafner's plane during the battle of Guernica.
Genre(s): Adventure Story.

Bradbury, Ray

◆ 2010. *Dandelion Wine.* Garden City, NY: Doubleday, 1957. 281 pp.
In 1928, Douglas Spaulding wanders around Green
Town, Illinois, with his brother and realizes that he is
alive.

Brand, Max

2011. *Murder Me!* New York: St. Martin's Press,
1995. 272 pp.
In the 1930s, New York police detectives Campbell and
O'Rourke investigate the suicide of a philanthropist,
which turns out to be murder.
Genre(s): Mystery.

Brautigan, Richard

2012. *The Hawkline Monster.* New York: Simon
and Schuster, 1974. 216 pp.
Two men meet two sisters in Oregon who entreat them to
rid the family mansion of a monster dwelling below in
ice caves.
Genre(s): Western Fiction; Gothic Fiction.

Breslin, Jimmy

2013. *Table Money.* New York: Ticknor and
Fields, 1986. 435 pp.
The Morrisons arrive in Queens in the late 19th century,
and their men continue drinking while their women ex-
haust themselves bearing children.

Bridgers, Sue Ellen

2014. *All We Know of Heaven.* Wilmington, NC:
Banks Channel, 1997. 212 pp.
After her mother dies and her father becomes an alcoholic, Bethany rushes into marriage with Joel, only to
have him become abusive and murder each family member.
Genre(s): Domestic Fiction.

Briskin, Jacqueline

2015. *The Onyx.* New York: Delacorte, 1982. 504 pp.
Tom Bridger founds an automobile company in Detroit and almost ruins his personal life.

2016. *Paloverde.* New York: McGraw Hill, 1978. 517 pp.
Two brothers fall in love with the same woman, and although one marries her, the other fathers her daughter in their saga beginning in the Los Angeles of the 1880s.
Genre(s): Family Saga.

Bristow, Gwen

2017. *This Side of Glory.* New York: Crowell, 1940. 400 pp.
The Larne family of *Deep Summer* and *The Handsome Road* become embroiled in the trials of World War I.
Genre(s): Family Saga.

Brody, Jean

2018. *Cleo.* New York: St. Martin's Press, 1995. 336 pp.
At 15 in 1927, Cleo, a Creek descendant, leaves her small town for Tulsa where she plays trumpet in a speakeasy and in a church while meeting the men that she will marry.
Genre(s): Musical Fiction; Bildungsroman (Coming of Age); Domestic Fiction.

Broome, H. B.

◆ 2019. *Dark Winter.* Garden City, NY: Doubleday, 1991. 193 pp.
Tom English, a rancher and well-known gunfighter, searches for Julian Haynes, murderer of ranch hands, and finds him with Elfego Baca, a Mexican who has decided to become the lawman of Frisco, New Mexico.
Genre(s): Biographical Fiction; Western Fiction.

Brough, James

2020. *Miss Lillian Russell.* New York: McGraw Hill, 1978. 307 pp.
Miss Lillian Russell's imaginary memoirs describe her relationship with the notorious Diamond Jim Brady and her experiences acting on Broadway.
Genre(s): Biographical Fiction.

Brown, Joe David

◆ 2021. *Addie Pray.* New York: Simon and Schuster, 1971. 313 pp.
Addie Pray, 11, and her father are con artists who travel the South before they join a more sophisticated schemer who plans their ultimate con.
Genre(s): Picaresque Fiction; Humorous Fiction.

Brown, John Gregory

◆ 2022. *The Wrecked, Blessed Body of Shelton Lafleur.* Boston: Houghton Mifflin, 1996. 257 pp.
Shelton La Fleur, an elderly black artist, recalls his early childhood with a white woman until age eight, when he twisted his limbs falling from a tree and was taken to a black orphanage.

Brown, Rita Mae

2023. *Southern Discomfort.* New York: Harper and Row, 1982. 249 pp.
A society matron, Hortensia Banastre, falls in love with a young black boxer of Montgomery in the early 20th century and raises their daughter in secret until her son figures out the relationship.
Genre(s): Domestic Fiction.

Brown, Sam

2024. *Devil's Rim.* New York: Walker, 1998. 224 pp.
When Concho Smith drifts into New Mexico, he meets Judyth Van, a mail-order bride whose husband was crippled weeks after their marriage, and helps her save the ranch from a greedy cattle baron.
Genre(s): Western Fiction.

Browne, Howard

2025. *Scotch on the Rocks.* New York: St. Martin's Press, 1991. 185 pp.
After family members auction their farm in 1932, they find a truck with illegal scotch and a dead driver, and later, they meet a hustler who knows the value of their discovery.
Genre(s): Mystery.

Bryant, Will

◆ 2026. *A Time for Heroes.* New York: St. Martin's Press, 1987. 308 pp.
The orphan Jason goes to live with his uncle Hector in the Arizona desert, and soon, he, his uncle, and a war buddy are chasing bandits into Mexico.
Genre(s): Adventure Story.

Buechner, Frederick

◆ 2027. *The Wizard's Tide.* New York: HarperCollins, 1990. 128 pp.
Teddy's family has difficulty adjusting to poverty during the Great Depression, and he, his sister, and mother move in with his mother's family.

Bunkley, Anita R.

2028. *Black Gold.* New York: Dutton, 1994. 404 pp.
Leela Brannon, a beautiful black woman living in 1920s Texas when the oil begins to flow, marries dependable T.J., but when T.J. dies, she rejects his brother, a man to whom she was previously attracted.
Genre(s): Domestic Fiction.

Burdett, David Llewellyn

2029. *Hix Nix Stix Pix.* Boston: Houghton Mifflin, 1984. 315 pp.
Between World Wars I and II, Philip Inshroin, a famous movie star, makes idiotic movies while Upton Sinclair runs for president.
Genre(s): Political Fiction.

Burgess, Anthony

2030. *Any Old Iron.* New York: Random House, 1989. 360 pp.
Welshman David Jones crosses the Atlantic on the *Titanic*, survives, and after arriving in New York, marries a Russian immigrant before he returns to London and service in World War I.
Genre(s): Family Saga.

Burkholz, Herbert

2031. *The Snow Gods.* New York: Atheneum, 1985. 256 pp.
Prior to World War I, two brothers, divided by a family rivalry, create business empires competing in the world of international skiing, one in Australia and one in New England.
Genre(s): Family Saga.

Burns, Olive Ann

2032. *Cold Sassy Tree.* New York: Ticknor and Fields, 1984. 391 pp.
Recent widower E. Rucker Blakeslee elopes with Cold Sassy's town milliner while his grandson, 14, falls in love with the new, lovely wife.
Genre(s): Humorous Fiction.

Burns, Olive Ann, and Katrina Kenison

2033. *Leaving Cold Sassy.* New York: Ticknor and Fields, 1992. 290 pp.
In 1917, Will Tweedy is 25 in the sequel to *Cold Sassy Tree*, and he courts Sanna Klein, the lovely new schoolteacher.
Genre(s): Domestic Fiction.

Burroway, Janet

2034. *Cutting Stone.* Boston: Houghton Mifflin, 1992. 404 pp.
In 1913, Baltimore socialite Eleanor Pointdexter accompanies her tubercular husband to Arizona, and after a tragic affair, she worries about friends fighting across the border in the Mexican Revolution.
Genre(s): Western Fiction.

Bush, Lawrence

2035. *Bessie.* New York: Seaview, 1983. 432 pp.
Bessie escapes to America from Russia and becomes involved in the radical events of the 20th century including the Triangle Factory Fire, the Sacco and Vanzetti trial, the McCarthy period, and the Civil Rights movement in the South.
Genre(s): Political Fiction.

Butler, Robert Olen

2036. *Wabash.* New York: Knopf, 1987. 207 pp.
After his child dies, Jeremy Cole participates in the violent labor reactions at the Wabash, Illinois, steel mill, and his wife must keep him from murder.
Genre(s): Domestic Fiction.

Cairney, John

2037. *Worlds Apart.* North Pomfret, VT: Trafalgar Square, 1992. 672 pp.
In 1900, Tina Keigh and Denis O'Neil meet and fall in love at Glasgow's docks as their families prepare to emigrate, but one family goes to America and the other to New Zealand.
Genre(s): Family Saga.

Caldwell, Taylor

2038. *Answer as a Man.* New York: Putnam, 1980. 445 pp.
Jason Garrity rises from a delivery boy to wealthy resort owner as he confronts all of the difficulties that threaten success.

2039. *Ceremony of the Innocent.* Garden City, NY: Doubleday, 1976. 422 pp.
A young servant girl meets and marries her prince, but her own children drive her to suicide in the early 20th century.

2040. *Dynasty of Death.* New York: Scribner's, 1938. 797 pp.
Ernest at 12 is cold and ruthless, and his life is in contrast to Martin, an inevitable abolitionist and pacifist during the Civil War.
Genre(s): Domestic Fiction; Family Saga.

2041. *The Eagles Gather.* New York: Scribner's, 1940. 498 pp.
In the sequel to *Dynasty of Death*, all of the the Bouchard munition factory males, except for Peter, hate each other and try to win supremacy over the business.
Genre(s): Domestic Fiction; Family Saga.

2042. *The Final Hour.* New York: Scribner's, 1944. 563 pp.
In the sequel to *Eagles Gather*, the Bourchard family bickers between business with Hitler and with the United States as World War II begins.
Genre(s): Domestic Fiction; Family Saga.

2043. *Testimony of Two Men.* Garden City, NY: Doubleday, 1968. 605 pp.
Jonathan Ferrier wants to perfect asepsis when few doctors understand the need for it in 1901, but his community shuns him because he demands perfection.
Genre(s): Medical Novel.

Callen, Paulette

2044. *Charity.* New York: Simon and Schuster, 1997. 320 pp.
The people in the small town of Charity, South Dakota, at the end of the 19th century exhibit racial prejudice, sexism, and violent behavior toward each other.
Genre(s): Domestic Fiction.

Campbell, R. Wright

2045. *Fat Tuesday.* Boston: Houghton Mifflin, 1983. 352 pp.
In 1916, a journalist comes to New Orleans searching for his daughter who has possibly become a prostitute in Storyville, the red-light district.

Capps, Benjamin

2046. *The White Man's Road.* New York: Harper and Row, 1969. 309 pp.
Joe Cowbone, half Comanche and half white, tries to follow his beliefs as the whites enforce their ideas on the Comanche in the 1890s.
Award(s): Western Writers of America Spur Award.
Genre(s): Western Fiction.

Carlile, Clancy

2047. *Children of the Dust.* New York: Random House, 1995. 428 pp.
Gypsy Smith, of Cherokee and African American heritage, is a lawman and gunfighter in Oklahoma after the Land Rush of 1889 where he must battle the Klan, Jim Crow laws, and racism.
Genre(s): Western Fiction.

2048. *Honkytonk Man.* New York: Simon and Schuster, 1981. 352 pp.
Red Stovall, a talented musician, travels from California to Oklahoma to Nashville during the Depression, while dying from tuberculosis, for a last chance to sing at The Grand Ole Opry.
Genre(s): Musical Fiction.

Carmichael, Emily

2049. *Gold Dust.* New York: Warner Books, 1996. 348 pp.
In 1897, Katy O'Connell of Willow Bend, Montana, wants to make her fortune panning gold.
Genre(s): Western Fiction; Romance.

Carr, Caleb

2050. *The Alienist.* New York: Random House, 1994. 496 pp.
In 1896, the New York reform police commissioner Theodore Roosevelt asks an upper class police reporter and a psychologist to investigate the serial killer of boy prostitutes, but crime bosses oppose their questions.
Genre(s): Mystery.

2051. *The Angel of Darkness.* New York: Random House, 1997. 400 pp.
In 1897 when someone kidnaps a Spanish diplomat's baby, Elspeth Hunter becomes the suspect, and Theodore Roosevelt must investigate her.
Genre(s): Mystery.

Carr, John Dickson

2052. *Deadly Hall.* New York: Harper, 1971. 251 pp.
Jeff Caldwell comes home from Paris to discuss a mysterious situation involving him and another person with the family lawyer.
Genre(s): Mystery.

Carr, Robyn

◆ 2053. *Woman's Own.* New York: St. Martin's Press, 1990. 480 pp.
The Armstrong women of Philadelphia in the late 19th century are unlucky in their love affairs and marriages, but they all try to live on their own terms.
Genre(s): Domestic Fiction.

Carroll, Gladys Hasty

2054. *As the Earth Turns.* New York: Norton, 1961. 339 pp.
Jen, Mark Shaw's oldest daughter, becomes the focus of the farm's life during a year in the 1930s.

Carroll, James

2055. *Memorial Bridge.* Boston: Houghton Mifflin, 1991. 495 pp.
When Sean Dillon works in the Chicago stockyards trying to pay for law school, he finds a murdered man in a blood drainage pipe, which sparks his decision to become an FBI agent.
Genre(s): Mystery.

Carton, Bernice

2056. *Beyond the Brooklyn Bridge.* Santa Fe, NM: Sunstone, 1998. 160 pp.
A young girl growing up in Brooklyn during the 1920s thinks that her street is the center of the world.
Genre(s): Domestic Fiction.

Cather, Willa

2057. *O Pioneers!* Boston: Houghton Mifflin, 1913. 308p pp.
Swedish farmer John Bergson's daughter Alexandra encourages the family members to help keep his dream alive after his death.
Genre(s): Western Fiction; Domestic Fiction.

Cavanaugh, Arthur

2058. *The Faithful.* New York: Morrow, 1986. 345 pp.
A nun wanting to educate Native Americans comes to the United States in 1908, but a young priest and an immigrant coerce her into becoming the headmistress of a school for affluent Catholic girls.
Genre(s): Domestic Fiction.

Cavanaugh, Jack

2059. *The Allies.* Wheaton, IL: Victor, 1997. 500 pp.
Katherine Morgan, 23, goes to Europe during World War I where she serves as a nurse, and her brother Johnnie is a pilot in the American Expeditionary Forces. (*Series:* American Family Portrait, 6)
Genre(s): Christian Fiction; War Story; Family Saga.

Chance, Megan

2060. *The Way Home.* New York: HarperCollins, 1997. 432 pp.
After Eliza Beaudry falls in love with Cole Wallace and becomes pregnant, he pairs her with his shy brother and

leaves, but when he returns Eliza's transformation surprises him.
Genre(s): Romance.

Charbonneau, Eileen

◆ 2061. *Waltzing in Ragtime.* New York: Forge, 1996. 477 pp.
Olana, a journalist, determines to have her own way for six years, refusing the loyal Matt until he is wounded in San Francisco before and during the earthquake of 1906.
Genre(s): Romance.

Charyn, Jerome

2062. *Panna Maria.* New York: Arbor House, 1982. 447 pp.
Panna Maria, a Polish tenement in New York's Hell's Kitchen, has a brothel on the top floor, and protagonist Stefan Wilde wants to woo the neighborhood's nurse.
Genre(s): Adventure Story.

Chase, Virginia

2063. *One Crow, Two Crow.* New York: Vanguard, 1971. 256 pp.
Laura and Joel get married in 1925 and live in a small Maine town, but the Depression weighs them down when Joel loses his job and Laura tries to keep things the same.
Genre(s): Domestic Fiction.

Chesnutt, Charles W.

2064. *Mandy Oxendine.* Champaign, IL: University of Illinois Press, 1997. 112 pp.
Mandy Oxendine, a light-skinned African American chooses to pass for white, but she has problems when a white landowner pursues her and she encounters her former black lover.
Genre(s): Domestic Fiction.

Chester, Laura

2065. *The Story of the Lake.* Boston: Faber And Faber, 1995. 382 pp.
Wealthy Midwestern families summer at Lake Nogowogotoc in Wisconsin as the business and social affairs of family members intertwine.
Genre(s): Family Saga.

Cheuse, Alan

2066. *The Bohemians: John Reed and His Friends Who Shook the World.* Cambridge, MA: Apple-Wood, 1982. 358 pp.
John Reed becomes involved with events in Mexico and Russia and has a relationship with Louise Bryant.
Genre(s): Biographical Fiction.

Clarke, Richard

2067. *The Peralta Country.* New York: Walker, 1987. 192 pp.
Constable Cutler must cope with a stranger who wants progress in Peralta, and he uses his two friends, Fred and Kelly, to help him.
Genre(s): Western Fiction; Romance.

Clouse, Loretta

2068. *Wilder.* Nashville, TN: Rutledge Hill, 1990. 256 pp.
Wilder, Tennessee, has little food during a coal miners' strike in 1932, while Lacey Conners weighs her feelings about her pursuers steady John and flashy Coy.
Genre(s): Domestic Fiction.

Coffman, Virginia

2069. *Pacific Cavalcade.* New York: Arbor House, 1981. 457 pp.
Between the two wars, Randi Lombard believes that she will be happy ever after in her marriage, but she finds otherwise.

Coleman, Lonnie

2070. *Orphan Jim.* Garden City, NY: Doubleday, 1975. 204 pp.
After motherless Trudy and Jim lose their father and an uncle's wife rejects them, they and a black prostitute form a family.

Collins, Max Allan

2071. *Blood and Thunder.* New York: Dutton, 1995. 320 pp.
When Nate Heller is hired to protect Huey Long of Louisiana from assassination, he fails, but when he returns a year later, he discovers that the man accused may not be the guilty party.
Genre(s): Mystery.

2072. *Carnal Hours.* New York: Dutton, 1994. 324 pp.
Nathan Heller goes to the Bahamas to find the killer of a Caribbean millionaire in the 1930s.
Genre(s): Mystery.

2073. *Damned in Paradise.* New York: Dutton, 1996. 308 pp.
Nathan Heller leaves Chicago in 1931 to help Clarence Darrow defend a group of men in Hawaii accused of killing a man thought to have been a rapist.
Genre(s): Mystery; Legal Story.

◆ 2074. *The Dark City.* New York: Bantam, 1987. 240 pp.
Elliott Ness tries to clean up Cleveland's corrupt police force and expose an official selling nonexistent cemetery plots in the 1930s.
Genre(s): Mystery.

◆ 2075. *Murder by the Numbers.* New York: St. Martin's Press, 1993. 210 pp.
During the 1930s, Eliot Ness works in Cleveland to put the Mayfield Road Gang behind bars, but he has to overcome political favorites and angry mobs.
Genre(s): Mystery.

2076. *True Detective.* New York: St. Martin's Press, 1984. 368 pp.
Nate Heller decides to resign his police appointment during Prohibition and work alone.
Award(s): Shamus Award.
Genre(s): Mystery.

Conley, Robert J.

2077. *Back to Malachi.* New York: Doubleday, 1986. 179 pp.
When Charlie Black, son of a prosperous Cherokee store-keeper, keeps company with the fullblooded Cherokee Malachi Pathkiller and his lawbreaking sons, his father becomes concerned, but after Malachi's sons die, Charlie finds Malachi, who teaches him about the Cherokee heritage.
Genre(s): Domestic Fiction; Western Fiction.

Connell, Evan S.

2078. *Mr. Bridge.* New York: Knopf, 1969. 369 pp.
A lawyer in Kansas City, in the sequel to *Mrs. Bridge,* Mr. Bridge lives the empty life of a middle class suburbanite.
Genre(s): Domestic Fiction.

2079. *Mrs. Bridge.* New York: Viking, 1959. 254 pp.
Mrs. Bridge, wife of a lawyer, brings up two daughters and a son in suburban Kansas City between the wars, but she has no respite from boredom or loneliness.
Genre(s): Domestic Fiction.

Cook, Thomas H.

2080. *The Chatham School Affair.* New York: Bantam, 1996. 304 pp.
In 1926, after Elizabeth Channing arrives at Chatham School for boys, she begins an affair with an unhappily married teacher and a chain of events leading to murder.
Award(s): Mystery Writers of America Edgar Award.
Genre(s): Mystery; Domestic Fiction.

2081. *Elena.* Boston: Houghton Mifflin, 1986. 435 pp.
Elena Franklin, daughter of a mother who died insane and a father who would not stay home, becomes a noted American author before she moves to Paris.

Cooke, Elizabeth

2082. *Zeena.* New York: St. Martin's Press, 1996. 352 pp.
Zenobia, Ethan Frome's wife, has had to temper her dreams of nursing others to live a lonely life with Frome on his farm.
Genre(s): Domestic Fiction.

Cooke, John Byrne

◆ 2083. *South of the Border.* New York: Bantam, 1989. 324 pp.
While managing a Hollywood boarding house in 1919 for movie extras, Charlie Siringo meets the supposedly dead Robert Leroy Parker (Butch Cassidy), who wants him to go to Mexico and film a movie about Pancho Villa.
Genre(s): Biographical Fiction; Western Fiction.

Cooke, John Peyton

2084. *Torsos.* New York: Mysterious Press, 1993. 359 pp.
In 1935, dismembered male bodies appear in Cleveland, and Elliott Ness, the new Safety Commissioner, works with Hank Lambert to find the homosexual killer, but Lambert himself is an unacknowledged homosexual.
Genre(s): Mystery.

Cooke, St. George

2085. *The Treasure of Rodolfo Fierro.* New York: Doubleday, 1990. 179 pp.
In 1923, Richard Henry Little comes to New Mexico for Pancho Villa's treasure using Villa's map, torn into eight pieces, as his only clue.
Genre(s): Western Fiction; Mystery.

Cooper, Jamie Lee

◆ 2086. *The Castaways.* Indianapolis: Bobbs Merrill, 1970. 212 pp.
Riff and his father wander throughout America on trains during the Depression after Riff's mother dies, and visit such places as a Seminole village in Florida.
Genre(s): Adventure Story.

Corbin, Steven

2087. *No Easy Place to Be.* New York: Simon and Schuster, 1989. 443 pp.
Three sisters in Harlem during the 1920s include a nurse who becomes committed to Marcus Garvey's movement, a dancer at the Cotton Club, and a student at Barnard College.
Genre(s): Domestic Fiction.

Corle, Edwin

2088. *Fig Tree John.* New York: Liveright and Boni, 1971. 310 pp.
When whites murder Agocho's wife in 1906 and his son later marries a white woman, Agocho loses his simple Apache way of life with its inner harmony.
Genre(s): Domestic Fiction.

Costello, Anthony

2089. *Jericho.* New York: Bantam, 1982. 497 pp.
When Harriet Hoskins finds out about her lover's secret life the night she becomes engaged to him, the knowledge causes her to examine her town's inhabitants and their lives.

Courter, Gay

2090. *The Midwife.* Boston: Houghton Mifflin, 1981. 559 pp.
In 1906, the midwife Hannah Blau's family flees from the anti-Semitism in Russia to New York, where she supports her family plying her trade in face of the medical establishment.

2091. *The Midwife's Advice.* New York: Dutton, 1992. 598 pp.
In the sequel to *The Midwife,* Hannah Sokolow helps women coming to Bellevue Hospital with their sexual

and medical conditions from 1913 to 1922 while trying to keep her family afloat.
Genre(s): Medical Novel.

Covin, Kelly

◆ 2092. *Hear that Train Blow: A Novel About the Scottsboro Case.* New York: Delacorte, 1970. 480 pp.
In 1931, a group of African Americans accused of raping two white girls on a train come to trial in Scottsboro, Alabama.
Genre(s): Legal Story.

Craven, Margaret

◆ 2093. *Walk Gently this Good Earth.* New York: Putnam, 1977. 172 pp.
During the first half of the 20th century, the Westcott family endures the Depression and the war because of their love of each other and of nature.
Genre(s): Domestic Fiction; War Story.

Crider, Bill

◆ 2094. *A Time for Hanging.* Boston: Little, Brown, 1989. 176 pp.
A Mexican teenager in the vicinity where Lizzie Randall is murdered is automatically accused of the crime and nearly lynched.
Genre(s): Western Fiction; Mystery.

Cummings, Jack

2095. *The Indian Fighter's Return.* New York: Walker, 1993. 184 pp.
Activist Ella Gordon's campaign against Jon Seaver for sheriff is successful, but when a Native American abducts her, the new sheriff asks Seaver to rescue her.
Genre(s): Western Fiction.

2096. *The Last Lawmen.* New York: Walker, 1994. 192 pp.
Rangers Wes Barnes and Jake Kenton work to rid Arizona of outlaws who rob and kill at will, but when Kenton seems too interested in killing, Barnes parts with him.
Genre(s): Western Fiction.

2097. *Once a Legend.* New York: Walker, 1988. 183 pp.
In 1915, the man that Frank Ladd captured and sent to prison 20 years before has been freed, and after killing the judge who sentenced him, he looks for Ladd.
Genre(s): Western Fiction.

2098. *The Rough Rider.* New York: Walker, 1988. 207 pp.
Lew Axford saves Jess Gault's life at San Juan Hill, and when they return to Nevada, Axford wants to become governor, and as Axford acts amorally to achieve his goal, Jess finds out the truth about San Juan Hill.
Genre(s): Western Fiction.

2099. *The Trick Shot.* New York: Walker, 1996. 171 pp.
John Drake, a trick shot artist in a traveling show, accidently kills his fiancé during a performance, and when he

goes into the desert to grieve, he has to rescue a young Native American girl from three escaped convicts.
Genre(s): Western Fiction.

Curtis, Jack

2100. *No Mercy.* New York: Walker, 1995. 160 pp.
Ranch hand Clint Durby wants to avenge the murder of his younger brother, who discovered the dishonesty of the Sawtooth Cattle syndicate before he died.
Genre(s): Western Fiction; Mystery.

Dailey, Janet

2101. *Stands a Calder Man.* New York: Pocket Books, 1983. 346 pp.
The 1909 Homestead Act in Montana causes major friction between the cowboys and the farmers, and Benjamin Calder becomes aware of the damage the farmers will do to the buffalo grass in the sequel to *This Calder Range.*
Genre(s): Romance; Family Saga.

Dallas, Sandra

2102. *Buster Midnight's Café.* New York: Random House, 1990. 288 pp.
Of friends in Butte, Montana, in the early 20th century, one becomes a Hollywood star and another becomes a world champion boxer.
Genre(s): Domestic Fiction.

2103. *The Persian Pickle Club.* New York: St. Martin's Press, 1995. 196 pp.
In Harveyville, Kansas, during the Depression, a quilting circle called the Persian Pickle Club meets weekly, and members help each other until Rita arrives and wants to solve the murder one of the member's husbands.
Genre(s): Mystery.

D'Angelo, Lou

2104. *What the Ancients Said.* New York: Doubleday, 1971. 237 pp.
In the early 1940s, Tommy and his brothers experience the disintegration of their mother's mental state but continue to base their decisions on the words of their Sicilian elders and their love of baseball.
Genre(s): Domestic Fiction.

Dash, Julie

2105. *Daughters of the Dust.* New York: Dutton, 1997. 336 pp.
Amelia Varnes, an anthropology student, goes to observe the Gullah society in the 1920s and rediscovers her heritage.
Genre(s): Domestic Fiction; Bildungsroman (Coming of Age).

Davis, Donald

◆ 2106. *Thirteen Miles From Suncrest.* Little Rock, AR: August House, 1994. 256 pp.
In 1910, Travis McGee looks at the world from a child's standpoint, but she does not understand how a schoolmate's father could murder his own daughter.
Genre(s): Bildungsroman (Coming of Age).

◆ May be suitable for young adult readers

Davis, H. L.

2107. *Honey in the Horn.* New York: Harper, 1935. 380 pp.
Clay Calvert meets Luce and becomes partners with her as they interact with a motley group of characters during Oregon's homesteading period in the early days of the 20th century.
Award(s): Pulitzer Prize.
Genre(s): Western Fiction.

Dawson, Carol

2108. *Body of Knowledge.* Chapel Hill, NC: Algonquin, 1994. 476 pp.
The Ransom dynasty's business partnership in the early 20th century leads to a feud which only Victoria, the last survivor in the family, has the information to end.
Genre(s): Domestic Fiction.

Day, Dianne

◆ 2109. *The Bohemian Murders.* New York: Doubleday, 1997. 256 pp.
Fremont Jones becomes the temporary lighthouse keeper at Point Pinos near Carmel after the San Francisco earthquake, and when a beautiful woman washes up on shore, she investigates.
Genre(s): Mystery.

◆ 2110. *Emperor Norton's Ghost.* New York: Doubleday, 1998. 230 pp.
Caroline Fremont Jones investigates a problem in California.
Genre(s): Mystery.

◆ 2111. *Fire and Fog.* New York: Doubleday, 1996. 241 pp.
Fremont Jones, 23, distracts other workers after the San Francisco earthquake of 1906 with her unconventional dress, but she investigates unusual deaths and helps her Chinese friend recover valuables.
Genre(s): Mystery.

◆ 2112. *The Strange Files of Fremont Jones.* New York: Doubleday, 1995. 229 pp.
In 1905, Caroline Fremont Jones leaves Boston for San Francisco to avoid an arranged marriage, and when she creates a secretarial business, she falls in love with her first client, a lawyer.
Award(s): Macavity Award.
Genre(s): Mystery.

Denker, Henry

◆ 2113. *Payment in Full.* New York: Morrow, 1991. 384 pp.
The Jewish Rebecca and David Rosen have no children, and when an African American domestic worker dies and leaves an eight-year-old daughter, they decide to form a loving family unit, against society's mores.
Genre(s): Domestic Fiction.

Dennis, Patrick

2114. *Around the World with Auntie Mame.* New York: Harcourt Brace, 1958. 286 pp.
A young man travels around the world with his wealthy widowed aunt before he attends college in 1937, in the sequel to *Auntie Mame.*
Genre(s): Humorous Fiction; Adventure Story.

2115. *Auntie Mame.* New York: Vanguard, 1955. 280 pp.
Patrick becomes the ward of his eccentric Auntie Mame in the 1920s, and he recalls the unusual aspects of their life together.
Genre(s): Adventure Story; Humorous Fiction.

Deveraux, Jude

2116. *The Awakening.* New York: Pocket Books, 1988. 348 pp.
Around 1913, Amanda Caulden falls in love with Hank Montgomery when he comes to unionize the Caulden field hands.
Genre(s): Romance; Western Fiction.

Di Donato, Georgia

2117. *Firebrand.* Garden City, NY: Doubleday, 1982. 336 pp.
Jospeh Pulitzer sends Amanda Lamar to Seattle in 1896 to report on the arrival of Chinese laborers, and during the next 20 years, she acquires four newspapers and a husband.
Genre(s): Adventure Story.

Dintenfass, Mark

2118. *Old World, New World.* New York: Morrow, 1982. 404 pp.
Jacob and Sophie Lieber arrive in New York City and try to raise their children in the Old World traditions.
Genre(s): Jewish Fiction.

Doctorow, E. L.

2119. *Billy Bathgate.* New York: Random House, 1989. 323 pp.
After young Billy Bathgate becomes a member of the mob, he begins to question its vengeful ways.
Award(s): PEN/Faulkner Award for Fiction; National Book Critics Circle Award; Howells Medal.

2120. *The Book of Daniel.* New York: Random House, 1971. 303 pp.
Daniel Isaacson recalls the espionage trial of the Rosenburgs, his parents, and from memory, examines their lives.
Genre(s): Legal Story; Domestic Fiction; Political Fiction.

2121. *Loon Lake.* New York: Random House, 1979. 258 pp.
In the 1930s, Joe, a poor son of mill hands, runs away and accidentally finds Loon Lake, the Adirondack estate of a tycoon.
Genre(s): Love Story.

◆ 2122. *Ragtime.* New York: Random House, 1975. 270 pp.
A Jewish immigrant, an African American musician, and a father trying to support his daughter find themselves intertwined during the early 20th century.
Award(s): National Book Critics Circle Award.

2123. *Welcome to Hard Times.* New York: Random House, 1960. 180 pp.
A criminal comes to Hard Times and destroys the town in one day.
Genre(s): Western Fiction.

◆ 2124. *World's Fair.* New York: Random House, 1985. 288 pp.
Edgar, nine, and his family have difficult times, but Edgar wins tickets for them to attend the New York World's Fair of 1939.
Award(s): National Book Award.
Genre(s): Domestic Fiction.

Doig, Ivan

2125. *Bucking the Sun.* New York: Simon and Schuster, 1996. 384 pp.
When construction of the Fort Peck Dam begins in the Montana countryside, the Duff family leaves its meager farm for a nearby boomtown for work during the Depression.

◆ 2126. *Dancing at the Rascal Fair.* New York: Atheneum, 1987. 405 pp.
Angus McCaskill travels with his friend to Montana from Scotland to settle in 1889.
Genre(s): Family Saga.

◆ 2127. *English Creek.* New York: Atheneum, 1984. 339 pp.
Jick McCaskill, 14, finds more about who he is by the end of the summer of 1939, in the sequel to *Dancing at the Rascal Fair*, than he expects.
Genre(s): Family Saga.

◆ 2128. *Ride with Me, Mariah Montana.* New York: Atheneum, 1996. 412 pp.
In the sequel to *English Creek*, Jick takes his daughter Mariah on a tour of Montana as the state leaves its pioneer past for an unknown future.
Genre(s): Domestic Fiction; Family Saga.

Donahue, Jack, and Michel T. Halbouty

2129. *Grady Barr.* New York: Arbor House, 1982. 349 pp.
After operating a Galveston brothel, Grady Barr becomes an oil entrepreneur when he goes to Venezuela in 1923.
Genre(s): Adventure Story.

Dos Passos, John

2130. *The 42nd Parallel.* New York: Harper, 1930. 426 pp.
The narrator presents life in the United States through a variety of methods, incidents, and characters.
Genre(s): Picaresque Fiction.

2131. *1919.* New York: Harcourt Brace, 1932. 473 pp.
The second volume of the U.S.A. trilogy, which begins with *The 42nd Parallel*, shows America in the war years through the eyes of five disparate people.
Genre(s): Picaresque Fiction.

2132. *Three Soldiers.* New York: Penguin, 1997. 410 pp.
Three soldiers fight together in World War I, one of them especially disenchanted with the aimlessness and boredom between battles.
Genre(s): War Story.

Douglas, John

2133. *Blind Spring Rambler.* New York: St. Martin's Press, 1988. 240 pp.
In 1923, Frank Grant and his young partner, Bill Edmonson, come to Blind Spring, West Virginia, to investigate a murder, but Grant keeps details of the case from Edmonson, and someone murders Grant as soon as they arrive.
Genre(s): Mystery.

Douglass, Thea Coy

2134. *Royal Poinciana.* New York: Donald I. Fine, 1988. 429 pp.
Madeleine Memory, head housekeeper at Palm Beach's Royal Poinciana Hotel meets Harry Loring, professional gambler, in the early 20th century.
Genre(s): Adventure Story.

Downing, Sybil

2135. *Fire in the Hole.* Niwot, CO: University Press of Colorado, 1996. 239 pp.
When Alex MacFarlane goes to Trinidad, Colorado, she and a former foe in law school unite to fight for better conditions in the coal mines that lead to the strike of 1913 and the Ludlow Massacre in 1914.
Genre(s): Western Fiction.

◆ 2136. *Ladies of the Goldfield Stock Exchange.* New York: Tor, 1997. 352 pp.
Meg Kendall, Tess Wallace, and Verna Bates have come to Goldfield for different reasons, but they realize that people with too little money for large holdings want to buy shares in goldmines, so they start a stock exchange.
Genre(s): Western Fiction.

Doxey, William

2137. *Cousins to the Kudzu.* Baton Rouge: Louisana State University Press, 1985. 255 pp.
In 1933, Doc Spaulding settles in Oughton, Georgia, and the town's residents reveal their quirks and characters back to the times of the Civil War.
Genre(s): Medical Novel.

Dreiser, Theodore

2138. *An American Tragedy.* New York: Boni and Liveright, 1925. 152 pp.
Clyde Griffiths falls in love with and impregnates Roberta, but realizing that another girl will help him succeed, he drowns Roberta.
Genre(s): Legal Story; Love Story.

◆ May be suitable for young adult readers

2139. *The Financier.* 1912. New York: New American Library, 1967. 463 pp.
Frank Cowperwood works to become a financier.

Drury, Allen

2140. *Toward What Bright Glory?* New York: Morrow, 1990. 496 pp.
Typical college students ignore social problems, but in 1939, they can no longer ignore anti-Semitism, racism, and war.
Genre(s): War Story; Bildungsroman (Coming of Age).

Dubus, Elizabeth Nell

2141. *Where Love Rules.* New York: Putnam, 1985. 414 pp.
Caroline Livaudais's parents object to her marrying Beau Langlinais in the 1920s, and she happily marries another, but Beau's wife is unpleasant, and he becomes a political figure.
Genre(s): Political Fiction.

Dunphy, Jack

2142. *The Murderous McLaughlins.* New York: McGraw Hill, 1988. 238 pp.
When a young boy goes to visit his grandmother to bring his father home, he experiences her domination of all the men in her life and the violent tempers that have earned the family an unsavory reputation.
Genre(s): Domestic Fiction.

Dykewomon, Elana

2143. *Beyond the Pale.* Chicago: Press Gang, 1997. 400 pp.
Chava emigrates to New York in the early 20th century and meets the woman who delivered her in Russia in 1889 and who now lives with a woman disguised as a man.
Genre(s): Domestic Fiction.

Edgerton, Clyde

◆ 2144. *Redeye.* Chapel Hill, NC: Algonquin, 1995. 256 pp.
In 1892, a group of explorers arrive at the cliff dwellings in southwest Colorado, each with a different agenda.
Genre(s): Western Fiction.

Edmonds, Walter D.

◆ 2145. *The Boyds of Black River.* New York: Dodd Mead, 1953. 248 pp.
A young visitor from the city at the Boyd family's horse farm admires their lifestyle in the early 1900s.

◆ 2146. *The South African Quirt.* Boston: Little, Brown, 1985. 186 pp.
Natty, 12, believes that his tyrannical father would like to use his South African quirt (whip) on Natty's mongrel dog in the summer of 1915.
Genre(s): Domestic Fiction.

Ehle, John

◆ 2147. *Last One Home.* New York: Harper and Row, 1984. 345 pp.
In the sequel to *The Road*, Pinkney Wright's family expects him to become a farmer, but he and his wife move to Asheville where he enters the business world.
Genre(s): Family Saga.

2148. *The Winter People.* New York: Harper and Row, 1982. 256 pp.
When Wayland Jackson comes to Appalachia during the Depression in the sequel to *The Lion of the Hearth*, he falls in love with Collie, but she has a son by another man who has refused to marry her.
Genre(s): Domestic Fiction; Family Saga.

Ehrlich, Max

2149. *The Big Boys.* Boston: Houghton Mifflin, 1981. 302 pp.
Four employees embezzle money from a bank to speculate on the stock market, and then decide to rob the bank to hide their misdeeds, but the crash of 1929 interrupts their plans.
Genre(s): Adventure Story.

Ellis, Julie

2150. *A Daughter's Promise.* New York: Arbor House, 1988. 470 pp.
Two orphaned sisters try to gain entrance into other social and economic classes between the 1920s and 1950s after their Southern Jewish shopkeeper father is convicted and lynched for a rape he did not commit.
Genre(s): Domestic Fiction.

2151. *Lasting Treasures.* New York: Putnam, 1993. 446 pp.
After escaping from Petrograd, Jewish Viktoria meets American Gary Barton in Paris, marries him, and returns with him to Virginia and his wealthy tobacco business family, where they raise their own family before Gary commits suicide and one of the children dies in World War II.
Genre(s): Family Saga.

◆ 2152. *No Greater Love.* New York: Morrow, 1991. 480 pp.
Idealistic teenagers Harry Newhouse and Katie Freeman marry in 1923 and move to Texas where they make money until Harry loses it in the stock market crash.
Genre(s): Romance.

Ellison, Ralph

2153. *Invisible Man.* New York: Random House, 1952. 429 pp.
The narrator traces his life from college and into Harlem where he becomes invisible like other African Americans.
Award(s): National Book Award.

Emshwiller, Carol

2154. *Ledoyt.* San Francisco: Mercury House, 1995. 232 pp.
Oriana runs West when unmarried and pregnant, planning to establish a home without men, but six years later,

a drifter comes by and wins her heart, and later, Lotti, her daughter, follows in her path.
Genre(s): Domestic Fiction; Family Saga.

Ephron, Amy

◆ 2155. *A Cup of Tea.* New York: Morrow, 1997. 200 pp.
Happily expecting to marry Philip Alsop, Rosemary Fell invites poor Eleanor Smith home with her in 1917, and Philip immediately falls in love with Eleanor.
Genre(s): Domestic Fiction.

Erdrich, Louise

2156. *Love Medicine.* New York: Henry Holt, 1984. 272 pp.
The members of the Chippewa Kaspaw and Lamartine families describe their simple existence as they both deny and discover their native heritages.
Award(s): National Book Award; *Los Angeles Times* Book Prize.
Genre(s): Family Saga.

Esstman, Barbara

2157. *The Other Anna.* New York: Harcourt Brace, 1993. 370 pp.
Anna Berter, 12, spends time with the old Scottish housekeeper and her granddaughter against her parents' wishes, and when the granddaughter has a child by one of their houseguests, Anna's parents adopt the child but drive out her grandmother.
Genre(s): Bildungsroman (Coming of Age).

Estes, Winston

◆ 2158. *Another Part of the House.* Philadelphia: Lippincott, 1970. 256 pp.
Larry Morrison, nine, remains optimistic during the Depression because of the closeness of his family until his favorite brother dies.
Genre(s): Domestic Fiction.

Estleman, Loren D.

◆ 2159. *The Hider.* Garden City, NY: Doubleday, 1978. 184 pp.
In 1898, a buffalo hunter, a young man sorry to have missed the Wild West, and a Native American trying to outrun justice team up in the Pacific Northwest.
Genre(s): Western Fiction.

◆ 2160. *Sudden Country.* Garden City, NY: Doubleday, 1991. 182 pp.
In the 1890s, David Grayle's mother supports the family by running a Texas rooming house, and when David meets a judge who comes to town and finds a map to a trove of gold, he begins his own search.
Genre(s): Western Fiction.

2161. *Whiskey River.* New York: Bantam, 1990. 262 pp.
Gangs and gangsters control bootlegger Jack Dance's life as a result of the 18th Amendment.
Genre(s): Adventure Story.

Evanier, David

2162. *Red Love.* New York: Scribner's, 1991. 322 pp.
The Communists in America seem to devote themselves blindly to their cause beginning in the 1930s, leading to the execution of the Rosenbergs in the 1950s.
Genre(s): Political Fiction.

Evans, Max

2163. *Bluefeather Fellini.* Niwot, CO: University Press of Colorado, 1993. 340 pp.
Bluefeather, half Native American and half Italian, wanders throughout the Southwest in the 1930s and 1940s but keeps returning to his spiritual home in Taos, New Mexico, with his Pueblo mother.
Genre(s): Bildungsroman (Coming of Age); Picaresque Fiction.

Fackler, Elizabeth

2164. *Backtrail.* New York: M. Evans, 1993. 320 pp.
In the sequel to *Blood Kin*, after asking a friend to look after Johanna, Seth tries to escape after robbing a bank.
Genre(s): Western Fiction.

Fair, Ronald

2165. *We Can't Breathe.* New York: Harper, 1971. 185 pp.
African American families go north to Chicago in the late 1930s hoping for a better life and find slums with roaches but people who help each other.
Genre(s): Domestic Fiction.

Fairbairn, Ann

2166. *Five Smooth Stones.* New York: Crown, 1966. 756 pp.
From his birth in the Depression to his interracial marriage to Sara and participation as a civil rights leader, David Champlin demonstrates courage and integrity, and he sacrifices everything in his devotion to larger causes at the cost of his own happiness.

Fante, John

◆ 2167. *1933 Was a Bad Year.* Santa Rosa, CA: Black Sparrow, 1985. 127 pp.
During the Depression, high school senior Dominic Molise worries about sex and being too short at the same time that he has concerns about his family's mental and economic welfare.
Genre(s): Domestic Fiction.

Farrell, James T.

2168. *The Dunne Family.* Garden City, NY: Doubleday, 1976. 326 pp.
In the sequel to *Judith*, the Dunnes gather in Chicago at the death of their mother during the early 20th century to plan her funeral and review family history.

◆ 2169. *Face of Time.* New York: Vanguard, 1953. 240 pp.
Danny O'Neill begins his story as a child in Chicago. (*Series:* Danny O'Neill Tetralogy, 1)

◆ 2170. *No Star is Lost.* New York: Vanguard, 1938. 474 pp.
Danny O'Neill's family continues life in Chicago. (*Series:* Danny O'Neill Tetralogy, 3)

2171. *Sam Holman.* New York: Prometheus, 1983. 276 pp.
Jewish intellectual Sam Holman joins the Communist party in the 1930s but leaves it for something else when it does not fulfill his needs.
Genre(s): Political Fiction.

2172. *Studs Lonigan.* New York: The Modern Library, 1938. 1113 pp.
In the three novels, *Young Lonigan*, *The Young Manhood of Studs Lonigan*, and *Judgment Day*, the Irish Lonigan leaves school, works as a house painter, and then faces the Depression with no job and declining health.

◆ 2173. *A World I Never Made.* New York: Vanguard, 1936. 516 pp.
Danny O'Neill lives with his grandmother in Chicago because his own parents are too poor to feed him, as he begins adolescence. (Danny O'Neill Tetralogy, 2)

Fast, Howard

◆ 2174. *The Immigrants.* Boston: Houghton Mifflin, 1977. 389 pp.
Three California families interact from the time of the San Francisco earthquake through World War I and the Depression.
Genre(s): Domestic Fiction; Family Saga.

◆ 2175. *Max.* Boston: Houghton Mifflin, 1982. 395 pp.
The industrious Max becomes an entrepreneur on the Lower East Side of New York and works his way through a series of businesses that make him a wealthy movie mogul.

◆ 2176. *Second Generation.* Boston: Houghton Mifflin, 1978. 441 pp.
In the sequel to *The Immigrants*, the Lavette family's Barbara becomes involved with the troubles of the 1930s.
Genre(s): Domestic Fiction; Family Saga.

Fast, Julius

2177. *What Should We Do about Davey?* New York: St. Martin's Press, 1988. 227 pp.
Davey, 16, seems bumbling to his friends, but an attractive, muscular older woman wants to educate him sexually during the Depression.
Genre(s): Humorous Fiction.

Faulkner, William

2178. *Absalom, Absalom!* New York: Random House, 1936. 384 pp.
When Thomas Sutpen returns from the war, he tries to continue his family name and complete his design to be a Southern aristocrat, but his children thwart his plan.
Genre(s): Family Saga.

2179. *The Reivers, a Reminiscence.* New York: Random House, 1962. 305 pp.
Boon Hogganbeck persuades Lucius Priest, 11, to borrow his grandfather's car in 1905, and after they arrive at a bordello, the black Ned McCaslin trades the car for a horse.
Genre(s): Humorous Fiction; Bildungsroman (Coming of Age).

2180. *Sartoris.* New York: Random House, 1929. 370 pp.
In the sequel to *The Unvanquished*, after Bayard Sartoris returns from World War I where his twin brother died, his urge for self-destruction becomes reckless.

2181. *Soldier's Pay.* New York: Boni and Liveright, 1926. 319 pp.
Two people who find Donald Mahon on a train help him return home from World War I with a mutilated face and little memory.
Genre(s): War Story.

Faust, Irvin

2182. *Jim Dandy.* New York: Carroll and Graf, 1994. 297 pp.
Hollis Cleveland, known as Jim Dandy, dances for his father's musical review in 1915, but after college 20 years later, he runs from a Harlem numbers boss, and ends up in Ethiopia during its war with Italy.
Genre(s): War Story.

Federspiel, Jurg

2183. *The Ballad of Typhoid Mary.* New York: Dutton, 1983. 171 pp.
A doctor brings a German immigrant girl into New York at the turn of the 20th century and she spreads typhoid throughout the city.
Genre(s): Biographical Fiction; Medical Novel.

Feldhake, Susan C.

2184. *The Darkness and the Dawn.* Grand Rapids, MI: Zondervan, 1996. 208 pp.
A gypsy girl staying in a small town's hotel delves into occultism that causes the inhabitants to question their beliefs. (*Series:* Enduring Faith, 8)
Genre(s): Christian Fiction; Western Fiction.

2185. *Joy in the Morning.* Grand Rapids, MI: Zondervan, 1995. 208 pp.
When Lester and Harmony Childers move to northern Minnesota from Illinois, Lester works in the timber business while Harmony becomes a nurse for Dr. Marcus Wellingham. (*Series:* Enduring Faith, 6)
Genre(s): Christian Fiction.

2186. *Serenity in the Storm.* Grand Rapids, MI: Zondervan, 1996. 288 pp.
When a couple has difficulty conceiving, they fight a custody battle for orphans. (*Series:* Enduring Faith, 7)
Genre(s): Christian Fiction.

Fenady, Andrew J.

2187. *The Summer of Jack London.* New York: Walker, 1985. 173 pp.
In 1896, after several years of sea voyage adventures, Jack London, 20, spends the summer in Oakland, where he meets Felicity, a woman who adores him but whose mother is horrified by London's illegitimate birth.
Genre(s): Biographical Fiction.

Ferber, Edna

2188. *Cimarron.* Garden City, NY: Doubleday, 1930. 388 pp.
Yancey Cravat arrives in Osage during the 1889 land rush, and his wife develops her business sense to take care of them before she goes to Congress.
Genre(s): Western Fiction; Political Fiction.

2189. *Giant.* Garden City, NY: Doubleday, 1952. 447 pp.
Leslie comes from Virignia to marry Bick Benedict and live on his huge ranch, but she never adjusts to the Texas way of life.
Genre(s): Domestic Fiction.

Fergus, Charles

2190. *Shadow Catcher.* New York: Soho, 1991. 308 pp.
An expedition visits 75 reservations in 1913 in an attempt to unite the tribes in appreciation of the government and to encourage contributions for a statue in New York Harbor.
Genre(s): Political Fiction.

Finley, Joseph E.

2191. *Missouri Blue.* New York: Putnam, 1976. 255 pp.
During the Depression, Braz Marvin loses his job as a railroad crewman and begins working in his wife's family's Missouri cotton fields.

Finney, Ernest J.

2192. *California Time.* Reno: University of Nevada Press, 1998. 240 pp.
In California's Great Central Valley, children of Japanese, Italians, and Portuguese relate their experiences during the Depression and World War II.
Genre(s): Domestic Fiction.

Finney, Jack

2193. *From Time to Time.* New York: Simon and Schuster, 1995. 303 pp.
In the sequel to *Time and Again*, Simon Morley leaves the 19th century and tries to stop World War I.
Genre(s): Fantastic Literature; Time Travel.

Fitzgerald, F. Scott

2194. *The Beautiful and Damned.* New York: Scribner's, 1922. 449 pp.
Anthony Patch expects to inherit millions from his grandfather in the 1920s, and when he and his wife spend without restraint, they do not receive the inheritance.
Genre(s): Domestic Fiction.

2195. *The Great Gatsby.* New York: Scribner's, 1925. 182 pp.
Jay Gatsby still adores Daisy Buchanan although she has married someone else, and he risks everything to lure her back.
Genre(s): Love Story.

2196. *This Side of Paradise.* New York: Scribner's, 1920. 282 pp.
Amory Blaine wanders through his early years falling in love with a variety of women and attempting to use the power of his personality to woo them.
Genre(s): Bildungsroman (Coming of Age).

Fitzgerald, Juliet

◆ **2197.** *Belle Haven.* New York: Viking, 1990. 209 pp.
Dabney Beale, 19, must live with her aunt after being expelled from college in the 1920s, and she finds a sinister woman whose alcoholic husband does not seem to see her unusual relationship with her lawyer.
Genre(s): Romance; Gothic Fiction.

Fleming, David L.

2198. *Border Crossings.* Fort Worth: Texas Christian University Press, 1993. 304 pp.
Salazar captures Mary Wells when Pancho Villa attacks Columbus, New Mexico, in 1916, and when her father's foreman rescues her, Salazar has brutally tortured her.
Genre(s): Western Fiction.

Flowers, Arthur

2199. *Another Good Loving Blues.* New York: Viking, 1993. 217 pp.
In 1919, Lucas Bodeen, a blues pianist, leaves Arkansas for Memphis with Melvira Dupree (a conjurer), but instead of searching for Melvira's mother, he stops on Beale Street, becoming enamored of the blues music scene.
Genre(s): Musical Fiction.

Fox, Charles

2200. *Portrait in Oil.* New York: Doubleday, 1984. 699 pp.
Tom Scott makes a fortune in oil before he is 21 in 1933, and he negotiates with large oil companies in his quest for more.
Genre(s): Family Saga.

Fox, Paula

2201. *The Western Coast.* New York: Harcourt Brace, 1972. 352 pp.
Not until she goes to California and suffers through marriage and affairs in the late 1930s does Annie Gianfala be-

gin to assert her individuality, and with her new feeling of independence, she goes to England to start over.
Genre(s): Bildungsroman (Coming of Age).

Frederikson, Edna

◆ 2202. *Three Parts Earth.* Susanville, CA: Threshold, 1972. 305 pp.
Delphie Doud grows up in poverty as her family moves to increasingly smaller homes in Arkansas and then in Oklahoma in pre-World War I times, and attending school is a luxury.
Genre(s): Bildungsroman (Coming of Age).

Freeman, Cynthia

◆ 2203. *Portraits.* New York: Arbor House, 1979. 677 pp.
After Esther Sandsonitsky arrives from Poland, immigration officials call her Sanders, and she and her family move from Cleveland to San Francisco.
Genre(s): Domestic Fiction; Jewish Fiction.

2204. *A World Full of Strangers.* New York: Arbor House, 1975. 450 pp.
David Rezinetsky changes his name in the 1930s so that he can become wealthy, but after sacrificing his marriage, he meets Jews in California who have become successful while maintaining their identities.
Genre(s): Domestic Fiction; Jewish Fiction.

Freeman, James A.

2205. *Ishi's journey.* Happy Camp, CA: Naturegraph, 1992. 224 pp.
In 1911, Ishi, the last of the Yahis, survives the genocide of his tribe and the ruin of his California environment.
Genre(s): Biographical Fiction.

French, Albert

◆ 2206. *Billy.* New York: Viking, 1993. 214 pp.
In the 1930s, Billy, a 10-year-old African American, is sentenced for killing a white girl who beat him up.

Fuller, Henry Blake

2207. *Bertram Cope's Year.* Chappaqua, NY: Turtle Point, 1998. 320 pp.
When homosexual professor Edmund Cope arrives in an Illinois town during the early 20th century, citizens welcome him, but he writes letters to the man he loves, asking him to join him.
Genre(s): Domestic Fiction.

Funderburk, Robert

2208. *These Golden Days.* Minneapolis, MN: Bethany House, 1995. 301 pp.
Although Catherine and Lane Temple have held their marriage together, they wonder if they will be able to handle daughter Jessie's fight to become independent in Hollywood. (Innocent Years, 2)
Genre(s): Domestic Fiction; Christian Fiction.

Gaffney, Patricia

2209. *Sweet Everlasting.* New York: Topaz, 1993. 384 pp.
Mute Carrie, 18, cures animals in the woods where she lives with her religious stepfather, and Tyler Wilkes, who comes to the town as the physician, hears her singing when alone and becomes enchanted.
Genre(s): Romance.

Gage, Elizabeth

2210. *Taboo.* New York: Pocket Books, 1992. 465 pp.
In the late 1930s, Eve Sinclair builds her movie career by sleeping with the men who can help her succeed, but when Kate arrives in Hollywood, she enthralls Eve's producer and takes a role already promised to Eve.
Genre(s): Romance.

Gambino, Richard

2211. *Bread and Roses.* New York: Seaview, 1981. 474 pp.
The Trinacrias of Sicily arrive in America in 1890, and the father of the family becomes a wealthy banker, and other family members include an Olympic champion and an anarchist.
Genre(s): Domestic Fiction; Family Saga.

Gann, Ernest Kellogg

◆ 2212. *The Aviator.* New York: Arbor House, 1981. 189 pp.
In 1928, while flying over the Columbia plateau, an aviator tries to save a passenger after the plane crashes.

2213. *Gentlemen of Adventure.* New York: Arbor House, 1983. 445 pp.
Toby Bryant and Kiffin Draper became involved in an experiment to stay aloft in 1905, and they continue their aviation exploits through World War I into the jet age.
Genre(s): Adventure Story.

Garcia, Lionel G.

2214. *To a Widow with Children.* Houston, TX: Arte Publico, 1994. 236 pp.
Because the sheriff hated Maria's dead husband, he sends her four children to an orphanage, but the children gain allies in the townspeople against him.
Genre(s): Western Fiction.

Gardner, Mary

2215. *Milkweed.* Watsonville, CA: Papier-Mache, 1994. 320 pp.
Susan Carson studies an old set of encyclopedias in the early 20th century that allows her to cope with serious loses in her family and finally leaves to open her own boarding house in Minnesota.
Genre(s): Domestic Fiction.

Garlock, Dorothy

2216. *Ribbon in the Sky.* New York: Warner Books, 1993. 352 pp.
Letty Pringle becomes pregnant by her boyfriend Mike, and her minister father sends her away to her grandpar-

ents, saying that she has died, and when Mike returns from war and finds her, he tries to make up the lost time.
Genre(s): Romance; War Story.

2217. *Sins of Summer.* New York: Warner Books, 1994. 400 pp.
Dory Callahan, an unwed mother, keeps the Idaho logging community homestead for her kind brother James and two half brothers until Ben Waller arrives with his deaf daughter, Odette.
Genre(s): Romance; Western Fiction.

Gast, Kelly P.

◆ 2218. *Dil Dies Hard.* New York: Doubleday, 1975. 164 pp.
In Washington during 1915, Dil Reeves struggles to settle his homesteading claim near Bear Creek while those around him are either murdered or kidnapped.
Genre(s): Western Fiction.

Gathje, Curtis

2219. *A Model Crime.* New York: Donald I. Fine, 1995. 208 pp.
A mentally disturbed artist confesses to the murder of New York nude model Ronnie Gideon on Easter Sunday in 1937.
Genre(s): Mystery.

Gerard, Philip

2220. *Cape Fear Rising.* Winston-Salem, NC: John F. Blair, 1994. 420 pp.
In 1898, Sam Jenks and his wife come to Wilmington, North Carolina's, largest city, where he works for the newspaper and finds whites disturbed about the large middle-class black population.

2221. *Hatteras Light.* New York: Scribner's, 1986. 240 pp.
In 1918, a U-boat spotted off Hatteras Island makes the water even more treacherous, and the Navy gives the people who live there no help in identifying it.
Genre(s): War Story.

Gerson, Noel B.

2222. *The Crusader.* Boston: Little, Brown, 1970. 375 pp.
Margaret Sanger campaigns for the right to planned parenthood for all social and economic classes.
Genre(s): Biographical Fiction.

Giardina, Denise

2223. *The Unquiet Earth.* New York: Norton, 1992. 480 pp.
Union organizer Dillion Freeman must cope with the sophisticated ploys of mine owners as he tries to help the coal miners in West Virginia after the Depression in this sequel to *Storming Heaven.*
Genre(s): Political Fiction.

Gibbons, Kaye

◆ 2224. *Charms for the Easy Life.* New York: Putnam, 1993. 256 pp.
Charlie Kate travels around the country with her herb bag as a midwife and healer, delivering her own daughter Sophia, but in 1904, her marriage ends, and she and Sophia live alone until her daughter gives birth to Margaret, the narrator.
Genre(s): Medical Novel.

2225. *A Cure for Dreams.* Chapel Hill, NC: Algonquin, 1991. 170 pp.
Betty Davies Randolph tells about her childhood and the people she knew on Milk Farm Road during the Depression.
Genre(s): Domestic Fiction.

Gibbons, Reginald

◆ 2226. *Sweetbitter.* Seattle, WA: Broken Moon, 1994. 420 pp.
In 1910, Reuben Sweetbitter, half Choctaw, falls in love with a white woman, but they are forbidden to see each other.
Genre(s): Bildungsroman (Coming of Age).

Giles, Janice Holt

2227. *Miss Willie.* 1951. Boston: Houghton Mifflin, 1971. 268 pp.
In the sequel to *The Enduring Hills,* Miss Willie comes from Texas to be the new schoolteacher in Piney Ridge, but the town refuses to accept her ways until she marries a local man.
Genre(s): Domestic Fiction.

2228. *Tara's Healing.* Boston: Houghton Mifflin, 1951. 253 pp.
In the sequel to *Miss Willie,* a doctor finds a new reason for living when he goes to the Kentucky mountains to serve the local people.
Genre(s): Romance; Domestic Fiction; Medical Novel.

Gilman, Charlotte Perkins

2229. *Unpunished.* 1929. New York: Feminist Press, 1997. 192 pp.
When a man hated by all dies in his locked study, a husband-and-wife team of detectives investigates.
Genre(s): Mystery.

Gloss, Molly

◆ 2230. *The Jump-Off Creek.* Boston: Houghton Mifflin, 1989. 194 pp.
Widow Lydia Sanderson travels to Oregon during the Depression of 1895 and begins to work the land in a community where neighbors feel bound to each other by their will to survive.
Genre(s): Domestic Fiction.

Godwin, Rebecca T.

2231. *Keeper of the House.* New York: St. Martin's Press, 1994. 288 pp.
When Minyon Manigault is 14 during the Depression, her grandmother gives her to Miss Addie to do housework in her high-class whorehouse, and Minyon listens

carefully enough to Miss Addie's business plan to run the house herself.
Genre(s): Bildungsroman (Coming of Age); Domestic Fiction.

Gold, Herbert

2232. *Fathers.* New York: Random House, 1967. 308 pp.
When a poor young boy of 13 escapes czarist Russia for the United States, racketeers try to control him before he finds success.

Goldreich, Gloria

2233. *Leah's Journey.* New York: Harcourt Brace, 1978. 450 pp.
Leah and her husband flee from pogroms in Russia to New York City where her family goes through a series of changes.
Award(s): National Jewish Book Award.
Genre(s): Jewish Fiction.

Goodman, Jo

2234. *Only in My Arms.* New York: Kensington, 1997. 432 pp.
Mary Francis, the oldest of five Dennehy sisters, leaves the convent after 13 years and goes west to Fort Union, Arizona, where she discovers that the man unjustly accused of raiding an Army supply train and killing soldiers is Ryder McKay, someone she met while still a nun.
Genre(s): Western Fiction; Romance.

Goodman, Mark

2235. *Hurrah for the Next Man Who Dies.* New York: Atheneum, 1985. 274 pp.
Princeton football hero Hobey Baker dies in World War I a month after the Armistice, and his life as an aviator in the army seems to have mirrored his life in college playing football.
Genre(s): Biographical Fiction; War Story.

Gores, Joe

2236. *Hammett.* New York: Putnam, 1975. 251 pp.
In the 1920s, Dashiell Hammett must help find the criminal who killed an honest cop, even though Hammett prefers to continue his writing.
Genre(s): Mystery.

Gorman, Edward

2237. *Blood Game.* New York: Henry Holt, 1989. 172 pp.
In 1892, bounty hunter Leo Guild becomes involved with a dishonest boxing promoter who pits blacks against whites with a fixed outcome that the blacks will be either beaten badly or killed.
Genre(s): Sports Fiction.

◆ 2238. *Night of Shadows.* New York: Doubleday, 1990. 180 pp.
Ann Tolan, the first policewoman in Cedar Rapids, Iowa, expects to be watching an alcoholic's actions, but a murder occures that diverts her attention.
Genre(s): Western Fiction.

◆ 2239. *What the Dead Men Say.* New York: M. Evans, 1990. 130 pp.
In 1901, James Hogan, 16, goes with his uncle to the Iowa State Fair, but on the way, they stop in a town where the uncle plans to avenge his daughter's death which occurred during a foiled bank robbery three years before.
Genre(s): Bildungsroman (Coming of Age).

Goulart, Ron

2240. *Groucho Marx, Master Detective.* New York: St. Martin's Press, 1998. 272 pp.
Groucho Marx and his assistant, scriptwriter Frank Denby, track a dead actress's murderer.
Genre(s): Mystery.

Grau, Shirley Ann

2241. *Roadwalkers.* New York: Knopf, 1994. 336 pp.
Someone finds Baby abandoned in the woods during the Depression, and Rita names her Mary Woods, teaching her how to be human, and with a salesman from India, Mary has her own daughter Nanda.
Genre(s): Family Saga.

Greeley, Andrew M.

◆ 2242. *Irish Whiskey.* New York: Tor, 1998. 304 pp.
Nuala Anne McGrail uses her psychic ability in an investigation of Al Capone's rival.
Genre(s): Mystery.

Greenberg, Eric Rolfe

2243. *The Celebrant.* New York: Everest House, 1993. 272 pp.
A young Jewish merchant tries to keep people from exploiting New York Giants pitcher Christy Mathewson, but the 1919 Black Sox scandal occurs anyway.
Genre(s): Biographical Fiction; Sports Fiction.

Griffin, W. E. B.

2244. *Call to Arms.* New York: Jove, 1987. 356 pp.
Ken McCoy returns to the United States to attend officers' training school before World War II begins where he is assigned to spy on one of the students who seems to have an affinity for Red China. (*Series:* The Corps, 2)
Genre(s): War Story.

Gross, Joel

2245. *Maura's Dream.* New York: Seaview, 1981. 427 pp.
Maura, 17, leaves Ireland with a man she does not love in 1897 to escape to America, but he dies soon after arrival, and someone sells her into prostitution.

Grubb, Davis

2246. *Fools' Parade.* New York: World, 1969. 306 pp.
When Mattie is released from a West Virginia prison after 47 years, he has enough money accrued from savings

to open a store, but townspeople want to thwart his honest endeavors.
Genre(s): Humorous Fiction.

Guthrie, A. B.

2247. *Arfive.* Boston: Houghton Mifflin, 1971. 278 pp.
When disciplined Benton Collingsworth arrives in Arfive, a small Montana town, to be the principle of the high school, he clashes with the loose attitude of the west, in the sequel to *These Thousand Hills.*
Genre(s): Western Fiction.

◆ 2248. *The Genuine Article.* Boston: Houghton Mifflin, 1977. 172 pp.
A rancher dies after cattle rustlers arrive, and Old Eagle Charlie is a prime suspect until he dies the same way.
Genre(s): Western Fiction; Mystery.

◆ 2249. *The Last Valley.* New York: Houghton Mifflin, 1975. 293 pp.
Ben Tate buys the Arfive local weekly and makes it into a respectable newspaper, in this sequel to *Arfive.*
Genre(s): Western Fiction.

2250. *No Second Wind.* New York: Houghton Mifflin, 1980. 216 pp.
In a cold winter in Montana, a group of strip miners wait to start their jobs, and those opposed to the mine cause problems.
Genre(s): Western Fiction.

Guy, Rosa

2251. *A Measure of Time.* New York: Holt, Rinehart, and Winston, 1983. 365 pp.
Dorine Davis, a young African American teenager, arrives in Harlem in the 1920s and becomes involved with department store boosters.
Genre(s): Bildungsroman (Coming of Age).

Hailey, Elizabeth Forsythe

2252. *A Woman of Independent Means.* New York: Viking, 1978. 256 pp.
Bess Alcott writes letters to and about her family to describe her life in the early 20th century.
Genre(s): Domestic Fiction.

Haines, Carolyn

2253. *Touched.* New York: Dutton, 1996. 371 pp.
In 1926, Mattie Mills comes to a small Mississippi town as the mail-order bride of an abusive man and meets the feminist JoHanna McVay and her daughter.
Genre(s): Domestic Fiction.

Halacy, Dan

◆ 2254. *Empire in the Dust.* New York: Walker, 1990. 168 pp.
Frank and Emily Cullen have a large Texas ranch around 1890, but the weather and external factors almost destroy their holdings.
Genre(s): Western Fiction.

Hall, Robert Lee

◆ 2255. *Murder at San Simeon.* New York: St. Martin's Press, 1988. 343 pp.
William Randolph Hearst invites people to his San Simeon house party, and someone is murdered.
Genre(s): Mystery.

Hammonds, Michael

2256. *Concerning the Death of Charlie Bowman.* New York: Doubleday, 1971. 179 pp.
An old ranch hand finds Charlie Bowman, a half-Native American homesteader, dead, in 1899, and becomes implicated in his death.
Genre(s): Western Fiction.

2257. *A Gathering of Wolves.* New York: Doubleday, 1975. 160 pp.
Walt Canfield plans to extort money for Pancho Villa from profiteer Linus Ballard in 1913 by kidnapping Ballard's daughter Addie, but a mountain man on the stage with Addie has other ideas.
Genre(s): Western Fiction.

Hamner, Earl

2258. *The Homecoming; a Novel About Spencer's Mountain.* New York: Random House, 1970. 115 pp.
Clay-Boy's siblings wait for their father to return from his out-of-town job one Christmas Eve in the 1930s in the sequel to *Spencer's Mountain.*
Genre(s): Domestic Fiction.

2259. *Spencer's Mountain.* New York: Dial, 1961. 247 pp.
Clay-Boy, whose father thinks college is unnecessary, grows up in the Blue Ridge Mountains of Virginia.
Genre(s): Domestic Fiction.

Hannah, Kristin

2260. *When Lightning Strikes.* New York: Fawcett, 1994. 384 pp.
Alaina Cozstanza falls asleep one night while working at her computer and wakes up in Fortune Flats, the town in her latest novel, 100 years earlier, where she falls in love with the villain rather than with the sheriff.
Genre(s): Romance; Time Travel; Western Fiction.

Hansen, Ron

◆ 2261. *Desperadoes.* New York: Knopf, 1979. 273 pp.
By 1937, Emmett Dalton has become a rich Hollywood resident from money made on books and movies about his outlaw days.
Genre(s): Biographical Fiction; Western Fiction.

Harington, Donald

2262. *The Choiring of the Trees.* San Diego, CA: Harcourt Brace, 1991. 388 pp.
Corrupt politicians of Stay More, Arkansas, frame Nail Chism for rape and sentence him to death in 1914, while Viridis Monday, an artist trained in Paris, draws trial sketches and decides that Chism is not guilty.
Genre(s): Political Fiction; Legal Story.

◆ May be suitable for young adult readers

Harris, Jana

2263. *The Pearl of Ruby City.* New York: St. Martin's Press, 1998. 368 pp.
In the 1890s, Pearl Ryan works to save money for nursing school, but when the mayor and two others are poisoned, she tries to solve the crime before her own secrets are exposed.
Genre(s): Mystery; Western Fiction.

Harris, Julie

2264. *The Longest Winter.* New York: St. Martin's Press, 1995. 306 pp.
An aviator, John Robert Shaw, crashes in Alaska's Aleutian Islands in the 1920s, and Eskimos help him survive for 17 years.
Genre(s): Biographical Fiction.

Harris, Marilyn

◆ 2265. *Lost and Found.* New York: Crown, 1991. 438 pp.
After her stepbrother puts Belle Drusso on the wrong train when she is three, her devoted foster mother tries to find her.
Genre(s): War Story.

Hartog, Diana

2266. *The Photographer's Sweethearts.* Woodstock, NY: Overlook, 1996. 240 pp.
Danish Louie Olsen goes to California in the early 1900s and sees the sequoias, and he enjoys taking pictures of both them and children, as he begins his pedophile career.

Hayden, Sterling

2267. *Voyage: A Novel of 1896.* New York: Putnam, 1976. 700 pp.
Two ships and their passengers, one a rigger from Maine and the other a private yacht, meet in San Francisco on the eve of the Bryan-McKinley presidential election.
Genre(s): Sea Story.

Hayes, J. M.

2268. *The Grey Pilgrim.* New York: Walker, 1990. 236 pp.
When a small band of Papago Indians refuses to register for the draft in 1940, Marshall J.D. Fitzpatrick tries to defuse the situation.
Genre(s): Western Fiction.

Hayes, Penny

2269. *Grassy Flats.* Tallahassee, FL: Naiad, 1992. 237 pp.
Aggie and Nell struggle to hold on to their Idaho potato farm in the years after the Depression, while Tessie and Clara, two married women, discover that they might love each other.
Genre(s): Domestic Fiction.

Heck, Peter J.

2270. *Death on the Mississippi.* New York: Berkeley, 1995. 290 pp.
Samuel Clemens goes on a speaking tour during the 1890s with his new travel secretary and investigates a murder involving his experience on the Mississippi River.
Genre(s): Mystery.

Helm, Thomas Monroe

2271. *Iron Skillet Bill.* New York: Doubleday, 1975. 155 pp.
Ambrose Patch, 14 and half Choctaw, and his aunt Miss Maggie have no money when they drive a 1911 Model-T Ford across the country in 1915, until they meet William Trevelyn Murphy, known as Iron Skillet Bill.
Genre(s): Western Fiction.

Hennessy, Max

◆ 2272. *The Bright Blue Sky.* New York: Atheneum, 1983. 250 pp.
Dickon Quinney, 17, becomes enamoured with airplanes, enlists in the military, and begins flying in World War I.
Genre(s): War Story; Adventure Story.

Henry, Will

2273. *Mackenna's Gold.* New York: Random House, 1963. 276 pp.
In 1897, a dying Apache tells a young prospector where to find gold.
Genre(s): Western Fiction.

2274. *San Juan Hill.* New York: Random House, 1962. 314 pp.
An Arizona cowboy joins Theodore Roosevelt and his Rough Riders in battle at San Juan Hill, Puerto Rico.
Genre(s): War Story; Adventure Story.

Henslee, Helen

2275. *Pretty Redwing.* New York: Henry Holt, 1983. 200 pp.
Flora marries a wealthy widower in the Blue Ridge during the 1930s and falls in love with her stepson.
Genre(s): Love Story.

Herr, Michael

2276. *Walter Winchell.* New York: Vintage, 1991. 157 pp.
Walter Winchell grows to prominence in journalism by pandering to those in power and disregarding those without it.
Genre(s): Biographical Fiction.

Herron, Carolivia

2277. *Thereafter Johnnie.* New York: Random House, 1991. 240 pp.
Johnnie, the result of an incestuous relationship between her mother and grandfather, examines African American life in her family and in the community.
Genre(s): Domestic Fiction.

Hewat, Alan V.

2278. *Lady's Time.* New York: Harper and Row, 1985. 338 pp.
Lady Winslow, a ragtime piano player in the early 20th century, faces the racial prejudices of the era.
Award(s): Ernest Hemingway Foundation Award.
Genre(s): Musical Fiction.

Heyward, DuBose

2279. *Porgy.* New York: Doran, 1925. 196 pp.
The African American Porgy becomes involved in a waterfront murder, and a white detective imprisons him as a witness in Charleston.
Genre(s): Love Story.

Hijuelos, Oscar

2280. *The Fourteen Sisters of Emilio Montez O'Brien.* New York: Farrar, Straus and Giroux, 1993. 480 pp.
In the early 20th century Emilio, with an Irish father, a Cuban mother, and 14 sisters in a small Pennsylvania town, becomes a movie star with Errol Flynn as his friend.
Genre(s): Domestic Fiction.

Hill, Weldon

2281. *Jefferson McGraw.* New York: Morrow, 1972. 288 pp.
Jeff, 12, feels that he has to do more than his share for the family and feels other conflicting emotions about girls and siblings and his friendship with an escaped prisoner hiding near his fishing hole.
Genre(s): Domestic Fiction.

Hjortsberg, William

2282. *Nevermore.* New York: Grove/Atlantic, 1994. 320 pp.
The aged Sir Arthur Conan Doyle begins believing in the occult, and Houdini wants to expose him as a fraud, but murders resembling those in Edgar Allan Poe's stories draw them together when the victims all have connections to Houdini.
Genre(s): Mystery; Gothic Fiction.

Hoagland, Edward

2283. *Seven Rivers West.* New York: Summit Books, 1986. 296 pp.
In the late 19th century, Cecil Roop travels west to find a grizzly bear for his vaudeville act, and accompanying him is Sutton, a high diver seeking gold.
Genre(s): Western Fiction.

Hobson, Laura Z.

2284. *First Papers.* New York: Random House, 1964. 502 pp.
Two families of immigrants struggle with the socialist liberal movement of 1911 to 1920.
Genre(s): Political Fiction.

Hoff, B. J.

2285. *The Penny Whistle.* Minneapolis, MN: Bethany House, 1996. 192 pp.
Two students plan to take a collection to replace their beloved teacher's stolen flute in the late 19th century, but one of them dies before they succeed.
Genre(s): Christian Fiction.

Hogan, Linda

◆ 2286. *Mean Spirit.* New York: Atheneum, 1990. 448 pp.
In 1922, Grace Blanket chooses supposedly worthless land allotted to Native Americans by the Dawes Act, but when the land is found to have oil, she and her family have to protect themselves from greedy white government officials.
Genre(s): Domestic Fiction; Political Fiction.

Horan, James David

2287. *The Blue Messiah.* New York: Crown, 1971. 504 pp.
Two boys from New York's west side slums rise to power in a sinister Italian American group.

Horgan, Paul

2288. *Everything to Live For.* New York: Farrar, Straus and Giroux, 1968. 215 pp.
Max Chittenden, wealthy Harvard undergraduate, has difficulty adjusting to the public watching everything his family does.
Genre(s): Domestic Fiction.

2289. *The Thin Mountain Air.* New York: Farrar, Straus and Giroux, 1977. 311 pp.
In the 1920s, Richard leaves college and works on a New Mexico ranch as a way to rebuild his health.
Genre(s): Domestic Fiction; Western Fiction; Bildungsroman (Coming of Age).

Hotchner, A. E.

2290. *King of the Hill.* New York: Harper and Row, 1972. 240 pp.
Aaron, 12, helps his family through illness and unemployment during the Depression.
Genre(s): Bildungsroman (Coming of Age).

Houston, Robert

2291. *Bisbee '17.* New York: Pantheon, 1979. 287 pp.
The men striking the copper mine in Bisbee, Arizona, during 1917, want to disrupt the war effort and begin a general nation-wide strike for workers throughout the country.

Howard, Clark

2292. *Dirt Rich.* New York: St. Martin's Press, 1986. 519 pp.
Sam Sheridan and his bride go to Dane, Texas, to claim the land left him by a man he never met, and after they discover oil fields, Sheridan joins the others in the Patman family in their fight against the Spence family.
Genre(s): Family Saga.

Howard, Fred

2293. *Charlie Flowers and the Melody Garden.*
New York: Liveright and Boni, 1972. 206 pp.
Maggie, a society girl who has had to get a job, and Char-
lie, an innocent but interesting male, come together dur-
ing the Depression in Chicago.
Genre(s): Love Story.

Howatch, Susan

2294. *The Rich Are Different.* New York: Simon
and Schuster, 1977. 658 pp.
The Van Zales own a large New York City bank with
Paul heading the family and the bank in 1920.
Genre(s): Family Saga; Domestic Fiction.

Humphrey, William

2295. *The Ordways.* New York: Knopf, 1964. 326
pp.
When the Ordway family gathers to clean their graveyard
in the 1930s, one of the sons recounts the life of the family since the Civil War.
Genre(s): Domestic Fiction; Family Saga.

Hunt, Marsha

2296. *Free.* New York: Dutton, 1993. 277 pp.
Freed slaves and their children live in Germantown, Pennsylvania, and timid Teenotchy, 19, works for Quakers after seeing his mother raped and killed when he was five.
Genre(s): Domestic Fiction.

Hunter, Evan

2297. *Sons.* Garden City, NY: Doubleday, 1969.
396 pp.
The Tyler family males fight in three wars, two of them
gladly, and one with grave doubts.
Genre(s): War Story.

Hurd, Jerrie

2298. *Kate Burke Shoots the Old West.* New
York: Pocket Books, 1997. 384 pp.
In 1891, married photographer Kate Burke wants to cap-
ture the West on film, and she defies Colonel Elliot
George when he tells her to stop taking photographs.
Genre(s): Western Fiction.

2299. *Miss Ellie's Purple Sage Saloon.* New
York: Pocket Books, 1995. 375 pp.
Miss Ellie, con artist, refuses to marry her lover Seth Watkins, and Seth's new bride ignores him, but when temperance women try to change the town, the two females join
forces.
Genre(s): Romance; Western Fiction.

Ingram, Bowen

◆ 2300. *Milbry.* New York: Crown, 1972. 224 pp.
Milbry grows from six to 16 in a small Tennessee town
beginning in 1910.
Genre(s): Domestic Fiction; Bildungsroman (Coming of
Age).

Ivory, Judith

2301. *Beast.* New York: Avon, 1997. 375 pp.
Louise Vandermeer agrees to marry an aristocrat in
Europe, but she has an affair with an Arab pasha on
board a ship, and later discovers that he is her intended
spouse.
Genre(s): Sea Story; Romance.

Jacobson, Sidney

2302. *Another Time.* New York: St. Martin's
Press, 1989. 368 pp.
When widower Congressman Will Jaffe wants to become
a senator, his family and political events seem to thwart
his progress.
Genre(s): Political Fiction; Romance.

Jakes, John

2303. *American Dreams.* New York: Dutton,
1998. 464 pp.
Chicago beer baron Joe Crown's daughter Fritzi fails on
the New York stage and goes to Hollywood for a movie
career while her brother drops out of Princeton and her
cousin photographer records the horrors of World War I.
Genre(s): Domestic Fiction; War Story.

2304. *California Gold.* New York: Random
House, 1989. 658 pp.
Mack Chance leaves the Appalachian coal mine for San
Francisco in 1886 and becomes a real estate tycoon be-
fore the earthquake in 1906.

2305. *Homeland.* New York: Doubleday, 1993.
785 pp.
Pauli Kroner arrives from Berlin, Germany, having been
robbed on the way, but has the opportunity to work in
cinematography with the newly invented camera.
Genre(s): Domestic Fiction.

Jamison, Janelle

2306. *A Light in the Window.* Uhrichsville, OH:
Barbour, 1997. 192 pp.
When Julie Erikson returns to Alaska in 1925 after studying nursing in Seattle for five years, she refuses to encourage the advances of Sam Curtiss because of her desire to
provide health care.
Genre(s): Christian Fiction; Romance.

Janus, Christopher G.

◆ 2307. *Miss 4th of July, Goodbye.* Chicago: Lake
View, 1986. 223 pp.
Niki migrates from Greece to a small town in West Virginia near the end of World War I, and she writes her
grandfather about the narrow-mindedness of those who
live there.
Genre(s): Domestic Fiction.

Jenkins, Dan

2308. *Fast Copy.* New York: Simon and Schuster,
1988. 396 pp.
Betsy Throckmorton returns to Texas from the east in
1935, takes over her father's newspaper and radio station,

and becomes an investigator after someone kills her husband.
Genre(s): Mystery.

Jennings, Gary

◆ 2309. *The Terrible Teague Bunch.* New York: Norton, 1975. 256 pp.
When four men meet at a brothel in east Texas during 1905, they conspire to earn an instant fortune.
Genre(s): Western Fiction.

Johnson, Guy

2310. *Standing at the Scratch Line.* New York: Random House, 1998. 432 pp.
After killing two white deputies raiding an African American smuggling operation, LeRoi Boudreaux escapes Louisiana at 17 and goes to France to fight in World War I.
Genre(s): War Story; Adventure Story.

Johnston, Mary

2311. *Hagar.* Boston: Houghton Mifflin, 1913. 390 pp.
Hagar Ashendyne grows up in Virignia, refusing to accept the old conventions of the South as her grandmother desires and making her own name as a novelist before marrying.
Genre(s): Domestic Fiction.

Johnston, Velda

◆ 2312. *The Fateful Summer.* New York: Dodd, Mead, 1981. 225 pp.
In 1910, after Amanda Dorrance falls in love with an Irish American, someone murders her father.
Genre(s): Romance.

Jones, Douglas C.

◆ 2313. *A Creek Called Wounded Knee.* New York: Scribner's, 1978. 236 pp.
The sequel to *Arrest Sitting Bull* reveals the tragedy of Wounded Knee.
Genre(s): Western Fiction; War Story.

2314. *A Spider for Loco Shoat.* New York: Henry Holt, 1997. 288 pp.
In 1907, the people of Fort Smith, Arkansas, are concerned about a body found on the river bank, and deputy marshall Oscar Schiller is especially surprised at how rapidly the sheriff closes the case.
Genre(s): Western Fiction; Mystery.

◆ 2315. *Weedy Rough.* New York: Holt, Rinehart, and Winston, 1981. 345 pp.
In the sequel to *Come Winter*, Duny Gene Pay and Hoadie Renkin are best friends in a small Arkansas town during the Depression, but the arrival of a woman changes their lives.
Genre(s): Domestic Fiction.

Jones, Nettie

2316. *Mischief Makers.* New York: Weidenfeld and Nicolson, 1989. 160 pp.
The daughter of physicians who have founded a hospital for African Americans in Detroit during the 1920s is light-skinned, and after she falls in love with a dark-skinned man, they send her East to act as white.
Genre(s): Domestic Fiction.

Jones, Rod

2317. *Billy Sunday.* New York: Henry Holt, 1996. 255 pp.
In 1892, Charles Van Schaick, Billy Sunday, and Frederick Jackson Turner come to the village of Balsam Point, Wisconsin, in the summer, and while Schaick tries to photograph the surrounding spirits, murders occur.
Genre(s): Mystery.

Joyce, Brenda

2318. *Secrets.* New York: Avon, 1993. 406 pp.
While Regina travels on a train through California, bandits intrude, and she falls in love with her rescuer after getting amnesia.
Genre(s): Romance.

Just, Ward S.

2319. *A Family Trust.* Boston: Little, Brown, 1978. 346 pp.
Even after his death, the editor of a daily newspaper in the midwest tries to control his children and grandchildren through the terms of his will.
Genre(s): Domestic Fiction.

Kalpakian, Laura

2320. *Caveat.* Winston-Salem, NC: John F. Blair, 1998. 258 pp.
In 1916, the town of St. Elmo, California, invites Hank Beecham, a prodigal son, to return and stop the drought which has lasted for 302 straight days.
Genre(s): Domestic Fiction.

2321. *These Latter Days.* New York: Times, 1985. 371 pp.
Ruth Mason, a Mormon, refuses to marry without love, but as her chances dwindle, she must settle for much less.
Genre(s): Religious Fiction.

Kaplan, Barry Jay

2322. *Biscayne.* New York: Simon and Schuster, 1988. 504 pp.
When Clara Reade returns to Biscayne Bay after her husband's death in the early 20th century, she and her son join a railroad magnate in creating a resort area that later became Miami.
Genre(s): Domestic Fiction.

Katkov, Norman

2323. *Blood and Orchids.* New York: St. Martin's Press, 1983. 503 pp.
When a naval officer's wife is beaten and raped in Hawaii during the 1930s, four boys are tried and acquitted,

but the community's subsequent rage reveals racial tensions.
Genre(s): Mystery.

2324. *Millionaires Row.* New York: Dutton, 1996. 371 pp.
Tobacco magnate Kyle Castleton's older wife Faith murders him in the 1930s, but the sheriff's son loves her and clears her of the murder charges.
Genre(s): Domestic Fiction.

Kaufelt, David A.

2325. *The Wine and the Music.* New York: Delacorte, 1981. 368 pp.
Immigrant Bessie Meyer wants to marry an American, but instead she becomes the mistress of an Irish gangster, which enables her to bring other family members from Poland during the first half of the 20th century.
Genre(s): Jewish Fiction.

Kavaler, Lucy

2326. *The Secret Lives of the Edmonts.* New York: Dutton, 1989. 432 pp.
Melanie Edmont's affairs relieve her from the tedium of limitations imposed upon women during the 1890s, but even through society abhors divorce, her husband decides that he wants one.
Genre(s): Domestic Fiction.

Kay, Terry

2327. *After Eli.* Boston: Houghton Mifflin, 1981. 271 pp.
Eli Pettit supposedly left treasure on his farm before disappearing, and a wandering Irishman tries to become part of the Pettit family's life in order to find it.
Genre(s): Domestic Fiction.

Kazan, Elia

2328. *The Anatolian.* New York: Knopf, 1982. 436 pp.
In 1909, in the sequel to *America, America,* Stavros Topouzoglou's family of seven brothers and sisters arrives in New York, and he has to assume the patriarchal role.

Kelly, Jack

2329. *Mad Dog.* New York: Atheneum, 1992. 292 pp.
An actor tries to portray John Dillinger, known as Mad Dog, in a carnival act touring the Midwest while the audience still admires Dillinger's daring.
Genre(s): Biographical Fiction; Western Fiction.

Kelton, Elmer

◆ 2330. *Honor at Daybreak.* New York: Doubleday, 1991. 390 pp.
In the 1920s, Sheriff Dave Buckalew tries to keep racketeers from destroying honest oilmen in Caprock.
Genre(s): Western Fiction.

Kennedy, William

2331. *Billy Phelan's Greatest Game.* New York: Viking, 1978. 282 pp.
Billy Phelan tries to make a deal with the local gangsters in the sequel to *Legs,* but he has no chance of success.
Genre(s): Adventure Story.

2332. *The Flaming Corsage.* New York: Viking, 1996. 205 pp.
Edward Daugherty, an Irish working-class playwright, and Katrina Taylor, his Albany upper-class wife, struggle with their marriage in the 20th century's first decade.
Genre(s): Domestic Fiction.

2333. *Ironweed.* New York: Viking, 1983. 227 pp.
In the sequel to *Billy Phelan's Greatest Game,* Francis Phelan, an old hobo, comes home to Albany, New York, during the Depression.
Award(s): National Book Critics Circle Award; Pulitzer Prize.
Genre(s): Domestic Fiction; Family Saga.

2334. *Legs.* New York: Coward-McCann, 1975. 317 pp.
Francis Phelan becomes a hobo after accidentally killing his son, but when he returns 22 years later, he cannot reunite his family.
Genre(s): Adventure Story.

Kennelly, Ardyth

2335. *Up Home.* Boston: Houghton Mifflin, 1955. 376 pp.
When Linnea Ecklund finally gets her own home in the sequel to *The Peaceable Kingdom,* she and friends help with the opening of the Mormon Temple and work to abolish polygamy.
Genre(s): Domestic Fiction.

Kesey, Ken, and Ken Babbs

2336. *Last Go Round.* New York: Viking, 1994. 237 pp.
Three men compete for the Pendleton, Oregon, round-up champion broncobuster title in 1911, and although Jonathan E. Lee Spain wins, controversy surrounds his selection when the Nez Percé and the African American entrants are also very good.
Genre(s): Western Fiction.

Keyes, Daniel

2337. *The River Road.* New York: Messner, 1945. 747 pp.
The d'Alvery family owns a sugar plantation in Louisiana after World War I, and faces adversity and wins.
Genre(s): Domestic Fiction; Family Saga.

Keyes, Frances Parkinson

2338. *Victorine.* New York: Messner, 1958. 272 pp.
In the sequel to *Blue Camellia,* Lavinia, Brent Wislow's daughter, has a son, Prosper, who manages a family rice plant.
Genre(s): Family Saga; Romance.

Kiefer, Warren

2339. *Outlaw.* New York: Donald I. Fine, 1989. 518 pp.

After Apaches kill Lee Garland's parents, he serves in several wars, makes more than one fortune, and falls in love until he dies at the hands of marshalls when he refuses to leave his home at age 89.
Genre(s): Family Saga; Western Fiction.

Kilgo, James

2340. *Daughter of my People.* Athens, GA: University of Georgia Press, 1998. 288 pp.

In 1918, Hart Bonner, heir in a white South Carolina family, begins a secret affair with Jennie Grant, his half white cousin.
Genre(s): Domestic Fiction.

Killens, John Oliver

2341. *Youngblood.* 1954. Athens: University of Georgia Press, 1982. 475 pp.

A labor union for African American hotel workers begins to gain strength in Georgia in the 1920s and 1930s, but white Georgians continue to repress the union members in their communities.
Genre(s): Bildungsroman (Coming of Age); Political Fiction.

Kimball, Philip

2342. *Harvesting Ballads.* New York: Simon and Schuster, 1984. 448 pp.

Sorry learns about his parents when he is 18 and ultimately refuses the sense of family that his uncle offers him.
Genre(s): Bildungsroman (Coming of Age).

Kinsolving, William

2343. *Raven.* New York: Putnam, 1983. 352 pp.

After attempting an Atlantic solo flight in 1927, Buck Faulkner begins an aircraft manufacturing business in which intrigue and bribery play a part.
Genre(s): Political Fiction.

Kirby, Susan

2344. *When the Lilacs Bloom.* New York: Avon, 1997. 256 pp.

Libby and Ike Galloway start their marriage together in their Edgewood cabin, and after scandal, hostility, and difficulty, have a family celebration 11 years later.
Genre(s): Romance; Christian Fiction.

Kluger, Richard

◆ 2345. *Members of the Tribe.* Garden City, NY: Doubleday, 1977. 471 pp.

In 1913, Seth Adler defends the Jew Noah Berg in his trial after he is accused of murdering a young woman in Savannah, Georgia.
Genre(s): Legal Story.

2346. *Un-American Activities.* Garden City, NY: Doubleday, 1982. 696 pp.

Toby Ronan goes to Harvard expecting life to be easy, but he graduates during the Depression and faces leftist politics, the New Deal, and the Communist party.
Genre(s): Bildungsroman (Coming of Age); Political Fiction.

Konecky, Edith

◆ 2347. *Allegra Maud Goldman.* New York: Harper and Row, 1976. 174 pp.

Allegra Maud Goldman grows up in Brooklyn during the 1930s and finds that girls do not get the credit they deserve.
Genre(s): Jewish Fiction.

Korman, Keith

2348. *Archangel.* New York: Viking, 1983. 300 pp.

Buck, 16, sees two railroad policeman kill a hobo, and they intimidate him into silence.
Genre(s): Gothic Fiction.

Kraft, Gabrielle

2349. *Hollywood Hills.* New York: Pocket Books, 1993. 330 pp.

Katherine Ransome comes to Hollywood in 1936, falls in love with a handsome actor, and becomes pregnant, and fter he abandons her, she marries the Hungarian Jew refugee, Leo, and starts her family.
Genre(s): Family Saga.

Kruger, Mary

2350. *No Honeymoon for Death.* New York: Kensington, 1995. 288 pp.

In 1896, Matt Devlin and his socialite wife honeymoon at sea, and on the first night, a friend goes overboard, but after the ship's detective arrests the wrong man for the deed, Devlin must become involved.
Genre(s): Mystery.

Kubicki, Jan

◆ 2351. *Breaker Boys.* Boston: Atlantic Monthly, 1986. 390 pp.

In Jeddoh, the Poles and the Welsh distrust each other but work together in the coal mines, and Euan Morgan, 11, reveals their concerns and helps Mother Jones overcome their employer.
Genre(s): Biographical Fiction; Bildungsroman (Coming of Age).

Kurland, Michael

2352. *Too Soon Dead.* New York: St. Martin's Press, 1997. 238 pp.

Alexander Brass receives scandalous photos in 1935 from an anonymous source, and after a murder occurs, he elicits help from a widow and his secretary.
Genre(s): Mystery.

Kwasny, Melissa

2353. *Trees Call for What They Need.* Minneapolis, MN: Spinsters Ink, 1993. 249 pp.
Cynic Nettie meets Marie, a Polish immigrant, when they are girls in their small Indiana town, and although the town changes, their friendship remains steady.
Genre(s): Domestic Fiction.

Lambert, Gavin

2354. *Running Time.* New York: Macmillan, 1983. 410 pp.
In 1919, Elva Kay takes her seven-year-old daughter to Hollywood for fame and fortune but also succeeds at selling real estate during six decades of Hollywood culture.

Landis, Jill Marie

2355. *Day Dreamer.* New York: Jove, 1996. 399 pp.
To escape accusation for a murder she did not commit, Celine Winters offers to exchange places with another woman in a marriage to Cord Moreau, and she must leave New Orleans for the West Indies.
Genre(s): Romance.

Langley, Dorothy

2356. *Swamp Angel.* Chicago: Academy, 1982. 172 pp.
Bertha Mallory, married to an abusive husband and mother of six children, falls in love with a young schoolteacher and defies her town's mores to be with him while he encourages her oldest son's musical abilities.
Genre(s): Domestic Fiction; Musical Fiction.

Larsen, Nella

2357. *Passing.* 1929. New York: Penguin, 1997. 122 pp.
Two light-skinned African American women try to pass for white to escape racism, and Clare Kendry cuts her ties to the past and to Irene Redfield, ignoring the fact that that racism exists.
Genre(s): Domestic Fiction.

Laxalt, Robert

2358. *The Basque Hotel.* Reno: University of Nevada Press, 1993. 136 pp.
During the Depression in Nevada, a young boy learns about his immigrant family's heritage. (*Series:* Basque 1)
Genre(s): Domestic Fiction; Bildungsroman (Coming of Age).

2359. *Child of the Holy Ghost.* Reno: University of Nevada Press, 1997. 168 pp.
Maitia, an illegitimate child in Spain, keeps the stigma of this situation throughout her life, and although she moves to America, her son retains it when he returns to her home.
Genre(s): Domestic Fiction.

◆ 2360. *Dust Devils.* Reno: University of Nevada Press, 1997. 120 pp.
In the early 1900s, Ira Hamilton relates better to his Paiute friend Crickett than to his parents, but when he falls

in love with Crickett's sister, he has to placate both his father and hers.
Genre(s): Bildungsroman (Coming of Age).

Lea, Tom

2361. *The Wonderful Country.* Boston: Little, Brown, 1952. 387 pp.
Martin Brady returns to Texas from Mexico where he has stayed since killing his father's murderer when he was 16.
Genre(s): Western Fiction; Love Story.

Leaf, Paul

2362. *Comrades.* New York: New American Library, 1985. 368 pp.
A writer, his wife, and an actor fight in the Spanish Civil War, go to France to help in the underground, and return to Hollywood for successful careers before being summoned to the House Committee on Un-American Activities.
Genre(s): War Story.

Leahy, Syrell Rogovin

2363. *Family Ties.* New York: Putnam, 1982. 319 pp.
Regina wants to marry her cousin, but the family expects her to marry an uncle and raise her family in pre-World War I America.
Genre(s): Jewish Fiction.

2364. *Family Truths.* New York: Putnam, 1984. 287 pp.
Judith decides to quit law school when she finds out about the inherited disease plaguing her family.
Genre(s): Jewish Fiction.

Lee, Harper

◆ 2365. *To Kill a Mockingbird.* Philadelphia: Lippincott, 1960. 296 pp.
Scout's father defends a black man accused of raping a white woman in a small Alabama town during the 1930s.
Genre(s): Legal Story; Bildungsroman (Coming of Age); Domestic Fiction.

Lee, Helen Elaine

2366. *The Serpent's Gift.* New York: Atheneum, 1994. 384 pp.
After Eula Smalls's husband dies in 1910, the Staples family asks her and her children to join their family, but the Smalls family withdraws when faced with pain while the Staples family tells stories and participates in the community.
Genre(s): Domestic Fiction.

Leland, Christopher T.

2367. *Mrs. Randall.* Boston: Houghton Mifflin, 1987. 234 pp.
The narrator leaves his small southern hometown for California after it and his family begin to disintegrate following the end of World War I.
Genre(s): Domestic Fiction; Bildungsroman (Coming of Age).

Leonard, Elmore

2368. *Cuba Libra.* New York: Delacorte, 1998. 343 pp.

Ben Tyler's old partner recruits him to sell guns to Cubans under the guise of horse trading, and when they arrive in 1898 to find the *U.S.S. Maine* wrecked in the Havana harbor, they have to revise their plans.
Genre(s): War Story; Adventure Story.

Lester, Julius

♦ 2369. *Do Lord Remember Me.* New York: Holt, Rinehart, And, 1985. 210 pp.

A dying minister recalls his boyhood and the life of his African American people in their churches throughout the South at the beginning of the 20th century.
Genre(s): Family Saga.

Levin, Meyer

2370. *The Old Bunch.* New York: Viking, 1937. 964 pp.

In 1921, a group of Jewish high school students graduate and begin their careers.
Genre(s): Jewish Fiction.

Lincoln, C. Eric

2371. *The Avenue, Clayton City.* New York: Morrow, 1988. 345 pp.

Southern African Americans segregate from whites except in situations in which they can benefit from each other, but many of the African Americans have no prospects for opportunity.
Genre(s): Domestic Fiction; Political Fiction.

Lipman, Elinor

2372. *The Inn at Lake Devine.* New York: Random House, 1998. 272 pp.

When Natalie Marx is 13, she arranges to visit a gentile vacation spot with a camp friend, and years later, the two meet again.
Genre(s): Domestic Fiction.

Litvin, Martin

2373. *The Impresario.* Woodston, KA: Western, 1995. 160 pp.

In 1901, Ed Jackson, a black man, stabs Charley Rowe in response to a racial slur in an Illinois tavern, and a Jewish junk dealer saves him from a lynch mob.
Genre(s): Western Fiction.

Liu, Aimee E.

♦ 2374. *Cloud Mountain.* New York: Warner Books, 1997. 176 pp.

Hope, an English tutor, meets Liang Poyu, a Chinese student, in Berkeley, and although Hope is engaged to someone else, she decides to marry Liang even though mixed marriage is illegal at the beginning of the 20th century.
Genre(s): Family Saga.

Livingston, Harold

2375. *Touch the Sky.* New York: Morrow, 1991. 484 pp.

When Simon Conway returns from World War I all he wants to do is fly, and he and others found Conway Aviation Industries in Los Angeles and nurture its growth.
Genre(s): War Story.

Lockridge, Ross

2376. *Raintree County.* Boston: Houghton Mifflin, 1948. 1066 pp.

On July 4, 1892, schoolteacher Johnny Shawnessy meets two old boyhood friends who remind him of his past, including his Civil War experiences.
Genre(s): Bildungsroman (Coming of Age); Epic Literature.

Logan, Ben

2377. *The Empty Meadow.* Sauk City, WI: Arkham, 1983. 232 pp.

In the late 1930s, a Wisconsin boy loses his innocence.
Genre(s): Bildungsroman (Coming of Age).

Longfellow, Pamela

2378. *China Blues.* New York: Doubleday, 1989. 389 pp.

Lizzie Stafford discovers that her husband is having an affair, and she retaliates by taking Chinese bootlegger Li Kwan Won as her lover.
Genre(s): Domestic Fiction.

Lorimer, George Horace

2379. *Letters From a Self-Made Merchant to His Son.* Washington, DC: Regnery Gateway, 1995. 266 pp.

At the beginning of the 20th century, a father's letters to his son describe life in a small American town.
Genre(s): Domestic Fiction.

Lovesey, Peter

2380. *Keystone.* New York: Pantheon, 1983. 255 pp.

Warwick Easton, a British vaudevillian, becomes involved with burglary and Mack Sennett's Keystone Cops around 1915.

Lowell, Elizabeth

2381. *Autumn Lover.* New York: Avon, 1996. 416 pp.

Elyssa Sutton wants someone to help her protect her Nevada ranch, and she hires Hunter, a man searching for the killers of his family.
Genre(s): Western Fiction; Romance.

Lumpkin, Grace

2382. *To Make My Bread.* Urbana: University of Illinois, 1932. 384 pp.

A family of mountaineers who become farmers, hunters, and moonshiners must leave their homes for the mill

♦ May be suitable for young adult readers

town for economic reasons, but they refuse to acquiesce to the conditions and strike in 1929.
Genre(s): Political Fiction.

Lupoff, Richard A.

◆ 2383. *Lovecraft's Book.* Sauk City, WI: Arkham House, 1985. 260 pp.
In 1927, Nazis create a plot to take the United States either through propaganda or invasion, and they hire a horror writer, H.P. Lovecraft, to write a book.
Genre(s): Biographical Fiction; Adventure Story.

2384. *The Sepia Siren Killer.* New York: St. Martin's Press, 1994. 304 pp.
In Hollywood during the 1930s, Speedy MacReedy, an African American film maker, submits an insurance claim for which Hobart Lindsey has to investigate arson, mistaken identity, and old tragedies.
Genre(s): Mystery.

Lynn, Jack

2385. *The Hallelujah Flight.* New York: St. Martin's Press, 1990. 240 pp.
In 1932, two black Americans with no money, no flight plan, and a makeshift plane decide to fly across the United States to New York.
Genre(s): Adventure Story.

Macdonald, Elisabeth

◆ 2386. *The House at Gray Eagle.* New York: Scribner's, 1976. 201 pp.
Hoping to escape looking after a bedridden old woman, a young girl marries a handsome man but finds herself helping his father on an isolated Colorado ranch.
Genre(s): Domestic Fiction.

Mackey, Mary

2387. *The Kindness of Strangers.* New York: Simon and Schuster, 1988. 588 pp.
Viola Kessler matures during the days of vaudeville in New York City, takes her talents to the German stage while Hitler is rising to power, and sees her daughter and granddaughter find success in television and the movies.
Genre(s): War Story; Family Saga.

Magill, Kathleen

◆ 2388. *Megan.* New York: Dodd, Mead, 1983. 224 pp.
Megan leaves her father in 1899 to go to Idaho where, as a cook in a house of prostitution, she realizes that both prostitution and marriage involve slavery.
Genre(s): Adventure Story.

Malamud, Bernard

2389. *The Natural.* New York: Harcourt Brace, 1952. 217 pp.
A girl shoots Roy Hobbs, 19, at the beginning of his promising baseball career.
Genre(s): Sports Fiction.

Mamet, David

2390. *The Old Religion.* New York: Simon and Schuster, 1997. 208 pp.
When Leo Frank, a Jewish factory owner, is wrongfully accused of raping and murdering a white southern girl in 1914, his attorney knows that an acquittal will damn him instead of Frank.
Genre(s): Legal Story.

Manfred, Frederick Feikema

2391. *Green Earth.* New York: Crown, 1977. 721 pp.
Three generations of German immigrants work the land of Iowa in the beginning of the 20th century.
Genre(s): Western Fiction.

2392. *No Fun on Sunday.* Norman: University of Oklahoma Press, 1990. 287 pp.
In the 1920s, Sherman Engleking works on his baseball so that he can try out for the Chicago Cubs, but his religion does not approve of Sunday sports.
Genre(s): Sports Fiction.

Marius, Richard

2393. *After the War.* New York: Knopf, 1992. 640 pp.
Greek refugee Paul is in Bourbonville, Tennessee, after World War I, and he finds himself the focus of the townspeople's many fears.
Genre(s): Domestic Fiction.

Mark, Grace

2394. *The Dream Seekers.* New York: Morrow, 1992. 412 pp.
Immigrants Josef and Hannah arrive in Chicago in the 1890s, and Josef becomes involved with unions during organization of the Pullman Strike of 1894.
Genre(s): Legal Story.

Markfield, Wallace

2395. *Teitlebaum's Window.* New York: Knopf, 1970. 387 pp.
Brighton Beach in the 1930s is the setting for Simon Sloan's growth from ages eight to 18, and his attitudes reflect those of the times in which he lives.
Genre(s): Domestic Fiction; Bildungsroman (Coming of Age).

Marquand, John P.

2396. *H. M. Pulham, Esquire.* Boston: Little, Brown, 1941. 431 pp.
Harry Pulham has a charmed life but realizes he only felt alive when he fought in World War I and loved the wrong woman.

Marshall, Catherine

2397. *Christy.* New York: McGraw Hill, 1967. 496 pp.
Christy, 19, goes to a mission in Cutter Gap, Kentucky, in 1912, and begins teaching in the local school.
Genre(s): Biographical Fiction; Christian Fiction.

Martin, William

2398. *The Rising of the Moon.* New York: Crown, 1987. 474 pp.
In 1916, three supporters of the Irish rebellion leave Boston with guns and ammunition for the Easter Rising.
Genre(s): Political Fiction.

Mason, Bobbie Ann

2399. *Feather Crowns.* New York: HarperCollins, 1993. 464 pp.
In 1900, Chrissie Wheeler, a Kentucky farmer's wife, gives birth to the first recorded quintuplets, but they die, and promoters pay Chrissie and her husband to take the painted bodies of the dead babies on tour.
Genre(s): Gothic Fiction.

Matheson, Richard

2400. *Bid Time Return.* New York: Viking, 1975. 278 pp.
A writer with an incurable brain tumor falls in love with a young woman who lives in the late 19th century.
Genre(s): Time Travel; Love Story.

◆ 2401. *Gunfight.* New York: M. Evans, 1993. 224 pp.
Louisa Harper, 16, makes her boyfriend jealous by lying that ex-Texas Ranger John Benton made a pass at her.
Genre(s): Western Fiction.

Matthiessen, Peter

◆ 2402. *Killing Mister Watson.* New York: Random House, 1990. 372 pp.
Edgar J. Watson, a successful sugar-cane farmer whom people like, lives in the Everglades, but when murders occur nearby, police suspect his involvement.
Genre(s): Biographical Fiction; Mystery.

Maxwell, A. E.

2403. *Steal the Sun.* New York: Richard Marek, 1981. 288 pp.
While Truman awaits the results of the atomic bomb test, U.S. agent Finn tries to get a Japanese agent to witness the explosion so that he will want peace, while someone else tries to steal the uranium.
Genre(s): Adventure Story; Mystery.

McCann, Colum

2404. *This Side of Brightness.* New York: Henry Holt, 1998. 288 pp.
In 1916, Con O'Leary dies constructing the New York subway tunnels, and a young African American man looks after Con's wife and child, marrying her against all odds.
Genre(s): Family Saga.

McCarthy, Cormac

2405. *The Crossing.* New York: Knopf: 1994. 425 pp.
Billy Parham, 16, tries desperately to catch a wolf threatening his father's cattle ranch, but when he does, he cannot bring himself to kill it, so he returns it to the mountains, only to return home to tragedy in the sequel to *All the Pretty Horses.*
Genre(s): Bildungsroman (Coming of Age); Adventure Story.

McCunn, Ruthanne Lum

2406. *Wooden Fish Songs.* New York: Dutton, 1995. 384 pp.
Lue Gim Gong's mother in China, a New England spinster, and the daughter of a slave tell the story of Lue Ginn Gong's coming to America to study botany and develop superior citrus fruit.
Genre(s): Biographical Fiction.

McGehee, Nicole

2407. *Regret Not a Moment.* Boston: Little, Brown, 1993. 432 pp.
Wealthy Devon Richmond marries a New York businessman and survives the 20th century through World War II, Ku Klux Klan encounters, and divorce.
Genre(s): Domestic Fiction.

McGinnis, Bruce

2408. *Sweet Cane.* New York: Vanguard, 1982. 256 pp.
The Sedley family of rural Texas endures enormous misfortune in 1923.
Genre(s): Domestic Fiction.

McKay, Allis

2409. *The Women at Pine Creek.* New York: Macmillan, 1966. 374 pp.
After their father dies and leaves them land in Pine Creek, Washington, Althea and Mary Hollister travel by train and steamboat to the land and begin to cultivate it.

McKenney, Ruth

2410. *Industrial Valley.* 1939. Westport, CT: Greenwood, 1969. 379 pp.
From 1932 until 1936, the rubber workers in Akron, Ohio, stage and win their first strike.
Genre(s): Political Fiction.

McLarey, Myra

◆ 2411. *Water from the Well.* New York: Atlantic Monthly, 1995. 232 pp.
In the beginning of the 20th century, blacks and whites live in Sugar Springs, Arkansas, each group with its own history and hostilities.
Genre(s): Family Saga.

McMurtry, Larry, and Diana Ossana

◆ 2412. *Pretty Boy Floyd.* New York: Simon and Schuster, 1994. 448 pp.
Charles Arthur "Pretty Boy" Floyd goes to jail for his first crime in 1925, but when he gets out, he improves his methods, and after agents kill Dillinger, he becomes the most important target.
Genre(s): Biographical Fiction.

◆ May be suitable for young adult readers

2413. *Zeke and Ned.* New York: Simon and Schuster, 1997. 592 pp.
Zeke Proctor and Ned Christic earn their Cherokee folk hero status in the 1890s after fighting federal takeovers of their tribe's land and customs.
Genre(s): Western Fiction; Biographical Fiction.

McNab, Tom

◆ 2414. *Flanagan's Run.* New York: Morrow, 1982. 444 pp.
A promoter plans a 3000-mile marathon from Los Angeles to New York in 1931 in which 2000 participants compete.
Genre(s): Adventure Story; Sports Fiction.

McNamer, Deirdre

2415. *One Sweet Quarrel.* New York: HarperCollins, 1994. 280 pp.
During Prohibition, Jerry Malone goes West, where he disovers that frontier life is very difficult, but his sister decides to come from New York to join him in 1923.
Genre(s): Western Fiction.

McPherson, William

2416. *Testing the Current.* New York: Simon and Schuster, 1984. 348 pp.
When Tommy MacAlister is seven in 1939, he watches his wealthy parents and their friends reveal that they are not always what they seem.
Genre(s): Bildungsroman (Coming of Age).

McReynolds, Mary

◆ 2417. *Wells of Glory.* Wheaton, IL: Crossway, 1996. 302 pp.
When Ben Reuben's wife Lillie dies during childbirth, he listlessly raises their four children in the wilds of Oklahoma until he meets a wealthy Jew and a new schoolteacher.
Genre(s): Western Fiction; Christian Fiction.

Melnyczuk, Askold

2418. *What Is Told.* Boston: Faber and Faber, 1995. 201 pp.
The Zabobon family, inhabitants of the Ukraine since the time of the Tartars, has to flee during World War I, and its members find that life in New Jersey has its own dangers.
Genre(s): Domestic Fiction; War Story.

Meriwether, Louise

2419. *Daddy Was a Number Runner.* Englewood Cliffs, NJ: Prentice Hall, 1970. 240 pp.
When 12-year-old Francie learns that her father is a number runner in Harlem in the late 1930s, it adds to her coming-of-age crisis.
Genre(s): Domestic Fiction; Bildungsroman (Coming of Age).

Meyers, Maan

◆ 2420. *The House on Mulberry Street.* New York: Bantam, 1996. 305 pp.
In 1895, John (Dutch) Tonneman helps the police commissioner try to stop graft, but at a Union Square labor parade, after John meets and falls in love with Jewish immigrant photographer Esther Breslau, her friend, reporter Robert Roman, is murdered.
Genre(s): Mystery.

Meynell, Laurence

2421. *Death by Arrangement.* New York: McKay, 1972. 221 pp.
In the 1930s, an English eccentric hires a private investigator of ill repute to keep him from being kidnapped or murdered.
Genre(s): Mystery.

Miles, Franklin

2422. *On Dearborn Street.* St. Lucia, Queensland: University of Queensland Press, 1982. 219 pp.
Sybyl Penelo, manager of a Chicago editorial-stenographic firm, and her friends reveal reactions to World War I and to the roles of women in the 20th century's first decade.
Genre(s): War Story.

Miles, Keith

◆ 2423. *Murder in Perspective.* New York: Walker, 1997. 264 pp.
Merlin Richards comes to America to meet Frank Lloyd Wright on the site of one of his new buildings in Arizona, and although Wright ignores him, he meets a young designer who is soon murdered.
Genre(s): Mystery.

Miller, Calvin

2424. *The Book of Seven Truths.* New York: St. Martin's Press, 1997. 154 pp.
Soon after Anton Beaufort's father leaves Anton, 10, and his mother for Duluth, a truck hits Anton and paralyzes him below the waist, but a stranger named Hajji Rhovee helps Anton by giving him a book containing seven truths.
Genre(s): Christian Fiction.

Millhauser, Steven

2425. *Martin Dressler.* New York: Crown, 1996. 294 pp.
Martin Dressler dreams of becoming successful as he carefully and systematically rises from clerk in his father's 1890s cigar store to bellhop, hotel manager, owner of his own cigar store, a large hotel, and a resort.
Genre(s): Bildungsroman (Coming of Age).

Mills, Hobie

2426. *The Song Comes Native.* Countryman, 1982. 189 pp.
Ocie Wiggins, pretty and poor African American, becomes pregnant in the summer of 1926 but refuses to re-

veal the father; however, the Ku Klux Klan decides to implicate someone.
Genre(s): Domestic Fiction.

Miner, Valerie

2427. *All Good Women.* Freedom, CA: Crossing, 1987. 464 pp.
Four young women meet in San Francisco and board together in 1938, but when World War II starts, one of them is interned with other Japanese Americans, a second goes to London to help Jewish refugee children, and the other two form a lesbian relationship.
Genre(s): Domestic Fiction; War Story.

Mink, Charles

2428. *Princess of the Everglades.* Sarasota, FL: Pineapple, 1991. 207 pp.
When Kirk Quintaine's Progressive Mandolin Orchestra tours Florida in the 1920s, one of Quintaine's 10-year-old twins disappears in the Everglades during a hurricane.
Genre(s): Musical Fiction; Adventure Story.

Mitchell, Paige

2429. *The Covenant.* New York: Atheneum, 1973. 436 pp.
When a Jewish lawyer defends an unpopular client, he defines himself as a man, a Jew, and a Southerner.
Genre(s): Legal Story; Jewish Fiction.

Mitchell, Sara

2430. *In the Midst of Lions.* Minneapolis, MN: Bethany House, 1996. 320 pp.
Elizabeth discovers a predator and jeopardizes her and Pinkerton detective Simon Kincaid's happiness. (*Series:* Shadow Catchers, 2)
Genre(s): Romance; Christian Fiction; Mystery.

2431. *Trial of the Innocent.* Minneapolis, MN: Bethany House, 1995. 336 pp.
In the 1890s, Eve Sheridan and Pinkerton detective Alexander MacKay, face a situation in which Eve is threatened. (*Series:* Shadowcatchers, 1)
Genre(s): Christian Fiction; Mystery.

Mohin, Ann

2432. *The Farm She Was.* Bridgehampton, NY: Bridge Work, 1998. 256 pp.
As Irene Reeni Leahy reflects about her life in the early 20th century, she recalls having to take over the management of the farm at her father's early death and the major changes that the Rural Electrification Act of 1935 brought.
Genre(s): Domestic Fiction.

Montecino, Marcel

2433. *Sacred Heart.* New York: Pocket Books, 1997. 375 pp.
In 1926, Tommy Coyne, a New York gangster, goes to Mexico to hide with his priest brother after an unscrupulous policeman accuses him of a murder he did not commit, and when he avoids execution, he becomes a hero who must make choices.
Genre(s): Mystery.

Moore, Dulce D.

2434. *A Place in Mind.* Dallas: Baskerville, 1992. 265 pp.
After the death of her husband from cancer, Mavis Maddox retreats to childhood memories of her life in Texas during the Depression.
Genre(s): Domestic Fiction.

Morgan, Robert

2435. *The Truest Pleasure.* Chapel Hill, NC: Algonquin, 1995. 334 pp.
Pentecostal worship ideals attract Ginny while her husband Tom disapproves, but they keep their marriage intact in the early-20th-century Blue Ridge mountains through a series of difficulties.
Genre(s): Domestic Fiction.

Morgan, Speer

2436. *The Whipping Boy.* Boston: Houghton Mifflin, 1994. 326 pp.
A hardware store salesman, a half-Native American orphan, and a secretive young woman contrive to steal land from poor Native Americans and farmers in Oklahoma during 1894.
Genre(s): Western Fiction.

Morrell, David

2437. *Last Reveille.* New York: Evans, 1977. 257 pp.
In 1916, Miles Calendar, 65 and a scout on the Mexico/New Mexico border, joins General Black Jack Pershing in his raid to punish Pancho Villa for marauding in New Mexico and Arizona, and while on the trail, Calendar becomes a mentor to the young cavalryman, Prentice.
Genre(s): Western Fiction; Adventure Story.

Morris, Gilbert

2438. *The Gallant Outlaw.* Minneapolis, MN: Bethany House, 1994. 288 pp.
Lanie Winslow goes to Oklahoma Territory in the 1890s to rescue her sister from an outlaw gang. (*Series:* House of Winslow, 15)
Genre(s): Christian Fiction; Domestic Fiction.

2439. *The Iron Lady.* Minneapolis, MN: Bethany House, 1996. 320 pp.
When the three Winslow cousins, Ruth, Priscilla, and Esther, come to New York to pursue their careers of nursing, show business, and news photography, they find life different than they expected. (House of Winslow, 17)
Genre(s): Christian Fiction; Domestic Fiction; Family Saga.

2440. *The Rough Rider.* Minneapolis, MN: Bethany House, 1995. 304 pp.
Aaron Winslow leaves the gold fields of the Klondike for the glory of war at San Juan Hill in 1898 but discovers that it is not enough to satisfy him. (*Series:* House of Winslow, 18)
Genre(s): War Story; Christian Fiction.

◆ May be suitable for young adult readers

2441. *The Shadow Portrait.* Minneapolis, MN: Bethany House, 1998. 304 pp.
After Peter Winslow arrives in New York, he becomes a race car driver and attracts two beautiful women while Phil Winslow meets an artist who lives as an invalid with her father. (*Series:* House of Winslow, 21)
Genre(s): Christian Fiction; Romance.

◆ **2442.** *A Time to Be Born.* Grand Rapids, MI: Revell, 1994. 312 pp.
The Stuart family have a variety of experiences at the turn of the 20th century. (*Series:* The American Odyssey, 2)
Genre(s): Domestic Fiction; Christian Fiction.

◆ **2443.** *A Time to Die.* Grand Rapids, MI: Revell, 1995. 296 pp.
Jerry Stuart becomes a pilot during World War I. (The American Odyssey, 2)
Genre(s): War Story; Christian Fiction.

2444. *A Time to Laugh.* Grand Rapids, MI: Revell, 1995. 296 pp.
The Stuart family's life changes after Jerry Stuart serves in World War I and they begin to face the 1920s. (*Series:* The American Odyssey, 3)
Genre(s): Domestic Fiction; Christian Fiction.

2445. *A Time to Weep.* Grand Rapids, MI: Revell, 1996. 336 pp.
The Ballard and Stuart families travel from Oklahoma to Hollywood and Chicago trying to escape poverty during 1931 and 1932, but their faith sustains them.
Genre(s): Domestic Fiction; Christian Fiction.

◆ **2446.** *The Yukon Queen.* Minneapolis, MN: Bethany House, 1995. 320 pp.
When Cassidy Winslow leaves his family's Wyoming ranch, he visits several cities and depletes his funds, but an elderly man he nurses offers to pay his way to Alaska's gold fields if he will find the man's daughter and take her with him. (*Series:* House of Winslow, 17)
Genre(s): Christian Fiction.

Morrison, Toni

2447. *Jazz.* New York: Knopf, 1992. 229 pp.
After Joe Trace shoots his 18-year-old lover in Harlem during 1926, his wife Violet slashes the dead girl's face and then desperately searches for information about the woman to find out why Joe was unfaithful.
Genre(s): Love Story.

Morsi, Pamela

2448. *No Ordinary Princess.* New York: Avon, 1997. 375 pp.
Penniless Tom Walker convinces Princess Calhoun, daughter of Oklahoma oilman King Calhoun, that he is Yale-educated (he is a half-Native American former Rough Rider), and she marries him, but when he has to fight fire in the oilfields, his heroism leads to the revelation of his past.
Genre(s): Western Fiction; Romance.

2449. *Sealed with a Kiss.* New York: Avon, 1998. 400 pp.
In the 1890s, Gidry Chais returns to his Texas hometown to see his dying father and encounters determined Prudence Belmont, the woman he jilted eight years before.
Genre(s): Romance; Western Fiction.

2450. *Simple Jess.* New York: Jove, 1996. 325 pp.
In 1906, widow Althea Winsloe has a son and a farm, but she needs a husband, and the Arkansas town gives her until Christmas to choose one.
Genre(s): Romance.

Mosby, Katherine

2451. *Private Altars.* New York: Random House, 1995. 322 pp.
When Vienna Daniels's husband abandons her in the early 1930s with two small children in a West Virginia town she lies to them about their father as she befriends a graduate student.
Genre(s): Domestic Fiction.

Mosley, Walter

2452. *Gone Fishin'.* New York: Black Classics, 1997. 244 pp.
Easy Rawlins is 19 when he goes on a trip with Mouse to Pariah, Texas, to get money from Mouse's stepfather, and there they encounter troubles that include dead bodies and a killer.
Genre(s): Mystery; Bildungsroman (Coming of Age).

Murayama, Milton

2453. *Five Years on a Rock.* Honolulu: University of Hawaii Press, 1994. 144 pp.
Sano goes from Japan to Hawaii in 1914 as a picture bride and finds that she is little more than a slave in her husband's family.
Genre(s): Domestic Fiction.

Murdoch, Anna

2454. *Family Business.* New York: Morrow, 1988. 592 pp.
Yarrow McLean leads the McLean newspaper as it grows from the 1920s through the Depression and into the Vietnam War era.
Genre(s): Family Saga.

Murray, Albert

◆ **2455.** *The Spyglass Tree.* New York: Pantheon, 1991. 209 pp.
In the 1930s, Scooter is an African American college student who remembers his youth as the adored son of both his natural and his adopted mother.
Genre(s): Bildungsroman (Coming of Age).

2456. *Train Whistle Guitar.* New York: Vintage, 1998. 208 pp.
His schoolteacher, the barber, older girls, and a train-hopping musician teach Scooter just about all he needs to know in Gasoline Point, Alabama, during the 1920s.
Genre(s): Bildungsroman (Coming of Age).

Murray, Earl

2457. *Song of Wovoka.* New York: Tor, 1992. 404 pp.
Mark Thomas, a Jesuit, becomes a Lakota Sioux named Two Robes and fights at Wounded Knee in 1890.
Genre(s): War Story; Political Fiction.

Myrdal, Jan

◆ 2458. *Another World.* Chicago: Ravenswood, 1994. 198 pp.
Jan Myrdal immigrates to the United States with his parents at age 11 and feels isolated because of their wealth and their disregard for him, in the sequel to *Childhood.*
Award(s): Grand Prize for the Novel.
Genre(s): Biographical Fiction.

Myrer, Anton

2459. *A Green Desire.* New York: Putnam, 1981. 511 pp.
When brothers fall in love with the daughter of a Portuguese sailor before World War I, their situation places them within the major historical events of the century through the aftermath of World War II.
Genre(s): War Story.

2460. *Once an Eagle.* New York: Holt, Rinehart and Winston, 1968. 817 pp.
Two military officers with differing viewpoints about the treatment of soldiers serving them fight during several wars.

Nason, Tema

2461. *Ethel.* New York: Delacorte, 1990. 320 pp.
While in prison, Ethel Rosenberg keeps a journal in which she wonders if she should lie and betray her husband so that she can live with her young sons or if she should be true to herself and die with him.
Genre(s): Biographical Fiction.

Nathan, Robert

2462. *One More Spring.* New York: Knopf, 1933. 212 pp.
Mr. Nathan loses everything from his antique business in the Depression except a bed, so he and three others spend the winter in a Central Park toolshed.

Nelson, Betty Palmer

2463. *Pursuit of Bliss.* New York: St. Martin's Press, 1994. 256 pp.
Annie Bee, 16, wants to marry farm worker and horse trainer, Ral, but afterwards, she needs to work to help support the family, which he opposes. (*Series:* Honest Women, 3)

2464. *Uncertain April: 1909-1950.* New York: St. Martin's Press, 1993. 336 pp.
A mother and her son's wife learn to adapt and accept the ways of their spouses in the early 20th century in the sequel to *The Pursuit of Bliss.*
Genre(s): Domestic Fiction.

Newcomb, Kerry, and Frank Schaefer

2465. *The Ghosts of Elkhorn.* New York: Viking, 1982. 291 pp.
An an old ex-gangster lives in a Rocky Mountain ghost town, and a young man and his girlfriend, having robbed a Denver gangster, seek asylum with him in 1927.
Genre(s): Western Fiction.

Ng, Fae Myenne

2466. *Bone.* New York: HarperPerennial, 1994. 193 pp.
A Chinese American family in San Francisco's Chinatown must face hostility as it aspires to improve its lot.
Genre(s): Domestic Fiction.

Noble, Marguerite

2467. *Filaree.* New York: Random House, 1979. 243 pp.
Melissa Baker survives childbirth and a loveless marriage to succeed in Arizona territory during the early 20th century.
Genre(s): Western Fiction.

Nolan, Frederick W.

2468. *Kill Petrosino!* London: Barker, 1975. 181 pp.
Joseph Petrosino, a lieutenant in the New York City police department, searches for Black Hand extortioners from Sicily and Italy in American cities before the group kills him on a visit to Sicily in 1909.
Genre(s): Biographical Fiction.

Nolan, William F.

2469. *The Black Mask Murders.* New York: St. Martin's Press, 1994. 214 pp.
As Dashiell Hammett delivers a ruby to a mobster, a shootout occurs, and the villain gets the stone and kidnaps the girl who was to receive it, so Erle Stanley Gardner and Raymond Chandler help Hammett search.
Genre(s): Mystery.

2470. *The Marble Orchard.* New York: St. Martin's Press, 1996. 230 pp.
The Black Mask Boys, Dashiell Hammett, Raymond Chandler, and Erle Stanley Gardner, investigate the supposed suicide of Cissy Chandler's former husband in the 1930s.
Genre(s): Mystery.

2471. *Sharks Never Sleep.* New York: St. Martin's Press, 1998. 288 pp.
When someone charges Erle Stanley Gardner with murder, Dashiel Hammett and Raymond Chandler help him find the killer.
Genre(s): Mystery.

Norman, Marc

2472. *Oklahoma Crude.* New York: Dutton, 1973. 251 pp.
In 1915, Lena Doyle owns an oil rig on a piece of land she calls Apache Dome, and she fights for her rights as an independent owner against the oil company.
Genre(s): Political Fiction.

◆ May be suitable for young adult readers

Nye, Nelson

2473. *Deadly Companions.* New York: Walker, 1987. 168 pp.
Wendy Eldridge decides to take a gunman as a partner so that she will not lose her ranch to creditors, promising him shares in a gold mine before she finds one.
Genre(s): Western Fiction.

Oates, Joyce Carol

2474. *Bellefleur.* New York: Dutton, 1980. 558 pp.
The first Bellefleur, Jean-Pierre, amasses a fortune, but when his namesake is accused of mass murder, the family flounders.
Genre(s): Domestic Fiction.

2475. *I Lock My Door Upon Myself.* Hopeland, NJ: Ecco, 1990. 98 pp.
Calla lives a boring life in rural America at the beginning of the 20th century until the African American water dowser Tyrell Thompson arrives.
Genre(s): Love Story.

2476. *Them.* New York: Vanguard, 1969. 508 pp.
Loretta Wendall and her two children experience violence and poverty in Detroit from the Depression in the 1930s to the riots of 1967.
Award(s): National Book Award.
Genre(s): Domestic Fiction.

Ogilvie, Elisabeth

2477. *The World of Jennie G.* New York: McGraw Hill, 1986. 355 pp.
In the sequel to *Jennie About to Be,* the widow Jennie carries her dead husband's child while pretending to be Alick Gilroy's wife so that he can escape execution in Scotland and come to America.
Genre(s): Domestic Fiction; Adventure Story.

O'Hara, John

2478. *Ten North Frederick.* New York: Random House, 1955. 408 pp.
Through Joe Chapin's wife, the hypocrisy and evil in the life of a small Pennsylvania town become exposed.
Award(s): National Book Award.
Genre(s): Domestic Fiction.

Oke, Janette

◆ 2479. *The Bluebird and the Sparrow.* Minneapolis, MN: Bethany House, 1994. 251 pp.
Berta Berdette becomes jealous of her lovely younger sister, and mentally and emotionally separates from her especially when they fall in love with the same man.
Genre(s): Christian Fiction.

2480. *Julia's Last Hope.* Minneapolis, MN: Bethany House, 1990. 204 pp.
One woman tries to comfort people in her town and her family during hard times. (*Series:* Women of the West, 2)
Genre(s): Christian Fiction.

◆ 2481. *Love Finds a Home.* Minneapolis, MN: Bethany House, 1989. 219 pp.
Belinda must face decisions about her future again, but she asks for God's help. (*Series:* Love Comes Softly, 8)
Genre(s): Christian Fiction; Romance; Family Saga.

◆ 2482. *Love Takes Wing.* Minneapolis, MN: Bethany House, 1985. 222 pp.
Brenda has a chance to visit Boston and goes gladly. (*Series:* Love Comes Softly, 7)
Genre(s): Christian Fiction; Romance; Family Saga.

◆ 2483. *Love's Abiding Joy.* Minneapolis, MN: Bethany House, 1983. 217 pp.
Belinda continues her life on the prairie. (*Series:* Love Comes Softly, 4)
Genre(s): Christian Fiction; Romance; Family Saga.

◆ 2484. *Love's Unending Legacy.* Minneapolis, MN: Bethany House, 1984. 222 pp.
The family continues to work and live on the prairie. (*Series:* Love Comes Softly, 5)
Genre(s): Christian Fiction; Romance; Family Saga.

◆ 2485. *Love's Unfolding Dream.* Minneapolis, MN: Bethany House, 1987. 222 pp.
Belinda, the youngest child, continues the family's traditions. (*Series:* Love Comes Softly, 6)
Genre(s): Christian Fiction; Family Saga; Romance.

2486. *The Winds of Autumn.* Minneapolis, MN: Bethany House, 1987. 220 pp.
Josh faces questions about his life and God. (*Series:* Seasons of the Heart, 2)
Genre(s): Christian Fiction.

Oke, Janette, and T. Davis Bunn

◆ 2487. *Return to Harmony.* Minneapolis, MN: Bethany Hosue, 1996. 223 pp.
Around 1915, in Harmony, North Carolina, Jodie and Bethan are best friends, but Jodie loses her faith until she realizes that science, her chosen career, and religion can coexist.
Genre(s): Domestic Fiction; Christian Fiction.

Olsen, Theodore V.

◆ 2488. *Rattlesnake.* New York: Doubleday, 1979. 182 pp.
Jim Izancho, an Apache, tries to make a home for his family, but the father-in-law of his friend, the sheriff, has different ideas about the land that Izancho uses.
Genre(s): Western Fiction.

Olsen, Tillie

2489. *Yonnondio: From the Thirties.* New York: Delacorte, 1974. 196 pp.
In the 1920s, the Holbrook family tries to survive by mining in Wyoming, farming in South Dakota, and scavenging in Chicago.
Genre(s): Domestic Fiction.

O'Malley, Richard K.

2490. *Mile High, Mile Deep.* Missoula, MT: Mountain, 1971. 304 pp.
Dick and Frank work in the copper mines of Butte, Montana, during the 1920s, but after enjoying all that Butte has to offer, Dick leaves and Frank dies in a mine.
Genre(s): Adventure Story.

Ondaatje, Michael

2491. *Coming Through Slaughter.* New York: Norton, 1976. 156 pp.
Buddy Bolden, a New Orleans barber, cornet player, and full-time editor of a gossip sheet, disappears for two years, and when he returns, he goes berserk and spends his final years in the East Louisiana State Hospital.
Genre(s): Biographical Fiction; Musical Fiction.

O'Neal, Charles

2492. *Three Wishes for Jamie.* Sagaponack, NY: Second Chance, 1980. 248 pp.
Jamie McRuin goes from Ireland to Georgia for a life of horsetrading, taking with him his Irish customs.
Genre(s): Domestic Fiction.

O'Rourke, Frank

2493. *The Swift Runner.* Philadelphia: Lippincott, 1969. 352 pp.
After serving seven years in prison for stealing horses, Doc Neely plans a horse chase over the plains for all to enjoy.
Genre(s): Humorous Fiction; Western Fiction.

Overholser, Stephen

◆ 2494. *Field of Death.* Garden City, NY: Doubleday, 1977. 178 pp.
When the daughter of a wealthy man and her three female servants are murdered in Colorado at the end of the 19th century, Aaron Mills tires to find who did it and why.
Genre(s): Western Fiction.

◆ 2495. *Track of a Killer.* New York: Walker, 1982. 165 pp.
A loyal foreman defends his boss's land against cattle rustlers and gold miners in the 1890s.
Genre(s): Western Fiction.

Owen, Guy

◆ 2496. *Journey for Joedel.* New York: Crown, 1970. 160 pp.
Joedel, 13, helps his sharecropper father bring in the tobacco during the 1930s, and although others taunt him for being part Croatian, he learns that he has value.
Genre(s): Bildungsroman (Coming of Age).

Paretti, Sandra

2497. *The Magic Ship.* New York: St. Martin's Press, 1979. 342 pp.
A German luxury liner stranded off Bar Harbor, Maine, at the onset of World War I cannot depart until the United States declares war on Germany.
Genre(s): War Story.

Parini, Jay

◆ 2498. *The Patch Boys.* New York: Henry Holt, 1986. 218 pp.
In the summer of 1924, Sammy di Contini, 15, grows up after his brother is shot while trying to organize the miners, and his underworld brother's girlfriend in New York seduces him.
Genre(s): Bildungsroman (Coming of Age).

Parks, Gordon

◆ 2499. *The Learning Tree.* New York: Harper and Row, 1963. 303 pp.
During the 1920s, Newt grows up as a young minority boy in a Kansas community.
Genre(s): Bildungsroman (Coming of Age).

Parry, Richard

2500. *The Wolf's Cub.* New York: Forge, 1997. 384 pp.
Nathan Blaylock and his partner go to Alaska, in the sequel to *The Winter Wolf*, to search for his son left there after the mother's death in childbirth.
Genre(s): Adventure Story; Western Fiction.

Patten, Lewis B.

2501. *Cheyenne Captives.* Garden City, NY: Doubleday, 1978. 183 pp.
Settlers search desperately for a pregnant rancher's wife kidnapped by the Cheyenne.
Genre(s): Western Fiction.

Paul, Barbara

2502. *A Cadenza for Caruso.* New York: St. Martin's Press, 1984. 146 pp.
Luigi Davila blackmails G. Puccini when he comes to New York in 1910 for the premiere of *Girl of the Golden West* starring Enrico Caruso, but someone murders Davila, and Puccini becomes the suspect.
Genre(s): Mystery.

◆ 2503. *A Chorus of Detectives.* New York: St. Martin's Press, 1987. 234 pp.
The New York police department tries to find out who is killing members of the Metropolitan Opera chorus, one at the time, and the soloists, including Enrico Caruso, Geraldine Farrar, and Rosa Ponselle, almost ruin his work.
Genre(s): Mystery.

2504. *Prima Donna at Large.* New York: St. Martin's Press, 1985. 246 pp.
When the French baritone Philippe Duchon takes over for an ill opera singer during World War I at the Metropolitan, someone adds ammonia to his throat spray, and soprano Geraldine Farrar investigates his death.
Genre(s): Musical Fiction; Mystery.

Paul, Charlotte

◆ 2505. *A Child Is Missing.* New York: Putnam, 1978. 259 pp.
When the Lindbergh child is taken, different people try to find the kidnappers.
Genre(s): Biographical Fiction.

Peart, Jane

2506. *Daring Bride.* Grand Rapids, MI: Zondervan, 1997. 288 pp.
Three women in the Montrose and Cameron families have become widows at a young age, and during the Depression, they try to rebuild their lives. (*Series:* Brides of Montclair, 13)
Genre(s): Domestic Fiction; Christian Fiction.

2507. *Hero's Bride.* Grand Rapids, MI: Zondervan, 1993. 108 pp.
The eldest son at Montclair must go to France to fight in World War I, leaving those behind to worry about his fate. (*Series:* Brides of Montclair, 11)
Genre(s): War Story; Christian Fiction.

◆ 2508. *Jubilee Bride.* Grand Rapids, MI: Zondervan, 1992. 207 pp.
During Queen Victoria's Diamond Jubilee, Garnet invites her aristocratic family from Virginia to England for a reunion. (*Series:* Brides of Montclair, 9)
Genre(s): Romance; Satire; Christian Fiction.

2509. *Mirror Bride.* Grand Rapids, MI: Zondervan, 1993. 206 pp.
Of wealthy identical twins, Cara and Kitty Cameron, Cara wants to reject the advances of a quiet ministerial student while Kitty falls in love with someone pining after Cara. (*Series:* Brides of Montclair, 10)
Genre(s): Romance; Domestic Fiction.

Peck, Robert Newton

◆ 2510. *A Day No Pigs Would Die.* New York: Knopf, 1972. 150 pp.
In the 1920s, Rob worries about his pig when it does not produce an expected litter.
Genre(s): Domestic Fiction; Bildungsroman (Coming of Age).

2511. *Hallapoosa.* New York: Walker, 1988. 215 pp.
Justice of the Peace Hiram MacHugh lives happily in Hallapoosa, Florida, but when his brother and his brother's wife are killed, he takes their children and gives up drinking and women.
Genre(s): Domestic Fiction.

2512. *A Part of the Sky.* New York: Knopf, 1994. 176 pp.
In the sequel to *A Day No Pigs Would Die*, Rob, 13, must take responsibility for his family and the farm, but during the Depression, he cannot make enough money to meet the mortgage payments.
Genre(s): Bildungsroman (Coming of Age); Domestic Fiction.

Peeples, Samuel Anthony

2513. *The Man Who Died Twice.* New York: Putnam, 1976. 252 pp.
A policeman hit in the head in 1976 finds himself in the body of a famous movie star of early films, William Desmond Taylor, who was a notorious womanizer.
Genre(s): Time Travel; Mystery.

Pelecanos, George P.

2514. *The Big Blowdown.* New York: St. Martin's Press, 1996. 304 pp.
Peter Karras, a Greek, and Joe Recevo, an Italian, grow up together in Washington, DC, during the 1930s, fight in World War II, and meet again when Joe is involved in organized crime against immigrants.

Peterson, Norma

◆ 2515. *Rhonda the Rubber Woman.* Sag Harbor, NY: Permanent Press, 1998. 248 pp.
Illegitimate Rhonda dislikes her mother's carefree lifestyle, but when the new boyfriend notices that Rhonda is double-jointed, he hires her as a carnival contortionist.
Genre(s): Domestic Fiction; Bildungsroman (Coming of Age).

Petrakis, Harry Mark

2516. *Days of Vengeance.* Garden City, NY: Doubleday, 1983. 279 pp.
Manolis follows his brother's murderer from Crete to the United States, where they both become involved with Americans.

Pharr, Robert Deane

2517. *The Book of Numbers.* Garden City, NY: Doubleday, 1969. 374 pp.
Two African American waiters in the 1930s make money on a numbers game but eventually suffer the consequences of Southern retribution.

Phillips, Jayne Anne

2518. *Machine Dreams.* New York: Dutton, 1984. 331 pp.
An American family transforms itself as it survives the Depression, World War II, and the Vietnam War.
Genre(s): War Story; Family Saga.

Phillips, Michael R.

◆ 2519. *The Braxtons of Miracle Springs.* Minneapolis, MN: Bethany House, 1996. 256 pp.
Corrie Belle Hollister and Christopher begin their married life. (*Series:* Journals of Corrie and Christopher, 1)
Genre(s): Christian Fiction.

2520. *A Dangerous Love.* Wheaton, IL: Tyndale House, 1997. 345 pp.
Jeremiah Eagleflight hopes that Mercy Randolph, a Kansas evangelist in the 1890s, will marry him, but his nephew arrives, looking for sapphires hoisted in a previous robbery. (*Series:* Mercy and Eagleflight, 2)
Genre(s): Western Fiction; Christian Fiction.

2521. *Mercy and Eagleflight.* Wheaton, IL: Tyndale, 1997. 192 pp.
Mercy Randolph, Kansas evangelist in the 1890s, starts an unlikely partnership with a wandering cowboy, Jeremiah Eagleflight. (*Series:* Mercy and Eagleflight, 1)
Genre(s): Western Fiction; Christian Fiction.

2522. *A New Beginning.* Minneapolis, MN: Bethany House, 1997. 231 pp.
Christopher suggests to Corrie that they should return to the East. (*Series:* Journals of Corrie and Christopher, 2)
Genre(s): Western Fiction; Christian Fiction.

Picken, Nellie Buxton

2523. *Fireweed.* Spokane, WA: Melior, 1989. 400 pp.
Ed McLaren arrives in Okanogan Valley in 1897 and observes the changes in the land and the policies between the government and Native Americans until 1954.
Genre(s): Family Saga.

Pickens, Lynne

◆ 2524. *Taking Chances.* New York: M. Evans, 1991. 258 pp.
In the 1890s, Lou Ferrance's illegitimate daughter becomes a cat burglar like her father, and he falls in love with Lena, a high-class prostitute, before he is kidnapped and presumed killed.
Genre(s): Adventure Story.

Plain, Belva

◆ 2525. *Evergreen.* New York: Delacorte, 1978. 593 pp.
The orphan Anna leaves Poland for the United States at the beginning of the 20th century, and after choosing to become a domestic, she marries and begins to guide her family through the next decades.
Genre(s): Domestic Fiction; Romance; Family Saga.

◆ 2526. *The Golden Cup.* New York: Delacorte, 1986. 399 pp.
While Hennie DeRivera, aunt of Paul in *Evergreen*, teaches at a settlement house in 1891, she meets Daniel, becomes pregnant, and marries him.
Genre(s): Domestic Fiction.

Popkin, Zelda

2527. *Dear Once.* Philadelphia: Lippincott, 1975. 382 pp.
A Russian Jewish family immigrates to the U.S. in 1899, and during the McCarthy era of communist-hunting, one of the granddaughters realizes that she must acknowledge her heritage.
Genre(s): Jewish Fiction; Family Saga.

Potok, Chaim

◆ 2528. *Davita's Harp.* New York: Knopf, 1985. 371 pp.
After her father is killed covering the Spanish Civil War, Ilana decides to attend yeshiva, rejecting both communism and Christianity.
Genre(s): Domestic Fiction.

2529. *In the Beginning.* New York: Knopf, 1975. 454 pp.
David Lurie has annoying childhood illnesses that lead other children into bullying him, and while he grows as a Biblical scholar, he must grow in his personal life during the Depression and World War II.
Genre(s): Jewish Fiction.

Pressfield, Steven

2530. *The Legend of Bagger Vance.* New York: Morrow, 1995. 245 pp.
African American Bagger Vance, middle-aged caddy to war hero and former golf champion Rannulph Junah in 1931, explains to Junah how golf resembles life, and Junah's game improves.
Genre(s): Sports Fiction.

Price, Nancy

2531. *An Accomplished Woman.* New York: Coward-McCann, 1979. 288 pp.
After Catherine Buckingham's parents are killed in the 1920s, her stepuncle becomes her guardian and keeps her in isolation until World War II starts, when he is reported killed.
Genre(s): War Story.

Price, Reynolds

2532. *Roxanna Slade.* New York: Scribner's, 1998. 304 pp.
A woman born in 1900 reflects on her life and her family.
Genre(s): Domestic Fiction.

2533. *The Surface of Earth.* New York: Atheneum, 1975. 491 pp.
Eva Kendal, 16, elopes with her Latin teacher, twice her age, in 1903 and begins a dysfunctional family line in North Carolina.
Genre(s): Family Saga.

Pronzini, Bill

2534. *Quincannon.* New York: Walker, 1985. 157 pp.
Quincannon, a Secret Service agent, pretends to be a patent medicine salesman in the 1890s in order to locate counterfeiters in Silver City, Idaho.
Genre(s): Western Fiction; Mystery.

Proulx, Annie

2535. *Accordion Crimes.* New York: Scribner's, 1996. 381 pp.
After a Sicilian immigrant comes to New Orleans with his son in 1890 and is murdered by an anti-Italian mob, his accordion passes through several immigrant families who suffer dislocation.
Genre(s): Musical Fiction; Family Saga.

Purdy, James

2536. *In the Hollow of His Hand.* New York: Weidenfeld and Nichols, 1986. 247 pp.
Illegitimate Chad's legal father, an Ojibwa, kidnaps Chad from his society matron mother in the 1920s.
Genre(s): Adventure Story.

2537. *On Glory's Course.* New York: Viking, 1984. 378 pp.
Adele Bevington, a wealthy aristocrat in a small town, searches in 1930 for the illegitmate son that she gave up 30 years before.
Genre(s): Domestic Fiction.

◆ May be suitable for young adult readers

Puzo, Mario

2538. *The Fortunate Pilgrim.* New York: Random House, 1997. 985 pp.
Larry, a "dummy" boy on horseback, guides the New York central trains through New York in 1928 while his mother, Lucia Santa Angeluzzi-Corbo, preserves their Italian family.
Genre(s): Biographical Fiction; Domestic Fiction; Family Saga.

Quinlan, Sterling

2539. *Something in Between.* New York: Braziller, 1994. 201 pp.
Polish immigrant Keltor leaves Chicago during the Depression and travels through America.
Genre(s): Picaresque Fiction.

Rølvaag, O. E.

2540. *The Third Life of Per Smevik.* Trans. Ella Valborg Tweet and Solveig Zempel. Minneapolis, MN: Dillon, 1971. 136 pp.
Per Smevik writes letters home to Norway from South Dakota from 1896 to 1901 in which he describes the work, customs, and social life of the state.
Genre(s): Family Saga.

Rae, Catherine M.

◆ 2541. *Afterward.* New York: St. Martin's Press, 1992. 182 pp.
When an excursion boat, the *General Slocum*, sinks on the Hudson River, two daughters must help their father and younger siblings after the death of their mother.
Genre(s): Romance.

2542. *Brownstone Facade.* New York: St. Martin's Press, 1987. 176 pp.
In the 1920s, Grace's siblings have moved out of their Manhattan brownstone, but they begin to return and strange things begin to happen in the house, including murder.
Genre(s): Domestic Fiction.

2543. *Flight from Fifth Avenue.* New York: St. Martin's Press, 1995. 186 pp.
Maida Jardine flees her New York home to avoid an arranged marriage to Viscount Ormley by taking the orphan train west, but she must eventually face him in a courtroom after physically injuring him.
Genre(s): Bildungsroman (Coming of Age).

2544. *Sunlight on a Broken Column.* New York: St. Martin's Press, 1997. 192 pp.
In 1892, the Slade parents die in an accident, and since the three upper-class children no longer have financial support, each finds a different path to adulthood.
Genre(s): Romance.

Randisi, Robert J.

2545. *The Ham Reporter.* Garden City, NY: Doubleday, 1986. 178 pp.
After Bat Masterson goes to New York to become a newspaperman, he finds out that his fellow journalist Ink-spot Jones has vanished, and Masterson investigates in 1912.
Genre(s): Mystery.

Redon, Joel

2546. *If Not On Earth, Then in Heaven.* New York: St. Martin's Press, 1991. 208 pp.
In 1905, Neoma lives in a Portland hotel for women and works as a seamstress, and although she becomes friends with Alan, a library clerk, and Birdie, another seamstress, none of them change.
Genre(s): Love Story.

2547. *The Road to Zena.* New York: St. Martin's Press, 1992. 320 pp.
As he prepares to go to college in the sequel to *If Not on Earth, Then in Heaven*, Viv meets the new schoolteacher Mae and falls in love.
Genre(s): Love Story.

Reed, Ishmael

2548. *Mumbo Jumbo.* New York: Doubleday, 1972. 223 pp.
In Harlem during the 1920s, two voodoo detectives track a plot to kill Jes Grew, a type of music containing soul, rhythm and blues, and boogie woogie.
Genre(s): Humorous Fiction.

Reid, Van

2549. *Cordelia Underwood.* New York: Viking, 1998. 480 pp.
In 1896, after Cordelia Underwood inherits land from her uncle and Tobias Walton, unusual incidents begin to happen.
Genre(s): Adventure Story.

Reinhart, Robert C.

2550. *A History of Shadows.* New York: Avon, 1982. 288 pp.
Four gay men, an interior designer, an accountant, a composer, and an actor, support each other like family when society will not tolerate their choices.
Genre(s): Domestic Fiction.

Rice, Clyde

2551. *Night Freight.* Portland, OR: Breitenbush, 1987. 156 pp.
Hobos, drifters, and homeless persons hop freight trains from Eureka, California, to San Francisco during the Depression, making friends with each other.

Rice, Keith

2552. *Out of Canaan.* New York: Scribner's, 1983. 192 pp.
A woman leaves her husband and eight children in 1892, only to return a year later with a child in her arms, either her husband's or that of a wealthy Florida man with whom she lived.
Genre(s): Domestic Fiction.

Richards, Emilie

2553. *Iron Lace.* New York: Harlequin, 1996. 480 pp.

Aurore Gerritsen, an elderly white socialite, asks African American journalist Phillip Benedict to ghostwrite her autobiography, and although at first he is suspicious, he discovers interesting and unexpected connections.
Genre(s): Romance.

Richards, Judith

2554. *Summer Lightning.* New York: St. Martin's Press, 1968. 271 pp.

In the days before Pearl Harbor, Terry, six, loves to visit Mr. McCree who lives next to a Florida swamp with its rattlesnakes and crocodile skins.
Genre(s): Adventure Story.

Richter, Conrad

◆ 2555. *A Simple Honorable Man.* New York: Knopf, 1962. 309 pp.

Harry Donner leaves storekeeping to become a Lutheran preacher in rural Pennsylvania.
Genre(s): Religious Fiction.

Ripley, Alexandra

2556. *From Fields of Gold.* New York: Warner Books, 1994. 467 pp.

Nate Richardson, 18, is attracted to his preacher brother's wife, but they move away, and he spends time trying to take over the cigarette industry until they return.
Genre(s): Domestic Fiction.

2557. *On Leaving Charleston.* Garden City, NY: Doubleday, 1984. 519 pp.

The sequel to *Charleston* begins in 1900, when Stuart Tradd marries Margaret Garden after impregnating a girl on a neighboring plantation.
Genre(s): Family Saga.

Ritter, Margaret

2558. *Women in the Wind.* New York: Simon and Schuster, 1985. 685 pp.

In 1905, Reanna Lovell marries a cattle rancher against her family's judgment and moves with him out West, where she finds a different and difficult culture.
Genre(s): Romance; Western Fiction.

Rivers, Francine

2559. *Redeeming Love.* Sisters, OR: Questar, 1997. 500 pp.

After being beaten, Angel, a young prostitute, decides to accept devout Christian Michael Hosea's offer of marriage and falls in love not only with him, but also with God.
Genre(s): Christian Fiction; Romance.

Roberts, Patricia

2560. *Tender Prey.* Garden City, NY: Doubleday, 1983. 263 pp.

John James has been imprisoned for sexual offenses, and after he fills an advertisement for companions, he and a young girl disappear and Dectective Hackett must find him.
Genre(s): Mystery.

Robinson, Margaret A.

◆ 2561. *Courting Emma Howe.* New York: Harper and Row, 1987. 212 pp.

In 1905, Emma Howe leaves Vermont and her family for Washington state and marriage to Arthur Smollett after a short correspondence with him, only to find after she arrives that they may have made a mistake.
Genre(s): Romance.

Rodgers, Alan

2562. *Bone Music.* Stamford, CT: Longmeadow, 1995. 302 pp.

When Robert Johnson sings the song Judgment Day at the funeral of Santeria, evil forces unleash themselves on the contemporary world and extend back to the south in 1938.
Genre(s): Biographical Fiction; Musical Fiction.

Roiphe, Anne

2563. *The Pursuit of Happiness.* New York: Simon and Schuster, 1991. 528 pp.

In 1892, the Gruenbaum family immigrates to America, and after making a fortune and losing it, they move to Israel.
Genre(s): Family Saga.

Rollo, Naomi June

2564. *Goldy Lark.* Santa Barbara, CA: Fithian, 1992. 240 pp.

Goldy Lark, 15, falls in love with unsuitable males living in the Ozarks during the Depression until one finally comes along who will fulfill her dreams.
Genre(s): Domestic Fiction.

Roosevelt, Elliott

◆ 2565. *A First Class Murder.* New York: St. Martin's Press, 1991. 261 pp.

Eleanor Roosevelt takes the *Normandie* back to America, happy to have several interesting companions aboard, but the Russian ambassador dies of strychnine poisoning.
Genre(s): Mystery.

◆ 2566. *The Hyde Park Murder.* New York: St. Martin's Press, 1985. 231 pp.

When Bob Hannah's father is indicted, his fiancé's father tries to separate the two, and Mrs. Roosevelt suspects murder when Bob's mother supposedly commits suicide.
Genre(s): Mystery.

◆ 2567. *Murder and the First Lady.* New York: St. Martin's Press, 1984. 277 pp.

When a lowly secretary, Philip Garber, is found dead in the room of her British secretary, Eleanor Roosevelt begins to investigate.
Genre(s): Mystery.

◆ May be suitable for young adult readers

◆ 2568. *Murder at Hobcaw Barony.* New York: St. Martin's Press, 1986. 233 pp.
While vacationing in South Carolina, Mrs. Roosevelt meets several Hollywood stars who all become suspects when a movie producer is found dead in his bedroom.
Genre(s): Mystery.

2569. *Murder at Midnight.* New York: St. Martin's Press, 1997. 224 pp.
Horace Lackwell comes to Washington in 1933 and stays in the White House across the hall from the Roosevelt suite, and when a maid finds Horace's naked and stabbed body, she is accused of the murder until Eleanor Roosevelt intervenes.
Genre(s): Mystery.

◆ 2570. *Murder in the Executive Mansion.* New York: St. Martin's Press, 1995. 197 pp.
While preparing for the visit of King George VI and Queen Elizabeth in 1939, Mrs. Roosevelt's social secretary disappears, and after the royal visit ends, her body is found stuffed in a linen closet.
Genre(s): Mystery.

◆ 2571. *Murder in the Map Room.* New York: St. Martin's Press, 1998. 256 pp.
Wholesale shoe salesman George Shen dies in the Map Room of the White House, and since no record of his entry in the White House can be found, Eleanor Roosevelt must defer much of her sleuthing to the Secret Service.
Genre(s): Mystery.

◆ 2572. *Murder in the Oval Office.* New York: St. Martin's Press, 1989. 247 pp.
A Southern Congressman is murdered during a White House party, and Mrs. Roosevelt helps to solve the crime.
Genre(s): Mystery.

◆ 2573. *Murder in the Red Room.* New York: St. Martin's Press, 1992. 249 pp.
In 1937, a Cleveland criminal is murdered in the Red Room while the Roosevelts host seven Supreme Court justices in the State Dining Room next door, and Eleanor Roosevelt investigates.
Genre(s): Mystery.

◆ 2574. *Murder in the Rose Garden.* New York: St. Martin's Press, 1989. 232 pp.
Vivian Taliafero is strangled in the White House Rose Garden in 1936, and Mrs. Roosevelt helps to gather information about the famous hostess.
Genre(s): Mystery.

◆ 2575. *Murder in the West Wing.* New York: St. Martin's Press, 1992. 247 pp.
Although Therese seems to be the murderer of President Roosevelt's special assistant, Mrs. Roosevelt disagrees and begins her investigation.
Genre(s): Mystery.

◆ 2576. *New Deal for Death.* New York: St. Martin's Press, 1993. 251 pp.
Blackjack Endicott travels to Hollywood to keep film producers and unpleasant union leaders from stopping Roosevelt's labor reforms.
Genre(s): Mystery.

◆ 2577. *The President's Man.* New York: St. Martin's Press, 1991. 345 pp.
Blackjack Endicott, a millionaire, investigates a death threat relayed to President Roosevelt from a Tammany Hall politician.
Genre(s): Mystery.

◆ 2578. *A Royal Murder.* New York: St. Martin's Press, 1994. 234 pp.
Mrs. Roosevelt goes to the Bahamas on a diplomatic mission to discourage the Duke and Duchess of Windsor from visiting the United States and becomes involved in a murder case.
Genre(s): Mystery.

Rose, Marcia

2579. *Like Mother, Like Daughter.* New York: Ballantine, 1994. 414 pp.
Leah writes for radical magazines in the early 20th century, and her daughter becomes a photographer, her granddaughter a singer, and her great-granddaughter a comedienne.
Genre(s): Domestic Fiction; War Story; Family Saga.

Rosen, Charley

2580. *The House of Moses All-Stars.* New York: Seven Stories, 1997. 496 pp.
During the Depression, a Jewish basketball team leaves the Bronx to tour across America where the team members have a chance to see the country and learn about one another.
Genre(s): Sports Fiction.

Rosen, Norma

2581. *John and Anzia.* New York: Dutton, 1989. 177 pp.
In 1917, John Dewey has an affair with Anzia Yezierska, a Polish immigrant half his age.
Genre(s): Biographical Fiction; Love Story.

Ross, Dana Fuller

◆ 2582. *Pacific Destiny.* New York: Bantam, 1994. 353 pp.
As the Pacific Northwest attracts unsavory characters, the Holt family tries to keep order in the area. (*Series:* An American Dynasty, 8)
Genre(s): Domestic Fiction; Western Fiction.

Roth, Henry

2583. *A Diving Rock in the Hudson.* New York: St. Martin's Press, 1995. 418 pp.
In the sequel to *A Star Shines over Mt. Morris Park*, Ira Stigman, the teenage son of Orthodox Jewish immigrants in the 1920s, gathers strength to focus on writing even while the sin of incest gnaws at his soul.
Genre(s): Bildungsroman (Coming of Age).

2584. *From Bondage.* New York: St. Martin's Press, 1996. 432 pp.
Ira Stigman works toward manhood in Manhattan in the 1920s, during which time he has an affair with his college professor.
Genre(s): Bildungsroman (Coming of Age).

2585. *Requiem for Harlem.* New York: St. Martin's Press, 1998. 304 pp.
Ira Stigman begins an affair with Edith, his English professor at NYU, after having an incestuous relationship with both his sister and his cousin. (*Series:* Mercy of a Rude Stream, 4)
Genre(s): Bildungsroman (Coming of Age).

◆ **2586.** *A Star Shines over Mt. Morris Park.* New York: St. Martin's Press, 1994. 290 pp.
Ira Stigman, nine, moves into Harlem with his Jewish family and faces anti-Semitism from the Irish in World War I as well as a sense of dislocation when other family members arrive from Austria.
Genre(s): Bildungsroman (Coming of Age).

Rowe, Jack

2587. *Dominion.* New York: Watts, 1986. 372 pp.
The second part of the du Pont family story presents the friendship of Lamont du Pont and Irish immigrant Michael Farrell and describes how they take the munitions industry from Henry du Pont.
Genre(s): Biographical Fiction.

Rubin, Louis D., Jr.

2588. *The Heat of the Sun.* Marietta, GA: Longstreet, 1995. 448 pp.
In Charlestown, South Carolina, during 1940, an English professor and a young reporter follow their careers and their love affairs.
Genre(s): Domestic Fiction.

Ruiz, Ronald L.

2589. *Guiseppe Rocco.* Houston, TX: Arte Publico, 1998. 272 pp.
While Italian immigrant Giuseppe Rocco works to become a wealthy man, he prefers the company of Mexican workers to that of the governors.
Genre(s): Domestic Fiction.

Rushing, Jane Gilmore

2590. *Tamzen.* New York: Doubleday, 1972. 318 pp.
Tamzen Greer, strong-willed and capable, becomes involved with the conflicts between the ranchers and the farmers in West Texas during the 1890s.
Genre(s): Western Fiction.

2591. *Winds of Blame.* Garden City, NY: Doubleday, 1983. 304 pp.
In a small Texas town in 1916, Ray Deane decides that he must kill his father after the man brings a prostitute into their home to live.
Genre(s): Domestic Fiction.

Sachs, Barbara Turner

2592. *The Rainbow Box.* New York: St. Martin's Press, 1984. 240 pp.
Poor Mary James and rich Edward Wyck marry quickly in the 1920s, but Edward's family tries to sue her for fraud when it discovers that she is one-eighth black.
Genre(s): Legal Story.

Salerno, Nan F., and Rosa Vandenburgh

◆ **2593.** *Shaman's Daughter.* Englewood Cliffs, NJ: Prentice Hall, 1980. 404 pp.
Supaya Cedar, a woman of the Ojibwa clan on Lake Huron, is the last shaman of the tribe in the early 20th century.
Genre(s): Biographical Fiction.

Sams, Ferrol

2594. *Run with the Horsemen.* San Diego, CA: Harcourt Brace, 1982. 118 pp.
A young boy grows up in rural Georgia as the son of an abusive school superintendent father during the Depression.
Genre(s): Bildungsroman (Coming of Age).

Santayana, George

2595. *The Last Puritan: A Memoir in the Form of a Novel.* New York: Scribner's, 1936. 602 pp.
A young man living in New England during the 1890s thinks that being a Puritan was wrong but finds that he himself is one.
Genre(s): Bildungsroman (Coming of Age).

Saroyan, William

2596. *The Human Comedy.* New York: Harcourt Brace, 1943. 242 pp.
Homer is a night messenger for the Postal Telegraph Office in a small California town during World War II after his father dies and his brother serves in the army.
Genre(s): War Story.

Sarrantonio, Al

◆ **2597.** *Kitt Peak.* New York: M. Evans, 1993. 160 pp.
Although Thomas Mullins, an African American cavalry officer, has retired in Boston, he returns to Arizona to help his friend find his daughter, and by the time he arrives, he must find his friend as well.
Genre(s): Mystery.

Satterthwait, Walter

◆ **2598.** *Miss Lizzie.* New York: St. Martin's Press, 1989. 336 pp.
In 1921, 13-year-old Amanda Burton lives next door to Lizzie Borden, and although Amanda's stepmother warns Amanda to avoid Lizzie, they become friends, and then someone murders Amanda's stepmother with an ax.
Genre(s): Mystery.

2599. *Wilde West.* New York: St. Martin's Press, 1991. 374 pp.
Oscar Wilde, the Irish poet lecturing in the United States, helps to investigate the brutal murders of redheads in the cities that he visits.
Genre(s): Mystery; Western Fiction.

Saunders, Raymond M.

2600. *Fenwick Travers and the Forbidden Kingdom.* Novato, CA: Lyford, 1994. 352 pp.
Fenwick Travers becomes a captain and is sent to the Philippines to stop a rebellion gainst the Americans.
Genre(s): War Story.

2601. *Fenwick Travers and the Years of Empire.* Novato, CA: Lyford, 1993. 360 pp.
Fenwick is posted to Cuba and to China after graduating from West Point in 1897, but he despises combat and creates unsubstantiated heroics for himself, which President McKinley rewards by sending him on a special mission to the Philippines.
Genre(s): Picaresque Fiction.

Savage, Elizabeth

2602. *Happy Ending.* Boston: Little, Brown, 1972. 308 pp.
Four people fight to survive on a Montana ranch during the Depression.
Genre(s): Domestic Fiction; Love Story.

Savage, Les

◆ 2603. *Table Rock.* New York: Walker, 1993. 156 pp.
Although unable to stand gunfire, Gordon Conner slowly changes so that he can pursue his father's killers.
Genre(s): Western Fiction.

Savage, Thomas

2604. *The Corner of Rife and Pacific.* New York: Morrow, 1988. 288 pp.
As developers arrive in Grayling, Montana, the Metlen family begins to lose status, but Zack begins to develop radio entertainment.
Genre(s): Domestic Fiction.

Schaeffer, Susan Fromberg

2605. *Time in Its Flight.* Garden City, NY: Doubleday, 1978. 782 pp.
Dr. John Steele, a widower, marries a 16-year-old girl, and they begin their family while he continues to see his Vermont patients.
Genre(s): Domestic Fiction; Family Saga.

Schofield, Susan Clark

2606. *Telluride.* Chapel Hill, NC: Algonquin, 1993. 328 pp.
Zachary Coleman (Cole) returns to Telluride in 1892 after a 14-year absence to investigate his father's strange death.
Genre(s): Western Fiction.

Schorr, Mark

2607. *Bully.* New York: St. Martin's Press, 1985. 196 pp.
Jim White answers Theodore Roosevelt's request in 1903 to investigate a secret conspiracy against him
Genre(s): Mystery.

Schreiner, Samuel Agnew

2608. *The Van Alens.* New York: Arbor House, 1981. 427 pp.
The Van Alen family battles with the Rockefellers for ascendancy in New York as some of the children become involved in politics.
Genre(s): Biographical Fiction.

Schulberg, Budd

2609. *The Disenchanted.* New York: Viking, 1950. 388 pp.
Manley Halliday, a literary genius of the 1920s, tries to recreate his talent in later life but instead embodies all of the attibutes of F. Scott Fitzgerald's "lost generation."

Schweitzer, Gertrude

2610. *Stand Before Kings.* New York: Putnam, 1982. 336 pp.
Terrance McNally's son rejects the magazine Terrance has founded, but his granddaughter takes his place in the early 20th century during times of anti-Irish and anti-Semitic attitudes.

Scofield, Sandra

2611. *Plain Seeing.* New York: HarperCollins, 1997. 304 pp.
Emma, 17 and beautiful, meets a screenwriter in New Mexico during the 1930s who encourages her to go to Hollywood, but she returns to New Mexico when she is pregnant, and gives birth to Lucy as their family story begins.
Genre(s): Domestic Fiction; Family Saga.

Seton, Cynthia Propper

◆ 2612. *The Half-Sisters.* New York: Norton, 1974. 213 pp.
Two 11-year-old girls spend August of 1937 together but separate for nine years when their one common relative dies.

Settle, Mary Lee

2613. *Choices.* New York: Nan A. Talese, 1995. 376 pp.
Melinda Kregg, a member of Virginia society, refuses to accept her station and spends the 20th century committed to social activism in America and in Europe.
Genre(s): Family Saga; Political Fiction; War Story.

2614. *The Clam Shell.* New York: Delacorte, 1972. 255 pp.
A young girl born in West Virginia into the family of a self-made man never gains acceptance in the town's society, but she attempts to fit herself into the roles that others have made for her.
Genre(s): Domestic Fiction.

2615. *The Scapegoat.* New York: Random House, 1980. 278 pp.
In the sequel to *Know Nothing*, set in June of 1912, the possibility of a miners' strike in a small West Virginia town concerns several groups of people.
Genre(s): Family Saga.

Shawhan, Dorothy

2616. *Lizzie.* Marietta, GA: Longstreet, 1995. 352 pp.
Members of Lizzie Dunbar's family and her friends relate the story of her life in Mississippi and her establishment of the first newspaper for women in the 1920s.
Genre(s): Domestic Fiction.

Sherburne, James

2617. *Death's Clenched Fist.* Boston: Houghton Mifflin, 1982. 194 pp.
Paddy Moretti covers horse racing for a sporting newspaper, but when an exploding cigar kills Tammany Hall leader Kanady, Moretti's investigation reveals the confrontation among politicians, radicals, and police in the 1890s.
Genre(s): Mystery; Political Fiction.

2618. *Death's Gray Angel.* Boston: Houghton Mifflin, 1981. 206 pp.
In the 1890s, Paddy Moretti starts to investigate con men who may have fixed a fight and finds a larger story in buried money linked to local politicians.
Genre(s): Mystery.

2619. *Poor Boy and a Long Way from Home.* Boston: Houghton Mifflin, 1984. 361 pp.
Glen Hatton has no responsibilities as a teenager in California during 1909 as he becomes involved in the early movie industry and in the plots against China in San Francisco's Chinatown.
Genre(s): Adventure Story.

2620. *Stand Like Men.* Boston: Houghton Mifflin, 1973. 268 pp.
In the 1930s, the United Mine Workers fail to support the Harlan County miners in a strike and the communist National Miners' Association takes over, but both strikers and owners show their brutality.
Genre(s): Political Fiction.

Sherman, Jory

2621. *Grass Kingdom.* New York: Forge, 1994. 412 pp.
In the 1920s, Matt Baron must find out who cut the throat of one of the hired hands on his Texas ranch and emasculated one of his prize stud bulls.
Genre(s): Western Fiction.

Shivers, Louise

2622. *Here to Get My Baby out of Jail.* New York: Random House, 1983. 136 pp.
Roxy Walston already has a child in 1937 when a stranger comes to town and changes her life.

Shuken, Julia

◆ 2623. *Day of the East Wind.* Wheaton, IL: Crossway, 1993. 256 pp.
To escape persecution and the unsettled climate in Russia at the beginning of the 20th century, Piotr Voloshin escapes to California.
Genre(s): War Story; Christian Fiction.

◆ 2624. *In the House of My Pilgrimage.* Wheaton, IL: Crossway, 1995. 252 pp.
In the sequel to *Day of the East Wind*, Piotr Voloshin marries Fenya, also an emigrant, and together they struggle with cultural changes and the difficulties of marriage.
Genre(s): Christian Fiction.

Silber, Joan

2625. *In the City.* New York: Viking, 1987. 232 pp.
Pauline Samuels comes of age in Greenwich Village during the 1920s, encountering speakeasies and flappers as part of her maturation.
Genre(s): Bildungsroman (Coming of Age).

Sinclair, Upton

2626. *Boston.* New York: Boni and Liveright, 1928. 799 pp.
Wealthy Cornelia Thornwell decides to work in a Boston factory where she meets Sacco and Vanzetti in 1920 and tries to save them.
Genre(s): Legal Story.

2627. *The Coal War.* Boulder, CO: Colorado Associated Universities, 1976. 417 pp.
In the sequel to *King Coal*, coal miners lead a strike in Colorado during 1913 and 1914 to reveal capitalist greed.

2628. *The Flivver King.* New York: Phaedra, 1969. 155 pp.
Henry Ford, congenial and quixotic, begins to make his cars, and three generations of both his family and the Shutts family (who work for him) tell about his foibles.
Genre(s): Biographical Fiction.

2629. *The Jungle.* Garden City, NY: Doubleday, 1906. 373 pp.
Jurgis Rudkus, a Slav immigrant lured by appealing advertisements, comes to Chicago to make money in the stockyards, but the reality is different from what he expects.

2630. *King Coal.* 1921. New York: AMS, 1980. 396 pp.
Hal Warner, a wealthy playboy, becomes a miner to study the coal industry, and then he becomes a union organizer.
Genre(s): Political Fiction.

2631. *Oil!* New York: Boni and Liveright, 1927. 527 pp.
The life of Bunny Ross, son of an oil magnate, reveals practices of those who have become wealthy from their oil wells during the Teapot Dome scandal.
Genre(s): Political Fiction.

Skimin, Robert

2632. *Chikara.* New York: St. Martin's Press, 1984. 541 pp.
Sataro Hoshi leaves Japan in 1907 for California, where he faces rising anti-Japanese feelings, the Depression, and both of the world wars.
Genre(s): Family Saga.

Skinner, Margaret

2633. *Old Jim Canaan.* Chapel Hill, NC: Algonquin, 1990. 287 pp.

As Jim Canaan's grandson recalls the summer of 1914 and his grandfather's actions as a political boss in Memphis, he tends to remember only the private man upon whom his family depended.

Genre(s): Political Fiction.

Skinner, Robert E.

2634. *Cat-Eyed Trouble.* New York: Kensington, 1998. 256 pp.

Creole nightclub owner Wesley Farrell still passes for white in the 1930s, but he does not want underworld figures to know that his father is a white policeman when he tracks a woman in a heroin-smuggling operation.

Genre(s): Mystery.

Skvorecky, Josef

◆ 2635. *Dvorak in Love.* New York: Norton, 1987. 544 pp.

In the 1890s, Antonin Dvorak stays in New York and Spillville, Iowa, where Americans influence his music.

Genre(s): Biographical Fiction; Musical Fiction.

Slone, Verna Mae

2636. *Rennie's Way.* Lexington, KY: University Press of Kentucky, 1994. 220 pp.

In 1917 when Rennie Slone is 12, her mother dies, and she begins to care for her infant sister and her father in the Kentucky mountains.

Genre(s): Domestic Fiction; Bildungsroman (Coming of Age).

Slotkin, Richard

2637. *The Return of Henry Starr.* New York: Atheneum, 1988. 576 pp.

Against an early 1920s backdrop of Prohibition and race problems in Tulsa, Oklahoma, Henry Starr dies in 1921 while seeking justice through a life of crime.

Genre(s): Western Fiction.

Smith, Bert Kruger

2638. *A Teaspoon of Honey.* Nashville, TN: Aurora, 1970. 223 pp.

Herschel Malinsky is fun-loving and successful in Russia at the turn of the century until pogroms force him to leave for America, where he eventually earns money in oil but loses it listening to poor advice.

Genre(s): Jewish Fiction.

Smith, Betty

◆ 2639. *Joy in the Morning.* New York: Harper and Row, 1963. 308 pp.

Annie McGairy, 18, elopes with a young law student in the late 1920s, and her husband continues to attend school.

Genre(s): Bildungsroman (Coming of Age).

◆ 2640. *A Tree Grows in Brooklyn.* New York: Harper and Row, 1943. 443 pp.

Francie Nolan grows up in Williamsburg, a slum section of Brooklyn, during the early 20th century.

Genre(s): Bildungsroman (Coming of Age).

Smith, C. W.

2641. *Buffalo Nickel.* New York: Simon and Schuster, 1989. 397 pp.

Went on a Journey attends an Oklahoma missionary school in 1904 where he is renamed David Copperfield, and he meets Iola, a young woman with whom he forms a strong bond lasting more than 25 years.

Genre(s): Bildungsroman (Coming of Age).

2642. *Hunter's Trap.* Fort Worth: Texas Christian University Press, 1996. 255 pp.

In the sequel to *Buffalo Nickel*, Will Hunter comes to El Paso in 1930 to avenge the deaths of his wife and his Kiowa employer that were ordered by a wealthy banker.

Genre(s): Western Fiction.

Smith, Eunice Young

2643. *A Trumpet Sounds.* Westport, CT: Lawrence Hill, 1985. 263 pp.

Amon and his saintly mother struggle as African Americans in a white world, but he overcomes indignity and gains fame as a singer.

Genre(s): Biographical Fiction; Musical Fiction.

Smith, Larry

2644. *The Original.* New York: McGraw Hill, 1972. 331 pp.

Jelm Garrett, the oldest son in his farm family, begins to work for an older woman, and although he has aspirations of a different future, he works well with his hands, and literally works himself to death.

Genre(s): Domestic Fiction.

Smith, Lee

2645. *Fair and Tender Ladies.* New York: Putnam, 1988. 336 pp.

Ivy Rowe wants to be a writer, but poverty and motherhood in World War I and then the Depression limit her to colorful letters describing those in her Appalachian family and community.

Genre(s): Domestic Fiction.

Smith, Lillian

2646. *Strange Fruit.* San Diego: Harcourt Brace, 1944. 371 pp.

Nonnie, a light-skinned and educated black woman, becomes beloved mistress of a white male in a small Georgia town.

Snow, Richard

2647. *The Burning.* Garden City, NY: Doubleday, 1981. 240 pp.

In 1894, the lumber town of Hinckley, Minnesota, goes up in flames in just a few hours.

Genre(s): Domestic Fiction.

Sondheim, Victor

2648. *Inheritors of the Storm.* New York: Dell, 1981. 832 pp.
During the 20 years after their banker father commits suicide, the five Sinclair children each choose a way, some legal and some illegal, to regain status.
Genre(s): Family Saga.

Soos, Troy

2649. *Cincinnati Red Stalkings.* New York: Kensington, 1998. 336 pp.
Mickey Rawlings, playing for the Cincinnati Reds, meets Oliver Perriman, organizer of a memorabilia show, and after Perriman gives Rawlings an 1869 baseball, Perriman is murdered, and Rawlings investigates.
Genre(s): Mystery; Sports Fiction.

2650. *Murder at Wrigley Field.* New York: Kensington, 1996. 304 pp.
Mickey Rawlings, the Chicago Cubs' second baseman, must find the murderer of his German friend Willie Kaiser at Wrigley Field in 1918.
Genre(s): Mystery.

Sorrentino, Gilbert

2651. *Steelwork.* New York: Pantheon, 1970. 256 pp.
The denizens of Brooklyn, including immigrants, families, gangs, alcoholics, and others, face World War II with the same attitudes with which they live their daily lives.
Genre(s): Domestic Fiction; War Story.

Sparks, Nicholas

2652. *The Notebook.* New York: Warner Books, 1996. 268 pp.
In 1932, Allie Nelson meets visitor Noah Calhoun in New Bern, and since her mother thinks Noah is from the slums she hides his letters, but 14 years later they meet again, and although Allie is engaged, they fall in love and marry, a story that Noah retells Allie when he is 80 and she has Alzheimer's.
Genre(s): Romance.

Spellman, Cathy Cash

2653. *So Many Partings.* New York: Delacorte, 1983. 519 pp.
When Tom Dalton, first abandoned in Ireland by his parents in 1875, emigrates to New York and becomes wealthy, family members first welcome and then abandon him again.
Genre(s): Domestic Fiction.

Spencer, LaVyrle

2654. *The Fulfillment.* New York: Avon, 1979. 266 pp.
In Minnesota in 1910, Jonathan Gray decides for his young wife and unmarried brother to sire him an heir, and when his scheme works, everyone seems somewhat pleased.
Genre(s): Romance; Domestic Fiction.

2655. *Morning Glory.* New York: Putnam, 1989. 384 pp.
A young widowed mother in the South advertises for a husband.
Genre(s): Domestic Fiction; Romance.

2656. *That Camden Summer.* New York: Putnam, 1996. 368 pp.
At the turn of the century, Roberta Jewett divorces her wandering husband, returns to Maine with her three daughters, gets a job, and learns to drive, much to the shock and chagrin of her family and neighbors.
Genre(s): Domestic Fiction.

Stallworth, Anne Nall

2657. *This Time Next Year.* New York: Vanguard, 1972. 288 pp.
In the mid-1930s, Florrie Birdson's father is a tenant farmer who digs graves for extra money, her mother saves for a house in town that she hopes to have by the next year, and Florrie at 15 seems to want to keep things as they are.
Genre(s): Domestic Fiction.

Starbuck, Marjorie

2658. *They Came in from the Road.* Vista, CA: Marbet, 1992. 319 pp.
In 1926, Spec and Wilma Boden begin living on the deserted prairie in Horse Creek Camp, Wyoming, where Wilma's love of art and music suffers for two years.
Genre(s): Biographical Fiction; Domestic Fiction.

Stead, Christina

2659. *I'm Dying Laughing.* New York: Henry Holt, 1987. 447 pp.
Her husband, his friends, and the postwar political climate slowly destroy writer Emily Wilkes Howard.
Genre(s): Domestic Fiction.

Steel, Danielle

2660. *No Greater Love.* Garden City, NY: Doubleday, 1991. 392 pp.
The Winfield parents stay aboard the *Titanic* after placing their six children on lifeboats, and Edwina, 20, raises the children for the next 12 years.
Genre(s): Sea Story.

◆ **2661.** *Wings.* New York: Delacorte, 1994. 400 pp.
Cassie O'Malley's father refuses to let her fly planes at his small private airport, but a new employee teaches her to fly, and she begins to test planes and set world records.
Genre(s): Adventure Story.

Steen, Marguerite

2662. *Jehovah Blues.* New York: Doubleday, 1952. 282 pp.
Aldebran Flood, last in her powerful shipping family, becomes involved in a racial situation. (*Series:* Flood Trilogy, 3)
Genre(s): Family Saga.

Stegner, Wallace Earle

2663. *The Big Rock Candy Mountain.* New York: Duell, Sloane, and Pearce, 1943. 733 pp.
Bo Mason and his family move from place to place as he endlessly searches for his fortune from 1906 to 1942.
Genre(s): Domestic Fiction.

2664. *Joe Hill.* 1950. New York: Penguin, 1990. 381 pp.
Joe Hill, labor leader and songwriter, becomes a martyr to the labor cause in 1915 when he is executed for a murder he did not commit.
Genre(s): Biographical Fiction.

Steinbeck, John

2665. *East of Eden.* New York: Viking, 1952. 602 pp.
The Trasks and the Hamiltons live and work together in Salinas during the early 20th century.
Genre(s): Domestic Fiction; Western Fiction.

2666. *The Grapes of Wrath.* New York: Viking, 1939. 559 pp.
The Joad family, Okie farmers forced from their dust-bowl home during the Depression, try to find work as migrant fruitpickers in California.
Award(s): Pulitzer Prize.

2667. *In Dubious Battle.* New York: Viking, 1938. 313 pp.
Radical leaders try to help striking California fruit pickers during the early 20th century.

Stern, Steve

2668. *Harry Kaplan's Adventures Underground.* New York: Ticknor and Fields, 1991. 310 pp.
Harry Kaplan's poor family must leave Brooklyn for Memphis in the 1930s, and Harry becomes friends with African American twins who expose him to the underside of the city.
Genre(s): Bildungsroman (Coming of Age).

Stewart, Fred Mustard

2669. *Century.* New York: Morrow, 1981. 576 pp.
Franco's family's fortunes begin before World War I with the kidnapping of an Italian princess and continue through World War II with the Mafia in pursuit.

2670. *The Mannings.* New York: Arbor House, 1973. 648 pp.
Mark Manning rises from bicycle shop owner to rubber magnate in the early 20th century.

2671. *The Titan.* New York: Simon and Schuster, 1985. 509 pp.
Nick Fleming becomes involved in the munitions industry and becomes very wealthy from trade during the Russian Revolution and World War II.
Genre(s): Love Story.

Stone, Irving

2672. *The Passionate Journey.* Garden City, NY: Doubleday, 1949. 337 pp.
The artist John Noble searches for beauty during his late 19th century travels to France, England, Provincetown, and New York.

Straight, Susan

◆ 2673. *The Gettin Place.* New York: Hyperion, 1996. 488 pp.
When a contemporary teenager in California tries to sort out his family's hostilities, his search leads him to the race riots in Tulsa during the 1920s.
Genre(s): Domestic Fiction.

Straley, John

2674. *Death and the Language of Happiness.* New York: Bantam, 1997. 210 pp.
When an old man is accused of killing a young mother, the man hires Cecil Younger to kill the witness, and Younger finds himself in 1916 working on an earlier case in which two boys mysteriously disappeared.
Genre(s): Mystery.

Streshinsky, Shirley

2675. *The Shores of Paradise.* New York: Putnam, 1991. 416 pp.
Beginning in 1898, True Lindstrom and Martha Moon form a friendship in a home for unwanted children before befriending the dwarf Liko and the child Princess Kaiulani in Hawaii.
Genre(s): Domestic Fiction.

Strong, Albertine

2676. *Deluge.* New York: Crown, 1997. 288 pp.
Aja tells about her grandfather who was pushed off a train in 1907 on his way to college and rescued by a Swedish immigrant who became her grandmother, and about resulting incidents that created the family's mixed heritage legacy.
Genre(s): Family Saga.

Strunk, Frank C.

2677. *Jordon's Showdown.* New York: Walker, 1993. 252 pp.
A professional murderer poses as a union organizer in Kentucky during the Depression while methodically killing union supporters, and when he kills Berkley Jordon's friend, Jordon goes into action.
Genre(s): Mystery.

Stuart, Colin

2678. *Shoot An Arrow to Stop the Wind.* New York: Dial, 1970. 248 pp.
Colin visits his mother's people in Montana in the summer of 1926 and meets his Blackfoot great-grandmother.
Genre(s): Domestic Fiction.

Stubbs, Jean

2679. *The Golden Crucible.* New York: Stein and Day, 1976. 287 pp.
Following the abductor Barak to San Francisco from London, Inspector Lintott is trying to rescue the kidnapped Alicia when the 1906 earthquake hinders his progress.
Genre(s): Mystery.

Sullivan, Faith

◆ 2680. *The Cape Ann.* New York: Crown, 1988. 342 pp.
Prior to World War II, the Erhardts live in a storage room adjacent to the depot, but Lark's growing makes the room too small, and they have no money, because of Lark's father's drinking and gambling, to purchase a house.
Genre(s): Domestic Fiction.

Swados, Harvey

2681. *Standing Fast.* New York: Doubleday, 1970. 648 pp.
From the 1930s to the 1960s, radicals try to change the status quo of America.
Genre(s): Epic Literature.

Swarthout, Glendon

2682. *The Old Colts.* New York: Donald I. Fine, 1985. 239 pp.
In 1916, Wyatt Earp goes to visit Bat Masterson in New York City, and, both needing money, they decide to return to Dodge City to rob a bank and collect what they think the West owes them.
Genre(s): Biographical Fiction; Western Fiction.

◆ 2683. *The Shootist.* Garden City, NY: Doubleday, 1975. 186 pp.
John Bernard Books survives his gunfighting battles in 1901, but when he goes to El Paso to consult a doctor about his pain and finds that he has incurable cancer, he engineers his own demise.
Award(s): Western Writers of America Spur Award.
Genre(s): Western Fiction.

2684. *The Tin Lizzie Troop.* New York: Doubleday, 1972. 240 pp.
In 1916, during a skirmish on the Texas-Mexican border, soldiers from Main Line Philadelphia chase a Mexican bandit in a Model T Ford.
Genre(s): Western Fiction.

Swift, Edward

2685. *A Place with Promise.* Garden City, NY: Doubleday, 1987. 205 pp.
Zeda Earl Overstreet wants to escape from Camp Ruby, Texas, but years later she returns to its familiarity for contentment.
Genre(s): Domestic Fiction.

Tatlock, Ann

2686. *A Room of My Own.* Minneapolis, MN: Bethany House, 1998. 400 pp.
Virginia's young teenaged daydreams stop when her uncle's family moves in, but when she sees homeless people on the edge of the city during the Depression, she begins to understand why her uncle Jim cannot get a job.
Genre(s): Domestic Fiction.

Tax, Meredith

◆ 2687. *Rivington Street.* New York: Morrow, 1982. 431 pp.
Russian women immigrate to the Lower East Side of New York in the early 20th century and work hard in the garment district for low pay.

2688. *Union Square.* New York: Morrow, 1988. 437 pp.
The sequel to *Rivington Street* finds Sarah, of the socialist worker and Marxist Levy family, married to Avi Spector, whose family is ideologically opposed to hers.
Genre(s): Domestic Fiction; Political Fiction.

Taylor, Robert B.

2689. *Long Road Home.* New York: Henry Holt, 1989. 420 pp.
The Robertson family, migrants from Texas, come into contact with Titus Wardlow, a man interested only in obtaining more money in any way possible.
Genre(s): Political Fiction.

Taylor, Robert Love

2690. *The Lost Sister.* Chapel Hill, NC: Algonquin, 1989. 280 pp.
Marshall Monroe moves to Oklahoma City, but life does not improve much for the family during the 1930s and the Depression.
Genre(s): Domestic Fiction.

Thane, Elswyth

2691. *Ever After.* New York: Duell, Sloan, and Pearce, 1945. 334 pp.
The sequel to *Yankee Stranger* continues the story of the Day/Murray/Sprague family in Williamsburg with journalist Bracken Murray traveling to England for Victoria's Jubilee and covering the Spanish-American war.
Genre(s): Domestic Fiction; Family Saga; War Story.

2692. *Kissing Kin.* New York: Duell, Sloan, and Pearce, 1948. 374 pp.
In the sequel to *The Light Heart*, Camilla and Calvert are twins who take part in World War I, with Calvert on a gun crew and Camilla in England at her cousin's hospital.
Genre(s): War Story; Family Saga.

Thayer, Steve

2693. *Saint Mudd.* New York: Viking, 1992. 387 pp.
In the early 1930s, Grover Mudd, newspaper columnist in St. Paul, alerts citizens to the crime surrounding them.
Genre(s): Mystery.

Thoene, Bodie

2694. *In My Father's House.* Minneapolis, MN: Bethany House, 1993. 589 pp.
Between the wars, ordinary people in Arkansas become caught in the difficulties of the Depression. (*Series:* Shiloh Legacy, 1)
Genre(s): War Story; Christian Fiction.

2695. *Say to this Mountain.* Minneapolis, MN: Bethany House, 1993. 447 pp.
During the Depression, people in Shiloh have to look deep within themselves for sustenance that is unavailable elsewhere. (*Series:* Shiloh Legacy, 3)
Genre(s): Christian Fiction.

2696. *A Thousand Shall Fall.* Minneapolis, MN: Bethany House, 1992. 428 pp.
Families become caught up in the 1920s before the stock market crashes in 1929. (*Series:* Shiloh Legacy, 2)
Genre(s): Christian Fiction.

Thoene, Bodie, and Brock Thoene

2697. *Shiloh Autumn.* Nashville, TN: Nelson, 1996. 470 pp.
While their husbands have gone to the Veterans' March in Washington during the early 1930s, Trudy and Willa Mae try to hold their Arkansas families together through poverty and disease.
Genre(s): Domestic Fiction; Christian Fiction.

Thomas, Bob

2698. *Weekend '33.* New York: Doubleday, 1972. 288 pp.
On Labor Day weekend of 1933, a group of filmmakers go to the castle of a newspaper tycoon, where he tries to gain control of the Depression-era film industry.
Genre(s): Political Fiction.

Thomas, Michael M

2699. *Hanover Place.* New York: Warner Books, 1990. 749 pp.
Hanover Place, the Warringtons's brokerage house in New York City is the site of stock market activity in 1924.

Thompson, Joan

2700. *Interesting Times.* New York: St. Martin's Press, 1981. 313 pp.
Two Harvard graduates decide to fight in France during World War I, and they become adults during the fray and manage to maintain their lives and their relationships.
Genre(s): War Story; Bildungsroman (Coming of Age).

Thornton, Lawrence

2701. *Under the Gypsy Moon.* New York: Doubleday, 1990. 212 pp.
Two writers succumb to the lures of fascism when Federico García Lorca meets Joaqun Wolf and transforms Wolf's life before the Guardia Civil murders García Lorca, and Wolf destroys Guernica in the Spanish Civil War.
Genre(s): War Story.

Thum, Marcella

2702. *Fernwood.* New York: Doubleday, 1973. 183 pp.
When Abigail comes to Fernwood, a dilapidated Virginia plantation in the 1890s, she discovers a secret about a death that occurred a few years earlier and endangers herself.
Genre(s): Romance; Mystery; Gothic Fiction.

Tilghman, Christopher

2703. *Mason's Retreat.* New York: Random House, 1996. 274 pp.
When Edward Mason inherits an estate on the Eastern Shore of Maryland in 1937, he brings his family from England, hoping to recoup business losses.
Genre(s): Domestic Fiction.

Tippette, Giles

2704. *Heaven's Gold.* New York: Forge, 1996.
In 1916, retired bank robber Wilson Young decides to steal over one million dollars in gold as a political statement about the country's turn toward consumerism.
Genre(s): Adventure Story.

2705. *The Trojan Cow.* New York: Macmillan, 1971. 256 pp.
As Oklahoma Territory prepares to become a state in the 20th century's first decade, residents of a small town worry about their land, their courthouse, and how to use a milking machine.
Genre(s): Western Fiction.

Treitel, Jonathan

2706. *The Red Cabbage Café.* New York: Pantheon, 1991. 185 pp.
In the 1920s, Humphrey Veil, an American engineer of German and English heritage, is devoted to Lenin and the building of the Moscow subway, but when Stalin comes to power, he faces unexpected hardship.
Genre(s): Political Fiction.

Tryon, Thomas

2707. *Lady.* New York: Knopf, 1974. 341 pp.
An eight-year-old boy falls hopelessly in love with a woman in his small town, whose kindness masks her own problems during the Depression.

2708. *The Other.* New York: Knopf, 1971. 280 pp.
In a small New England country town, a variety of mishaps disrupt the family life of Niles and Holland Perry.
Genre(s): Domestic Fiction.

Tucker, Augusta

2709. *Miss Susie Slagle's.* 1939. Baltimore: Johns Hopkins University Press, 1987. 332 pp.
Medical students live in Miss Susie Slagle's boarding house while attending Johns Hopkins University during World War I.
Genre(s): War Story.

Tucker, Helen

2710. *The Guilt of August Fielding.* New York: Stein and Day, 1971. 320 pp.
Repelled by the fire and brimstone sermons he hears in the 1890s, August Fielding decides to bring dignity to religion, but before he can become an effective teacher of religion, he first must overcome his guilt about his affair with a professor's wife.
Genre(s): Family Saga; Christian Fiction.

Turnbull, Agnes Sligh

2711. *Gown of Glory.* Boston: Houghton Mifflin, 1952. 403 pp.
Although clergyman David Lyall wants a more prestigious position in another church, he never receives it, and he finally realizes he is in the right place.
Genre(s): Christian Fiction.

Turner, Steven

2712. *A Measure of Dust.* New York: Simon and Schuster, 1970. 190 pp.
In one week during the 1930s, Mark, 13, sees his parents' weaknesses, is seduced by a girl, and looks for his own place in the adult world.
Genre(s): Bildungsroman (Coming of Age).

Uchida, Yoshiko

2713. *Picture Bride.* Flagstaff, AZ: Northland, 1987. 216 pp.
After Hana Omija arrives in San Francisco prior to World War II to marry Taro Takeda, she betrays him with his best friend before realizing his qualities and before they are interned at Topaz.
Genre(s): Domestic Fiction; War Story.

Ude, Wayne

2714. *Becoming Coyote.* Amherst, MA: Lynx House, 1981. 165 pp.
A white man confronts his Coyote figure, Charlie Two Rivers, in Belknap, and begins to understand the convergence between the real world and the shadow world.
Genre(s): Western Fiction.

Updike, John

2715. *In the Beauty of the Lilies.* New York: Knopf, 1996. 528 pp.
The generations of the Wilmot family become more and more secular during the 20th century from the time that Clarence Wilmot, a Presbyterian minister, loses his faith in 1910.
Genre(s): Family Saga.

Van Every, Dale

2716. *The Day the Sun Died.* Boston: Little, Brown, 1971. 320 pp.
The Native Americans of the Great Plains expect a Messiah beginning in 1889, and they begin wearing a ghost shirt, thought to be impervious to the white man's bullets, but the massacre at Wounded Knee in 1891 proves them wrong.
Genre(s): War Story; Political Fiction.

Van-Loon, Antonia

2717. *Sunshine and Shadow.* New York: St. Martin's Press, 1981. 280 pp.
Tracy Sullivan decides to marry a man she does not love in order to take her family and herself out of poverty in New York, but she and her true love meet too often at weddings and funerals.
Genre(s): Romance.

Vanderbilt, Gloria

2718. *The Memory Book of Starr Faithfull.* New York: Knopf, 1994. 309 pp.
In June of 1931, Starr Faithfull's body washes up on the shore of a New York beach, and her diary, discovered by police, describes her history of sexual abuse at age 11 and her encounters with members of the upper class in 1920s New York City.
Genre(s): Erotic Literature.

Victor, Daniel D.

◆ 2719. *The Seventh Bullet.* New York: St. Martin's Press, 1992. 186 pp.
Sherlock Holmes and Dr. Watson leave retirement for America, where they search for the killer of famous journalist David Graham Phillips.
Genre(s): Mystery.

Vidal, Gore

◆ 2720. *Empire.* New York: Random House, 1987. 486 pp.
Caroline Sanford owns an important newspaper that she uses as the key to enter social circles in Washington, DC, which include Abraham Lincoln's friend John Hay. (*Series:* American Chronicle, 4)
Genre(s): Political Fiction.

◆ 2721. *The Smithsonian Institution.* New York: Random House, 1998. 240 pp.
In 1939, someone summons prep school student T to the Smithsonian via telephone, and when he arrives, the place is closed, but the exhibit dummies come alive, and he discovers that his knowledge of numbers might help the country build better bombs.
Genre(s): Time Travel.

2722. *Washington, D.C.* New York: Random House, 1976. 377 pp.
In the sequel to *1876*, a senator's ambitions are defeated when Franklin Roosevelt decides to run for a third term. (*Series:* American Chronicle, 5)
Genre(s): Political Fiction.

Villars, Elizabeth

2723. *One Night in Newport.* Garden City, NY: Doubleday, 1981. 360 pp.
Socially pretentious Mrs. Elias Leighton tries to marry off her three daughters in Newport society before World War I.
Genre(s): Romance.

◆ May be suitable for young adult readers

von Herzen, Lane

◆ 2724. *Copper Crown.* New York: Morrow, 1991. 288 pp.
In 1913, two women, one white and one black, become friends in their Texas town, and remain so throughout their lives.
Genre(s): Domestic Fiction.

Wagoner, David

◆ 2725. *Where Is My Wandering Boy Tonight?* New York: Farrar, Straus and Giroux, 1970. 272 pp.
A boy in Wyoming during the 1890s has a variety of experiences, mostly positive, that lead him to leave town and become a cowboy.
Genre(s): Western Fiction.

Walker, Alice

2726. *The Color Purple.* New York: Harcourt Brace, 1982. 245 pp.
Two African American sisters, one a missionary in Africa and the other a child-wife living in the South, support each other through their correspondence, beginning in the 1920s.
Award(s): Pulitzer Prize; American Book Award.
Genre(s): Domestic Fiction.

2727. *The Third Life of Grange Copeland.* New York: Harcourt Brace, 1970. 256 pp.
In Georgia during the 1920s, Grange Copeland creates and sustains a dream for his granddaughter in the midst of African American dehumanization.
Genre(s): Family Saga.

Walker, Jack

◆ 2728. *Boomer's Gold.* Berkeley, CA: Thorp Springs, 1978. 313 pp.
In the 1920s, Texas cattlemen and oil barons vie for power in the towns they build.
Genre(s): Western Fiction.

Ward, Robert

2729. *Cattle Annie and Little Britches.* New York: Morrow, 1978. 240 pp.
Jenny (Little Britches) and Annie join the Doolin-Dalton gang of bank robbers in the 1890s.
Genre(s): Biographical Fiction; Western Fiction.

Warren, Robert Penn

2730. *All the King's Men.* New York: Harcourt Brace, 1946. 464 pp.
Jack Burden, a young journalist, becomes involved with Willie Stark's quest for power while serving as a Southern governor.
Award(s): Pulitzer Prize.
Genre(s): Political Fiction.

2731. *A Place to Come To.* New York: Random House, 1977. 401 pp.
Jed Tewksbury hates his hometown and his life and escapes to college and World War II.
Genre(s): Bildungsroman (Coming of Age); War Story.

Wathen, Richard B.

◆ 2732. *The Only Yankee.* Washington, DC: Regnery, 1970. 240 pp.
Silas Fant lives on the north side of the Ohio River and has to cross by ferry to school, where people see him as different because he is a Yankee.
Genre(s): Humorous Fiction; Adventure Story.

Watson, Larry

◆ 2733. *Justice.* Minneapolis, MN: Milkweed, 1995. 226 pp.
In 1924, Sheriff Julian Hayden's sons get into trouble on a hunting trip in the badlands of South Dakota.
Genre(s): Domestic Fiction.

Weidman, Jerome

2734. *Fourth Street East.* New York: Random House, 1970. 239 pp.
Benny Kramer lives with his Jewish immigrant parents in New York's Lower East Side in the 1920s, where his neighbors assert their rights so that Benny can feel safe.
Genre(s): Bildungsroman (Coming of Age).

2735. *Last Respects.* New York: Random House, 1971. 381 pp.
In the sequel to *Fourth Street East*, Benny Kramer, a bootlegger in the 1920s, has difficulty finding the body of his mother after it disappears between the hospital and the morgue.
Genre(s): Bildungsroman (Coming of Age).

2736. *Tiffany Street.* New York: Random House, 1974. 429 pp.
Benjamin Kramer, a successful attorney, sees himself as a failure before he realizes that he has raised a moral son who, instead of avoiding the draft for the Vietnam war, decides to become a conscientious objector.
Genre(s): Domestic Fiction.

Woloh, James

2737. *Winter in the Blood.* New York: Harper and Row, 1974. 176 pp.
When a Blackfoot misfit returns to his Montana home, he realizes that he longer belongs in that environment.
Genre(s): Adventure Story.

Wells, Lawrence

2738. *Let the Band Play Dixie.* Garden City, NY: Doubleday, 1987. 391 pp.
At the first North-South All-Star Football Game in Philadelphia during 1896, Civil War veterans and speculators gamble for their sides.
Genre(s): Sports Fiction.

Welty, Eudora

2739. *Losing Battles.* New York: Random House, 1970. 436 pp.
On a hot August weekend in the 1930s, family members attend Granny Vaughan's 90th birthday on Sunday and the funeral of a former teacher on Monday.
Genre(s): Domestic Fiction.

2740. *The Robber Bridegroom.* Garden City, NY: Doubleday, 1942. 185 pp.
Rosamond, daughter of a Mississippi planter, falls in love with a bandit chief.
Genre(s): Adventure Story.

Wertenbaker, Lael

2741. *Unbidden Guests.* Boston: Little, Brown, 1970. 287 pp.
During Prohibition on a small Georgia island, an Episcopalian minister arrives who disturbs the balance of life that its inhabitants have created through the years.
Genre(s): Domestic Fiction.

West, Jessamyn

2742. *The State of Stony Lonesome.* San Diego: Harcourt Brace, 1984. 184 pp.
Ginerva Chalmers remembers her youth in a 1919 discussion with Uncle Zen.
Genre(s): Domestic Fiction.

West, Michael Lee

2743. *Crazy Ladies.* Marietta, GA: Longstreet, 1990. 352 pp.
When someone tries to rape Gussie in her own kitchen during the Depression, her infant daughter becomes traumatized, and the event affects future generations.
Genre(s): Domestic Fiction.

Westervelt, Virginia Veeder

2744. *Pearl Buck.* New York: Elsevier, 1979. 297 pp.
Pearl Buck grows up in China as the daughter of missionaries and returns to America to write about her experiences in her novels.
Genre(s): Biographical Fiction.

Westin, Jeane

2745. *Swing Sisters.* New York: Scribner's, 1991. 576 pp.
In the 1930s, women in an all-female jazz band have a variety of relationships with men and other women as they perform around New York City.
Genre(s): Musical Fiction.

Wharton, Edith

2746. *The Buccaneers.* New York: Viking, 1993. 384 pp.
When the wealthy St. George girls and their friend are rejected by New York society because their bloodlines are too short, they go to England and make superb marriages, but Nan St. George finds that being a duchess does not necessarily bring happiness.
Genre(s): Domestic Fiction.

2747. *The Gods Arrive.* 1932. New York: Scribner's, 1985. 439 pp.
In the sequel to *Hudson River Bracketed*, Vance Weston's wife dies, and until Halo Tarrant is free to marry him, they go abroad.
Genre(s): Domestic Fiction.

2748. *The House of Mirth.* New York: Scribner's, 1905. 532 pp.
Orphaned Lily Bart, 29, finds herself falling in society because of situations outside her control.
Genre(s): Domestic Fiction.

2749. *Hudson River Bracketed.* New York: Appleton, 1929. 536 pp.
When Vance Weston comes to New York City from the midwest, he meets people who live in a house with Hudson River bracketed architecture, and the treasures of their library expose him to a depth of culture that he has never known.
Genre(s): Domestic Fiction.

Wheaton, Philip D.

◆ 2750. *Razzmatazz.* New York: Everest House, 1980. 310 pp.
Willis Winston, 12, tells of his difficult 16-year-old sister Penny, who tries to uncover family secrets.
Genre(s): Bildungsroman (Coming of Age).

Wheeler, Richard S.

2751. *Goldfield.* New York: Forge, 1995. 379 pp.
Thousands of people, including con men, prospectors, gold diggers, and others, converge on the boom camp of Goldfield, Nevada, in the early 1900s.
Genre(s): Western Fiction.

White, Walter

2752. *The Fire in the Flint.* Athens: University of Georgia Press, 1996. 300 pp.
When Kenneth Harper returns to his southern home in the 1920s after having received his medical degree, the Ku Klux Klan tries to stifle his accomplishments.
Genre(s): Medical Novel.

Wick, Lori

2753. *Promise Me Tomorrow.* Eugene, OR: Harvest House, 1997. 400 pp.
Katherine Taggart (Rusty) loves children and works with them in her family's orphanage, and when she takes two orphans to their new home, she falls in love with their new father.
Genre(s): Christian Fiction.

Wiley, Richard

◆ 2754. *Fools' Gold.* New York: Knopf, 1988. 304 pp.
In Nome, Alaska, during the gold rush, the Irishman Finn and two young women arrive, unexpectedly finding that many others have preceded them.
Genre(s): Western Fiction.

Willard, Tom

2755. *The Sable Doughboys.* New York: Forge, 1997. 319 pp.
After Augustus Talbot serves in the Spanish-American War with his sons, the sons attend Officer Candidate School so that they can lead African American troops in France during World War I.
Genre(s): War Story.

◆ May be suitable for young adult readers

Williams, Gordon

2756. *Pomeroy.* New York: Arbor House, 1982. 299 pp.
John Stockley Pomeroy becomes the first secret service agent for the United States while Theodore Roosevelt is president, and on his way to London, he meets spies and cardsharks.
Genre(s): Mystery; Spy Fiction.

Williams, Jeanne

◆ 2757. *Home Station.* New York: St. Martin's Press, 1995. 321 pp.
After Lesley Morland's father dies preventing a robbery in their new railroad town, she becomes the station agent and adopts three orphans, but when she chooses a wagon driver over the railroad owner, she faces possible disaster.
Genre(s): Bildungsroman (Coming of Age).

◆ 2758. *The Longest Road.* New York: St. Martin's Press, 1993. 389 pp.
After their mother's death, two children hop a freight car to California to find their father, but when they discover that he drowned trying to save another, they must find a way to save themselves.
Genre(s): Love Story; Musical Fiction.

◆ 2759. *The Unplowed Sky.* New York: St. Martin's Press, 1994. 307 pp.
Hallie Meredith, 19, becomes a cook with the MacLeod threshing outfit in the 1920s to support her five-year-old brother after her widowed stepmother abandons them, and she becomes interested in the two MacLeod brothers.
Genre(s): Western Fiction; Romance.

Winther, Sophus Keith

2760. *Take All to Nebraska.* New York: Macmillan, 1936. 305 pp.
Peter Grimsen emigrates from Denmark to Massachusetts and then Nebraska in 1898, hoping for a better life.
Genre(s): Western Fiction.

Wise, Tad

◆ 2761. *Tesla.* Atlanta: Turner, 1994. 381 pp.
Nikola Tesla invents radio, solar cells, X-ray generators, sonar, and fluorescent lighting, but his personal attitudes make Thomas Edison and many others hate him.
Genre(s): Biographical Fiction.

Woiwode, Larry

2762. *Beyond the Bedroom Wall.* New York: Farrar, Straus and Giroux, 1975. 619 pp.
The Neumiller family represents the history of the Midwestern family as change occurs during the 20th century.
Genre(s): Domestic Fiction; Family Saga.

2763. *Born Brothers.* New York: Farrar, Straus and Giroux, 1988. 610 pp.
In the sequel to *Beyond the Bedroom Wall*, the five Neumiller children grow up and marry but recall their childhood together.
Genre(s): Family Saga.

Wolfe, Thomas

2764. *The Web and the Rock.* New York: Harper and Row, 1939. 695 pp.
As George Webber grows up and attends college, he tries to understand the meaning of life, but is unsuccessful.
Genre(s): Bildungsroman (Coming of Age).

Wood, Jane Roberts

2765. *Dance a Little Longer.* New York: Delacorte, 1993. 233 pp.
Lucy Richards Arnold is happy with her husband and her four-year-old son in west Texas where they move in 1931, but when her son dies, she loses interest in life until one of the Depression victims helps her find renewal, in the sequel to *A Place Called Sweet Shrub.*
Genre(s): Domestic Fiction; Romance.

◆ 2766. *A Place Called Sweet Shrub.* New York: Delacorte, 1990. 307 pp.
In the sequel to *The Train to Estelline*, Lucinda Richards marries Josh Roberts, and they move to Arkansas, unaware of the racial hostilities in their new small town.
Genre(s): Romance.

2767. *The Train to Estelline.* Lufkin, TX: Ellen C. Temple, 1987. 240 pp.
In 1911, Lucinda Richards begins teaching in Estelline, Texas, where she finds much prejudice and ignorance in her one-room schoolhouse.
Genre(s): Romance.

Woodworth, Deborah

2768. *A Deadly Shaker Spring.* New York: Avon, 1998. 304 pp.
At first Sister Rose Callahan thinks that pranksters have disrupted Shaker village life in North Homage, until she discovers journals noting the occurrence of similar events 25 years previously.
Genre(s): Mystery.

2769. *Death of a Winter Shaker.* New York: Avon, 1997. 352 pp.
In the 1930s, during the Depression, a winter shaker (someone who needs food and shelter and pretends to be a Believer) dies, and the sheriff of a nearby town tries to blame the murder on someone in the Shaker community.
Genre(s): Mystery.

Wouk, Herman

2770. *The Winds of War.* Boston: Little, Brown, 1971. 885 pp.
Pug Henry and his family prepare for World War II as he progresses toward his own command and interaction with Franklin Roosevelt and Hitler.

Wright, Sarah E.

2771. *This Child's Gonna Live.* New York: Delacorte, 1969. 276 pp.
Mariah Upshur tries to keep her children alive in a black ghetto during the 1930s.
Genre(s): Domestic Fiction.

Wubbels, Lance

2772. *The Bridge over Flatwillow Creek.* Minneapolis, MN: Bethany House, 1998. 320 pp.
In 1901, Stuart Gray arrives at the scene of an accident and decides that medicine is his calling rather than the ministry, and he also meets Annie Harding, a young woman new to town, who is courting the town banker's son.
Genre(s): Christian Fiction; Romance.

2773. *Whispers In The Valley.* Minneapolis, MN: Bethany House, 1995. 304 pp.
Jerry and Marjie Macmillan are finally reunited when Jerry returns from the war, but they worry about raising their child and keeping their farm. (*Series:* Gentle Hills, 2)
Genre(s): Christian Fiction; Domestic Fiction.

Wyckoff, James

2774. *Slater's Book.* New York: Doubleday, 1976. 152 pp.
In the 1890s, cattle barons expect to take prime lands in Wyoming, but Slater leads a group of men against them.
Genre(s): Western Fiction.

Wyden, Barbara

2775. *A Rich Wife.* New York: Macmillan, 1985. 292 pp.
Wealthy but plain Fredericka Schumacher meets a fortune hunter in New York City in the early 20th century, and after their marriage she becomes a force in pre World War I society.
Genre(s): Domestic Fiction.

Yamaguchi, Yoji

2776. *Face of a Stranger.* New York: HarperCollins, 1995. 208 pp.
Wealthy Arai Takashi is banished from Japan to the United States in the early 20th century for his unseemly conduct, and he becomes a houseboy and discovers that someone is using his photograph to lure unsuspecting mail-order brides into prostitution.

Yglesias, Helen

2777. *Family Feeling.* New York: Dial, 1976. 309 pp.
Anne Goddard leaves her Jewish immigrant family in the ghetto to join left-wing intellectual circles in New York City.
Genre(s): Domestic Fiction.

Young, I. S.

2778. *Uncle Herschel, Dr. Padilsky, and the Evil Eye.* New York: Harcourt Brace, 1973. 264 pp.
In 1900, Uncle Herschel emigrates from Russia, and Yankel, 10, who admires his uncle, often becomes his interpreter as he tries to establish a medicinal shop against the wishes of a local gangster and a doctor.
Genre(s): Domestic Fiction.

Yount, John

2779. *Hardcastle.* New York: Marek, 1980. 287 pp.
A poor young man hired as a guard for a coal mine becomes sympathetic to the strikers in 1931.
Genre(s): Political Fiction.

Yount, Steven

◆ 2780. *Wandering Star.* New York: Ballantine, 1994. 395 pp.
Tom Greer remembers 1910 in Texas when he was 12 and the fear of some that the world was ending when Halley's comet appeared.
Genre(s): Western Fiction.

Zagst, Michael

2781. *M.H. Meets President Harding.* New York: D. I. Fine, 1987. 247 pp.
In 1923, Thomas Edison invites Sidney Halverton, a tentmaker, on one of his West Virginia picnics with President Harding, and Sidney meets the lovely Margarete Fabry, who, after inciting him to help her kidnap Harding, turns out to be Mata Hari in disguise.
Genre(s): Biographical Fiction; Mystery.

Zaroulis, N. L.

2782. *The Last Waltz.* Garden City, NY: Doubleday, 1984. 398 pp.
Marian Childs's mother pushes her to become a companion to various members of the January family in Boston until she eventually inherits from an old uncle.
Genre(s): Domestic Fiction.

2783. *The Poe Papers.* New York: Putnam, 1977. 252 pp.
In the 1890s, a Poe scholar acquires love letters from an old woman supposedly written by Poe, and when the man visits with the woman, he begins using drugs.
Genre(s): Mystery.

Zuckerman, George

2784. *The Last Flapper.* Boston: Little, Brown, 1969. 439 pp.
Zelda Fitzgerald finally marries Scott and wanders around Europe with him in the 1920s.
Genre(s): Biographical Fiction; Domestic Fiction.

1941-1945
World War II

Adams, Alice

2785. *Families and Survivors.* New York: Knopf, 1975. 211 pp.
After attending a Virginia college, Louisa Calloway moves to California where she experiences many family difficulties but manages to survive.
Genre(s): Bildungsroman (Coming of Age).

Appel, Allen

2786. *Till the End of Time.* New York: Doubleday, 1990. 412 pp.
Alex Balfour travels into the Pacific and the attack on Pearl Harbor during World War II.
Genre(s): Time Travel; War Story.

Appleman, Philip

2787. *Apes and Angels.* New York: Doubleday, 1989. 320 pp.
In the months before Pearl Harbor in 1941, some people in a small Indiana town become involved in guilty relationships that lead them directly to the war and December 7.
Genre(s): War Story.

Baxt, George

2788. *The Greta Garbo Murder Case.* New York: St. Martin's Press, 1992. 197 pp.
Erich Von Stroheim directs a movie starring Greta Garbo about Joan of Arc as World War II begins, while Garbo investigates the poisoned bodies that collect as part a possible Nazi plot surrounding the movie's financial backer.
Genre(s): Mystery.

Beach, Edward Latimer

2789. *Dust on the Sea.* New York: Holt, Rinehart and Winston, 1972. 351 pp.
In the sequel to *Run Silent Run Deep*, Commander Richardson takes a submarine to the Yellow Sea in an attempt to prevent the Japanese transfer of troops from Manchuria to Okinawa.
Genre(s): Sea Story; War Story; Adventure Story.

2790. *Run Silent, Run Deep.* New York: Holt, Rinehart and Winston, 1955. 364 pp.
Richardson, an Annapolis graduate, takes his submarine *Walrus* deep while avoiding depth charges of enemy destroyers in World War II.
Genre(s): Sea Story; War Story; Adventure Story.

Berger, Thomas

2791. *Orrie's Story.* Boston: Little, Brown, 1990. 276 pp.
At the end of World War II, Orrie, Augie, Esther, and others recreate the Oresteia tragedy when Augie pretends to go to war and sends postcards to get way from his wife.
Genre(s): War Story; Domestic Fiction.

Berry, Wendell

2792. *A World Lost.* Washington, DC: Counterpoint, 1996. 160 pp.
Andy Catlett is still distressed by his uncle's murder in 1944 when he becomes an adult, and when he investigates, he learns much about his family and life during the 1940s.
Genre(s): Domestic Fiction.

Bickham, Jack M.

◆ 2793. *All the Days Were Summer.* Garden City, NY: Doubleday, 1981. 192 pp.
Danny, 12, becomes involved with both POWs and a blind dog while his father is director of a German prisoner-of-war camp in the Midwest during 1943.
Genre(s): War Story.

Bogin, Magda

2794. *Natalya, God's Messenger.* New York: Scribner's, 1994. 288 pp.
Knowing that she will lose her job as a riveter after World War II, Rita buys a palmistry business in New York City, and afterwards, she finds that she is clairvoyant and can foretell events in the future.
Genre(s): Fantastic Literature; Love Story.

Boyd, William Young

◆ 2795. *The Gentle Infantryman.* New York: St. Martin's Press, 1985. 384 pp.
Will Hope, 18 and drafted into the army, learns how to be a combat soldier serving in France and Austria during World War II.
Genre(s): War Story.

Boyne, Walter J.

◆ 2796. *Eagles at War.* New York: Crown, 1991. 392 pp.
Frank Bandfield and Hadley Roget begin the Allied aviation force during World War II to fight the German air

force led by Bruno Hafner, in the sequel to *Trophy for Eagles*.
Genre(s): War Story; Adventure Story.

Bradford, Richard

◆ 2797. *Red Sky at Morning.* Philadelphia: Lippincott, 1968. 256 pp.
Josh, 17, goes with his mother from Mobile, Alabama, to Sagrado, New Mexico, while his father serves in the navy during World War II.
Genre(s): War Story; Biographical Fiction; Humorous Fiction.

Brautigan, Richard

2798. *Dreaming of Babylon.* New York: Delacorte, 1977. 220 pp.
C. Card is an inept private eye in San Francisco who dreams of Babylon in 596 BC and has to figure out how to steal a body from a morgue.
Genre(s): Mystery; Fantastic Literature; Humorous Fiction.

Cauley, Harry

2799. *Bridie and Finn.* San Diego, CA: Harcourt Brace, 1994. 356 pp.
In 1942, Bridie moves into Finn's Irish neighborhood, announces that she hates nuns more than the Japanese, and becomes best friends with Finn, who is embarrassed by his twisted leg.
Genre(s): War Story; Domestic Fiction.

Cavanaugh, Jack

2800. *The Victors.* Wheaton, IL: Victor, 1998. 500 pp.
The Morgan siblings, Nat, Walt, Alex, and Lily, take part in World War II, and each handles the experience differently. (*Series:* American Family Portrait, 7)
Genre(s): Christian Fiction; Family Saga; War Story.

Chalker, Jack L.

◆ 2801. *The Devil's Voyage.* New York: Doubleday, 1981. 328 pp.
The *Indianapolis* takes 1,200 men and the bomb for Hiroshima from San Francisco to a Pacific launch site, but on its return, the Japanese torpedo it.
Genre(s): Adventure Story.

Chappell, Fred

◆ 2802. *I Am One of You Forever.* Baton Rouge: Louisiana State University Press, 1985. 184 pp.
Young Jess finds his unusual relatives intriguing and suffers when a farmhand dies in World War II.
Genre(s): Domestic Fiction; War Story.

Coe, Marian

2803. *Legacy.* Little Switzerland, NC: South, 1993. 370 pp.
Lelia Eliot, raised by her Alabama kin, wants to know about her family as World War II ends.
Genre(s): War Story; Bildungsroman (Coming of Age).

Covington, Vicki

◆ 2804. *Night Ride Home.* New York: Simon and Schuster, 1992. 288 pp.
In a small Alabama mining town, everyone has secrets that they forget when they must join together during a mine collapse even while news of Pearl Harbor comes on the radio.
Genre(s): Domestic Fiction; War Story.

Cozzens, James Gould

2805. *Guard of Honor.* New York: Harcourt Brace, 1948. 631 pp.
In 1943, a series of incidents at an air base in Florida leads every one to guard the honor of the others.
Genre(s): War Story.

Davis, Don

2806. *Appointment with the Squire.* Annapolis, MD: Naval Institute, 1995. 327 pp.
A German infiltrator plans to assassinate President Roosevelt with FBI agents unwittingly helping, but only one man can positively identify the German.
Genre(s): Adventure Story; War Story; Biographical Fiction.

Davis, J. Madison

◆ 2807. *And the Angels Sing.* Sag Harbor, NY: Permanent Press, 1996. 303 pp.
Carl Walthers, known as the Carolina Crooner, plans to become a star with the help of a Cleveland mafia member, but World War II interrupts, and when Carl returns, too many murders interfere with his progress.
Genre(s): War Story; Mystery.

Deighton, Len

2808. *Close-Up.* New York: Atheneum, 1972. 381 pp.
As Peter Anson, married to Marshall Stone's ex-wife, writes Stone's biography, he exposes all of the sham of the movie industry during the 1940s and 1950s.

Delston, Ethel

2809. *Of Love Remembered.* New York: Delacorte, 1972. 224 pp.
After meeting at a Naval Academy dance, Charlotte and Matt marry, and during World War II, after the birth of their son, he dies in a poorly organized campaign.
Genre(s): Love Story; War Story.

DeMarinis, Rick

2810. *The Year of the Zinc Penny.* New York: Norton, 1989. 175 pp.
Trygve Napoli, 11, is reunited with his mother during World War II after three years apart, and he has to learn to deal with her and with other relatives.
Genre(s): War Story; Domestic Fiction; Bildungsroman (Coming of Age).

Denny, Robert

2811. *Aces.* New York: Donald I. Fine, 1991. 291 pp.

In World War II, pilots Mitchell M. Robinson and Lon Amundson, who come from a small Pennsylvania town, become part of the skies over Germany as they fly B-17s through flak and bad weather.
Genre(s): War Story.

2812. *Night Run.* New York: Donald I. Fine, 1992. 387 pp.

Mike Gavin, an American pilot, flies with the Soviets at night, but during a raid, he has to abandon his B-17 behind Soviet lines.
Genre(s): War Story.

Dubus, Elizabeth Nell

2813. *To Love and to Dream.* New York: Putnam, 1986. 359 pp.

From the years 1941 to 1950, the children of Caroline and Beau in *Where Love Rules* leave home; Skye becomes a bomber pilot in England during World War II and Caro quits school to work in a New Orleans shipyard.
Genre(s): War Story; Domestic Fiction.

Ehrlich, Gretel

2814. *Heart Mountain.* New York: Viking, 1988. 377 pp.

McKay runs his family's ranch near the Heart Mountain Relocation Camp in Wyoming for interning Japanese Americans, including his cook, Bobby Korematsu, while his brothers fight in the Pacific.
Genre(s): War Story.

Epstein, Leslie

2815. *Pandaemonium.* New York: St. Martin's Press, 1997. 384 pp.

Peter Lorre wants to terminate his studio contract because he hates the character he plays, and he tells the story of a group of actors in Austria at the time of the Anschluss that gets into trouble because of its Jewish members.
Genre(s): War Story; Allegory; Political Fiction.

Epstein, Seymour

2816. *A Special Destiny.* New York: Donald I. Fine, 1986. 327 pp.

Eugene, a German Jewish refugee, and Saul, the oldest son in an unhappy Jewish family, are friends but they have different views of World War II, one concerned about Europe's Jews and the other worried only about his play writing.
Genre(s): War Story.

Finney, Ernest J.

2817. *Words of My Roaring.* New York: Crown, 1993. 380 pp.

During World War II in San Bruno, California, a teacher and others face the traumas of wartime.
Genre(s): War Story.

Flagg, Fannie

2818. *Fried Green Tomatoes at the Whistle-Stop Cafe.* New York: Random House, 1987. 403 pp.

Vinnie remembers the gossip from a newsletter published in their small Alabama town during the 1940s which reveals their feelings before and during World War II.
Genre(s): Domestic Fiction.

Fleming, Thomas

2819. *Time and Tide.* New York: Simon and Schuster, 1987. 734 pp.

An Annapolis man relieves his friend from command of the USS *Jefferson City* after his ship leaves the Battle of Savo under suspicion in 1942.
Genre(s): Epic Literature; Sea Story; Adventure Story.

Follett, Ken

2820. *Night over Water.* New York: Morrow, 1991. 400 pp.

A Nazi, Jew, filmstar, jewel thief, unfaithful housewife, and a Russian princess are on board a Pan American flight that crash lands off the coast of Maine during World War II.
Genre(s): Adventure Story; War Story.

Ford, Robert E.

2821. *Sergeant Sutton.* New York: Hawthorn, 1970. 320 pp.

From Oklahoma, Sutton joins the Marines and enjoys a series of promotions during World War II until the war destroys his sense of humanity.
Genre(s): War Story.

Forester, C. S.

2822. *The Good Shepherd.* Boston: Little, Brown, 1955. 310 pp.

Captain Krause takes the *Keeling* with only four ships to protect 37 merchantmen during a harrowing 48 hours on the Atlantic in 1942.
Genre(s): War Story; Sea Story.

Freeman, Cynthia

2823. *Seasons of the Heart.* New York: Putnam, 1986. 399 pp.

The Japanese inter Ann Coulter's husband during World War II, and she improves the family finances by becoming a realtor.
Genre(s): Family Saga; Love Story.

French, Albert

◆ 2824. *Holly.* New York: Viking, 1995. 307 pp.

In the last year of World War II, Holly wonders if she wants to marry Billy when he returns from the Pacific, but she receives word that he is dead, her brother returns changed with a head wound, and a discharged black amputee begins to console her.
Genre(s): War Story; Love Story.

Gannon, Michael

2825. *Secret Missions.* New York: HarperCollins, 1994. 384 pp.
Peter Krug, a Nazi spy in Florida trying to find information about war planes, confesses to Father D'Angelo, who must decide how to stop murder within the confines of the Catholic Church.
Genre(s): War Story; Spy Fiction.

Garcia, Lionel G.

2826. *Leaving Home.* Houston, TX: Arte Publico, 1985. 249 pp.
Mexican-American Adolfo, a former baseball player, wanders around California with his friend, having sexual encounters with women who have lived difficult lives.
Genre(s): War Story.

Gilroy, Frank Daniel

2827. *Private.* New York: Harcourt Brace, 1970. 160 pp.
A draftee learns that the army is not democratic as World War II ends, and he returns from the European front.
Genre(s): War Story; Bildungsroman (Coming of Age).

Glover, Vivian

◆ 2828. *The First Fig Tree.* New York: St. Martin's Press, 1988. 224 pp.
While her father fights in World War II and her mother works, a young girl becomes acquainted with her great grandmother Ellen who moves into the same house and tells about her days as a slave and as a free woman.
Genre(s): War Story; Domestic Fiction.

Goldreich, Gloria

◆ 2829. *That Year of Our War.* Boston: Little, Brown, 1994. 368 pp.
On D-Day, 1944, Sharon Grossberg's mother dies, and since her physician father is overseas, she lives with various members of her family, but as they go through their daily lives, they are always thinking of the war.
Genre(s): War Story; Bildungsroman (Coming of Age).

Grant, Pete

2830. *Night Flying Avenger.* South Windsor, CT: Newmark, 1990. 297 pp.
World War II pilots attend flying school and experience combat aboard the aircraft carrier *Saratoga* during 1944 and 1945.
Genre(s): War Story.

Grattan-Dominguez, Alejandro

◆ 2831. *The Dark Side of the Dream.* Houston, TX: Arte Publico, 1995. 434 pp.
A migrant family moves to Texas in 1942 and suffers the problems of immigrants as one son fights the Nazis in Italy and another tries to unite the migrant workers in the Rio Grande Valley.
Genre(s): War Story; Family Saga.

Green, Gerald

2832. *East and West.* New York: D. I. Fine, 1986. 476 pp.
Japanese Kenji Tamba studies in the United States and marries an American girl before he is sent to the Manzanar detention camp after the bombing of Pearl Harbor.
Genre(s): War Story.

Griffin, W. E. B.

2833. *Battleground.* New York: Putnam, 1991. 414 pp.
Marines fight in Midway and continue to Guadalcanal with those on the edges of the battle doing the planning. (*Series:* The Corps, 4)
Genre(s): War Story.

2834. *Behind the Lines.* New York: Putnam, 1995. 384 pp.
Generals in the Philippines struggle for power during World War II. (*Series:* The Corps, 8)
Genre(s): War Story.

2835. *Counterattack.* New York: Putnam, 1990. 444 pp.
Marines fighting after Pearl Harbor but before Guadalacanal must adjust to situations for which they are unprepared, including promotions. (*Series:* The Corps, 3)
Genre(s): War Story.

2836. *Line of Fire.* New York: Putnam, 1992. 414 pp.
Marines fight on Guadalcanal in August and September of 1942 while other events occur around the globe involving people they know. (*Series:* The Corps, 5)
Genre(s): Adventure Story; War Story.

Hassler, Jon

2837. *Grand Opening.* New York: Morrow, 1987. 368 pp.
In 1944, the Foster family members move to Plum, Minnesota, to start a supermarket, but first they have to overcome the townspeople's prejudice against outsiders.
Genre(s): Bildungsroman (Coming of Age).

Heggen, Thomas

2838. *Mister Roberts.* Boston: Houghton Mifflin, 1946. 221 pp.
A man on an American naval cargo ship plays several roles for the men on his ship while crossing and recrossing the Pacific during World War II.
Genre(s): War Story; Sea Story.

Himes, Chester B.

2839. *If He Hollers Let Him Go.* Garden City, NY: Doubleday, 1945. 203 pp.
A young African American describes his wartime experiences in Los Angeles before he finally joins the military.

Homewood, Harry

2840. *O, God of Battles.* New York: Morrow, 1983. 360 pp.
Two brothers, a submariner and a fighter pilot, try to rise in the military during World War II and bring home honors.
Genre(s): War Story.

2841. *Silent Sea.* New York: McGraw Hill, 1981. 368 pp.
In 1943, the *USS Eelfish* patrols the Leyte Gulf with a talented crew that sinks ships and delivers supplies.
Genre(s): War Story; Sea Story.

Honig, Donald

2842. *The Last Great Season.* New York: Simon and Schuster, 1979. 384 pp.
A baseball team rises from obscurity under its new owner while World War II rages in the background.
Genre(s): Sea Story; War Story; Sports Fiction.

Hyman, John H.

2843. *The Relationship.* Manassas, VA: E. M. Press, 1995. 251 pp.
In 1944, an African American child of nine becomes close friends with a poor white boy of the same age, and after a first encounter with German POWs working in the area, they experience a series of mishaps.
Genre(s): War Story; Domestic Fiction.

Ikeda, Stewart David

2844. *What the Scarecrow Said.* New York: Regan, 1996. 445 pp.
Prosperous William Fujita, a Japanese American born as soon as his mother arrives on the mainland in 1897, must go with his family and other Japanese to the internment camps in 1942.
Genre(s): Domestic Fiction; War Story.

Inman, Robert

2845. *Home Fires Burning.* Boston: Little, Brown, 1987. 392 pp.
Jake Tibbetts, editor of a southern town's newspaper, harbors a grudge against his son Henry for killing Jake's best friend's daughter in a car accident and escaping to World War II, but when Henry dies and the coffin comes home, Jake tears off the top in anguish, only to find that the body inside is not Henry.
Genre(s): War Story.

Jacobs, Harvey

2846. *Summer on a Mountain of Spices.* New York: Harper, 1974. 352 pp.
A Catskill summer at the end of World War II allows Jews to relax at a resort and cope with the international news.
Genre(s): War Story; Humorous Fiction.

Jessup, Richard

2847. *Sailor.* Boston: Little, Brown, 1969. 471 pp.
Howard Cadiz, cabin boy at 14, captains a merchant marine vessel in World War II.
Genre(s): Sea Story; War Story.

Jones, James

2848. *From Here to Eternity.* New York: Delacorte, 1951. 861 pp.
Two soldiers have love affairs in the early months of 1941.
Award(s): National Book Award.
Genre(s): Love Story.

2849. *The Thin Red Line.* New York: Scribner's, 1962. 495 pp.
In a companion novel to *From Here to Eternity*, Company C engages in the Guadalcanal campaign of World War II.
Genre(s): War Story.

2850. *Whistle.* New York: Delacorte, 1978. 457 pp.
In the sequel to *The Thin Red Line*, four soldiers from an infantry company in the Pacific receive treatment in a Tennessee hospital before being released in an insecure world.
Genre(s): War Story.

Kaminsky, Stuart M.

2851. *Buried Caesars.* New York: Mysterious Press, 1989. 179 pp.
Toby Peters works for General Douglas MacArthur in 1942 to find incriminating papers which an aide has stolen, and Dashiell Hammett, hiding from Lillian Hellman, offers his services.
Genre(s): Mystery.

2852. *Dancing in the Dark.* New York: Mysterious Press, 1996. 228 pp.
Luna Martin wants to dance with Fred Astaire, but after Astaire hires Toby Peters to stand in for him, someone murders Luna, and her gangster boyfriend wants Peters to quickly find out who did it.
Genre(s): Mystery.

2853. *The Devil Met a Lady.* New York: Mysterious Press, 1993. 194 pp.
Bette Davis's husband hires Toby Peters to protect her when Nazis threaten to kidnap her and play a tape of her indiscretion with Howard Hughes.
Genre(s): Mystery.

2854. *A Fatal Glass of Beer.* New York: Mysterious Press, 1997. 256 pp.
In 1943, when someone steals W.C. Fields's bankbooks and crosses the country emptying his accounts, Toby Peters has to find him.
Genre(s): Mystery.

2855. *He Done Her Wrong.* New York: St. Martin's Press, 1983. 168 pp.
In 1942, Mae West's biography has been stolen from her apartment, and when Toby Peters searches for it, he encounters violence.
Genre(s): Mystery.

2856. *The Howard Hughes Affair.* New York: St. Martin's Press, 1979. 207 pp.
Someone steals military secrets from Howard Hughes, and Toby Peters tries to find the criminal in the 1940s.
Genre(s): Mystery.

2857. *The Man Who Shot Lewis Vance.* New York: St. Martin's Press, 1986. 194 pp.
Toby Peters tries to retrieve his stolen gun from a known killer, and at the same time, secures employment with John Wayne and Charlie Chaplin.
Genre(s): Mystery.

2858. *Never Cross a Vampire.* New York: St. Martin's Press, 1980. 182 pp.
Toby Peters tries to solve vampire threats against Bela Lugosi while someone frames William Faulkner for murder in 1942.
Genre(s): Mystery.

2859. *Poor Butterfly.* New York: Mysterious Press, 1990. 179 pp.
The San Francisco performance of *Madame Butterfly* in 1942 causes problems that only Toby Peters and his odd associates can solve.
Genre(s): Mystery.

◆ 2860. *Smart Moves.* New York: St. Martin's Press, 1986. 212 pp.
Toby Peters goes to Princeton, New Jersey, in 1942 to help Albert Einstein find who is accusing him of being a traitor, and the climax comes during a Sunday afternoon concert as Albert Einstein plays accompaniment for singer Paul Robeson.
Genre(s): Mystery.

2861. *Think Fast, Mr. Peters.* New York: St. Martin's Press, 1987. 198 pp.
In Los Angeles during the 1940s, Toby Peters searches for his client's wife who has supposedly run away with Peter Lorre.
Genre(s): Mystery.

2862. *Tomorrow Is Another Day.* New York: Mysterious Press, 1995. 201 pp.
While extras act dead on the set of *Gone with the Wind*, one does not pretend, and Clark Gable asks Toby Peters to help him find the murderer.
Genre(s): Mystery.

2863. *You Bet Your Life.* New York: St. Martin's Press, 1978. 215 pp.
Toby Peters has to save Chico Marx from the Mafia and he asks Al Capone from Chicago to help him.
Genre(s): Mystery.

Kanon, Joseph

2864. *Los Alamos.* New York: Bantam, 1997. 416 pp.
A Manhattan Project security officer is murdered in Los Alamos near the end of World War II, and a civilian intelligence officer, reporting directly to J. Robert Oppenheimer, investigates the crime.
Genre(s): War Story; Mystery.

Kluger, Steve

◆ 2865. *Last Days of Summer.* New York: Avon, 1998. 352 pp.
After Jewish Joey Margolis's father leaves their Brooklyn home, Joey wants a father, and he begins writing New York Giants player Charlie Banks.
Genre(s): War Story; Domestic Fiction; Bildungsroman (Coming of Age).

Knowles, John

◆ 2866. *Peace Breaks Out.* New York: Holt, Rinehart, and Winston, 1981. 192 pp.
At the end of World War II, graduates of the Devon School in New Hampshire are disappointed because they cannot fight in the war.

◆ 2867. *A Separate Peace.* New York: Macmillan, 1960. 186 pp.
Gene Forrester remembers a World War II year in prep school and the unexpected events of that year.
Genre(s): Bildungsroman (Coming of Age).

Kotlowitz, Robert

2868. *His Master's Voice.* New York: Knopf, 1992. 337 pp.
Baltimore cantor Sigmund Safer balances his work and his teenage daughter with a sense of humor while trying to forget his early life in Poland.
Genre(s): Humorous Fiction; War Story.

Larson, Elsie J.

◆ 2869. *Dawn's Early Light.* Nashville, TN: Nelson, 1996. 240 pp.
Jean Thornton begins hating Japanese Americans when her fiancé is killed at Pearl Harbor, but after she works as a teacher and spy in the Tule Lake internment camp, she changes her opinion.
Genre(s): Christian Fiction; War Story.

Laurents, Arthur

2870. *The Way We Were.* New York: Harper, 1972. 256 pp.
When committed Communist Katie Morosky meets Hubbell Gardiner in World War II, she gives up her political activity to marry him, but in the 1950s, during the McCarthy era, her past threatens his career.
Genre(s): War Story; Political Fiction; Love Story.

Lee, John

2871. *The Ninth Man.* Garden City, NY: Doubleday, 1976. 306 pp.
When Germans land nine saboteurs in the United States, eight are apprehended, but the ninth escapes and an army officer searches for him.
Genre(s): War Story; Spy Fiction.

Leffland, Ella

◆ 2872. *Rumors of Peace.* New York: Harper and Row, 1979. 389 pp.
Suse grows through adolescence with World War II in the background.
Genre(s): War Story.

Lieberman, Gerald F.

2873. *The Sea Lepers.* New York: Doubleday, 1971. 360 pp.
At the end of World War II, when the Merchant Marine is ordered to bring home army troops, a ship's commander has an altercation with an army officer who wants to take charge.
Genre(s): War Story; Humorous Fiction.

Lindau, Joan

◆ 2874. *Mrs. Cooper's Boardinghouse.* New York: McGraw Hill, 1980. 210 pp.
In 1944, Kat, 10, becomes friends with an aging artist who owns the town's boardinghouse.

MacInnes, Patricia

2875. *The Last Night on Bikini.* New York: Morrow, 1995. 171 pp.
Lucky's father works on atomic and hydrogen bombs in the 1940s and 1950s and inadvertently destroys his family with his obsessions.
Genre(s): Domestic Fiction.

Mailer, Norman

2876. *The Naked and the Dead.* New York: Holt, Rinehart and Winston, 1948. 721 pp.
In World War II, an American general and a lieutenant try to lead American soldiers in a Pacific Island invasion.
Genre(s): War Story.

Marquand, John P.

2877. *B. F.'s Daughter.* Boston: Little, Brown, 1946. 439 pp.
A wealthy woman controls her husband's life until he leaves for the war.
Genre(s): War Story; Domestic Fiction.

2878. *So Little Time.* Boston: Little, Brown, 1943. 594 pp.
Jeffrey Wilson, successful before World War II, has to examine the various worlds in which he lives during the war.

Matthews, Greg

2879. *Come to Dust.* New York: Walker, 1998. 336 pp.
In 1944, Keith Moody is adapting a novel for the cinema when someone kidnaps his wife, and he must find out why her stamp collection is so important.
Genre(s): Mystery.

Mayerson, Evelyn Wilde

2880. *No Enemy But Time.* Garden City, NY: Doubleday, 1983. 396 pp.
Hilary spends her years from 10 to 14 during World War II in a Miami Beach hotel where her Jewish immigrant mother and Catholic father manage the kitchen.
Genre(s): War Story; Bildungsroman (Coming of Age).

McCormick, John

2881. *The Right Kind of War.* Annapolis, MD: Naval Institute, 1992. 352 pp.
Marines fighting the Japanese in the Pacific during World War II also fight fear, illness, and boredom.
Genre(s): War Story.

Mercer, Charles

2882. *Pacific.* New York: Simon and Schuster, 1981. 320 pp.
World War II servicemen have a series of unexpected and entertaining adventures on the Pacific.
Genre(s): War Story; Humorous Fiction.

Michaels, Fern

2883. *Texas Rich.* New York: Ballantine, 1985. 568 pp.
Billie Ames meets Moss Coleman, a wealthy Texan, in Philadelphia during World War II, and after she marries him, she goes with him to Texas.
Genre(s): Romance; Family Saga.

Michener, James A.

2884. *Space.* New York: Random House, 1982. 622 pp.
During World War II, scientists and politicians become involved in the program that eventually takes humans into space.

Millhauser, Steven

2885. *Edwin Mullhouse.* New York: Knopf, 1972. 305 pp.
Edwin Mullhouse considers himself a superb author, and a fictious biographer presents his story during the period between 1943 and 1954.
Genre(s): Biographical Fiction.

Morris, Gilbert

◆ 2886. *A Time of War.* Ada, MI: Revell, 1997. 384 pp.
Members of the Stuart family have different reasons for wanting to serve the Allies in World War II. (*Series:* American Odyssey, 5)
Genre(s): War Story; Christian Fiction.

Morrison, Toni

2887. *The Bluest Eye.* New York: Henry Holt, 1970. 192 pp.
Two African American girls and their friend Pecola, who was raped and impregnated by her father, live a year in the 1940s before Pecola bears a dead child.
Genre(s): Domestic Fiction; Bildungsroman (Coming of Age).

Murayama, Atsushi

2888. *Plantation Boy.* Honolulu: University of Hawaii Press, 1998. 180 pp.
A young boy works his way through life from the attack on Pearl Harbor through Hawaii's statehood.
Genre(s): War Story; Bildungsroman (Coming of Age).

Myrdal, Jan

2889. *12 Going On 13.* Trans. Christine Swanson. Chicago: Ravenswood, 1995. 192 pp.
After Jan Myrdal moves to New York, one of his teachers tells him to doubt everything at least once, and he uses this motto to learn about his new home in New York, as well as to understand his old home of Stockholm at the beginning of World War II, in the sequel to *Another World.*
Award(s): Esselte Prize for Literature in Sweden.
Genre(s): Biographical Fiction.

Nash, N. Richard

◆ 2890. *East Wind, Rain.* New York: Atheneum, 1977. 371 pp.
When Tokan's wife has an affair with an American naval officer, Tokan castrates him and disappears into the Hawaiian jungle in the autumn of 1941.

Nazarian, Barry A.

2891. *Final Reckoning.* New York: Putnam, 1983. 256 pp.
Sam fails his physical when he tries to enlist in World War II and he feels guilty while getting rich on black market trading.
Genre(s): War Story.

Niven, David

2892. *Go Slowly, Come Back Quickly.* Garden City, NY: Doubleday, 1981. 327 pp.
Stani Skolimowski and Pandora Bryce go to Hollywood searching for success in the movies during World War II.
Genre(s): War Story.

Norman, Rick

2893. *Fielder's Choice.* Little Rock, AR: August, 1991. 192 pp.
Andrew Jackson Fielder fails to play baseball in the majors because he hesitates during a game, but a Japanese admiral admires his pitching in a Japanese POW camp, leading to his American trial for treason.
Genre(s): War Story; Bildungsroman (Coming of Age).

O'Hehir, Diana

2894. *I Wish This War Was Over.* New York: Atheneum, 1984. 278 pp.
Helen travels across America from California to Washington, DC, in 1944 to rescue her attractive but alcoholic mother.

Oke, Janette, and T. Davis Bunn

◆ 2895. *Another Homecoming.* Minneapolis, MN: Bethany House, 1997. 224 pp.
When Kyle's pregnant mother hears that her husband has died in North Africa during World War II, she decides to give up her child for adoption, and when Kyle is older, she searches for her real mother and finds that her father is not dead.
Genre(s): Christian Fiction.

O'Nan, Stewart

2896. *A World Away.* New York: Henry Holt, 1998. 338 pp.
After James has an affair with one of his high-school students, his marriage and his family suffers that as well as the trauma of World War II and the news that their conscientious-objector son is missing in the Pacific.
Genre(s): War Story.

Petry, Ann Lane

2897. *The Street.* Boston: Houghton Mifflin, 1936. 435 pp.
Lutie Johnson tries to raise her son with integrity in Harlem during the 1940s.
Genre(s): Domestic Fiction.

Piercy, Marge

2898. *Gone to Soldiers.* New York: Summit Books, 1987. 703 pp.
Women serve in World War II in a variety of roles, and a female journalist is finally allowed to cover the war.
Genre(s): War Story.

Plain, Belva

2899. *Tapestry.* New York: Delacorte, 1988. 448 pp.
Paul Werner, concerned about World War II and his German-Jewish relatives and friends, struggles with his bad marriage and memories of his first love, in the sequel to *The Golden Cup.*
Genre(s): War Story; Family Saga.

◆ May be suitable for young adult readers

Pratt, James Michael

2900. *The Last Valentine.* New York: St. Martin's Press, 1998. 272 pp.
In 1944, Caroline Thomas awaits the birth of her child while her husband serves in the Pacific, and 50 years later, their son tells their story to a reporter.
Genre(s): War Story; Domestic Fiction.

Raucher, Herman

2901. *Summer of '42.* New York: Putnam, 1971. 251 pp.
Three innocent Brooklyn boys summer in Maine during 1942 where Hermie meets a war widow who introduces him to sex.
Genre(s): Bildungsroman (Coming of Age).

Robbins, Harold

2902. *The Predators.* New York: Forge, 1998. 352 pp.
Jerry Cooper's parents die in an accident when he is 18 in 1941, and after he goes to work for his disreputable uncle, he is drafted and sent to France, where he begins to make money to recover what his uncle took from him.
Genre(s): War Story; Bildungsroman (Coming of Age).

Robertson, Don

◆ 2903. *The Greatest Thing Since Sliced Bread.* New York: Putnam, 1965. 255 pp.
Determined to see his good friend, nine-year-old Morris Bird III travels across Cleveland and becomes a hero in the East Ohio Gas Company explosion of October 1944.
Genre(s): Bildungsroman (Coming of Age).

Roget, Elizabeth

2904. *Shagbark Hill.* New York: McGraw Hill, 1970. 320 pp.
The war seems far away from the small Pennsylvania town in which Rachel Gervasi lives until her companion Ione decides to go into the empty quarry to sketch in the summer of 1945.
Genre(s): War Story; Domestic Fiction.

Roosevelt, Elliott

◆ 2905. *Murder in the Blue Room.* New York: St. Martin's Press, 1990. 215 pp.
In 1942, the Soviet Foreign minister secretly visits the White House, and Eleanor Roosevelt must solve a double murder and fight racial discrimination in the military.
Genre(s): Mystery.

◆ 2906. *Murder in the Chateau.* New York: St. Martin's Press, 1996. 200 pp.
In 1941, Eleanor Roosevelt goes to Vichy, France, to meet with French and German citizens against Hitler, representing her husband, but while at the meeting, someone is murdered, and she must help investigate.
Genre(s): Mystery; War Story.

◆ 2907. *Murder in the East Room.* New York: St. Martin's Press, 1993. 201 pp.
A controversial senator comes to dinner at the White House and is murdered in the East Room, and when the local police have no clues, Mrs. Roosevelt helps them solve the case.
Genre(s): Mystery.

◆ 2908. *The White House Pantry Murder.* New York: St. Martin's Press, 1987. 231 pp.
While Winston Churchill is visiting the White House in 1941, someone finds an unidentified man in the freezer and weapons in a storm sewer, spurring Mrs. Roosevelt into action.
Genre(s): Mystery.

Rosten, Leo

2909. *Captain Newman, M.D.* New York: Harper and Row, 1961. 331 pp.
Captain Newman, the antithesis of military mentality, is chief of the psychiatric ward on an Air Force base during World War II.
Genre(s): War Story; Medical Novel.

Roth, Philip

2910. *The Great American Novel.* New York: Holt, Rinehart and Winston, 1973. 382 pp.
A third major baseball league tries to survive, but World War II decimates it by 1943.
Genre(s): Sports Fiction; Humorous Fiction; Picaresque Fiction.

Sams, Ferrol

2911. *When All the World Was Young.* Atlanta, GA: Longstreet, 1991. 610 pp.
Porter Osborne flunks out of medical school so that he can join the military during World War II, and he goes to Normandy where his strong Baptist upbringing helps him cope.
Genre(s): War Story; Bildungsroman (Coming of Age); Christian Fiction.

Sanchez, Thomas

2912. *Zoot-Suit Murders.* New York: Dutton, 1978. 230 pp.
During World War II, people in the Los Angeles barrios suspect everyone else, especially the Zoot-Suiters, for drugs, robberies, and spying.
Genre(s): War Story.

Sanders, Dori

2913. *Her Own Place.* Chapel Hill, NC: Algonquin, 1993. 252 pp.
African American Mae Lee Barnes goes to high school during World War II, marries, and when her husband deserts her, raises five children in a rural South Carolina town.
Genre(s): Domestic Fiction.

Sanders, Leonard

2914. *Act of War.* New York: Simon and Schuster, 1982. 368 pp.
After the *Normandie* sinks in New York harbor, the U-boat captain sent by Hitler to sink it says that Roosevelt sank it first for political reasons.
Genre(s): War Story; Political Fiction.

Scott, Justin

2915. *Normandie Triangle.* New York: Arbor House, 1981. 475 pp.
When the French ship *Normandie* sinks in New York Harbor during World War II, Steve Gates, a naval architect, suspects sabotage although the Navy says it was an accident.
Genre(s): War Story.

Shands, Linda

◆ 2916. *A Time to Embrace.* Downers Grove, IL: InterVarsity, 1995. 232 pp.
While her husband fights in the Pacific, Cella Freeman stays at home worrying about him.
Genre(s): Christian Fiction; War Story; Domestic Fiction.

Shreve, Susan Richards

2917. *A Country of Strangers.* New York: Simon and Schuster, 1989. 239 pp.
Charley Fletcher wants his family to live in a rural area near Washington, DC, during World War II, but when he encounters a black family on his land, he must decide how to remove them without hostility.
Genre(s): War Story; Domestic Fiction.

Silman, Roberta

2918. *Beginning the World Again.* New York: Viking, 1990. 410 pp.
Lily Fialka reports that those working on the bomb in Los Alamos, including her husband, see it as a creative activity to stop the enemy while women around her continue to create children in defiance of such a weapon.
Genre(s): War Story.

Smith, Lee

2919. *The Christmas Letters.* Chapel Hill, NC: Algonquin, 1996. 128 pp.
Birdie, a World War II bride, writes about her experiences of moving from a farm to the business world, and her daughter and granddaughter add their letters about their experiences over the next 30 years.
Genre(s): Domestic Fiction; Family Saga.

Smith, Martin Cruz

2920. *Stallion Gate.* New York: Random House, 1986. 321 pp.
Sergeant Joe Pena, a Pueblo Indian assigned as a chauffeur and bodyguard to J. Robert Oppenheimer, describes the events leading to the Los Alamos A-bomb test in July of 1945.
Genre(s): War Story.

Smith, Mary-Ann Tirone

2921. *Masters of Illusion.* New York: Warner Books, 1994. 210 pp.
In 1944, a fire in the Barnum and Bailey circus tent in Hartford, Connecticut, kills 150 people and wounds over 1,000, and Charlie, then 10, grows up to be a firefighter and investigate who set the fire and why.
Genre(s): Mystery.

Spencer, Scott

2922. *Secret Anniversaries.* New York: Knopf, 1990. 257 pp.
During World War II, young Caitlin Van Fleet comes to Washington to work for a senator and realizes that the political belief of "America First" with those who have pro-Nazi leanings is inappropriate.
Genre(s): Political Fiction; War Story.

Stansbury, Domenic

2923. *The Last Days of Il Duce.* Sag Harbor, NY: Permanent Press, 1998. 168 pp.
Niccol Jones tells the story from prison of San Francisco during World War II when the Italian Fascists had connections in the city.
Genre(s): War Story; Domestic Fiction.

Starbird, Kaye

2924. *The Lion in the Lei Shop.* New York: Harcourt Brace, 1970. 288 pp.
Marty, five, has to leave her father for the mainland after the bombing of Pearl Harbor, and an older boy on the ship frightens her further with the announcement that a lion would be waiting to eat her in the lei shop where she had enjoyed watching the women work with the lovely flowers.
Genre(s): War Story; Domestic Fiction; Bildungsroman (Coming of Age).

Steel, Danielle

2925. *Crossings.* New York: Delacorte, 1982. 433 pp.
On a luxury liner going to France before World War II, Liane and her husband meet another couple, and Liane and Nick begin an affair in the following years.
Genre(s): Love Story; Romance.

2926. *Family Album.* New York: Delacorte, 1985. 399 pp.
After Hollywood actress and director Fay Price Thayer performs for troops during World War II, she develops her motion picture career.
Genre(s): Domestic Fiction.

2927. *Silent Honor.* New York: Delacorte, 1996. 353 pp.
A Japanese couple sends their daughter to America to stay with a cousin who is a political science professor at Stanford, and when she arrives, she falls in love with his white assistant, but World War II starts, and the family is interned with other Japanese Americans.
Genre(s): War Story; Romance.

Stein, Benjamin J.

2928. *The Manhattan Gambit.* Garden City, NY: Doubleday, 1983. 326 pp.
In 1943, a Nazi officer escapes from a POW camp in California, and he and his companion cross the country trying to kidnap or kill people for Himmler.
Genre(s): War Story.

Stokes, Penelope J.

2929. *Home Fires Burning.* Wheaton, IL: Tyndale House, 1996. 333 pp.
Link Winsom and Owen Slaughter fight in France during World War II while the women they love remain at home in Mississippi waiting anxiously for their return. (*Series:* Faith on the Home Front, 1)
Genre(s): War Story; Christian Fiction; Romance.

2930. *Remembering You.* Wheaton, IL: Tyndale House, 1997. 300 pp.
Owen Slaughter loses his memory after he returns home from France and World War II, but in his search for his past, he finds his God. (*Series:* Faith on the Home Front, 3)
Genre(s): Christian Fiction; War Story.

2931. *Till We Meet Again.* Wheaton, IL: Tyndale, 1997. 327 pp.
Libba Coltrain is happily reunited with her fiancé but his battle wounds may leave him permanently paralyzed, while Owen Slaughter returns to his wife, child, and nagging mother. (*Series:* Faith on the Home Front, 2)
Genre(s): Christian Fiction; War Story.

Taylor, Theodore

2932. *To Kill the Leopard.* San Diego, CA: Harcourt Brace, 1993. 288 pp.
Horst Kammerer, German submariner, and Sullivan Jordan, Merchant Marine officer, fight a final sea battle in the Battle of the Atlantic.
Genre(s): War Story; Sea Story.

Thackara, James

2933. *America's Children.* London: Chatto and Windus, 1984. 330 pp.
J. Robert Oppenheimer, friend to communists and husband of one, helps develop the atomic bomb but has difficulty perceiving reality, for which diplomats destroy him.
Genre(s): Biographical Fiction; War Story; Political Fiction.

Thayer, James Stewart

◆ 2934. *The Hess Cross.* New York: Putnam, 1977. 240 pp.
Rudolf Hess agrees to meet with intelligence agents and Enrico Fermi in Chicago to discuss secrets about the atomic bomb during World War II.
Genre(s): War Story.

Tillman, Barrett

2935. *Dauntless.* New York: Bantam, 1992. 412 pp.
Representatives of different military branches prepare to fight at Guadalcanal and Midway during World War II.
Genre(s): Adventure Story; War Story.

Toland, John

◆ 2936. *Gods of War.* Garden City, NY: Doubleday, 1985. 598 pp.
The McGlynns and the Todas are friends who have intermarried but who must separate during the political and cultural upheaval of World War II.
Genre(s): War Story; Family Saga.

Unger, Douglas

2937. *Leaving the Land.* New York: Harper and Row, 1984. 277 pp.
Marge Hogan tries to escape the labor and loneliness of her father's Dakota farm during World War II, and her son finally escapes by attending college and joining the Navy.
Genre(s): War Story.

Uris, Leon

2938. *Battle Cry.* New York: Putnam, 1953. 505 pp.
In the Pacific islands during World War II, American marines train and fight for their country.
Genre(s): War Story.

Villars, Elizabeth

2939. *Wars of the Heart.* Garden City, NY: Doubleday, 1986. 346 pp.
Three women form friendships with each other and find personal escapes during World War II, one becoming a radio reporter; another, an advertising executive; and a third, an actress.
Genre(s): War Story.

Volk, Toni

◆ 2940. *Montana Women.* New York: Farrar, Straus and Giroux, 1992. 310 pp.
Sisters whose men die in World War II try to fill their lives in Montana until of them decides to marry a farmer and have a child, who later tells their story.
Genre(s): Domestic Fiction.

Vonnegut, Kurt

2941. *Slaughterhouse Five.* New York: Delacorte, 1969. 186 pp.
Billy Pilgrim, an American soldier captured by the Germans, witnesses firebombing and destruction in Dresden.
Genre(s): War Story.

Wakefield, Dan

◆ 2942. *Under the Apple Tree.* New York: Delacorte, 1982. 352 pp.
Artie Garber, 10, tries to do his part for the war effort by identifying spies in his home town, and one that he chooses is a stranger claiming to be a Guadalcanal veteran.
Genre(s): War Story; Bildungsroman (Coming of Age).

Westin, Jeane

2943. *Love and Glory.* New York: Simon and Schuster, 1986. 524 pp.
Four women from disparate backgrounds decide to join the Women's Army Corps during World War II; three go overseas.
Genre(s): War Story.

Wharton, William

2944. *Pride.* New York: Knopf, 1985. 304 pp.
Dicki Kettleson's family survives the Depression in the late 1930s and his father returns to work but faces threats because of his dealings with the union.
Genre(s): Domestic Fiction.

Wheaton, Philip D.

◆ 2945. *The Best Is Yet to Be.* New York: Dodd, Mead, 1983. 279 pp.
In the sequel to *Razzmatazz*, set in the late 1930s, Willie and Penny Winston, living with their aunt in Connecticut, find out that they are probably not even cousins, much less brother and sister, and when they go to Europe during World War II, they are free to interact as they desire.
Genre(s): War Story; Bildungsroman (Coming of Age).

Wilson, Sloan

◆ 2946. *Pacific Interlude.* New York: Arbor House, 1982. 256 pp.
Coast Guard Lieutenant Sylvester Grant assumes command of a gas tanker when he is 24 in support of MacArthur's attempt to retake the Philippines.
Genre(s): War Story; Sea Story.

Wouk, Herman

2947. *The Caine Mutiny.* Garden City, NY: Doubleday, 1952. 498 pp.
An American mine sweeper, the *Caine*, patrols in the Pacific during World War II under a tyrannical skipper until an ensign leads a mutiny against him.
Award(s): Pulitzer Prize.
Genre(s): Sea Story; War Story.

2948. *War and Remembrance.* Boston: Little, Brown, 1978. 1042 pp.
In the sequel to *The Winds of War*, as the father of the Henry family becomes an admiral in World War II, but other aspects of his life unravel.
Genre(s): War Story.

Wubbels, Lance

2949. *Far from the Dream.* Minneapolis, MN: Bethany House, 1994. 303 pp.
After Jerry and Marjie are married for two days, Jerry leaves for World War II. (*Series:* The Gentle Hills, 1)
Genre(s): War Story; Christian Fiction.

2950. *Keeper of the Harvest.* Minneapolis, MN: Bethany House, 1995. 286 pp.
Jerry and Marjie Macmillan become the owners of the family farm, but they must try to make a success of it. (*Series:* Gentle Hills, 3)
Genre(s): Christian Fiction; War Story.

Wylie, James

◆ 2951. *The Homestead Grays.* New York: Putnam, 1977. 382 pp.
A squadron of African American fighter pilots battles both the Germans and racism among the Allies in World War II.
Genre(s): War Story.

Yates, Richard

2952. *Cold Spring Harbor.* New York: Delacorte, 1986. 182 pp.
Evan fails his military physical and resents his life enough to start an affair with his ex-wife while expecting a child with his second wife at the beginning of World War II .
Genre(s): War Story.

1946-1975
The Mid-20th Century

Albert, Bill

◆ 2953. *Desert Blues.* Sag Harbor, NY: Permanent Press, 1994. 188 pp.
Harold Abelstein's parents die in a freeway accident when he is 16 in 1957, and he goes to live with his aunt, a high-class prostitute in Palm Springs.
Genre(s): Humorous Fiction; Bildungsroman (Coming of Age).

Albert, Mimi

2954. *Skirts.* Dallas: Baskerville, 1994. 259 pp.
Ruth and Helene both choose Zalman Finster, a character from the Village, to help them escape their restrictive lower middle-class Bronx families in the 1960s.
Genre(s): Bildungsroman (Coming of Age).

Allison, Dorothy

2955. *Bastard out of Carolina.* New York: Dutton, 1993. 320 pp.
Bone, an illegitimate child in a family of social outcasts, sees her mother's happiness with her new husband and will not tell when the stepfather begins abusing her in the 1950s.
Genre(s): Family Saga.

Alther, Lisa

2956. *Original Sins.* New York: Knopf, 1981. 592 pp.
Daughters of a white mill owner, sons of a white mill foreman, and the African American son of a maid in the mill owner's house grow up in Tennessee during the 1960s.
Genre(s): Domestic Fiction; Bildungsroman (Coming of Age); Satire.

Alvarez, Julia

2957. *How the Garcia Girls Lost Their Accents.* Chapel Hill, NC: Algonquin, 1991. 290 pp.
The four Garcia girls escape the Dominican Republic and a life of privilege in the 1960s to come to the United States and difficult adjustment.
Genre(s): Domestic Fiction.

Anaya, Rudolfo

2958. *Bless Me, Ultima.* 1973. New York: Warner Books, 1994. 277 pp.
A young New Mexico boy comes of age.
Award(s): Premio Quinto Sol Award.

Genre(s): Bildungsroman (Coming of Age).

Anderson, Ken

2959. *Sympathy for the Devil.* Garden City, NY: Doubleday, 1987. 500 pp.
Hanson enjoys the chase and killing in the Vietnam War, but in the end when his buddies Quinn and Silver die, he realizes that he is doomed to live.
Genre(s): War Story.

Argo, Ronald

2960. *Year of the Monkey.* New York: Simon and Schuster, 1989. 387 pp.
Payne goes to Vietnam as an army journalist, and at the request of the CIA, he reports on another man's activities, but when he is court-martialed for that man's murder, he becomes aware of multiple layers of duplicity.
Genre(s): War Story; Spy Fiction.

Ascher, Carol

◆ 2961. *The Flood.* Freedom, CA: Crossing, 1987. 191 pp.
Eva Hoffman, 10, lives with her parents in Kansas during the 1950s after fleeing from the Nazis, and during a severe flood, her family helps the Willigers, who make racial slurs against the Jews.
Genre(s): Domestic Fiction.

Auchincloss, Louis

2962. *The Dark Lady.* Boston: Houghton Mifflin, 1977. 246 pp.
After Ivy Trask rescues Elesina Dart from alcohol and gets her married to a wealthy judge, Elesina eyes a seat in the House of Representatives and perfects her own manipulative ways.

Babitz, Eve

2963. *L. A. Woman.* New York: Simon and Schuster, 1982. 165 pp.
Sophie, 17, experiences the fast life of Los Angeles in the 1960s when she has an affair with Jim Morrison of The Doors.
Genre(s): Adventure Story.

Bache, Ellyn

◆ 2964. *The Activist's Daughter.* Duluth, MN: Spinsters Ink, 1997. 264 pp.
Beryl Rosinsky decides to defy her activist mother and formerly blacklisted father by enrolling in the University of North Carolina in 1963.
Genre(s): Bildungsroman (Coming of Age).

Baker, Kenneth Waymon

2965. *Alone in the Valley.* Sag Harbor, NY: Permanent Press, 1992. 296 pp.
Daniel Purdue, 18, goes to Vietnam, where he gains self-confidence as a leader of his squad.
Genre(s): War Story.

Baker, Larry

◆ 2966. *The Flamingo Rising.* New York: Knopf, 1997. 384 pp.
Abraham Isaac Lee, adopted son of an outdoor movie theater owner, falls in love with the daughter of his father's enemy, the mortician whose funeral parlor is next door to the movie theater.
Genre(s): Bildungsroman (Coming of Age); Love Story.

Barlay, Stephen

2967. *In the Company of Spies.* New York: Summit Books, 1981. 379 pp.
Russians convince Helm Rust, an ex-CIA agent smuggling in the Florida Keys, to come to the Soviet Union to rescue his father, and they tell him Khrushchev's plan for Cuba.
Genre(s): Spy Fiction.

Battle, Lois

2968. *War Brides.* New York: St. Martin's Press, 1982. 384 pp.
Three women, Dawn, Gaynor, and Shelia, leave Australia with soldiers for America during and after World War II and must either adjust to change or separate from their husbands.
Genre(s): War Story; Domestic Fiction.

Bausch, Richard

2969. *Good Evening Mr. and Mrs. America, and All the Ships at Sea.* New York: HarperCollins, 1996. 320 pp.
In 1964, devout Catholic Walter Marshall worships the memory of Kennedy as he attends night school, works in Washington, DC, and gets himself engaged to two different women.

Baxt, George

2970. *The Noel Coward Murder Case.* New York: St. Martin's Press, 1992. 199 pp.
Noel Coward helps the New York police solve the murder of an American woman in Shanghai who was investigating white slavery, and when another murder occurs in New York City, he must help there as well.
Genre(s): Mystery.

2971. *The Tallulah Bankhead Murder Case.* New York: St. Martin's Press, 1987. 228 pp.
As someone kills the friendly witnesses for the House Committee on Un-American Activities in the 1950s, Tallulah Bankhead teams with policeman Jacob Singer to find the murderer.
Genre(s): Mystery.

Beach, Edward Latimer

2972. *Cold Is the Sea.* New York: Holt, Rinehart and Winston, 1978. 348 pp.
Three World War II naval veterans meet again in 1960, in the sequel to *Dust on the Sea*, at a nuclear submarine school and unexpectedly fight the Russians while testing a submarine.
Genre(s): Sea Story.

Bell, Christine

2973. *The Pérez Family.* New York: Norton, 1990. 261 pp.
After Juan Pérez escapes to Florida, he meets a woman who loves America's excesses, and the two enjoy life together.
Genre(s): Political Fiction.

Benz, Maudy

2974. *Oh, Jackie.* Brownsville, OR: Story Line, 1998. 224 pp.
When North Waggoner is 15, her parents leave her with her aunt and uncle while they fly to Europe, and when her uncle begins to act strangely toward her, she finds solace in racing cars.
Genre(s): Bildungsroman (Coming of Age).

Berent, Mark

◆ 2975. *Phantom Leader.* New York: Putnam, 1991. 414 pp.
In the sequel to *Steel Tiger*, Viet Cong shoot down Flak's airplane and imprison him, but with help of another pilot he escapes.
Genre(s): War Story.

◆ 2976. *Rolling Thunder.* New York: Putnam, 1989. 382 pp.
Three Air Force pilots go to Vietnam in 1965 and face the horrors of the jungle, but when they return home, they face the hostility of Americans against the war.
Genre(s): War Story.

Bergman, Andrew

◆ 2977. *Hollywood and LeVine.* New York: Henry Holt, 1975. 216 pp.
A Hollywood writer fingered by McCarthy's committee in the 1940s commits suicide, and Jack LeVine teams with Humphrey Bogart to investigate.
Genre(s): Mystery.

Berne, Suzanne

2978. *A Crime in the Neighborhood.* Chapel Hill, NC: Algonquin, 1997. 285 pp.
While Watergate unfolds on television in Spring Hill, Maryland, Marsha's father has an affair with her aunt,

and a young boy is found raped and murdered behind the local mall.
Genre(s): Domestic Fiction; Mystery.

Bingham, Sallie

◆ 2979. *Matron of Honor.* Cambridge, MA: Zoland, 1994. 192 pp.
On the day before Apple's wedding in 1970 to Billy, her sister Cory arrives home, having left her husband, and their family problems begin to surface.
Genre(s): Domestic Fiction.

◆ 2980. *Small Victories.* Cambridge, MA: Zoland, 1992. 298 pp.
After the deaths of her parents, Louise cares for her epileptic sister at home in the 1950s although her brother disapproves, and Louise writes her nephew about the family's past.

Bittle, Camilla R.

2981. *Friends of the Family.* New York: St. Martin's Press, 1994. 230 pp.
Although Alice Dwire has used most of her money by the 1950s, she continues to pretend and to impose upon the Richards family because of a scholarship she gave their son John for his education.
Genre(s): Domestic Fiction.

Blaine, Richard

2982. *The Silver Setup.* New York: Pageant, 1988. 256 pp.
In 1948, Michael Garrett, a Los Angeles private detective, visits a small town and finds his beautiful client's wealthy husband dead in a disreputable hotel.
Genre(s): Mystery.

Blair, Leona

2983. *A Woman's Place.* New York: Delacorte, 1981. 397 pp.
Four American women become involved in the establishment of a homeland for the Jews in Palestine.
Genre(s): Family Saga.

Bledsoe, Jerry

◆ 2984. *The Angel Doll.* New York: St. Martin's Press, 1997. 103 pp.
Fatherless Whitey Black, 10, new in Thomasville in the 1950s, has a sister with polio who wants an angel doll for Christmas, and Whitey meets a friend who enlists others to help Whitey find the doll.
Genre(s): Domestic Fiction.

Bosworth, Sheila

2985. *Slow Poison.* New York: Knopf, 1992. 352 pp.
The Cade family meets again in Louisana for a crisis during the Vietnam War and for the King and Kennedy assassinations in 1968.
Genre(s): Domestic Fiction; War Story.

Bourjaily, Vance Nye

2986. *A Game Men Play.* New York: Dial, 1980. 311 pp.
Chink Peters, son of a Mongolian Buddhist and a White Russian soldier, earns the name the Meatgrinder in World War II, and afterward, he travels the world fulfilling a variety of undercover contracts.
Genre(s): War Story; Adventure Story; Mystery.

Boutell, Cleve

2987. *A Certain Discontent.* Tallahassee, FL: Naiad, 1992. 233 pp.
Raised to enjoy male activities as a young girl in the late 1940s, Joanna finds herself barred from equal treatment in society and in law school.
Genre(s): Bildungsroman (Coming of Age).

Bowers, John

2988. *No More Reunions.* New York: Dutton, 1973. 224 pp.
In the 1940s, John (Boney) and his friends enjoy high school, with one of them taking any dare, but another one becomes a gambler.
Genre(s): Bildungsroman (Coming of Age).

Boyd, Blanche McCrary

2989. *The Revolution of Little Girls.* New York: Knopf, 1991. 192 pp.
In the South during the 1960s, Ellen seems to enjoy her redneck qualities as she adds spirits of ammonia to her cokes and then wants stronger substances, including drugs and alcohol.
Genre(s): Bildungsroman (Coming of Age).

Boyne, Walter J.

◆ 2990. *Air Force Eagles.* New York: Crown, 1992. 455 pp.
John Marshall from *Eagles at War* returns home after the Korean War, and he and another pilot go to Arkansas to rescue friends from the Ku Klux Klan in 1957.
Genre(s): War Story; Adventure Story.

Boyne, Walter J., and Steven L. Thompson

◆ 2991. *The Wild Blue.* New York: Crown, 1986. 757 pp.
Six men serve in the Air Force and interact beginning in 1947.
Genre(s): Adventure Story.

Brand, Millen

2992. *Savage Sleep.* New York: Crown, 1968. 465 pp.
Dr. Marks, a young psychiatrist, tries to change treatment methods from electric shock to psychoanalysis in his hospital.
Genre(s): Medical Novel.

Briskin, Jacqueline

2993. *Everything and More.* New York: Putnam, 1983. 476 pp.
Three women in Los Angeles have careers and convoluted love affairs during the 1950s.
Genre(s): Romance.

2994. *Rich Friends.* New York: Delacorte, 1976. 461 pp.
In the sequel to *Paloverde*, the families of Bud, Amelia, and 3Vee cannot find love even though they have all the money they want.
Genre(s): Family Saga.

Britton, Christopher

2995. *Paybacks.* New York: Donald I. Fine, 1985. 264 pp.
Michael Taggart, an inexperienced military lawyer, must defend the drill instructor Sergeant Markey, who is charged with beating a young Marine to death near the end of the Vietnam War.
Genre(s): War Story.

Bryan, C. D. B.

2996. *P.S. Wilkinson.* New York: Harper and Row, 1965. 441 pp.
P. S. Wilkinson serves his last year in Korea but comes home to find that his life is no less a muddle.
Genre(s): Adventure Story; War Story.

Buck, Pearl S.

2997. *Kinfolk.* New York: John Day, 1949. 406 pp.
After a professor from China teaching in New York City extols the wonders of his country to his four children, two go to China, stay, and excel while the others return to their American home.
Genre(s): Domestic Fiction.

Buckley, William F.

2998. *Mongoose, R.I.P.* New York: Random House, 1987. 322 pp.
Blackford Oakes links Lee Harvey Oswald to the Castro regime of Cuba after Kennedy's assassination.
Genre(s): Spy Fiction.

Budhos, Marina Tamar

2999. *House of Waiting.* New York: Consortium, 1995. 220 pp.
After Sarah Weisberg's adopted family disowns her for marrying a native of British Guiana, she, pregnant, makes friends with his people while he returns home, and when she joins him, she discovers that he has a daughter.
Genre(s): Domestic Fiction.

Burke, Martyn

◆ 3000. *Ivory Joe.* New York: Bantam, 1991. 320 pp.
Christie and her sister Ruthie enjoy 1950s Brooklyn, watching their father as he tries to stay legitimate while keeping ties to the Mob and their mother as she manages the rock group Ivory Joe and the Classics.
Genre(s): Musical Fiction.

Burke, Phyllis

3001. *Atomic Candy.* New York: Atlantic Monthly, 1989. 367 pp.
In 1952, Kate Albion becomes so upset at Nixon's "Checkers" speech that she gives birth early, and her husband, smitten with Marilyn Monroe, wants to name their daughter after her.
Genre(s): Biographical Fiction; Political Fiction.

Butler, Robert Olen

3002. *Alleys of Eden.* New York: Henry Holt, 1994. 256 pp.
Cliff Butler enjoys Vietnam since he speaks the language, but after his marriage fails, he lives with a bar girl in Saigon before escaping with her in one of the last available helicopters for an unsatisfactory life in Illinois.
Genre(s): War Story.

◆ 3003. *On Distant Ground.* New York: Knopf, 1985. 218 pp.
After letting a Viet Cong suspect escape, a soldier faces a court-martial, but during the trial, he realizes that he may have left a child behind, and he returns to Vietnam.
Genre(s): War Story; Legal Story.

Cady, Jack

3004. *Inagehi.* Seattle, WA: Broken Moon, 1994. 272 pp.
As Harriette Johnson investigates the murder of her father years before in Asheville, North Carolina, she begins to understand her Cherokee heritage.
Genre(s): Domestic Fiction.

Calisher, Hortense

3005. *The New Yorkers.* Boston: Little, Brown, 1969. 559 pp.
Each member of the affluent Mannix family of New York, during the years 1943-1955, lives under the shadow of a dark secret involving the death of their mother.
Genre(s): Jewish Fiction.

Campbell, Bebe Moore

◆ 3006. *Your Blues Ain't Like Mine.* New York: Putnam, 1992. 332 pp.
When African American Armstrong Todd visits Hopewell, Mississippi, in 1955, Floyd Cox murders him, and following the trial, both families try to rebuild their lives.
Genre(s): Bildungsroman (Coming of Age).

Caraganis, Lynn

3007. *Cousin It.* New York: Ticknor and Fields, 1991. 224 pp.
Vickie Fowler, 17, is an orphan recently moved into her cousin's home, where a stream of people with values and social mores different from Vickie's try to converse with her about something other than cosmetics.
Genre(s): Domestic Fiction.

Carroll, Gerry

3008. *Ghostrider One.* New York: Pocket Books, 1993. 458 pp.
A Marine air controller inside Khe Sanh and others recreate life during the Vietnam War during 1968 before the Tet Offensive.
Genre(s): War Story.

3009. *North SAR.* New York: Pocket Books, 1991. 323 pp.
In June of 1972, Tim Boyle flies from an aircraft carrier in the South China Sea to rescue air crews crashed in North Vietnam, and his best friend, Mike Santy, is an attack pilot.
Genre(s): War Story.

Carroll, James

3010. *Firebird.* New York: Dutton, 1989. 437 pp.
The FBI and the State Department compete against each other rather than working together to defeat the Soviets when Christopher Malone, an agent, arrives in Washington in 1949.
Genre(s): Spy Fiction.

Chao, Evelina

◆ 3011. *Gates of Grace.* New York: Warner Books, 1985. 372 pp.
Upper-class Mei-yu marries peasant Wong Kung-chaio in China after World War II, and they flee to America and raise a daughter in Manhattan, but Kung-chaio is murdered while celebrating with fellow students who reveal their racial prejudices.
Genre(s): Domestic Fiction.

Charters, Samuel Barclay

3012. *Elvis Presley Calls His Mother After the Ed Sullivan Show.* Minneapolis, MN: Coffee House, 1992. 104 pp.
In 1957, after Elvis Presley appears on *The Ed Sullivan Show*, he calls his mother, not understanding why his physical movements cause such an uproar.
Genre(s): Biographical Fiction; Musical Fiction.

Chase, Joan

3013. *During the Reign of the Queen of Persia.* New York: Harper and Row, 1983. 215 pp.
In Ohio during the 1950s, two cousins tell the stories of three generations of women under the matriarch, Gram, called Queen of Persia.
Award(s): Ernest Hemingway Foundation Award.
Genre(s): Domestic Fiction.

Clark, Robert

3014. *In the Deep Midwinter.* New York: Picador, 1997. 278 pp.
In 1949, wealthy Richard and Sarah MacEwan, married for 30 years, see their world crumble after Richard's brother is killed in a hunting accident and their divorced daughter becomes pregnant.
Genre(s): Domestic Fiction.

Cleary, Jon

3015. *The Beaufort Sisters.* New York: Morrow, 1979. 417 pp.
A Kansas cattle rancher's four daughters marry or live with a variety of male and female lovers as they become involved in several intrigues.
Genre(s): Western Fiction.

Clement, Mickey

◆ 3016. *The Irish Princess.* New York: Putnam, 1994. 224 pp.
With news of war in Southeast Asia during 1964, Mike Malloy and his wife try to raise two daughters with their values in Troy, New York.

Cobb, William

◆ 3017. *A Walk Through Fire.* New York: Morrow, 1992. 416 pp.
In 1961, the Civil Rights movement comes to the black community of Hammond, Alabama, and both blacks and whites must take sides.
Genre(s): Domestic Fiction.

Collins, Max Allan

3018. *Neon Mirage.* New York: St. Martin's Press, 1988. 275 pp.
Nate Heller cannot save gambling boss James Ragen in Chicago during the 1940s so he has to find out who killed him.
Genre(s): Mystery.

Colter, Cyrus

3019. *A Chocolate Soldier.* St. Paul, MN: Thunder's Mouth, 1988. 278 pp.
Meshach Barry tells about his friend Cager, who killed a white woman during the 1940s and was later murdered in segregated and intolerant Tennessee.
Genre(s): Domestic Fiction.

Conroy, Frank

3020. *Body and Soul.* Boston: Houghton Mifflin, 1993. 450 pp.
Claude Rawlings, a street urchin, finds a mentor who nourishes his talent so that he eventually plays his own concerto with the London Symphony Orchestra.
Genre(s): Musical Fiction; Bildungsroman (Coming of Age).

Conroy, Pat

3021. *The Lords of Discipline.* Boston: Houghton Mifflin, 1980. 499 pp.
Will McLean spends four years at a Carolina military academy where he is responsible for shepherding the first black cadet.

Conteris, Hiber

3022. *Ten Percent of Life.* New York: Simon and Schuster, 1987. 200 pp.
In 1956, a *Los Angeles Times* reporter hires Philip Marlowe to investigate a suicide who represented writers on Hollywood's blacklist.
Genre(s): Mystery.

Cook-Lynn, Elizabeth

3023. *From the River's Edge.* Boston: Little, Brown, 1991. 160 pp.
When John Tatekeya wins a court case against a white cattle rustler in 1967, he receives no compensation, and some of his people betray him to the white culture.
Genre(s): Legal Story.

Cook, Thomas H.

3024. *Streets of Fire.* New York: Putnam, 1981. 319 pp.
Ben Wellman carefully investigates the death of a young black girl found in a shallow grave during the 1963 freedom marches.

Coonts, Stephen

◆ 3025. *Flight of the Intruder.* Annapolis, MD: Naval Institute, 1986. 329 pp.
During the war in Vietnam, Jack Grafton loves to fly and beat the enemy with his A-6 Intruder.
Genre(s): War Story.

Cooper, Michael H.

3026. *Dues.* Willimantic, CT: Curbstone, 1994. 248 pp.
David Thorne, the smartest in his family, drops out of college in 1967 and ends up in Vietnam where he uses drugs to escape both the boredom and the terror.
Genre(s): War Story.

Coulter, Hope Norman

3027. *The Errand of the Eye.* New York: August House, 1988. 256 pp.
When a girl moves to Louisiana in 1966 at six, she watches the integration around her, and she becomes friends with a black African teacher during her high school years.
Genre(s): Bildungsroman (Coming of Age).

Covington, Vicki

3028. *The Last Hotel for Women.* New York: Simon and Schuster, 1996. 300 pp.
In Birmingham, Alabama, during 1961, Diana and her husband Pete try to escape their former lives, but Sheriff Bull Connor refuses to cope with the changes that racial equality require.
Genre(s): Domestic Fiction.

Cox, Elizabeth

◆ 3029. *Night Talk.* St. Paul, MN: Graywolf, 1997. 270 pp.
In 1949, after African American Janey Louise and Volusia, her mother, move into Evie's house, Janey Louise starts sleeping in Evie's bedroom, and they begin sharing their secrets at night, even after Janey Louise becomes one of the girls who integrates Evie's white high school in 1956.
Genre(s): Domestic Fiction; Political Fiction.

Coyle, Neva

3030. *Close to the Father's Heart.* Minneapolis, MN: Bethany House, 1996. 288 pp.
In 1957, Amy Weaver's mother dies suddenly, and as she sorts through the family's old files, she discovers secrets that lead her to Owen Sampson, an arson investigator. (*Series:* Summerwind, 3)
Genre(s): Christian Fiction.

3031. *A Door of Hope.* Minneapolis, MN: Bethany House, 1995. 272 pp.
After finding the man who seems perfect, Karissa Hill marries in 1957, but her marriage is everything that she fears. (*Series:* Summerwind, 1)
Genre(s): Christian Fiction.

3032. *Inside the Privet Hedge.* Minneapolis, MN: Bethany House, 1996. 256 pp.
In California during 1957, Retta wants the orange grove to stay in the family, but a seemingly ambitious young man buys it and falls in love with Retta. (*Series:* Summerwind, 2)
Genre(s): Christian Fiction; Romance.

D'Amato, Barbara

3033. *Good Cop Bad Cop.* New York: St. Martin's Press, 1998. 320 pp.
In 1969, Chicago police raid the Black Panthers and kill Fred Hampton, and when Nick Bertolucci, who participated, becomes the superintendent of police, his angry brother Aldo targets him.
Genre(s): Political Fiction; Mystery.

Danziger, Jeff

◆ 3034. *Rising Like the Tucson.* New York: Doubleday, 1991. 368 pp.
Uninformed enlisted men and unqualified officers try to win in Vietnam using whatever scheme someone thinks will work.
Genre(s): War Story.

Daugharty, Janice

3035. *Earl in the Yellow Shirt.* New York: HarperCollins, 1997. 224 pp.
When Louella Lay dies, her family scrounges to find money to bury her properly in rural Georgia during the 1960s.
Genre(s): Domestic Fiction.

3036. *Necessary Lies.* New York: HarperCollins, 1995. 176 pp.
In the 1950s, Cliffie, 17, becomes pregnant by a local boy whom her father had asked her to avoid, and while hoping that he will take her away, she finds out that the boy has also seduced her younger sister.
Genre(s): Domestic Fiction.

◆ May be suitable for young adult readers

3037. *Whistle.* New York: HarperCollins, 1998. 224 pp.
In the early 1960s, Roper Rackard discovers the body of his boss's wife in the hay, and he hides the corpse, making himself the prime suspect in the murder.
Genre(s): Domestic Fiction; Mystery.

Davidson, Donald

3038. *The Big Ballad Jamboree.* Jackson: University Press of Mississippi, 1996. 295 pp.
In 1949, folk music in the North Carolina Appalachians changes from folk to hillbilly, and Cissie Timberlake decides to get her master's degree codifying the tradition.
Genre(s): Musical Fiction.

Davis, Kathryn

3039. *Hell.* New York: Ecco, 1998. 192 pp.
In the 1950s, two parents and two daughters living in a decaying Philadelphia house become involved with Napoleon's chef and a 19th-century expert on home management.
Genre(s): Domestic Fiction; Time Travel.

Davis, Patrick A.

3040. *The General.* New York: Putnam, 1998. 384 pp.
During the Vietnam War, Air Force officer Charles Jensen investigates the death of an Air Force chief and connects it to the one officer who escaped from a prisoner-of-war camp.
Genre(s): War Story; Mystery.

Davis, Thulani

◆ 3041. *1959.* New York: Grove Weidenfeld, 1992. 297 pp.
After 12-year-old Willie Tarrant guides Martin Luther King around the black college where her father teaches, she is chosen to integrate the white high school in 1959.
Genre(s): Bildungsroman (Coming of Age).

De Rosa, Tina

3042. *Paper Fish.* New York: Feminist, 1996. 176 pp.
Carmolina, 8, hears her family speak of institutionalizing her older mute sister, and she runs away from her Italian American home in the 1940s.
Genre(s): Domestic Fiction.

Del Vecchio, John M.

3043. *Carry Me Home.* New York: Bantam, 1995. 719 pp.
In the sequel to *For the Sake of All Living Things,* veterans return home from Vietnam in the 1960s to a hostility through which they must rebuild their lives.
Genre(s): War Story.

3044. *The 13th Valley.* New York: Bantam, 1982. 606 pp.
Two whites and one African American in an infantry unit fight in a major combat assault during August 1970.
Genre(s): War Story.

DeLillo, Don

3045. *Libra.* New York: Penguin, 1989. 456 pp.
Lee Harvey Oswald, the plotters who enlisted him, and an undercover historian explore the day of Kennedy's assassination.
Genre(s): Political Fiction.

DeMarinis, Rick

3046. *The Mortician's Apprentice.* New York: Norton, 1994. 300 pp.
Ozzie Santee, 18, thinks that he would like to live on the beach with his jazz records while his friends discuss college or marriage in order to avoid the draft, but then he meets Colleen, who wants him to marry her and work for her mortician father.
Genre(s): Bildungsroman (Coming of Age).

DeMille, Nelson

◆ 3047. *Word of Honor.* New York: Warner Books, 1985. 518 pp.
After an account of the My Lai massacre appears in book form, the army decides to investigate Ben Tyson, an electronics executive, for his part in the murders.
Genre(s): Mystery; War Story.

Deutermann, P. T.

3048. *The Edge of Honor.* New York: St. Martin's Press, 1994. 544 pp.
In 1969, Lt. Brian Holcomb is trying to reverse his fitness report, but while serving as the weapons officer on a ship going to the Gulf of Tonkin, he discovers that drug use is rampant.
Genre(s): War Story.

Dick, Philip K.

3049. *The Broken Bubble.* New York: Arbor House, 1988. 288 pp.
Married teenagers Art and Rachel idolize the older Jim because he is a disk jockey in the 1950s, but when Jim's ex-wife seduces Art, Jim and Rachel have to work together.
Genre(s): Domestic Fiction; Musical Fiction.

3050. *Mary and the Giant.* New York: Arbor House, 1987. 209 pp.
In 1953, Mary Anne Reynolds, 20, wants to find a man whom she can love in Pacific Park, California.

Dobyns, Stephen

3051. *The House on Alexandrine.* Detroit, MI: Wayne State University Press, 1990. 224 pp.
Duane, a Canadian farm boy, searches for his wandering sister in Detroit in 1973, and people in his lodging house who had not previously communicated begin to help him search and to bond with each other.
Genre(s): Bildungsroman (Coming of Age).

Dodge, Ed

3052. *Dau.* New York: Macmillan, 1984. 208 pp.
Morgan Preston goes from his Michigan high school to
the Air Force and Vietnam in 1965, and at his discharge,
he harbors many psychological scars.
Genre(s): War Story.

Douglas, Ellen

3053. *Can't Quit You, Baby.* New York:
Atheneum, 1988. 256 pp.
In the early 1960s, Cornelia, a white woman, and her
black employee, Julia, while making preserves, talk about
their pasts.

Dreher, Sarah

3054. *Solitaire and Brahms.* Norwich, VT: New
Victoria, 1997. 292 pp.
In the 1960s, Shelby, 25, has all that she could want, but
she contemplates suicide as she starts to realize her homo-
sexuality.
Genre(s): Bildungsroman (Coming of Age).

Drown, Merle

3055. *Plowing Up a Snake.* New York: Dial,
1982. 288 pp.
After Forest Langley is murdered on New Year's Day in
the mid-1950s, only his wife and cousin want to find the
killers in their small New Hampshire town.
Genre(s): Mystery.

Ducker, Bruce

◆ 3056. *Lead Us Not into Penn Station.* Sag Harbor,
NY: Permanent Press, 1994. 224 pp.
Danny Meadoff comes of age during his 16th summer
during which he worries about the Dodgers leaving town,
hears of his friend's father running away with his secretary, and learns of his own father's dealings with a loan
shark.
Genre(s): Bildungsroman (Coming of Age).

Duncan, David James

◆ 3057. *The Brothers K.* New York: Doubleday,
1992. 672 pp.
The Chance brothers live in the 1960s, asking about God,
moral behavior, and other unanswerable questions.
Genre(s): Humorous Fiction.

Duncan, Julia Coley

◆ 3058. *Halfway Home.* New York: St. Martin's
Press, 1979. 322 pp.
Annie Trammell, a white girl of 12, has to struggle be-
tween the Old South and the New South when her closest
friends are African Americans.
Genre(s): Domestic Fiction.

Dunne, John Gregory

3059. *True Confessions.* New York: Dutton, 1977.
341 pp.
Two Irish Catholic brothers, a policeman and a priest, become involved in investigating the death of a prostitute.
Genre(s): Mystery.

Edgerton, Clyde

3060. *Where Trouble Sleeps.* Chapel Hill, NC: Al-
gonquin, 1997. 260 pp.
When the stranger Jack Umstead shows up in Listre,
North Carolina, during the 1950s, the town soon realizes
that he has ulterior motives for being there.
Genre(s): Mystery.

Edwards-Yearwood, Grace

3061. *In the Shadow of the Peacock.* New York:
McGraw Hill, 1987. 192 pp.
African Americans continue to be exploited from World
War II through the Vietnam War, but some black women
seem to accept their roles.
Genre(s): War Story.

Egan, Jennifer

3062. *The Invisible Circus.* New York: Dou-
bleday, 1995. 338 pp.
Phoebe O'Connor wants to know what happened to her
sister in the 1960s, so she leaves San Francisco for
Europe in 1978 to trace her sister's last steps.
Genre(s): Bildungsroman (Coming of Age).

Ellis, Erika

3063. *Good Fences.* New York: Random House,
1998. 208 pp.
In 1972, the African American Spader family moves into
a Greenwich, Connecticut, neighborhood, and after someone mistakes Mabel for a maid, she decides that the family should retreat behind their fences, but her husband disagrees.
Genre(s): Domestic Fiction.

Ellroy, James

3064. *The Big Nowhere.* New York: Mysterious
Press, 1988. 406 pp.
A few years after World War II, in the sequel to *The
Black Dahlia*, Deputy Danny Upshaw probes homosex-
ual murders while another investigator checks on Holly-
wood leftists.
Genre(s): Mystery.

3065. *The Black Dahlia.* New York: Mysterious
Press, 1987. 325 pp.
Bucky Bleichert, ex-prize fighter and policeman, investi-
gates when a young woman's mutilated body appears in a
vacant Los Angeles lot.
Genre(s): Mystery.

3066. *LA Confidential.* New York: Mysterious
Press, 1990. 496 pp.
In Los Angeles during the 1950s, three policemen in-
volved in a Bloody Christmas precinct house riot become
involved in drugs and prostitution in the sequel to *The
Big Nowhere*.
Genre(s): Mystery.

3067. *White Jazz.* New York: Knopf, 1992. 349 pp.
In the late 1950s, in the sequel to *LA Confidential*, David
Klein makes his own rules in the Los Angeles police de-
partment, but he becomes a scapegoat for the other cor-
rupt officers.
Genre(s): Mystery.

◆ May be suitable for young adult readers

Erhart, Margaret

◆ 3068. *Augusta Cotton.* Cambridge, MA: Zoland, 1992. 289 pp.
Augusta, 11, makes friends with Helen and learns about her family and that Helen has lupus, a serious illness.

Esstman, Barbara

3069. *Night Ride Home.* San Diego, CA: Harcourt Brace, 1997. 332 pp.
Nora's husband threatens that he will take ownership of a ranch passed from Nora's mother, and for the first time, she and her daughter demand their rights.
Genre(s): Domestic Fiction.

Estleman, Loren D.

3070. *Edsel: A Novel of Detroit.* New York: Mysterious Press, 1995. 291 pp.
When Henry Ford II picks Connie Minor, a discarded journalist, for his Edsel advertising campaign, Minor is blackmailed by a local politician searching for Communists in 1950s Detroit.
Genre(s): Mystery.

3071. *Motown.* New York: Bantam, 1991. 292 pp.
An ex-policeman, an inspector, and a numbers racketeer reveal the problems in Detroit leading to the 1966 riots, in the sequel to *Whiskey River.*
Genre(s): Mystery.

3072. *Stress.* New York: Mysterious Press, 1996. 276 pp.
Charlie Battle, an African American policeman in Detroit during the early 1970s, must struggle in a racist department while black militant groups proliferate.
Genre(s): Mystery.

Evanier, David

3073. *The One-Star Jew.* New York: North Point, 1983. 256 pp.
Bruce, a Jewish boy, grows up in the 1950s and begins adulthood in the 1960s in New York.
Genre(s): Jewish Fiction; Domestic Fiction.

Evans, Elizabeth

3074. *The Blue Hour.* Chapel Hill, NC: Algonquin, 1994. 350 pp.
Penny Powell, 10, moves with her family to a large Illinois town in the 1950s and watches her father fail at his new business venture.
Genre(s): Domestic Fiction; Bildungsroman (Coming of Age).

Eyre, David

3075. *Float.* New York: Doubleday, 1991. 400 pp.
On a U.S. Navy gunboat in the Mekong delta in 1966, Lieutenant Dubecheck tries to relax and enjoy himself between battles.
Genre(s): War Story.

Faherty, Terence

3076. *Come Back Dead.* New York: Simon and Schuster, 1997. 320 pp.
Scott Elliott helps provide security for movie studios in 1955 Hollywood, and as television gains momentum, he has to save a film and its crew from sabotage and attempted murder.
Genre(s): Mystery.

3077. *Kill Me Again.* New York: Simon and Schuster, 1996. 304 pp.
As Scott Elliott, a movie studio security employee, investigates a screenwriter in the 1950s, the man is murdered, and Elliott finds jealousy and blackmail related to the McCarthy Red Scare.
Genre(s): Mystery.

Farrell, James T.

3078. *The Death of Nora Ryan.* Garden City, NY: Doubleday, 1978. 402 pp.
In the sequel to *The Dunne Family*, adult children gather in Chicago at the sickbed of their mother in 1946 and recall the family and the city of their past.
Genre(s): Family Saga.

Fast, Howard

◆ 3079. *The Establishment.* Boston: Houghton Mifflin, 1979. 365 pp.
In 1948, in the sequel to *Second Generation*, Barbara Lavette's husband dies in Israel, and she becomes involved in the McCarthy witch-hunt.
Genre(s): Domestic Fiction; War Story; Family Saga.

◆ 3080. *The Legacy.* New York: Houghton Mifflin, 1981. 359 pp.
In the sequel to *The Establishment*, members of the Lavette family function during the civil rights struggle, the Vietnam War, and the Six-Day War in the Middle East.
Genre(s): Family Saga.

◆ 3081. *The Outsider.* Boston: Houghton Mifflin, 1984. 311 pp.
When David Hartman returns from World War II, he becomes a rabbi in Connecticut.
Genre(s): Religious Fiction.

◆ 3082. *The Pledge.* Boston: Houghton Mifflin, 1988. 324 pp.
After World War II, Bruce Bacon goes to India where Indians report that the British have starved them, and then he returns to the United States and becomes involved with a Communist-front organization.
Genre(s): Political Fiction.

Fennelly, Tony

3083. *The Hippie in the Wall.* New York: St. Martin's Press, 1994. 240 pp.
In 1970, Margo Fortier, a society writer for a New Orleans newspaper, helps police with a murder in a strip club in which she used to work.
Genre(s): Mystery.

Ferber, Edna

3084. *Ice Palace.* Garden City, NY: Doubleday, 1958. 411 pp.
One leading citizen of Baranof wants Alaska's statehood, and the other wants it to remain a territory.
Genre(s): Love Story.

Fields, Jeff

3085. *A Cry of Angels.* New York: Atheneum, 1974. 383 pp.
Earl Whitaker helps his great-aunt run her boarding house in Quarrytown where a group of eccentric elderly people live.

Filene, Peter

◆ 3086. *Home and Away.* Cambridge, MA: Zoland, 1992. 322 pp.
When Murray Baum's father leaves New York for California in December 1950, Murray does not know if he will return, and he spends his 17th year studying himself, his family, and his relationships.
Genre(s): Jewish Fiction; Bildungsroman (Coming of Age).

Flagg, Fannie

◆ 3087. *Coming Attractions.* New York: Morrow, 1981. 344 pp.
Daisy Fay Harper turns 17 during the 1950s, and her experiences evoke the time in the deep South of strapless net evening gowns and Red Ryder.
Genre(s): Domestic Fiction.

Fleming, Thomas

◆ 3088. *The Officers' Wives.* Garden City, NY: Doubleday, 1981. 645 pp.
In the 1950s, wives of West Point graduate officers react to their social position in various ways while their husbands fight in Southeast Asia.
Genre(s): War Story.

Flood, John

3089. *Bag Men.* New York: Norton, 1997. 240 pp.
Father Sedgewick is murdered on New Year's Day after arriving at Logan Airport with pope-blessed communion wafers that disappear, and Ray Dunn has the responsibility of finding the murderer.
Genre(s): Mystery.

Flynn, Robert

3090. *The Last Klick.* Dallas: Baskerville, 1994. 363 pp.
A college professor's daughter dies, and in an attempt to find meaning in life, he goes to Vietnam as a reporter for a conservative men's magazine, but his stories seem too intellectual until he has a war experience that changes him.
Genre(s): War Story.

Ford, Elaine

3091. *Missed Connections.* New York: Random House, 1983. 230 pp.
Christine Scarpa tries to separate from her Italian Catholic blue-collar family in Boston, but her first love eventually lures her back.
Genre(s): Domestic Fiction.

Freed, Donald, and Mark Lane

3092. *Executive Action.* New York: Dell, 1973. 251 pp.
Based on actions of a variety of people and discrepancies in the Warren Report, a new theory evolves about the assassination of John F. Kennedy in 1963.
Genre(s): Biographical Fiction; Mystery.

French, Marilyn

3093. *The Women's Room.* New York: Summit Books, 1977. 471 pp.
Mira, a suburban housewife, becomes divorced and returns to Harvard for graduate school where she meets others in her predicament.

Friedman, Mickey

3094. *Hurricane Season.* New York: Dutton, 1983. 204 pp.
In the 1950s on the northwest coast of Florida, a young seminarian seems the likely murderer of the promiscuous daughter of a local politician.
Genre(s): Mystery.

Fuller, Jack

3095. *Fragments.* New York: Morrow, 1984. 225 pp.
Morgan's friend Neumann is possibly involved in an atrocity against Vietnamese citizens, and when he returns to the States, Morgan tries to identify the events surrounding the situation.
Genre(s): War Story.

Funderburk, Robert

◆ 3096. *Love and Glory.* Minneapolis, MN: Bethany House, 1994. 304 pp.
When Lane Temple returns from Japan after World War II, he moves his family to Baton Rouge, hoping for more opportunities as a lawyer. (*Series:* Innocent Years, 1)
Genre(s): Christian Fiction.

3097. *The Rainbow's End.* Minneapolis, MN: Bethany House, 1997. 256 pp.
Although Cassidy Temple believes in the war in Vietnam in which he fights, he must return home to find something in which to trust. (*Series:* Innocent Years, 6)
Genre(s): Christian Fiction; War Story.

Gabriel, Eric

◆ 3098. *Waterboys.* San Francisco: Mercury House, 1989. 235 pp.
In the 1960s, three boys, Asa, Matthew, and Justin, try to come to terms with the men in their lives who either are or represent their fathers.
Genre(s): Bildungsroman (Coming of Age).

◆ May be suitable for young adult readers

Gaines, Ernest J.

3099. *A Lesson before Dying.* New York: Knopf, 1993. 256p pp.

A young illiterate African American man witnesses two black robbers kill a white store owner in Louisiana in the late 1940s, and he is the one convicted.

Award(s): National Book Critics Circle Award.

Genre(s): Political Fiction.

Garcia, Cristina

3100. *Dreaming in Cuban.* New York: Knopf, 1992. 245 pp.

While Celia del Pino supports Fidel Castro, her daughter Lourdes lives in New York and blames Castro for her rape by a revolutionary, and her daughter Pilar laughs at her way of fighting Communisim.

Genre(s): Political Fiction; Family Saga.

Garrett, George P.

3101. *The King of Babylon Shall Not Come against You.* New York: Harcourt Brace, 1996. 336 pp.

Billy Tone visits Florida to look into a double murder/suicide that occurred in 1968 at the time Martin Luther King was assassinated.

Genre(s): Mystery.

Giardina, Anthony

3102. *Men with Debts.* New York: Knopf, 1984. 280 pp.

In the mid-1950s, Jack, one of a group of insurance salesmen, falls in love with the widow of one of his former clients and, at 43, decides to leave his wife and two children.

Gilden, Katya, and Bert Gilden

3103. *Between the Hills and the Sea.* New York: Doubleday, 1971. 552 pp.

Although Mish Lunin works hard as a trade unionist from 1946, trying to organize the workers at United Vacuum, he eventually loses his job when the hysteria of the McCarthy era infiltrates everyone's psyche.

Genre(s): Political Fiction.

Giles, Janice Holt

3104. *Shady Grove.* Boston: Houghton Mifflin, 1968. 260 pp.

In the sequel to *The Great Adventure*, in Broke Neck, Kentucky, the Appalachian natives disapprove of denominations and believe the minister ought to live without pay in the mid-20th century.

Genre(s): Family Saga.

Gingher, Marianne

◆ 3105. *Bobby Rex's Greatest Hit.* New York: Atheneum, 1986. 320 pp.

Bobby Rex's song "Pally Thompson" becomes a hit record in 1961, and even though Bobby Rex never even kissed Pally, the song's namesake, the town thinks that much more happened.

Genre(s): Musical Fiction; Adventure Story.

Glasser, Ronald J.

3106. *Another War/ Another Peace.* New York: Simon and Schuster, 1985. 247 pp.

David is sent to Vietnam as an inexperienced physician, and although he disdains his driver when he first arrives, he finds that Tom is more than a mere soldier.

Genre(s): War Story; Medical Novel.

Gold, Herbert

3107. *Family.* New York: Arbor House, 1981. 192 pp.

A young boy grows to middle-age before he realizes that his mother's Old World Ukranian customs and values are not truly embarrassing in this sequel to *Fathers.*

Genre(s): Domestic Fiction.

Goldberg, Philip

◆ 3108. *This Is Next Year.* New York: Ballantine, 1992. 302 pp.

In the 1955 pennant race, Roger Stone thinks that his cap is the lucky charm to help the Dodgers win the World series.

Genre(s): Sports Fiction.

Golden, Marita

◆ 3109. *And Do Remember Me.* New York: Doubleday, 1992. 208 pp.

In 1964, during Freedom Summer, Jessie Foster runs from her Mississippi home to New York to become an actress and discovers that she can forget her past and her present when she performs.

Genre(s): Bildungsroman (Coming of Age).

◆ 3110. *Long Distance Life.* New York: Doubleday, 1989. 312 pp.

Naomi leaves North Carolina for Washington, DC, her daughter returns to the South during the Civil Rights movement, and her children separate from her.

Genre(s): Domestic Fiction.

Goldreich, Gloria

3111. *Leah's Children.* New York: Macmillan, 1985. 320 pp.

In the sequel to *Leah's Journey,* Leah Goldfeder's three grown children, Aaron, Michael, and Rebecca, engage in their own political struggles of human rights, political refugees, and civil rights.

Genre(s): Family Saga; Political Fiction.

3112. *Years of Dreams.* Boston: Little, Brown, 1992. 464 pp.

Young women who attended college together meet at the death of a friend and find that their personal lives are as unsatisfying as the political problems of the 1960s and 1970s.

Genre(s): Domestic Fiction.

Good, Paul

3113. *Once to Every Man.* New York: Putnam, 1970. 320 pp.

In 1964, a civil rights campaign disturbs the equilibrium of a small Florida town.

Genre(s): Political Fiction.

Goudge, Eileen

3114. *Garden of Lies.* New York: Viking, 1989. 534 pp.

Sylvia switches her child during a hospital fire with another girl and raises Rachel to become a physician, and her real daughter defends Rachel in court while the Vietnam War rages in the background.
Genre(s): Medical Novel; Legal Story; Domestic Fiction; Romance.

Green, Hannah

3115. *The Dead of the House.* Garden City, NY: Doubleday, 1972. 180 pp.

In trying to understand herself in the 1940s, Vanessa Nye examines her family for two centuries previous.
Genre(s): Domestic Fiction.

Greenfeld, Josh, and Paul Mazursky

3116. *Harry and Tonto.* New York: Saturday Review, 1974. 183 pp.

In the 1970s, an old man in New York and his cat are removed from an apartment building slated to be demolished, and they wander across country looking for a new home.

Greer, Ben

3117. *The Loss of Heaven.* Garden City, NY: Doubleday, 1988. 456 pp.

Four orphaned brothers go from South Carolina to Vietnam to Washington beginning in the mid-1960s as their grandmother tries to keep the family newspaper fortune intact for them.
Genre(s): Family Saga.

Griffin, W. E. B.

◆ 3118. *The Colonels.* New York: Berkley, 1983. 470 pp.

Although Major Craig Lowell becomes involved with other military officers' wives between wars from 1958 to 1961, he is willing to fight honorably with his colleagues against the foreign enemy. (*Series:* Brotherhood of War, 4)
Genre(s): War Story; Adventure Story.

3119. *The Murderers.* New York: Putnam, 1994. 396 pp.

When Jerry Kellog of the Philadelphia police department is one of three people murdered in 1975, detective Matt Payne and Sergeant Jason Washington must investigate. (*Series:* Badge of Honor, 6)
Genre(s): Mystery.

Griffith, Lois

3120. *Among Others.* New York: Crown, 1998. 288 pp.

Dark-skinned Della feels like an outsider in her own lighter-hued family during the 1960s, and when white policemen kill her father, she decides to join black activists.
Genre(s): Bildungsroman (Coming of Age); Political Fiction.

Grinstead, David

3121. *Promises of Freedom.* New York: Crown, 1991. 448 pp.

Five college graduates during the Vietnam War experience fears of fighting and the politics over which they have no control.
Genre(s): War Story; Political Fiction.

Groom, Winston

3122. *As Summers Die.* New York: Summit Books, 1980. 319 pp.

When oil is discovered under the Holt land, the Holts believe they own it, until a lawyer reminds them that earlier generations in the family had given deeds for miscellaneous plots to black families.

3123. *Better Times than These.* New York: Summit Books, 1978. 411 pp.

In Vietnam in 1966, Bravo Company has great difficulties under an inexperienced leader.
Genre(s): War Story.

◆ 3124. *Forrest Gump.* Garden City, NY: Doubleday, 1986. 228 pp.

In the 1960s, Forrest Gump, a pleasant and obedient son with low intelligence, joins the army, returns from Vietnam famous for his heroics, and makes millions on a Louisiana shrimp boat while steadfastly loving a girl from his childhood.
Genre(s): War Story; Adventure Story; Love Story.

Guterson, David

3125. *Snow Falling on Cedars.* San Diego: Harcourt Brace, 1994. 345 pp.

After returning from internment and trying to get his land back, Kabuo Miyomoto is arrested and tried for the murder of Carl Heine.
Genre(s): Legal Story.

Haeger, Diane

3126. *Pieces of April.* New York: HarperCollins, 1998. 352 pp.

In the 1950s, Isabelle Maguire falls in love with her childhood friend Stephen, who happens to be a priest, and her father takes her to Scotland to have their child before taking the child from her for adoption.
Genre(s): Romance; Family Saga.

Hamill, Pete

3127. *Snow in August.* Boston: Little, Brown, 1997. 336 pp.

Michael Devlin, an 11-year-old Irish American, meets Rabbi Hirsch, recently arrived from Europe, and in return for teaching the rabbi about baseball and English, the rabbi teaches Michael Yiddish and tells him about Prague, until an Irish gang becomes violent in its anti-Semitism.
Genre(s): Bildungsroman (Coming of Age).

Hamilton, Jane

3128. *The Short History of a Prince.* New York: Random House, 1998. 320 pp.
Walter McCloud's brother Daniel lies dying of cancer while Walter attends high school in 1972 and learns of his homosexuality and his inability to communicate with his parents.
Genre(s): Domestic Fiction.

Hampton, Georgia

3129. *Desire.* New York: Dutton, 1988. 352 pp.
Maisie Green, recently moved to New York in the 1950s, experiences the bohemian life of poets and painters searching for beauty.
Genre(s): Domestic Fiction.

Harris, Mark

◆ 3130. *Speed.* New York: Donald I. Fine, 1990. 260 pp.
A young man comes of age in upstate New York following World War II as he remembers his brother Speed, who parted from the family forever.
Genre(s): Bildungsroman (Coming of Age).

Harrison, Marshall

3131. *Cadillac Flight.* San Francisco: Presidio, 1990. 344 pp.
Captain Jim Broussard flies over Hanoi with other pilots.
Genre(s): War Story.

Hasford, Gustav

◆ 3132. *The Phantom Blooper.* New York: Bantam, 1990. 256 pp.
While searching for a marine who supposedly deserted to the Vietcong, Joker Davis is captured, but he is freed and returns to the U.S. where he faces hatred toward those who fought in Vietnam.
Genre(s): War Story.

Hassler, Jon

3133. *Rookery Blues.* New York: Ballantine, 1995. 484 pp.
In 1969, faculty members at Rookery State College form a jazz quintet, and the lives of those in the group reflect the trials of the times including the Vietnam War and campus problems.
Genre(s): Musical Fiction.

Heath, Layne

3134. *The Blue Deep.* New York: Morrow, 1993. 382 pp.
Marsh McCall and his men go to Vietnam to train French helicopter pilots, but he suspects a black market for weapons that he investigates before the war actually begins.
Genre(s): War Story.

3135. *CW2.* New York: Morrow, 1990. 400 pp.
Helicopter pilot Billy Roark applies for reassignment as a scout in the Vietnam War and searches the jungle for Viet Cong troops.
Genre(s): War Story.

Heath, William

3136. *The Children Bob Moses Led.* Minneapolis, MN: Milkweed, 1995. 350 pp.
Tom Morton joins the Civil Rights Movement and travels to Mississippi during Freedom Summer in 1964 to help disenfranchised African Americans.
Genre(s): Bildungsroman (Coming of Age).

Heckler, Jonellen

3137. *Safekeeping.* New York: Putnam, 1983. 192 pp.
After her husband has been a POW for five years and she has participated in antiwar demonstrations, a mother worries about her son Kevin, 12, and a major on temporary duty helps them.
Genre(s): War Story.

Hedges, Peter

◆ 3138. *An Ocean in Iowa.* New York: Hyperion, 1997. 256 pp.
Scotty Ocean grows up in Iowa during 1969, and as his parents' relationship deteriorates, he has difficulty reconciling the situation.
Genre(s): Domestic Fiction; Bildungsroman (Coming of Age).

Heinemann, Larry

3139. *Close Quarters.* New York: Farrar, Straus and Giroux, 1977. 335 pp.
Philip Dosier goes to Vietnam with images of John Wayne's war movies in his mind, and when the Viet Cong do not wage war with the same rules, he has to develop a ruthlessness that he has never known.
Genre(s): War Story.

3140. *Paco's Story.* New York: Farrar, Straus and Giroux, 1986. 209 pp.
After Paco Sullivan is the lone survivor from Alpha Company's Viet Cong attack, he returns home and survives on Valium and Librium while employed as a dishwasher.
Award(s): National Book Award.
Genre(s): War Story.

Hemley, Robin

3141. *The Last Studebaker.* St. Paul, MN: Graywolf, 1992. 256 pp.
In the early 1960s, Lois's family is in a state of flux when the Studebaker plant of South Bend, Indiana, closes, and when her landlord returns to live in his house with her and her daughters, they forge a new family.
Genre(s): Domestic Fiction.

Hemphill, Paul

3142. *The Sixkiller Chronicles.* New York: Macmillan, 1985. 243 pp.
Grandfather Bluejay Clay from Sixkiller Gap in North Carolina sings in Nashville during the 1940s, his son never rises to stardom, but a grandson attends Harvard Medical School before returning to practice in the area.
Genre(s): Family Saga.

Henderson, William McCranor

3143. *I Killed Hemingway*. New York: St. Martin's Press, 1993. 320 pp.

A biographer, Elliot McGuire, tries to ghostwrite for Eric Pappy Markham, the man who says he killed Hemingway for stealing his stories in the 1920s.
Genre(s): Biographical Fiction.

Herman, John

3144. *The Light of Common Day*. New York: Doubleday, 1997. 304 pp.

In 1962, Paul Werth attends a private high school in New York, feeling unsure about himself and those around him, until he remembers his father's comment before he died that all are not as they seem.
Genre(s): Bildungsroman (Coming of Age).

Hijuelos, Oscar

3145. *The Mambo Kings Play Songs of Love*. New York: Farrar, Straus and Giroux, 1989. 407 pp.

Brothers emigrate to New York City in 1949 and form a band with their popularity peaking in 1956 when they get to perform on *I Love Lucy*.
Genre(s): Domestic Fiction; Musical Fiction.

Hill, Richard

3146. *Riding Solo with the Golden Horde*. Athens, GA: University of Georgia Press, 1994. 143 pp.

In Florida, during the 1950s, Vic Messenger loves jazz and has great ability on the saxophone, but his interest in things other than school frustrates the adults in his life.
Genre(s): Musical Fiction; Bildungsroman (Coming of Age).

Hillerman, Tony

3147. *Finding Moon*. New York: HarperCollins, 1995. 320 pp.

Moon Mathias, editor of a minor Colorado newspaper, reluctantly goes to Vietnam to search for the child of his brother who was killed in Southeast Asia.
Genre(s): War Story.

Hoffman, Ray

3148. *Almost Family*. New York: Dial, 1983. 288 pp.

Before and during the Civil Rights period, a black domestic worker is employed by a Jewish woman in the South for over 30 years.
Genre(s): Domestic Fiction.

Honig, Donald

3149. *Last Man Out*. New York: Dutton, 1993. 240 pp.

When police accuse a rookie Brooklyn Dodger of murder in 1946, a New York sportswriter thinks he is innocent and delays going to spring training in order to help him.
Genre(s): Mystery.

3150. *The Plot to Kill Jackie Robinson*. New York: Dutton, 1992. 261 pp.

In 1946, a racist determines that he will not let Jackie Robinson play for the Brooklyn Dodgers, but Joe Tinker, a *New York Daily News* sportswriter, is impressed by Robinson's behavior.
Genre(s): Sports Fiction.

Horgan, Paul

◆ 3151. *Whitewater*. New York: Farrar, Straus and Giroux, 1970. 337 pp.

In the late 1940s, three teenagers live in a western Texas town during their last year of high school.
Genre(s): Bildungsroman (Coming of Age)

Howard, Maureen

3152. *Natural History*. New York: Norton, 1992. 512 pp.

After World War II, James and Catherine live in their own home, but they cannot become independent from their parents.
Genre(s): Domestic Fiction.

Howatch, Susan

3153. *Sins of the Fathers*. New York: Simon and Schuster, 1980. 608 pp.

The sequel to *The Rich Are Different* finds the Van Zales still using their wealth as a means to achieve what they want.
Genre(s): Domestic Fiction; Family Saga.

Hudson, Helen

◆ 3154. *Criminal Trespass*. New York: Putnam, 1985. 256 pp.

Rannee tries to escape the restriction of criminal trespass which the whites use in the South during the 1940s to control the African American communities.

Iida, Deborah

3155. *Middle Son*. New York: Algonquin, 1996. 238 pp.

Spencer Fujii returns to Maui as an adult and recalls the sacrifice of his brother, arranged with his adopted younger brother, while they were children on a sugarcane plantation in the 1950s.
Genre(s): Bildungsroman (Coming of Age).

Inge, William

3156. *Good Luck, Miss Wyckoff*. Boston: Little, Brown, 1970. 179 pp.

Miss Evelyn Wyckoff teaches Latin in Freedom, Kansas, and by the age of 35, she is very interested in trying sex.
Genre(s): Domestic Fiction.

Ison, Tara

3157. *A Child out of Alcatraz*. New York: Faber and Faber, 1997. 264 pp.

When Olivia hears of her father, an Alcatraz prison guard, beating a man senseless in the 1950s, she loses her

innocence like her mother, who has become isolated since her marriage.
Genre(s): Domestic Fiction; Bildungsroman (Coming of Age).

Jen, Gish

◆ 3158. *Typical American.* Boston: Houghton Mifflin, 1991. 296 pp.
When exchange students Ralph and Teresa Chang and their friend Helen have to stay in the United States after the Communists take control of China in 1948, they decide to follow the American dream while retaining their Chinese values.

Johnson, Charles

3159. *Dreamer.* New York: Scribner's, 1998. 256 pp.
Martin Luther King Jr.'s last two years would have been different if he had had other dreams.
Genre(s): Political Fiction; Domestic Fiction.

Johnson, Wayne

3160. *The Snake Game.* New York: Knopf, 1990. 257 pp.
Three young men, including one white who wants to live in the Ojibwa community and a Native American who wants to escape it, face white American culture during the years after 1951.
Genre(s): Political Fiction.

Jones, Simmons

3161. *Show Me the Way to Go Home.* Chapel Hill, NC: Algonquin, 1991. 323 pp.
In the 1960s, after North Carolina real estate agent Julian Warren and his wife separate, he goes with his cousin's husband on a rescue mission in Italy.
Genre(s): Domestic Fiction.

Kadohata, Cynthia

◆ 3162. *The Floating World.* New York: Ballantine, 1989. 176 pp.
In the 1950s, Olivia and her extended family travel along California's coast while her stepfather works at transient jobs, and although her grandmother annoys her with her stories, after her grandmother's death, the stories continue to guide Olivia in her life.

Kagan, Elaine

◆ 3163. *Somebody's Baby.* New York: Morrow, 1998. 256 pp.
In 1959, the Jewish Jenny Jaffe, 16, falls in love with Will McDonald, recently released from San Quentin, and becomes pregnant by him to the horror of her friends and family.
Genre(s): Domestic Fiction; Love Story.

Kalb, Bernard, and Marvin Kalb

3164. *The Last Ambassador.* Boston: Little, Brown, 1981. 267 pp.
Hadden Walker, Washington's last ambassador to South Vietnam, tries to save the United States's position in 1975.
Genre(s): War Story.

Kaminsky, Stuart M.

3165. *Catch a Falling Clown.* New York: St. Martin's Press, 1982. 182 pp.
Toby Peters must investigate the electrocution of an elephant at the Rose and Elder Circus, and Emmett Kelly fears for his own life.
Genre(s): Mystery.

3166. *Down for the Count.* New York: St. Martin's Press, 1985. 178 pp.
In the 1940s, Toby Peters uses heavyweight boxing champion Joe Louis to help him find out why Ralph Howard, current husband of Peters' ex-wife, has been murdered.
Genre(s): Mystery.

◆ 3167. *The Fala Factor.* New York: St. Martin's Press, 1984. 174 pp.
Eleanor Roosevelt consults Toby Peters about a dog that she thinks has been secretly exchanged for her husband's Scottish terrier Fala, and chaos follows.
Genre(s): Mystery.

3168. *High Midnight.* New York: St. Martin's Press, 1981. 188 pp.
Toby Peters helps Gary Cooper overcome a blackmailer who wants him to play in a B cowboy movie called *High Midnight.*
Genre(s): Mystery.

Kay, Terry

◆ 3169. *The Runaway.* New York: Morrow, 1997. 448 pp.
Tom, 12, does not understand why people condemn his friendship with Sonny Jesus, an African American boy, but after Sonny is critically injured, they cement their friendship, and simultaneously, several racially motivated murders occur.
Genre(s): Mystery.

Keegan, John E.

3170. *Clearwater Summer.* New York: Carroll and Graf, 1994. 320 pp.
Will Bradford and his friends seem safe from any changes during the Eisenhower era until they discover their town's sexual side through a violent death.
Genre(s): Bildungsroman (Coming of Age).

Kennedy, William

3171. *Very Old Bones.* New York: Viking, 1992. 292 pp.
In the sequel to *Ironweed,* Orson Purcell, the bastard son of Peter Phelan, tells stories about members of the family, based on information from a family gathering in 1958.
Genre(s): Domestic Fiction; Family Saga.

Kerouac, Jack

3172. *Visions of Cody.* New York: McGraw Hill, 1973. 398 pp.
In the 1950s, the Beat Generation evolved, and the author's friend Cody Pomeray illustrates the attitudes of those who participated in this social movement.
Genre(s): Adventure Story.

Kincaid, Nanci

3173. *Crossing Blood.* New York: Putnam, 1992. 288 pp.
Lucy lives next door to an African American family in Tallahassee, Florida, and when she falls in love with the son in the family, she must face the attitudes of southerners toward such a relationship.
Genre(s): Domestic Fiction.

Kinder, Chuck

◆ 3174. *The Silver Ghost.* New York: Harcourt Brace, 1979. 256 pp.
Jimbo, impressed with his own masculinity, emulates James Dean in the late 1950s as he drives his silver Porsche along the East Coast.
Genre(s): Bildungsroman (Coming of Age).

King, Kathleen Wallace

3175. *The True Story of Isobel Roundtree.* Little Rock, AR: August House, 1993. 178 pp.
After Isobel's mother leaves the night before John Kennedy was assassinated in 1963, Isobel and her father find her in a small town trying to start a singing career, and as a result of several incidents, including a devastating fire, Isobel finds her own strength.
Genre(s): Domestic Fiction.

Kingston, Maxine Hong

3176. *Tripmaster Monkey.* New York: Knopf, 1989. 340 pp.
Wittman Ah Sing tries to find his place in San Francisco as a Chinese American during the 1960s while fighting Chinese stereotypes.

Korda, Michael

3177. *The Immortals.* New York: Poseidon, 1992. 559 pp.
Marilyn Monroe and John F. Kennedy meet and have a love affair.
Genre(s): Biographical Fiction.

Kricorian, Nancy

3178. *Zabelle.* New York: Atlantic Monthly, 1998. 256 pp.
When grandmother Zabelle dies, her family wonders what was special about her, and then they discover that the Turks massacred her Armenian family in 1916.
Genre(s): War Story; Political Fiction; Domestic Fiction.

Kuban, Karla

3179. *Marchlands.* New York: Scribner's, 1998. 270 pp.
While a Guatemalan ranch hand impregnates Sophie Behr, 15, her mother watches news on television to see if her son appears in footage of the Vietnam War.
Genre(s): Bildungsroman (Coming of Age); War Story.

Kuhlken, Ken

3180. *The Angel Gang.* New York: St. Martin's Press, 1994. 261 pp.
Tom Hickey, private investigator, leaves Lake Tahoe at his pregnant wife's request to help a San Diego singer accused of killing her brother in law, but while his is gone villains kidnap Tom's wife.
Genre(s): War Story; Mystery.

La Puma, Salvatore

3181. *A Time for Wedding Cake.* New York: Norton, 1991. 288 pp.
Members of a Sicilian American community in Brooklyn readjust to life and to each other after World War II.
Genre(s): Domestic Fiction.

Labro, Philippe R.

3182. *One Summer Out West.* Trans. William Byron. New York: Ballantine, 1991. 272 pp.
In 1955, a French exchange student travels across the country, where he discovers the myth of the American West along with its realities, including syphilis.
Genre(s): Bildungsroman (Coming of Age).

Lane, Abbe

3183. *But Where Is Love?* New York: Warner Books, 1993. 448 pp.
When Julie Lauren, a Brooklyn teenager, meets famous Latin bandleader Paco Castell in the 1940s she becomes famous, but he soon changes into a tyrant.
Genre(s): Musical Fiction; Biographical Fiction.

Lapin, Mark

3184. *Pledge of Allegiance.* New York: Dutton, 1991. 288 pp.
In 1958, an FBI agent lures nine-year-old Josh to meet Pee Wee Reese because he wants information about Josh's busy Communist parents and their friends.
Genre(s): Political Fiction.

Lawton, David

3185. *A Lovely Country.* San Diego, CA: Harcourt Brace, 1995. 226 pp.
Giles Trent serves as the American ambassador in Vietnam during America's last years there, and he thinks that government leaders have become amoral.
Genre(s): War Story.

Laxalt, Robert

3186. *The Governor's Mansion.* Reno: University of Nevada Press, 1994. 227 pp.
Pete tells of his older brother Leon's change in political plans when the cowboy with whom he runs drops dead,

and Leon uses the new medium of television to advertise his candidacy to both Mormons and crime syndicates (*Series:* Basque, 2)
Genre(s): Political Fiction.

Learmon, Warren

◆ 3187. *Unheard Melodies.* Marietta, GA: Longstreet, 1990. 214 pp.
In 1948, as the narrator hears stories about his uncle who has returned from the war and passes through high school rituals, he begins to realize that what he thinks is real may be merely illusion.

Lee, Gus

◆ 3188. *China Boy.* New York: Dutton, 1991. 322 pp.
In the 1950s, Kai Ting and his family come to San Francisco, but his mother dies shortly thereafter, and his new stepmother wants to erase everything Chinese from his life.
Genre(s): Domestic Fiction.

◆ 3189. *Honor and Duty.* New York: Knopf, 1994. 425 pp.
Kai Ting from *China Boy* enters West Point as an Asian while America fights in Vietnam.
Genre(s): Bildungsroman (Coming of Age).

Lehrer, Jim

3190. *White Widow.* New York: Random House, 1996. 224 pp.
Although faithful to his wife for years, Jack T. Oliver becomes enamoured with a white widow (beautiful woman) who boards his bus one night in the 1950s.
Genre(s): Adventure Story.

Lelchuk, Alan

◆ 3191. *Brooklyn Boy.* New York: McGraw Hill, 1989. 304 pp.
Aaron Schlossberg, son of immigrants, enjoys his life in Brooklyn during the 1940s even though his parents are breaking up and anti-Semitism pervades.
Genre(s): Bildungsroman (Coming of Age).

Lester, Julius

3192. *And All Our Wounds Forgiven.* New York: Arcade, 1994. 228 pp.
The dead John Calvin Marshall, a Harvard-educated civil rights leader, shares his thoughts on his wife, his white mistress, and a friend in Mississippi.
Genre(s): Fantastic Literature.

Levy, Burt

3193. *Last Open Road.* New York: St. Martin's Press, 1998. 400 pp.
Buddy Palumbo discovers his enjoyment of open-road racing in the 1950s, and to avoid working in the local chemical plant, he learns to become an expert mechanic for sport racing stars and their cars.
Genre(s): Adventure Story.

Liotta, P. H.

3194. *Diamond's Compass.* Chapel Hill, NC: Algonquin, 1993. 353 pp.
Dante Diamond leaves the Air Force Academy and wonders how to tell his father, who is stationed in Iran with the Shah, but within three years, Dante returns to Iran to face two different foes.
Genre(s): Political Fiction; War Story.

Logue, John

3195. *Boats against the Current.* Boston: Little, Brown, 1987. 231 pp.
Jack Harris returns to Montgomery, Alabama, in 1967 to edit the local newspaper, and he must reconcile the segregationist policies and the political corruption of the town.
Genre(s): Political Fiction.

Lovisi, Gary

3196. *Hellbent on Homicide.* Chester Springs, PA: Dufour, 1997. 192 pp.
In 1962, Bill Griffin and his partner Fats investigate the murder of a rich girl and find a similarity to the unsolved murders of seven streetwalkers.
Genre(s): Mystery.

MacDougall, Ruth Doan

◆ 3197. *The Cheerleader.* New York: Putnam, 1973. 288 pp.
Snowy and her group of elite friends in a New Hampshire high school during the 1950s are more interested in being popular than in academic pursuits.
Genre(s): Domestic Fiction.

Mackey, Mary

3198. *Season of Shadows.* New York: Bantam, 1991. 509 pp.
After she goes through college at Radcliffe and marries a prince, Lucy Constable becomes a fugitive in Mexico during the 1960s student movement.
Genre(s): Political Fiction.

Madden, David

3199. *Bijou.* New York: Crown, 1974. 500 pp.
Lucius Hutchfield, 13, envelops himself in the dream world of the movies in the 1940s as he grows up in Tennessee.
Genre(s): Bildungsroman (Coming of Age).

Major, Clarence

3200. *Dirty Bird Blues.* San Francisco: Mercury House, 1996. 256 pp.
Manfred Banks tries to support his family playing blues music throughout the midwest in the 1940s using Dirty Bird (Old Crow whiskey) as a way to raise himself in performance.
Genre(s): Musical Fiction.

Malamud, Bernard

3201. *The Assistant.* New York: Farrar, Straus and Giroux, 1957. 246 pp.
A Jewish grocer's assistant robs him and then helps him and his family.
Genre(s): Jewish Fiction.

3202. *A New Life.* New York: Farrar, Straus and Cuhady, 1961. 367 pp.
Seymour Levin goes to the Pacific Northwest to take a teaching job and to change his life in 1950.

Mallon, Thomas

3203. *Aurora 7.* New York: Ticknor and Fields, 1991. 238 pp.
When Scott Carpenter orbits the earth three times in 1962, Gregory Noonan, a fifth-grader, becomes entranced.
Genre(s): Domestic Fiction.

3204. *Dewey Defeats Truman.* New York: Pantheon, 1997. 355 pp.
During the campaign for president in 1948, the people in Dewey's hometown of Owosso, Michigan, react to the situation and anticipate the fame their town will receive when Dewey wins.
Genre(s): Biographical Fiction; Love Story.

Margolis, David

3205. *Change of Partners.* Sag Harbor, NY: Permanent Press, 1997. 231 pp.
In the 1960s, Sam moves to San Francisco and then to a commune in southern Oregon called The Farm, where he lives in the counterculture of the time.
Genre(s): Domestic Fiction.

Marlowe, Katherine

3206. *Heart's Desires.* New York: Donald I. Fine, 1991. 307 pp.
Alyssa tries to avoid her mother's mistakes as she muddles through her teenage years in the 1950s.
Genre(s): Domestic Fiction.

Marquand, John P.

3207. *Women and Thomas Harrow.* Boston: Little, Brown, 1958. 497 pp.
Although Thomas Harrow has remarried after his wife divorced him during World War II, he spends much time recalling the social and theatrical life in New York City during the 1920s that he loved.

Martin, Ron

3208. *To Be Free!* New York: Vanguard, 1986. 256 pp.
Ramsey plans his escape as a Marine prisoner of war while following his daily routine of work and torture until he finally succeeds.
Genre(s): War Story.

Martinez, Max

◆ **3209.** *Schoolland.* Houston, TX: Arte Publico, 1988. 250 pp.
A Mexican American boy in a family of nine grows up in a close family in rural Texas during the 1950s.
Genre(s): Domestic Fiction.

Masterton, Graham

3210. *Headlines.* New York: St. Martin's Press, 1987. 446 pp.
In Chicago during 1949, Morgana discovers that she will inherit her father's newspaper, but when he refuses to support the mayor in exposing slum landlords and helping the tenants, something seems wrong at the paper.
Genre(s): Political Fiction.

Matlin, David.

3211. *How the Night Is Divided.* Kingston, NY: McPherson, 1993. 201 pp.
Tom Green, a Kiowa Indian working for a Jewish rose farmer in southern California shortly after World War II, realizes that his past parallels that of his employers.
Genre(s): Domestic Fiction.

Matthews, Greg

3212. *Far from Heaven.* New York: Walker, 1997. 306 pp.
In the 1940s, Keith Moody's Hollywood script is a biography of his cousin, a war hero, but as the movie begins filming, his cousin disappears, and Moody must find him before filming can continue.
Genre(s): Mystery.

McAfee, John P.

3213. *On Rims of Empty Moons.* Lubbock, TX: Texas Tech University Press, 1997. 288 pp.
In the 1960s, Johnny McBride survives his abusive father who wants to kill him while he loves wealthy Sarah Eberhard, and he gets the help of the wise foreman on the Eberhard ranch before going to Vietnam.
Genre(s): Bildungsroman (Coming of Age); War Story.

◆ **3214.** *Slow Walk in a Sad Rain.* New York: Warner Books, 1993. 239 pp.
As the narrator watches his son play in the water, he remembers with guilt his participation in the Vietnam war and the mother and child he killed.
Genre(s): War Story.

McAleer, John J., and Billy Dickson

3215. *Unit Pride.* Garden City, NY: Doubleday, 1981. 515 pp.
Billy, 17, and his best friend Dewey fight together during the war in Korea, facing the danger and the horror.
Genre(s): War Story.

McCall, Dan

3216. *Messenger Bird.* San Diego, CA: Harcourt Brace, 1993. 187 pp.
A public health services physician works on the Mescalero Apache reservation in the early 1970s and falls in love with a nurse who gets cancer.
Genre(s): Medical Novel.

McCammon, Robert R.

3217. *Boy's Life.* New York: Pocket Books, 1991. 440 pp.
Twelve-year-old Cory Mackenson's father finds a dead man handcuffed to a car's steering wheel that has plunged into Zephyr's Lake in 1964, and they realize that all is not as it seems in their quiet town.
Genre(s): Bildungsroman (Coming of Age); Mystery.

McCarry, Charles

3218. *Lucky Bastard.* New York: Random House, 1998. 416 pp.
A subversive organization wants to begin a revolution against the government during the Vietnam War, and it recruits a young man from the anti-war movement who thinks he is John F. Kennedy's illegitimate son.
Genre(s): Political Fiction.

◆ 3219. *The Tears of Autumn.* New York: Saturday Review, 1975. 276 pp.
Paul Christopher begins to investigate the assassination of John Kennedy in 1963, thinking it results from the Vietnamese assassination of Ngo Dinh Diem.
Genre(s): Spy Fiction.

McCarthy, Cormac

3220. *Cities of the Plain.* New York: Knopf, 1998. 289 pp.
In the final volume of the Border trilogy, John Grady Cole works as a cowhand outside El Paso after World War II where he falls in love with a prostitute whose pimp becomes unhappy at the thought of losing her.
Genre(s): Adventure Story; Love Story.

McCorkle, Jill

3221. *Ferris Beach.* Chapel Hill, NC: Algonquin, 1990. 380 pp.
Young Katie Burns thinks of the small town which is home to her cousin Angela in the mid-1960s as a place of secrets when she begins to mature.
Genre(s): Bildungsroman (Coming of Age).

McDermott, Alice

3222. *At Weddings and Wakes.* New York: Farrar, Straus and Giroux, 1992. 213 pp.
Children in an Irish-American family in the 1960s tell about their activities and the stories of Irish immigrants they have heard.
Genre(s): Domestic Fiction.

McDowell, Edwin

3223. *To Keep Our Honor Clean.* New York: Vanguard, 1980. 313 pp.
Soldiers serving in a Marine boot camp before the Korean War wonder how much brutality is necessary to train them for war.
Genre(s): War Story.

McFather, Nelle

3224. *Southern Secrets.* New York: St. Martin's Press, 1991. 464 pp.
Off the coast of Georgia during the period from 1951 to 1964, inhabitants meet, fall in love, and become involved in intrigue and sexual irregularities.
Genre(s): Romance.

McGarry, Jean

3225. *Gallagher's Travels.* Baltimore, MD: Johns Hopkins University Press, 1998. 224 pp.
Cathy irritates everyone at a small New England newspaper in the early 1970s by refusing to stick to the expected subjects of the Women's Page in her articles.
Genre(s): Adventure Story.

McGehee, Nicole

3226. *No More Lonely Nights.* Boston: Little, Brown, 1995. 480 pp.
Dominique Avalon leaves Cairo and her wealthy family after the Suez crisis with an American for San Francisco, but he fails her as she moves from New York to New Orleans to Washington, DC in the 1950s and 60s.
Genre(s): Romance.

McInerney-Whiteford, Merry

◆ 3227. *Dog People.* New York: Tor, 1998. 288 pp.
In 1968, Trisha, 12, tries to adjust to the disintegration of her family by dwelling on the family story of a relative who was hung in Salem as a witch.
Genre(s): Bildungsroman (Coming of Age); Domestic Fiction.

McKinney-Whetstone, Diane

◆ 3228. *Tempest Rising.* New York: HarperCollins, 1998. 288 pp.
When their father disappears and their mother has a nervous breakdown in the 1960s, three sisters come under the care of Mae and her daughter Ramona.
Genre(s): Domestic Fiction.

McNamer, Deirdre

◆ 3229. *Rima in the Weeds.* New York: HarperCollins, 1991. 288 pp.
When a young girl goes to the city, she has to return to Madrid, Montana, in the early 1960s pregnant and unmarried.
Genre(s): Domestic Fiction; Bildungsroman (Coming of Age).

McPhee, Martha A.

◆ 3230. *Bright Angel Time.* New York: Random House, 1997. 246 pp.
After Kate's parents divorce in 1969, Kate, eight, and her two sisters have to go with their mother and her new love and his five children on a cross-country vacation during which Kate is exposed to sex, drugs, and irresponsible adults.

Mee, Susie

◆ 3231. *The Girl Who Loved Elvis.* Atlanta, GA: Peachtree, 1993. 215 pp.
LaVonne Grubbs works in a Georgia textile mill in the 1950s and fantasizes about Elvis Presley, even hoping to see him at his mother's funeral.
Genre(s): Bildungsroman (Coming of Age).

Meeter, Glenn

3232. *Letters to Barbara.* Grand Rapids, MI: Eerdmans, 1982. 263 pp.
In the 1950s, Adrian visits his grandmother and realizes that he wants to pass on his heritage to his own daughter.
Genre(s): Domestic Fiction.

Michaels, Fern

3233. *Texas Fury.* New York: Ballantine, 1989. 499 pp.
In the sequel to *Texas Heat,* the Coleman family continues to increase its holdings.
Genre(s): Family Saga; Romance.

3234. *Texas Heat.* New York: Ballantine, 1986. 502 pp.
In the sequel to *Texas Rich,* Maggie Coleman Tanner inherits Sunbridge, the Texas ranch she loves more than her family.
Genre(s): Family Saga; Romance.

Mickle, Shelley Fraser

◆ 3235. *The Queen of October.* Chapel Hill, NC: Algonquin, 1989. 301 pp.
In 1959, Sally Maulden, 13, goes to live with her grandparents in Coldwater, Arkansas, while her parents are considering a divorce, and she discovers an eccentric group with their own agendas.
Genre(s): Domestic Fiction; Bildungsroman (Coming of Age).

Miller, Isabel

◆ 3236. *Side by Side.* Tallahassee, FL: Naiad, 1991. 256 pp.
Girls who become lovers in adolescence are separated by their parents, but they reunite in the 1960s.

Momaday, N. Scott

3237. *House Made of Dawn.* New York: Harper and Row, 1968. 212 pp.
After Abel returns from the army and World War II to San Ysidro, he has difficulty re-adapting to the reservation or accepting the white ways.
Award(s): Pulitzer Prize.
Genre(s): Western Fiction.

Moore, Susanna

3238. *My Old Sweetheart.* Boston: Houghton Mifflin, 1982. 211 pp.
In Hawaii, Lily, 12, helps her mother through her drugs and delusions but faces the same dependency herself as an adult.
Genre(s): Bildungsroman (Coming of Age).

Morris, Bill

3239. *Motor City.* New York: Knopf, 1992. 320 pp.
Ted Mackey of General Motors plans for Buick to be the third leading make of cars in 1954, and he uses any marketing ploy available to reach his goal.

Morris, Gilbert

3240. *The Silver Star.* Minneapolis, MN: Bethany House, 1997. 304 pp.
Priscilla Winslow goes to Hollywood to star in a serial, and when she becomes involved in the base lifestyle of those around her, Jason Ballad, a rancher, helps. (*Series:* House of Winslow, 20)
Genre(s): Christian Fiction; Western Fiction.

Morrison, Toni

3241. *Paradise.* New York: Knopf, 1998. 320 pp.
Four young African American women living in a convent near an all-black town are attacked in the 1970s, and the narrator reviews the events leading to this horror.
Genre(s): Domestic Fiction.

Morrow, Bradford

3242. *Trinity Fields.* New York: Viking, 1995. 448 pp.
When friends in college realize what their fathers did in Los Alamos during World War II, they react differently, and separate, but they reunite later in life and discuss their choices.
Genre(s): War Story; Bildungsroman (Coming of Age).

Moses, Edwin

◆ 3243. *One Smart Kid.* New York: Macmillan, 1982. 256 pp.
In the 1950s the McCarthy trials fuel Fox Creek's prejudices, and the small town believes the lie of a young boy.
Genre(s): Domestic Fiction; Bildungsroman (Coming of Age).

Mosher, Howard Frank

◆ 3244. *A Stranger in the Kingdom.* New York: Doubleday, 1989. 456 pp.
Jim Kinnison, 13, discovers the intolerance of small towns in 1952 when the new Presbyterian minister turns out to be African American.
Genre(s): Bildungsroman (Coming of Age); Mystery.

Mosley, Walter

3245. *Black Betty.* New York: Norton, 1994. 255 pp.
In the Los Angeles of the early 1960s, Easy Rawlins looks for a woman he had known in Houston.
Genre(s): Mystery.

3246. *Devil in a Blue Dress.* New York: Norton, 1990. 219 pp.
Easy Rawlins is fired from his factory job in 1948 and after working for a mobster, he finds that he has skills as an investigator.
Award(s): Shamus Award; Creasey Award.
Genre(s): Mystery.

3247. *A Little Yellow Dog.* New York: Norton, 1996. 288 pp.
Easy Rawlins is working in a high school as head custodian after he has stopped drinking when he discovers a corpse on the grounds and becomes involved in the investigation during the 1960s.
Genre(s): Mystery.

3248. *A Red Death.* New York: Norton, 1991. 284 pp.
In the 1950s, the IRS, the FBI, and the local police pursue Easy Rawlins for different reasons.
Genre(s): Mystery.

3249. *White Butterfly.* New York: Norton, 1992. 272 pp.
Easy Rawlins helps his loyal friend Mouse in 1958 when Mouse is accused of killing bar girls in Los Angeles.
Genre(s): Mystery.

Myrer, Anton

3250. *The Last Convertible.* New York: Putnam, 1978. 526 pp.
After five Harvard students share a car in 1938, they continue to stay in touch through the war, their marriages, and their times as parents.

Noonan, David

◆ 3251. *Memoirs of a Caddy.* New York: Simon and Schuster, 1991. 173 pp.
In a small New Jersey town, Jim Mooney, 17, works as a caddy in the late 1960s and reveals how the volatile politics and the undercurrent of the Vietnam War affect people around him.
Genre(s): Sports Fiction; Political Fiction; War Story.

Nordan, Lewis

3252. *Wolf Whistle.* Chapel Hill, NC: Algonquin, 1993. 308 pp.
After Bobo, a black Chicago teenager, whistles at the wife of Arrow Catcher's most prominent citizen, he is murdered, an event that reveals the interdependence of blacks and whites in the Mississippi delta.
Genre(s): Political Fiction.

Oates, Joyce Carol

3253. *Because It Is Bitter, and Because It Is My Heart.* New York: Dutton, 1990. 405 pp.
Jinx Fairchild fights and kills a boy who bothers Iris Courtney in a western New York racial incident during the 1950s.
Genre(s): Domestic Fiction.

◆ 3254. *Foxfire: Confessions of a Girl Gang.* New York: Dutton, 1993. 328 pp.
Legs Sadovsky leads a girl gang called Foxfire during 1955 in her upstate New York hometown.
Genre(s): Adventure Story.

3255. *You Must Remember This.* New York: Dutton, 1987. 436 pp.
With a 1950s background of national and international events, Enid continues to become involved with her Uncle Felix.
Genre(s): Domestic Fiction.

Oates, Marylouise

3256. *Making Peace.* New York: Warner Books, 1991. 327 pp.
In 1967, organizers work on the Offensive Against the War in Washington, DC, and when they find that their leader, a Yale dropout, has CIA ties, they begin to wonder about the funding for their endeavor.
Genre(s): Political Fiction; War Story.

Oeste, Bob

3257. *The Last Pumpkin Paper.* New York: Random House, 1996. 224 pp.
Joe Pope investigates for Congressman Richard Nixon in 1948 during the Alger Hiss investigation and is recalled from retirement in 1989 as the Berlin Wall falls.
Genre(s): Mystery; Political Fiction.

O'Hagan, Christine

3258. *Benediction At the Savoia.* San Diego, CA: Harcourt Brace, 1992. 336 pp.
Delia Delaney feels the constrictions of a meddling mother, an alcoholic husband, and a church that imposes guilt upon her in the 1960s.
Genre(s): Domestic Fiction.

O'Sullivan, Bill

3259. *Precious Blood.* New York: Soho, 1992. 208 pp.
Mike Driscoll and his friends from Precious Blood parish in Brooklyn find their lives vastly different from those of their parents in rural Ireland, and when Mike learns of premeditated violence, he must decide whether or not to tell.
Genre(s): Domestic Fiction.

Palmer, Bruce

◆ 3260. *The Karma Charmer.* New York: Crown, 1994. 256 pp.
Dick Howser, an ex-hippie in Woodstock, New York, falls in love with a student who is displaced from her dormitory and moves into his house in 1969, but his son Howard, 10, arrives, and is irritated at his dad's lack of attention.

Parker, Gwendolyn M.

3261. *These Same Long Bones.* Boston: Houghton Mifflin, 1994. 260 pp.
Although Sirus MacDougald is a leader in the Hay-Ti section of Durham, North Carolina, after World War II, he

loses the ability to bring the community together after the death of his daughter.
Genre(s): Domestic Fiction.

Parker, Michael

◆ 3262. *Hello Down There.* New York: Scribner's, 1993. 288 pp.
In the early 1950s, Edwin Keane breaks his back, and in a town where social divisions still loom large, Eureka Speight, daughter of a farmer, helps him recover.
Genre(s): Domestic Fiction.

Parker, Robert B.

3263. *Perchance to Dream.* New York: Putnam, 1991. 271 pp.
In the early 1950s, Philip Marlowe must search for the psychotic Carmen Sternwood, who is missing from a sanatorium for the wealthy.
Genre(s): Mystery.

Parrish, Richard

3264. *Defending the Truth.* New York: Onyx, 1998. 416 pp.
In 1951, as Joseph McCarthy's trials lead to hysteria, lawyer Joshua Rabb finds that his clients and family are on McCarthy's list.
Genre(s): Political Fiction; Legal Story.

3265. *The Dividing Line.* New York: Dutton, 1993. 368 pp.
Brooklyn Jew Joshua Rabb loses his arm in World War II and his wife to an accident before he comes to work in Tucson in 1946, and he immediately must investigate the murder of a nun, for which the son of the Papago chief is accused.
Genre(s): Mystery.

Patton, Frances Gray

3266. *Good Morning, Miss Dove.* New York: Dodd, Mead, 1954. 218 pp.
Miss Dove's influence as a teacher in her small town goes unappreciated until she becomes ill.
Genre(s): Domestic Fiction.

Perry, Richard

3267. *No Other Tale to Tell.* New York: Morrow, 1994. 356 pp.
Carla March, 44, starts an affair in 1966 with a golf caddy passing through Kingston, New York, but she breaks it off when she decides to continue waiting for Max, the white foundling her parents adopted who burned the house after teenaged Carla had his half-white child.
Genre(s): Domestic Fiction.

Petersen, Ray

3268. *Cowkind.* New York: St. Martin's Press, 1996. 195 pp.
A herd of dairy cows relates the actions and concerns of Farmer Bob's family from the restlessness of Renee to Gerry's concern about being drafted into the Vietnam War in 1969.
Genre(s): Domestic Fiction.

Peterson, Michael

3269. *A Time of War.* New York: Pocket Books, 1990. 580 pp.
President Johnson sends Bradley Marshall to Vietnam to discuss the withdrawal of troops, but he fails before the Tet Offensive occurs.
Genre(s): War Story.

Petrakis, Harry Mark

3270. *In the Land of Morning.* New York: D. McKay, 1973. 290 pp.
Alex Rifakis returns from the Vietnam War and starts to rebuild his life.
Genre(s): Love Story.

Pierce, Constance

◆ 3271. *Hope Mills.* New York: Pushcart, 1997. 311 pp.
Tollie, a high school freshman, tries to find her way through casual sex and friendship while her mother mourns the death of her little brother and her stepfather worries about his job during 1959 in Hope Mill, North Carolina.
Genre(s): Bildungsroman (Coming of Age).

Piercy, Marge

3272. *Vida.* New York: Summit Books, 1979. 412 pp.
Vida, an antiwar activist during the 1960s, goes underground in 1970 after being associated with a bombing.
Genre(s): Political Fiction.

Pinckney, Darryl

3273. *High Cotton.* New York: Farrar, Straus and Giroux, 1992. 309 pp.
In the 1950s and 1960s, blacks growing up in Indianapolis have their own pockets of pride and hyprocrisy as "upper shadies."
Genre(s): Bildungsroman (Coming of Age).

Plain, Belva

3274. *Harvest.* New York: Delacorte, 1990. 409 pp.
The Werners affirm their Jewish heritage during the 1960s while the children assert their individuality, and Steve becomes an anarchist and another child goes to Israel in the sequel to *Tapestry*.
Genre(s): Domestic Fiction; Love Story.

Plante, David

◆ 3275. *The Family.* New York: Farrar, Straus and Giroux, 1978. 301 pp.
Daniel, 12, views his family dispassionately until he drops out of college and realizes that he appreciates them.
Genre(s): Bildungsroman (Coming of Age).

Plesko, Les

3276. *The Last Bongo Sunset.* New York: Simon and Schuster, 1995. 269 pp.
College leaves Boston University for Venice, California, in the 1970s where his decadent lifestyle belies the rea-

◆ May be suitable for young adult readers

sons his mother sent him away from Hungary during the 1956 revolution.
Genre(s): Bildungsroman (Coming of Age).

Pomeranz, Gary

◆ 3277. *Out at Home.* Boston: Houghton Mifflin, 1985. 231 pp.
Arnie Barzov, dismissed from college for gambling, returns to Chicago, where he begins betting on the Cubs who are competing for the baseball pennant.
Genre(s): Sports Fiction.

Porcelli, Joe

◆ 3278. *The Photograph.* Charleston, SC: Wyrick, 1995. 346 pp.
Bok Chang Kimboy, orphaned at six in Korea and adopted by an American officer, lives in Charleston, South Carolina, but returns to Southeast Asia to fight in Vietnam.
Genre(s): War Story.

Porter, Connie Rose

◆ 3279. *All-Bright Court.* Boston: Houghton Mifflin, 1991. 224 pp.
Black families inhabit Buffalo's All-Bright Court in the 1950s when they come north to work in the steel industry.
Genre(s): Domestic Fiction.

Potok, Andrew

3280. *My Life with Goya.* New York: Arbor House, 1986. 304 pp.
After the Nazis murder his parents, Adam Krinsky comes from Poland to New York to live with his uncle and become an artist.
Genre(s): Bildungsroman (Coming of Age).

Potok, Chaim

3281. *The Book of Lights.* New York: Knopf, 1981. 369 pp.
Rabbi Gershon Loran becomes drawn to Jewish mysticism after having a vision on an apartment roof and before going to Korea as a chaplain.
Genre(s): Jewish Fiction.

Powers, James F.

3282. *Wheat that Springeth Green.* New York: Knopf, 1988. 335 pp.
In the turbulence of the last months of the 1960s, a Catholic parish priest rebels against the church.

Powers, John R.

3283. *Do Black Patent-Leather Shoes Really Reflect Up?* Chicago: Regnery, 1975. 227 pp.
In the sequel to *The Last Catholic in America*, a student spends four years in a Catholic high school during the 1950s, where rules seem to have little reason behind them.
Genre(s): Bildungsroman (Coming of Age); Humorous Fiction.

3284. *The Last Catholic in America.* New York: Saturday Review, 1973. 228 pp.
Eddie Ryan recalls his 1950s youth in a South Side Chicago Catholic neighborhood.
Genre(s): Humorous Fiction.

Price, Reynolds

3285. *Blue Calhoun.* New York: Atheneum, 1992. 364 pp.
In the 1950s, when husband and father Blue Calhoun, sees the daughter of a high school acquaintance from the wrong side of the tracks, he cannot control himself.
Genre(s): Domestic Fiction.

3286. *The Source of Light.* New York: Atheneum, 1981. 318 pp.
The sequel to *The Surface of the Earth* reveals that Rob Mayfield, dying of cancer, has let his son leave for Oxford in 1955 without telling him about his condition.
Genre(s): Family Saga.

Price, Richard

3287. *Bloodbrothers.* Boston: Houghton Mifflin, 1976. 271 pp.
Stony DeCoca, ineligible for college and uninterested in hard labor, tries to make something of his life in the Bronx's Co-Op City.
Genre(s): Bildungsroman (Coming of Age).

Proffitt, Nicholas

3288. *Gardens of Stone.* New York: Carroll and Graf, 1983. 373 pp.
Jack Willow's idealization of war leads him to join the Army, but after completion of Officer Candidate School and a trip to Vietnam, he changes.
Genre(s): War Story.

Proulx, Annie

3289. *Postcards.* New York: Scribner's, 1992. 308 pp.
Loyal Blood leaves his family in Vermont and carries the secret with across the country that he accidentally killed his girlfriend, and he continually sends postcards back home.
Award(s): PEN/Faulkner Award for Fiction.

Puzo, Mario

3290. *Fools Die.* New York: Putnam, 1978. 572 pp.
After surviving World War II and other events, John Merlyn thinks that he is a modern-day Merlin while traversing the globe from Las Vegas to New York to Tokyo.
Genre(s): Love Story.

3291. *The Godfather.* New York: Putnam, 1969. 446 pp.
Don Vito Corleone controls a major mafia family in the 1940s, but when one of his sons is murdered, he fights to dominate all of the other families as well.
Genre(s): Family Saga.

◆ 3292. *The Sicilian.* New York: Linden Press, 1984. 410 pp.
Turi Guilliano works to enhance his romantic image, but in the mid-1940s the Sicilian Mafia forces him to escape to the American Mafia, in the sequel to *The Godfather.*
Genre(s): Family Saga.

Quindlen, Anna

3293. *Object Lessons.* New York: Random House, 1991. 262 pp.
Maggie, 12, tells the story of her family in the 1960s in which her grandfather, although dying, still tries to control his children and grandchildren.
Genre(s): Bildungsroman (Coming of Age).

Remarque, Erich Maria

3294. *Shadows in Paradise.* Trans. Ralph Manheim. Boston: Harcourt Brace, 1972. 305 pp.
Refugees from World War II come to the United States to start new lives with false names and passports but discover that Hitler's effect on them never ends.

Reynolds, Marjorie

◆ 3295. *The Starlite Drive-in.* New York: Morrow, 1997. 256 pp.
In the summer of 1956, Callie Anne Benton is 13, and her mother's agoraphobia strands her and her father at the drive-in he runs until a drifter draws her mother out of the house and then out of their lives.
Genre(s): Domestic Fiction; Bildungsroman (Coming of Age).

Robertson, Don

◆ 3296. *The Greatest Thing that Almost Happened.* New York: Putnam, 1970. 284 pp.
Morris Bird III becomes 17, and after seeing his grandmother die, he must deal with his own death when he is diagnosed with leukemia, in the sequel to *The Sum and Total of Now.*
Genre(s): Bildungsroman (Coming of Age).

◆ 3297. *The Sum and Total of Now.* New York: Putnam, 1966. 251 pp.
In the sequel to *The Greatest Thing Since Sliced Bread,* Morris Bird III becomes a Cleveland adolescent who watches his family fight over his grandmother's possessions after her death.
Genre(s): Bildungsroman (Coming of Age).

Rockcastle, Mary Francois

3298. *Rainy Lake.* St. Paul, MN: Graywolf, 1994. 278 pp.
Danny and her friend spend summers in the 1960s at Rainy Lake, and one summer, she falls in love with a boy of mixed parentage, and her brother brings anti-Vietnam radicalism home from college and conflicts with her father.
Genre(s): Bildungsroman (Coming of Age).

Rodriguez, Victor

3299. *Eldorado in East Harlem.* Houston, TX: Arte Publico, 1992. 160 pp.
Rene Gomez, 17, and his widowed mother live in East Harlem in 1960, where he becomes involved in petty crime.

Rosen, Charley

3300. *Barney Polan's Game.* New York: Seven Stories, 1998. 336 pp.
In August 1950, sportswriter Barney Polan has heard rumors of fixed college basketball games, but he does not pay much attention until he observes a major scandal unfolding.
Genre(s): Sports Fiction.

Rosen, Gerald

3301. *Mahatma Gandhi in a Cadillac.* Berkeley, CA: North Atlantic, 1995. 275 pp.
Danny Schwartz, a Jew from the Bronx working on a master's degree at Wharton, goes to Seattle for a summer job in 1961, where he meets Leslie, a Catholic who also is looking to be educated about life.
Genre(s): Bildungsroman (Coming of Age).

Ross, Joann

3302. *No Regrets.* New York: Harlequin, 1997. 475 pp.
After their parents' murder-suicide in 1972, three sisters follow different paths, one as a nun who is an emergency room nurse, another as a doctor's wife, and another as a would-be actress.
Genre(s): Domestic Fiction.

Ryan, Kathryn Morgan

3303. *The Betty Tree.* New York: Trident, 1972. 432 pp.
The generations of the Lansing family live in a small Iowa town in the 1940s, where they reveal their individual and collective foibles and illnesses.
Genre(s): Family Saga.

Saiter, Susan Sullivan

3304. *Moira's Way.* New York: Donald I. Fine, 1993. 343 pp.
In the 1950s, Moira grows up in South Dakota with a sullen mother and an alcoholic father who tells her that she is worthless, until something happens that finally frees her, her sister, and her mother.
Genre(s): Bildungsroman (Coming of Age); Domestic Fiction.

Sallis, James

3305. *Black Hornet.* New York: Carroll and Graf, 1994. 208 pp.
In the early 1960s, a rooftop sniper kills African American Lewis Griffin's friend in front of him, and with the help of a white policeman and others, he searches for the murderer.
Genre(s): Mystery.

Salter, James

3306. *The Hunters.* Washington, DC: Counterpoint, 1997. 244 pp.
In the Korean War, Captain Steve Connell is a rocket
ace, but the more missions he flies, the more his courage
ebbs.
Genre(s): War Story.

Sammons, Sonny

3307. *The Keepers of Echowah.* Marietta, GA:
Cherokee, 1995. 240 pp.
Twin brothers Patty and Matty MacDonald grow up in
south Georgia during the 1950s, and in the 1960s, they go
to Vietnam, where one of them dies.
Genre(s): Bildungsroman (Coming of Age); War Story.

Sayers, Valerie

3308. *Who Do You Love?* New York: Doubleday,
1991. 336 pp.
The Rooney family, unaware of the world outside Due
East, South Carolina, awaken from their petty hostilities
on November 22, 1963, when President Kennedy is assassinated.
Genre(s): Domestic Fiction.

Schaeffer, Susan Fromberg

◆ 3309. *Buffalo Afternoon.* New York: Knopf,
1989. 535 pp.
While serving in Vietnam, Pete Bravado meets Li, whose
water buffalo have been shot by American soldiers.
Genre(s): War Story.

Schneider, Bart

3310. *Blue Bossa.* New York: Viking, 1998. 244
pp.
Ronnie Reboulet, a drug-addicted jazz trumpet player,
tries a comeback as a musician in the 1970s.
Genre(s): Musical Fiction.

Schott, Penelope Scambly

3311. *A Little Ignorance.* New York: Clarkson N.
Potter, 1986. 208 pp.
While Alison grows from eight to 14 in the 1950s, she
learns to accept her stepmother while spending summers
with her grandparents in the Midwest and winters with
her widowed father in New York City.
Genre(s): Domestic Fiction.

Scofield, Sandra

◆ 3312. *Walking Dunes.* San Francisco: Permanent
Press, 1992. 247 pp.
Tennis star David Puckett, 18, is from the wrong side of
the tracks, but he wants to make something of his life al-
though he is not sure how to proceed.
Genre(s): Bildungsroman (Coming of Age).

Segal, Lore

3313. *Her First American.* New York: Knopf,
1985. 285 pp.
After Ilka Weissnix arrives in America and begins to assimilate by learning the language, she meets Carter Bay-
oux, a middle-aged African American author.
Genre(s): Domestic Fiction.

Senna, Danzy

◆ 3314. *Caucasia.* New York: Putnam, 1998. 368 pp.
In the 1960s, Birdie and her sister Cole try to support
each other when their black father and white mother finally separate, and when Cole goes with her father to Bra-
zil, Birdie has to face a federal investigation of her
mother's political activities.
Genre(s): Political Fiction.

Settle, Mary Lee

3315. *Charley Bland.* New York: Farrar, Straus
and Giroux, 1989. 207 pp.
A widow returns to West Virginia after living in postwar
Paris, renews acquaintance with the man she worshipped
as a child, and loses her independence to him.
Genre(s): Domestic Fiction.

Shah, Diane K.

3316. *Dying Cheek to Cheek.* New York: Doubleday, 1992. 384 pp.
While Paris Chandler, a gossip columnist in Hollywood
during the 1940s, searches for the murderer of her lover,
she uncovers other scandals.
Genre(s): Mystery.

Shange, Ntozake

◆ 3317. *Betsey Brown.* New York: St. Martin's
Press, 1985. 207 pp.
In 1957, Betsey Brown, 13, desegregates a school with
the support of her mother and grandmother.
Genre(s): Bildungsroman (Coming of Age); Domestic
Fiction.

Siddons, Anne Rivers

3318. *Downtown.* New York: HarperCollins,
1994. 352 pp.
Maureen Smoky O'Donnell goes to Atlanta to write for a
magazine in the 1960s, and after writing about the city's
war on poverty, she falls in love with a man who leaves
for Vietnam.
Genre(s): Romance.

Sinclair, Andrew

3319. *The Facts in the Case of E.A. Poe.* New
York: Henry Holt, 1980. 181 pp.
After Ernest Albert Pons arrives in New York and feels
terrible guilt about the death of his family in Hitler's
death camps, he starts to believe that he is Edgar Allan
Poe.
Genre(s): Biographical Fiction.

Sinclair, April

◆ 3320. *Coffee Will Make Me Black.* New York: Hyperion, 1994. 239 pp.
Jean Stevie Stevenson is 11 in 1965, and while growing up in Chicago, she becomes influenced by Martin Luther King Jr. and Malcolm X.
Genre(s): Bildungsroman (Coming of Age).

Singer, Isaac Bashevis

3321. *Enemies: A Love Story.* Trans. Aliza Shevrin and Elizabeth Shub. New York: Farrar, Straus and Giroux, 1972. 280 pp.
Yadwiga helps Herman Broder reach New York to escape from Poland and the Nazis, and when Broder thinks his wife has died, he marries Yadwiga.
Genre(s): Love Story.

3322. *Shadows on the Hudson.* New York: Farrar, Straus and Giroux, 1998. 544 pp.
Boris Makaver, a wealthy and religious Jew in New York City faces a scandal after World War II when his daughter leaves her second husband.
Genre(s): Domestic Fiction.

Skinner, Margaret

3323. *Molly Flanagan and the Holy Ghost.* Chapel Hill, NC: Algonquin, 1995. 242 pp.
In Memphis, Tennessee, during the 1950s, Molly lives under the shadow of her brother as she tries to see with her "lazy" eye and tries to free herself from the stern control of her grandmother who wants her to play "Spinning Song" for her music recital instead of the racy "Tarantella."
Genre(s): Bildungsroman (Coming of Age).

Skinner, Robert E.

3324. *Skin Deep, Blood Red.* New York: Kensington, 1997. 256 pp.
In New Orleans during 1936, a gangster blackmails a small-time criminal into finding the murderer of the cop he supported, and Wesley Farrell unwillingly teams with detective Francis Casey for the investigation.
Genre(s): Mystery.

Smith, Mary Burnett

◆ 3325. *Miss Ophelia.* New York: Morrow, 1997. 288 pp.
In the summer of 1948, Belly Anderson goes to her mean Aunt Rachel to help her recover from surgery, because she wants to get away from home and to take piano lessons from Miss Ophelia Love, and while there, she learns a lot about adults.
Genre(s): Bildungsroman (Coming of Age).

Solomita, Stephen

3326. *A Piece of the Action.* New York: Putnam, 1992. 271 pp.
In 1957, Moodrow wins a boxing match for his police department and receives both a promotion and the favors of another policeman's daughter, but he hesitates to investigate a homicide.
Genre(s): Mystery.

Soos, Troy

3327. *Hunting a Detroit Tiger.* New York: Kensington, 1997. 346 pp.
Detroit Tiger infielder Mackey Rawlings is blamed for shooting organizer Emmett Siever, but Mackey denies the charge.
Genre(s): Mystery; Biographical Fiction.

Spanbauer, Tom

3328. *Faraway Places.* New York: Putnam, 1988. 114 pp.
A boy on an isolated rural Idaho farm during the 1950s tells about a murder.
Genre(s): Mystery.

Spencer, LaVyrle

3329. *Then Came Heaven.* New York: Putnam, 1997. 352 pp.
In 1950, Eddie Olczak, St. Joseph's Church janitor, has two daughters to raise after his wife dies in an accident, and when Sister Regina helps him, she begins to feel more than just compassion.
Genre(s): Romance; Christian Fiction.

Spencer, Scott

◆ 3330. *The Rich Man's Table.* New York: Knopf, 1998. 272 pp.
Billy Rothschild tracks legendary singer Luke Fairchild who left Billy's mother Esther before his birth in the 1960s, and confronts him with patrimony.
Genre(s): Bildungsroman (Coming of Age).

Stallworth, Anne Nall

3331. *Go, Go, Said the Bird.* New York: Vanguard, 1984. 384 pp.
Bird Lasseter, 17 in 1964, has passed for white as the son of a pale black woman and a white man, but after he falls in love with the doctor's daughter, his life changes.
Genre(s): Love Story.

Steadman, Mark

3332. *Bang-Up Season.* Marietta, GA: Longstreet, 1990. 162 pp.
In 1947, Jack Lynch comes to St. Boniface High and inspires the football team to its first winning season in five years.
Genre(s): Sports Fiction.

Steel, Danielle

3333. *Full Circle.* New York: Delacorte, 1980. 323 pp.
Tana Roberts, raped at 18, becomes a radical during the 1960s and a prosecutor in the 1970s.
Genre(s): Love Story.

◆ 3334. *Message from Nam.* New York: Delacorte, 1990. 416 pp.
College student Paxton Andrews goes to Vietnam to report on the war for a San Francisco paper after her fiancé dies there, and she meets another soldier with whom she falls in love.
Genre(s): War Story; Romance.

◆ May be suitable for young adult readers

Stone, Scott C. S.

3335. *Song of the Wolf.* New York: Arbor House, 1985. 377 pp.
As a half Cherokee growing up in the South, John Dane kills a rapist, and realizes that he wants to be a fighter, so he serves in Korea and Asia.
Genre(s): War Story; Political Fiction.

Straight, Susan

◆ 3336. *I Been in Sorrow's Kitchen and Licked Out All the Pots.* New York: Hyperion, 1992. 355 pp.
When Marietta's mother dies, Marietta, 15, leaves for Charleston, but when she becomes pregnant, she returns home to have her twins and find work on a plantation being restored for tourists.
Genre(s): Domestic Fiction.

Swaim, Don

3337. *The H.L. Mencken Murder Case.* New York: St. Martin's Press, 1988. 174 pp.
In the 1940s, Howard's friend Lenny offers him a valuable manuscript to sell in Howard's father's secondhand bookstore, but someone murders Lenny, and H.L. Mencken, one of the bookstore's customers, offers to help the investigation.
Genre(s): Mystery.

Swick, Marly A.

3338. *Paper Wings.* New York: HarperCollins, 1996. 276 pp.
Suzanne Keller, 12, watches her mother become depressed after President Kennedy is assassinated in 1963 and tries to understand the value in life.
Genre(s): Domestic Fiction.

Tate, Donald

3339. *Bravo Burning.* New York: Scribner's, 1986. 216 pp.
While stationed in Vietnam during 1967, Mike Ripp learns that his wife has left him just before a big battle occurs.
Genre(s): War Story.

Taylor, Laura

3340. *Honorbound.* New York: Watts, 1988. 367 pp.
The Viet Cong shoot down Matthew Benedict and his jet in 1967 just after he has married Eden and he becomes a prisoner of war for whom Eden must wait for five miserable years.
Genre(s): War Story; Romance.

Taylor, Robert

3341. *The Innocent.* Santa Barbara, CA: Fithian, 1997. 256 pp.
When Captain Matthew Fairchild serves in Vietnam, he falls in love with a Vietnamese busboy who gives him an understanding of Vietnamese culture before Fairchild discovers secret information about the massacre of citizens in a village.
Genre(s): War Story; Bildungsroman (Coming of Age).

Thames, Susan

◆ 3342. *I'll Be Home Late Tonight.* New York: Villard, 1997. 256 pp.
Lily, 12, and her mother June drift through the South with no aim in 1957, and when Lily is 14 and realizes that all she has is her unreliable mother, she begins supporting herself through sex.
Genre(s): Bildungsroman (Coming of Age).

Thomas, Abigail

3343. *An Actual Life.* Chapel Hill, NC: Algonquin, 1996. 236 pp.
Virginia, 19, and her husband Buddy return to Buddy's hometown with their child in 1960, and Buddy seems to still love his high school girlfriend.
Genre(s): Domestic Fiction.

Thomas, D.M.

3344. *Flying in to Love.* New York: Scribner's, 1992. 242 pp.
When John F. Kennedy is assassinated in 1963, the American myth changes.
Genre(s): Biographical Fiction.

Truscott, Lucian K.

3345. *Army Blue.* New York: Crown, 1989. 436 pp.
Lieutenant Blue IV is charged in 1969 with desertion and cowardice against the North Vietnamese, but he claims that his superiors ordered actions that would have harmed the men in his charge.
Genre(s): War Story.

Updike, John

3346. *Memories of the Ford Administration.* New York: Knopf, 1992. 371 pp.
A college professor includes information from his research on James Buchanan, the president preceding Lincoln from 1857 to 1861, while relating his experiences during the Ford administration of 1974 to 1977.
Genre(s): Political Fiction.

Urrea, Luis Alberto

3347. *In Search of Snow.* New York: HarperCollins, 1994. 258 pp.
After his mother dies when he is seven, Mike and his amateur boxer father run a gas station in Arizona, and when his father dies while boxing a younger man, Mike must form new relationships.
Genre(s): Domestic Fiction.

Valtorta, Laura P.

3348. *Family Meal.* Durham, NC: Carolina Wren, 1993. 127 pp.
Sally Linden's 1950s family is silly and sexist, and not until she goes to college and meets her roommate, who wants to be Annette Funicello, does she assert her independence.
Genre(s): Domestic Fiction.

Van Peebles, Melvin

3349. *Panther.* New York: Thunder's Mouth, 1995. 230 pp.
In the 1960s, Judge Taylor drops out of college after serving in Vietnam to join the Black Panther Party for Self-Defense and become its personal spy.
Genre(s): Political Fiction.

Van Slyke, Helen

3350. *Public Smiles, Private Tears.* New York: Harper and Row, 1982. 250 pp.
Beverly Richmon devotes her life to her retailing career in the 1940s and 1950s rather than attend college.

Vea, Alfredo

◆ 3351. *La Maravilla.* New York: Dutton, 1993. 320 pp.
Beto, nine, lives in an adobe hut in a small Arizona community as the grandchild of a Yaqui Indian and a Mexican woman of Spanish descent.
Genre(s): Domestic Fiction.

Wakefield, Dan

3352. *Going All the Way.* New York: Delacorte, 1970. 307 pp.
In 1954, men who have returned to Indianapolis from army duty meet, and one of them begins to question all of the emptiness and prejudices of their conventional lives.

Watson, Larry

◆ 3353. *Montana 1948.* Minneapolis, MN: Milkweed, 1993. 200 pp.
David, 12, comes of age during 1948 when his uncle is accused of molesting and murdering Native Americans in his small Montana town.
Award(s): Milkweed National Fiction Prize.
Genre(s): Western Fiction; Bildungsroman (Coming of Age).

Webb, James H.

3354. *A Sense of Honor.* Englewood Cliffs, NJ: Prentice Hall, 1981. 308 pp.
In 1968, as midshipmen at Annapolis continue their rituals with the threat of service in Vietnam, one freshman questions the tradition.
Genre(s): War Story.

Weber, Joe

3355. *Targets of Opportunity.* New York: Jove, 1994. 335 pp.
Austin, an American pilot, uses a North Vietnamese Mig-17 to fly into Vietnam and infiltrate the Air Force, but once there, he has a difficult, additional assignment.
Genre(s): War Story.

Weitz, John

3356. *Friends in High Places.* New York: Macmillan, 1982. 384 pp.
After Charly, baptized Karl-Heinz Dorn, comes to New York after World War II, he tries to obtain citizenship, but a Jewish congressman tries to thwart his request.
Genre(s): War Story; Political Fiction.

West, Dorothy

3357. *The Wedding.* New York: Doubleday, 1995. 208 pp.
As the distinguished African American Cole family prepares for a daughter's wedding on Martha's Vineyard in the 1950s, tensions lead to tragedy.
Genre(s): Domestic Fiction.

West, Michael Lee

3358. *She Flew the Coop.* New York: HarperCollins, 1994. 390 pp.
In a small Mississippi town during the spring of 1952, the attempted suicide of a 16-year-old girl, impregnated by the Baptist preacher begins revelations about several improper liaisons.
Genre(s): Humorous Fiction.

Wharton, William

◆ 3359. *Birdy.* New York: Knopf, 1979. 309 pp.
Al Colombato goes to an army hospital at the end of World War II to try to bring his childhood friend Birdy out of a catatonic state.
Genre(s): War Story.

Wheeler, Amanda

3360. *Beyond the Fire.* New York: Fawcett, 1996. 260 pp.
In the early 1970s, law student Nina Lewis becomes entangled with both a lover and a mayor's campaign.
Genre(s): Romance; Political Fiction.

Wilkinson, Sylvia

3361. *Bone of My Bones.* New York: Putnam, 1982. 252 pp.
Ella Ruth Higgins recalls her days of maturation in North Carolina during the 1940s and 1950s.
Genre(s): Domestic Fiction; Bildungsroman (Coming of Age).

Williams, Joan

3362. *Country Woman.* Boston: Little, Brown, 1982. 288 pp.
Allie McCall gains meaning in her life by defending the black man falsely accused of murdering her mother during the early 1960s in Mississippi.
Genre(s): Domestic Fiction.

Williams, Thomas

3363. *The Moon Pinnace.* Garden City, NY: Doubleday, 1986. 352 pp.
After John Hearne returns from World War II, he decides to travel across the country to find his father rather than

marry a high school senior with whom he has had a relationship.
Genre(s): Bildungsroman (Coming of Age).

Wiseman, Thomas

3364. *A Game of Secrets.* New York: Delacorte, 1979. 370 pp.
After the war, lawyer Bill Hardtman helps President Truman create the Central Intelligence Agency, but he becomes perturbed by the disappearance and death of his acupuncturist.
Genre(s): Spy Fiction.

Witherspoon, Mary Elizabeth

3365. *The Morning Cool.* New York: Macmillan, 1972. 320 pp.
Maggie Cole Hill becomes involved with Communist activism through her first marriage, and in her second marriage, she and her husband avoid politics, but the McCarthy hearings refuse to let them live quietly.
Genre(s): Political Fiction.

Wolfe, Swain

3366. *The Lake Dreams the Sky.* New York: HarperCollins, 1998. 352 pp.
A real estate demographer returns to her Montana town and discovers the love affair of Rose, a half-Native American waitress, and the artist Cody, which occurred just after World War II and evoked the town's prejudices.
Genre(s): Love Story.

Wolff, Miles

◆ 3367. *Season of the Owl.* New York: Stein and Day, 1981. 181 pp.
A boy living with his uncle in the summer of 1957 grows up when a body is found behind the baseball stadium scoreboard and racially motivated picket lines form outside.
Genre(s): Bildungsroman (Coming of Age).

Wood, Jane

3368. *Josey Rose.* New York: Simon and Schuster, 1998. 304 pp.
In the early 1960s, Josey Rose befriends a young woman living in the woods, and when he sees his alcoholic father rape her, he goes to the priest for help, but the priest tries to molest him.
Genre(s): Domestic Fiction; Bildungsroman (Coming of Age).

Woods, Stuart

3369. *Chiefs.* New York: Norton, 1981. 427 pp.
Three police chiefs in Delano, Georgia, must deal with a case in which a number of white teenage boys have disappeared over 40 years.
Genre(s): Mystery.

Woodson, Jacqueline

3370. *Autobiography of a Family Photo.* New York: Dutton, 1995. 113 pp.
The young female narrator grows up in Brooklyn in a family of a drag queen who has gone to Vietnam to prove

his manhood, a sister, and a half-white brother who reveals her mother's infidelity.
Genre(s): Domestic Fiction; Bildungsroman (Coming of Age).

Wouk, Herman

◆ 3371. *Inside, Outside.* Boston: Little, Brown, 1985. 644 pp.
To fill his time while working as a consultant for President Nixon, tax lawyer David Goodkind writes about his Russian immigrant family and his life as a young man.
Genre(s): Legal Story.

Yamanaka, Lois-Ann

3372. *Wild Meat and the Bully Burgers.* New York: Putnam, 1995. 368 pp.
Lovey Nariyoshi grows up in white culture on the island of Hawaii where her Japanese American family is racially segregated from the others.
Genre(s): Bildungsroman (Coming of Age).

Young, John

◆ 3373. *Thief of Dreams.* New York: Viking, 1991. 240 pp.
After his parents separate in 1948 and someone beats up a friend instead of him, James, 13, runs away to be with nature but suffers from hypothermia.
Genre(s): Domestic Fiction; Bildungsroman (Coming of Age).

Youngblood, Shaw

3374. *Soul Kiss.* New York: Putnam, 1997. 224 pp.
Mariah Kin Santos grows up on a military base where her Cherokee, black, and Mexican descent is unimportant, but at seven, when her mother disappears, she faces the hostile outside world.
Genre(s): Domestic Fiction; Bildungsroman (Coming of Age).

Zacharias, Lee

3375. *Lessons.* Boston: Houghton Mifflin, 1981. 342 pp.
Jane Hurdle wants to be a concert clarinetist, but circumstances cause her to return home from college and become the lover of her former music teacher in the early 1960s.
Genre(s): Domestic Fiction; Bildungsroman (Coming of Age).

Zimmerman, R.

3376. *Deadfall in Berlin.* New York: Donald I. Fine, 1990. 279 pp.
In 1975, Will Walker, a Chicago actor born Willi Berndt, tries regression to remember who murdered his mother and his past in Berlin during the final days of World War II.
Genre(s): War Story; Time Travel.

After 1975
The Late 20th Century

Connolly, Edward

3377. *Deer Run.* New York: Scribner's, 1971. 186 pp.

When the Vermont community distrusts the commune formed by Vietnam war veterans, one of its members responds violently.

De Hartog, Jan

3378. *The Outer Buoy.* New York: Pantheon, 1994. 272 pp.

Harinxma and other World War II retirees agree to have out-of-body experiences for space station study with NASA in the sequel to *The Centurian*.

Genre(s): Adventure Story.

Dye, Dale

3379. *Outrage.* Boston: Little, Brown, 1988. 200 pp.

In 1983, Marines suffer a bomb attack in Beirut, Lebanon, because bureaucrats ignore warnings.

Genre(s): War Story.

Estleman, Loren D.

3380. *King of the Corner.* New York: Bantam, 1992. 304 pp.

In the 1980s, in the sequel to *Motown*, the civil unrest in Detroit turns into drug wars and rule by the minority.

Genre(s): Mystery.

Fast, Howard

◆ 3381. *The Immigrant's Daughter.* Boston: Houghton Mifflin, 1985. 321 pp.

In the sequel to *The Legacy*, Barbara Lavette continues her activist career by running for Congress.

Genre(s): Domestic Fiction; Family Saga.

Goodman, Allegra

3382. *Kaaterskill Falls.* New York: Dial, 1998. 352 pp.

A small Orthodox Jewish sect spends summers in a Dutch community, and in 1976, the townspeople begin to resent the intrusion, and female members of the group chafe under its laws and restrictions.

Genre(s): Domestic Fiction; Jewish Fiction.

Lan, Cao

3383. *Monkey Bridge.* New York: Viking, 1997. 260 pp.

Although Mai Nguyen adjusts to her new life in Farmington, Connecticut, after being airlifted from Saigon, her mother cannot recover from the losses of her Vietnamese past.

Genre(s): Domestic Fiction.

Mason, Bobbie Ann

3384. *In Country.* New York: Harper and Row, 1985. 247 pp.

Sam resents the effects of the Vietnam War, especially the death of her father and her uncle's suffering from Agent Orange ingestion.

Genre(s): War Story.

Sayles, John

3385. *Los Gusanos.* New York: HarperCollins, 1991. 480 pp.

In the early 1980s, Marta de la Pena, a Cuban exile in Miami, plans to avenge her brother's death during the Bay of Pigs invasion in Cuba by gathering her own guerrillas.

Genre(s): Political Fiction.

Settle, Mary Lee

3386. *The Killing Ground.* New York: Farrar, Straus and Giroux, 1982. 385 pp.

In the sequel to *The Scapegoat*, Hannah McKarkle returns to her West Virginia home after pursing a writing career in New York and finds that a distant relative has killed her brother.

Genre(s): Family Saga.

Sidhwa, Bapsi

◆ 3387. *An American Brat.* Minneapolis, MN: Milkweed, 1993. 320 pp.

When she begins to rebel at women's clothing requirements in increasingly fundamentalist Pakistan, Feroza Ginwalla comes to the United States to spend a few months with her uncle at MIT in 1978 and decides to stay.

Genre(s): Bildungsroman (Coming of Age).

APPENDIXES

Appendix I
Book Awards

Note: Numbers refer to entry numbers.

Capps, Benjamin, *The White Man's Road*, 2046
Cooke, John Byrne, *The Snowblind Moon*, 1193
Eidson, Tom, *St. Agnes' Stand*, 638
Fisher, Vardis, *Mountain Man*, 642
Grove, Fred, *The Great Horse Race*, 1357
Hackenberry, Charles, *Friends*, 1363
Henry, Will, *The Gates of the Mountains*, 327; *From Where the Sun Now Stands*, 1394

Jones, Douglas C., *Roman*, 1445; *Gone the Dreams and Dancing*, 1444
Kelton, Elmer, *The Far Canyon*, 1458; *Slaughter*, 1462
Long, Jeff, *Empire of Bones*, 490
Matheson, Richard, *Journal of the Gun Years*, 1531
McMurtry, Larry, *Lonesome Dove*, 1552; *Comanche Moon*, 1551
Robson, Lucia St. Clair, *Ride the Wind*, 525
Sherman, Jory, *The Medicine Horn*, 383

Svee, Gary D., *Sanctuary*, 1816
Swarthout, Glendon, *The Shootist*, 2683; *The Homesman*, 550
Thom, James Alexander, *Panther in the Sky*, 390
Wheeler, Richard S., *Sierra*, 803
Williams, Jeanne, *Home Mountain*, 1884
Wister, Owen, *The Virginian*, 1896

Whitbread Book of the Year Award

Brady, Joan, *Theory of War*, 832
D'Aguiar, Fred, *The Longest Memory*, 621

Appendix II
Books Suitable for Young Adult Readers

Note: Books in this list may be appropriate for or of interest to young adult readers (ninth grade in high school and up). The selection of most of the books noted as young adult come from lists in *School Library Journal* and *Booklist* provided by professional educators and reviewers. Numbers refer to entry numbers.

Adams, Clifton, *Hassle and the Medicine Man*, 1020

Adams, Harold, *The Ditched Blonde*, 1913; *Hatchet Job*, 1915; *The Man Who Missed the Party*, 1917; *The Man Who Was Taller Than God*, 1918; *The Naked Liar*, 1919; *A Way with Widows*, 1920

Adams, Jane, *Seattle Green*, 573

Adicks, Richard, *A Court for Owls*, 819

Agee, James, *A Death in the Family*, 1922

Albert, Bill, *Castle Garden*, 1923; *Desert Blues*, 2953

Aldrich, Bess Streeter, *Miss Bishop*, 1924; *Spring Came on Forever*, 1025; *A White Bird Flying*, 575

Alexander, Lawrence, *The Big Stick*, 1925; *The Strenuous Life*, 1926

Allen, Clay, *Range Trouble*, 1026

Alter, Judy, *Cherokee Rose*, 1931

Ames, Francis H., *The Callahans' Gamble*, 1932

Anderson, Edward, *Hungry Men*, 1934

Anderson, Sherwood, *Poor White*, 1935; *Tar: A Midwest Childhood*, 1031

Appel, Allen, *Twice Upon a Time*, 1032

Armen, M.A., *The Hanging of Father Miguel*, 1035

Arnow, Harriette Louisa Simpson, *The Kentucky Trace: A Novel of the American Revolution*, 198

Ascher, Carol, *The Flood*, 2961

Bache, Ellyn, *The Activist's Daughter*, 2964

Bahr, Howard, *The Black Flower*, 822

Baker, Calvin, *Naming the New World*, 581

Baker, Elliott, *The Penny Wars*, 1955

Baker, Larry, *The Flamingo Rising*, 2966

Bakst, Harold, *Prairie Widow*, 1041

Barr, Nevada, *Bittersweet*, 1045

Barrett, Bob, *Pembrook vs. the West*, 1046

Barry, Jane, *The Carolinians*, 200; *The Long March*, 201; *Maximilian's Gold*, 1047; *A Shadow of Eagles*, 1048; *A Time in the Sun*, 1049

Bass, Cynthia, *Maiden Voyage*, 1961; *Sherman's March*, 824

Bass, Milton, *Mistr Jory*, 1054

Bean, Amelia, *The Feud*, 1055

Bechko, P. A., *Blown to Hell*, 584; *The Winged Warrior*, 1059

Beck, K. K., *Peril Under the Palms*, 1975

Berent, Mark, *Phantom Leader*, 2975; *Rolling Thunder*, 2976

Bergman, Andrew, *Hollywood and LeVine*, 2977

Bernhard, Virginia, *A Durable Fire*, 44

Bickham, Jack M., *All the Days Were Summer*, 2793

Bigsby, Christopher, *Hester*, 45

Bingham, Sallie, *Matron of Honor*, 2979; *Small Victories*, 2980

Bjorn, Thyra Ferre, *Papa's Wife*, 1995

Blair, Clifford, *The Guns of Sacred Heart*, 1070

Bledsoe, Jerry, *The Angel Doll*, 2984

Bly, Stephen, *Standoff at Sunrise Creek*, 1083

Bohnaker, Joseph J., *Of Arms I Sing*, 1

Bonds, Parris Afton, *Blue Moon*, 2001

Bonner, Cindy, *Lily*, 1089; *Looking after Lily*, 1090; *The Passion of Dellie O'Barr*, 1091

Borland, Hal, *The Seventh Winter*, 1092; *When the Legends Die*, 2003

Bowering, George, *Caprice*, 1095

Bowers, Terrell L., *Ride Against the Wind*, 596; *The Secret of Snake Canyon*, 2005

Boyd, Brendan C., *Blue Ruin*, 2006

Boyd, William Young, *The Gentle Infantryman*, 2795

Boyne, Walter J., *Air Force Eagles*, 2990; *Eagles at War*, 2796; *Trophy for Eagles*, 2009

Boyne, Walter J., and Steven L. Thompson, *The Wild Blue*, 2991

Bradbury, Ray, *Dandelion Wine*, 2010

Bradford, Richard, *Red Sky at Morning*, 2797

Brady, Joan, *Theory of War*, 832

Brand, Max, *The Last Showdown*, 1105; *Mountain Guns*, 1110; *Wild Freedom*, 1117

Bristow, Gwen, *Calico Palace*, 599

Broome, H. B., *Dark Winter*, 2019

Brouwer, S. W., *Moon Basket*, 1132; *Morning Star*, 1133

Brown, Dee Alexander, *Conspiracy of Knaves*, 837; *Killdeer Mountain*, 1134; *The Way to Bright Star*, 838

Brown, Diana, *The Hand of a Woman*, 1135

Brown, Joe David, *Addie Pray*, 2021

Brown, John Gregory, *The Wrecked, Blessed Body of Shelton Lafleur*, 2022

Brown, Rita Mae, *Dolley*, 295

Brown, Sam, *The Long Season*, 1139; *The Trail to Honk Ballard's Bones*, 1140

Bryant, Will, *The Big Lonesome*, 1144; *A Time for Heroes*, 2026

Buechner, Frederick, *The Wizard's Tide*, 2027

Burke, Martyn, *Ivory Joe*, 3000

Butler, Robert Olen, *On Distant Ground*, 3003

Byrd, Max, *Jackson*, 408; *Jefferson*, 110

Campbell, Bebe Moore, *Your Blues Ain't Like Mine*, 3006

Carr, Robyn, *Woman's Own*, 2053

INDEXES

Author Index

Note: Numbers refer to entry numbers. Books with joint authors are listed under each author. Joint authors are listed individually.

Epstein, Seymour, *A Special Destiny*, 2816

Erdman, Loula Grace, *The Edge of Time*, 1274; *The Far Journey*, 1275; *Many a Voyage*, 437

Erdrich, Louise, *The Antelope Wife*, 1276; *Love Medicine*, 2156

Erhart, Margaret, *Augusta Cotton*, 3068

Erickson, Steve, *Arc D'X*, 127

Esstman, Barbara, *Night Ride Home*, 3069; *The Other Anna*, 2157

Estes, Winston, *Another Part of the House*, 2158

Estleman, Loren D., *Billy Gashade*, 868; *Bloody Season*, 1277; *City of Widows*, 1278; *Edsel: A Novel of Detroit*, 3070; *The Hider*, 2159; *Journey of the Dead*, 1279; *King of the Corner*, 3380; *Motown*, 3071; *Murdock's Law*, 438; *Stress*, 3072; *Sudden Country*, 2160; *This Old Bill*, 1280; *Whiskey River*, 2161

Eulo, Elena Yates, *A Southern Woman*, 869

Evanier, David, *The One-Star Jew*, 3073; *Red Love*, 2162

Evans, Elizabeth, *The Blue Hour*, 3074

Evans, Max, *Bluefeather Fellini*, 2163

Everett, Percival, *God's Country*, 1281

Eyre, David, *Float*, 3075

Fackler, Elizabeth, *Backtrail*, 2164; *Billy the Kid*, 1282; *Blood Kin*, 1283; *Road From Betrayal*, 1284

Faherty, Terence, *Come Back Dead*, 3076; *Kill Me Again*, 3077

Fair, Ronald, *We Can't Breathe*, 2165

Fairbairn, Ann, *Five Smooth Stones*, 2166

Fall, Thomas, *The Ordeal of Running Standing*, 1285

Fante, John, *1933 Was a Bad Year*, 2167

Farr, Judith, *I Never Came to You in White*, 640

Farraday, Tess, *Shadows in the Flame*, 1286

Farrell, Cliff, *Patchsaddle Drive*, 1287

Farrell, James T., *The Death of Nora Ryan*, 3078; *The Dunne Family*, 2168; *Face of Time*, 2169; *No Star is Lost*, 2170; *Sam Holman*, 2171; *Studs Lonigan*, 2172; *A World I Never Made*, 2173

Farris, Jack, *Me and Gallagher*, 870

Fast, Howard, *April Morning*, 226; *Citizen Tom Paine*, 128; *The Establishment*, 3079; *Freedom Road*, 1288; *The Hessian*, 227; *The Immigrants*, 2174; *The Immigrant's Daughter*, 3381; *The Legacy*, 3080; *Max*, 2175; *The Outsider*, 3081; *The Pledge*, 3082;

Second Generation, 2176; *Seven Days in June*, 228

Fast, Julius, *What Should We Do about Davey?* 2177

Faulkner, Colleen, *Fire Dancer*, 129

Faulkner, William, *Absalom, Absalom!* 2178; *The Reivers, a Reminiscence*, 2179; *Sartoris*, 2180; *Soldier's Pay*, 2181; *The Unvanquished*, 871

Faust, Irvin, *Jim Dandy*, 2182

Federspiel, Jurg, *The Ballad of Typhoid Mary*, 2183

Feldhake, Susan C., *The Darkness and the Dawn*, 2184; *For Ever and Ever*, 1289; *From This Day Forward*, 1290; *Hope for the Morrow*, 1291; *In Love's Own Time*, 641; *Joy in the Morning*, 2185; *Seasons of the Heart*, 1292; *Serenity in the Storm*, 2186

Fenady, Andrew J., *Claws of the Eagle*, 1293; *The Summer of Jack London*, 2187

Fennelly, Tony, *The Hippie in the Wall*, 3083

Ferber, Edna, *Cimarron*, 2188; *Giant*, 2189; *Ice Palace*, 3084; *Saratoga Trunk*, 1294; *Show Boat*, 1295; *So Big*, 1296

Fergus, Charles, *Shadow Catcher*, 2190

Fergus, Jim, *One Thousand White Women*, 1297

Ferro, Robert, *The Blue Star*, 1298

Few, Mary Dodgen, *Azilie of Bordeaux*, 59

Fickett, Harold, *Daybreak*, 130; *First Light*, 60

Field, Rachel, *All This, and Heaven Too*, 439; *And Now Tomorrow*, 440; *Time Out of Mind*, 1299

Fields, Jeff, *A Cry of Angels*, 3085

Filene, Peter, *Home and Away*, 3086

Finch, Phillip, *Birthright*, 1300

Fine, Warren, *In the Animal Kingdom*, 314

Finley, Joseph E., *Missouri Blue*, 2191

Finney, Ernest J., *California Time*, 2192; *Words of My Roaring*, 2817

Finney, Jack, *From Time to Time*, 2193; *Time and Again*, 1301

Fisher, Vardis, *Children of God*, 441; *Mountain Man*, 642

Fitzgerald, F. Scott, *The Beautiful and Damned*, 2194; *The Great Gatsby*, 2195; *This Side of Paradise*, 2196

Fitzgerald, Juliet, *Belle Haven*, 2197

Flagg, Fannie, *Coming Attractions*, 3087; *Fried Green Tomatoes at the Whistle-Stop Cafe*, 2818

Fleming, David L., *Border Crossings*, 2198

Fleming, Thomas, *Liberty Tavern*, 229; *The Officers' Wives*, 3088; *Remember the Morning*, 131; *The*

Spoils of War, 1302; *Time and Tide*, 2819

Fletcher, Inglis, *Bennett's Welcome*, 61; *Cormorant's Brood*, 132; *Lusty Wind for Carolina*, 62; *Men of Albemarle*, 133; *Raleigh's Eden*, 134; *Roanoke Hundred*, 7; *Rogue's Harbor*, 63; *The Scotswoman*, 135; *Toil of the Brave*, 230; *Wicked Lady*, 231; *The Wind in the Forest*, 136

Flood, John, *Bag Men*, 3089

Flowers, Arthur, *Another Good Loving Blues*, 2199

Flynn, Robert, *The Last Klick*, 3090

Follett, Ken, *Night over Water*, 2820; *A Place Called Freedom*, 137

Forbes, Esther, *O, Genteel Lady!* 442; *The Running of the Tide*, 315

Ford, Elaine, *Missed Connections*, 3091

Ford, Paul Leicester, *Janice Meredith*, 232

Ford, Robert E., *Sergeant Sutton*, 2821

Foreman, Paul, *Quanah, the Serpent Eagle*, 643

Forester, C. S., *The Good Shepherd*, 2822

Forman, James, *The Cow Neck Rebels*, 233; *So Ends this Day*, 443

Fowler, Karen Joy, *Sarah Canary*, 1303

Fowler, Robert H., *Jason McGee*, 138; *Jeremiah Martin*, 139; *Jim Mundy*, 872; *Voyage to Honor*, 316

Fox, Charles, *Portrait in Oil*, 2200

Fox, John, Jr., *The Heart of the Hills*, 1304; *The Little Shepherd of Kingdom Come*, 1305; *The Trail of the Lonesome Pine*, 873

Fox, Paula, *The Western Coast*, 2201

Fraser, George MacDonald, *Flashman and the Angel of the Lord*, 644

Frazier, Charles, *Cold Mountain*, 874

Frederikson, Edna, *Three Parts Earth*, 2202

Freed, Donald, *Executive Action*, 3092

Freeman, Cynthia, *Portraits*, 2203; *Seasons of the Heart*, 2823; *A World Full of Strangers*, 2204

Freeman, James A., *Ishi's journey*, 2205

French, Albert, *Billy*, 2206; *Holly*, 2824

French, Marilyn, *The Women's Room*, 3093

Fried, Albert, *The Prescott Chronicles*, 64

Friedman, Mickey, *Hurricane Season*, 3094

Friend, Charles E., *The Savage Trail*, 1306

Fuller, Henry Blake, *Bertram Cope's Year*, 2207

MacInnes, Patricia, *The Last Night on Bikini*, 2875

Mackey, Mary, *The Kindness of Strangers*, 2387; *Season of Shadows*, 3198

Mackin, Jeanne, *The Frenchwoman*, 349

MacLean, Alistair, *Breakheart Pass*, 1523

MacLean, Amanda, *Everlasting*, 697

Madden, David, *Bijou*, 3199; *Sharpshooter*, 925

Magill, Kathleen, *Megan*, 2388

Magnuson, James, *Orphan Train*, 698

Mailer, Norman, *The Naked and the Dead*, 2876

Major, Clarence, *Dirty Bird Blues*, 3200

Malamud, Bernard, *The Assistant*, 3201; *The Natural*, 2389; *A New Life*, 3202

Mallon, Thomas, *Aurora 7*, 3203; *Dewey Defeats Truman*, 3204; *Henry and Clara*, 926

Mamet, David, *The Old Religion*, 2390

Manfred, Frederick Feikema, *Green Earth*, 2391; *No Fun on Sunday*, 2392; *Scarlet Plume*, 927

Margason, Roger, *Stagecoach to Nowhere*, 1524

Margolis, David, *Change of Partners*, 3205

Marius, Richard, *After the War*, 2393

Mark, Grace, *The Dream Seekers*, 2394

Markfield, Wallace, *Teitlebaum's Window*, 2395

Marlowe, Katherine, *Heart's Desires*, 3206

Marlowe, Stephen, *The Lighthouse at the End of the World*, 699

Marquand, John P., *B. F.'s Daughter*, 2877; *H. M. Pulham, Esquire*, 2396; *The Late George Apley*, 1525; *Sincerely, Willis Wayde*, 1526; *So Little Time*, 2878; *Women and Thomas Harrow*, 3207

Marshall, Catherine, *Christy*, 2397; *Julie*, 1527

Marshall, Joe, *Winter of the Holy Iron*, 159

Marshall, William Leonard, *The New York Detective*, 1528

Martin, Kat, *Midnight Rider*, 700

Martin, Larry Jay, *Against the 7th Flag*, 492; *El Lazo*, 701

Martin, Ron, *To Be Free!* 3208

Martin, William, *Annapolis*, 248; *Cape Cod*, 78; *The Rising of the Moon*, 2398

Martinez, Max, *Schoolland*, 3209

Mason, Bobbie Ann, *Feather Crowns*, 2399; *In Country*, 3384

Mason, Connie, *To Love a Stranger*, 1529

Mason, David P., *Five Dollars a Scalp*, 350

Mason, F. Van Wyck, *Brimstone Club*, 160; *Eagle in the Sky*, 249; *Guns for Rebellion*, 250; *Our Valiant Few*, 928; *Proud New Flags*, 929; *Rivers of Glory*, 251; *The Sea Venture*, 79; *Stars on the Sea*, 252; *Three Harbours*, 161; *Trumpets Sound No More*, 1530; *Wild Horizon*, 253

Masterton, Graham, *Headlines*, 3210; *A Man of Destiny*, 702

Matheson, Richard, *Bid Time Return*, 2400; *Gunfight*, 2401; *Journal of the Gun Years*, 1531

Mathews, John Joseph, *Sundown*, 1532

Matlin, David., *How the Night Is Divided*, 3211

Matthews, Greg, *Come to Dust*, 2879; *Far from Heaven*, 3212; *The Further Adventures of Huckleberry Finn*, 703; *Heart of the Country*, 704; *Power in the Blood*, 1533

Matthews, Jack, *Sassafras*, 493

Matthiessen, Peter, *Killing Mister Watson*, 2402

Maxwell, A. E., *Steal the Sun*, 2403

May, Karl Friedrich, *Winnetou*, 1534

Mayerson, Evelyn Wilde, *Dade County Pine*, 1535; *Miami*, 1536; *No Enemy But Time*, 2880

Mazursky, Paul, *Harry and Tonto*, 3116

McAfee, John P., *On Rims of Empty Moons*, 3213; *Slow Walk in a Sad Rain*, 3214

McAleer, John J., *Unit Pride*, 3215

McBride, Mary, *Darling Jack*, 1537

McCaig, Donald, *Jacob's Ladder*, 930

McCall, Dan, *Messenger Bird*, 3216

McCammon, Robert R., *Boy's Life*, 3217

McCann, Colum, *This Side of Brightness*, 2404

McCarry, Charles, *The Bride of the Wilderness*, 162; *Lucky Bastard*, 3218; *The Tears of Autumn*, 3219

McCarthy, Cormac, *Blood Meridian, or, The Evening Redness in the West*, 705; *Cities of the Plain*, 3220; *The Crossing*, 2405

McCarthy, Gary, *The Gringo Amigo*, 706; *The Mustangers*, 931; *Sodbuster*, 1538

McCarver, Aaron, *Beyond the Quiet Hills*, 354; *Over the Misty Mountain*, 355

McCord, Christian, *Across the Shining Mountains*, 494

McCord, John S., *Montana Horseman*, 1539; *Texas Comebacker*, 1540; *Walking Hawk*, 1541; *Wyoming Giant*, 1542

McCorkle, Jill, *Ferris Beach*, 3221

McCormick, John, *The Right Kind of War*, 2881

McCrumb, Sharyn, *Ballad of Frankie Silver*, 495; *If I'd Killed Him When I Met Him*, 1543; *MacPherson's Lament*, 932; *She Walks These Hills*, 254

McCunn, Ruthanne Lum, *Thousand Pieces of Gold*, 1544; *Wooden Fish Songs*, 2406

McDermott, Alice, *At Weddings and Wakes*, 3222

McDowell, Edwin, *To Keep Our Honor Clean*, 3223

McEachin, James, *Tell Me a Tale*, 1545

McElroy, Lee, *Eyes of the Hawk*, 496

McFarland, Philip, *Seasons of Fear*, 163

McFather, Nelle, *Southern Secrets*, 3224

McGarry, Jean, *Gallagher's Travels*, 3225

McGehee, Nicole, *No More Lonely Nights*, 3226; *Regret Not a Moment*, 2407

McGinnis, Bruce, *Reflections in Dark Glass*, 1546; *Sweet Cane*, 2408

McInerney-Whiteford, Merry, *Dog People*, 3227

McKay, Allis, *The Women at Pine Creek*, 2409

McKenney, Ruth, *Industrial Valley*, 2410

McKinney, Meagan, *Fair Is the Rose*, 1547; *The Fortune Hunter*, 1548

McKinney-Whetstone, Diane, *Tempest Rising*, 3228

McLarey, Myra, *Water from the Well*, 2411

McLeay, Alison, *Sea Change*, 933

McLellon, Waldron Murrill, *Leather and Soul*, 934

McMurtry, Larry, *Anything for Billy*, 1549; *Buffalo Girls*, 1550; *Comanche Moon*, 1551; *Dead Man's Walk*, 497; *Lonesome Dove*, 1552; *Pretty Boy Floyd*, 2412; *Streets of Laredo*, 1553; *Zeke and Ned*, 2413

McNab, Tom, *The Fast Men*, 1554; *Flanagan's Run*, 2414

McNamee, Thomas, *A Story of Deep Delight*, 1555

McNamer, Deirdre, *One Sweet Quarrel*, 2415; *Rima in the Weeds*, 3229

McNickle, D'Arcy, *The Surrounded*, 1556; *Wind from an Enemy Sky*, 1557

McPhee, Martha A., *Bright Angel Time*, 3230

McPherson, William, *Testing the Current*, 2416

McReynolds, Mary, *Wells of Glory*, 2417

Mead, Robert Douglas, *Heartland*, 707

Title Index

Note: Numbers refer to entry numbers.

Genre Index

Note: Numbers refer to entry numbers.

Adventure Story

Adleman, Robert H., *Sweetwater Fever,* 574

Agnew, James B., *Eggnog Riot,* 402

Allen, Hervey, *The Forest and the Fort,* 103; *Toward the Morning,* 104

Ames, Francis H., *The Callahans' Gamble,* 1932

Babitz, Eve, *L. A. Woman,* 2963

Bart, Sheldon, *Ruby Sweetwater and the Ringo Kid,* 1960

Barton, Wayne, and Stan Williams, *Lockhart's Nightmare,* 1052

Beach, Edward Latimer, *Dust on the Sea,* 2789; *Run Silent, Run Deep,* 2790

Benchley, Nathaniel, *All Over Again,* 1981

Berger, Thomas, *Little Big Man,* 1062

Berry, Don, *Moontrap,* 404; *To Build a Ship,* 405; *Trask,* 406

Blakely, Mike, *Baron of the Sacramentos,* 1077

Blevins, Winfred, *The Misadventures of Silk and Shakespeare,* 1079

Bohnaker, Joseph J., *Of Arms I Sing,* 1

Bourjaily, Vance Nye, *A Game Men Play,* 2986

Bowen, Peter, *Imperial Kelly,* 2004; *Yellowstone Kelly,* 1094

Boyne, Walter J., *Air Force Eagles,* 2990; *Eagles at War,* 2796; *Trophy for Eagles,* 2009

Boyne, Walter J., and Steven L. Thompson, *The Wild Blue,* 2991

Brand, Max, *Wild Freedom,* 1117

Bristow, Gwen, *Jubilee Trail,* 1127

Brunner, John, *The Great Steamboat Race,* 1143

Bryan, C. D. B., *P.S. Wilkinson,* 2996

Bryant, Will, *The Big Lonesome,* 1144; *A Time for Heroes,* 2026

Buchan, John, *Salute to Adventurers,* 108

Chalker, Jack L., *The Devil's Voyage,* 2801

Charbonneau, Louis, *Trail,* 301

Charyn, Jerome, *Panna Maria,* 2062

Churchill, Winston, *The Crossing,* 214

Coffman, Virginia, *Mistress Devon,* 116

Conley, Robert J., *The Dark Way,* 4

Cooper, James Fenimore, *The Deerslayer, or, the First War-Path,* 118; *The Pathfinder,* 120; *The Pioneers,* 121; *The Red Rover,* 216; *The Spy,* 217

Cooper, Jamie Lee, *The Castaways,* 2086

Cotton, Ralph W., *Powder River,* 849

Culp, John H., *The Bright Feathers,* 1214; *Oh, Valley Green!* 1215; *The Restless Land,* 1216

Davis, Don, *Appointment with the Squire,* 2806

Day, Robert, *The Last Cattle Drive,* 1235

De Hartog, Jan, *The Outer Buoy,* 3378

Dempsey, Al, *Path of the Sun,* 1240

Dennis, Patrick, *Around the World with Auntie Mame,* 2114; *Auntie Mame,* 2115

Di Donato, Georgia, *Firebrand,* 2117

Donahue, Jack, and Michel T. Halbouty, *Grady Barr,* 2129

Douglass, Thea Coy, *Royal Poinciana,* 2134

Downes, Anne Miller, *The Pilgrim Soul,* 431

Edmonds, Janet, *Rivers of Gold,* 1265

Edmonds, Walter D., *In the Hands of the Senecas,* 224; *Rome Haul,* 634

Ehrlich, Max, *The Big Boys,* 2149

Epstein, Leslie, *Pinto and Sons,* 639

Erickson, Steve, *Arc D'X,* 127

Estleman, Loren D., *Whiskey River,* 2161

Ferro, Robert, *The Blue Star,* 1298

Fickett, Harold, *First Light,* 60

Fine, Warren, *In the Animal Kingdom,* 314

Fleming, Thomas, *Time and Tide,* 2819

Follett, Ken, *Night over Water,* 2820; *A Place Called Freedom,* 137

Fowler, Karen Joy, *Sarah Canary,* 1303

Fraser, George MacDonald, *Flashman and the Angel of the Lord,* 644

Gabbert, Dean, *The Log of the Jessie Bill,* 1307

Gann, Ernest Kellogg, *Gentlemen of Adventure,* 2213

Gear, Kathleen O'Neal, and W. Michael Gear, *People of the Lakes,* 8; *People of the Lightning,* 9; *People of the Mist,* 10; *People of the Silence,* 11

Gear, W. Michael, and Kathleen O'Neal Gear, *People of the Earth,* 12; *People of the Fire,* 13; *People of the River,* 14; *People of the Sea,* 15; *People of the Wolf,* 16

Giles, Janice Holt, *The Enduring Hills,* 142; *Johnny Osage,* 320; *Six-Horse Hitch,* 649; *Voyage to Santa Fe,* 452

Gingher, Marianne, *Bobby Rex's Greatest Hit,* 3105

Gray, Robert Steele, *Survivor,* 17

Green, Julian, *The Distant Lands,* 656

Griffin, W. E. B., *The Colonels,* 3118; *Line of Fire,* 2836

Groom, Winston, *Forrest Gump,* 3124

Guthrie, A. B., *The Big Sky,* 1361

Hall, Oakley, *Apaches,* 1365; *Separations,* 1366

Hennessy, Max, *The Bright Blue Sky,* 2272

Henry, Will, *The Gates of the Mountains,* 327; *San Juan Hill,* 2274

House, R. C., *Warhawk,* 335

Jakes, John, *The Americans,* 1430; *Heaven and Hell,* 1431

Jennings, Gary, *Spangle,* 1434

Johnson, Charles Richard, *Middle Passage,* 471; *Oxherding Tale,* 676

Johnson, Guy, *Standing at the Scratch Line,* 2310

Johnston, Terry C., *Cry of the Hawk,* 898; *Winter Rain,* 1440

Jones, Robert F., *Deadville,* 476; *Tie My Bones to Her Back,* 1449

Kelley, Leo P., *Morgan,* 680

Kelton, Elmer, *Slaughter,* 1462

Kennedy, William, *Billy Phelan's Greatest Game,* 2331; *Legs,* 2334

Kerouac, Jack, *Visions of Cody,* 3172

Kevan, Martin, *Racing Tides,* 72

Kilian, Michael, *Major Washington,* 151

Kipling, Rudyard, *Captains Courageous,* 483

Kunstler, James Howard, *An Embarrassment of Riches,* 344

L'Amour, Louis, *The Ferguson Rifle,* 1481; *Jubal Sackett,* 73; *Lonely on the Mountain,* 1483

Lancaster, Bruce, *The Big Knives,* 245

Lehrer, Jim, *White Widow,* 3190

Lehrer, Kate, *Out of Eden,* 1500

Leonard, Elmore, *Cuba Libra,* 2368

Levy, Burt, *Last Open Road,* 3193

Lupoff, Richard A., *Lovecraft's Book,* 2383

Lynn, Jack, *The Hallelujah Flight,* 2385

MacLean, Alistair, *Breakheart Pass,* 1523

Magill, Kathleen, *Megan,* 2388

Allegory

Bildungsroman (Coming of Age)

Domestic Fiction

Picaresque Fiction

Political Fiction

Religious Fiction

Romance

Satire

Sea Story

Western Fiction

Geographic Index

Note: Numbers refer to entry numbers. The action of stories may take place in several different states or regions or across the United States as a whole. This index lists the setting or settings in which the predominant action occurs. For each state also check under corresponding cities (e.g., for settings in "Louisiana" see also under "New Orleans"). Also check the Subject Index for place names (e.g., "Mississippi River") and for more specific locales. Stories that involve specific settings outside the United States (e.g., "Vietnam") will be listed in the subject index.

Lawrence, Margaret K., *Blood Red Roses*, 347; *Hearts and Bones*, 348

Moore, Ruth, *Sarah Walked over the Mountain*, 353

Ogilvie, Elisabeth, *Jennie Glenroy*, 504; *The World of Jennie G*, 2477

Paretti, Sandra, *The Magic Ship*, 2497

Raucher, Herman, *Summer of '42*, 2901

Roberts, Kenneth Lewis, *Arundel*, 271; *Boon Island*, 179; *Captain Caution*, 376; *The Lively Lady*, 377; *Lydia Bailey*, 378; *Northwest Passage*, 180; *Rabble in Arms*, 272

Spencer, LaVyrle, *That Camden Summer*, 2656

Stuart, Anne, *Cameron's Landing*, 1812

Williams, Ben Ames, *Come Spring*, 281

Maryland

Barth, John, *The Sot-Weed Factor*, 42

Berne, Suzanne, *A Crime in the Neighborhood*, 2978

Churchill, Winston, *Richard Carvel*, 114

Cornwell, Bernard, *The Bloody Ground*, 846

De Blasis, Celeste, *A Season of Swans*, 1236; *Swan's Chance*, 626; *Wild Swan*, 309

Eagle, Sarah, *Lady Vengeance*, 312

Hatvary, George Egon, *The Murder of Edgar Allan Poe*, 665

Heidish, Marcy, *A Woman Called Moses*, 666

Kotlowitz, Robert, *His Master's Voice*, 2868

Marlowe, Stephen, *The Lighthouse at the End of the World*, 699

Martin, William, *Annapolis*, 248

Michener, James A., *Chesapeake*, 28

Noble, Hollister, *Woman with a Sword*, 959

Robertson, Don, *By Antietam Creek*, 979

Robson, Lucia St. Clair, *Mary's Land*, 89

Tilghman, Christopher, *Mason's Retreat*, 2703

Tucker, Augusta, *Miss Susie Slagle's*, 2709

Webb, James H., *A Sense of Honor*, 3354

Wright, Sarah E., *This Child's Gonna Live*, 2771

Massachusetts

Benchley, Nathaniel, *Portrait of a Scoundrel*, 289

Bigsby, Christopher, *Hester*, 45

Bittle, Camilla R., *Dear Family*, 1991; *Friends of the Family*, 2981

Burke, Phyllis, *Atomic Candy*, 3001

Cavanaugh, Jack, *The Colonists*, 113; *The Puritans*, 48

Child, Lydia Maria Francis, *Hobomok*, 49

Coleman, Terry, *Thanksgiving*, 50

Condé, Maryse, *I, Tituba, Black Witch of Salem*, 51

Cook, Thomas H., *The Chatham School Affair*, 2080

Copeland, Lori, *Angelface and Amazing Grace*, 1196

Costello, Anthony, *Jericho*, 2089

Dillon, Eilís, *The Seekers*, 56

Elliott, Edward E., *The Devil and the Mathers*, 58

Engstrom, Elizabeth, *Lizzie Borden*, 1273

Farr, Judith, *I Never Came to You in White*, 640

Fast, Howard, *April Morning*, 226; *Seven Days in June*, 228

Fickett, Harold, *Daybreak*, 130

Field, Rachel, *All This, and Heaven Too*, 439

Forbes, Esther, *The Running of the Tide*, 315

French, Marilyn, *The Women's Room*, 3093

Fuller, Jamie, *The Diary of Emily Dickinson*, 645

Gambino, Richard, *Bread and Roses*, 2211

Gerson, Noel B., *The Land Is Bright*, 65

Giardina, Anthony, *Men with Debts*, 3102

Graver, Elizabeth, *Unravelling*, 655

Hawthorne, Nathaniel, *The Blithedale Romance*, 462; *The House of the Seven Gables*, 463; *The Scarlet Letter*, 68

Heidish, Marcy, *Witnesses*, 69

Hodge, Jane Aiken, *Judas Flowering*, 238; *Wide Is the Water*, 239

Hoff, B. J., *Cloth of Heaven*, 330

Hunter, Evan, *Lizzie*, 1427

Ikeda, Stewart David, *What the Scarecrow Said*, 2844

Jarrett, Miranda, *The Secrets of Catie Hazard*, 149

Kipling, Rudyard, *Captains Courageous*, 483

Kricorian, Nancy, *Zabelle*, 3178

Laity, Sally, and Dianna Crawford, *Fires of Freedom*, 153; *The Gathering Dawn*, 154; *The Kindled Flame*, 155

Larson, Charles R., *Arthur Dimmesdale*, 74

Lipman, Elinor, *The Inn at Lake Devine*, 2372

Marquand, John P., *Sincerely, Willis Wayde*, 1526

Martin, William, *Cape Cod*, 78

Mason, F. Van Wyck, *Guns for Rebellion*, 250; *Three Harbours*, 161

McInerney-Whiteford, Merry, *Dog People*, 3227

Morris, Gilbert, *The Captive Bride*, 82; *The Honorable Imposter*, 83; *The Indentured Heart*, 166

Myrer, Anton, *The Last Convertible*, 3250

Porter, Donald Clayton, *White Indian*, 86

Riefe, Barbara, *For Love of Two Eagles*, 176

Rossner, Judith, *Emmeline*, 536

Rushing, Jane Gilmore, *Covenant of Grace*, 90

Satterthwait, Walter, *Miss Lizzie*, 2598

Sedgwick, Catharine Maria, *Hope Leslie, or, Early Times in the Massachusetts*, 92

Seton, Anya, *The Hearth and Eagle*, 1778; *The Winthrop Woman*, 93

Sidhwa, Bapsi, *An American Brat*, 3387

Sinclair, Upton, *Boston*, 2626

Smith, Claude Clayton, *The Stratford Devil*, 95

Stone, Irving, *Those Who Love*, 185

Swann, Lois, *The Mists of Manittoo*, 186; *Torn Covenants*, 187

Thompson, Joan, *Interesting Times*, 2700

Walker, Mildred, *If a Lion Could Talk*, 796

West, Dorothy, *The Wedding*, 3357

Williams, Lawrence, *I, James McNeill Whistler*, 569

Winston, Daoma, *The Fall River Line*, 814

Zaroulis, N. L., *Call the Darkness Light*, 572

Miami

Aronson, Harvey, *The Golden Shore*, 1940

Kaplan, Barry Jay, *Biscayne*, 2322

Mayerson, Evelyn Wilde, *Dade County Pine*, 1535; *Miami*, 1536

Sayles, John, *Los Gusanos*, 3385

Michigan

Benz, Maudy, *Oh, Jackie*, 2974

Boyle, T. Coraghessan, *The Road to Wellville*, 2008

Briskin, Jacqueline, *The Onyx*, 2015

Dobyns, Stephen, *The House on Alexandrine*, 3051

Dodge, Ed, *Dau*, 3052

Estleman, Loren D., *Edsel: A Novel of Detroit*, 3070; *King of the Corner*, 3380; *Motown*, 3071; *Stress*, 3072; *Whiskey River*, 2161

Fuller, Iola, *The Loon Feather*, 317

Groseclose, Elgin Earl, *The Kiowa*, 1352

Jones, Nettie, *Mischief Makers*, 2316

Lancaster, Bruce, *The Big Knives*, 245

Mallon, Thomas, *Dewey Defeats Truman*, 3204

Morris, Bill, *Motor City*, 3239

Oates, Joyce Carol, *Them*, 2476

Price, Nancy, *An Accomplished Woman*, 2531

Salerno, Nan F., and Rosa Vandenburgh, *Shaman's Daughter*, 2593

Sinclair, Upton, *The Flivver King*, 2628

Smith, Larry, *The Original*, 2644

Soos, Troy, *Hunting a Detroit Tiger*, 3327

Traver, Robert, *Laughing Whitefish*, 1835

Midwest

Allen, Clay, *Range Trouble*, 1026

Bechko, P. A., *The Eye of the Hawk*, 1058

Washington

West

Subject Index

Note: Numbers refer to entry numbers.

Denker, Henry, *Payment in Full*, 2113
Eckert, Allan W., *Johnny Logan*, 1263
Oke, Janette, and T. Davis Bunn, *Another Homecoming*, 2895

Advertising

Estleman, Loren D., *Edsel: A Novel of Detroit*, 3070

Aerospace industry

Kinsolving, William, *Raven*, 2343

Africa

Baker, Calvin, *Naming the New World*, 581
Bowen, Peter, *Yellowstone Kelly*, 1094
Haley, Alex, *Roots*, 146

African Americans

Appel, Allen, *Twice Upon a Time*, 1032
Austin, Doris Jean, *After the Garden*, 1952
Baker, Calvin, *Naming the New World*, 581
Blakely, Mike, *Shortgrass Song*, 592
Bontemps, Arna, *Black Thunder*, 291
Boyne, Walter J., *Air Force Eagles*, 2990
Brown, John Gregory, *The Wrecked, Blessed Body of Shelton Lafleur*, 2022
Brown, Linda Beatrice, *Crossing over Jordan*, 1136
Brown, Wesley, *Darktown Strutters*, 600
Bunkley, Anita R., *Black Gold*, 2028
Burchardt, Bill, *Black Marshal*, 1146
Burke, Martyn, *Ivory Joe*, 3000
Campbell, Bebe Moore, *Your Blues Ain't Like Mine*, 3006
Cary, Lorene, *The Price of a Child*, 604
Chase-Riboud, Barbara, *Sally Hemings*, 303
Chesnutt, Charles W., *Mandy Oxendine*, 2064
Cliff, Michelle, *Free Enterprise*, 610
Cobb, William, *A Walk Through Fire*, 3017
Coldsmith, Don, *South Wind*, 615
Colter, Cyrus, *A Chocolate Soldier*, 3019
Corbin, Steven, *No Easy Place to Be*, 2087
Courlander, Harold, *The African*, 307
Covin, Kelly, *Hear that Train Blow: A Novel About the Scottsboro Case*, 2092
Cox, Elizabeth, *Night Talk*, 3029
D'Aguiar, Fred, *The Longest Memory*, 621
Daugharty, Janice, *Whistle*, 3037
Davis, Thulani, *1959*, 3041
Denker, Henry, *Payment in Full*, 2113
Douglas, Thorne, *Night Riders*, 1256
Edwards-Yearwood, Grace, *In the Shadow of the Peacock*, 3061
Ell, Flynn J., *Dakota Scouts*, 1271
Ellison, Ralph, *Invisible Man*, 2153
Erickson, Steve, *Arc D'X*, 127
Estleman, Loren D., *King of the Corner*, 3380; *Motown*, 3071; *Stress*, 3072

Fair, Ronald, *We Can't Breathe*, 2165
Fast, Howard, *Freedom Road*, 1288
Faust, Irvin, *Jim Dandy*, 2182
French, Albert, *Billy*, 2206
Gaines, Ernest J., *The Autobiography of Miss Jane Pittman*, 879; *A Lesson before Dying*, 3099
Gerard, Philip, *Cape Fear Rising*, 2220
Golden, Marita, *And Do Remember Me*, 3109; *Long Distance Life*, 3110
Grau, Shirley Ann, *Roadwalkers*, 2241
Guy, Rosa, *A Measure of Time*, 2251
Haley, Alex, *Roots*, 146
Hambly, Barbara, *Fever Season*, 458; *A Free Man of Color*, 459
Harvey, James Alphonsus, *Blood Hunt*, 1375
Henry, Will, *One More River to Cross*, 1396
Herron, Carolivia, *Thereafter Johnnie*, 2277
Himes, Chester B., *If He Hollers Let Him Go*, 2839
Hoffman, Ray, *Almost Family*, 3148
Honig, Donald, *The Plot to Kill Jackie Robinson*, 3150
Hotchkiss, Bill, *Ammahabas*, 332; *The Medicine Calf*, 333
Hudson, Helen, *Criminal Trespass*, 3154
Hunt, Marsha, *Free*, 2296
Johnson, Charles Richard, *Middle Passage*, 471; *Oxherding Tale*, 676
Johnson, Guy, *Standing at the Scratch Line*, 2310
Kelton, Elmer, *The Wolf and the Buffalo*, 1463
Killens, John Oliver, *Youngblood*, 2341
Larsen, Nella, *Passing*, 2357
Lentz, Perry, *The Falling Hills*, 921
Lester, Julius, *And All Our Wounds Forgiven*, 3192
Lincoln, C. Eric, *The Avenue, Clayton City*, 2371
Litvin, Martin, *The Impresario*, 2373
Lupoff, Richard A., *The Sepia Siren Killer*, 2384
Lynn, Jack, *The Hallelujah Flight*, 2385
Major, Clarence, *Dirty Bird Blues*, 3200
McCann, Colum, *This Side of Brightness*, 2404
McEachin, James, *Tell Me a Tale*, 1545
McFarland, Philip, *Seasons of Fear*, 163
McKinney-Whetstone, Diane, *Tempest Rising*, 3228
Meriwether, Louise, *Daddy Was a Number Runner*, 2419; *Fragments of the Ark*, 935
Morrison, Toni, *Beloved*, 1603; *The Bluest Eye*, 2887; *Jazz*, 2447; *Paradise*, 3241
Mosher, Howard Frank, *A Stranger in the Kingdom*, 3244

Mosley, Walter, *Black Betty*, 3245; *Devil in a Blue Dress*, 3246; *Gone Fishin'*, 2452; *A Little Yellow Dog*, 3247; *A Red Death*, 3248; *White Butterfly*, 3249
Murray, Albert, *The Spyglass Tree*, 2455; *Train Whistle Guitar*, 2456
Parker, Gwendolyn M., *These Same Long Bones*, 3261
Parks, Gordon, *The Learning Tree*, 2499
Petry, Ann Lane, *The Street*, 2897
Pharr, Robert Deane, *The Book of Numbers*, 2517
Phillips, Caryl, *Crossing the River*, 362
Pinckney, Darryl, *High Cotton*, 3273
Porter, Connie Rose, *All-Bright Court*, 3279
Pressfield, Steven, *The Legend of Bagger Vance*, 2530
Prose, Francine, *Marie Laveau*, 367
Reed, Ishmael, *Flight to Canada*, 973; *Mumbo Jumbo*, 2548
Rhodes, Jewell Parker, *Voodoo Dreams*, 371
Richards, Emilie, *Iron Lace*, 2553
Sallis, James, *Black Hornet*, 3305
Sanders, Dori, *Her Own Place*, 2913
Sarrantonio, Al, *Kitt Peak*, 2597
Seelye, John, *The Kid*, 1775
Segal, Lore, *Her First American*, 3313
Shange, Ntozake, *Betsey Brown*, 3317
Sinclair, April, *Coffee Will Make Me Black*, 3320
Skinner, Robert E., *Cat-Eyed Trouble*, 2634
Smith, Eunice Young, *A Trumpet Sounds*, 2643
Smith, Lillian, *Strange Fruit*, 2646
Smith, Mary Burnett, *Miss Ophelia*, 3325
Stern, Steve, *Harry Kaplan's Adventures Underground*, 2668
Stowe, Harriet Beecher, *Uncle Tom's Cabin*, 548
Straight, Susan, *The Gettin Place*, 2673
Styron, William, *The Confessions of Nat Turner*, 549
Tallant, Robert, *The Voodoo Queen*, 389
Vea, Alfredo, *La Maravilla*, 3351
von Herzen, Lane, *Copper Crown*, 2724
Walker, Alice, *The Color Purple*, 2726; *The Third Life of Grange Copeland*, 2727
Walker, Jack, *West of Fort Worth*, 1004
Walker, Margaret, *Jubilee*, 1859
Watkins, Emerson, *The Story of a Forgotten Hero*, 1863
West, Dorothy, *The Wedding*, 3357
Wheeler, Amanda, *Beyond the Fire*, 3360
White, Richard, *Jordan Freeman Was My Friend*, 280; *Mister Grey of the Further Adventures of Huckleberry Finn*, 805

Hatvary, George Egon, *The Murder of Edgar Allan Poe*, 665

Heck, Peter J., *A Connecticut Yankee in Criminal Court*, 1384; *Death on the Mississippi*, 2270; *The Prince and the Prosecutor*, 1385

Henderson, William McCranor, *I Killed Hemingway*, 3143

Johnston, Mary, *Hagar*, 2311

Jones, Kathy, *Wild Western Desire*, 1448

Lupoff, Richard A., *Lovecraft's Book*, 2383

Matheson, Richard, *Bid Time Return*, 2400

Millhauser, Steven, *Edwin Mullhouse*, 2885

Moore, Barbara, *The Fever Called Living*, 500

Puzo, Mario, *Fools Die*, 3290

Rosen, Norma, *John and Anzia*, 2581

Satterthwait, Walter, *Wilde West*, 2599

Schulberg, Budd, *The Disenchanted*, 2609

Sinclair, Andrew, *The Facts in the Case of E.A. Poe*, 3319

Stead, Christina, *I'm Dying Laughing*, 2659

Steward, Barbara, and Dwight Steward, *Evermore*, 546

Thomas, Jodi, *To Tame a Texan's Heart*, 1831

Zaroulis, N. L., *The Poe Papers*, 2783

Automatons

Gavin, Thomas, *Kingkill*, 446

Automobile industry

Briskin, Jacqueline, *The Onyx*, 2015

Estleman, Loren D., *Edsel: A Novel of Detroit*, 3070

Morris, Bill, *Motor City*, 3239

Sinclair, Upton, *The Flivver King*, 2628

Automobile racing

Morris, Gilbert, *The Shadow Portrait*, 2441

Aviation industry

Livingston, Harold, *Touch the Sky*, 2375

Bachelors

Reid, Van, *Cordelia Underwood*, 2549

Bahamas

Collins, Max Allan, *Carnal Hours*, 2072

Bank robbery and robbers *see also* Criminals

Brand, Max, *The Last Showdown*, 1105

Bromael, Robert, *The Bank Robber*, 1129

Fackler, Elizabeth, *Backtrail*, 2164; *Blood Kin*, 1283; *Road From Betrayal*, 1284

Gorman, Edward, *What the Dead Men Say*, 2239

Hoffman, Lee, *Sheriff of Jack Hollow*, 1402

Hogan, Ray, *Solitude's Lawman*, 1409

La Fountaine, George, *The Scott-Dunlap Ring*, 1476

Overholser, Stephen, *Search for the Fox*, 1642

Paine, Lauran, *Custer Meadow*, 1647; *The Prairieton Raid*, 1652

Rhode, Robert, *Sandstone*, 1727

Swarthout, Glendon, *The Old Colts*, 2682

Tippette, Giles, *The Bank Robber*, 1833

Bankhead, Tallulah

Baxt, George, *The Tallulah Bankhead Murder Case*, 2971

Banks and banking

Parker, Laura, *Beguiled*, 1661

Barnum, P. T. *see also* Ringling Brothers Barnum and Bailey

Thorp, Roderick, *Jenny and Barnum*, 791

Trell, Max, *The Small Gods and Mr. Barnum*, 392

Barrios

Sanchez, Thomas, *Zoot-Suit Murders*, 2912

Baseball

Boyd, Brendan C., *Blue Ruin*, 2006

Brock, Darryl, *If I Never Get Back*, 1128

Ducker, Bruce, *Lead Us Not into Penn Station*, 3056

Duncan, David James, *The Brothers K*, 3057

Dyja, Tom, *Play for a Kingdom*, 864

Goldberg, Philip, *This Is Next Year*, 3108

Greenberg, Eric Rolfe, *The Celebrant*, 2243

Honig, Donald, *The Last Great Season*, 2842; *Last Man Out*, 3149; *The Plot to Kill Jackie Robinson*, 3150

Kluger, Steve, *Last Days of Summer*, 2865

Lapin, Mark, *Pledge of Allegiance*, 3184

Lelchuk, Alan, *Brooklyn Boy*, 3191

Malamud, Bernard, *The Natural*, 2389

Manfred, Frederick Feikema, *No Fun on Sunday*, 2392

Norman, Rick, *Fielder's Choice*, 2893

Pomeranz, Gary, *Out at Home*, 3277

Roth, Philip, *The Great American Novel*, 2910

Soos, Troy, *Cincinnati Red Stalkings*, 2649; *Hunting a Detroit Tiger*, 3327; *Murder at Wrigley Field*, 2650

Wolff, Miles, *Season of the Owl*, 3367

Basketball

Rosen, Charley, *Barney Polan's Game*, 3300; *The House of Moses All-Stars*, 2580

Basque Americans

Laxalt, Robert, *Child of the Holy Ghost*, 2359; *The Governor's Mansion*, 3186

Bay of Pigs

Sayles, John, *Los Gusanos*, 3385

Beat generation

Albert, Mimi, *Skirts*, 2954

Kerouac, Jack, *Visions of Cody*, 3172

Beckwourth, James Pierson

Hotchkiss, Bill, *Ammahabas*, 332; *The Medicine Calf*, 333

Jones, Robert F., *Deadville*, 476

Berlin

Zimmerman, R., *Deadfall in Berlin*, 3376

Between the Wars

Bryant, Will, *A Time for Heroes*, 2026

Ellis, Julie, *No Greater Love*, 2152

Fox, Paula, *The Western Coast*, 2201

Leland, Christopher T., *Mrs. Randall*, 2367

Lincoln, C. Eric, *The Avenue, Clayton City*, 2371

Spencer, LaVyrle, *Morning Glory*, 2655

Sullivan, Faith, *The Cape Ann*, 2680

Bikini Atoll

MacInnes, Patricia, *The Last Night on Bikini*, 2875

Billy the Kid

Estleman, Loren D., *Journey of the Dead*, 1279

Fackler, Elizabeth, *Billy the Kid*, 1282

McMurtry, Larry, *Anything for Billy*, 1549

Birth control

Gerson, Noel B., *The Crusader*, 2222

Black Hand

Nolan, Frederick W., *Kill Petrosino!*, 2468

Black Hawk

Fuller, Iola, *The Shining Trail*, 444

Black Hawk Wars

Derleth, August William, *Wind over Wisconsin*, 430

Olsen, Theodore V., *Summer of the Drums*, 505

Black market

Nazarian, Barry A., *Final Reckoning*, 2891

Black Panthers

D'Amato, Barbara, *Good Cop Bad Cop*, 3033

Van Peebles, Melvin, *Panther*, 3349

Blackfoot

Brand, Max, *Mountain Guns*, 1110

Johnston, Terry C., *Buffalo Palace*, 473

Stuart, Colin, *Shoot An Arrow to Stop the Wind*, 2678; *Walks Far Woman*, 1813

Walker, Mildred, *If a Lion Could Talk*, 796

Welch, James, *Fools Crow*, 40; *Winter in the Blood*, 2737

Wheeler, Richard S., *Richard Lamb*, 1875

Zelazny, Roger, and Gerald Hausman, *Wilderness*, 400

Clark, George Rogers

Clatsop

Clergy

Cleveland

Clothing workers, women

Coal mines and mining

Drowning victims
Haines, Carolyn, *Touched*, 2253

Drugs and drug trade
Deutermann, P. T., *The Edge of Honor*, 3048

Flood, John, *Bag Men*, 3089

Plesko, Les, *The Last Bongo Sunset*, 3276

Wolfe, Lois, *Mask of Night*, 1897

Du Pont family
Rowe, Jack, *Brandywine*, 762; *Dominion*, 2587; *Fortune's Legacy*, 1757

Dutch Americans
Boyle, T. Coraghessan, *World's End*, 47

Meyers, Maan, *The Dutchman*, 80

Pye, Michael, *The Drowning Room*, 87

Seton, Anya, *Dragonwyck*, 538

Dvorak, Antonin
Skvorecky, Josef, *Dvorak in Love*, 2635

Earp, Wyatt
Aggeler, Geoffrey, *Confessions of Johnny Ringo*, 1022

Eickhoff, Randy Lee, *The Fourth Horseman*, 1268

Jones, Kathy, *Wild Western Desire*, 1448

Parry, Richard, *The Winter Wolf*, 1663

Swarthout, Glendon, *The Old Colts*, 2682

Earthquakes
Benchley, Nathaniel, *All Over Again*, 1981

Jones, Douglas C., *This Savage Race*, 342

Stubbs, Jean, *The Golden Crucible*, 2679

East, Jim
Shelton, Gene, *Tascosa Gun*, 1779

Easter Rising
Martin, William, *The Rising of the Moon*, 2398

Edison, Thomas A.
Zagst, Michael, *M.H. Meets President Harding*, 2781

Edsel automobile
Estleman, Loren D., *Edsel: A Novel of Detroit*, 3070

Egypt
McGehee, Nicole, *No More Lonely Nights*, 3226

Einstein, Albert
Kaminsky, Stuart M., *Smart Moves*, 2860

Elder, Kate
Coleman, Jane Candia, *Doc Holliday's Woman*, 616

Elections, presidential
Vidal, Gore, *Washington, D.C.*, 2722

Electric engineers
Wise, Tad, *Tesla*, 2761

Emerson, Ralph Waldo
Forbes, Esther, *O, Genteel Lady!*, 442

Emigration and immigration
see also **Immigrants**

Bojer, Johan, *The Emigrants*, 1087

Moberg, Vilhelm, *The Settlers*, 1576; *Unto a Good Land*, 941

Shuken, Julia, *In the House of My Pilgrimage*, 2624

Engineers
Bickham, Jack M., *Jilly's Canal*, 1065

England
Bigsby, Christopher, *Hester*, 45

Cavanaugh, Jack, *The Allies*, 2059

Coffman, Elaine, *If You Love Me*, 415

Dubus, Elizabeth Nell, *To Love and to Dream*, 2813

Eagle, Sarah, *Lady Vengeance*, 312

Edmonds, Janet, *Sarah Camberwell Tring*, 124

Peart, Jane, *Jubilee Bride*, 2508

Wharton, Edith, *The Buccaneers*, 2746

Epilepsy
Perks, Micah, *We Are Gathered Here*, 1696

Erie Canal
Adams, Samuel Hopkins, *Canal Town*, 401

Edmonds, Walter D., *The Big Barn*, 433; *Erie Water*, 435; *Rome Haul*, 634; *The Wedding Journey*, 436

Eskimos
Harris, Julie, *The Longest Winter*, 2264

Espionage
Austell, Diane, *While the Music Plays*, 821

Bailey, Anthony, *Major André*, 105

Batchelor, John Calvin, *American Falls*, 826

Bristow, Gwen, *Celia Garth*, 210

Buckley, William F., *Mongoose, R.I.P.*, 2998

Doctorow, E. L., *The Book of Daniel*, 2120

Douglas, Barbara, *Fair Wind of Love*, 1255

Gannon, Michael, *Secret Missions*, 2825

Jones, Ted, *The Fifth Conspiracy*, 902

King, Benjamin, *A Bullet for Stonewall*, 912

Nason, Tema, *Ethel*, 2461

Oeste, Bob, *The Last Pumpkin Paper*, 3257

Sherman, Dan, *The Traitor*, 274

Steelman, Robert J., *The Galvanized Reb*, 994

Ethan Frome
Cooke, Elizabeth, *Zeena*, 2082

Ethiopia
Faust, Irvin, *Jim Dandy*, 2182

Europe
Fox, Charles, *Portrait in Oil*, 2200

Settle, Mary Lee, *Choices*, 2613

Evangelists, women
Phillips, Michael R., *A Dangerous Love*, 2520; *Mercy and Eagleflight*, 2521

Everglades
Matthiessen, Peter, *Killing Mister Watson*, 2402

Executions
Doctorow, E. L., *The Book of Daniel*, 2120

French, Albert, *Billy*, 2206

Stegner, Wallace Earle, *Joe Hill*, 2664

Exiles
Hale, Edward Everett, *Man Without a Country*, 322

Expatriates
Cook, Thomas H., *Elena*, 2081

Williams, Lawrence, *I, James McNeill Whistler*, 569

Explorers
Atherton, Gertrude Franklin Horn, *Rezanov*, 288

Bohnaker, Joseph J., *Of Arms I Sing*, 1

Burns, Ron, *The Mysterious Death of Meriwether Lewis*, 299

Charbonneau, Louis, *Trail*, 301

Coldsmith, Don, *Runestone*, 3

Hall, Oakley, *The Children of the Sun*, 67

Henry, Will, *The Gates of the Mountains*, 327

Kaufelt, David A., *American Tropic*, 25

Lytle, Andrew Nelson, *At the Moon's Inn*, 26

Panger, Daniel, *Black Ulysses*, 31

Pitre, Glen, and Michelle Benoit, *Great River*, 84

Roberts, Kenneth Lewis, *Northwest Passage*, 180

Steelman, Robert J., *Call of the Arctic*, 545

Thom, James Alexander, *The Children of First Man*, 38

Vernon, John, *La Salle*, 98

Wohl, Burton, *Soldier in Paradise*, 99

Factory workers
Gilden, Katya, and Bert Gilden, *Between the Hills and the Sea*, 3103

Graver, Elizabeth, *Unravelling*, 655

The Fall of the House of Usher
Kiraly, Marie, *Madeline*, 684

Family
Adams, Alice, *A Southern Exposure*, 1910

Adams, Jane, *Seattle Green*, 573

Agee, James, *A Death in the Family*, 1922

Aldrich, Bess Streeter, *A Lantern In Her Hand*, 1023; *Spring Came on Forever*, 1025; *A White Bird Flying*, 575

Alther, Lisa, *Original Sins*, 2956

Askew, Rilla, *The Mercy Seat*, 1038

Atwell, Lester, *Life with its Sorrow, Life with its Tear*, 1942

Austin, Doris Jean, *After the Garden*, 1952

Bakst, Harold, *Prairie Widow*, 1041

Banis, Victor, *The Earth and All It Holds*, 1957

Barnes, Joanna, *Silverwood*, 1959

Battle, Lois, *War Brides*, 2968

Farm life